Modern Germany

Recent Titles in Understanding Modern Nations

Modern China
Xiaobing Li

Modern Spain
Enrique Ávila López

Modern Mexico
James D. Huck Jr.

Modern India
John McLeod

Modern Saudi Arabia
Valerie Anishchenkova

Modern Brazil
Javier A. Galván

Modern Greece
Elaine Thomopoulos, Editor

MODERN GERMANY

Wendell G. Johnson and Katharina Barbe

Understanding Modern Nations

BLOOMSBURY ACADEMIC

NEW YORK • LONDON • OXFORD • NEW DELHI • SYDNEY

BLOOMSBURY ACADEMIC
Bloomsbury Publishing Inc
1385 Broadway, New York, NY 10018, USA
50 Bedford Square, London, WC1B 3DP, UK
29 Earlsfort Terrace, Dublin 2, Ireland

BLOOMSBURY, BLOOMSBURY ACADEMIC and the Diana logo
are trademarks of Bloomsbury Publishing Plc

First published in the United States of America by ABC-CLIO 2022
Paperback edition published by Bloomsbury Academic 2025

COVER PHOTOS: Neuschwanstein fairytale castle, Bavaria, Germany. (Minnystock/ Dreamstime);
Germany vs. Austria, September 2, 2011. (dpa picture alliance archive/Alamy Stock Photo);
Holocaust Memorial, Berlin, Germany. (Peter Schickert/Alamy Stock Photo);
Subway riders traveling to Oktoberfest. (AS/Alamy Stock Photo)

Library of Congress Cataloging-in-Publication Data
Names: Johnson, Wendell G., author. | Barbe, Katharina, author.
Title: Modern Germany / Wendell G. Johnson and Katharina Barbe.
Description: Santa Barbara : ABC-CLIO, [2022] | Series: Understanding modern nations |
Includes bibliographical references and index.
Identifiers: LCCN 2021042056 (print) | LCCN 2021042057 (ebook) |
ISBN 9781440864537 (cloth) | ISBN 9781440864544 (ebook)
Subjects: LCSH: Germany—Encyclopedias.
Classification: LCC DD14 .J64 2022 (print) | LCC DD14 (ebook) |
DDC 943.003—dc23/eng/20211028
LC record available at https://lccn.loc.gov/2021042056
LC ebook record available at https://lccn.loc.gov/2021042057

ISBN: HB: 978-1-4408-6453-7
PB: 979-8-7651-4111-3
ePDF: 978-1-4408-6454-4
eBook: 979-8-2161-1855-8

Series: Understanding Modern Nation

It is with a heavy heart we write that during the writing of this book, Cord Yorrick Barbe, our nephew, passed away tragically on September 22, 2019, at the age of twenty-one. Yorrick was a proud member of the German army (Bundeswehr) and served with the Einsatz- und Ausbildungszentrum für Tragtierwesen 230 in Bad Reichenhall.

We dedicate this volume to Yorrick, his parents, Christian and Nicole, and sisters, Alina and Lisabelle.

CONTENTS

SERIES FOREWORD

We live in an evolving world, a world that is becoming increasingly globalized by the minute. Cultures collide and blend, leading to new customs and practices that exist alongside long-standing traditions. Advancing technologies connect lives across the globe, affecting those from densely populated urban areas to those who dwell in the most remote locations in the world. Governments are changing, leading to war and violence but also to new opportunities for those who have been oppressed. The *Understanding Modern Nations* series seeks to answer questions about cultures, societies, and customs in various countries around the world.

Understanding Modern Nations is geared toward readers wanting to expand their knowledge of the world, ideal for high school students researching specific countries, undergraduates preparing for studies abroad, and general readers interested in learning more about the world around them. Each volume in the series focuses on a single country, with coverage on Africa, the Americas, Asia and the Pacific, and Europe.

Each country volume contains 16 chapters focusing on various aspects of culture and society in each country. The chapters begin with an Overview, which is followed by short entries on key topics, concepts, ideas, and biographies pertaining to the chapter's theme. In a way, these volumes serve as "thematic encyclopedias," with entries organized for the reader's benefit. Following a general Preface and Introduction, each volume contains chapters on the following themes:

- Geography
- History
- Government and Politics
- Economy
- Religion and Thought
- Social Classes and Ethnicity
- Gender, Marriage, and Sexuality
- Education
- Language
- Etiquette
- Literature and Drama
- Art and Architecture

- Music and Dance
- Food
- Leisure and Sports
- Media and Popular Culture

Each entry concludes with a list of cross references and Further Readings, pointing readers to additional print and electronic resources that might prove useful.

Following the chapters are appendices, including "A Day in the Life" feature, which depicts "typical" days in the lives of people living in that country, from students to farmers to factory workers to stay-at-home and working mothers. A Glossary, Facts and Figures section, and Holidays chart round out the appendices. Volumes include a Selected Bibliography, as well as sidebars that are scattered throughout the text.

The volumes in the *Understanding Modern Nations* series are not intended to be comprehensive compendiums about every nation of the world, but instead are meant to serve as introductory texts for readers, examining key topics from major countries studied in the high school curriculum as well as important transitioning countries that make headlines daily. It is our hope that readers will gain an understanding and appreciation for cultures and histories outside of their own.

PREFACE

This book, *Modern Germany*, is an intensely personal project for us. I made my first trip to Berlin in the spring of 1986 when Katharina Barbe and I were *Lebensabschnittsgefährten* (a convoluted German term roughly translated as "fellow travelers during this period of our life"). I took the overnight train from Paris and arrived at the East German border the following afternoon. The border formalities at the inner-German border were elaborate and contrived. I was ordered to remove my glasses, and the border guard held my passport up to my face to make sure that I resembled the photo in it. I remember thinking how ridiculous this process was—no one in his or her right mind wanted to sneak *into* East Germany, least of all a graduate student in theology (I was and am no Bonhoeffer). Katharina, a native of West Berlin, met me at Berlin *Zoologischer Garten*, the depot for trains in and out of the western sector of the divided city. *Bahnhof Zoo*, though located in West Berlin a stone's throw from Kurfürstendamm (the main shopping drag in the western section of the divided city), was managed by the Deutsche Reichsbahn (DR), the East German rail authority. The DR operated an Intershop (a government-owned retail outlet that accepted only hard currencies) in the station, although most customers crossed the street to McDonald's.

We were both graduate students at Rice University at the time. Katharina had a summer job teaching German at the Goethe-Institut in West Berlin, and I did dissertation research in the library at the Free University. My future father-in-law, Professor Helmut Barbe (1927–2021), lived in Spandau, a couple of blocks from the old East German border. After dinner we would stroll down to the *Mauer* (the Berlin Wall) and wave at the surly East German border patrol manning the watchtower. During my time in Berlin, I crossed through (or under) the Berlin Wall several times, both that portion dividing East and West Berlin and the inner-German border separating West Berlin from East Germany. In order to visit East Berlin, I merely showed up at the border crossing in the Friedrichstrasse train station, paid 5 DM (*deutsche mark*) for a visa, exchanged the obligatory 25 West Marks for 25 East Marks, and was on my way. Katharina, as a registered resident of West Berlin, had to apply for a visa ahead of time. That particular border crossing is now a museum, the *Tränenpalast* (Palace of Tears).

We were married in the St. Nikolai-Kirche in Spandau on July 7, 1990 (the day before Germany defeated Argentina in the final of the FIFA World Cup). Our first daughter, Hannah Barbe Johnson, a dual citizen of the United States and Germany, was born the following year. Helmut Barbe, Hannah's grandfather and a veteran of the Wehrmacht in the Second World War, came to visit us in DeKalb, Illinois, shortly after her birth. He said (my translation), "I think back to the war, when I had to shoot at the Americans and they had to shoot at me, and now I see this little girl, and I know that I have found peace in my time."

We have returned to Berlin many times in the intervening three decades. Berlin is not only Katharina's home (and Hannah moved there after finishing college), it is also my hobby—seemingly all my spare time and change are spent in the city. And herein lies the challenge for us: we have first-person experience of the material covered in this book. *Modern Germany*, however, is not a book about Berlin. We did not include an entry on the Berlin Airlift of 1948–1949, when 300 planes made 277,000 flights to Tempelhof Airport during the Russian blockade. Tempelhof is no longer an airport. The last flight departed from it October 31, 2008, and it is now a park where Berliners can spend Sunday afternoons. Rather, *Modern Germany* is about a nation nearly the size of the state of Montana with a population approaching 83 million. Germany has the world's fourth-largest economy in terms of nominal gross domestic product ($4 trillion) and is home to the world's largest automaker: the Volkswagen Group.

When writing and editing this book, we did so with the expectation that it would find a home in both school libraries and the reference shelves in college and university libraries. High school students can consult it for various social studies projects. Undergraduates will find it useful in their second-language acquisition courses. We hope our readers will want to visit Germany and consult this book before doing so. If *Modern Germany* is meaningful, we have accomplished our purpose.

ACKNOWLEDGMENTS

Modern Germany is the second project I have edited for ABC-CLIO (the first was *End of Days: An Encyclopedia of the Apocalypse in World Religions*, 2017). It has been our pleasure to work with Kaitlin Ciarmiello, Senior Acquisitions Editor at ABC-CLIO. Kaitlin offered us the contract to work on *Modern Germany* over two years ago and graciously provided us an extension when medical inconveniences on our part delayed the project. She responded to all our queries and assisted us with editorial questions and contract issues. We also owe our thanks to her unknown (by us) associates at ABC-CLIO who helped see this project to completion. It is our sincere hope that we can cross paths again and work on another project with Kaitlin and ABC-CLIO.

Modern Germany would not have been possible without the conscientious scholarship of our roster of contributors. Three people have contributed numerous entries to both of my projects for ABC-CLIO: Josianne Campbell, William Burns, William Kladky, and I look forward to working with them again. The editors want to thank three of our colleagues who contributed entire chapters to Modern Germany. Wayne Finley, associate professor and business librarian in the University Libraries, Northern Illinois University, wrote **Chapter 4: Economy**. James Lund, library director at Westminster Seminary, California, wrote **Chapter 5: Religion and Thought**.

Mr. Lund and I serve on the editorial board of the *Journal of Religious and Theological Information*, published by Taylor and Francis. Jessamine Cooke-Plagwitz, associate professor of German and director of undergraduate studies in the Department of World Languages and Cultures at Northern Illinois University, wrote **Chapter 11: Literature and Drama**. In addition to her very fine chapter, Professor Cooke-Plagwitz assisted with the headword list. It is with great pride that we thank our daughter, Hannah Barbe Johnson, for her contributions to *Modern Germany*. Hannah was living in Berlin when we started the project and moved to Copenhagen (where she was quarantined during the COVID-19 pandemic) when we were finishing the project. While residing in these two great European capitals, Hannah acted as our target audience and proofreader. We finished this project while under a stay-at-home order during the spring semester 2020. Our younger daughter, Aletta Barbe Johnson (also a dual citizen), kindly looked after us and suffered through hours of conversation regarding this project.

We would be remiss if we did not mention Fred Barnhart and Leanne VandeCreek from the administration of Founders Memorial Library at Northern Illinois University in these acknowledgments. They provided me with research leave and Katharina with a carrel in the library.

INTRODUCTION

Modern Germany is an economic and cultural powerhouse. The nation boasts the fourth-largest nominal GDP in the world and accounts for 28% of economic activity in the Euro zone. It is home to the Bayreuth Festival, dedicated to the works of the composer Richard Wagner, and the Oberammergau Passion, which has been performed every ten years since 1634. Germany is burdened with a complicated history, however. Both the Third Reich (1933–1945) and the postwar division of Germany are alive in the memory of the nation. No book bearing the title *Modern Germany* can go to press without accounting for these two periods. The terms "World War I" and "First World War" are used interchangeably, as are "World War II" and "Second World War." A note to researchers (and reference librarians): The Library of Congress subject headings for these two wars are *Great War, 1914–1918* and *Great War, 1939–1945,* respectively. Following the Second World War, the victorious powers (France, Great Britain, the Soviet Union, and the United States) divided Germany and its capital, Berlin, into four zones of occupation. The Soviet Union occupied the northeastern section of the country as well as the eastern portion of Berlin. In October 1949, the Soviet zone became the German Democratic Republic (GDR) or Die Deutsche Demokratische Republik (DDR), known colloquially as "East Germany." The rest of the country previously occupied by the Americans, British, and French became the Federal Republic of Germany (FRG) or Die Bundesrepublik Deutschland (BRD), often referred to as "West Germany" in May 1949. The eastern portion of Berlin ("East Berlin") became the capital of the GDR. The capital of the FRG was established in Bonn.

Excursus: From the Nazi seizure of power (*Machtergreifung*) to zero hour (*Stunde Null*) to reunification (*Wiedervereinigung*)

The Third Reich. The Third Reich refers to the National Socialist Regime (the Nazis) dating from Adolf Hitler's ascension to power as Chancellor on January 30, 1933 (*Machtergreifung*) until the Allied defeat of Germany in May 1945. Hitler saw his regime as the successor to two great German empires, the first marked by the coronation of Charlemagne as the Holy Roman Emperor in 800 CE and the second with the foundation of the Imperial German Empire in 1871. The First Reich existed in name only following the Peace of Westphalia in 1648 and was finally dissolved upon the abdication of the emperor Franz II in 1806. The Second Reich was ushered in by the foundation of the German Empire in 1871 and endured, albeit briefly, until

Germany's defeat in the First World War in 1918. The literature on the Third Reich is immense and continues to grow. A well-known standard on the period is William Shirer's *The Rise and Fall of the Third Reich*, first published in 1960. More contemporary works admirably frame the Third Reich, from Rüdiger Barth's *The Last Winter of the Weimar Republic: The Rise of the Third Reich* (2020) to Ian Kershaw's *The End: The Defiance and Destruction of Hitler's Germany, 1944–1945* (2011).

Stunde Null (literally "zero hour") refers to midnight, May 8, 1945, when the Second World War came to an end. The term implies a break with the nation's Nazi past and the desire for a new beginning. However, the specter of the Holocaust haunted Germany society. Over 300,000 Jews emigrated from Germany from the time that Hitler assumed power on January 30, 1933, and the start of World War II on September 1, 1939. By the time the Third Reich had been destroyed, over 6 million European Jews had been murdered. The tragedy of the Holocaust is not glossed over with euphemisms in Germany. It is against the law in Germany to deny the Holocaust (*Holocaustleugnung*). English historian David Irving was fined in Germany for stating that only 30,000 people died in Auschwitz between 1940 and 1945 and was banned from entering the country. The constitutional protection of free speech in Germany does not extend to Holocaust denials. In May 2018, the "Nazi Grandma" Ursula Haverbeck, age eighty-nine, began serving a two-year prison sentence for declaring on television that the Holocaust was a lie and that it had not been historically proven that Auschwitz was a death camp. Perhaps the best-known Holocaust denier from the United States is Arthur Butz, a faculty member in the Department of Electrical and Computer Engineering at Northwestern University in Evanston, Illinois.

Holocaust sites and memorials are scattered throughout Germany.

- Sachsenhausen, located thirty miles north of Berlin near Oranienburg, was built in 1936 and served as a model for future camps. Sachsenhausen was the administrative headquarters of all concentration camps and served as a training center for SS officers. The camp originally housed political prisoners, but soon included Jews, Jehovah's Witnesses, Roma, homosexuals, and other individuals deemed "asocial" by the Nazi regime. Approximately 200,000 detainees (including 11,000 Jews) were either incarcerated or transited through Sachsenhausen.
- Bergen-Belsen, located in northwest Germany, was originally built as a prison for prisoners of war and was converted into a concentration camp in 1943. The guards at Bergen-Belsen were notoriously brutal, and many prisoners starved to death. When Bergen-Belsen was liberated by the British army in 1945, it held nearly 80,000 prisoners. The British soldiers also discovered 35,000 corpses in the camp.
- Buchenwald, located south of Berlin near Weimar, was the largest concentration camp on German soil. Buchenwald was not an extermination camp (like Auschwitz in Poland), but a forced labor camp. However, the camp was the scene of gruesome medical experiments. Buchenwald was liberated by American troops in April 1945. At that time, the camp held 25,000 prisoners, 4,000 of whom were Jews.
- Dachau, located in a suburb of Munich, was the first concentration camp built in Germany. It was the scene of mass executions of Soviet and French prisoners of

war. Upon its liberation by the American Seventh Army, the American commanding officer ordered the residents of Dachau to march through the camp to witness the unspeakable inhumanity in its midst. Forty staff members of the camp were tried after the war, thirty-six of whom were sentenced to death.

- The Memorial to the Murdered Jews of Europe covers 19,000 square meters in the heart of Berlin. Architect Peter Eisenman placed 2711 concrete slabs of different heights throughout the memorial, creating an accessible spatial structure. An underground information center on the grounds contains documentation of the individuals killed in the Holocaust. Throughout Germany, *Stolpersteine* (stumbling stones) have been placed in the pavement outside of apartment houses; in Berlin, for example, there are more than 9,000. The *Stolpersteine* are brass plaques bearing the names, birthday, and day of death (if known) of previous tenants who were murdered in the Holocaust.

- The Nuremberg Palace of Justice was selected as the site for war crimes trials held initially November 20, 1945–October 1, 1946. The Allies were determined to hold the German civilian and military authorities responsible for the mass murder carried out in the areas of Europe occupied by Germany. The first set of trials involved twenty-two defendants. Twelve defendants were sentenced to death, ten of whom were hanged on October 16, 1949 (Martin Bormann was convicted *in absentia*, and Hermann Goering committed suicide shortly before his execution).

Wiedergutmachmachung refers to the reparations the West German government agreed to pay to the survivors of the Holocaust. Israel and the FRG signed the Reparations Agreement on September 10, 1952. The East German government initially refused to accept responsibility for the Holocaust and placed the blame on the West Germans. Finally, in 1990, following the fall of the Berlin Wall but before reunification, the GDR recognized that the entirety of the German people were responsible for the past, and it pledged to do everything in its power to combat anti-Semitism. By the time of reunification, the FRG had paid an estimated $37 billion in reparations to Israel and ca. 170,000 victims of the Nazis were receiving regular checks from the West German government.

Wiedervereinigung (reunification) of Germany took place officially on October 3, 1990, when a treaty between the governments of the Federal Republic of Germany and the German Democratic Republic went into effect. In hindsight, the GDR's fate was sealed on November 9, 1989, when an East German official, Günter Schabowski, announced that citizens were permitted to apply for permission to travel abroad. According to the treaty on reunification, the German Democratic Republic was absorbed by the Federal Republic of Germany and a unified Berlin named the capital of the reunited nation. United Germany became a fully sovereign nation on March 15, 1991.

As the former capital of the GDR, Berlin contains many relics of the Cold War that are now museums.

- Checkpoint Charlie was the name given by the Western Allies to the border crossing between East and West Berlin. The original building, featured in numerous movies and television shows, was removed from the border on June 22, 1990, and now resides in the Allied Museum in western Berlin.

- The Tränenpalast ("Palace of Tears") at the Friedrichstrasse station is the former border crossing for trains going between East and West Berlin. The border post had separate checkpoints for West Berliners, West Germans, other foreigners, and East Germans. The border crossing is called so because it was the scene for tearful good-byes between Westerners heading home and East Germans who were not permitted to leave the country.
- The former Stasi (Ministry for State Security) Headquarters and Prison are both located in East Berlin. The Stasi was one of the most hated and feared organizations in East Germany. One of its main tasks was spying on its citizens. The Stasi's Hohenschönhausen prison, portrayed in the opening scenes of the Oscar winning film *The Lives of Others*, was the site of physical and psychological torture.

The reunification of the two Germanies marked the end of the geographic and political division of the country. However, during the forty years that Germany was divided, social and economic divisions also arose. These divisions are reflected in entries devoted to the German Democratic Republic: "Erich Honecker" (Ch. 2), "Government and Politics in the German Democratic Republic" (Ch. 3), "Education in the German Democratic Republic" (Ch. 8); "Language Development in Divided Germany" (Ch. 9); "Literature of the German Democratic Republic" (Ch. 11), "Food and Drink in the German Democratic Republic" (Ch. 14), "Leisure and Sports in the German Democratic Republic" (Ch. 15), and "*Ostalgie*" (Ch. 16). In addition, many of the chapter overviews contain information on (the former) East Germany.

As our contributors point out, modern-day Germany is much more than the collected national experience of these two periods. Wayne Finley wrote the chapter on the German economy. Germany has the world's fourth-largest economy in terms of nominal gross domestic product. The country is the largest net contributor to the budget of the European Union. In 2018, Germany contributed €25.267 billion to the EU's coffers, and in turn, the EU spent €12.054 billion in Germany. *Modern Germany* includes an entry on the German automotive industry. Indeed, Germany is the home to numerous automobile companies: Daimler (Mercedes-Benz), Bavarian Motor Works (BMS), Volkswagen, and Audi. Other large companies include Deutsche Post DHL Group, the largest courier mail/logistics company in the world; BASF, the world's largest chemical producing company; Deutsche Telekom, parent company of T-Mobile, and others.

James Lund provided the chapter on Religion and Thought. Germany is the home of Martin Luther (born in Eisleben in 1483) and the Protestant Reformation (Wittenberg), and both are represented here. An influential figure of the time, and one not widely known to a general audience, is Philip Melanchthon (1497–1560), who is buried alongside Luther in All Saints' Church in Wittenberg. Given the scope of the project, *Modern Germany* contains only a single entry on a philosopher: a sidebar on Immanuel Kant (1724–1804).

Jessamine Cooke-Plagwitz wrote the extensive chapter on German Literature (Chapter 11). Germany has a proud literary tradition. Thirteen winners of the Nobel

Prize for Literature hail from the German-speaking world. The first German laureate (and second overall) was Theodor Mommsen in 1902. Mommsen taught in Berlin at the Friedrich-Wilhelms University, present-day Humboldt University. He spent thirty years researching and writing his three-volume *History of Rome*, which influenced German research for nearly a century. Other German Nobel Laureates familiar to American audiences include Thomas Mann (1929), Hermann Hesse (1946), Heinrich Böll (1972), and Günter Grass (1999).

Katharina Barbe wrote chapters 8–10 (Education, Language, and Etiquette) in their entirety, reflecting her experience as a *Schülerin/Studentin* in Berlin, her field of study at Rice University in Houston, Texas, and her daily life growing up in postwar West Berlin. Chapter 14 ("Food") was a collaborative effort . . . and the result of forty years of field work in Germany.

The bibliography cites English-language books available from most colleges and universities, which are on their shelves or available through interlibrary loan. German-language books and pertinent websites are listed at the end of the entries.

Academic works of all stripes often include a section "Further Research," or something to that effect. *Modern Germany* is no different. In the course of producing this manuscript, it became obvious that three individuals are in need of an authoritative, English-language biography. Konrad Duden (1829–1911) was a gymnasium (college preparatory) teacher who became a philologist. Duden developed the German dictionary that bears his name. The twenty-seventh edition, published in August 2017, contains twelve volumes. Erich Honecker (1912–1994) was the security secretary for the Socialist Unity Party in the GDR in 1961, and as such was the person in charge of the construction of the Berlin in August of that year. He served as leader of the Party from 1971 until he was removed in October 1989—three weeks before the fall of the Berlin Wall. Axel Springer (1912–1985) founded Springer SE, which publishes the tabloid *Bild*, Europe's largest-circulation newspaper, and *Die Welt*, an influential national daily.

Further Reading

Barth, Rüdiger, Hauke Friederichs, and Caroline Waight. *The Last Winter of the Weimar Republic: The Rise of the Third Reich*. New York: Pegasus Books, 2020.

Bartrop, Paul R., and Michael Dickerman. *The Holocaust: An Encyclopedia and Document Collection*. Santa Barbara, CA: ABC-CLIO, 2017.

Bromley, Joyce E. *German Reunification: Unfinished Business*. London; New York: Routledge, 2017.

Evans, Richard J. *Lying about Hitler: History, Holocaust, and the David Irving Trial*. New York: Basic Books, 2001.

Giles, Geoffrey J. *Stunde Null: The End and the Beginning Fifty Years Ago*. Washington, DC: German Historical Institute, 1997.

Goldman, Ari L. "Upheaval in the East: East Germany; East Germany Agrees to Pay Reparations to the Jewish Victims of the Nazis." *New York Times*, Section A, p. 10, February 9, 1990.

Heller, Kevin Jon. *The Nuremberg Military Tribunals and the Origins of International Criminal Law*. Oxford; New York: Oxford University Press, 2011.

Kershaw, Ian. *The End: The Defiance and Destruction of Hitler's Germany, 1944–1945.* New York: Penguin Group USA, 2012.

Manschreck, Clyde Leonard. *Melanchthon, the Quiet Reformer.* Westport, CT: Greenwood Press, 1975.

McManus, John C. *Hell Before Their Very Eyes: American Soldiers Liberate Concentration Camps in Germany, April 1945.* Baltimore: Johns Hopkins University Press, 2015.

Niven, Bill, and J. K. Thomaneck. *Dividing and Uniting Germany.* New York; Florence: Routledge, 2000.

Pötzl, Norbert F. *Erich Honecker: Eine deutsche Biographie.* Stuttgart: Deutsche Verlags-Anstalt, 2002.

Sharet, Yaʻakov. *The Reparations Controversy: The Jewish State and German Money in the Shadow of the Holocaust, 1951–1952.* Berlin; Boston: De Gruyter, 2011.

Stone, Dan. *The Liberation of the Camps: The End of the Holocaust and Its Aftermath.* New Haven, CT: Yale University Press, 2015.

Wistrich, Robert S. *Holocaust Denial: The Politics of Perfidy.* Berlin; Boston; Jerusalem: De Gruyter; The Hebrew University Magnes Press, 2012.

GERMANY

CHAPTER 1

GEOGRAPHY

OVERVIEW

Germany, the fourth-largest country in the European Union after France, Spain, and Sweden, has a surface area of 357,022 km^2 and a land area of 349,223 km^2. In comparison, the U.S. state of Montana is slightly larger than Germany with 380,832 km^2. Germany is the most densely populated country in Europe, with a population of 83.78 million (2020), or 240 persons per square kilometer. In comparison, Montana has 2.73 persons per square kilometer. With a total border of 3,757 km, Germany, in the middle of Europe, borders on nine countries: Denmark, Poland, Czech Republic, Austria, Switzerland, France, Luxembourg, Belgium, and the Netherlands. The country extends from the Baltic and North Seas in the north to the Alps in the south.

Politically, Germany is a federal state divided into sixteen states (*Länder*). They are Baden-Württemberg, Bayern (Bavaria), Berlin, Brandenburg, Bremen, Hamburg, Hessen (Hesse), Mecklenburg-Vorpommern (Mecklenburg-Western Pomerania), Niedersachsen (Lower Saxony), Nordrhein-Westfalen (North Rhine-Westphalia), Rheinland-Pfalz (Rhineland-Palatinate), Saarland, Sachsen (Saxony), Sachsen-Anhalt (Saxony-Anhalt), Schleswig-Holstein, and Thüringen (Thuringia).

Germany's physical features are astonishingly diverse and can be divided into four different topographical areas: the North German Lowland, the Central Uplands, the

---

GERMAN *LÄNDER*/STATES

The Federal Republic of Germany consists of sixteen semi-sovereign states. The cities of Berlin and Hamburg are called "city-states" (*Stadtstaaten*), as is the Free Hanseatic City of Bremen, which also includes the city of Bremerhaven. The other thirteen states are known as "area states" (*Flächenländer*). Prior to reunification in 1990, the western states of Baden-Württemberg, Bavaria, Bremen, Hamburg, Hesse, Lower Saxony, North Rhine-Westphalia, Rhineland-Palatinate, Schleswig-Holstein, and the Saarland formed West Germany, with Berlin having a special status. After reunification, the eastern *Länder* of Mecklenburg-Western Pomerania, Brandenburg, Saxony, Saxony-Anhalt, and Thuringia, dubbed the *neue Länder* or "new states," were incorporated into the Federal Republic of Germany, and Berlin became the new capital after Bonn.

Table 1.1

Land State	Capital	Size (km²/mi²)	Inhabitants (2018, in 1,000)
Baden-Württemberg (also Baden-Wuerttemberg)	Stuttgart	35,748/13,802	11,070
Bayern Bavaria	München Munich	70,542/27,236	13,077
Berlin	City-state	891/344	3,645
Brandenburg	Potsdam	29,654/11,449	2,512
Bremen	City-state	419/162	683
Hamburg	City-state	755/292	1,841
Hessen Hesse	Wiesbaden	21,116/8,153	6,266
Mecklenburg-Vorpommern Mecklenburg-Western Pomerania	Schwerin	23,295/8,994	1,610
Niedersachsen Lower Saxony	Hannover Hanover	47,710/18,421	7,982
Nordrhein-Westfalen North Rhine-Westphalia	Düsseldorf	34,112/13,171	17,933
Rheinland-Pfalz Rhineland-Palatinate	Mainz	19,846/7,663	4,085
Saarland	Saarbrücken	2,571/993	991
Sachsen Saxony	Dresden	18,450/7,124	4,078
Sachsen-Anhalt Saxony-Anhalt	Magdeburg	20,454/7,897	2,208
Schleswig-Holstein	Kiel	15,804/6,102	2,897
Thüringen Thuringia	Erfurt	16,202/6,256	2,143

Sources: https://de.statista.com/statistik/daten/studie/71085/umfrage/verteilung-der-einwohnerzahl
-nach-bundeslaendern/
https://de.statista.com/statistik/daten/studie/154868/umfrage/flaeche-der-deutschen-bundeslaender/

Alpine Foothills, and the southern Alpine area. The first three are approximately equal in size, with the Alpine area a sliver along the south German frontier with Austria and Switzerland.

Germany's coastline along the Baltic and North Seas extends for 2,389 km (1,484 mi). The East Frisian and North Frisian Islands are situated along the German North Sea coast. The three main North Frisian Island are Föhr, Amrum, and Sylt; the latter contains the northernmost point in Germany. There are several islets referred to as Halligen, which are marsh islands situated in the *Wattenmeer* (mud flats) that do not have a lot of protections and are, therefore, prone to floods. These islands extend from the German–Danish border southward. The East Frisian Islands from west to east are Wangerooge, Langeoog, Norderney, Juist, and Borkum; all are popular summer vacation destinations for German tourists. Helgoland (Heligoland) is the only German island at a distance from the mainland; it belonged to the United Kingdom until 1890, when it was transferred to Germany. The island is situated about 70 km from Bremerhaven and Cuxhaven and consists of a massive cliff on the northwest side and a low-lying sandy beach on the southeast side. Its size is 4.2 km² and its population of 1,300 is eclipsed when summer visitors swell the population. In 2016, 357,089 tourists visited the island, most of them for day visits as Helgoland is a duty-free zone; about 85,000 spent the night.

The Baltic Sea coast, which extends from the border with Denmark to the Polish frontier, also consists of a series of islands. From Fehmarn in the west to Usedom in the east, the chain of islands includes Rügen, the largest island with an area of 926 km². Rügen is the home to the Jasmund National Park, a World Heritage Site. The island is renowned for its chalk cliffs and beech tree forests. The North German Lowland is relatively flat, with rolling grasslands, heathlands, bogs, and forested areas.

The Lüneburger Heide (Lüneburg Heath) in Lower Saxony is Germany's oldest national park. At 169.2 meters, the Wilseder Berg (Mound) in the middle of the park is the highest elevation in the North German Lowland. Situated in south central Mecklenburg-Western Pomerania is the largest contiguous lake area in Germany. Canals link many of the lakes, including the Müritz See, which is Germany's largest lake that is entirely in Germany. While the Bodensee (Lake Constance) in southern Germany is larger than the Müritz See, it is only partially in Germany and also borders on Switzerland and Austria.

The Central German Uplands rise south of the North German Lowlands. The demarcation line between the two areas is an irregular arc that begins at the German Belgian border, bows to the north and follows the northern edge of the Harz Mountains, and continues to the southeast to the Polish–German frontier. The Porta Westfalica, the gate to Westphalia, which separates the northern lowlands from the central uplands, is the geographical midpoint of the east–west boundary. The forested hills are of moderate height, but in several instances reach 1,000 meters. The lower-lying areas are suitable for various types of agriculture such as grain, potatoes, and fruit. Rivers, such as the Rhine, Weser, and Elbe and their tributaries, traverse the valleys of the region.

Forests play an outsized role in Germany, not only as a part of the environment, but their importance is also reflected in German culture and the German mentality. Expressions like *ins Grüne gehen* (to go out into the green) or *Waldeinsamkeit* (forest solitude), and the Grimm brothers' fairy tales such as "Hänsel und Gretel" or "Rotkäppchen" (Little Red Riding Hood) attest to the importance of the forest. The Green movement also has its roots in the reverence of the forests. Almost one-third of Germany consists of forests, situated mostly in central and southern Germany. Sixty percent of the forests are coniferous, the remaining 40% deciduous.

The North German forests include Müritz, Ruppiner Heide, Grünewald, Havelland, Spreewald, and the Lüneburger Heide. The Spreewald is an area east of Berlin. It was settled by Sorbs in the sixth century, and Sorbian culture is still alive there. The area was formed during the last ice age, which resulted in a web of little rivers comprising 1,575 km of which 267 are navigable. Today the Spreewald is a popular tourist destination.

The middle German forests (Mittelgebirge) consist of the Erzgebirge, Thüringer Wald, Frankenwald, Fränkische Schweiz, Fichtelgebirge, Rhön, Spessart, Odenwald, Taunus, Sauerland, Eifel-Venn, Hunsrück, and Westerwald. Christmas decorations originate from the Erzgebirge. When mining could no longer sustain families, miners turned to woodcarving. The Christmas pyramid has its origin there; its design was based on the hoisting plant in the mining shafts. *Räuchermännchen* (incense smokers) and the iconic *Nussknacker* (nutcrackers) are also produced there.

The southern German forests include the Bayerischer Wald, Bayerische Alpen, Schwäbische Alb, and Schwarzwald. The Schwarzwald is actually not a black forest; it gets its name from the dense growth of spruce trees and the associated darkness in the woods. Already in Roman times it was called *silva nigra* (wood black), and in 868 CE it was first documented as Swarzwald. Today, deciduous trees are planted there, too, as the bark beetle has attacked the spruce trees, so the forest is now of many colors.

The rivers in Germany not only shape the landscape, but also play a significant economic and cultural role. Most rivers flow from south to north, emptying either in the North Sea or the Baltic Sea. The exception, the Danube, flows in a southeasterly direction. The main rivers in Germany are the Rhine (Rhein), Danube (Donau), Oder, Weser, and Elbe. Each of these rivers forms a river system, which consists of a network of tributaries that flow into the main branch of the river. The primary tributaries of the Rhine are the Neckar, Main, and Mosel rivers. The Main at 535 km (326 mi) is Germany's longest river entirely in Germany. The Rhine (865 km) empties into the North Sea in the Netherlands after leaving Germany. The Danube (647 km in Germany), which has its source in Donaueschingen, flows through ten European countries before it empties into the Black Sea 2,250 km (1,700 mi) from its source. Its largest tributaries are the Isar, Lech, Altmühl, and Naab as well as the Inn, which flows through Austria, Switzerland, and Germany.

The Weser is formed by the confluence of the Fulda and Werra rivers. It flows in a north-northwesterly direction and ultimately empties into the North Sea at Bremerhaven. The overall length of the Weser is 452 km (281 mi). With its Werra tributary it reaches a length of 744 km (462 mi), which makes it the longest river in Germany that empties into a sea. The Oder and its tributary the Neisse form the border between Germany and Poland, while the Elbe flows in a northwesterly direction ultimately flowing into the North Sea at Cuxhaven about 100 km beyond Hamburg. The Elbe, which has its source in the Czech Republic, flows 700 km in a northwesterly direction into the North Sea at Cuxhaven.

While the climate is rather moderate without extremes of cold and hot conditions, Germany has seen recent changes to its climate in the form of very hot and dry summers. The northwest and coastal areas are influenced by the North Sea and north Atlantic Gulf Stream resulting in moderate temperatures throughout the year.

Farther inland, Germany has a continental climate with warmer summers and colder winters. The alpine areas, as well as the highest mountains in the central uplands, have colder temperatures due to altitude.

Germany is home to a vast assortment of animal species originating from European habitats. Animals associated with the country include alpine ibex, badger, buzzard, chamois, deer, European hamster, fox, harbor seal, hare, hedgehog, heron, mallard, marmot, marten, mole, mouse, muskrat, mute swan, owl, pheasant, rabbit, rat, shrew, squirrel, stork, and wild boar. Some animals were introduced to Germany as pets and then escaped into nature; one example is the raccoon.

Compared to industrial production and service industries, agriculture is a very small part of the German economy. Less than 2% of GDP is attributed to agriculture. While over 80% of Germany's land area is used for agriculture and forestry, in the last half century, the number of farmers has decreased drastically, giving way to automation and the greater efficiency of larger enterprises. Chief agricultural products include milk, pork, beef, poultry, potatoes, wheat, barley, cabbage, and sugar beets. Beer and wine are two main agricultural export items. The European Union regulates agricultural production not only in Germany but throughout the EU member states. The objective is to provide high income for farmers while assuring low prices for consumers, which is done through subsidies.

John Stark

Further Reading

Federal Ministry of Food and Agriculture. *The Forests in Germany. Selected Results of the Third National Forest Survey.* Bonn: BMEL, 2015.

Käthe Wohlfahrt. "Traditionally Erzgebirge Items." https://kaethe-wohlfahrt.com/en/Christmas-World/Traditionally-Erzgebirge-Items/. Accessed July 11, 2020.

Murphy, Alexander B., Terry G. Jordan-Bychkov, and Bella Bychkova Jordan. *The European Culture Area: A Systematic Geography*, 6th ed. Lanham, MD: Rowman & Littlefield, 2014.

Statista. "Bevölkerung—Anzahl der Einwohner in den Bundesländern in Deutschland am 31. Dezember 2018." https://de.statista.com/statistik/daten/studie/71085/umfrage/verteilung-der-einwohnerzahl-nach-bundeslaendern/. Accessed July 11, 2020.

Wohlleben, Peter. *The Hidden Life of Trees: What They Feel, How They Communicate: Discoveries from a Secret World.* New York: Greystone Books, 2016.

Biosphere Reserves and National Parks

Biosphere Reserves

The United Nations Educational, Scientific, and Cultural Organization's (UNESCO) program called "The Man and the Biosphere Program" designates areas meant to preserve biodiversity and promote the sustainable use of the ecosystem. The seventeen biosphere reserves in Germany measure 1,994,276 hectares

Table 1.2: GERMAN BIOSPHERE RESERVES

Name	Bundesland	Area in ha	Recognized since
Flußlandschaft Elbe	Brandenburg Mecklenburg-Vorpommern Niedersachsen Schleswig-Holstein Sachsen-Anhalt	282,250	1997
Rhön	Bayern Hessen Thüringen	243,323	1991
Schleswig-Holstein Wattenmeer und Halligen	Schleswig-Holstein	443,100	1990
Hamburgisches Wattenmeer	Hamburg	11,700	1992
Niedersächsisches Wattenmeer	Niedersachsen	24,000	1993
Südost-Rügen	Mecklenburg-Vorpommern	22,800	1991
Schaalsee	Mecklenburg-Vorpommern	31,000	2000
Schorfheide Chorin	Brandenburg	129,160	1990
Spreewald	Brandenburg	47,509	1991
Karstlandschaft Südharz	Sachsen-Anhalt	30,034	2009
Oberlausitzer Heide- und Teichlandschaft	Sachsen	30,102	1996
Thüringer Wald	Thüringen	33,672	1997
Bliesgau	Saarland	36,152	2009
Pfälzerwald-Nordvogesen	Rheinland-Pfalz	180,969	1992
Schwäbische Alb	Baden-Württemberg	85,269	2009
Schwarzwald	Baden-Württemberg	63,236	2017
Berchtesgardener Land	Bayern	84,000	1990

(19,942.76 km^2/7,701.8 mi^2), which, excluding the vast North Sea and Baltic marine and mudflat areas, represents 3.7% of German territory. The Schleswig-Holstein Wadden Sea and Halligen Biosphere Reserve is the largest in the country. This particular reserve, parts of which also lie in Denmark and the Netherlands, plays a vital role in the livelihoods of the local population, combining tourism, fishing, and agriculture. A trilateral commission of the three nations, the SEM (Socio-Economic Monitoring) Wadden Sea, was established to identify avenues for further economic development and find new approaches for conflict resolution between environmental and business concerns. The Wadden Sea project is an environmental hybrid, claiming designation as a bioreserve by UNESCO and protection as a German national park. The Wadden Sea reserve includes enclaves in Hamburg, Lower Saxony, and Schleswig-Holstein.

National Parks

Germany has sixteen national parks. The Black Forest National Park (established in 2014) is one of the best-known locales in Germany. The national park is located between Baden-Baden and Freudenstadt and covers an area of approximately 10,000 hectares. It is the home of the world's fastest bird, the peregrine falcon, and Europe's smallest owl, the pygmy owl. Trees that normally survive only one-third of their natural life span in managed forests can survive for several hundred years in the Black Forest National Park. The Jasmund National Park located in Mecklenburg-Western Pomerania is Germany's smallest national park. Its chalk cliffs (on the island of Rügen) provided the backdrop to *Chalk Cliffs of Rügen* by Caspar David Friedrich (1774–1840), perhaps the most famous painting of German Romanticism. In addition to the Wadden Sea enclaves, other national parks include, for example, the Bayerischer Wald (Bavarian Forest) and Berchtesgarden (an alpine retreat on the Austrian border that also served as Adolf Hitler's vacation home). Germany also contains 98 "nature parks," established by Federal Nature Conservation Act, which comprise approximately 25% of the nation's territory. The act strengthens protections of wild living species of flora (such as ferns and wildflowers) and fauna (e.g., beetles and birds) within the designated areas, like the Arnberg Forest in North Rhine-Westphalia or the Mecklenburg Elbe Valley in Mecklenburg-Vorpommern.

Wendell G. Johnson

See also: Chapter 1: Overview; Bodies of Water; Climate Policy and Recycling. Chapter 2: Hitler, Adolf (1889–1945). Chapter 3: Overview; Regional Government/ Federalism. Chapter 4: Agriculture. Chapter 12: Artists.

Further Reading

Deutsche Nationalparks. "Information zu den Nationalparks in Deutschland." http://deutsche-nationalparks.com/. Accessed July 11, 2020.

Federal Agency for Nature Conservation (BfN—Bundesschutz für Natur). "Biosphere Reserves." https://www.bfn.de/en/activities/protected-areas/biosphere-reserves.html. Accessed July 11, 2020.

Full of Life: UNESCO Biosphere Reserves, Model Regions for Sustainable Development. Berlin; New York: Springer, 2003.

Robbins, Paul. *Encyclopedia of Environment and Society*. Thousand Oaks, CA: Sage Publications, 2007.

Rosing, Norbert, Sarah Fuchs, and Klaus Nigge. *Deutsche Nationalparks*, 1st ed. Steinfurt, Germany: Tecklenborg, 1997.

Bodies of Water

Sea Coast

Germany has 1,484 miles of coastline along the North (Nordsee) and Baltic Seas (known as the East Sea or Ostsee in German). Hamburg, situated 75 miles from the open sea at the head of the Elbe estuary, is Germany's largest port. Kiel, home port of the German naval yards, and Lübeck are the busiest German ports—by tonnage—on the Baltic Sea. Other noteworthy ports include Rostock and the World Heritage Sites of Stralsund and Wismar. The Kiel Canal extends eastward for 61 miles from Brunsbüttelkoog at the mouth of the Elbe to the Kiel Harbor on the Baltic. The canal was originally constructed (between 1887 and 1895) to provide the German military with a shortcut between the two seas, thus eliminating the need to sail around the Danish Peninsula. Today, the Kiel Canal provides the shortest shipping route between the North and Baltic Seas.

Rivers

Three great rivers of Germany, the Rhine, Danube, and Elbe, dominate the nation's waterways and are connected by a series of canals in the north (including the Kiel Canal) and by the Rhine-Main-Danube Canal in the south. The Rhine (Rhein) River, ca. 820 miles in length, flows from the Swiss Alps to the North Sea. Humans have inhabited the Rhine-Meuse delta for at least 200,000 years. Cologne is the largest city on the Rhine, and in modern times the river has been considered a symbol of the German nation. The Danube (Donau) River, ca. 1,770 miles in length, is the second-longest river in Europe. It is the only major European river that flows from west to east (from the Black Forest in southwest Germany to the Black Sea). The Elbe River, 725 miles long, flows through Dresden and Wittenberg before emptying into the North Sea.

Lakes

Thousands of lakes dot the German landscape. The state of Brandenburg alone has 3,000 lakes and 30,000 kilometers of waterways, forming the largest inland water system in Europe. The Bodensee (or Lake Constance), a popular vacation destination, with a total area of 207 square miles, is the third-largest lake in Central and Western Europe, after Lakes Geneva (Lac de Genève in Switzerland) and Balaton (Hungary). Located at the northern foot of the Alps, its shoreline lies in the German *Länder* of Bavaria and Baden-Württemberg as well as along the Austrian and Swiss borders. Prehistoric lakeside dwellings have been discovered along its shores. With 45 square miles, Lake Muritz (Müritzsee) is the largest inland lake located entirely in Germany. The lake in the former German Democratic Republic provides breeding grounds for rare and endangered birds such as white-tailed eagles, ospreys, and cranes. Chiemsee is the largest lake in Bavaria (40 square miles). In 1873, King Ludwig of Bavaria (1845–1886) purchased the largest of the lake's three islands, the Herreninsel, in order to build Schloss Herrenchiemsee, modeled after the palace in Versailles.

Wendell G. Johnson

See also: Chapter 1: Cities; Transportation. Chapter 3: Armed Forces. Chapter 4: Trade.

Further Reading

Bristow, Philip. *Through the German Waterways*, new rev ed. London: Nautical Books, 1988.

Germany Waterways Map. https://www.eurocanals.com/Waterways/germanywaterways .html. Accessed July 11, 2020.

Gresswell, R. Kay, and Anthony Julian Huxley. *Standard Encyclopedia of the World's Rivers and Lakes*. New York: Putnam, 1966.

Miller, Gary. *The Rhine: Europe's River Highway*. New York: Crabtree Pub. Company, 2010.

Penn, James R. *Rivers of the World: A Social, Geographical, and Environmental Sourcebook*. Santa Barbara, CA: ABC-CLIO, 2001.

Cities

Germany has four cities with a population of at least 1 million inhabitants: Berlin, Hamburg, Munich (München), and Cologne (Köln). Berlin (3.8 million), corresponding with the state (*Land*) of Berlin and located on the Spree and Havel Rivers, is both Germany's largest city and since 1990 again its capital. After the Second World War, Berlin was divided into four zones of occupations. The British, French, and American sectors (186 square miles) became West Berlin, and the Soviet sector (155 square miles) in the east was known as Berlin, Capital of the German Democratic Republic. During the Cold War, Berlin was a divided city. West Berlin was completely surrounded by the Wall and cut off from the Federal Republic of Germany (FRG). Bonn (population 318,000) was capital of the FRG. The Wall finally fell in a peaceful revolution on November 9, 1989, a date that changed European history.

The other three large cities are found in western Germany. Hamburg (population ca. 1,800,000), officially the Free and Hanseatic City of Hamburg, is, like Berlin, a city and a state (*Land*). The city was nearly destroyed during the Second World War. Operation Gomorrah, a firebombing carried out by the British Royal Air Force, resulted in over 40,000 civilian deaths. Hamburg is located near the mouth of the Elbe River on the North Sea. It is Germany's largest port and handles approximately half of the nation's foreign trade. *Die Zeit* and *Der Spiegel,* two internationally influential periodicals, have their main editorial offices there. Hamburg is also the home of the Reeperbahn, a street in Hamburg's St. Pauli district, which teems with nightlife of all kinds, including a red-light district. In the 1960s, the Beatles performed there in clubs, and Hamburg now boasts a Beatles Platz (place) and claims to be the birthplace of the Beatles' career.

Munich (population ca. 1,500,000), the capital of Bavaria, is located on the Isar River near the Bavarian Alps. The city boasts a robust business climate, with BMW (**B**ayerische **M**otorenwerke—Bavarian Motor Works) as its largest employer with 34,500 employees. Other large employers include Siemens, an industrial manufacturing company, and Allianz, an insurance company, with 9,000 and 8,500 employees respectively. Munich is the home of Oktoberfest, which takes place annually from the third Saturday in September through the first Sunday in October, canceled for 2020 and 2021 due to the pandemic. The festival is held on the Theresienwiese fairground under huge tents that can seat several thousand revelers. Tourist attractions in central Munich include the Marienplatz, where the town hall features a glockenspiel show, and the Hofbräuhaus, the self-claimed most famous beer hall in the world. Just outside of Munich, tourists can visit Neuschwanstein Castle, the inspiration for Walt Disney's Magic Kingdom, and the Dachau concentration camp, liberated by American troops on April 29, 1945.

Cologne, with a population of ca. 1,100,000, is the largest city in the *Land* of North Rhine-Westphalia. Thirty-six percent of the population are migrants. The city's commercial importance arose as a result of its location: it lies along the Rhine River, where it intersects one of the major trade routes between western and eastern Europe. Cologne is the European headquarters of the Ford Motor Company and the home of the eponymous Eau de Cologne or Köllnisch Wasser. The Cologne Cathedral, a UNESCO World Heritage site, is the largest Gothic church in Europe. Located nearby is the Roman-Germanic Museum, which displays the city's archaeological heritage.

Two cities in Germany share the name "Frankfurt." In the west, Frankfurt (Main) (nicknamed "Bankfurt") is considered the financial capital of Germany, and as such the home of the European Central Bank and the Deutsche Bank (DB). The DB holds assets greater than the annual budget of the German government. Frankfurt's train station is Germany's busiest with a daily volume of about 350,000 travelers and commuters. The city's airport, Flughafen Frankfurt am Main, served as the gateway for air travel in and out of West Berlin when that city was divided and remains Lufthansa's primary hub. In the east, Frankfurt (Oder) lies on the Polish border, roughly 50 miles from Berlin. Since reunification, Frankfurt (Oder) has experienced high unemployment and sluggish economic growth.

Several smaller yet notable cities can be found in the former German Democratic Republic. Like Hamburg, Dresden was firebombed during the Second World War (the background to Kurt Vonnegut's novel *Slaughterhouse Five*) and largely destroyed. The Baroque Quarter of Dresden contains numerous architectural gems, such as the rebuilt Frauenkirche (reduced to rubble by the firebombing), the Zwinger Museums (housing paintings by Titian, Rembrandt, and Vermeer as well as a famous collection of Meissen porcelain), and the Royal Palace. Leipzig is closely associated with Baroque music. It was here that Johann Sebastian Bach composed many of his cantatas and motets while employed as the cantor in the Thomaskirche, where he is buried. The Leipzig Bach Museum is located across the street from the church. The world-renowned Gewandhaus Orchestra also hails from Leipzig. The period of German history following the First World War up until the Nazi seizure of power is known as the Weimar Republic because it was here that the nation's constitution was drafted. Weimar was a center of art and literature. Walter Gropius founded Bauhaus in Weimar, and both Goethe and Schiller are buried in the city.

Lutherstadt (Luther city) refers to a city where the Reformer Martin Luther either visited or his teaching played a significant role. Luther cities are scattered throughout Germany. According to legend, Luther posted his *Ninety-Five Theses* on the door of All Saints' Church (where he is buried) in Wittenberg in 1517. The Union of Luther Cities is comprised of sixteen towns, including Augsburg, Eisenach, Eisleben (where Luther was born and died), Erfurt, and Torgau, where Soviet and American troops met for the first time in Germany on April 25, 1945.

Wendell G. Johnson

See also: Chapter 1: Overview; Bodies of Water; Transportation. Chapter 2: Overview; Berlin Wall. Chapter 4: Banking; Frankfurt Stock Exchange; German Automobile Industry; Manufacturing; Trade. Chapter 5: Holocaust; Luther, Martin (1483–1546); The Reformation. Chapter 11: Overview; Romanticism (*Romantik*) (1788–1835); Weimar Classicism (*Weimarer Klassik*) (ca. 1772–1805). Chapter 12: Overview; Architecture; Museums. Chapter 13: Overview; Musical Periods and Composers; Orchestras. Chapter 14: Beer; Oktoberfest. Chapter 16: Overview; Springer, Axel (1912–1985).

Further Reading

Gaab, Jeffrey S. *Munich: Hofbräuhaus & History: Beer, Culture, & Politics.* New York: Peter Lang, 2006.

Kater, Michael H. *Weimar: From Enlightenment to the Present.* New Haven, CT: Yale University Press, 2014.

Large, David Clay. *Berlin.* New York: Basic Books, 2000.

Steves, Rick. *Best of Germany.* Berkeley, CA: Avalon Travel, 2018.

Climate Policy and Recycling

Climate Policy

Germany's Basic Law (the Grundgesetz) stresses the importance of environmental protection for the country. The Federal Ministry for the Environment, Nature Conservation and Nuclear Safety is tasked with enforcing Germany's climate policy. Its "Integrated Energy and Climate Programme of 2007" set targets for reducing greenhouse gas emissions, expanding renewable resources, and increasing energy efficiency. Germany is a signatory to the Kyoto Protocol (1997), an international treaty that commits nations to reduce greenhouse gas emissions. By 2020, Germany pledged to reduce emissions by 40% when compared to 1990 levels and 80–95% by 2050. In 2012, the share of renewable energy consumption in Germany from electricity, heat, and fuels was 12.7%. By 2050, the German government intends that 60% of the nation's energy needs derive from renewable resources. Germany also seeks to increase energy efficiency, which in addition to its positive impact on the environment, will cut both energy costs and imports.

Germany is also a signatory to the Paris Climate Agreement (2015), which seeks to curb global warming (the United States started to withdraw from the accord in 2017, but joined again in 2021). According to a survey on public attitudes toward climate change in European countries conducted by the National Centre for Social Research, 44% of Germans are either "very" or "extremely" worried about global warming, which constitutes the highest percentage in Europe. Germany has adopted many strategies to deal with global warming. In 2011, seventeen nuclear power plants were online; all of these are slated to close by 2022. An update to the Renewable Energy Act of 2014 gives preference to renewables on the nation's energy grid. Germany also levies an "eco-tax" on fossil fuels, which currently runs at €0.65 per liter.

Recycling

Germany produces 412 million tons of garbage annually (roughly 455 kg domestic waste and 187 kg bulky waste per inhabitant) and recycles approximately 70% of its waste (the comparable figure is 30% for the United States). One reason for this relatively high rate of recycling is the "polluter pays" principle mandated by the Packaging Ordinance of 1991. Manufacturers and retailers in Germany pay to have a "Green Dot" (*Grüner Punkt*) placed on their products. The more packaging on the product, the higher the fee (and more expensive the product). The Green Dot system has led to

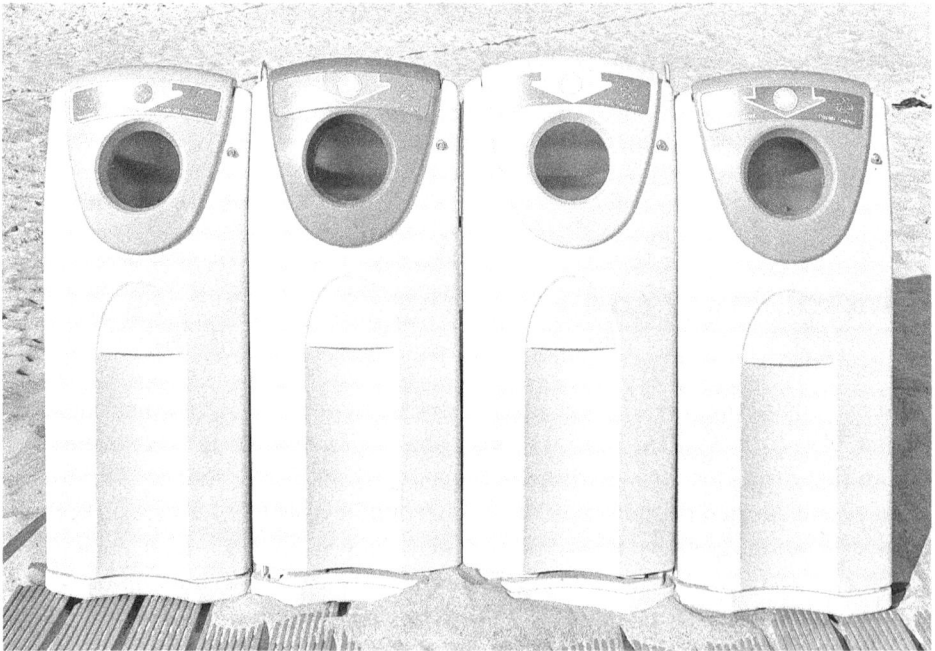

Germany recycles approximately 70% of its waste, with separate receptacles here for clear glass, colored glass, plastic, and paper. (DRpics24/Dreamstime.com)

less paper, thinner glass, and less metal being used in the packaging of goods. It is not unusual to find six different recycling bins outside of German residences: for Green Point packaging, paper, bio waste (compost), and separate receptacles for green, white, and brown glass. Many bottles and cans in Germany are sold with a redeemable deposit (*Pfand*) between €0.08 and €0.25. Retailers are obligated to refund the deposit regardless of where it was purchased. In many large shopping areas, the refund is automated: the customer returns the bottle or can to the designated automat and in return receives a receipt that can be redeemed.

Wendell G. Johnson

See also: Chapter 3: Overview; Constitutions; Political Parties; Tax Policy. Chapter 4: Energy. Chapter 10: Shopping. Chapter 14: Overview; Food Laws in Germany.

Further Reading

Federal Ministry for the Environment, Nature Conservation and Nuclear Safety. "German Climate Policy." https://www. https://www.bmu.de/en/topics/climate-adaptation/climate-protection/national-climate-policy/. Accessed June 16, 2020.

Federal Ministry for the Environment, Nature Conservation and Nuclear Safety. "Key Elements of an Integrated Energy and Climate Programme." https://www.bmu.de/fileadmin/bmu-import/files/english/pdf/application/pdf/klimapaket_aug2007_en.pdf. Accessed June 16, 2020.

How to Germany. "All About Recycling in Germany." https://www.howtogermany.com/pages/recycling.html. Accessed June 16, 2020.

"Ten Things Germany Is Doing for the Environment." https://www.deutschland.de/en/topic/environment/10-things-germany-is-doing-for-the-environment. Accessed June 16, 2020.

Timperley, Jocelyn. "People Living in Germany Are the Most Worried about Climate Change, According to a New Analysis of 18 Countries Published This Week." https://www.carbonbrief.org/germans-worried-climate-change-analysis-shows. Accessed June 16, 2020.

Demographics

Unlike the United States, Germany does not conduct a regular census of its population. The last survey of Germany's population (in 2011) was not a national census but was carried out by the European Union. At that time, Germany's population was 80,291,695. Official estimates in 2016 were 82,521,653. The most populous city in Germany is Berlin (ca. 3.86 million), and the nation's largest metropolitan region is the Rhine-Ruhr area (ca. 10 million).

Across the nation, life expectancy is highest in the *Land* of Baden-Württemberg (83.96 years for women; 79.54 for men) and lowest in Thuringia (83.02 year for women; 77.24 for men). Approximately 17.7 million people in Germany are aged sixty-five or over, accounting for 21.4% of the population. The number of senior citizens has increased by 36.6% in the past twenty years. Germany's population is aging. By the year 2060, the nation's population is expected to fall to 68–73 million people. The implications for Germany's workforce (and by extension its economy) are sobering. At present, 60% of Germans are between the ages of twenty and sixty-four, and this figure is expected to drop to 50% by 2060.

Germany has a highly educated workforce. Eighty-six percent of Germans aged twenty-five to sixty-four have attained an upper secondary education. Given present trends, this figure is expected to rise to 95% for German youth (one of the highest rates in the world). Germany has been more successful than most countries in battling unemployment during the recent financial crisis. It is one of the few countries where the unemployment rate (3.3% in December 2018) has actually declined across all educational levels. However, due to COVID-19, it has risen to over 6% as of June 2020 and fallen to 4.5% in March 2021.

The average adjusted disposable per capita income in Germany is $33,652 (compared to the OECD average of $30,563). A considerable gap exists between the richest and poorest Germans: the top 20% of the population earn at least four times as much as the bottom 20%.

Eighty percent of the population in Germany are ethnic Germans. Four groups are considered national minorities: Sorbs, Danes, Frisians, and Roma. With about 4 million, Turks are the largest ethnic minority. Other minority groups include Poles (1.7% of the population), Russians (1.5%), and Afro-Germans (1%). Recently, about 600,000 Syrian refugees have settled in the country.

Forty-seven million Germans identify as Christians. Catholics outnumber Protestants 24 million to 23 million, a surprising statistic, perhaps, given that the Protestant Reformation took root on German soil. Fully one-third of Germans claim no religious affiliation, and a majority of East Germans claim to be atheist. The German population also includes 4–5 million Muslims and approximately 200,000 Jews.

Wendell G. Johnson

See also: Chapter 1: Cities. Chapter 4: Guest Workers; Gross Domestic Product (GDP). Chapter 5: Overview; The Reformation. Chapter 6: The Grey Culture; Immigration; Refugees; Roma and Sinti; Turks in Germany.

Further Reading

Coulmas, Florian, and Ralph Lützeler. *Imploding Populations in Japan and Germany: A Comparison.* Leiden, Netherlands: Brill, 2011.

DeStatis (Statistisches Bundesamt). "Society and Environment: Population." https://www.destatis.de/EN/FactsFigures/SocietyState/Population/Population.html. Accessed June 18, 2020.

The Europa World Yearbook. London: Europa Publications, 1989.

Kibele, Eva U. B. *Regional Mortality Differences in Germany.* Dordrecht, Netherlands; New York: Springer, 2012.

Mountain Ranges

Three significant mountain ranges dot the German landscape: The Alps (in Bavaria), Harz (Lower Saxony), and Ore (Lower Saxony, Erzgebirge) Mountains. The Alps are Europe's most extensive mountain range, extending 1,200 miles from Nice, France, across southern Germany to Vienna, Austria. Six countries share the Alps: Germany, Austria, Slovenia, Liechtenstein, Switzerland, and France. The tallest peak in Germany, the Zugspitze (elevation 9,718 ft.), is in the Wetterstein Mountains, a group of mountains in the Eastern Alps. The three main Alpine subgroups in Germany are the Bavarian, Allgäu, and Berchtesgaden Alps. In the broad sense, "Bavarian Alps" refers to the mountains between the Lech and Saalach Rivers. The Bavarian Alps are also the home of Schloss Neuschwanstein, the inspiration for the castle at Walt Disney's Magic Kingdom, the biggest tourist destination in the German Alps (attracting 1.4 million visitors each year). The Berchtesgaden Alps feature the Eagle's Nest, a mountain retreat built by the Nazi party to host social gatherings and business meetings; legend has it that the Eagle's Nest was built as a fiftieth-birthday present to Adolf Hitler. The Alps are known as "the playground of Europe," and the twentieth century gave rise to a proliferation of mountain railways, ski resorts, and so on. The continued

The Titan RT suspension bridge is the longest suspended walking bridge in the world, extending over 1,500 feet. It was opened in 2017 and affords those who cross it beautiful views of the Harz Mountains. (Joppi/Dreamstime.com)

development of the tourist industry in the Alps has led to economic and social change in the Alpine region.

Until unification in 1990, the Inner German border (between the Federal Republic of Germany and the German Democratic Republic) ran through the Harz. The Harz Mountains have long been associated with German legends, including Goethe's *Faust*. Well-known tourist destinations in the Harz include the Harz National Park and the towns of Quedlinburg (a World Heritage Site) and Wernigerode. The highest peak is the Brocken or Blocksberg (1,141 m). It is said to be a meeting point for all witches, and the Walpurgisnacht is still celebrated there yearly on April 30–May 1, observing the start of summer and also the meeting of witches. Legends and stories abound. "Bibi Blocksberg," for example, is a children's story about a little girl who is also a witch. It started as an audio drama and has now expanded into movies and TV Shows.

The Ore Mountains (Erzgebirge) straddle the border between Germany and the Czech Republic. Geographically, the Ore Mountains played a prominent role in the Bronze Age (ca. 3200 BCE to 500 CE), contributing to the development of early mining technologies and metallurgy. By the time of the Industrial Revolution, the importance of mining had declined in the region and manufacturing developed in its place. Artisans started to carve wood in the seventeenth century and still sell Christmas pyramids (patterned after the ore shafts), nutcrackers, and incense smokers.

Wendell G. Johnson

See also: Chapter 1: Overview; Biosphere Reserves and National Parks. Chapter 2: Hitler, Adolf (1889–1945).

Further Reading

Huxley, Anthony Julian. *Standard Encyclopedia of the World's Mountains*. New York: Putnam, 1962.

Richins, Harold, and John Hull. *Mountain Tourism: Experiences, Communities, Environments and Sustainable Futures*. Oxfordshire, UK: CABI, 2016.

Transportation

Germany possesses a diverse and highly developed transportation infrastructure. The German highway system, known as the *Autobahn*, is ca. 8,000 miles long. The *Autobahn* has no federally mandated speed limit, although an advisory limit of 130 kilometers per hour (81 mph) is posted on over half of it. The construction and maintenance standards of German highways far exceed those of their American counterparts (the *Autobahn* is constructed with multiple layers of concrete). Further, rusted-out cars are not permitted on German roads: cars in Germany are required to undergo regular and thorough inspections to ensure their safety, the dreaded so-called TÜV (Technischer Überwachungsverein or Technical Inspection Association). In the United States, inspections are handled at the state level.

Rail traffic in Germany is predominantly operated by the Deutsche Bahn (German Railway, abbreviated DB in German), a joint venture between private investors and the federal government. With over 2 billion passengers yearly, the Deutsche Bahn is the largest railway operator in Europe and the largest railway company in Europe by revenue. The 5,400 railway stations in Germany are divided into seven categories. Category 1 stations, located in large cities, are considered traffic hubs, and often have a shopping mall inside the terminal. Germany's four largest cities, Berlin, Hamburg, Munich, and Cologne, each have more than one Category 1 station. Category 2 stations connect to airports and are stops for InterCity (IC) and EuroCity (EC) trains. At the other end of the spectrum, Category 7 stations are generally located in rural areas and often have only one platform.

Public mass transportation in Germany's larger cities is served by four interconnected systems: subway (U-Bahn), suburban express train (S-Bahn), trolley (Strassenbahn), and bus (Bus). Most public transportation in Germany is operated on a regional level, so a ticket for one means of public transportation is also valid for the others. In Berlin, for example, a ticket for the subway can also be used to transfer to a Bus, S-Bahn, or Strassenbahn for use within a two-hour window. Passengers can buy tickets for a single journey (*Einzelfahrkarte*) or passes valid for 24 hours (*Tageskarte*), a week (*Wochenkarte*), a month (*Monatskarte*), or a year (*Jahreskarte*). Each city has its own unique ticketing system, and tourists are often seen puzzling over the intricate system in Munich. Using public transportation without a ticket results in hefty fines. So-called *Schwarzfahrer* (people riding without a ticket) can be caught through regular controls. In 2017, the BVG (Berliner Verkehrsbetriebe) ticketed nearly half a million *Schwarzfahrer*, each of whom paid a fine of €60. Pepe Danquart's 1992 short film *Der Schwarzfahrer*, dealing with daily racism, won an Oscar for best short subject.

Germany is also known as a land of bicycles. Many German roads have bicycle lanes as part of their sidewalks (and not part of the streets). The country has ca. 70,000 km (43,496 mi) of bicycle paths, including 200 long-distance routes. Münster in North Rhine-Westphalia can be considered the bicycle capital of Germany; it has twice as many bicycles (500,000) as inhabitants (250,000), and each day 100,000 people travel via bicycle. In Freiburg, bicycles outnumber cars. Each day, 10,000 two-wheeled commuters pass over its Blaue Brücke (Blue Bridge), creating bottlenecks.

Germany is a partner in Airbus SE, the European aerospace agency. Frankfurt am Main Flughafen, Germany's busiest airport, serves over 60 million passengers a year, which also makes it the fourth busiest in Europe, and the twelfth busiest worldwide. Frankfurt is the central hub for Lufthansa, Germany's largest airline. When combined with its subsidiaries, it is the largest airline in Europe in terms of both fleet size and passenger load. During the Cold War, Berlin was served by Tegel (closed in 2020) and Tempelhof Airports (closed in 2008) in West Berlin and Schönefeld in East Berlin, neither of which are able to meet the demands of contemporary air travel in the unified capital. City (Berlin), state (Brandenburg), and federal (Federal Republic) authorities planned a modern airport located adjacent to Schönefeld. The ground breaking for the new airport, Berlin Brandenburg Willy Brandt (BER), took place in 2006 with the understanding that Tegel and Schönefeld would close when it opened. The grand opening of BER, originally scheduled for 2012, had to be postponed due to construction failures; not only were 90,000 meters of cable installed incorrectly, but the escalators were also too short, flight paths were incorrectly calculated, and so on. The project's original budget of €2 billion is now expected to soar to at least €7.5 billion. Berlin Brandenburg airport finally opened October 31, 2020. Willy Brandt's family, embarrassed by this fiasco, has requested that his name be removed from the project.

Wendell G. Johnson

See also: Chapter 1: Cities. Chapter 3: *Die Wende.*

Further Reading

BBC. "Whatever Happened to Berlin's Deserted 'Ghost' Airport?" http://www.bbc.com /capital/story/20181030-what-happened-to-berlins-ghost-airport. Accessed February 16, 2019.

Brown, Aaron. "8 Reasons That Germany's Autobahn Is So Much Better than US Highways." *Business Insider.* https://www.businessinsider.com/germanys-autobahn-vs -us-highways-compared-2016-3. Accessed February 18, 2019.

The German Way and More. "Public Transport in Germany." https://www.german-way .com/travel-and-tourism/public-transport-in-germany/. Accessed February 18, 2019.

Hackelsberger, Christoph. *U-Bahn-Architektur in München/Subway Architecture in Munich.* Munich; New York: Prestel, 1997.

Horn, Roland, Klaus Grewe, and Bernd Timmers. *Der Ingenieurbahnhof: Der Bau Des Neuen Berliner Hauptbahnhofs/A Feat of Engineering: Constructing the New Berlin Central Station.* Wiesbaden, Germany: Nelte, 2005.

Merrill, Samuel. *Networked Remembrance: Excavating Buried Memories in the Railways Beneath London and Berlin.* Oxford, UK; Berlin: Peter Lang, 2017.

Newhouse, John. *Boeing versus Airbus: The Inside Story of the Greatest International Competition in Business.* New York: Vintage, 2008.

Zeller, Thomas. *Driving Germany: The Landscape of the German Autobahn, 1930–1970.* New York; Oxford, UK: Berghahn Books, 2007.

CHAPTER 2

HISTORY

OVERVIEW

Germania was the Roman term for the geographical area extending from the Danube River in the south to the Baltic Sea in the north, and from the Rhine River in the west to the Vistula River in the east. Julius Caesar was the first to describe the inhabitants of this area as the *Germani*. Human ancestors were present in what is now modern-day Germany at least 500,000 years ago. Neanderthals, named after fossils discovered in the Neander Valley near Düsseldorf, inhabited Germany over 40,000 years ago. A figurine created from mammoth ivory between 40,000 and 35,000 BCE was found in 2008 in Schelklingen in Germany. This Venus of Hohle Fels appears to be the oldest depiction of a human worldwide. The oldest Homo sapiens, a double grave from about 14,000 years ago, were discovered in 1914 in Kassel, Hesse. By the fifth century CE, Ostrogoths, Visigoths, Vandals, Lombards, Alemanni, and Burgundians had settled the areas around the Rhine River. Germanic peoples from northwest Europe, the Saxons, Angles, and Jutes, sailed to Britain and attacked its inhabitants.

Medieval Germany

Many scholars date the beginning of German history to 771 CE, when the Carolingian Charlemagne (742–814) became the sole ruler of the Franks. Charlemagne sought to revive the Roman Empire and unite Christian Europe. Even though he was not able to read and write, Charlemagne sought to restore the Latin language, strongly supported the liberal arts, and had convents built. The Carolingian Empire was not a homogenous state, but a disparate group held together by force of arms. Charlemagne waged over fifty military campaigns, which he considered crusades in defense of Christendom. During a visit to Rome, he was crowned Holy Roman Emperor on Christmas day 800 by Pope Leo III, who considered him the protector of Rome. After the death of Charlemagne and the demise of the Carolingian Empire, Germany was ruled by a series of dynasties.

The next great German ruler was the *Saxon* king Otto the Great (912–973), who was crowned Holy Roman Emperor by Pope John XII in 962, which marks the beginning of the First Reich in German history. In domestic affairs, Otto relied on the advice of his youngest brother, Bruno. Under Otto and Bruno, the Church increased its wealth and influence, and soon, Otto's influence in the empire superseded that of the pope. Otto converted the Slavs to Christianity, Germanized the area of present-day Austria, and seized many of the port cities of Italy.

The *Salian Dynasty* (1024–1125) came to power after the German kings and Holy Roman Emperors of the Saxon Dynasty had died out by 1024. The first Salian monarch, Konrad of Swabia, was crowned in 1027. He reasserted German power in Italy and created a new class of officials (the ministerial) attached to the crown. Conrad's son, Heinrich (Henry) III (reigned 1039–1056), managed to control the papacy, which enabled him to establish the strongest central government in medieval Germany.

The Salian line came to an end in 1125 when Heinrich's grandson, Heinrich V, died without an heir. They were succeeded by the *Hohenstaufen Dynasty*, a series of six kings who ruled the Holy Roman Empire from 1138 to 1208 and again from 1212 to 1254. Middle High German literature reached its peak in lyrical poetry during this period, and one of the Hohenstaufen kings, Friedrich Barbarossa (1122–1190), so named because of his red beard, died in Turkey during the Third Crusade (1190). The early death of Konrad IV, son of Frederick II (1194–1250), in 1254 brought an end to the Hohenstaufen Dynasty, which was followed by the *House of Habsburg*, who ruled over Germany through the Protestant Reformation.

Protestant Reformation and Religious Wars (1517–1648)

The Protestant Reformation dates to 1517, when, as legend has it, Martin Luther (1483–1546) nailed his Ninety-Five Theses to the door of All Saints Church in Wittenberg (Saxony). The sale of "indulgences" by the Roman Catholic Church, a means by which an individual could purchase a reduction of the time spent in purgatory, particularly provoked Luther. There were three main points to Luther's theology. In his view, justification, or favor in the eyes of God, resulted from faith alone and not by works (such as the purchase of an indulgence) sanctioned by the Catholic Church. Second, Luther emphasized the Bible, and not the pope or General Councils of the Catholic Church, as the sole authority in matters of faith and practice. He also translated the Bible into German, and thus, German became the language of the Reformation. Finally, Luther promulgated the idea of the priesthood of all believers.

Luther's theology represented a threat to both the hegemony of the Roman Catholic Church and the prerogatives of the Catholic rulers of Europe. The Catholic response is known as the Counter-Reformation, which included the Council of Trent, held in Trento, Italy, 1545–1563. The Council of Trent served to harden the distinction between the Protestant and Catholic Churches. The upheaval of the Reformation was addressed, in part, by the Peace of Augsburg (1555), which stated *Cuius regio, eius religio* (Whose realm, his religion). In other words, religious confession and creedal adherence were to be determined by the religious affiliation of the ruling prince rather than by individual conscience.

Ferdinand II of Bohemia, emperor of the Holy Roman Empire, attempted to curtail the religious activities of his subjects. His actions led to the outbreak of the Thirty Years War (1618–1648), one of the most destructive wars in European history. The Thirty Years War finally ended with the Peace of Westphalia (1648), which effectively marked the end of the Holy Roman Empire as a European power. Germany suffered significant economic harm during the war. In Bavaria, the population fell by 50%, and 900 towns and villages were devastated. As a result, by 1760, there were fewer farms in the region than in 1616. The economies of the German states continued to languish until the time of the French Revolution.

Enlightenment and French Invasion

The fine arts and intellectual pursuits flourished in Germany in the eighteenth and nineteenth centuries. Notable composers during this period included Johann Sebastian Bach (1685–1750), Ludwig van Beethoven (1712–1827), Georg Friedrich Händel (1685–1759), and Georg Philipp Telemann (1681–1767). In literature, Johann Wolfgang von Goethe (1749–1832) achieved international acclaim and is considered Germany's greatest modern writer. Famous German philosophers of this period include Immanuel Kant (1724–1804), Schopenhauer (1788–1860), Georg Hegel (1770–1831) and Friedrich Nietzsche (1844–1900).

"Germany" emerged from the Thirty Years War as a collection of ca. 250 smaller states. Prussia distinguished itself from many other states by virtue of its religious toleration. Frederick the Great (1712–1786, Friedrich der Große) announced that Turks and heathens (Catholics) were welcome in Prussia, and he promised to build mosques and churches for them. Frederick engaged in a series of costly wars, conducting campaigns against Austria, France, Russia, and Sweden. By 1763, nearly 180,000 Prussian soldiers had lost their lives in Frederick's campaigns. The Prussian economy was in tatters, its currency debased, and inflation ran rampant (Kitchen, 1996). Frederick managed to stabilize the Prussian economy, but in the decades after his death, the Prussian rulers continued to meddle in European affairs. Prussia declared war on France October 9, 1806, and Napoleon made quick work of the Prussian armies, crushing them at the battles of Jena and Auerstedt. On October 27, 1806, Napoleon and his generals held a victory parade in Berlin, marching through the Brandenburg Gate.

Revolution and German Unification (1815–1870)

The German Federation, consisting of thirty-four states and four cities (Bremen, Frankfurt am Main, Hamburg, and Bremen) arose after the Napoleonic Wars. A number of German states adopted limited constitutional reforms, including representational government, a written constitution, and guarantees of freedom of speech at this time. In 1818, tariffs were abolished in Prussia. A number of neighboring states followed suit, and on January 1, 1834, the German customs union (*Zollverein*) came into being. A period of rapid industrialization ensued, and soon Germany could boast of Europe's most extensive railroad network. Industrialization led to income inequality, and many parts of Germany suffered appalling social conditions, including mass unemployment, poverty, and hunger. Failed harvests in 1845 led to food riots in Berlin, Stuttgart, and Ulm. Germany was not immune from the revolutionary fervor that gripped much of Europe in 1848. Moderate governments replaced authoritarian ones in several German principalities, including Württemberg, Hanover, and Saxony.

Imperial Germany 1871–1918

Otto von Bismarck, the Prussian envoy in Paris, was appointed minister-president of Prussia by Wilhelm I (1797–1888) in 1862. Bismarck was known as the "Iron Chancellor." Upon taking office, he gave his famous "Blood and Iron" (*Blut und Eisen*) speech. Under his leadership, Prussia waged a series of wars, culminating with the Franco-Prussian War of 1870–1871. The French army was soon overwhelmed, and German troops occupied parts of France until 1873. Bismarck negotiated with Bavaria, Saxony, and Württemberg over the formation of a new German confederation, and on January 1, 1871, William I of Prussia was proclaimed the German emperor in the Palace of Versailles. The south German states joined the North German Federation. The kingdoms of Bavaria, Saxony, and Württemberg retained their own armies (under the command of the emperor during wartime). The Wilhelmine Empire, or Kaiserreich, is also known as the Second Reich in Germany history. Upon his death on March 9, 1888, Wilhelm I was succeeded by his son, Frederick III, who was terminally ill when he assumed the throne. Wilhelm II was subsequently crowned Emperor on June 15, 1888.

Wilhelm II was thus emperor when Archduke Ferdinand (heir to the throne of Austria-Hungary) was assassinated in Sarajevo, Serbia, on June 28, 1914. The Austro-Hungarian Empire declared war on Serbia. Russia mobilized in support of its ally, Serbia; and Germany mobilized in support of Austria. Germany declared war on Russia, and soon thereafter, France and the United Kingdom declared war on Germany, thereby inaugurating the Great War, or World War I. Germany soon defeated Russia on the eastern front, but the fighting on the western front came to a standstill. The United States, originally neutral in the conflict, eventually declared war on Germany on April 6, 1917. Germany, attempting to end the war before the influence of the United States could be brought to bear on the conflict, launched a spring offensive in March 1918. The offensive failed, and Germany sued for peace. After the armistice, Wilhelm II abdicated the throne and went into exile in the Netherlands, marking the end of Imperial Germany. He died in Doorn, Holland, on June 4, 1941.

Germany after the Great War

The Weimar Republic (1918–1933), which arose from the devastation of the First World War, gave rise to two related momentous events, both pivotal in the history of the twentieth century: the hyperinflation of the 1920s and the subsequent emergence of Adolf Hitler and the Nazi (Nationalsozialistische Deutsche Arbeiterpartei or NSDAP) party. Two factors led to German hyperinflation: the government's failure to pay for its war expenditures through taxation and the onerous reparations placed on Germany by the Treaty of Versailles. In January 1919, the German mark was trading 8.9 to the dollar; by late 1923, 200 *billion* marks equaled about one American cent. The collapse of the German currency caused widespread economic hardship. Hitler promised to end unemployment and revive the German economy. By 1932, the Nazis were Germany's strongest political party.

The Third Reich (1933–1945) lasted from the appointment of Adolf Hitler as German chancellor in 1933 until the end of the Second World War in 1945. During the

Third Reich, the Nazis conducted state-sponsored genocide primarily against the Jewish people, but also against the Sinti and Roma people, the disabled, and homosexuals. This program of mass murder, known as the Holocaust, resulted in the deaths of 6 million Jews (and as many as 500,000 Sinti and Roma, 270,000 disabled, and between 5,000 and 15,000 homosexuals) and many others, such as nearly 6 million Soviet civilians. On September 1, 1939, German forces invaded Poland. In response, Great Britain and France declared war on Germany, inaugurating the Second World War. German forces soon overran much of Western Europe and invaded the Soviet Union on June 22, 1941. After the Japanese bombed Pearl Harbor (December 7, 1941), Germany declared war on the United States. While Germany enjoyed early success in the war, two events turned the tide against it: the Battle of Stalingrad (August 1942–February 1943) in the east and the allied landing in Normandy, France (June 6, 1944). Germany surrendered to the Allies on May 7, 1945.

After the Second World War, Germany was divided into four zones of occupation: British (northwest Germany), French (southwest Germany), American (southern Germany), and Soviet (eastern Germany). Berlin, the capital, was also divided: the French, British, and Americans occupied the western half of Berlin, while the Soviets occupied the eastern half. Berlin soon became the front line of the Cold War. In 1948, the Soviets cut off western access to the western half of Berlin. In response, the Allies organized an airlift (*Luftbrücke*) into West Berlin. During the course of the blockade, the Allies flew over 200,000 flights into West Berlin, supplying the city with over 8,000 tons of supplies per day until the Soviets lifted the blockade in September 1949.

That same year, postwar Germany became two separate countries. The western sectors formed the Federal Republic of Germany (or West Germany), based on the principles of western democracy, and the Soviet sector became the German Democratic Republic (or East Germany), a Soviet-style Stalinist state. The two nations soon joined separate defense organizations. West Germany joined the North Atlantic Treaty Organization (NATO), while East Germany became a member of the Warsaw Pact.

The divided city of Berlin continued to be a flash point in relations not only between NATO and the Warsaw Pact, but also between East and West Germany. Many East German citizens fled to West Berlin, causing a drain on the East German economy. In response, the East German authorities walled off West Berlin in August 1961.

Construction of the *Innerdeutsche Grenze* (Inner German Border) between East and West Germany had begun in 1952. Following the construction of the Berlin Wall, the 1,378 km long border between the two countries was expanded and became nearly insurmountable. The Cold War effectively ended on November 9, 1989, when the East German government opened border crossings between East and West Berlin, permitting East German citizens to travel freely to the western part of the once-divided city. The East and West German governments signed the Reunification Treaty (Wiedervereinigungsvertrag) on August 23, 1990, and East and West Germany officially united as the Bundesrepublik Deutschland on October 3, 1990.

Wendell G. Johnson

Further Reading

Clark, Christopher M. *Iron Kingdom: The Rise and Downfall of Prussia, 1600–1947.* Cambridge, MA: Belknap Press of Harvard University Press, 2006.

Dennis, Mike. *The Rise and Fall of the German Democratic Republic, 1945–1990.* Harlow, UK: Longman, 2000.

Evans, Richard J. *The Third Reich in History and Memory.* Oxford, UK: Oxford University Press, 2015.

Fried, Johannes, and Peter Lewis. *Charlemagne.* Cambridge, UK: Harvard University Press, 2016.

Fulbrook, Mary. *A Concise History of Germany.* Cambridge, UK: Cambridge University Press, 2004.

Kitchen, Martin. *The Cambridge Illustrated History of Germany.* Cambridge, UK: Cambridge University Press, 1996.

Kolb, Eberhard. *The Weimar Republic.* London: Routledge, 2005.

Lebendiges Museum Online. https://www.dhm.de/lemo/. Accessed June 27, 2020.

Leiby, Richard A. *The Unification of Germany, 1989–1990.* Westport, CT: Greenwood Press, 1999.

Metaxas, Eric. *Martin Luther: The Man Who Rediscovered God and Changed the World.* New York: Viking, 2017.

Nipperdey, Thomas. *Germany from Napoleon to Bismarck, 1800–1866.* Princeton, NJ: Princeton University Press, 1996.

Scales, Len. *The Shaping of German Identity: Authority and Crisis, 1245–1414.* Cambridge, UK: Cambridge University Press, 2012.

Smyser, W. R. *From Yalta to Berlin: The Cold War Struggle over Germany.* New York: St. Martin's Press, 1999.

Steinberg, Jonathan. *Bismarck: A Life.* Oxford, UK: Oxford University Press, 2011.

Todd, Malcolm. *The Early Germans.* Malden, MA: Blackwell, 2004.

Watson, Alexander. *Ring of Steel: Germany and Austria-Hungary in World War I.* New York: Basic Books, 2014.

Weinfurter, Stefan. *The Salian Century: Main Currents in an Age of Transition.* Philadelphia: University of Pennsylvania Press, 1999.

Whaley, Joachim. *Germany and the Holy Roman Empire.* Oxford, UK: Oxford University Press, 2012.

Wilson, Peter H. *The Thirty Years War: Europe's Tragedy.* Cambridge, MA: Belknap Press of Harvard University Press, 2009.

TIMELINE

Prehistoric Germany

500,000 BCE	Human ancestors were present in what is now modern-day Germany.
40,000 BCE	Neanderthals settled in the Neander Valley during the Middle Paleolithic period.

| 35,000 BCE | Venus of Hohle Fels probably created from ivory (found in a cave near Schelklingen, 2008). |
| 4,100 BCE | Agriculture is adopted in Germany during the late Neolithic period. |

Roman Germany

| 9 | Under the leadership of Herman (Arminius the Cheruscan), the Germanic tribes defeated the Roman army at "Teutoburg Forest." |
| 98 | *Germania* was written by Tacitus. |

Medieval Germany

400	Jewish immigrants settled along the trade routes in the German cities of Worms, Speyer, and Mainz.
508	Baptism of King Clovis I, initiating the Christianization of the Frankish peoples.
600	Start of Old High German.
675	Birth of Saint Boniface, known as the "Apostle of the Germans."
718	Saint Boniface was granted authority by Pope Gregory II to evangelize in the Frisian regions.
722	Charles Martel, the grandfather of Charlemagne, defeated a Muslim army at the Battle of Tours.
742	Saint Boniface convened the first council held in German lands.
752	Pepin the Younger founded the Carolingian Dynasty.
753	Saint Boniface and fifty-three companions were martyred by the Frisians.
768	Birth of Charles the Great, or Charlemagne.
800	Charlemagne crowned Emperor of the Holy Roman Empire by Pope Leo.
962	Otto the Great was crowned emperor by Pope John XII, uniting German royalty and the (Holy) Roman Empire.
1027	Conrad II, the first Salian monarch crowned.
1050	Start of Middle High German.
1205	Publication of Wolfram von Eschenbach's *Parzival*, the best-known German courtly epic.
1220	The Icelandic historian Snorri Sturluson wrote the *Edda*, the best-known account of Germanic mythology.
1322	The second-largest (after Milan) Gothic cathedral in the world was consecrated in Cologne.
1254	Death of Konrad IV marked the end of the Hohenstaufen dynasty.
1348	Jewish communities were ransacked during the time of the bubonic plague.
1350	Start of early New High German.

Reformation to Enlightenment

| 1440 | Johannes Gutenberg invented the printing press. |
| 1483 | Martin Luther, the father of the Protestant Reformation, was born in Eisleben. |

1497	Philip Melanchthon, the first systematic theologian of the Protestant Reformation, was born in Bretten (near Karlsruhe).
1517	Martin Luther nailed his Ninety-Five Theses on the door of All Saint's Church in Wittenberg, setting off the Protestant Reformation.
1520	Luther appealed to the German princes to oppose the papacy.
1521	The Diet of Worms condemned Luther as a heretic. Luther subsequently went into exile in Wartburg Castle.
1522	While in exile, Luther finished the translation of the New Testament into German. The translation was published the same year.
1524	Inspired by the Reformation, German-speaking peasants staged an uprising. Luther spoke out against the uprising and thousands of peasants were killed.
1529	Luther met the Swiss reformer Ulrich Zwingli in Marburg. The two were unable to agree on the nature of the Lord's Supper.
1530	Emperor Charles V called the Diet of Augsburg to deal with "the German question" of the Reformation.
	Publication of the Augsburg Confession.
1545	In response to the events of the Reformation, the Roman Catholic Church convened the Council of Trent in Trento, Italy, which marked the beginning of the Counter-Reformation.
1546	Luther died in Eisleben.
1555	The Peace of Augsburg established the principle *Cuius regio, eius religio* (whose reign, his religion), granting the princes of the Holy Roman Empire the right to determine the state religion within their domains.
1608	A group of Protestant princes formed the Protestant Union.
1609	The German Catholic princes formed the Catholic League.
1617	The Fruchtbringende Gesellschaft (Fruitbearing Society), dedicated to the purity of the German language, was founded.
1618	The Protestant Union and Catholic League fought each other in the Thirty Years War (1618–1648).
1634	First performance of the Passion Play in Oberammergau.
1648	The Peace of Westphalia brought an end to the Thirty Years War. Eight million people lost their lives in the war. Germany became a loose confederation of quasi-sovereign states.
1650	Approximate start of New High German (Hochdeutsch).
1681	Birth of composer Philip Telemann.
1685	Birth of composers Johann Sebastian Bach (Eisenach) and George Friedrich Händel (Halle).
1687	The German language was first used in a lecture in a German University.
1700	The Duchy of Prussia became the Kingdom of Prussia.
	Frederick I crowned himself King.
1712	Birth of Frederick the Great (Friedrich II or Der alte Fritz).
	Birth of Ludwig van Beethoven.

1724	Birth of Immanuel Kant.
1729	Birth of Catherine the Great.
1731	The first congregation of Muslims in Germany met in Potsdam.
1749	Birth of Johann Wolfgang von Goethe, Germany's greatest modern writer.
1762	Catherine the Great assumed the Russian throne.
1770	Birth of philosopher Georg Hegel.
1786	Death of Frederick the Great.
1788	The *Abitur* (university admission exam) established in Prussia.
	Adolf Freiherr von Knigge (1752–1796) published *Über den Umgang mit Menschen* (On Human Relations).

Revolution and German Unification (1815–1870)

1806	Prussia declared war on France. Later that year Napoleon and his general marched through the Brandenburg Gate.
1810	Prussia introduced state certification requirements for teachers.
1815	Napoleon Bonaparte was defeated by British and Prussian forces at the Battle of Waterloo.
	Congress of Vienna established the German Confederation of 39 independent German states.
	Birth of Otto von Bismarck.
1832	Publication of *On War*, the classic treaty on military strategy, by Carl von Clausewitz.
1834	The foundation of the *Zollverein* (customs union) under Prussian leadership.
1847	Karl Marx and Friedrich Engels presented the *Communist Manifesto* at a conference in London.
1848	The Frankfurt Parliament passed the Imperial Act, guaranteeing certain rights to the German people.
1862	Otto von Bismarck appointed minister-president of Prussia. Bismarck gave his famous "Blood and Iron" speech.
1866	Austro-Prussian War.
1870	France declared war on Germany (July 19), setting off the Franco-Prussian War.

Imperial Germany (1871–1918)

1871	Germany captured Paris. France and Germany signed an armistice, officially ending the Franco-Prussian War. Germany annexed the French territories of Alsace and Lorraine.
	Wilhelm I crowned as the first kaiser of the German Empire, uniting the German states.
	Paragraph 175 of the Prussian Civil Code criminalized the male homosexual act.
1876	First performance of Richard Wagner's *The Ring of the Nibelungen*.

1880	Publication of Konrad Duden's first dictionary (*Vollständiges Orthographisches Wörterbuch der deutschen Sprache*).
1888	Bismarck forced from office by Emperor Wilhelm II.
1889	Birth of Adolf Hitler.
1900	Sütterlin script adopted in many German schools.
1902	Publication of *Regeln für die deutsche Rechtschreibung nebst Wortverzeichnis,* the first authoritative Germany orthography and glossary.
1905	Field Marshall Alfred von Schlieffen developed the Schlieffen Plan, which involved the invasion of France and Belgium in the event of a two-front war.
1908	Women permitted to take the *Abitur* (university entrance exam).
1911	The Kaiser Wilhelm Society, forerunner of the Max Planck Institute, was founded in Berlin.
1913	The German National Library was founded in Leipzig.
1914	Archbishop Ferdinand (heir to the throne of Austria and Hungary) was assassinated in Sarajevo, leading to the First World War. The United Kingdom declared war on Germany (August 4). The Royal Navy blockaded German ports.
	The German Eighth Army under Field Marshall Paul von Hindenburg defeated the Russian Second Army at the Battle of Tannenberg (August 30).
	Coeducational secondary education was introduced in the country.
1915	The German army deployed chlorine gas against French troops during the Second Battle of Ypres in Belgium.
1916	The Battle of Verdun resulted in nearly 1 million French and German casualties.
	The 1916 Summer Olympic Games, scheduled to be held in Berlin, were cancelled.
1917	The German navy introduced unrestricted submarine warfare, which led the United States to declare war on Germany.
1918	Kaiser Wilhelm abdicated.
	Germany signed an armistice with the Allies (November 11), bringing an end to the First World War.
	Women were granted the right to vote.

Weimar Republic (1918–1933)

1919	The Spartacist Uprising, a power struggle between the Social Democratic Party (led by Ebert) and the Communist Party (led by Karl Liebknecht and Rosa Luxemburg).
	The Treaty of Versailles ending the First World War was signed.
	The Weimar Constitution replaced the Imperial Constitution.
	The Bauhaus was founded in Weimar by Walter Gropius.
1921	The Allied Reparations Committee levied reparations on Germany: 33 billion marks and 26% of the value of German exports.

The Weimar Republic experienced a period of hyperinflation.

1923   The Beer Hall Putsch: Adolf Hitler and the Nazi Party attempted to overthrow the German government (November 8).

1925   Paul von Hindenburg elected president of Germany.

1929   Birth of Anne Frank, who died in the Bergen-Belsen concentration camp in 1945.

Third Reich (1933–1945)

1933   Adolf Hitler appointed chancellor of Germany by President Paul von Hindenburg, inaugurating the Third Reich.

The Reichstag was burned and civil liberties were suspended as a result.

The first concentration camp (Sachsenhausen) was built at Oranienburg, near Berlin.

Germany quit both the Disarmament Conference and the League of Nations.

1934   Night of the Long Knives (June 30): SS paramilitary units killed many member of the SA (Brownshirts), eliminating a threat to Hitler's power.

Death of Hindenburg.

The Nazis murdered Austrian chancellor Dolfuβ.

1935   The Nuremburg Laws relegated Jews in Germany to second-class status in the country.

Hitler announced that Germany would rearm, in violation of the Treaty of Versailles.

1936   German troops entered the Rhineland, in violation of the Treaty of Versailles.

Both the Winter (Garmisch-Partenkirchen) and Summer (Berlin) Olympic Games were held in Germany.

1937   Hitler revealed his war plans during the Hossbach Conference.

The Degenerate Art Law devastated modern art collections in Germany.

1938   *Anschluss*—Austria was annexed to Germany.

The Munich Agreement granted the Sudetenland region of Czechoslovakia to Germany in exchange for peace.

Jewish shops and synagogues were destroyed overnight during the Kristallnacht (November 9–10).

1939   Hitler predicted that a war in Europe would lead to the annihilation of the Jewish race in Europe.

The Nazi-Soviet Non-aggression Pact was signed in Moscow.

Germany invaded Poland on September 1, and two days later, Britain and France declared war on Germany.

1940   Germany launched a blitzkrieg against France, Belgium, and Holland.

The Battle of Britain failed to subdue Great Britain.

1941   Germany launched Operation Barbarossa (June 22). Three million German troops invaded the Soviet Union.

Following the Japanese attack on Pearl Harbor, Hitler declared war on the United States (December 11).

1942   The Wannsee Conference, held on the outskirts of Berlin, approved plans for the "Final Solution," the state-sponsored systematic extermination of European Jews.

1943   The German army surrendered in Stalingrad, Russia, marking the turning point of the war in the east.

1944   The Allies landed on the Normandy coast (June 6). Paris fell to the Allies two months later.

Hitler survived an assassination attempt (July 20).

The German army launched its last major offensive of the war, the Battle of the Bulge, but was turned back.

1945   Dietrich Bonhoeffer was hanged (April 9).

The Soviet army attacked Berlin (April 23).

Hitler committed suicide (April 30).

Germany surrendered unconditionally (May 8), ending the Second World War in Europe.

At the Potsdam Conference (July 17–August 2), the victorious allies divided Germany into four zones of occupation: France in the southwest, Great Britain in the northwest, the United States in the south, and the Soviet Union in the east. Berlin, the capital, was also divided into four separate zones of occupation.

Postwar Division

1946   The Nuremburg war crimes trial commenced. The tribunal sentenced twelve defendants to death. Seven defendants received lengthy prison sentences, and three others were acquitted.

The German Academic Exchange Service (DAAD) was reconstituted by the Western occupying powers.

1947   The Gesellschaft für deutsche Sprache (GfdS) was founded as the successor to the General German Language Union.

1948   The Soviet Union blockaded West Berlin, cutting off western access to the city. In response, the United States and its allies began the "Berlin Airlift," supplying the city via cargo planes with food and fuel.

Germany was barred from competing in the London Summer Olympic Games.

1949   The Soviet Union lifted the Berlin Blockade. West Germany (Bundesrepublik or the Federal Republic) was founded on May 23 and East Germany (the Germany Democratic Republic) on October 7.

Konrad Adenauer became the first Chancellor of West Germany.

1950   Walter Ulbricht was named the first secretary of the Central Committee of the ruling SED party of East Germany.

1951   West Germany and six other European nations signed the Treaty of Paris, establishing a single market for coal and steel.

East Germany adopted its first Soviet-style five-year plan.

The Goethe Institute was founded.

The first East German edition of Duden's dictionary was published.

1952   West Germany was accorded status as a "sovereign state" by the General Treaty (signed by the United States, France, and Great Britain). Construction on the Inner German border began.

Germany became a founding member of the European Coal and Steel Community, the forerunner of the European Community.

German athletes were permitted to compete in the Olympic Games.

1953   The East German government increased work quotas, leading to a strike in East Berlin. The next day, thousands of protestors gathered in East Berlin in support of the strike. Soviet tanks fired on the crowd, killing many protestors and ending the strike.

1954   Germany won the FIFA World Cup ("the miracle at Bern"), upsetting the heavily favored Hungarians.

1955   West (NATO) and East (Warsaw Pact) joined separate collective defense organizations.

The Allies declared an end to the military occupation of West Berlin.

1957   Germany signed the Treaty of Rome, which established the European Economic Community (EEC).

1961   Construction began on the Berlin Wall, separating West and East Berlin.

1968   East German athletes competed for the first time in the Olympic Games under their own national banner.

1969   Willy Brandt elected Chancellor of West Germany.

1970   West Germany and the Soviet Union signed the Treaty of Moscow, in which the FRG recognized the GDR and renounced historical German territory east of the Oder-Neisse line.

The United States, the Soviet Union, France, and Great Britain signed the Four Power Agreement on Berlin, guaranteeing trade between West Berlin and West Germany.

Tatort, the longest running drama on German television, premiered.

1971   Erich Honecker was named first secretary of the SED of the GDR.

1972   East and West Germany signed the Basic Treaty (Grundlagenvertrag), in which each country recognized the sovereignty of the other.

The Summer Olympic Games were held in Munich. Eight members of the Black September Organization (a Palestinian terror organization) snuck into the Olympic village and killed eleven members of the Israeli Olympic team.

1973   East and West Germany were admitted to the United Nations.

1974   Helmut Schmidt was elected chancellor of West Germany.

Germany defeated the Netherlands for the FIFA World Cup in Munich.

1982	Helmut Kohl was elected chancellor of West Germany.
1987	Erich Honecker became the first general secretary of East Germany to pay a state visit to West Germany.
1989	"The Monday Demonstrations," a series of protests against the East German government, began in Leipzig, East Germany. By October, the number of weekly demonstrators grew to 70,000. Erich Honecker was forced out of office, and Egon Krenz was named first secretary of the SED. The checkpoints on the Berlin Wall were opened (November 9), effectively ending the division of the city.

(Re)Unified Germany

1990	The Treaty on the Final Settlement with Respect to Germany was signed by East and West Germany, the United States, the Soviet Union, the United Kingdom, and France. The four occupying powers renounced all rights they held in Germany after the Second World War. East and West Germany became a single nation, with Berlin as its capital.
	Germany defeated Argentina for the FIFA World Cup.
1992	The Maastricht Treaty created the European Union (EU), including Germany.
	Germany fielded a unified team for the Olympic Summer Games in Barcelona.
1994	The Federal Constitutional Court held that the *Bundeswehr* could partake in operations outside of NATO territory.
	Abolition of Paragraph 175 (criminalizing homosexual behavior).
1995	The Federal Constitutional Court ruled that German armed forces may be deployed outside of the country. The German air force entered combat for the first time since the Second World War.
1996	The Spelling Reform Act added 112 new rules governing German orthography in Germany, Austria, Switzerland, and other German-speaking areas of Europe.
1998	Gerhard Schröder was elected chancellor of Germany.
2001	Chancellor Gerhard Schröder announced that Germany would send 3,500 troops to Afghanistan in support of the U.S. mission after 9/11.
2002	The euro was introduced as the official currency of Germany, ending the legal status of the deutsche mark.
2003	The German women beat the host United States to claim the FIFA World Cup.
2005	Pope Benedict XVI (Cardinal Joseph Aloisius Ratzinger) was elected pope.
	Angela Merkel of the CDU was elected chancellor of Germany.
2006	The FIFA World Cup, won by Italy, was held in Germany.
2007	The German women repeated as FIFA World Cup champions.
2008	Germany signed the Kyoto Protocol (a pledge to reduce greenhouse gas emissions).

2011	Germany conducted its most recent census (population: ca. 80,300,000). Germany hosted the women's FIFA World Cup.
2012	Courses in Islam were introduced into German schools.
2013	Pope Benedict abdicated the papacy.
2014	Germany won the men's FIFA World Cup for the fourth time, defeating Argentina.
2015	The number of refugees in Germany reached 1.5 million as a result of the European migrant crisis. Germany signed the Paris Climate Accord (a pledge to curb global warming).
2016	A terror attack on a Christmas market in Berlin left twelve people dead and injured fifty-six others.
2017	Angela Merkel secured a fourth term as German Chancellor. The AfD (Alternative für Deutschland) won nearly 13% of the vote, making it the largest opposition in the Bundestag.
2018	The chemical and pharmaceutical giant Bayer acquired Monsanto. German soccer exited the World Cup at the group stage.
2019	Ursula von der Leyen, the former German minister of defense, became president of the European Commission.
2020	In response to the COVID-19 pandemic, Germany closed its borders. Germany assumed the presidency of the Council of the European Union (July–December). The Federal Office for the Protection of the Constitution declared a faction of the Alternative fur Deutschland an extremist endeavor and placed it under surveillance.
2021	Angela Merkel stepped down as chancellor after sixteen years in office. Olaf Scholz was elected as the new chancellor.

Adenauer, Konrad (1876–1967)

Konrad Adenauer, affectionately known as *Der Alte* ("the Old Man"), was the first chancellor of the Federal Republic of Germany after the Second World War. Adenauer was born into a devoutly Catholic family in the Rhineland. His father, Johann Adenauer, served in the Prussian army and became a chancery official in a regional court in Cologne. Adenauer received a classical Catholic education and went on to study at the Universities of Freiburg, Munich, and Bonn. He worked in the public prosecutor's office in Cologne in 1903 and two years later became an assistant judge in the regional court. He was elected mayor of Cologne in 1917 and had the title Lord Mayor bestowed on him by Emperor Wilhelm II.

After the Nazis came to power in 1933, Adenauer was dismissed from office. He went into self-imposed exile in the Benedictine Abbey of Maria Laach. In 1934, he moved to Neubabelsberg, Brandenburg, and was imprisoned for two days in connection with the Röhm Putsch. In 1936, he and his family build a house in Rhöndorf, North Rhine-Westphalia, where he lived until his death. He was again imprisoned, this

Konrad Adenauer (1876–1967) was the first post-war chancellor of West Germany. He was in office from 1949 to 1963, and his economic policies placed Germany on the path to prosperity. (Library of Congress)

time for several months, in 1944 following an attempt on Hitler's life. His second wife, Auguste "Gussi" Adenauer (1895–1948), was also imprisoned, put under tremendous pressure to disclose Adenauer's hiding place, and tried to commit suicide in prison.

Immediately after the end of the war, American military officials reinstated Adenauer as lord mayor of Cologne. However, his relations were strained with the British military command, who removed him from office. Out of office, Adenauer joined the Christian Democratic Union (CDU) and turned his attention to the reconstruction of Germany.

Beginning in 1945, Adenauer played an outsized role in German politics when he was influential in drafting the constitution of the new West Germany and in the choice of Bonn as its capital. In August 1949, he formed a coalition with the Federal Democratic Party and the now-defunct German Party and was elected chancellor of the country. Adenauer helped Germany recover from the shame of the Nazi era, ignominy of occupation, and pain of reconstruction. He was chancellor during the postwar economic boom of the 1950s and saw his country reclaim its full sovereignty in 1955. The economic boom, known as the *Wirtschaftswunder* (Economic Miracle), included currency reform, investment, anti-cartel activities, foreign trade, and an aggressive social policy (which benefitted the working and middles classes). Gross national product grew at an annual rate of 9 to 10% per year from 1950 to 1957 (Bryson, 1998).

Adenauer was also minister of Foreign Affairs from 1951 to 1955. He was a fervent anti-Bolshevik and an avowed foe of the expansionist aims of the Soviet Union. His overarching goal was to obtain equal status for the Federal Republic within a united Western Europe. In 1952, Germany became a founding member of the European Coal and Steel Community (the forerunner of the European Community) and signed the Reconciliation Pact with Israel. He obtained an annulment of the occupation statutes in 1954, and the following year Germany was accepted as a full member of NATO. Adenauer was roundly criticized in 1961 when the East German government began construction of the Berlin Wall on August 13. He was campaigning for office at the time and did not visit the city until nine days later. Perhaps his crowning achievement in diplomacy was the German-French Treaty of 1962, which ended a century of hostility between the two nations. Adenauer formed five governments before he resigned in 1963.

After leaving office, Adenauer traveled widely and wrote his memoirs. He died in 1967 and is buried in Rhöndorf (North Rhine-Westphalia). His property in Rhöndorf was gifted by his heirs to the Federal Republic and now houses the Stiftung Bundeskanzler-Adenauer-Haus, the Chancellor Adenauer Foundation.

Wendell G. Johnson

See also: Chapter 2: Overview; Berlin Wall; Hitler, Adolf (1889–1945); Honecker, Erich (1912–1994); Wilhelm II (1859–1941). Chapter 3: Overview; Armed Forces; Constitutions; Foreign Policy; Germany and the European Union; Political Parties. Chapter 4: Overview; Gross Domestic Product (GDP).

Further Reading

Bryson, Philip. J. "Economic Miracle (Wirtschaftswunder)." In Dieter K. Buse and Juergen Doerr, eds. *Modern Germany: An Encyclopedia of History, People, and Culture, 1871–1990*, 258–259. New York: Garland, 1998.

Konrad Adenauer Stiftung. "Konrad Adenauer 1876–1967." https://www.konrad-adenauer.de/. Accessed June 27, 2020.

Morsey, Rudolf. "Adenauer, Konrad." In Walther Killy and Rudolf Vierhaus, eds. *Dictionary of German Biography (DGB)*. München: K. G. Saur, 2001.

Williams, Charles. *Adenauer: The Father of the New Germany*. New York: John Wiley, 2000.

Berlin Wall

West Germany's astonishing postwar economic growth outpaced that of East Germany, which struggled with food shortages and a lack of consumer goods. Many East Germans "voted with their feet," seeking a better future in the west. As many as 3 million East Germans fled through West Berlin and on to West Germany, draining the economy of the German Democratic Republic (GDR). In response, SED Party

Construction on the Berlin Wall commenced August 13, 1961. It surrounded the western sectors of Berlin and divided the city into two. The fall of the Berlin Wall on November 9, 1989, followed months of civil unrest. (Department of Defense)

security secretary Erich Honecker, GDR head of state Walter Ulbricht (1893–1973), and the authorities of the GDR started to construct the Berlin Wall, after Ulbricht had said on June 15, 1961, "*Niemand hat die Absicht eine Mauer zu errichten*" (Nobody intends to erect a wall).

The Berlin Wall went up nearly overnight. The citizens of Berlin awoke on Sunday morning, August 13, 1961, to find that access points between East and West Berlin had been sealed off with barbed wire and were guarded by sentries. In the upcoming weeks, construction on a concrete wall took place that encircled West Berlin and physically divided it from East Berlin. When completed, the wall was fifteen feet tall, topped with barbed wire, and guarded by a series of watchtowers, gun emplacements, and land mines. The wall extended twenty-eight miles through Berlin and seventy-five miles around West Berlin. Faced with a *fait accompli*, the Western allies stood by helplessly as Berlin was divided between East and West and West Berlin was sealed off.

The East German authorities referred to the wall as the *Antifaschistischer Schutzwall*, or the "Anti-Fascist Protective Barrier," whose avowed purpose was to keep Western fascists from entering East Berlin and undermining the German Democratic Republic. Its true purpose, of course, was to staunch the flow of defections from East Germany to West Germany. Already while the wall was being built, East Germans attempted to escape to the west. The wall claimed its first victim on August 22, 1961, when Ida Siekmann was killed in an accident trying to escape. Perhaps the wall's most famous victim is Peter Fechter, who was shot on August 17, 1962, attempting to scale the wall. The East German border guards left Fechter to bleed to death in view of hundreds of witnesses, including journalists.

Two American presidents visited the Berlin Wall. John F. Kennedy visited on June 26, 1963, when he gave his famous *"Ich bin ein Berliner"* (I am a Berliner) speech at the Rathaus Schöneberg, accompanied by the then-mayor Willy Brandt and the chancellor Konrad Adenauer. *Ich bin ein Berliner* can also be translated as "I am a jelly doughnut," and this sentence has spawned a whole cottage industry of t-shirts, postcards, and so on. During his visit on June 11, 1985, Ronald Reagan, speaking in front of the wall, challenged the Russian premier Mikhail Gorbachev to "tear down this wall."

The Berlin Wall remained standing until the evening of November 9, 1989, when Günter Schabowski, spokesman for the SED, announced new travel regulations. Answering the question of a journalist about the timeline, Schabowski looked at his handwritten notes and said *"Das tritt nach meiner Kenntnis . . . ist das sofort, unverzüglich"* (According to my knowledge . . . it is immediately, forthwith), which had not been intended. Following this announcement, throngs of East Berliners crossed into West Berlin that night, ushering in the inevitable demise of the German Democratic Republic. According to the Berlin Wall Memorial, located on the old border between East and West Berlin, ninety people were killed trying to cross the wall between 1961 and 1989.

Wendell G. Johnson

See also: Chapter 2: Honecker, Erich (1912–1994). Chapter 3: Government and Politics in the German Democratic Republic. Chapter 4: Overview. Chapter 14: Food and Drink in the German Democratic Republic.

Further Reading

Ahonen, Pertti. *Death at the Berlin Wall*. Oxford, UK: Oxford University Press, 2011.

Berlin Wall Memorial. https://www.berliner-mauer-gedenkstaette.de/en/berlin-wall -memorial-12.html. Accessed July 11, 2020.

Engel, Jeffrey A., ed. *The Fall of the Berlin Wall: The Revolutionary Legacy of 1989*. Oxford, UK: Oxford University Press, 2009.

Major, Patrick. *Behind the Berlin Wall: East Germany and the Frontiers of Power*. Oxford, UK: Oxford University Press, 2010.

Sarotte, M. E. *The Collapse: The Accidental Opening of the Berlin Wall*. New York: Basic Books, 2014.

Bismarck, Otto Von (1815–1898)

Otto von Bismarck, known as the Iron Chancellor, was one of the most influential European statesmen of the nineteenth century. He was the architect of German unification, but his policies on modernization ultimately led to two world wars in Europe.

Otto Eduard Leopold von Bismarck was born April 1, 1815, in Schönhausen, west of Berlin. He was the son of Ferdinand von Bismarck, a member of the Prussian land-owning nobility, and Wilhelmine Louise Mencken, the daughter of a bureaucrat. Bismarck married Johanna von Puttkamer in 1847, and the couple had three children: Marie (1848–1926), Herbert (1849–1904), and Wilhelm (1851–1901). Bismarck studied law at the Universities of Göttingen and Berlin and entered the Prussian civil service in 1836. He left government work soon thereafter to pursue life as a country *Junker* (a member of the landed nobility in Prussia).

Bismarck began his political career as an ultraconservative member of the United Diet, the Prussian national assembly. He served as the Prussian envoy to Saint Petersburg and Paris and in September 1862 was appointed as the Prussian minister-president. Shortly after taking office, he gave his famous "Blood and Iron" (*Blut und Eisen*) speech: "The great questions of our day are not decided by speeches and majority decisions . . . but by blood and iron" (Steinberg, 2011, p. 465). Bismarck consolidated his power the following month by also assuming the office of Prussian foreign minister. His main objective as foreign minister was to secure Prussian influence in Germany and Europe. Under his leadership, Prussia waged war successfully against Denmark, Austria, and France.

Bismarck negotiated with Bavaria, Saxony, and Württemberg over the formation of a new German confederation, and on January 1, 1871, William I of Prussia was proclaimed the German emperor in the Palace of Versailles. Bismarck was named chancellor of the new empire, and his tenure was characterized by anticlericalism and authoritarianism. Domestically, he levied tariffs on iron and grain imports, and promoted social welfare legislation, including old-age pensions, unemployment benefits, and universal health insurance in Germany, a model subsequently adopted by many European nations. During Bismarck's time as chancellor, Germany established colonies in Africa, New Guinea, and the Pacific Islands. He hoped that the colonies would provide markets for German goods

Otto von Bismarck was one of the most significant European statesmen of the nineteenth century. As Minister President of Prussia, he was instrumental in the creation of the German Empire. As German Chancellor, he promoted social welfare, including access to health care and pensions for senior citizens. (Chaiba Media)

and a source of raw materials for the country. However, the colonies were expensive to maintain and proved a drain on German resources.

In 1888, Wilhelm I's grandson, Wilhelm II, ascended to the German throne. A power struggle ensued between the emperor and the chancellor, and in 1890 Bismarck was forced to resign from office. He retired to his estate near Hamburg and wrote his memoirs. However, his continued opposition to Wilhelm II brought on a protracted period of political instability in Germany.

Wendell G. Johnson

See also: Chapter 2: Wilhelm II (1859–1941). Chapter 3: Tax Policy. Chapter 6: Aristocracy and the Elites; The Grey Culture.

Further Reading

Bismarck, Otto. *The Memoirs: Being the Reflections and Reminiscences of Otto, Prince Von Bismarck, Written and Dictated by Himself after His Retirement from Office.* New York: H. Fertig, 1966.

Lebendiges Museum Online. "The Era of Reaction and Nation Building." https://www .dhm.de/lemo/kapitel/reaktionszeit. Accessed July 11, 2020.

Röhl, John C. G. *Wilhelm II: The Kaiser's Personal Monarchy, 1888–1900.* New York: Cambridge University Press, 2004.

Showalter, Dennis E. *The Wars of German Unification.* London: Arnold, 2004.

Steinberg, Jonathan. *Bismarck: A Life.* Oxford, UK: Oxford University Press, 2011.

Catherine the Great (1729–1796)

Catherine the Great, born as Princess Sophie Auguste Friederike of Anhalt-Zerbst in Germany (1729–1796), came to Russia in 1744 to marry her second cousin, Grand Duke Peter III. The relationship was not a happy one: Peter was an alcoholic and humiliated his wife at court. Catherine learned Russian but was struck by the backwardness of the country. She studied history, ethics, and the writings of famous Enlightenment philosophers and corresponded with the likes of Voltaire, Montesquieu, and Diderot.

Peter acceded to the Russian throne in 1762. Six months into his reign, Catherine connived with the military to arrest Peter in the Winter Palace in Saint Petersburg and throw him into prison, where he was murdered six weeks later. On the day of the coup d'état (July 8, 1762), Catherine forced Peter to sign his own abdication and convinced the Russian clergy to recognize her accession to the throne. Her coronation was held in the Russian Orthodox Cathedral of the Assumption in Moscow.

Domestically, after consolidating her power, Catherine addressed Russia's poor financial situation. She established the Assignation Bank in 1769 (a type of federal reserve bank), which allowed Russia to trade foreign currencies without tapping into its reserves of precious metals. She convened a legislative commission in 1767, which she instructed to devise new legal codes. The Provincial Reform of 1785 regularized local government and reformed Russia's central administration. She also granted individuals the right to establish printing presses and promoted the expansion of a public national school network providing free access to schooling.

Catherine converted from Lutheranism to the Russian Orthodoxy and began a secularization of Russian society. She nationalized the holdings of the Russian Orthodox Church and closed hundreds of monasteries. She attempted to revise clerical studies, excluding religious instruction from public education.

Catherine's imperial success in international affairs earned her the sobriquet "The Great." Her policies greatly increased the size of the Russian empire and permitted it to play a major role in European affairs. She gained territories in the Baltics, Moldavia, the Ukraine, and Romania and was instrumental in the partition of Poland (with Austria and Prussia). To encourage economic development, Catherine issued a manifesto to invite foreigners to settle in her empire in 1763. For this purpose, she created the Guardianship Chancellery office and sent agents to central Europe. Farmers and tradesmen from Germany, Holland and France settled in the Volga River Valley, the Crimea, and along the western coastlines of the Black Sea. These farmers introduced modern agricultural methods to the hinterlands and became the most productive grain producers in the empire. A new port built on the Black Sea became a hub of mercantile activities.

She extended Russian influence in Siberia and founded colonies in Alaska. During her reign, Russia waged a series of campaigns against the Turks and fought a war with Persia.

Until her death in 1796, she reigned as Her Imperial Majesty the Empress and Autocrat of All the Russias. Catherine died of a stroke in 1796. A so-called "enlightened despot," she is widely considered the most literate of all Russian leaders and was greatly admired by the Soviet authorities.

Christiane Grieb

See also: Chapter 5: Overview.

Further Reading

Alexander, John T. "Catherine II." In James R. Millar, ed. *Encyclopedia of Russia*, 205–209. New York: Macmillan Reference, 2004.

Giesinger, Adam. *The Story of Russia's Germans: From Catherine to Khrushchev.* Battleford, SK, Canada: Marian Press, 1974.

Massie, Robert K. *Catherine the Great: Portrait of a Woman.* New York: Random House, 2012.

Charlemagne (748–814)

Charlemagne, heir to the kingdom of the Franks and the titular founder of the Carolingian Empire, was the son of Pepin the Short and the grandson of Charles Martel, who defeated the Muslim army at the Battle of Tours in 722. Upon the death of Pepin in 768, the Frankish Kingdom was divided between Charlemagne and his brother

Carloman. Carloman died three years later, leaving Charlemagne as the sole ruler of the Franks. He inherited a centralized, feudal state in which each count or royal official oversaw an administrative district. He maintained his authority through a series of special envoys, the *missi dominici*, and elite warriors, the *vassi dominici*.

After assuming the Frankish throne, Charlemagne began a series of military campaigns, raiding the Saxons in 772 and conquering Lombardy in 774. After a Saxon counterattack, Charlemagne executed 4,500 Saxon prisoners *en masse*. He began the construction of a palace in Aachen in 777 and made a pilgrimage to Rome in 781, where he had his son Pepin proclaimed King of Italy. Charlemagne took control of Bavaria in 788, thereby uniting all of the territory of the Germans under his rule. He launched a campaign against the Avars in the areas of Austria and Hungary, eventually destroying them.

During one of his journeys, Charlemagne met the Northumbrian monk Alcuin (735–804) in the Italian city of Parma and convinced him to join his court. Alcuin became the head of the palace school at Aachen and introduced the liberal arts in a personalized atmosphere of scholarship and teaching (Duckett, 1951). Although Charlemagne himself was not literate, he introduced a system of spelling and handwriting in his kingdom and restored Latin to its previous position as a literary language. Throughout his rule, Charlemagne considered it his duty to protect the Church and condemn heresy. He insisted that the churches in the kingdom follow the lead of Rome in administering rites. Every bishop was required to set up a school in his diocese to instruct their congregants in the basics of Christianity.

In 799, after being attacked in the streets in Rome, Pope Leo III appealed to Charlemagne for protection. Charlemagne met Leo in Paderborn and went to Rome to help the pope clear his name. While in Rome, Charlemagne was crowned Holy Roman Emperor (HRE) by Leo on Christmas Day, 800. This made Charlemagne the political master of Rome, and he exercised dominion over Christianized Western Europe, with the exception of the British Isles and portions of Spain. The coronation, however, created tension with the Eastern (Byzantine) emperors, who did not recognize Charlemagne as HRE until 812. The following year, he conferred the title of HRE on his son Louis. According to his biographer Einhard (770–840), Charlemagne died on January 28, 814, from a high fever.

Throughout the Middle Ages, Charlemagne was celebrated as a hero and was the central figure in a number of epic poems. Since 1950, the city of Aachen has awarded the Charlemagne Prize for distinguished service on behalf of European unification. Previous winners include Konrad Adenauer, Winston Churchill, and Bill Clinton.

Wendell G. Johnson

See also: Chapter 2: Adenauer, Konrad (1876–1967). Chapter 5: Overview. Chapter 11: The Middle Ages (ca. 718–1500). Chapter 12: Overview; Carolingian Renaissance.

Further Reading

Duckett, Eleanor Shipley. *Alcuin: Friend of Charlemagne, His World and His Work*. New York: Macmillan, 1951.

Einhard and Notker the Stammerer. *Two Lives of Charlemagne*. David Ganz, trans. London: Penguin, 2008.

Fichtenau, Heinrich. *The Carolingian Empire*. Peter Munz, trans. Toronto: University of Toronto Press in Association with The Medieval Academy of America, 1995.

Fried, Johannes. *Charlemagne*. Peter Lewis, trans. Cambridge, MA: Harvard University Press, 2016.

Clausewitz, Carl Von (1780–1831)

Carl Philipp Gottlieb von Clausewitz (1780–1831) was a Prussian general and military theorist. He was born in Burg near Magdeburg, Prussia, and died in Wrocław (then Silesia and now Poland). Von Clausewitz became known into the present era for his classic treatise on military strategy, his book *On War* (*Vom Kriege*) published in 1832.

As did his father, who fought in the Seven Years War, Clausewitz enrolled in the Prussian General Staff College (later the General War College or Kriegsakademie) in Berlin, served in the Prussian army, and ultimately became an experienced general in his own right. After the war against France in 1806, when Napoleon defeated the Prussian army in the twin battles of Jena and Auerstädt, von Clausewitz joined General Gerhard von Scharnhorst's staff, and participated in the work of this enigmatic reformer of military education. Under the tutelage of von Scharnhorst, von Clausewitz helped reform the Prussian Army and taught at the War College, thus shaping the careers of distinguished military leaders to come, notably von Moltke (1800–1891).

According to von Clausewitz, war is a social and military phenomenon that might — depending on circumstances—involve the entire population of a nation at war. His theories were based on his study of records of warfare, especially the Thirty Years War, his own war experiences, and from observations of human nature that he believed were a driving force of war. In von Clausewitz's opinion, military operations could not rely solely on the linear logic of strategic and tactical planning. Rather, the intellect of imperial and military leaders and the temperament of civilian population were factors that had to be considered before a nation embarked on a war.

War, according to von Clausewitz, was a national affair. Three major objectives were necessary to wage war successfully: (1) the opposing army must be destroyed, (2) the opposing country must be occupied, and (3) the will of its populace had to be subdued. It was von Clausewitz who issued the famous dictum "war being politics by other means." War was not conducted as an end in itself, but was meant to realign political power and spheres of influence. Hence, peace treaties are signed to prevent alliances between potential enemies.

Von Clausewitz established military strategy as a means of political ambition. He did not compare war to art, as did Sun Tzu in his own treatise *Art of War*. Rather, war resembles business activities, which seek to resolve conflicts of human interests and activities. Von Clausewitz died before concluding his treatise *On War*. It was due to his wife, Marie, that *On War* was published in 1832. Von Clausewitz's classic treatise on military strategy remains an essential reading for modern armies and a primary reference work for business strategists and politicians alike.

Christiane Grieb

See also: Chapter 2: Overview.

Further Reading

Bellinger, Vanya Eftimova. *Marie von Clausewitz: The Woman behind the Making of On War*. Oxford, UK: Oxford University Press, 2015.

Stoker, Donald. *Clausewitz: His Life and Work*. Oxford, UK: Oxford University Press, 2014.

Von Clausewitz, Carl. *On War*. James John Graham, trans. Overland Park, KS: Digireads. com Publishing, 2018.

Frank, Anne (1929–1945)

Anne Frank, perhaps the best-known victim of the Holocaust, died of typhus in the Bergen-Belsen concentration camp in February or March 1945. She was born in Frankfurt am Main on June 12, 1929, the daughter of Otto Frank and Edith Holländer.

Otto Frank served in the German army during the First World War and after the war went to work in the bank founded by his father. Edith Holländer was the daughter of a wealthy manufacturer. The couple married in 1925 and their first daughter, Margot, was born the following year.

The Franks were nonobservant Jews who settled in an apartment in the Marbachweg 307 in Frankfurt; their landlord, Otto Könitzer, was a Nazi sympathizer. The Nazis blamed Germany's postwar economic difficulties on its Jewish citizens. After the appointment of Adolf Hitler as chancellor in 1933, the situation of Jews in Germany dramatically worsened. In response, the Franks moved to Amsterdam, where Otto worked for Opekta, a pectin and spice company.

Anne Frank attended a Montessori school in Amsterdam, where she learned to speak Dutch and made many friends. On May 10, 1940, German troops invaded Holland. Soon thereafter, Arthur Seyss-Inquart (1892–1946), the Reichskommissar (Reich Commissioner) of the Netherlands, instituted anti-Semitic measures across the country. Life became increasingly difficult for Jewish people residing in Holland. On June 26, 1942, it was announced that all Jews between the ages of sixteen and forty were to be sent to

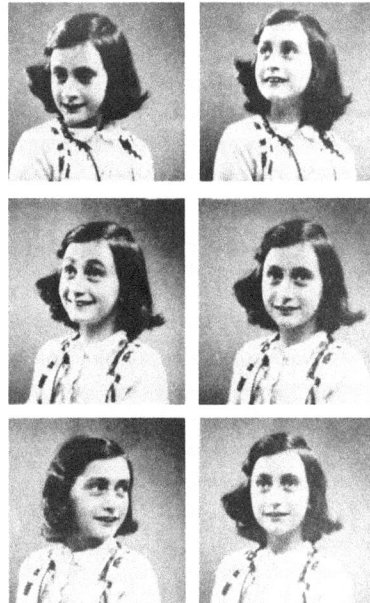

Anne Frank, a young Jewish German girl, hid with her family in Amsterdam during the Second World War. She died in the Bergen Belson concentration camp in 1945. Anne Frank's posthumously published diary documented her time in the Dutch capital. (Library of Congress)

labor camps. When Anne's sister Margot received a summons to report for duty, the family went into hiding.

The Franks resided in a hidden annex in the Opetka facility (located at 263 Prinsengracht), where they were sheltered by Jan and Miep Gies. During their travail, Anne Frank kept a diary, which she intended to turn into a novel after the war. The diary recounts feelings of melancholy and loneliness. Each resident of the annex was able to bathe once a week, and, as the war progressed, food became increasingly difficult to obtain. Anne took solace in reading and listening to BBC radio, where they learned that Jews were being gassed. As she noted in her diary on July 11, 1943, "ordinary people don't know how much books can mean to someone who is cooped up" (Frank, 1995, p. 11).

The last entry in Anne Frank's diary was dated August 1, 1944. Three days later, the Frank family was deported to a transitional detention facility in Westerbork and then on to Auschwitz, where Edith Frank died. At the end of October 1944, Margot and Anne Frank were transferred to Bergen-Belsen, located near Hannover, in Lower Saxony. A typhus outbreak that winter claimed the lives of both girls, who were probably buried in Bergen-Belsen's mass grave. Otto Frank was the only member of the family to survive the concentration camps. Today the building at 263 Prinsengracht, now known as the Anne Frank House, is one of Amsterdam's most popular tourist attractions.

Wendell G. Johnson

See also: Chapter 2: Hitler, Adolf (1889–1945). Chapter 5: Holocaust; Judaism in Germany. Chapter 6: Jews in Germany.

Further Reading

Anne Frank Haus. https://www.annefrank.org/en/. Accessed July 11, 2020.

Frank, Anne. *The Diary of a Young Girl: The Definitive Edition.* Frank Otto and Susan Massotty, eds. New York: Doubleday, 1995.

Miller, Melissa. *Anne Frank: The Biography.* New York: Metropolitan Books/Henry Holt and Company, 2013.

Hindenburg, Paul Von (1847–1934)

Paul von Beneckendorff und von Hindenburg was born in Posen, Prussia (in present-day Poland). The son of a *Junker*, a landowner, Hindenburg was destined for a career in the German military. He entered cadet school at the age of eleven and eventually was commissioned as a second lieutenant in the Third Regiment of Foot Guards. Hindenburg served in the Austro-Prussian war (1866) and was wounded at the Battle of Königgrätz. He also saw action in the Franco-Prussian war (1870–1871) and represented his regiment at the Palace of Versailles when the German Empire was proclaimed on January 18, 1871. After the Franco-Prussian War, Hindenburg attended the War Academy. He rose through the ranks before retiring as a lieutenant-general in 1911.

Hindenburg was recalled to duty after the outbreak of World War 1 and was placed in charge of the Eighth Army in East Prussia. Under his command, the German forces annihilated the Russian Second Army at the Battle of Tannenberg (August 26–30, 1914) and defeated the Russian First Army at the First Battle of Masurian Lakes (September 6–15, 1914), driving the Russians out of East Prussia. He received widespread acclaim after the battles, and statues in his honor were erected across Germany.

Kaiser Wilhelm II appointed Hindenburg as general chief of staff in August 1916. Hindenburg was strongly influenced by the quartermaster general, Erich Ludendorff. The two men endorsed the Germany policy of waging unrestricted submarine warfare in 1917 (which led to war with the United States) and imposed the Peace of Brest Litovsk on Russia in 1918. The First World War ended in defeat for Germany on November 11, 1918, and Hindenburg retired once again from military service in January 1919. During a parliamentary inquest regarding the outbreak of the war in 1914 and subsequent defeat in 1918, Hindenburg testified that Germany was on the verge of winning the war until it was stabbed in the back (*Dolchstoss*) by disloyal elements, a mantra subsequently repeated by the Nazis.

Hindenburg was elected president of Germany in 1925. By 1930, the Great Depression had taken hold in Germany, resulting in widespread unemployment and giving rise to the Nazi Party. Hindenburg won reelection in 1932, receiving 53% of the vote (Adolf Hitler came in second, with 36% of the vote). During his time in office, Germany became an increasingly authoritarian state. Article 48 of the Weimar Constitution permitted the president to take action under certain circumstances without obtaining permission from the Reichstag. When Hindenburg was unable to muster a parliamentary majority in support of his policies, he invoked Article 48 and governed by decree. Unable to form a new government after the 1932 election, Hindenburg installed Hitler as chancellor of Germany on January 30, 1933. Hindenburg died at his home in Neudeck (in present-day Poland) the following year and was initially buried at the Tannenberg Memorial; in 1945, his body was moved to the Saint Elizabeth's Church in Marburg. After his death, Hitler immediately consolidated and assumed the offices of president and chancellor.

Wendell G. Johnson

See also: Chapter 2: Overview; Hitler, Adolf (1889–1945); Wilhelm II (1859–1941). Chapter 3: Constitutions. Chapter 6: Aristocracy and the Elites.

Further Reading

Lebendiges Museum Online. "Paul von Hindenburg 1847–1934." https://www.dhm.de /lemo/biografie/biografie-paul-von-hindenburg.html. Accessed June 10, 2021.

Showalter, Dennis E. *Tannenberg: Clash of Empires*. Hamden, CT: Archon Books, 1991.

Von der Goltz, Anna. *Hindenburg: Power, Myth, and the Rise of the Nazis*. Oxford, UK: Oxford University Press, 2009.

Hitler, Adolf (1889–1945)

Adolf Hitler served as chancellor of Germany, 1933–1945. During this time, his expansionist policies launched World War II in Europe, and his hatred of the Jewish people led to the Holocaust, the state-sponsored genocide of 6 million Jews.

Hitler was born near Linz, Austria, on April 20, 1889, the son of Klara and Alois Hitler. He aspired to an artistic career and moved to Vienna in 1907, only to be rejected by the Viennese Academy of Arts. In 1913, Hitler moved to Germany and volunteered for the Bavarian army the next year. During the First World War, he was wounded at the Somme in 1916, temporarily blinded by a mustard gas attack in 1918, and decorated for bravery. Hitler reacted viscerally to Germany's World War I defeat. He contended that the German army did not lose the war; rather, it was "stabbed in the back" (*Dolchstoss*), betrayed by Jews, Bolsheviks, and the government in Berlin.

After the First World War, Hitler joined the German Worker's Party, before long renamed the National Socialist German Workers Party (NSDAP or Nazi Party). Hitler was a gifted politician, and he soon headed the party. He led an unsuccessful coup, the "Beer Hall Putsch," against the Bavarian government in 1923, which resulted in a five-year prison sentence for treason. While in prison he penned *Mein Kampf* (My Struggle), which laid out his ideology, including the philosophy of *Lebensraum*—the concept that Germany needed more "living space." Hitler was a candidate for the Office of Reich President in 1932 and garnered over 13 million votes, coming in second after Hindenburg. He was appointed chancellor of Germany on January 30, 1933.

The period 1933–1945 is known in German history as the Third Reich. Like other nations, Germany suffered the effects of the Great Depression, and the Nazi government took measures to combat unemployment. Among the public works projects undertaken during this time was the construction of the *Autobahn*, the national highway system. Employment was further bolstered by an increase in the production of armaments.

Hitler often referred to the "Jewish problem" during his time in office. On the evening of November 9, 1938, German paramilitary forces carried out a pogrom, termed Kristallnacht ("Crystal Night" or the "Night of Broken Glass"). A total of 7,500 Jewish businesses were destroyed, 171 synagogues burned down, and 91 Jews were murdered. The next year, in a speech to the Reichstag, Hitler rhetorically threatened to exterminate Jews. During the Third Reich, the Nazis established twenty-three concentration camps to carry out this threat, including Auschwitz, Buchenwald, Dachau, and Treblinka.

Adolf Hitler was not only the political head of Germany, he also assumed command of the German armed forces. On September 1, 1939, the German army invaded Poland, plunging Europe once again into war. Two days later, Great Britain and France declared war on Germany. In addition to Poland, German forces quickly overran the Netherlands, Luxembourg, France, Denmark, Yugoslavia, Greece, and Norway. On June 22, 1941, Hitler ordered the invasion of the Soviet Union (Operation Barbarossa). The German advance was halted at Stalingrad (modern-day Volgograd) on January 31, 1943, and they capitulated, marking the turning point of the war on the eastern front. Shortly after the Japanese attacked the American fleet in Pearl Harbor, Hitler also declared war on the United States on December 11, 1941.

In September 1944, Hitler ordered all men between the ages of sixteen and sixty who had so far not been drafted to form the so-called *Volkssturm* (People's Army) to defend the *Heimatboden* (native soil). By April 1945, the Red Army had surrounded Berlin. Hitler took up residency in a bunker in the Reich chancellery in the German capital. After marrying his long-term girlfriend Eva Braun on April 29, the couple committed suicide on April 30, when Soviet troops were within a couple of blocks of the chancellery.

Wendell G. Johnson

See also: Chapter 5: Holocaust; Judaism in Germany. Chapter 6: Jews in Germany.

Further Reading

Hitler, Adolf. *Mein Kampf.* Ralph Manheim, trans. Boston: Houghton Mifflin Company, 1943.

Kershaw, Ian. *Hitler,* 2 volumes. New York: W. W. Norton, 1999–2000.

Lebendiges Museum Online. "Adolf Hitler 1889–1945." https://www.dhm.de/lemo/biografie/biografie-adolf-hitler.html. October 23, 2021.

Honecker, Erich (1912–1994)

Erich Honecker was the general Secretary of the Socialist Unity Party (Sozialistische Einheitspartei, SED), the ruling party of the German Democratic Republic (GDR), from 1971 up until the weeks preceding the fall of the Berlin Wall in November 1989. He was born into a working-class family in the Saarland, in western Germany, and grew up during the turbulence of the Weimar Republic. Honecker became active in the Communist Party of Germany (KPD) at the age of ten and spent a year in Moscow at the international Lenin School of the Communist International (1930). Upon his return to Germany, he became the general secretary of the youth division of the KPD.

Honecker joined the anti-fascist resistance after the Nazis came to power in 1933. He was arrested several times. In 1937, he was sentenced to ten years for *Hochverrat* (high treason) and was imprisoned until 1945, when he was freed by Soviet troops. Honecker became a protégé of Walter Ulbricht (1893–1973), then the leader of the KPD. After the founding of the GDR, he was given a leadership position in the Socialist Unity Party of Germany. He led government campaigns against dissident writers and artists and supervised the construction of the Berlin Wall in 1961. The wall, termed the "anti-fascist barrier" by East German functionaries, effectively stanched the exodus of skilled labor from East to West Germany and permitted the GDR to survive as the poor cousin of the Federal Republic of Germany (FRG).

In 1971, Honecker succeeded Walter Ulbricht as the first secretary of the SED. Upon assuming power, Honecker emphasized the need for stringent party discipline. He insisted that each member personally represent the unity of the party's politics, ideology, and economics. He sought to align the SED closely with the Communist Party of the Soviet Union, and hoped, thereby, to secure a prominent role for the SED in the Eastern bloc. Honecker signed the Basic Treaty (Grundlagenvertrag) between East and West Germany in 1972, which normalized relations between the two nations, and in 1987 became the first East German head of state to visit West Germany. Domestically, he saw housing as a means of strengthening the state and oversaw the construction of thousands of apartments. Despite these efforts, the GDR continued to fall behind the FRG economically.

Under Honecker's leadership, East Germany became one of the east bloc's most repressive states. The Stasi, the East Germany Ministry for State Security (Ministerium für Staatssicherheit or MfS) exercised nearly complete control over the population of the nation. The Stasi's foreign intelligence wing, the HVA (Hauptverwaltung Aufklärung) carried out extensive espionage activity in the Federal Republic. When the Berlin Wall fell in 1989, the Stasi had over 91,000 full-time staff and over 175,000 collaborators within the GDR's general population of 16.4 million. Three days after the fall of the wall, Honecker was kicked out of the SED, ending his sixty-year affiliation with communism. After East Germany was absorbed by West Germany in 1990, the German government issued an arrest warrant for Honecker on homicide charges related to shooting deaths at the Berlin Wall; during his time in office, over 125 East Germans were killed trying to reach the west. The charges eventually were dropped due to his poor health, and he went into exile in Chile, where he died in 1994.

Wendell G. Johnson

See also: Chapter 2: Berlin Wall; Marx, Karl (1818–1883). Chapter 3: Government and Politics in the German Democratic Republic; Political Parties.

Further Reading

Friedrich-Ebert Stiftung. *Zur Geschichte der DDR: von Ulbricht zu Honecker.* Bonn: Verlag Neue Gesellschaft, 1986.

Fulbrook, Mary. *The People's State: East German Society from Hitler to Honecker.* New Haven, CT; London: Yale University Press, 2005.

Johnson, Wendell G. "Stasi." In Glenn P. Hastedt, ed. *Spies, Wiretaps, and Secret Operations: An Encyclopedia of American Espionage*, 736–738. Santa Barbara, CA: ABC-CLIO, 2011.

Lebendiges Museum Online. "Erich Honecker 1912–1994." https://www.hdg.de/lemo/biografie/erich-honecker.html. Accessed July 11, 2020.

Lorenzen, Jan N. *Erich Honecker: Eine Biographie.* Reinbek bei Hamburg: Rowohlt, 2001.

Pötzl, Norbert F. *Erich Honecker: Eine Deutsche Biographie.* Stuttgart: Deutsche Verlags-Anstalt, 2002.

Marx, Karl (1818–1883)

Karl Marx is considered one of the most influential social and political theorists of all time. Marxism, the philosophy that bears his name, includes a commitment to socialism, where production and consumption are determined according to need and ability, and advocates for working-class activism, which demands self-determination through suffrage.

Marx was born in Trier, in Rhenish Prussia, now Rhineland-Palatinate, one of nine children. His parents were Jewish but converted to Christianity, most likely as a response to the anti-Semitic legislation of the time. Marx studied briefly at the Universities of Bonn and Berlin (today's Humboldt Universität). Politically, he became involved with the Young Hegelians (after Georg W. F. Hegel, 1770–1831), a group that saw the historical development of liberalism within politics. Marx eventually submitted a dissertation on the ancient Greek philosophers Democritus and Epicurus to the University of Jena. In 1848, he married Jenny von Westphalen (1814–1881), and the couple had four children (three others died in infancy): Jenny Caroline (1844–1883), Jenny Laura (1845–1911), Edgar (1847–1855), and Jenny Julia Eleanor (1855–1898).

Marx took a job at a newspaper in Cologne and soon moved to Paris, where he met Friedrich Engels (1820–1895). The two men were asked by the Communist League to draft a treatise describing international socialism. The result, *The Communist Manifesto*, was presented at a conference in London in 1847. In the *Manifesto*, Marx and Engels described the development of industrial production in Europe. They predicted a series of ever-worsening economic crises that would lead to conflict between two great social classes: the bourgeoisie, who controlled capital and the means of production, and the proletariat, who provided the labor. Marx predicted that class struggle would lead to a revolution that would topple the German monarchy and reach tsarist Russia.

After the failure of revolutionary forces in France in 1848–49, Marx was expelled from Paris at the instigation of the Prussian authorities and settled in London, where he was supported financially by Engels. While in London, Marx served as the European correspondent of the *New York Tribune* and spent considerable time in the British Museum researching the capitalist means of production and the anatomy of bourgeois society, the results of which were published as *Das Kapital* in 1867.

Marx died in London in 1883. At his graveside, Engels said that Marx made two discoveries that transformed our understanding of the social world. First was his theory of the development of human history or historical materialism. Second, and this is perhaps his most striking contribution, was his theory of surplus value (*Mehrwert*), which shows that capitalism profits from the exploitation of the working class. It is important, perhaps, to differentiate between Marxism, the philosophy that bears Karl Marx's name, and communism. Marxism is the political ideology based on Marx's thought, whereas communism was the practical implementation of that thought by Lenin in revolutionary Russia.

Wendell G. Johnson

See also: Chapter 2: Honecker, Erich (1912–1994). Chapter 3: Government and Politics in the German Democratic Republic.

Further Reading

Carver, Terrell. "Marx, Karl." In John Merriman and Jay Winter, eds. *Europe 1789–1914: Encyclopedia of the Age of Industry and Empire*, 1461–1468. Detroit: Thomson Gale, 2006.

Marx, Karl, Friedrich Engels, and Ellen Meiksins Wood. *The Communist Manifesto*. New York: Monthly Review Press, 1998.

Wheen, Francis. *Karl Marx: A Life*. New York: Norton, 2000.

Wilhelm II (1859–1941)

Wilhelm II was the last king of Prussia and *kaiser* (emperor) of the German Empire. His autocratic philosophy of rule and impetuous diplomatic style are frequently blamed for Germany's diplomatic isolation and defeat in the First World War.

Wilhelm was the son of Frederick William of Prussia (1831–1888) and his wife Princess Victoria (1840–1901), the eldest daughter of Queen Victoria of the United Kingdom. A traumatic birth left him with a crippled left arm. In 1881, he married Princess Auguste Viktoria of Schleswig-Holstein (1858–1921). The couple would have six sons and one daughter.

Wilhelm succeeded his father as king and emperor on June 15, 1888. His first controversial decision was the forced resignation of Chancellor Otto von Bismarck, Europe and Germany's most respected statesman, in 1890. Although Wilhelm was widely blamed for this, Bismarck's behavior in the previous months had been growing more erratic and autocratic, and Wilhelm's decision was supported by the German elite, including the military leadership. However, the first major manifestation of Wilhelm's diplomatic impetuosity occurred a few years later, with the *Krüger Depesche* (telegram) of 1896. This expression of support of Boer Republic president Paul Krüger after the British-backed Jameson raid contributed to the deterioration of Anglo-German relations, which had been generally friendly under Bismarck. This was the first in a series of diplomatic blunders that contributed to hostility to Germany in foreign countries.

As kaiser, Wilhelm was a zealous proponent of the building of a navy strong enough to challenge Britain's domination of the seas and of the modernization of the German educational system. He was an anti-Semite who believed Jews were conspiring to bring down Germany, although he was capable of friendly relationships with Jewish individuals. The culture of the German court was highly militaristic, and the kaiser was known for his love of uniforms and parade-ground maneuvers. In 1914, Wilhelm hoped to avoid war, although his intransigence and blundering helped bring it about. During the First World War itself, Wilhelm was largely excluded from actual power, instead attending military parades and ceremonies designed to maintain German morale. His political ineffectiveness, however, did not protect him from being demonized as the embodiment of German militarism and expansionism in Allied propaganda. Wilhelm abdicated on November 9, 1918, after some confusion caused by the fact that he first tried to abdicate as kaiser while *retaining* the title of King of Prussia. This proved impossible, however.

On November 10, the ex-kaiser slipped across the border with the Netherlands, which had remained neutral during the war. He eventually settled in the Dutch community of Doorn. Despite the numerous cries of "Hang the kaiser" by the Allies, and the call for his trial in the Treaty of Versailles after the war, there was no serious effort made to extradite him, and he was allowed to live out his life in peace. In exile he composed self-serving memoirs and indulged his hobbies of hunting and chopping down trees. He observed the rise of the Nazis with some ambivalence, hoping for a restoration of the monarchy—never a serious possibility, as Hitler despised him—but was repulsed by Kristallnacht. Increasingly anti-Semitic, he applauded German victories early in the war, hoping for a cleansing of the European continent from British and Jewish corruption. Wilhelm died of a pulmonary embolism at Doorn on June 4, 1941. His tomb at Doorn remains a pilgrimage site for the small community of German monarchists.

William E. Burns

See also: Chapter 2: Bismarck, Otto von (1815–1898); Hitler, Adolf (1889–1945). Chapter 5: Judaism in Germany. Chapter 6: Aristocracy and the Elites; Jews in Germany.

Further Reading

Craig, Gordon A. *Germany 1866–1945.* New York: Oxford University Press, 1978.

Lebendiges Museum Online. "Wilhelm II 1859–1941." https://www.dhm.de/lemo /biografie/biografie-wilhelm-ii.html. Accessed July 11, 2020.

Röhl, John C. G. *Kaiser Wilhelm II: A Concise Life.* New York: Cambridge University Press, 2014.

CHAPTER 3

GOVERNMENT AND POLITICS

OVERVIEW

The Grundgesetz or Basic Law is the constitutional foundation of the Federal Republic of Germany (FRG). It was adopted in 1949 in response to National Socialism, the social dislocation of the postwar period, and the looming conflict between East and West. The Grundgesetz divides political power between federal and state (*Länder*) governments. At the federal level, it established Germany as a parliamentary democracy with three separate governmental branches: executive, legislative, and judicial. It created a multiparty democracy and, mindful of the role populism played in Hitler's rise to power, requires all state governments "to conform to the principles of a republican, democratic and social state governed by the rule of law" (Article 28). The Grundgesetz remains unamendable with regard to federalism, the separation of powers, and the role of political parties. After the fall of the Berlin Wall, it became the constitution of reunified Germany.

Political parties play an extremely significant role in German politics, and according to the Grundgesetz, form the political will of the people. Two parties dominate the political landscape in Germany: the center-right Christian Democratic Union (CDU, Christlich Demokratische Union) with its Bavarian affiliate the Christian Social Union (CSU, Christlich Soziale Union) and the center-left Social Democratic Party (SPD, Sozialdemokratische Partei Deutschlands). The Grundgesetz grants universal suffrage to citizens eighteen years of age and older. Over 60 million German citizens were eligible to vote in the 2021 federal election. Voter turnout is high in Germany; over 76% of eligible voters cast ballots in the last election (compared to 61% in the 2016 and nearly 69% in the 2020 U.S. presidential elections). Voters over seventy years of age make up nearly 21% of the electorate, the largest voter group by age.

The Legislative Branch

The Grundgesetz established a bicameral legislature. The central legislative power in Germany lies with the Bundestag (or parliament), which elects the chancellor, half the membership of the Federal Constitutional Court, and supervises the bureaucracy and military. Federal elections are held every four years. German voters elect their members to the Bundestag with two votes. The first vote is a direct vote for a specific candidate; the second vote is for the candidate-slate in each state established by the party caucus. Half of the members of the Bundestag are elected by the direct vote, and half are elected according to the proportion received by the slate of each party. A political party forms a government if it wins a majority of seats in the Bundestag. If no party wins a majority, a coalition government is formed. A party must receive at least 5% of the vote in order to be represented in the Bundestag. Generally speaking, political parties in Germany practice strict discipline and vote along party lines.

The key organizational components of the Bundestag are the caucuses (*Fraktionen*) of the members of the political parties. The size of a party's caucus determines its representation on parliamentary committees, and unlike the United States, opposition parties chair a proportional share of legislative committees. The Grundgesetz mandates four committees: Defense, Foreign Affairs, Affairs of the European Community, and Petitions. Other than these, the Bundestag itself decides how many committees it establishes; currently, there are twenty-three committees. The two largest committees are the Budget Committee and the Committee on Economic Affairs.

The Bundesrat, or the upper house of the German legislature, represents the sixteen states. Members of the Bundesrat are not popularly elected but are appointed by their respective state governments and tend to be state government ministers. There are, at present, sixty-nine members of the Bundesrat. States with at least 7 million inhabitants (Baden-Württemberg, Bavaria, Lower Saxony, and North Rhine-Westphalia) each have six seats, those with populations between 2 and 7 million (Berlin, Brandenburg, Hesse, Mecklenburg-Western Pomerania, Rhineland-Palatinate, Saxony, Saxony-Anhalt, Schleswig-Holstein, and Thuringia) each have four seats, and states with fewer than 2 million people (Bremen, Hamburg, and the Saarland) each receive three seats. In the Bundesrat, the individual states vote as a unit. According to the Grundgesetz, the Bundesrat must approve all laws related to the responsibilities of the *Länder*, giving it veto power over approximately 50% of legislation approved by the Bundestag.

The Executive Branch

The chancellor, or head of the German government, is elected by the Bundestag and is responsible for general policy guidelines. Although elected by a majority vote in the Bundestag, the chancellor cannot be brought down by a majority vote. The opposition must also have a majority vote in favor of a new chancellor before the incumbent can be replaced.

The chancellor appoints the members of the Cabinet (Bundeskabinett), who, along with the chancellor, constitute the chief executive body of the FRG. The chancellor has responsibility for the overall direction of government policy. However, within policy guidelines, each cabinet minister conducts departmental affairs independent from the chancellor. When forming the cabinet, the chancellor considers the commitments made to coalition partners and the demands of the factions within their own party. The size of the cabinet varies: At the present time, it includes fifteen federal ministers: Finance, Interior, Foreign Affairs, Economics and Energy, Justice and

Table 2.1:   CHANCELLORS OF THE FEDERAL REPUBLIC OF GERMANY

	Time in Office	Party Affiliation
Konrad Adenauer (1876–1967)	9/15/1949–10/16/1963	CDU
Ludwig Erhardt (1897–1977)	10/16/1963–12/1/1966	CDU
Kurt Georg Kiesinger (1904–1988)	12/1/1966–12/21/1969	CDU
Willy Brandt (1913–1992)	12/21/1969–5/7/1974	SPD
Walter Scheel (1919–2016) Scheel was the vice chancellor and was asked to be in a managing position until the new chancellor's assumption of office	5/7/1974–5/16/1974	FDP
Helmut Schmidt (1918–2015)	5/16/1974–10/1/1982	SPD
Helmut Kohl (1930–2017)	10/1/1982–10/27/1998	CDU
Gerhard Schröder (b. 1944)	10/27/1998–11/22/2005	SPD
Angela Merkel (b. 1954)	11/22/2005– 12/8/2021	CDU
Olaf Scholz (b. 1958)	12/8/2021–	SPD

Consumer Protection, Labor and Social Affairs, Defense, Food and Agriculture, Family Affairs, Health, Transport and Digital Infrastructure, Environment, Education and Research, Economic Cooperation and Development, and Special Affairs (the chief of staff of the chancellery).

The president (*Bundespräsident*), the head of state, is not directly elected but chosen every five years by a federal assembly consisting of Bundestag deputies and delegates elected by the state parliaments. The job of the German president is largely ceremonial, and he (no woman has yet been president) is clearly subordinate to the chancellor in matters of policy. The president appoints and dismisses federal judges, has the power to pardon criminals, and proposes candidates for the office of chancellor. The president exercises soft power in Germany, expressing the conscience of the nation on uncomfortable topics (such as its Nazi past). The official residence of the president is the Bellevue Palace in Berlin.

The Judicial Branch

The Federal Constitutional Court (FCC)

Articles 93 and 94 of the Grundgesetz established the Federal Constitutional Court, the Bundesverfassungsgericht, as the final arbiter of constitutional questions in Germany. The Court consists of two senates, each with eight members elected by the Bundestag and Bundesrat. Judges serve a single twelve-year term and face mandatory retirement at the age of sixty-eight. The main task of the FCC is judicial review. The *Bundesländer* (federal states) may appeal any federal law they deem unconstitutional to the Court. The Court also adjudicates disputes between the various *Länder* and the federal government. The FCC has the power to ban political parties, which it has done on two occasions. The Court banned the neo-Nazi Socialist Reich Party in 1952 and the German Communist Party in 1956. German officials attempted to outlaw the ultraright National Democratic Party of Germany (Nationaldemokratische Partei Deutschlands or NPD) in 2016. The Federal Constitutional Court rejected the attempt, basing its decision on the relative political insignificance of the NDP.

On more than one occasion, the Federal Constitutional Court has ruled on Germany's participation in the European Union. In 1998, the Court found the Maastricht Treaty (establishing the European Monetary Union) was constitutional. The FCC rendered one of the most important decisions in its history when it found no decisive constitutional objection to the Lisbon Treaty, which provides the constitutional basis of the European Union. However, the Court ruled that the German implementation of the Lisbon Treaty could proceed only with supplemental legislation allowing the states (through the Bundestag and Bundesrat) to give direction to Germany's representatives in the European Council.

Europe's migrant crisis has not spared the Federal Constitutional Court. In the Court's annual report for 2017, its president, Andreas Voßkuhle (b. 1963), mentioned an increase in constitutional complaints regarding asylum proceedings.

The Judiciary

German courts are organized according to their areas of jurisdiction (Lewis et al., 2001, p. 104):

- ordinary courts (*ordentliche Gerichte*) hear criminal and civil matters;
- industrial and labor courts (*Arbeitsgerichte*) rule on issues related to wages, working conditions, and labor disputes;
- administrative courts (*Allgemeine Verwaltungsgerichte*) deal with regional law and disputes between the states;
- social or welfare courts (*Sozialgerichte*) consider national insurance, pensions, and welfare legislation;
- finance and revenue courts (*Finanzgerichte*) resolve conflicts on taxation and customs.

In addition to this functional structure, German courts are organized hierarchically, with the federal courts (*Bundesgerichte*) at the apex, followed by state courts (*Landgerichte*), and then local or district courts (*Amtsgerichte*).

Federalism

Germany has a strong tradition of federal government dating back to the foundation of the empire in 1871. For the Federal Republic of Germany, the Grundgesetz stipulates that the constitutional order of the *Länder* must conform to the principles of republican, democratic, and social government (Article 28). The FRG is comprised of sixteen states, including the thirteen "area states" (*Flächenländer*) of Bavaria, Hesse, Baden-Württemberg, the Saarland, Schleswig-Holstein, Lower Saxony, Rhineland-Palatinate, North Rhine-Westphalia, Brandenburg, Thuringia, Saxony, Saxony-Anhalt, Mecklenburg-Western Pomerania, and the "city states" (*Stadtstaaten*) of Berlin, Bremen and Bremerhaven, and Hamburg.

Federalism is different in Germany compared to federal systems in other nations. In geographically larger countries such as the United States, Canada, and Australia, the federal system manages national diversity. In Germany, it is the opposite; the constitutional purpose of federalism is to foster national unity. The FRG is committed to the maintenance of a unity of living standards, the so-called *Länderfinanzausgleich* (financial equalization scheme between the federal government and the *Länder*) across the nation. Each *Land* has a similar per capita amount for education, infrastructure, health care, environmental protection, and so on. The unity of living standards is carried out vertically (federal payments to the states) and horizontally (poorer states receive a greater share of federal tax revenues than do wealthier ones). In contrast to the situation in the United States, where the individual states levy state income taxes, the *Länder* themselves generally do not have independent taxing authority. The horizontal transfer of tax revenues among states has proved controversial. Four *Länder*, Bavaria, Baden-Württemberg, Hamburg, and Hesse, contribute billions of Euros yearly to the coffers of the other twelve states.

The *Länder* have the right to legislate in areas not reserved for the federal government and have exclusive power in the areas of culture, education (including universities), matters of local authority, and the police. Recent federal reforms had given administrative authority to district or local authorities in maintaining local roads, issuing building permits, fire protection and disaster control, protection of green spaces, building and maintaining hospitals and secondary schools, waste collection, food safety, and the treatment of aliens (including entrance into the local area, residency permits, and surveillance).

Wendell G. Johnson

Further Reading

Bundesrat of Germany. http://germanculture.com.ua/germany-facts/bundesrat-of-germany/. Accessed May 26, 2018.

Conradt, David P., and Eric Langenbacher. *The German Polity*, 10th ed. Lanham, MD: Rowman & Littlefield, 2013.

Green, Simon, ed. *The Politics of the New Germany*. London: Routledge, 2008.

Gunlicks, Arthur B. *The Länder and German Federalism*. Manchester, UK: Manchester University Press; 2003.

Lewis, Derek, Johannes Schwitalla, and Ulrike Zitzlsperger. *Contemporary Germany: A Handbook*. London: Arnold, 2001.

Armed Forces

Germany was disarmed by the Allies following the Second World War and divided into four occupation zones. In 1955, East and West Germany joined different military alliances: West Germany joined NATO on May 5 and East Germany became part of the Warsaw Pact on May 14, which led to the reformulation of their respective militaries. After reunification in 1990, the East German military was dissolved. The German government suspended the military draft in 2011, and military service is no longer compulsory in the country. The unified armed forces of Germany are known as the *Bundeswehr* with three combat branches: the army (*Heer*), navy (*Marine*), and air force (*Luftwaffe*). All three combat branches are served by the Joint Support Service and Joint Medical Service. The German armed forces are under the titular command of the Minister for Defense (in 2021, Christine Lambrecht).

The German army has 60,000 active-duty soldiers. Its combat units include two armed divisions (*Panzerdivisionen*), a rapid deployment force (*Division Schnelle Kräfte*), and the Franco-German brigade headquartered in Strasbourg, France. The German navy has over sixty commissioned ships, including ten frigates and six submarines. Its primary mission is protecting German territorial waters (in the North and Baltic seas), and it participates in various NATO maritime groups. The German air force has trained with the U.S. Seventeenth Air Force in handling and delivering nuclear weapons. The reconstituted *Luftwaffe* experienced combat for the first time during the war in the Balkans in 1995. The German air force has fallen on hard times of late, as a significant portion of its aircraft are no longer serviceable.

In contrast to the United States, where each branch of the military has its own procurement and medical operations, these tasks are performed by a joint command in Germany. The ca. 41,000 personnel of the Joint Support Service (Streitkräftebasis or SKB) provide logistic and organizational support to the *Bundeswehr*. In 2002, the medical services of each branch of the *Bundeswehr* were merged into the Joint Medical Services (Zentraler Sanitätsdienst der Bundeswehr). A few specialized units, such as those for divers and aircraft crews, are not part of the Joint Medical Services. In 2016, a sixth branch of the German armed forces was commissioned, the Cyber and Information Domain Service (Kommando Cyber- und Informationsraum or KdoCIR). The KdoCIR oversees Germany's cyber warfare, information technology, and military intelligence. The Command is slated to be fully operational by 2025.

According to the German constitution (Grundgesetz or Basic Law), the *Bundeswehr* is limited to defensive operations. In 1995, the Federal Constitutional Court ruled that the *Bundeswehr*'s duties can be expanded to guarding the nation's security anywhere in the world. German troops are deployed in Afghanistan and, to a more limited degree, Syria and Iraq. However, the German public remains opposed to overseas military engagements, raising the question of what role the *Bundeswehr* will play in supporting NATO missions.

Wendell G. Johnson

See also: Chapter 2: Overview. Chapter 3: Constitutions; Germany and the United States.

Further Reading

Corum, James S., ed. *Rearming Germany*. Leiden, Netherlands; Boston: Brill, 2011.

Die Bundeswehr. https://www.bundeswehr.de/de/. Accessed July 3, 2020.

Kelleher, Catherine M. "Fundamentals of German Security: The Creation of the Bundeswehr: Continuity and Change." In Stephen F. Szabo, ed., *The Bundeswehr and Western Security*. New York: St. Martin's Press, 1990.

Citizenship

There are three paths to German citizenship: by right of blood (descended from a German parent), by right of soil (birth within the borders of Germany), and by naturalization. Prior to 1999, the Federal Republic of Germany had one of the strictest citizenship policies in Europe; these policies have been relaxed somewhat over the course of the past twenty years after a change to the German Nationality Law. The rights extended to German citizens include the right to vote, consular protection while traveling, and access to national health insurance and pension programs.

Permanent residents of Germany can apply for naturalization by fulfilling the following requirements:

- Live in Germany for at least seven years on a residency permit
- Attend an integration course (on German life and customs)
- Demonstrate German-language proficiency at the B1 level
- Be financially stable
- Have no criminal record
- Pass a citizenship test
- Renounce previous citizenship(s)

Individuals who marry a German citizen can also apply for naturalization after two years of marriage. The other requirements remain in effect.

Germany was a founding member of the European Union (EU). One of the pillars of the EU is the right of free movement, settlement, and employment across the European Union. Citizens of the EU as well as the European Economic Area (the EU plus Iceland, Liechtenstein, and Norway) and Switzerland do not need visas or permits to live, work, or study in Germany. People who have resided in Germany for five uninterrupted years may apply for a European Commission (EC) permanent resident permit.

American citizens can acquire German citizenship and become dual citizens of the United States and Germany. A child born to an American parent and a German parent acquires American and German citizenship at birth; they now no longer have to

SELECTION OF GERMAN CITIZENSHIP QUESTIONS

(All together there are 300)

Which law belongs to the basic laws in Germany?	• Possession of firearms • Private warfare • Freedom of expression✓ • Vigilante justice
What is the name of the German constitution?	• Public Law • Federal Law • German Law • Basic Law✓
Which basic right applies only to foreigners in Germany? The basic right to . . .	• Protection of the family • Human dignity • Asylum✓ • Freedom of speech
In Germany, freedom of speech means that I . . .	• can assert false facts on flyers. • can share my opinion in the form of letters to the editor. ✓ • am allowed to wear Nazi symbols. • can express my opinion as long as I don't contradict the government.
What form of government does Germany have?	• Monarchy • Dictatorship • Republic✓ • Principality
How many federal states does Germany have?	• 14 • 15 • 16✓ • 17
Which animal is Germany's national symbol?	• Lion • Eagle✓ • Bear • Horse
In Germany, you opened a letter on purpose that was addressed to another person. What did you neglect to consider?	• Right to silence • Secrecy of correspondence✓ • Official discretion • Freedom of expression
Which honorary office do German citizens have to accept when they are asked to do so?	• Club coach • Library supervisor • Election worker✓ • Teacher

Why do you have to indicate on your tax return if you belong to a church or not? Because	• that is important for German statistics. • there is a church tax that is connected to income and payroll taxes.✓ • you have to pay more taxes if you don't belong to a church. • the church is responsible for your tax return.
From which country did most of the German migrants come from?	• Italy • Poland • Morocco • Turkey✓
When were the National Socialists with Hitler in power in Germany?	• 1918–1923 • 1932–1950 • 1933–1945✓ • 1945–1989

Source: https://www.einbuergerungstest-online.eu/fragen/. Accessed October 23, 2021.

choose one or the other upon turning eighteen years of age. German citizens seeking naturalization in the United States forfeit their German citizenship unless they obtain a special permit (*Beibehaltungsgenehmigung*) before completing the naturalization process. Although Germany recognizes the validity of dual citizenship, while in Germany, the holder of dual passports is considered a German citizen only. Such individuals must enter and leave Germany on their German passports. By the same token, these individuals must present their American passports before being readmitted to the United States. American-German males must register with the United States Selective Service within three months of their eighteenth birthday. Dual citizens may have tax liabilities in both countries and are obligated to file tax returns with the U.S. Internal Revenue Service.

Wendell G. Johnson

See also: Chapter 3: Germany and the European Union; Germany and the United States. Chapter 6: Immigration. Chapter 7: Weddings and Divorce.

Further Reading

Bock, Jan-Jonathan, and Sharon Macdonald. *Refugees Welcome? Difference and Diversity in a Changing Germany.* New York: Berghahn Books, 2019.

How to Germany. "Dual Citizenship Germany/USA." https://www.howtogermany.com /pages/dualcitizen.html. Accessed July 3, 2020.

Constitutions

The constitutional history of Germany begins in 1848 when the Frankfurt Parliament passed the Imperial Act guaranteeing certain rights, including equality before the law, freedom of expression, and the abolition of capital punishment, to the German people. The following year, the parliament passed the Frankfurt Constitution, which included provisions for a hereditary emperor, a bicameral legislation, and jury trials for serious crimes and political offenses. Germany at that time was a loose amalgamation of thirty-nine separate states. The Frankfurt Constitution opens with the sentence "The German Empire consists of the lands of the German Confederation" (§1), thus answering the question as to the geographical boundaries of Germany.

The Constitution of the German Empire, often referred to as Bismarck's Imperial Constitution, came into effect after the founding of the German Empire in 1871. It established the Bundesrat, comprised of representatives of the German states; the Reichstag or Imperial Diet, elected by universal suffrage, that is, all male citizens over 25 years of age; and the office of *Reichskanzler* (imperial chancellor), who was appointed by the emperor. The chancellor Otto von Bismarck (1815–1898) acted as a one-person cabinet and was required to countersign all decrees issued by the emperor.

Emperor Wilhelm II abdicated his throne in 1918 following Germany's defeat in the First World War, and the Constitution of the German Empire was replaced by the Weimar Constitution (1919). The Weimar Constitution maintained the bicameral legislation of the previous constitution, granted women the right to vote, and established separate offices of president and chancellor. According to Article 48 of the Weimar Constitution, the president could take emergency measures without the prior consent of the Reichstag. Unfortunately, the economic challenges brought on by the Great Depression and the burdensome reparations placed on Germany by the victorious powers after World War I undermined the Weimar Republic and its constitution. After the Reichstag burned in February 1933, Chancellor Adolf Hitler claimed a Communist revolution was imminent and convinced President Hindenburg to invoke Article 48 and issue the Reichstag Fire Decree, which the government used as a pretext to curtail constitutional rights. During his time in office, Hitler based his authoritarian decrees on Article 48.

After the Second World War, the four victorious powers divided Germany into four zones of occupation. The unified western occupation zones of the United States, Great Britain, and France formed the Federal Republic of Germany (FRG) with its capital in Bonn. The eastern Soviet zone became the German Democratic Republic (GDR). Initially, each country identified itself as the representative of the German nation, and this notion was reflected in their respective constitutions.

FRG

The Basic Law for the Federal Republic of Germany (Grundgesetz) was approved by the West German states (*Länder*) and the Western Allies in 1949. The Basic Law was intended as a provisional document valid only in the West German states and was also enacted "on behalf of those Germans to whom participation was denied" (Preamble); it "loses its validity on the day in which the German people enact a constitution (*Verfassung*) on the basis of their own free decision" (§146). At the insistence of the Western Allies, Berlin was explicitly excluded from the Grundgesetz. The Grundgesetz mandated three branches of government:

- the legislative branch, a bicameral legislature (the Bundestag and Bundesrat)
- the executive branch (the chancellor, cabinet, and president)
- the judicial branch (the Federal Constitutional Court).

The Grundgesetz declared capital punishment unconstitutional, dictated that Germany was to participate in the European Union, and outlawed wars of aggression.

GDR

The GDR's first constitution, adopted in October 1949, was intended as a compromise to allow for the development of either a socialist state or a Western-style democracy. This constitution placed limits on state authority and granted citizens the right to emigrate and to strike. However, the lack of an independent constitutional judiciary seriously impaired its authority. The ruling party (the Sozialistische Einheitspartei Deutschlands or SED) issued a new constitution in April 1968, placing greater emphasis on the GDR as a socialist state and enshrining the political hegemony of the ruling party. The 1968 constitution emphasized the fraternal ties between the GDR and the Soviet Union. It identified the United States and West Germany as bastions of imperialism and sought the unification of the East and West Germany as a socialist German state. During Willy Brandt's time as chancellor, the Basic Treaty of 1972 was signed, in which the FRG and GDR recognized each other. The GDR amended its constitution once again in 1974. Gone were the hostile references to West Germany, and the GDR identified itself as a socialist state of farmers and workers. The constitution also dropped the notion that the GDR was the sole legitimate government of the German nation. In response to the upheaval brought on by the opening of the Berlin Wall, the GDR's constitution was amended for a final time in 1989 when it eliminated the SED's monopoly of power. On October 3, 1990, the Grundgesetz became the constitution of a united Germany.

Wendell G. Johnson

See also: Chapter 2: Overview; Berlin Wall; Bismarck, Otto von (1815–1898); Hitler, Adolf (1889–1945); Hindenburg, Paul von (1847–1934); Honecker, Erich (1912–1994); Wilhelm II (1859–1941). Chapter 3: *Die Wende*; Germany and the European Union; Germany and the United States; Government and Politics in the German Democratic Republic.

Further Reading

Basic Law for the Federal Republic of Germany. Berlin: German Bundestag, 2015.

Constitutional History of Germany. http://www.constitutionnet.org/country /constitutional-history-germany. Accessed October 1, 2019.

Crosby, Margaret Barber. *The Making of a German Constitution: A Slow Revolution.* Oxford, UK: Oxford University Press, 2008.

Deutscher Bundestag. "Grundgesetz." https://www.bundestag.de/parlament/aufgaben /rechtsgrundlagen/grundgesetz. Accessed October 1, 2019.

Herhoffer, Astrid. "Constitutions: GDR." In John Sandford, ed. *Encyclopedia of Contemporary German Culture*, 112. London: Routledge, 1999.

Die Wende

Die Wende, "the turnaround," refers to a series of events in 1989 and 1990 by which the German Democrat Republic (GDR) turned from the one-party rule of the Socialist Unity Party of Germany (SED, Sozialistische Einheitspartei Deutschlands) toward the parliamentary democracy of the Federal Republic of Germany (FRG).

The first of these events were the Monday demonstrations (*Montagsdemonstrationen*) held in Leipzig during October 1989. On October 2, 1989, more than 20,000 demonstrators called for democratic reforms. East German security forces broke up the demonstration and made several arrests. The following week, 70,000 marchers met while the security forces stood down. The crowds swelled to 120,000 protestors on October 16 and 300,000 on October 23. These enormous demonstrations served, in part, to force Erich Honecker (1912–1994), the general secretary (*Generalsekretär*) of the SED, from power. The demonstrations soon spread to other cities, and on November 4, 500,000 people demonstrated against the regime.

Certainly, the most dramatic event of the *Die Wende* was the fall of the Berlin Wall on November 9, 1989. That evening, Günter Schabowski (1929–2015), a spokesperson for the SED, announced that East German Citizens would be able to travel. Upon being asked about the timing for this new travel provision, he answered "*Sofort, unverzüglich*" (immediately), even though the government had planned a gradual implementation. Right away, throngs of East Berliners descended on the Berlin Wall and crossed into West Berlin, leading to the fall of the wall and the inevitable demise of the German Democratic Republic.

The first free election in eastern Germany in fifty-seven years was held on March 18, 1990, when the citizens of the GDR went to the polls to elect a parliament, the *Volkskammer*. The transcendent issue during the campaign was German reunification. An impressive 93% of the electorate turned out to vote, and the winners of the election, an Eastern affiliate of the West German Christian Democratic Union, pledged to work for the unification of the GDR and FRG.

The two German nations signed the treaty of reunification (*Einigungsvertrag*) on August 31, 1990. The treaty incorporated the five East German *Länder* (Brandenburg, Mecklenburg-Western Pomerania, Saxony, Saxony-Anhalt, and Thuringia) and the East German capital Berlin into the Federal Republic of Germany. The treaty further stipulated that the city of Berlin was to be the capital and the Basic Law (Grundgesetz) the constitution of the united land. Unified Germany became a member of the North Atlantic Treaty Organization and the European Economic Community (or Common Market, the forerunner of the European Community). The *Einigungsvertrag* also erased certain vestiges of the Second World War: Soviet armed forces withdrew from the territory of the GDR; France, Great Britain, and the United States terminated their rights and responsibilities related to Berlin and Germany (Leiby, 1999). The unification of East and West Germany was finalized on October 3, 1990; this Day of National Unity (Tag der Deutschen Einheit) is now a national holiday.

Wendell G. Johnson

See also: Chapter 2: Berlin Wall; Honecker, Erich (1912–1994). Chapter 3: Constitutions; Government and Politics in the German Democratic Republic; Political Parties; Regional Government/Federalism.

Further Reading

Leiby, Richard A. *The Unification of Germany, 1989–1990.* Westport, CT: Greenwood Press, 1999.

Wallach, H. G. Peter, and Ronald A. Francisco. *United Germany: The Past, Politics, Prospects.* Westport, CT: Greenwood Press, 1992.

Foreign Policy

The Federal Republic of Germany (FRG, Bundesrepublik Deutschland—BRD) was formally announced as an independent republic on May 5, 1949. Five months later, on October 7, 1949, the German Democratic Republic (GDR, Deutsche Demokratische Republik—DDR) was established. The two nations joined separate defense blocs in 1955: the North Atlantic Treaty Organization (FRG) and the Warsaw Treaty Organization (GDR). Together with Belgium, France, Italy, Luxembourg, and the Netherlands, the FRG was a founding member of the European Economic Community, the predecessor of the European Community. The GDR joined the Council for Mutual Economic Assistance (Comecon) under the leadership of the Soviet Union. From 1955 to 1970, the Federal Republic adhered to the Hallstein Doctrine, which stated that the FRG would regard it as an unfriendly act should any third countries (except for the Soviet Union) recognize the German Democratic Republic diplomatically. The Hallstein Doctrine eventually gave way to *Ostpolitik*, the normalization of relations between the FRG and Eastern Europe. The FRG and the GDR recognized each other with the Basic Treaty (Grundlagenvertag) of 1972, which also enabled the two German states to be recognized by the international diplomatic community. Both the FRG and GDR were admitted to the United Nations the following year (1973).

West German foreign policy employed a "culture of contrition," rebuilding relationships with countries that had been victimized during the Second World War, particularly France and the Netherlands. The West Germans also sought to make amends with Jewish communities worldwide. By 2010, the German government had paid at least $85 billion in reparations to victims of the Holocaust. The nation continues to take responsibility for the Holocaust: Holocaust denial in Germany is considered a crime of incitement to hatred and carries a prison sentence of up to five years.

Following reunification in 1990, the orientation of Germany's foreign policy generally followed that of the FRG. Germany uses soft power rather than military muscle-flexing in the conduct of its foreign policy. Foreign policy is conducted by the Foreign Ministry (Auswärtiges Amt), currently headed by Annalena Baerbock (b. 1980). Today, Germany maintains diplomatic relations with 195 countries and has permanent representatives at twelve international organizations. After the postwar economic boom of the 1950s, the FRG became one of the world's largest international donors, earmarking 0.4% of its gross national income for foreign aid (the comparative figure for the United States is 0.2%). The nation has invested heavily in soft-power infrastructure such as the German Academic Exchange Service (DAAD) and the Goethe-Institut.

Germany conducts its foreign policy multilaterally and remains committed to playing a leading role in the European Union, of which the FRG was a founding member. The eastward expansion of the European Union and NATO will increase the importance of Germany's relations with Russia.

Wendell G. Johnson

See also: Chapter 3: Armed Forces; Germany and the European Community; Germany and the United States; Government and Politics in the German Democratic Republic. Chapter 5: Holocaust. Chapter 8: DAAD; Goethe-Institut. Chapter 16: *Ostalgie.*

Further Reading

Conradt, David P., and Eric Langenbacher. *The German Polity*, 10th ed. Lanham, MD: Rowan & Littlefield, 2013.

Erb, Scott. *German Foreign Policy: Navigating a New Era*. Boulder, CO: Rienner, 2003.

Facts about Germany. "Peace and Security." https://www.tatsachen-ueber-deutschland .de/en/chapter/foreign-policy. Accessed July 3, 2020.

Maull, Hanns, ed. *Germany's Uncertain Power: Foreign Policy of the Berlin Republic.* Basingstoke, UK: Palgrave Macmillan, 2006.

The German Welfare State

Germany is regarded as a classic example of a high social-welfare state. The country provides its citizens with pensions, comprehensive health insurance, and unemployment benefits. People who are employed in Germany make payments to these parts of the social welfare systems:

(1) **Pension insurance (*Rentenversicherung*).** Contributions to pension insurance are currently nearly 18.7% of annual gross income (up to a maximum of €76,200 in the west and €68,400 in the east), split equally between employer and employee. Payments are made to pensioners when they reach the age of sixty-five; however, plans are in place to increase this to age sixty-seven over the next twenty years. Retirees collect 67% of their average net income. Low-income workers face difficult times when they retire.

(2) **Health insurance (*Krankenversicherung*).** Health insurance is considered a right and not a commodity in Germany; declaring bankruptcy because of medical expenses is unheard of in Germany. Approximately 85% of the German population is enrolled in the GKV (*Gesetzliche Krankenversicherung*), the national health care system. At the present time, the premiums are at 14.6% of monthly income, split evenly between employer and employee. However, the GKV occasionally assess a 1% co-pay to meet expenses, a cost borne entirely by the employee. Private, supplemental health plans (PKV) are also available in Germany for more deluxe coverage. Otherwise, the GKV covers pretty much all medical expenses deemed necessary by a physician.

(3) **Unemployment insurance (*Arbeitslosenversicherung*).** Unemployment insurance is presently 4.2% of the gross salary, split evenly between employer and employee. Employees who are laid off can collect up to 70% of their salaries up to one year.

German employers and employees make two additional contributions to the welfare state. Long-term nursing care insurance (*Pflegeversicherung*) was introduced in 1995 and includes both home care by caregivers and inpatient care. The present contribution is 1.7% of the gross salary, also split evenly between employer and employee. The final category of insurance is workers compensation insurance (*Unfallversicherung*), a cost borne entirely by the employers (the contribution varies by profession and averages 1.47% of employee salaries). Workers who are injured at work receive 80% of their wages for six weeks, after which they collect disability benefits. The total contributions of employers and employers to the statutory insurance plans corresponds to approximately 42% of the gross salary.

The cost of this system is severely straining the federal budget. Germany currently spends over 30% of GDP (the figure is closer to 50% in the east) on welfare. Of these funds, pensions consume 12% of GDP and health care a further 10%; the combined eclipsed the number of employed people paying into the system. The cost of reunification exacerbated the financial pressures on the social welfare network. Germany has admitted nearly 1 million refugees since 2015, and nearly half of them may qualify for social benefits. Germany's long-term commitments to its citizens leave little room for public spending on other priorities, such as national defense and education. Federal governments face the dilemma of containing the cost of social welfare without alienating the voters who depend on these benefits.

Wendell G. Johnson

See also: Chapter 2: Bismarck, Otto von (1815–1934). Chapter 3: Tax Policy. Chapter 6: The Grey Culture; Poverty.

Further Reading

Green, Simon, et al., eds. *The Politics of the New Germany*. London: Routledge, 2008.

How to Germany. "Social Security and Employee Benefits in Germany." https://www
.howtogermany.com/pages/working.html. Accessed July 3, 2020.

Germany and the European Union

Germany is a founding member of the European Union (EU). The roots of the EU go back to the Treaty of Paris (1952), which established the European Coal and Steel Community (ECSC). Along with Germany (West), the founding constituent members were France, Belgium, the Netherlands, Luxembourg, and Italy. The ECSC intended to address the devastation caused by the Second World War and announced that its main task was "to create and maintain conditions that will promote competition free from the bondage of national boundaries, obstructions and discriminations imposed by governments, and from restrictions imposed by private agreements in the form of cartels" (ECSC, 1954, p. 1). The Community originally attempted to accomplish this task by creating and expanding competitive markets for coal, iron ore, and steel. With the Treaty of Rome (1957), the six nations established the European Economic Community (EEC) or Common Market, a major step toward economic and political union on the continent. The Common Market itself evolved, offering membership to all democratic European countries. With the Treaty on European Union, signed in Maastricht (Netherlands) in 1993, the EEC officially became the European Union (EU), founded on the "four freedoms" of movement of goods, services, people, and capital. On January 1, 1999, the euro was introduced as the common currency in the EU, with the notable exceptions of Denmark, Sweden, and the United Kingdom. By 2016, twenty-eight nations had joined the EU. That same year, Great Britain announced its intention to leave the EU. Germany is acting within the framework provided by the European Union to deal with Great Britain's departure ("Brexit") from the EU.

Membership in the EU has yielded positive results for Germany. The EU functions as a vast internal market, and nearly 60% of German commerce is with other EU nations. Germany was the primary architect of the European Monetary Union, and its decision to adopt the euro was controversial domestically. With its annual contribution of €23 billion, Germany is the largest contributor to the EU's budget (in turn, the EU spends €10 billion annually in Germany). When the European sovereign debt crisis threatened the economies of several EU member states (especially Greece, but also Portugal, Ireland, and Spain) earlier this century, Germany provided 27% of the capital to keep their respective economies from defaulting on their national debt. Germany currently holds ninety-six seats in the European Parliament. In order to alleviate fears that it might use its size and wealth to dominate the

EU, Germany accepts chronic underrepresentation in the European Parliament and European Council.

Wendell G. Johnson

See also: Chapter 3: Citizenship. Chapter 4: Currency; Trade.

Further Reading

Crawford, Beverly. "German Power and 'Embedded Hegemony' in Europe." In Sarah Colvin and Mark Taplin, eds. *The Routledge Handbook of German Politics & Culture*, 329–348. London: Routledge, 2015.

Dinan, Desmond, ed. *Origins and Evolution of the European Union*. Oxford, UK: Oxford University Press, 2006.

ECSC. *Bulletin from the European Community*. October 1954.

Official Website of the European Union. https://europa.eu/european-union/index_en. Accessed July 3, 2020.

Germany and the United States

The diplomatic history of Germany and the United States has gone from violent confrontation to peaceful cooperation. Germany and the United States fought against each other in two wars in the twentieth century. The United States declared war on Imperial Germany on April 2, 1917. Up until this time, the United States was officially neutral in the Great War. The event that turned the American public against Germany was its announcement of unrestricted submarine warfare on February 1, 1917. On December 11, 1941, four days after the Japanese attack on the American naval base a Pearl Harbor, Germany declared war on the United States, dragging it into the Second World War.

Following the Second World War, the United States occupied the southern portion of Germany and the western sector of Berlin. American occupation policy pursued two main goals: the eradication of Nazism and the foundation of a Western-style democracy in Germany. Nineteen forty-eight was a pivotal year in the postwar relations between the two countries. First, in June 1948, the Soviet Union blockaded Western access to the Allied sectors of West Berlin. In response, Allied air forces established the *Luftbrücke* (Berlin Airlift) and flew over 200,000 cargo flights into West Berlin, delivering 8,800 tons of fuel and food each day until the Soviet Union lifted the blockade the following year. Second, from 1948 to 1952, the United States extended nearly $2 billion in aid to Germany under the European Recovery Program (better known as the Marshall Plan). In 1949, the United States cooperated with the West German people in the establishment of the Federal Republic of Germany.

Ten years after the end of the Second World War, Germany joined the North Atlantic Treaty Organization (NATO) in 1955. Although the formal occupation of

Germany had come to an end, the United States has continued to maintain military bases on German soil until today, including Ramstein Air Force Base, the headquarters of Air Force operations in Europe. Under NATO's weapons sharing agreement, the United States provided approximately sixty B61 nuclear bombs for use by the German armed forces (as many as twenty remain in the country).

After the terrorist attacks on September 11, 2001, German chancellor Gerhard Schröder (b. 1944) announced unlimited solidary with the United States and sent 3,500 troops to Afghanistan. However, Schröder opposed U.S. action in Iraq in 2003, resulting in strained personal relations between the chancellor and President Bush. Despite periodic disagreements, relations between President Barack Obama and Chancellor Angela Merkel were more pleasant. Obama described Merkel as "probably . . . my closest international partner these past eight years" (BBC News). Berlin and Washington were at odds over President Trump's efforts to withdraw from both the Iran nuclear deal and the Paris climate accord as well as the imposition of U.S. tariffs on steel and aluminum imports from Europe, and the withdrawal of American troops. Chancellor Merkel called President Trump's refusal to endorse the G-7 accord in June 2018 "disappointing." More recently, the former American ambassador to Germany, Richard Grenell (in office May 8, 2018 to June 1, 2020), had been criticized by German politicians for meddling in domestic affairs. "I know you are quite new at your post," said Lars Klingbeil, general secretary of the Social Democratic Party, "but it is not part of the job description of an ambassador to interfere in the politics of his guest country" (Eddy, 2018, p. A6). Upon his election, President Biden declared his intention to restore transatlantic ties between the United States and Europe.

Wendell G. Johnson

See also: Chapter 3: Armed Forces; Citizenship; Foreign Policy; Merkel, Angela (1954–).

Further Reading

BBC News. *In Pictures: Obama-Merkel Relationship.* https://www.bbc.com/news/world-europe-38010066, November 17, 2016. Accessed June 18, 2020.

Eddy, Melissa. "Promoting Europe's Conservatives, U.S. Envoy Upsets Germans." *New York Times*, June 4, 2018, A6. https://www.nytimes.com/2018/06/04/world/europe/richard-grenell-germany-us.html. Accessed August 26, 2021.

Jonas, Manfred. *The United States and Germany: A Diplomatic History.* Ithaca, NY: Cornell University Press, 1984.

Merritt, Richard L. "American Influences in the Occupation of Germany." *The Annals of the American Academy of Political and Social Science* 428(1): 91–103, 1976.

Pommerin, Reiner, eds. *The American Impact on Postwar Germany.* Providence, RI: Berghahn Books, 1995.

Schweigler, Gebhard, and Steven Muller, eds. *From Occupation to Cooperation: The United States and United Germany in a Changing World Order.* New York: Norton, 1992.

Steil, Benn. *The Marshall Plan: Dawn of the Cold War.* New York: Simon & Schuster, 2018.

Government and Politics in the German Democratic Republic

The German Democrat Republic (GDR) was created as a socialist republic on October 7, 1949, on the Stalinist model of the Soviet Union. Government functions were administered by the country's sole political party, the Socialist Unity Party of Germany (Sozialistische Einheitspartei Deutschlands or SED). The Council of State (Ministerrat) served to carry out the decisions of the SED. Its Presidium, or inner circle of the council, consisted of a chairman and eleven deputy chairs. The offices of general secretary of the SED and chairman of the Council of State were often held by a single individual. The longest-serving leaders of the GDR were Walter Ulbricht (general secretary of the SED, 1950–71; chairman of the Council of State, 1960–73) and Erich Honecker (general secretary of the SED, 1971–89; chairman of the Council of State, 1976–1989). After Honecker was forced from power in October 1989, Egon Krenz briefly held both positions.

The political history of the GDR can be divided into four distinct periods. During the initial period, from the founding of the regime in 1949 until the construction of the Berlin Wall in 1961, the government was building a socialist state and attempted to suppress all opposition. By 1950, courts in the GDR had meted out 78,000 prison sentences for political crimes. In order to maintain its hold on the power, the government established the Ministry for State Security (the Stasi, Staatssicherheitsdienst), an institution that proved crucial for the maintenance of the regime. The Stasi had over 90,000 full-time operatives (by comparison, the Nazi Gestapo had 65,000) and hundreds of thousands of informers.

In 1951, the GDR introduced its first Soviet-style five-year plan. However, economic output continued to lag, leading to the rationing of foodstuffs. In 1953, the East German authorities announced an increase in work quotas for many workers. In response, the first anti-government uprising in Eastern Europe took place in East Berlin on June 16, 1953. At least 30,000 disgruntled workers demonstrated against the new work regulations. Soviet forces quickly suppressed the uprising, killing a number of people (the exact number is not available) and wounding more than one hundred. Martial law was imposed in East Berlin on June 17. Fourteen hundred East Germans were sentenced to prison for their participation in a "fascist plot" against the government. To commemorate the victims of the uprising, the boulevard in West Berlin leading to the Brandenburg Gate was named Strasse des 17. Juni (Street of June 17th).

The construction of the Berlin Wall in 1961 inaugurated the second period of the GDR's political history, a time of stability and consolidation. The *Mauer* (wall) sealed the border between East and West Berlin and forced the East German populace to reconcile themselves with their political system. In return, the authorities introduced the "New Economic System," which promised higher wages and more consumer goods. During this period, the Berlin Quadripartite Agreement was concluded, which normalized the status of West Berlin and guaranteed access to the city through the

GDR. The agreement was opposed by East German leader Walter Ulbricht, who was subsequently forced from office. He was replaced by Erich Honecker.

During the Honecker era (1971–1989), the third period of the GDR's political history, the nation established diplomatic relations with the United States and was a signatory to the Helsinki Accord, which stabilized postwar boundaries. Domestically, Honecker sought to improve the living conditions of the GDR's citizens and accelerated the construction of mass apartment complexes to deal with the country's chronic housing shortage. To finance this program, Honecker greatly increased the nation's foreign debt and the GDR became dependent on West German aid.

Mikhail Gorbachev's introduction of *perestroika* (restructuring) in the Soviet Union introduced the final period of the GDR's political history. Throughout the 1980s, the GDR's economy continued to lag, and the supply of consumer goods worsened. Thousands of East Germans demonstrated on Monday evenings in September and October 1989, frustrated by the nation's economy and the government's refusal to allow them to leave the country. The GDR's identity was based on a single dictatorship with complete control of the economy and society. Without the wall, the nation's citizens would vote with their feet. On November 9, 1989, an SED spokesman announced that citizens of the GDR were free to cross the nation's border, and simultaneously, in effect, announcing the political and demise of East Germany. In 1990, social welfare systems and economies of East and West Germany were merged and the West German mark became the sole currency for both states. On October 3, 1990, the Day of German Unity, the former German Democrat Republic ceased to exist and formally merged with the Federal Republic of Germany.

Wendell G. Johnson

See also: Chapter 2: Overview; Berlin Wall; Honecker, Erich (1912–1994). Chapter 3: Overview. Chapter 4: Overview; Currency. Chapter 6: The Grey Culture.

Further Reading

Conradt, David P., and Eric Langenbacher. *The German Polity*. Lanham, MD: Rowman & Littlefield, 2013.

Johnson, Wendell G. "Stasi." In Glenn P. Hastedt, ed. *Spies, Wiretaps, and Secret Operations: An Encyclopedia of American Espionage*, 736–738. Santa Barbara, CA: ABC-CLIO, 2011.

Merkel, Angela (1954–)

Angela Merkel became Germany's first female chancellor following the 2005 federal election and is widely regarded as one of Europe's most influential political figures.

Growing up in the German Democratic Republic, Merkel joined the Free German Youth, the official youth organization of the ruling Social Unity Party of Germany (East) or SED. The catalyst for her political career was the fall of the Berlin Wall in

Angela Merkel was the first woman and first East German to serve as chancellor. She was originally elected in 2005 and reelected in 2009, 2013, and 2017. In 2021 she announced that she would not seek reelection to a fifth term. (European Commission)

1989. She joined the Democratic Awakening, a small independent party allied with Chancellor Helmut Kohl of the ruling conservative Christian Democratic Union (CDU). Merkel ran for a seat in the Bundestag in Germany's post-unity elections in December 1991. She won a seat representing Mecklenburg-Western Pomerania, and Kohl named her minister for women's affairs in January 1991, making Angela Merkel, at age thirty-six, postwar Germany's youngest cabinet minister.

Merkel was elected chairwomen of the CDU in 2000. The CDU lost the federal election of 2002 to the Social Democratic Party, but Merkel emerged as the CDU's opposition leader in the Bundestag. As a result of the federal election of 2005, the CDU, along with its partner the Christian Social Union (CSU), won 226 of the Bundestag's 614 seats and the SPD won 222. Neither party could form a majority government, so they formed a grand coalition with Merkel designated as chancellor, making her not only the first woman but also the first former citizen of the GDR to lead the country. During this term, Merkel sought to mitigate the effects of the meltdown of the world's financial markets on the German economy. In order to maintain confidence in the German banking system, the government announced it would guarantee private bank accounts. The government also sought to stimulate the economy by appropriating €80 billion in new spending.

Merkel retained the office of chancellor after the 2009 federal elections, this time in a coalition with the Free Democratic Party (FDP). The Greek economy collapsed the following year, threatening the integrity of the European Union and its currency, the euro. Merkel's government approved €22 billion in loans to Greece to prop up the struggling Greek economy, a move widely unpopular among German voters. In 2011, a violent xenophobic neo-Nazi group, the National Socialist Underground, emerged and murdered several members of Germany's Turkish community. In response, the government stiffened penalties for racially motivated crimes.

Merkel was named chancellor for a third term following the 2013 federal elections, once again joining with the SPD to form a coalition government. Immigration issues dominated her third term in office. Following a series of humanitarian crises in the Middle East and Africa, 800,000 refugees applied for asylum in Germany, severely straining the country's social services. This influx provided renewed momentum to the anti-immigration movement and extremist groups. In 2015, the Alternative fur Deutschland (AfD), an anti-immigration political party, won eight seats in a local legislative election in Hamburg. On December 19, 2016, a Tunisian immigrant, Anis Amri, drove a truck into a crowded Christmas market in central West Berlin, killing twelve people and injuring forty-nine others (Amri was shot and killed by police on December 23). The Islamic State claimed responsibility for the outrage, and Merkel's government reexamined security procedures in an effort to prevent further terrorist attacks.

The results of the federal election of 2017 mirrored those of the previous election of 2013. The CDU/CSU reached a coalition agreement with the SPD to form a government, thus granting Merkel her fourth term as chancellor. Merkel faces stiff challenges as chancellor. She has been a staunch supporter of the European Union during her time in office, but Euroskeptizism is on the rise across the continent and the nationalist AfD won nearly 13% of the vote, making it the largest opposition party in the Bundestag. In foreign affairs, relations with Turkey are at an all-time low and Russia continues to conduct military maneuvers on the eastern borders of the EU. Merkel stepped down as chancellor in 2021.

Merkel was born in Hamburg (in West Germany) in 1954, the daughter of Herlind and Horst Kasner, a Lutheran minister. Her father was called to a pastorate in Perleberg in East Germany, and soon thereafter, the family moved to Templin, fifty miles north of East Berlin. In high school, Angela Kasner excelled in math, but her favorite subjects were Russian and English. She studied physics from 1973–1978 at Karl Marx University in Leipzig. While there, she met her first husband, fellow student Ulrich Merkel. The couple moved to Berlin, where she worked on her doctorate at the Central Institute for Physical Chemistry of the (East) Berlin Academy of Sciences. The couple divorced in 1982. In 1998, she married Joachim Sauer (b. 1949), a professor of quantum chemistry at the Humboldt University of Berlin. She lives with her husband in an apartment in Berlin Mitte. Merkel is a huge soccer fan and can often be seen cheering on the German national soccer team.

Wendell G. Johnson

See also: Chapter 2: Berlin Wall. Chapter 3: Overview; Politics and Government in the German Democratic Republic; Political Parties. Chapter 4: Overview; Banking; Currency. Chapter 6: Immigration; Nationalism; Refugees. Chapter 7: Representation in Government; Women in the Workforce. Chapter 8: Education in the German Democratic Republic; German Universities and *Fachhochschulen*. Chapter 15: Bundesliga; FIFA World Cups.

Further Reading

Crawford, Alan, and Tony Czuczka. *Angela Merkel: A Chancellorship Forged in Crisis.* Chichester, UK: John Wiley & Sons, 2013.

The Federal Government. "Chancellor Angela Merkel." https://www.bundesregierung.de /breg-en/chancellor. Accessed July 3, 2020.

Mushaben, Joyce Marie. *Becoming Madam Chancellor: Angela Merkel and the Berlin Republic.* Cambridge, UK: Cambridge University Press, 2017.

Qvortrup, Matt. *Angela Merkel: Europe's Most Influential Leader.* New York: Overlook Duckworth, 2016.

Political Parties

Germany is a party-based parliamentary democracy. Political parties are required to garner at least 5% of the popular vote in the federal election in order to qualify for seats in the German Parliament or Bundestag. As a result of the federal election of 2021, seven parties are seated in the 20th Bundestag. No single party won a majority of seats, so the Social Democratic Party (206 seats), the Alliance 90/The Greens (118 seats), and the Free Democratic Party (92 seats) formed a coalition government after the election. This coalition is a so-called *Ampel* (stop light) coalition, signified through the colors red (SPD), yellow (FDP), and green (Alliance 90/The Greens).

The Ruling Coalition

The Social Democratic Party (Sozialdemokratische Partei Deutschlands or SPD), the strongest member of the coalition, was founded in 1875, making it Germany's oldest political party. Its strongholds are in the industrialized regions of western Germany, particularly the Ruhr area and the states of Hesse and Lower Saxony. The SPD seeks to foster social democracy, and its election manifesto called for higher taxes on wealthier citizens, investment in the nation's schools and infrastructure, and a minimum pension. SPD party chairs Willy Brandt (1969–1974), Helmut Schmidt (1974–1982), and Gerhard Schröder (1998–2005) have served as chancellors of Germany. The new chancellor is the SPD's Olaf Scholz, the former Finance Minister.

Alliance 90/The Greens (Bündnis 90/Die Grünen), a coalition of the West German Green Party and the East German protest movement Bündnis 90, won one hundred eighteen seats in the 2021 federal election, a huge increase from 2017's sixty-seven seats. The Green Party formed in 1980 as a grassroots movement comprised of environmental, peace, and human rights activists. The Greens also were a coalition partner with the ruling SPD following the 1998 federal election. The party selects two co-leaders: one male and one female, and requires that 50% of the party's elected posts be held by women.

The Free Democratic Party (Freie Demokratische Partei or FDP) is a center-right party with ninety-two seats in the Bundestag. The FDP also formed governing coalitions with the SPD following the elections of 1972, 1976, and 1980. The FDP generally advocates for free enterprise combined with social reform. It endured a disastrous election defeat in 2013, falling below the threshold of 5% of the popular vote and thus failing to win any seats in the Bundestag. In 2021, the party campaigned on a platform of calling for dramatic changes, especially following the pandemic.

Opposition Parties

The Christian Democratic Union (Christlich Demokratische Union or CDU), until 2021 headed by Chancellor Angela Merkel, is a conservative party with broad appeal in Germany. The CDU was founded shortly after the Second World War and was dominated by Konrad Adenauer, who served as chancellor of the FRG from its founding in 1949 until 1963. Helmut Kohl of the CDU was chancellor when the Berlin Wall fell on November 9, 1989, and presided over the reunification of Germany in 1990. More recently, the CDU under Merkel has been a strong supporter of the European Union, but her liberal stance on immigration has cost her support among the CDU's base electorate. In 2021 the CDU/CSU won 197 seats. The Christian Social Union (Christlich Soziale Union or CSU) is the Bavarian affiliate of the CDU. By mutual agreement, the CSU is unopposed by the CDU in Bavaria and does not present a slate of candidates outside of the state. For years, the CSU was headed by Franz-Josef Strauss (1915–1988), who was minister-president of Bavaria following the 1978 state election and the CDU/CSU candidate for chancellor in the 1980 federal election, which was won by Helmut Schmidt (1918–2015). The Alternative for Germany (Alternative für Deutschland or AfD) won eighty-three seats in 2021, losing 11 seats from the 2017 election. The AfD, a right-wing nationalist party, contends that Germany's national identity is under attack by European integration and the presence of refugees and immigrants. The party wants to close Germany's borders to refugees, encourages foreign residents to return to their countries of origin, rejects Islam as a component of German society, and questions the scientific validity of climate change. The AfD's electoral strength lies in the eastern states of Germany, particularly Thuringia and Saxony. Its supporters are predominantly male (69%) and with a median age of 51.4 years, slightly older than the average German voter.

The Left (Die Linke), with thirty-nine seats in the Bundestag, is an electoral alliance of two left-wing parties, the Party of Democratic Socialism and the Electoral Alternative for Labor and Social Justice. Die Linke is particularly strong in the former Communist states and among the working classes. The party has called for increases in pensions, the minimum wage, and unemployment benefits; proposes additional taxes on wealthier Germans to fund infrastructure and schools; and seeks to withdraw all German soldiers from foreign deployments. Die Linke has no natural coalition partners in the Bundestag, but at the state level, it heads the government in Thuringia under Premier Bodo Ramelow.

Wendell G. Johnson

See also: Chapter 1: Climate Policy and Recycling. Chapter 2: Adenauer, Konrad (1876–1967); Berlin Wall. Chapter 3: Armed Forces; The German Welfare State; Germany and the European Union; Merkel, Angela (1954–); Regional Government/Federalism. Chapter 6. Immigration; Nationalism; Refugees. Chapter 7: Representation in Government.

Further Reading

"Germany's Political Parties CDU, CSU, SPD, AfD, FDP, Left Party, Greens—What You Need to Know." *Deutsche Welle*, 2018. http://www.dw.com/en/germanys-political-parties-cdu-csu-spd-afd-fdp-left-party-greens-what-you-need-to-know/a-38085900. Accessed August 26, 2021.

Lansford, Tom, ed. *Political Handbook of the World 2016–2017*, vol. 1. Thousand Oaks, CA: Sage, 2017.

Regional Government/Federalism

German federalism dates back to the founding of the German Empire in 1871 and was written into the postwar constitution (the Grundgesetz or Basic Law) of the Federal Republic: "Except as otherwise provided or permitted by this Basic Law, the exercise of state powers and the discharge of state functions is a matter for the *Länder*" (§ 30). After the Second World War, Germany was divided into four zones of occupation: French, British, and American constituted the West and Soviet the East. The "area states" (the *Flächenländer*) in the western zone—Bavaria, Hesse, Baden-Württemberg, Schleswig-Holstein, Lower Saxony, Rhineland-Palatinate, North-Rhine-Westphalia, and the Saarland—along with the "city states" (*Stadtstaaten*) of Bremen and Bremerhaven, and Hamburg formed the basis of the Federal Republic of Germany. The status of Berlin, itself divided into four zones, remained a point of contention among the occupying powers. The five states in the eastern zone—Mecklenburg-Western Pomerania, Brandenburg, Saxony, Saxony-Anhalt, and Thuringia—were effectively dissolved in 1952 and subdivided into three administrative districts within the German Democratic Republic. After the reunification of Germany in 1990, the eastern *Länder* of the German Democratic Republic were reconstituted and were incorporated into the Federal Republic of Germany.

At the present time, all sixteen German states have a unicameral legislature (Bavaria had a bicameral legislature until 1999) with an executive *Ministerpräsident(in)* or prime minister for the area states and *Bürgermeister* or mayor for the city states) responsible to it. The states exercise broad discretion in the areas of education (including universities), cultural activities, and police authority. Recent federal reforms have extended this authority to maintaining local roads, issuing building permits, fire protection and disaster control, hospitals, garbage collection, food safety, and the treatment of foreign nationals (including residency permits and surveillance).

The German states influence national, federal policy through their representation in the Bundesrat (the upper house of the German legislature). Members of the Bundesrat are not elected by popular vote but are appointed by their respective state governments. There are, at present, sixty-nine members of the Bundesrat. States with at least 7 million inhabitants (Baden-Württemberg, Bavaria, Lower Saxony, and North Rhine-Westphalia) each have six seats, those with populations between 2 and 7 million (Berlin, Brandenburg, Hesse, Mecklenburg-Western Pomerania, Rhineland-Palatinate, Saxony, Saxony-Anhalt, Schleswig-Holstein, and Thuringia) each have four seats, and states with fewer than 2 million people (Bremen, Hamburg, and the Saarland) each receive three seats. In the Bundesrat, the individual states vote as a unit. According to the Grundgesetz, the Bundesrat must approve all laws related to the responsibilities of the *Länder*, giving it veto power over approximately 50% of legislation approved by the Bundestag. In contrast to the situation in the United States where the individual states levy state income taxes, the *Länder* themselves generally do not have independent taxing authority. Rather, the federal government transfers tax revenue to the states, and the poorer states receive a greater share of federal tax revenues than do wealthier ones.

Below the state level, German counties are governed by an elected council and a county manager (who is chosen by the council, except for Bavaria, where the executives are elected by popular vote). Local governments serve two functions: compulsory duties (education, sanitation, fire protection) and duties transferred to them by the *Länder* (health care, housing, revenue collection). Local communities are dependent on revenue transfers from the federal and *Länder* governments. As a result, many city governments are heavily indebted, particularly in the eastern part of the country where the development of urban infrastructure was neglected by the authorities of the German Democratic Republic.

Wendell G. Johnson

See also: Chapter 3: Overview; Constitutions; *Die Wende*; Tax Policy.

Further Reading

Conradt, David P., and Eric Langenbacher. *The German Polity*, 10th ed. Lanham, MD: Rowman & Littlefield, 2013.

Gunlicks, Arthur B. *The Länder and German Federalism*. Manchester, UK: Manchester University Press, 2003.

Rowe, Carolyn, and Wade Jacoby. *German Federalism in Transition: Reforms in a Consensual State*. London: Taylor & Francis Group, 2013.

Umbach, Maiken. *German Federalism: Past, Present, Future*. Basingstoke, UK; New York: Palgrave, 2002.

Sports and Government

Germany played a leading role in the use of sports for political ends throughout the twentieth century. The 1936 Summer Olympic Games, the so-called "Hitler Olympics" held in Berlin, remain perhaps the most blatant use of sports for political purposes. Joseph Goebbels, the propaganda minister of the Third Reich, sought to draw an aesthetic connection from the Greek origins of the Olympic Games to the Third Reich. Written, directed, and produced by Leni Riefenstahl, who was arrested and found to be a Nazi sympathizer after the Second World War, the 1936 Games were the subject of the first documentary feature film on the Olympic Games, *Olympia* (1938).

Following the war, East and West Germany established separate national sports organizations: the German Sport Federation (Deutscher Sportbund or DSB) in the West and the German Gymnastics and Sports Association (Deutscher Turn- und Sportbund der DDR or DTSB) in the East. The two nations also formed separate Olympic committees. It was not until 1968, that the East German Olympic committee was recognized by the International Olympic Committee, so the two nations competed together as the United Team of Germany (Équipe unifiée d'Allemagne or EUA) until that time.

Germany hosted the Summer Olympic Games twice, in Berlin (1936) and Munich (1972), and the Winter Olympic Games once, in Garmisch Partenkirchen (also in 1936). The American track and field athlete Jesse Owens achieved international fame by winning four gold medals in the 1936 Summer Games. (The Illustrated London News Picture Library)

In its effort to gain international recognition, the German Democratic Republic (GDR) elevated the politicization of sport to unparalleled heights. The GDR considered its athletes "diplomats in track suits" (Dennis, 1999, p. 577) and enjoyed widespread international success, becoming one of the world's top sporting nations. This success came at a price, however. After reunification, it was revealed that the government of the GDR promoted the widespread use of performance-enhancing drugs. The GDR's influence on the international athletic stage continues to this day. Its abiding contributions, since copied by many nations, include

- initiating a government policy on sports;
- providing government funding for full-time athletes;
- establishing a system for identifying athletic talent on a national scale;
- professionalizing the coaching ranks;
- integrating sports medicine into athletic performance (Grix, 2015).

Munich in West Germany was awarded the 1972 Summer Olympic Games. The nation hoped to stage the games as proof that it had successfully transformed itself from a defeated aggressor to a responsible member of the international community. Tragically, the 1972 Summer Games were marred by the murder of eleven members of the Israeli Olympic team and a West German policeman at the hands of Palestinian terrorists. An example of united Germany's use of international athletic competition for political ends was its successful bid to host the FIFA 2006 World Cup. In contrast to the calamity of the 1972 Summer Games, the 2006 World Cup improved the stereotypical and often negative international image of Germany.

At the present, the Federal Ministry of the Interior (Bundesministerium des Innern or BMI) is the government agency responsible for the promotion of high-performance sports as distinguished from recreational sports in Germany.

Wendell G. Johnson

See also: Chapter 15: FIFA World Cups; Leisure and Sports in the German Democratic Republic; Olympic Games. Chapter 16: Film.

Further Reading

Dennis, Mike. "Sport: GDR." In John Sandford, ed. *Encyclopedia of Contemporary German Culture*, 576–577. London: Routledge, 1999.

Grix, Jonathan. "Sport Politics." In Sarah Colvin and Mark Taplin, eds. *The Routledge Handbook of German Politics & Culture*, 441–456. London: Routledge, 2015.

Tax Policy

The German constitution (Grundgesetz, or Basic Law) dictates that the Federal Republic is to maintain "equal living conditions" across the states (*Länder*) (Art. 72 §). In order to further this goal, German tax policy operates on a system of financial

---

COMPULSORY SOCIAL INSURANCE TAXES

In addition to income taxes, Germany levies taxes to pay for various compulsory social insurance programs. The contributions are paid by both the employer and the employee. Below are the rates for 2021.

	Employer Contribution	Employee Contribution
Health Insurance	7.3%	7.3%
Nursing-care Insurance	1.525%	1.525%
Pension Insurance	9.3%	9.3%
Unemployment Insurance	2.4%	2.4%
Accident (Workers Comp) Insurance	1.25%	N/A

Source: https://www.expatica.com/de/ . . . /Income-tax-in-Germany-for-employees_108112. html. *Accessed October 23, 2021.*

---

equalization (*Finanzausgleich*), which allocates tax revenues on the basis of *vertical equalization* between the federal government and the states and *horizontal equalization* among the states themselves. According to this policy, each state receives similar per capita funding from the federal government for schools, hospitals, infrastructure, and so on.

Germany levies a progressive tax on personal incomes. In 2021, the first €9,744 are tax-free. Incomes above €57,918 are taxed at a rate of 42%; for incomes above €273,613, the rate rises to 45%. The taxes are made up of income tax and social contributions (*Sozialabgaben*). German incomes are also subject to an up to 5.5% surcharge used primarily to cover the costs of Germany reunification; however, since 2021, this tax is only paid on incomes above €61,700. This graduated "solidary surcharge" (*Solidaritätszuschlag* or *Soli*) is used to cover the debts and pension obligations owed by the East German government as well as costs associated with infrastructure upgrades and environmental remediation. According to the Organization for Economic Co-operation and Development (OECD), tax on personal income in Germany amounts to 10% of gross domestic product.

German tax policy, in part, is based on Article 20 of the German constitution, which stipulates that the Federal Republic of Germany is a democratic and social federal state obligated to "protect the natural foundations of life . . ." (Article 20). Accordingly, German tax revenue finances a very comprehensive social welfare system, consuming 29% of the national gross domestic product. In order to finance this social safety net, additional taxes are levied to cover insurance programs for health (obligatory in German), nursing care, pensions, unemployment, and workers' compensation.

Property owners in Germany pay property tax (*Grundsteuer*) that is based on the assessed value of the property. Property taxes in Germany tend to be quite low: the average tax for a private household is only €200 ($230 as of October 2018). By comparison, the average American household pays approximately $2,200 (€1,909) per annum. In lieu of sales taxes, Germany levels a 19% value-added tax (VAT) on the added value of an article at each state of production. The German rate is slightly below the European average (the rate in Spain, Belgium, and the Netherlands is 21%) and is reduced to 7% for certain consumer goods and services (such as food, public transportation, and hotel stays). Some services, such as banking and health care, remain VAT free.

Wendell G. Johnson

See also: Chapter 3: Constitutions; The German Welfare State. Chapter 4: Gross Domestic Product (GDP).

Further Reading

Colvin, Sarah, and Mark Taplin, eds. *The Routledge Handbook of German Politics & Culture*. London: Routledge, 2015.

Expatica. "How to File Your Income Taxes in Germany," 2021. https://www.expatica.com /de/finance/taxes/income-taxes-in-germany-108112/. Accessed October 23, 2021.

Lewis, Derek, Johannes Schwitalla, and Ulrike Zitzlsperger. *Contemporary Germany: A Handbook*. London: Arnold, 2001.

OECD iLibrary. "Tax on Goods and Services." https://www.oecd-ilibrary.org/taxation /tax-on-goods-and-services/indicator/english_40b85101-en. Accessed July 3, 2020.

CHAPTER 4

ECONOMY

Wayne Finley

OVERVIEW

The success of the modern German economy is impressive considering the country and its economy were devastated by World War II. The German economy was stifled in the years immediately following the war as Allied forces, wishing to both prevent another war and punish Germany, set out to dismantle German military manufacturing and the industries that could support the production of weapons. The framework for the rollback of German industry was set forth in the Potsdam Agreement in 1945. Not only were factories dismantled, but also sanctions on the production of steel were strangling German manufacturing. The effects of the Potsdam Agreement were short-lived, as the Marshall Plan of 1948 helped ease production restrictions and directed money toward rebuilding Germany's infrastructure and industrial sector, and compelled other European nations to trade with Germany.

Following the division of Germany into the Federal Republic of Germany (West Germany) and the German Democratic Republic (East Germany), different governments and economic policies led West Germany to a seemingly miraculous recovery, while the East German economy grew but faced hardships. But even years after reunification, the effects of World War II and the countries' respective postwar economic policies are still seen in the current economic conditions of states in the east and in the west. Taken as a whole, Germany now has one of the strongest economies in the world. Much of the current success of the German economy is due to the economic choices made in West Germany in the middle of the twentieth century.

From 1949 to 1959, West Germany's economy had a dramatic turnaround called the Economic Miracle (*Wirtschaftswunder*). During the Economic Miracle, Germany's gross domestic product grew at a rate of almost 10% per year. Ludwig Erhard, West Germany's minister of Economic Affairs from 1949 to 1963, implemented many of the reforms that led to the country's postwar success. Erhard promoted economic reforms that backed a "social market economy" philosophy. In a social market economy, businesses operate in a free market, but the government reserves the right to protect consumers through the use of regulations such as antitrust laws and price limits on certain goods and services. Citizens are protected by having access to social programs such as socialized health care, free education, and unemployment benefits. Employee rights are protected by government regulations such as minimum wage requirements, collective bargaining rights, and equal pay laws.

Immediately following the war, German citizens experienced rampant inflation, shortages of goods, and Allied-sanctioned price controls. As a result, black markets emerged. One of the first steps in the West German recovery was currency reform (*Währungsreform*). West Germany abandoned the *Reichsmark* and adopted the deutsche mark as its official currency on June 20, 1948. The exchange rate was set was set at 10 *Reichsmark* for 1 deutsche mark. At the same time, price controls were lifted. With this new, stable currency, West German citizens were now able to satisfy their demand for goods. These events are considered the starting point of the German Economic Miracle.

Despite the Allied dismantling of the German manufacturing industry, the country was able to quickly revitalize its manufacturing sector to accommodate a growing demand for goods. The adoption of the stable deutsche mark also increased the demand for German-produced goods from European countries and the United States. And demand for German industrial goods increased with the advent of the Korean War. This demand of goods from both German and foreign consumers caused a rapid increase in manufacturing. For centuries, Germany had a reputation for its skilled laborers, and its manufacturing sector was renowned for its ability to innovate. These characteristics were essential to the rebirth of the West German manufacturing sector and its ability to quickly meet the growing demand for manufactured goods.

With the growth of manufacturing came an increased need for unskilled labor in German factories and mines. The labor supply in Germany was not sufficient to fill the number of job vacancies. At the same time, many European countries were facing high levels of unemployment. To fill the increasing demand for laborers, the German government began recruiting unskilled guest workers from other European countries. Known as *Gastarbeiter* in German, these laborers came primarily from countries in Mediterranean Europe and North Africa. The German government even entered into treaties with Italy and Turkey that defined terms for guest workers. The practice of inviting unskilled laborers into Germany lasted until 1973, but Germany has recently started to recruit skilled, educated workers.

The ability for workers to form work councils and unions was abolished by the Nazis during World War II. The right for workers to organize was restored by the Allied Control Commission and was later codified in the Collective Bargaining Act of 1949. A fundamental ideal of German labor relations is the principle of codetermination (*Mitbestimmung*), in which labor is granted a say in the operations of a company through seats on company boards. This principle, although routinely practiced, was not part of German law until the Codetermination Act of 1951, which gave coal and steel workers representation on company boards. The representation of workers on corporate boards was extended to other industries and made mandatory for all companies employing 500 or more workers in the Works Constitution Act of 1952. The Works Constitution Act ensures that one-third of the seats on a company's supervisory board are reserved for employees. The Codetermination Act of 1976 gave even more representation to employees at larger firms. If a company has 2,000 or more employees, half of all supervisory board members must be employees.

Although the economy of East Germany grew significantly for nearly two decades after World War II, it never reached the same levels of growth as that of West Germany. While West Germany adopted the social market economy, East Germany operated under a centralized, planned economy that was guided by the Socialist Unity Party and was heavily influenced by the Soviet Union. In the new planned economy, many industries were nationalized and an emphasis was placed on the agriculture sector.

East Germany also underwent a dismantling of its military production facilities by the Soviet Union. However, it did not receive the same injection of aid from the Marshall Plan as did West Germany. Additionally, the Soviet Union demanded the payment of reparations, severely taxing the East German economy. Another factor that hurt the East German industry was the large-scale nationalization of private firms and industries. Large farms were also broken up, and the land was either absorbed by the government or redistributed to laborers. Eventually, most agriculture production in East Germany would come from large-scale farm cooperatives.

Despite not enjoying the same levels of economic success as West Germany, citizens of East Germany had one of the highest standards of living in the Eastern Bloc. At one point, East Germany was also one of Europe's most dominant industrial nations. The East German economy was still growing in the early 1980s. However, the latter half of that decade was a period of economic turmoil for Eastern Germany, as the country experienced slow growth and trade deficits.

By the time the East German border was opened to West Germany in 1989, the East German economy was suffering, as were the economies of Eastern Bloc nations. Immediately after the border opening, East Germans flocked to West Germany, leading to increased unemployment in the East. The dire economic conditions of the East made economic action from the West a necessity.

In 1990, the Federal Republic of Germany and the German Democratic Republic enacted a treaty establishing a Monetary, Economic and Social Union. The treaty effectively brought the formerly socialist economy of the East into the social market economy of the West. The deutsche mark became the official currency of both the East and West, replacing the East German currency at an exchange rate set at 1 to 1. The treaty also gave former East German citizens access to the social services of West Germany, and provided them with unemployment insurance and wage support payments. These drastic and immediate measures were put in place with the hope that they would prevent the further flow of immigration from East to West Germany.

The now unified economies of the East and West struggled shortly after reunification. The former East German states were not able to keep up with the West, and the industrial abilities of the East were vastly undeveloped compared to those of the West. Unified Germany faced massive unemployment rates and began taking on debt to pay for investments in infrastructure in the East, absorb East German debt, and pay for social programs such as the continuation of East German pension benefits. The new unified government also had to curb inflation, and, as a result, interest rates rose.

MITTELSTAND

Mittelstand firms are family-owned businesses or small and medium-sized enterprises (SMEs) with annual revenues under €50 million and fewer than 500 employees. Aside from their size, SMEs differ from other enterprises because they operate according to a relatively common set of values and management practices. They are often a family business that remains committed to its workers and region, are export oriented, and produce a business-to-business niche product. German SMEs are managed by thin hierarchies, practice social responsibility, and finance their operations with their own equity. They are known for high levels of productivity, quality control, and innovation. *Mittelstand* firms invest heavily in research and development and in the training and professional development of their workers.

Mittelstand firms have been and remain crucially important to Germany's economic success. Often referred to as "micro-multinationals," SMEs comprise 99.6% of all German companies. Some 70% are in small cities and rural areas, especially in the federal states of North Rhine-Westphalia (with 2,300 of the leading SMEs), Bavaria (1,997), and Baden-Württemberg (1,812). Critical to the nation's economy, SMEs employ 59.4% of all German workers and have 82.2% of job trainees. They employ over 90% of wholesale and retail trade workers, over 80% of those providing services, and over 60% of construction and transportation-storage jobs. Smaller numbers are in mining and manufacturing and energy and water supply.

William P. Kladky

Further Reading

Parella, Jordi Franch, and Gemma Carmona Hernández. "The German Business Model: The Role of the Mittelstand." *Journal of Management Policies and Practices* 6(1): 10–16, 2018.

Years after reunification, the effects of the postwar economic policy are still apparent in the former Eastern states, as demonstrated by their respective gross regional products. The new federal states of Germany contributed approximately 15% of the nation's gross domestic product (GDP). Unemployment in the East is higher than that in the West, and average incomes are also lower.

In 1992, Germany, along with other European nations, signed the Maastricht Treaty. The treaty, which created the European Union, went into effect on November 1, 1993. As a member of the European Economic and Monetary Union, Germany uses the euro (€) as its official currency. The euro was adopted as the official currency of Germany on January 1, 1999, replacing the deutsche mark.

In the last twenty years, Germany's GDP has increased steadily except for a short period between 2002 and 2003, and in 2009 when Germany and other countries experienced the economic effects of the Great Recession. Today, Germany has the largest economy in Europe and the fourth largest in the world based on GDP, which totaled nearly $4 trillion in 2019. The western and southern states contribute the most to the German economy. Of Germany's nearly $4 trillion GDP, the services sector is the largest economic sector, making up nearly 70% of the total economy, and employing nearly 75% of all workers.

Industry and manufacturing are still a vital part of the German economy. In 2020, 22% of Germany's GDP came from industrial activities, with almost 20% of total GDP coming from manufacturing. In 2019, over a quarter of German jobs came from the industry and manufacturing sectors. German workers have a long-standing reputation for their innovation, high levels of craftsmanship, and strong work ethic. This emphasis on manufacturing is demonstrated in Germany's trade statistics. Germany produces 16% of the world's supply of machinery and equipment and is the world's largest exporter of automobiles. Although Germany is home to some of the world's most well-known manufacturing companies such as Volkswagen, Daimler, BMW, and Siemens, it is small and medium-sized (*Mittelstand*) firms that are the heart of the German manufacturing sector. *Mittelstand* firms often produce specialized precuts and own a significant percentage of market shares in their respective industries.

The principle of codetermination is also still an essential part of the German business world. German corporations follow a two-tiered system of corporate governance. All large companies have two boards: a supervisory board and an executive board. A company's supervisory board is tasked with electing and advising the executive board, and the executive board oversees the operations of the company. The supervisory board is comprised of company employees and stock owners. The number of employees on the supervisory board is proportional to the total number of employees working in the organization.

The ideals of the social market economy are still alive in the German business world. Workers in Germany enjoy a high level of work–life balance. They are protected by numerous labor laws that grant guaranteed minimums for paid time off from work, numerous federal holidays, paid sick leave and family leave, and easy access to parental leave. One example of this type of law is the Working Hours Act, which sets limits on the number of hours a company can require an employee to work in a week and defines break times. Another example is the Transparency on Pay Act, which is intended to shrink the pay gap between men and women in Germany by compelling corporations to divulge information about difference in pay between the male and female employees working in the corporation.

Wayne Finley

Further Reading

Berghoff, Hartmut, and Uta A. Balbier. *The East German Economy, 1945–2010: Falling Behind or Catching Up?* Washington, DC; New York: German Historical Institute; Cambridge University Press, 2013.

Glossner, Christian Ludwig. *The Making of the German Post-war Economy: Political Communication and Public Reception of the Social Market Economy after World War II.* London; New York: Tauris Academic Studies, 2010.

Spicka, Mark E. *Selling the Economic Miracle: Reconstruction and Politics in West Germany, 1949–1957.* New York: Berghahn Books, 2007.

Agriculture

Although it makes up only 0.7% of Germany's GDP, agriculture, which includes forestry and fishing, is still an important part of the Germany economy (Statistisches Bundesamt, 2019a). In 2020, the agriculture sector employed 1.17% of all German workers (World Bank, 2019). Germany ranks as the number three exporter of agriculture products in the world (Federal Ministry of Food and Agriculture, 2020c), and is one of the four largest in the European Union (Federal Ministry of Food and Agriculture, 2020a). It is known for growing many of the ingredients of beer including hops, barley, and wheat. Germany is the world's largest producer of hops and is responsible for one-third of the world's supply. Other key agricultural products include sugar beets, potatoes, and wine. Germany is well known for its signature white wine, Riesling.

Over the past forty years, the number of agriculture-related business in Germany has diminished dramatically (Statistisches Bundesamt, 2019b). Despite the decrease in businesses, agriculture dominates the German landscape, as over 50% of all land in Germany is used for agriculture production (Federal Ministry of Food and Agriculture, 2020c). Ninety-nine percent of Germany's land used for agriculture is either arable land or permanent grasslands and meadows. The arable land is used mainly to produce cereal grains, animal feed, and industrial crops (Eurostat, 2018). Much of the grasslands and meadows in Germany are used to support animal production—specifically cattle for the dairy industry (Federal Ministry of Food and Agriculture, 2020c). Agricultural production differs significantly throughout Germany. Cereals are produced mainly in the west and southwest. Most of the cattle production takes place in the northwest and southwest, and the production of pigs is centered in the northwest. The majority of wine and hops production takes place in the south (Federal Ministry of Food and Agriculture, 2020c). The Hallertau region of Bavaria grows the majority of Germany's hops (Federal Ministry of Food and Agriculture, 2020c). The demand for organic food among German consumers is increasing, and Germany is now the largest market for organic food in the European Union (Zech, 2019). However, the domestic supply of organic food cannot keep up with demand, making Germany a net importer of organic food (ARC 2020, 2018). To help curb this imbalance and also reduce the amount of carbon emissions coming from agriculture production, the German government has set the goal of having 20% of all land used for agriculture farmed via organic processes by 2030 (ARC 2020, 2018). As of 2017, only 9.9% of land was farmed organically (Appunn, 2018). Bavaria and Baden-Württemberg are the two states with the most land used for organic agriculture (Federal Ministry of Food and Agriculture, 2020b).

Wayne Finley

See also: Chapter 1: Overview. Chapter 14: Overview; Beer; Wine.

Further Reading

Appunn, Kerstine. "Climate Impact of Farming, Land Use (Change) and Forestry in Germany," 2018. https://www.cleanenergywire.org/factsheets/climate-impact-farming -land-use-change-and-forestry-germany. Accessed October 23, 2021.

ARC 2020. "Germany—20% Organic by 2030?," 2018. https://www.arc2020.eu/germany -20-organic-2030/. Accessed October 23, 2021.

Eurostat. "Archive: Agricultural Census in Germany," 2018. https://ec.europa.eu/eurostat /statistics-explained/index.php?title=Agricultural_census_in_Germany&oldid =379544. Accessed October 23, 2021.

Federal Ministry of Food and Agriculture. "Farming," 2020a. https://www.bmel.de/EN /Agriculture/agriculture_node.html. Accessed October 23, 2021.

Federal Ministry of Food and Agriculture. "Organic Farming in Germany," 2020c. https:// www.bmel.de/EN/topics/farming/organic-farming/organic-farming_node.html .Accessed October 23, 2021.

Federal Ministry of Food and Agriculture. "Understanding Farming: Facts and Figures about German Farming," 2020b. https://www.bmel.de/SharedDocs/Downloads/EN /Publications/UnderstandingFarming.pdf;jsessionid=22BF2928B700E02CC6E9FCEA F1D9D277.1_cid385?__blob=publicationFile. Accessed October 23, 2021.

Statistisches Bundesamt. "Germany: Share of Economic Sectors in Gross Domestic Product (GDP) in 2018." In Statista, 2019a. https://www.statista.com/statistics/295519/germany- share-of-economic-sectors-in-gross-domestic-product/. Accessed October 23, 2021.

Statistisches Bundesamt. "Number of Businesses in German Agriculture from 1975 to 2019 (in 1,000s)." In Statista, 2019b. https://www.statista.com/statistics/1070967 /agriculture-number-businesses-germany/. Accessed October 23, 2021.

World Bank. "Germany: Distribution of Employment by Economic Sector from 2009 to 2019" [Graph]. In Statista, 2020. https://www.statista.com/statistics/624297 /employment-by-economic-sector-in-germany/. Accessed October 23, 2021.

Zech, Tanja. "More Organic Farming," 2019. https://www.deutschland.de/en/topic /environment/how-germany-is-promoting-organic-farming. Accessed October 23, 2021.

Banking

Germany's banking system is far-reaching and complicated compared to other developed nations. With over 36,000 banks (as of 2017), Germany has more banks than any other nation in Europe, and more banks per capita than any other country in the world. Germany uses a three-tiered banking system, with each type of bank differing in its ownership and purpose. The three types of banks are private commercial banks, public savings banks, and cooperative banks. Despite the differences in ownership and purpose, all three bank types are universal banks that offer both commercial and investment services. These banks also offer basic consumer services such as receiving customer deposits and granting loans.

Of the three types of banks, cooperative banks (*Kreditgenossenschaften*) are most numerous in terms of the number of individual institutions. The idea of the cooperative bank came about in Germany during the mid-nineteenth century. Similar to the credit unions of the United States, cooperative banks are owned by their members, who usually join by depositing money into the institution. Although cooperative banks are open to the public, their focus is on supporting the needs of local members.

While private commercial banks (*Private Geschäftsbanken*) do not have as many institutions as cooperative banks, they do hold 40% of Germany's banking assets. These large-scale banks, such as Deutsche Bank, are owned by private investors and focus on exports and foreign transactions.

Public savings banks are owned by either the federal, state, or municipal governments. The goal of these banks is to support the economic development of the areas they serve. There are two types of public savings banks—*Sparkassen* and *Landesbanken*. *Sparkassen* are located in cities and locally owned and managed. *Landesbanken* serve larger regions and are owned by the federal government. Although both banks provide typical individual bank accounts and loans, the larger *Landesbanken* supports the *Sparkassen* and provides financial services to larger organizations and state and local governments.

Personal banking operations at all three bank types are similar. Customers, both residents and expatriates, can open a *Giro* account (checking account) by depositing cash or making a money transfer. This account may incur a monthly fee. *Geldautomat* (ATM) transactions are conducted using a bank-issued *EC-Karte* (an ATM and credit card), and customers can also receive regular credit cards. In addition, customers of German banks have access to services that most American banks do not offer. These services include exchanging currencies, purchasing financial instruments such as stocks and bonds, and conducting real estate transactions. Banking hours usually run from 8:30 until 16:00 on weekdays, with longer hours on Thursdays. Many banks are also closed between 12:30 and 13:30 for lunch.

Wayne Finley

See also: Chapter 4: Currency.

Further Reading
Germany: Money & Banking. Petaluma, CA: World Trade Press, 2010.

Corporations in Germany

Corporations in Germany follow an organizational structure similar to those in the United States and some European countries. German corporations enjoy the protections of limited liability, and certain forms of incorporation allow companies to raise capital by issuing stock. In addition, German corporations are overseen by supervisory boards. Companies in Germany typically take two forms: the *Aktiengesellschaft* (*AG*) and the *Gesellschaft mit beschränkter Haftung* (*GmbH*).

Companies that are established as AGs allow for public ownership via stock and limit the personal liability of employees and executives. AGs are analogous to publicly traded companies in the United States (Inc., Co.). However, unlike their U.S. counterparts, which are governed by a single board of directors, German corporations follow a two-tiered system of corporate governance. The two boards are the *Aufsichtsrat* (supervisory board) and the *Vorstand* (executive board). A company's *Aufsichtsrat* is comprised in part by members elected by shareholders and representatives elected by employees. The proportion of employee representation on the *Aufsichtsrat* depends on the number of workers employed by the company. The purpose of the board is to elect, supervise, and advise the *Vorstand*, which oversees the operations of the company. Both boards meet regularly, but the *Vorstand* usually meets more often as it deals with day-to-day company operations. AGs have a minimum capital requirement of €50,000, must create articles of association, and register with the *Handelsregister* (commercial register). Many of Germany's largest companies operate as AGs. Examples include Volkswagen AG, Daimler AG, BMW AG, and Siemens AG.

The most common type of corporation in Germany is the GmbH (Hargrave, 2019). Like owners of AG stock, owners of companies operating as GmbHs enjoy limited liability. GmbHs are privately owned companies, similar to limited liability companies in the United States. Therefore, GmbHs do not issue stock and are not required to function under a two-tiered system of corporate governance. Instead, directors are responsible for running a GmbH, and, unless the company has more than 500 employees, a supervisory board is not required. German law requires all GmbH companies to start with at least €25,000 in capital (Hargrave, 2019). Germany's largest GmbH is Robert Bosch GmbH, which produces auto parts and consumer goods such a power tools and appliances.

Smaller companies may avoid the same capital requirement of AGs and GmbHs by operating as *Unternehmergesellschafts* (UG). UG companies may form with only €1, but are required to save 25% of their annual profits until they reach €25,000 in capital. Once the UG has reached the minimum capital requirements, it may convert to GmbH status (Germany Trade and Invest, 2019a).

Large, multinational, public corporations operating in Germany use the SE designation. SE (*Societas Europaea*) corporations were established by the European Union with the intent of making it easier for large corporations to operate in multiple European countries without having to establish numerous subsidiaries. SE corporations are required to establish their headquarters in the same country in which they register as a corporation, and they must operate in at least two European countries. And like companies incorporated in Germany, SEs have a minimum capital requirement, although larger at €120,000, and employees must be involved in the management of the organization, although the specific requirements vary from country to country (Your Europe European Union, 2019).

Wayne Finley

See also: Chapter 3: Germany and the European Union. Chapter 4: Frankfurt Stock Exchange.

Further Reading

Germany Trade and Invest "Mini GmbH" (Limited Liability Entrepreneurial Company), 2019a. https://www.gtai.de/gtai-en/invest/investment-guide/company-set-up-630302 Accessed October 23, 2021.

Hargrave, Marshall. "What Is GmbH?," 2019. https://www.investopedia.com/terms/g/gmbh.asp. Accessed October 23, 2021.

Your Europe European Union. (2019). "Setting Up a European Company (SE)." https://europa.eu/youreurope/business/running-business/developing-business/setting-up-european-company/index_en.htm. Accessed October 23, 2021.

Currency

As a member of the European Monetary Union, Germany uses the euro (€) as its official currency. Along with ten other countries, Germany adopted the euro on January 1, 1999. Today, the number of countries now using the euro as official currency has increased to 19.

Euro banknotes are issued by the European Central Bank (ECB) and the European System of Central Banks (ESCB). These paper bank notes come in denominations of €5, €10, €20, €50, €100, €200, and €500. Since no European Union member nation has the ability to issue their own banknotes, all euro banknotes feature the same design throughout the European Union.

While euro notes are issued by the ECB and ESCB, coins are issued and minted by individual member nations. One euro is divisible into 100 euro cents, and coins are available in denominations of €2, €1, 50 cents, 20 cents, 10 cents, 5 cents, 2 cents, and 1 cent. Although the reverse side of each denomination of coin has the same design regardless of where it is produced, each member nation is allowed to choose a design for the opposite (obverse) side. For example, starting in 2006, the Deutsche Bundesbank, the central bank of Germany, began issuing a series of commemorative 2€ coins featuring motifs representing the sixteen German federal states.

While the euro has served as Germany's only currency during the twenty-first century, the country's currency went through several changes during the twentieth century. From 1871 until 1914, the *Goldmark* was used as the currency of Germany. During that time, the German currency system, like the currency systems of many countries around the world, was based on the gold standard. The gold standard allowed bearers of *Goldmark* to exchange their currency for gold. The outbreak of World War I in 1914 led to a transition from the gold standard form of currency to banknotes. The first banknote used by Germany following the end of the gold standard was the *Papiermark* (paper mark).

Hyperinflation after World War I left the *Papiermark* almost worthless, and in 1923 the German government switched to the *Rentenmark* as a way to deal with the instability of the postwar economy. The *Rentenmark* was used only until 1924, when it was replaced by yet another currency, the *Reichsmark*. The *Reichsmark*, which reverted to the gold standard, stayed in use as the official currency of Germany throughout Nazi rule. Following World War II, East Germany moved to the East German mark. West Germany, however, created the deutsche mark in 1948 as its official currency.

The deutsche mark would remain the official currency of Unified Germany until the euro was used starting in 1999.

Since euro notes were not issued at the time of official adoption, deutsche marks were still used as payments for daily transactions until 2002. During that transitional time period, a fixed exchange rate from deutsche mark to euro was established, with one euro being the equivalent to 1.95583 deutsche marks. That rate still stands today, although deutsche marks are no longer legal tender. Those still holding deutsche marks may exchange them for euro through the Deutsche Bundesbank.

Wayne Finley

See also: Chapter 2: Overview. Chapter 3: Germany and the European Union; Government and Politics in the German Democratic Republic. Chapter 4: Banking.

Further Reading

Germany: Money & Banking. Petaluma, CA: World Trade Press, 2010.

Energy

Given Germany's status as the largest economy in Europe, it comes as no surprise that the country is also Europe's largest consumer of energy. In 2020, Germany's energy consumption was ranked at number seven in the world behind other industrial giants such as the United States and China (BP, 2021). But while Germany consumes a large amount of energy, it also produces a significant portion of Europe's energy supply, ranking third behind France and the United Kingdom (Eurostat, 2019b). Despite producing a high volume of energy, Germany still relies heavily on energy imports to fulfill the demands of consumers. In 2017, Germany had an energy dependency rate of over 60% (Eurostat, 2019c) and imported large amounts of oil, natural gas, and hard coal. The heavy reliance on imported fossil fuels as sources of energy stems from the fact that domestic sources are either becoming scarce or are too expensive to produce (Wettengel, 2019).

Like other countries in the EU and around the world, Germany is trying to reduce its carbon emissions and its reliance on fossil fuels in order to help combat climate change. And like these other countries, Germany is an active partner in the Paris Agreement. To help curb the country's reliance on fossil fuels, the German government enacted legislation in 2010 to support the concept of *Energiewende*, which translates to "energy turn" in English. *Energiewende* sets country-wide goals for reducing greenhouse gas emissions and sets goals for transitioning the country's sources of energy from fossil fuels to renewables and reducing overall energy consumption. These goals are moving targets, increasing by year and decade (Appunn and Wettengel, 2020). For example, Germany aims to have at least 65% of its energy come from renewables by 2030. It appears that the country is making progress toward this mark as renewables overtook coal as Germany's top source of energy in 2018, with 40% of electricity coming from renewable sources (Eckert, 2019).

Another key component of Germany's energy policy is the phaseout of nuclear and coal-burning power plants. Following the 2011 disaster at Japan's Fukushima Daiichi Nuclear Power Plant, the German government announced the plan to shut down all of the country's nuclear power plants by 2022 (International Atomic Energy Agency, 2019). As of 2021, only six nuclear power plants were actively producing electricity in Germany (International Atomic Energy Agency, 2019). Since Germany relied heavily on nuclear power plants for the production of electricity, the shutdown of the majority of the country's reactors shifted production to other resources, one of them being coal. Since the burning of coal produces more greenhouse gas emissions than nuclear power, Germany had an increase in CO_2 emissions in 2012 and 2013. This increase in CO_2 despite the measures set forth by the German government to fight climate change and carbon emissions is known as the *Energiewende Paradox* (Agora Energiewende, 2015). In 2019, the German government proposed legislation to phase out all coal-generated electricity by 2038 (U.S. Energy Information Administration, 2019).

Compared to other European countries, the cost of energy in Germany is high. In 2019, German households paid more for electricity than households in any other European nation. Forty-five percent of the total cost of household energy comes from taxes and levies (Eurostat, 2019a). As with many other goods and services, Germans pay a 19% value-added tax on energy (Thalman and Wehrmann, 2020). Additionally, the price of electricity for non-household consumers in Germany was the third highest in Europe (Eurostat, 2019a).

Wayne Finley

See also: Chapter 1: Climate Policy and Recycling; Transportation.

Further Reading

Agora Energiewende. "The German Energiewende and Its Climate Paradox," 2014. https://static.agora-energiewende.de/fileadmin/Projekte/2014/Energiewende-Paradox/Analysis_Energiewende_Paradox_web_EN.pdf. Accessed October 23, 2021.

Appunn, Kerstine, Freja Ericksen, and Julian Wettengel. "Germany's Greenhouse Gas Emissions and Energy Transition Targets, 2020." https://www.cleanenergywire.org/factsheets/germanys-greenhouse-gas-emissions-and-climate-targets. Accessed October 23, 2021.

Eckert, Vera. "Renewables Overtake Coal as Germany's Main Energy Source," 2019. https://www.reuters.com/article/us-germany-power-renewables/renewables-overtake-coal-as-germanys-main-energy-source-idUSKCN1OX0U2. Accessed October 23, 2021.

Eurostat. "Electricity Price Statistics," 2019a. https://ec.europa.eu/eurostat/statistics-explained/index.php/Electricity_price_statistics#Electricity_prices_for_non-household_consumers. Accessed October 23, 2021.

Eurostat. "Energy Production and Imports," 2019b. https://ec.europa.eu/eurostat/statistics-explained/index.php?title=Energy_production_and_imports. Accessed October 23, 2021.

Eurostat. "From Where Do We Import Energy," 2019c. https://ec.europa.eu/eurostat /cache/infographs/energy/bloc-2c.html. Accessed October 23, 2021.

International Atomic Energy Agency. "Country Nuclear Power Profiles: Germany," 2021. https://cnpp.iaea.org/countryprofiles/Germany/Germany.htm. Accessed October 23, 2021.

"Primary Energy Consumption Worldwide from 2000 to 2020 (in Exajoules)." In Statista, 2021. https://www.statista.com/statistics/265598/consumption-of-primary -energy-worldwide/. Accessed October 23, 2021.

Thalman, Ellen, and Benjamin Wehrmann. "What German Households Pay for Power," 2021. https://www.cleanenergywire.org/factsheets/what-german-households-pay-power. Accessed October 23, 2021.

U.S. Energy Information Administration. "Germany Announces Proposal to Phase Out Coal by 2038, Further Changing Its Generation Mix," 2019. https://www.eia.gov/today-inenergy/detail.php?id=39652. Accessed October 23, 2021.

Wettengel, Julian. "Germany's Dependence on Imported Fossil Fuels," 2020. https://www .cleanenergywire.org/factsheets/germanys-dependence-imported-fossil-fuels. Accessed October 23, 2021.

Equal Pay Act

The Transparency on Pay Act went into effect in Germany on July 6, 2017. The law was passed by the Bundesrat (Federal Council) with the intention of shrinking the pay gap between the genders. As of 2019, German men earned, on average, 21% more than German women (Statistisches Bundesamt, 2019). This is one of the highest disparities in pay among all European countries.

This law was not the first to define equality between the men and women of Germany. Article 3 of the German Basic Law (1949) explicitly granted equal rights for men and women and prohibited discrimination based on sex. However, it did not specifically address pay inequalities between genders. The Transparency on Pay Act shed light on the problem of pay inequality and combats discrimination by giving employees information on their respective salaries.

The act calls on employers to treat men and women equally and clearly states the ideal of equal pay for equal work. Companies are prohibited from discriminating against employees through either direct or indirect forms of compensation. The act does not require increased compensation for women. Rather, it focuses on how companies provide information regarding workers' salaries.

Part of the Transparency on Pay Act gives employees (under certain circumstances) the right to request information on the compensation provided to employees of the opposite gender who perform the same job in comparable positions. Employees may request that the employer provide the average gross monthly salary of full-time employees in the same position, along with information on additional forms of compensation. If the company fails to divulge the requested information within three months, the employee may file a lawsuit (*Entgeltgleichheitsklage*) under the act, and the burden of proof falls on the employer. The obligation to disclose salary information applies only to companies employing at least 200 workers and does not pertain to employees covered by a collective bargaining agreement (Herrmann, 2017). In cases where workers are covered by a collective bargaining agreement, the company and its employees are expected to use the process of collective bargaining to enforce the principles of the act (Bundesamt für Justiz, 2017).

The act levies additional stipulations on companies with at least 500 or more employees. Pursuant to the German Commercial Code, these companies must file a management report that describes the measures they have taken in order to promote both equality and pay equity between men and women. Companies with collective bargaining agreements are required to produce equity reports every five years. All other companies have a three-year requirement for reporting. Companies with more than 500 employees are also encouraged, but not required, to conduct pay audits. If a company chooses to perform an audit, it must inform employees of the results (Baker McKenzie, 2018).

Wayne Finley

See also: Chapter 7: Women in the Workforce.

Further Reading

Bundesamt für Justiz. "The Act to Promote Transparency in Wage Structures among Women and Men," 2017. https://www.gesetze-im-internet.de/englisch_entgtranspg /englisch_entgtranspg.html#p0048 Accessed October 23, 2021.

Häferer, Katja. "Spotlight on the Gender Pay Gap in Germany," 2018. https://www .bakermckenzie.com/en/insight/publications/2018/06/spotlight-on-the-gender-pay -gap-in-germany. Accessed October 23, 2021.

Herrmann, Kaja S. "Germany's Gender Pay Gap Law: What It Means for Employers," 2017. https://www.jonesday.com/en/insights/2017/06/germanys-gender-pay-gap-law -what-it-means-for-employers. Accessed October 23, 2021.

Statistisches Bundesamt. "Gender Pay Gap Remained Unchanged at 21% in 2018," 2019. https:// www.destatis.de/EN/Press/2019/03/PE19_098_621.html. Accessed October 23, 2021.

Frankfurt Stock Exchange

Just as New York City's New York Stock Exchange (NYSE) is the center of stock trading in the United States, Frankfurt's Frankfurter Wertpapierbörse (FWB), colloquially known as the Frankfurt Stock Exchange, is the center for stock trading in Germany. Due to the large amount of stock trading and other financial transactions that take place there, Frankfurt is one of the world's most prominent international financial centers along with New York, London, and Tokyo (Reinert and Ramkishen,

The Frankfurt Stock Exchange (FRA) is the third largest stock exchange in the world after the NYSE and NASDAQ. Approximately 3,300 North American companies are listed on the FRA. (Rodrigo Garrido/Dreamstime.com)

2009). Although there are several stock exchanges in Germany, the FWB is by far the largest. Its market capitalization of nearly $2 trillion (USD) makes the FWB the twelfth-largest stock exchange in the world.

The FWB traces its history back to the eleventh century when Frankfurt functioned as a center of trade for the region during autumn fairs. An official exchange would not open in Frankfurt until 1585, when merchants came together to exchange currency as a means to facilitate the flow of commodities through the region. However, it wasn't until 1820 that the first share of common stock was traded in Frankfurt, and 1896 when stock trading throughout Germany was uniformly regulated by the Stock Exchange Act of 1896 (Deutsche Börse Group, 2019).

Two World Wars stifled trading during the first half of the twentieth century, and the Frankfurt Stock Exchange Building was damaged from Allied bombing in 1944. The FWB reopened in 1945 and has since became one of the world's foremost stock exchanges. Today, oversight of the FWB falls under the purview of Deutsche Börse Group AG, which took control in 1992 (Deutsche Börse Group, 2019).

Trading takes place Monday through Friday from 8:00 until 20:00, and the FWB is closed on holidays. Trades may happen both in-person on the floor and electronically via Deutsche Börse Group's Xetra platform (Medleva, 2019). Traders can buy and sell shares of common (*Stammaktien*) and preferred (*Vorzugsaktien*) stock, in addition to stock futures and options. The most well-known index for tracking the FWB is the DAX (Deutscher Aktienindex), which consists of 30 blue-chip stocks, is comparable to the DOW Jones Industrial Average (DOW). Many of Germany's largest companies, including Volkswagen Group, BMW, Bayer, and Adidas, are listed on the DAX.

The FWB imposes strict regulations on companies listed on its exchange. German companies must submit a prospectus before they are listed on the FWB, and are required to issue annual financial statements. Such statements (and other financial disclosures) permit investors to make informed decisions when buying or selling a company's stock (Sheimo, 1999).

In contrast to the United States, the type of information disclosed by companies in Germany is based on the size of the firm (Sheimo, 1999). The two levels of financial disclosure are the Prime Standard and the General Standard. The Prime Standard requires companies to adhere to the highest standard of transparency and is intended for companies seeking to attract both German and international investors (Deutsche Börse Cash Market, 2020a). Companies listed on the DAX follow the Prime Standard. Companies that are traded under the General Standard have less stringent reporting requirements and are also required to disclose certain types of information (Deutsche Börse Cash Market, 2020b).

Wayne Finley

See also: Chapter 2: Overview. Chapter 4: Corporations in Germany; Currency.

Further Reading

Deutsche Börse Cash Market. "Prime Standard: The Premium Segment for Raising Equity," 2020a. https://www.deutsche-boerse-cash-market.com/dbcm-en/primary -market/market-structure/segments/prime-standard. Accessed October 23, 2021.

Deutsche Börse Cash Market. "General Standard," 2020b. https://www.deutsche-boerse -cash-market.com/dbcm-en/primary-market/market-structure/segments/General -Standard-16806. Accessed October 23, 2021.

Deutsche Börse Group. "History of the Frankfurt Stock Exchange," 2019. https://www .deutsche-boerse.com/dbg-en/our-company/frankfurt-stock-exchange/history-of-the -frankfurt-stock-exchange. Accessed October 23, 2021.

Medleva, Valerie. "The Frankfurt Stock Exchange: Everything You Need to Know to Invest in Germany Today," 2019. https://capital.com/the-frankfurt-stock-exchange. Accessed October 23, 2021.

Reinert, Kenneth A., and S. Rajan Ramkishen. "International Financial Centers." In Reinert, Kenneth et al. *The Princeton Encyclopedia of the World Economy*, vol. 2, 663– 665. Princeton, NJ: Princeton University Press, 2009.

Sheimo, Michael D., ed. "Germany, the Federal Republic Of." In Michael D. Sheimo and Andreas Loizou, eds. *International Encyclopedia of the Stock Market*, vol. 1, 446–454. Chicago: Fitzroy Dearborn, 1999.

German Automobile Industry

Automobile manufacturing is a vital part of Germany's economy and history. What started with Karl Benz's patenting of the first gasoline-powered automobile in 1886 has now become a multibillion-dollar industry and earned Germany a reputation for producing high-quality passenger cars. This is a remarkable accomplishment considering that the production of all civilian automobiles was halted during both World War I and World War II, and the economic crisis of the Great Depression resulted in a major blow to the German automobile industry. Remarkably, automobile production in Germany rebounded after all these setbacks, and the automobile industry currently accounts for a large percentage of the German economy.

During their one hundred-plus years of automobile manufacturing, German automobile manufacturers have earned a reputation for building high-quality, luxury passenger vehicles. Many of the world's premium automobile brands are German, including BMW, Mercedes-Benz, and Porsche. In 2019, the Volkswagen Group became the world's largest manufacturer of passenger vehicles—surpassing Renault-Nissan and Toyota in global sales. However, in 2020, Toyota produced more passenger vehicles. The Volkswagen Group produces cars in Germany under its flagship brand Volkswagen and its luxury brand Audi. The company also manufactures cars in other

Volkswagen, headquartered in Wolfsburg, is the world's largest car manufacturer. The company's ID.4 is the best selling electric car in Germany. (VanderWolfImages/Dreamstime.com)

countries under world-famous brand names including Lamborghini and Bentley. Examples of iconic German automobiles include the Volkswagen Beetle and Golf, and the Porsche 911.

German drivers appear to have an affinity for German-produced vehicles. In 2018, Volkswagen topped the list of new cars registered in Germany, with twice the number of the second-place manufacturer, Mercedes (KBA, 2019). Mercedes was followed by BMW and Audi (KBA, 2019). However, other global manufacturers produce and sell vehicles in Germany. For example, Ford, an American company, has a long history of producing cars in Germany dating back to the late 1920s. More recently, in 2019, electric car manufacturer Tesla announced it would build a production plant near Berlin, where it can take advantage of Germany's automobile manufacturing infrastructure and skilled labor pool.

As a whole, the automobile industry comprises a significant percentage of Germany's economy. Motor vehicles and motor vehicle parts accounted for 16.9% ($264 billion) of Germany's total exports, and 10.2% ($132 billion) of Germany's total imports in 2018 (globalEDGE, n.d.). Over 5 million passenger cars were produced in Germany during 2018, which makes it the fifth-largest producer of vehicles, behind China, the United States, Japan, and India, respectively, and the third-largest producer of cars. (International Organization of Motor Vehicle Manufacturers, n.d.). And it takes a robust network of auto parts suppliers to support the large numbers of automobiles produced in Germany each year. These auto parts suppliers totaled for €81.5 billion in revenue in 2018. Over half of that revenue came from Bosch (Berylls Strategy Advisors, 2019).

In addition to contributing to the overall success of the German economy, the automotive industry plays a key role in the individual lives of many Germans. Over 830,000 people were employed in the German automobile industry during 2018. These same employees worked a total of 1.18 million hours and received an average hourly wage of €47.80 (Statistisches Bundesamt 2021; Statistisches Bundesamt, 2020).

Wayne Finley

See also: Chapter 4: Manufacturing; Trade.

Further Reading

Berylls Strategy Advisors. "Leading German Automobile Suppliers in 2019, Based on Revenue (in Million Euros)." In Statista, 2019. https://www.statista.com/statistics/587798/leading-german-car-suppliers-by-revenue/. Accessed October 23, 2021.

globalEDGE. "Germany: Trade Statistics," n.d. https://globaledge.msu.edu/countries/germany/tradestats. Accessed October 23, 2021.

International Organization of Motor Vehicle Manufacturers. "2018 Production Statistics," n.d. http://www.oica.net/category/production-statistics/2018-statistics/. Accessed October 23, 2021.

KBA. "Most Popular Car Brands in Germany in 2019 and 2020, by Number of Registrations," 2021. https://www.statista.com/statistics/810637/passenger-cars-registrations-by-brand-germany/. Accessed October 23, 2021.

Statistisches Bundesamt. "Hourly Wage in the Automobile Industry in Germany from 2005 to 2019 (in Euros)." In Statista, 2020. https://www.statista.com/statistics/587603/hourly-wage-german-automobile-industry/. Accessed October 23, 2021.

Statistisches Bundesamt. "Total Hours Worked by Employees of the Automobile Industry in Germany from 2010 to 2020 (in Millions)." In Statista, 2021. https://www.statista.com/statistics/810443/automobile-industry-hours-worked-germany/. Accessed October 23, 2021.

Gross Domestic Product (GDP)

Germany is one of the five largest economies in the world, and the largest economy in Europe, based on gross domestic product (GDP). GDP is the monetary value of a country's total output of goods and services in a year and is often broken down into three major sectors: services, industry, and agriculture. Germany's standing as one of the world's largest economies is remarkable considering Germany is behind global economic giants such as the United States, China, and Japan, all of which have land-masses and populations larger than those of Germany (World Bank, n.d.). With the exception of small dips in 2002 and 2003, and a significant drop in 2009 during the Great Recession, Germany's GDP has steadily increased over the past twenty years. As with many nations, Germany's GDP shrank in 2020 by 4.9% as a result of the COVID-19 pandemic (IMF, 2021a).

The services sector (e.g., consulting, tourism, information technology) is the largest contributor to Germany's $4 trillion GDP. This sector alone accounted for 68.2% of Germany's total GDP in 2018 (Statistisches Bundesamt, 2019). The services sector also employs the majority of the nation's workers. In 2019, 71.86% of all employed Germans worked in service providing jobs (World Bank, 2019).

Industrial activities make up a significant portion of the German economy. Total industry accounted for almost 27% of Germany's GDP in 2019. And although manufacturing is included in the total industry calculations, it alone accounts for 19% of Germany's total GDP (globalEDGE, n.d.). This number is not surprising given Germany's reputation around the world as a leader in the manufacture of durable goods. Many Germans are employed in industry-related jobs. In 2019, 26.88% of all employment in Germany came from industry and manufacturing jobs (World Bank, 2019).

Agriculture is a small, yet important, part of Germany's GDP. In 2018, agriculture, forestry, and fishing made up only 0.7% of the German economy (Statistisches Bundesamt, 2021), but 1.27% of workers were employed in the sector (World Bank, 2019).

Other factors used by economists in examining a country's GDP are government spending as a percentage of GDP and GDP per capita. In 2018, 44.46% of Germany's GDP came from government expenditures (IMF, 2021b). As a point of comparison, the U.S. government spent 35.42% of the country's GDP in 2018 (IMF, 2021c), and Japan spent 38.9% in 2017 (Trading Economics, n.d.). Germany's GDP per capita was

$45,732.80 in 2020, while the United States had a GDP per capita of over $63,000 (IMF, 2021d).

A country's GDP can also be broken down by state or region. This calculation is referred to as gross regional product (GRP). The western and southern states contribute the most to the German economy. North Rhine-Westphalia contributes the largest percentage of the German economy. In 2016, 21.2% of the German GDP came from the region (Eurostat, 2018). Germany's southernmost states, Bavaria and Baden-Württemberg, accounted for 33.3% of Germany's total GDP. The economic divide between east and west is still apparent as the new federal states of Germany contributed approximately 15% of the nation's GDP (Eurostat, 2018). Berlin alone accounted for 4.1% of that total (Eurostat, 2018).

Wayne Finley

See also: Chapter 3: Germany and the European Union. Chapter 4: Agriculture; Manufacturing; Services Industry.

Further Reading

Eurostat. "GDP per Capita in 276 EU Regions," 2018. https://ec.europa.eu/eurostat /documents/2995521/8700651/1-28022018-BP-EN/15f5fd90-ce8b-4927-9a3b -07dc255dc42a. Accessed October 23, 2021.

globalEDGE. "Germany: Economy," n.d. https://globaledge.msu.edu/countries/germany /economy. Accessed October 23, 2021.

IMF. "Germany: Growth Rate of the Real Gross Domestic Product (GDP) from 2016 to 2026 (Compared to the Previous Year)" [Graph]. In Statista, 2021a. https://www .statista.com/statistics/375203/gross-domestic-product-gdp-growth-rate-in-germany/. Accessed October 23, 2021.

IMF. "Germany: Ratio of government expenditure to gross domestic product (GDP) from 2016 to 2026 [Graph]. In Statista, 2021b. https://www.statista.com/statistics/624182 /ratio-of-government-expenditure-to-gross-domestic-product-gdp-in-germany/. Accessed October 23, 2021.

IMF. "Ratio of Government Expenditure to Gross Domestic Product (GDP) in the United States from 2016 to 2026." In Statista, 2021c. https://www.statista.com/statistics/268356 /ratio-of-government-expenditure-to-gross-domestic-product-gdp-in-the-united-states/. Accessed October 23, 2021.

IMF. "The 20 Countries with the Largest Gross Domestic Product (GDP) per Capita in 2020 (in U.S. Dollars)." In Statista, 2021d. https://www.statista.com/statistics/270180 /countries-with-the-largest-gross-domestic-product-gdp-per-capita/. Accessed October 23, 2021.

Statistisches Bundesamt. "Germany: Distribution of Gross Domestic Product (GDP) across Economic Sectors from 2010 to 2020," 2021. https://www.statista.com/statistics /375569/germany-gdp-distribution-across-economic-sectors/. Accessed October 23, 2021.

Trading Economics. "Japan Government Spending to GDP," n.d. https://tradingeconomics.com/japan/government-spending-to-gdp. Accessed October 23, 2021.

World Bank. "GDP (Current US$)," n.d. https://data.worldbank.org/indicator/NY.GDP.MKTP.CD. Accessed October 23, 2021.

World Bank. "Germany: Distribution of Employment by Economic Sector from 2009 to 2019." In Statista, 2019. https://www.statista.com/statistics/624297/employment-by-economic-sector-in-germany/. Accessed October 23, 2021.

Guest Workers

Foreign workers have been an important part of the German economy since the middle of the twentieth century. In the years following World War II, West Germany was faced with a shortage of unskilled labor as a result of increased production in factories and mines, while countries in southern Europe had high unemployment rates. As a result of this labor imbalance, laborers from other countries came to West Germany seeking employment. These guest workers were referred to as *Gastarbeiter* (guest worker).

In 1955, Germany entered into an official agreement with Italy to recruit unskilled workers. Soon, treaties with other countries would follow, and laborers from Mediterranean Europe and North Africa came to West Germany seeking employment. In 1961, Germany ratified a treaty with the Turkish government allowing Turkish workers to stay for up to two years. After their stay in Germany was over, the Turkish laborers would return to Turkey, bringing their newly learned skills with them. After the first group of immigrant laborers left, new workers would replace them. However, the German government soon realized that training new workers would be costly, so changes were made allowing Turkish guest workers to stay permanently and bring their families (Prevezanos, 2011). The guest worker program was halted in 1973 after the German economy experienced a downturn, and the country shifted its focus to recruiting only skilled immigrants (OECD, 2013). Unemployment was high in unified Germany during the 1990s due to a struggling economy (Spitz-Oener, 2017). During that time period, immigrants working in Germany were primarily employed in agriculture, food service, health care, and construction, and many of these laborers came from Eastern Europe (Jurgens, 2010). Throughout the 2000s, Germany took advantage of provisions in EU treaties of accession to prevent workers from newly entered EU states—predominately those from Eastern Europe—from settling in Germany without work permits (OECD, 2013). As of 2015, all treaties of accession have expired, and citizens from member EU states have unfettered rights to reside and work in Germany as defined in EU Community legal documents.

A thriving economy in recent years has resulted in Germany's lowest unemployment rates and highest number of job vacancies since the 1990s ("Opening Up, a Crack," 2019). As of 2020, nearly 1.2 million jobs are vacant in Germany (Zech, 2020). These vacancies exist in fields requiring skilled labor such as information technology and medicine, and are affecting the economies of eastern and southern states (*Länder*) as they are the source of many service and industry sector businesses (Federal Ministry for Economic Affairs and Energy, n.d.). Because these positions are not being filled by workers who are from Germany or the EU, the German government voted the Skilled Labor Immigration Act into law in 2019. The law went into effect on March 1, 2020. The aim of the law is to recruit educated, skilled workers from outside the EU. It allows qualified workers from outside the EU with either a college or vocational degree to reside in Germany for a period of six months while they seek employment. They must also speak German and be able to provide for themselves prior to finding employment. Workers over forty-five years old must prove they can earn a minimum income. Once they have received an offer of employment, workers will receive a settlement permit. After working in Germany for four years, they may file for permanent residence. The law also allows workers with a degree from a German university or training from a German vocational program to apply for permanent residency after only two years (Gesley, 2019).

Wayne Finley

See also: Chapter 3: Citizenship; Germany and the European Union. Chapter 6: Immigration; Turks in Germany.

Further Reading

Federal Ministry for Economic Affairs and Energy. "Skilled Professionals for Germany," n.d. https://www.bmwi.de/Redaktion/EN/Dossier/skilled-professionals.html. Accessed October 23, 2021.

Gesley, Jenny. "Germany: New Immigration Acts to Attract and Retain Skilled Workers Published," 2019. https://www.loc.gov/item/global-legal-monitor/2019-10-28/germany-new-immigration-acts-to-attract-and-retain-skilled-workers-published/. Accessed October 23, 2021.

Jurgens, Jeffrey. "The Legacies of Labor Recruitment: The Guest Worker and Green Card Programs in the Federal Republic of Germany." Policy and Society 29(4), 345–355, 2010. https://doi.org/10.1016/j.polsoc.2010.09.010. Accessed October 23, 2021.

OECD. "Evolution of Labour Migration Policy," in *Recruiting Immigrant Workers: Germany 2013*. Paris: OECD Publishing. https://doi.org/10.1787/9789264189034-8-en. Accessed October 23, 2021.

"Opening Up, a Crack: Germany Is Cautiously Recruiting More Workers from outside the EU." *Economist*. May 18, 2019. https://www.economist.com/europe/2019/05/16/germany-is-cautiously-recruiting-more-workers-from-outside-the-eu. Accessed October 23, 2021.

Prevezanos, Klaudia. "Turkish Guest Workers Transformed German Society." DW, 2011. https://www.dw.com/en/turkish-guest-workers-transformed-german-society/a-15489210. Accessed October 23, 2021.

Spitz-Oener, Alexandra. "The Real Reason the German Labor Market Is Booming." *Harvard Business Review, 2017.* https://hbr.org/2017/03/the-real-reason-the-german-labor-market-is-booming. Accessed October 23, 2021.

Zech, Tanja. "Skilled Personnel Welcome," 2020. https://www.deutschland.de/en/topic/business/the-skilled-labour-immigration-act-working-in-germany. Accessed October 23, 2021.

Manufacturing

Germany's economy has placed a strong emphasis on manufacturing since World War II. For years, German workers have been recognized for their innovation, craftsmanship, and work ethic. These traits, combined with the bolstering of industry in the Federal Republic of Germany thanks to money from the Marshall Plan in the years after World War II, helped turn modern Germany into one of the world's leading manufacturers (Cook, 2013). This sudden economic growth is known as the "German Economic Miracle" (*Wirtschaftswunder*). Today, manufacturing and industry make up a large share of the German economy and employ millions of Germans.

Germany is the world's fourth-largest manufacturer, behind China, the United States, and Japan, respectively (World Bank, n.d.). In 2019, 26.7% of the entire German gross domestic product (GDP) came from industry and manufacturing activities (globalEDGE, n.d.). Manufacturing alone accounted for 19.11% of Germany's total GDP in 2019 (globalEDGE, n.d.). Germany's largest manufacturing sectors are machinery and equipment production, motor vehicle production, metal and fabricated metal production, and computers and electronics (Trading Economics, n.d.).

Of Germany's top five largest companies, four are manufacturers. These companies include automotive giants Volkswagen, Daimler (known for its Mercedes-Benz line of vehicles), and BMW, and the internationally renowned technology company Siemens (Orth, 2019). Large companies are not the only contributors to Germany's manufacturing success. Small and medium-sized enterprises (SMEs) make up the majority of Germany's manufacturing sector. These firms, called the German *Mittelstand*, are usually privately owned, family-operated companies that specialize in producing a specific product (Frangoul, 2014). It is common for these companies to control a high percentage of the market share in a specific industry, and much of their success comes from the flexibility that comes with being smaller companies and the relations they build with their employees and their local communities (Audretsch, 2018).

Industry and manufacturing have been a significant source of employment for Germans since the middle of the twentieth century. In the years following World War II, there was a significant shortage of labor needed to fill the demand for industrial and manufacturing jobs in Germany. As a result, many European and North African immigrants were hired as guest workers (see *Gastarbeiter*) to fill these positions, and the practice continued until the 1970s. Today, a large percentage of Germans are employed in industrial and manufacturing jobs. In 2019, 26.88% of all German employment came from the industry sector (World Bank, 2019). Although this is a significant amount, the number is steadily declining as the service sector continues to employ more Germans every year. Many of Germany's manufacturing jobs are provided by *Mittelstand* firms. Since manufacturing jobs often require skilled laborers, 90% of all apprenticeships in Germany are offered by *Mittelstand* companies (Storbeck, 2018).

Wayne Finley

See also: Chapter 4: German Automobile Industry; Gross Domestic Product (GDP). Chapter 6: Immigration; Turks in Germany.

Further Reading

Audretsch, D. B. "*Insights into Manufacturing Policy*: Why Is German So Strong in Manufacturing?" Policy Institute (4), 2018. https://policyinstitute.iu.edu/doc/mpi/insight/2018-03.pdf. Accessed October 23, 2021.

Cook, Bernard A. "Germany, Federal Republic of." In Cook, Bernard A. ed. *Europe since 1945: An Encyclopedia*. New York: Garland, 2013.

Frangoul, Anmar. "Meet 'the Mittelstand,'" 2014. https://www.cnbc.com/2014/10/24/meet-the-mittelstand.html. Accessed October 23, 2021.

globalEDGE. "Germany: Economy," n.d. https://globaledge.msu.edu/countries/germany/economy. Accessed October 23, 2021.

Orth, Martin. "German Industry's Big Five," 2019. https://www.deutschland.de/en/topic/business/ranking-germanys-five-largest-companies. Accessed October 23, 2021.

Storbeck, O. "Germany's Mittelstand Puts Happy Workers over Profits." *Financial Times*, 2018. https://www.ft.com/content/68417a94-cb0f-11e8-9fe5-24ad351828ab. Accessed October 23, 2021.

Trading Economics. "Germany Manufacturing Production," n.d. https://tradingeconomics.com/germany/manufacturing-production. Accessed October 23, 2021.

World Bank. "Germany: Distribution of Employment by Economic Sector from 2009 to 2019." In Statista, 2021. https://www.statista.com/statistics/624297/employment-by-economic-sector-in-germany/. Accessed October 23, 2021.

World Bank. "Manufacturing, Value Added (Current US$)," n.d. https://data.worldbank.org/indicator/NV.IND.MANF.CD?most_recent_value_desc=true. Accessed October 23, 2021.

Services Industry

Like many industrialized countries in the West, Germany's economy depends heavily on the services sector. The three main components of a country's gross domestic product are services, manufacturing, and agriculture. The services sector is made up of business activities that provide services, rather than material goods, and consists of industries such as financial services, information technology services, health care, and tourism. As a whole, the services sector accounted for 70.4% of Germany's total GDP in 2020 (Statistisches Bundesamt, 2021a).

The German labor force has seen a steady shift from agriculture and manufacturing jobs to service jobs, and the majority of German workers are employed in service industry jobs. In 2019, service sector jobs made up 71% of the German labor market (World Bank, 2019). Most service industry jobs in Germany are in the large cities of the West and in Berlin.

Germany's booming services and manufacturing sectors are powered by thriving financial services and insurance industries. The financial services industry alone contributed almost 4% to the nation's GDP in 2018 and employed approximately 1.2 million people. The main finance hub of Germany is Frankfurt. In addition to being home to the Frankfurt Stock Exchange, Frankfurt is the location for seventy-six banking company headquarters and twenty-one insurance company headquarters. And while financial markets are centered in Frankfurt, Munich is an important player in the world insurance market. Munich is home to fifty-six insurance company headquarters. Many of Germany's insurance companies are also headquartered in Cologne and Hamburg (Germany Trade and Invest, 2020a). Germany is the third-largest insurance market in Europe, and the second-largest reinsurance market in the world after the United States (Germany Trade and Invest, 2020b).

Germany is a world leader in logistics. In 2018, Germany was ranked number one on the World Bank's International Logistics Performance Index (globalEDGE, 2020). Germany's success in the logistical services field is due to its central location in Europe and well-developed infrastructure (German Convention Bureau, 2020). Germany's strength in logistics also contributes to its rank as both the world's third-largest importer and exporter of goods in 2018 (World Integrated Trade Solutions, n.d.).

Management consulting services are in high demand in Germany. In 2019, Germany was the world's third-largest management consulting market (Statista, 2020). This industry has been growing steadily for the last ten years. In 2018, the industry grew by 7%, generating total revenues of over €34 billion. The top management consulting companies in Germany are PwC, EY, KPMG, and Deloitte. Although these leading companies are all foreign firms, Germany has a large number of successful domestic consulting companies (Consultancy Europe, 2019).

Travel and tourism are an important part of the German economy (WTTC, 2018b), as they contribute about $350 billion to the economy annually, and employ well over 6 million people (WTTC, 2018a). Germany is a popular holiday destination because of its many cultural attractions. Germany's central location in Europe combined with its major cities and robust infrastructure contribute to its popularity as a destination for international conferences (German Convention Bureau, n.d.). Many Germans enjoy traveling on holiday within their own country, and over the past decade the number of international tourists spending time in Germany has increased steadily. In 2018, the country saw 478 million overnight stays at travel accommodations (Statistisches Bundesamt, 2021b), with 87 million of those stays coming from international travelers (Müller, 2019). The most popular German cities for overnight stays among both foreign and domestic travelers are Berlin, Munich, Frankfurt, and Hamburg (Statistisches Landesamt, 2018).

Wayne Finley

See also: Chapter 1: Cities; Transportation.

Further Reading

Consultancy Europe. "Germany's Management Consulting Industry Grows to €34 Billion," 2019. https://www.consultancy.eu/news/3018/germanys-management-consulting-industry-grows-to-34-billion. Accessed October 23, 2021.

German Convention Bureau. "Destination Germany Provides an Attractive Setting for Successful Business," n.d. https://www.gcb.de/en/why-germany/destination-germany/. Accessed October 23, 2021.

German Convention Bureau. "Transport and Logistics," 2020. https://www.gcb.de /discover-germany/discover-german-expertise/transport-and-logistics.html. Accessed October 23, 2021.

Germany Trade and Invest. "Financial Services," 2020a. https://www.gtai.de/gtai-en /invest/industries/financial-sector/financial-services. Accessed October 23, 2021.

Germany Trade and Invest. "Insurance Location Germany," 2020b. https://www.gtai.de /gtai-en/invest/industries/financial-sector/insurance-location-germany-75176. Accessed October 23, 2021.

globalEDGE. "Germany: Indices," 2020. https://globaledge.msu.edu/countries/germany /indices. Accessed October 23, 2021.

Müller, Frederike. "More Tourists in Germany than Ever in 2018," 2019. https://www .dw.com/en/more-tourists-in-germany-than-ever-in-2018/a-47774009. Accessed October 23, 2021.

Statista. "Size of the Global Consulting Market in 2019, by Country (in Billion U.S. Dollars) [Graph]. In Statista, 2020. https://www.statista.com/statistics/1065188 /management-consulting-market-size-country/. Accessed October 23, 2021.

Statistisches Bundesamt. "Germany: Share of Economic Sectors in Gross Domestic Product (GDP) in 2020." In Statista, 2021a. https://www.statista.com/statistics/295519 /germany-share-of-economic-sectors-in-gross-domestic-product. Accessed October 23, 2021.

Statistisches Bundesamt. "Number of Overnight Stays at Travel Accommodation in Germany from 1992 to 2020 in Millions)." In Statista, 2021b. https://www.statista.com /statistics/560792/overnight-stays-german-accommodation/. Accessed October 23, 2021.

Statistisches Landesamt. "Leading City Destinations in Germany from 2015 to 2017, by Inbound Overnight Stays (in 1,000)." In Statista, 2018. https://www.statista.com/statistics/561012 /popular-cities-germany-inbound-overnight-stays/. Accessed October 23, 2021.

World Bank. "Germany: Distribution of Employment by Economic Sector from 2009 to 2019." In Statista, 2021. https://www.statista.com/statistics/624297/employment-by -economic-sector-in-germany/. Accessed October 23, 2021.

World Integrated Trade Solutions. "Top Exporters and Importers by Country 2018," n.d. https://wits.worldbank.org/CountryProfile/en/Country/WLD/Year/2018/TradeFlow /EXPIMP/Partner/by-country. Accessed October 23, 2021.

WTTC. "Total Contribution of Travel and Tourism to Employment in Germany from 2012 to 2028 (in 1,000 Jobs)." In Statista, 2018a. https://www.statista.com/statistics /644731/travel-and-tourism-employment-contribution-germany/. Accessed October 23, 2021.

WTTC. "Total Contribution of Travel and Tourism to GDP in Germany from 2012 to 2028* (in Billion Euros)." In Statista, 2018b. https://www.statista.com/statistics /644714/travel-tourism-total-gdp-contribution-germany/. Accessed October 23, 2021.

Trade

With total exports and total imports in excess of $1 trillion, respectively, in 2019, Germany is among the top three nations in each category along with the United States and China (globalEDGE, n.d.). These numbers alone are even more impressive given Germany's number two ranking in terms of balance of trade—only China has a greater surplus of exports to imports (globalEDGE, n.d.). Germany's top trading partners are the United States, China, France, and the Netherlands. China tops the list by receiving $108 billion in German products in 2019 and supplying the country with $124 billion in goods, making it Germany's top supplier. The United States receives more German goods than any other nation. In 2019, the United States topped the list of German export nations by receiving over $134 billion in goods (World Integrated Trade Solutions, n.d.).

Trade statistics, both imports and exports, demonstrate Germany's emphasis on the manufacturing of industrial machinery, automobile parts and accessories, and pharmaceuticals. Industrial machinery is Germany's largest import and export sector. In 2018, 17.5% ($273 billion) of all German exports and 12.9% ($167 billion) of German imports were tied to the industrial machinery industry (globalEDGE, n.d.). Germany is the world leader in machinery and equipment manufacturing and produces 16% of the world's supply (Germany Trade & Invest, 2020b). Germany's domination in this field can be attributed to the focus of its manufacturers on engineering and design, and the country's diverse industrial base (Germany Trade & Invest, 2020b).

The automobile industry accounts for a large portion of Germany's imports and exports. In 2018, Germany exported over $264 billion in automobiles and automotive parts (16.9% of all exports) (globalEDGE, n.d.). Germany is the largest exporter of cars in the world, and cars are the top import in the country (The Observatory of Economic Complexity, 2020). Not only do German manufacturers build and export finished cars and SUVs, they also produce many of the parts that go into the production of cars around the world. In 2017, German companies accounted for sixteen of the world's top automotive parts suppliers (Germany Trade & Invest, 2020a). Automobile parts and accessories accounted for $132 billion in imports (10.2% of all imports) in 2018. Additionally, the import of automobile parts supports the production of domestically built automobiles and automobile parts.

Germany not only is known for its production of industrial machines and automobile parts, but also has a reputation as a leader in the pharmaceutical industry. The country's emphasis on research, innovation, and engineering, combined with its central location in Europe, have led to its success in the field of pharmaceuticals. In 2018, German manufacturers exported over $96 billion in pharmaceuticals (globalEDGE, n.d.). The United States is the single largest consumer of German pharmaceuticals, having imported over €14 billion of German pharmaceuticals in 2019 (BPI, 2020). Germany also exports billions of dollars in pharmaceuticals to the Netherlands, Switzerland, Ireland, Italy, France, and Great Britain.

Wayne Finley

See also: Chapter 3: Germany and the European Union; Germany and the United States. Chapter 4: German Automobile Industry; Manufacturing.

Further Reading

BPI. "Leading Countries for the Export of Pharmaceuticals from Germany in 2019 (in Billion Euros)." In Statista, 2020. https://www.statista.com/statistics/458585/ leadingcountries-pharmaceuticals-exports-from-germany/. Accessed October 23, 2021.

Germany Trade & Invest. "Automotive Industry," 2020a. https://www.gtai.de/gtai-en /invest/industries/mobility/automotive. Accessed October 23, 2021.

Germany Trade & Invest. "Machinery & Equipment Industry," 2020b. https://www.gtai .de/gtai-en/invest/industries/machinery-equipment. Accessed October 23, 2021.

globalEDGE. n.d. "Germany: Trade Statistics," n.d. https://globaledge.msu.edu/countries /germany/tradestats#source_1. Accessed October 23, 2021.

The Observatory of Economic Complexity. "Cars," 2020. https://oec.world/en/profile /hs92/cars#Profile. Accessed October 23, 2021.

World Integrated Trade Solutions. "Germany Trade Balance, Exports and Imports by Country and Region 2019," n.d. https://wits.worldbank.org/CountryProfile/en /Country/DEU/Year/2019/tradeFlow/EXPIMP. Accessed October 23, 2021.

Working in Germany

Germans enjoy a high level of work–life balance. Germans have shorter working hours compared to those of their European neighbors, while still demonstrating high levels of productivity (I Am Expat, n.d.). This is attributed to the numerous laws that protect employees' hours spent working (OECD, n.d.). Although several key laws define the working conditions of workers in Germany, the Working Hours Act (Arbeitszeitgesetz) is one of the most important, as it defines the workweek, limits the number of hours an employee can work during a day and a week, and sets standards for break time during a workday (Passport to Trade 2.0, 2019). Although the Working Hours Act applies to most workers in the country, certain classifications of workers, such as clergy, doctors, and civil servants, are covered under different laws.

A workweek in Germany is defined by law as Monday through Saturday, and employees, under most circumstances, may not work more than forty-eight hours per week (Fürnthaler, n.d.). An eight-hour days is typical, and employers may ask employees to work ten-hour days (The Press and Information Office of the Federal Government, n.d.). However, the average number of hours an employee works over a six-month period may not exceed eight hours per day (Passport to Trade 2.0, 2019). Most full-time employees in Germany work seven to eight hours a day, five days a week, for a total time spent working during the week between thirty-six and forty hours. Many employers in Germany also allow their employees flexible working conditions including the ability to work from home and the option of working longer days over a shorter workweek (I Am Expat, n.d.). German employment law also dictates that workers in select industries who are required to work on Sundays must receive compensatory time off for their work.

During a full workday of six to nine hours, employees are guaranteed at least one thirty-minute work break, which may be split into two fifteen-minute breaks. For those working more than nine hours, a forty-five-minute break is required. Unlike workers in the United States, German employees also have protections for rest periods between working days. For most jobs, eleven hours must elapse before the next work-day may begin, but there are exceptions to this rule for those working in select industries (Fürnthaler, n.d.).

Time away from work helps Germans maintain their healthy work-life balance. In addition to numerous federal holidays, German workers are entitled to a considerable amount of vacation leave. After working in a position for six months, full-time employees are entitled to a minimum of twenty-four working days of paid leave per calendar year (The Press and Information Office of the Federal Government, n.d.). It is not uncommon for employers to exceed the minimum amount of vacation time required by law and offer their employees up to thirty days (Fürnthaler, n.d.). In most cases, to use their vacation leave, employees submit requests, and the employer grants the absences. Unused holiday leave may be carried forward to the first three months of the next calendar year in the event that the employer did not grant the vacation leave due to operational reasons (The Press and Information Office of the Federal Government, n.d.).

Full-time workers in Germany are eligible for sick leave, leave for special occasions, and parental leave. After working for an employer for more than four weeks, an employee is eligible for up to six weeks of paid leave for either physical or mental illness (Fürnthaler, n.d.). A medical certificate documenting the illness or injury is required if the leave is for more than three consecutive days (Federal Government Commissioner for Migration, Refugees and Integration—Office for the Equal Treatment of EU Workers, n.d.). Workers are also entitled to special leave for events such as a death or birth in the family, or the serious illness of a close relative (Ibid, n.d.).

Parental leave in Germany is also quite generous. Women are entitled to paid leave six week before the birth of a child, and for eight weeks after (Fürnthaler, n.d.). The rate of pay is based on the mother's last three months of employment prior to taking the maternity leave (Fürnthaler, n.d.). In addition, the employment of a mother on maternity leave may not be terminated during pregnancy for four months after giving birth, save for extreme circumstances that must be approved by public authorities (Fürnthaler, n.d.). Both the mother and father of a newborn child are entitled to up to three years of parental leave. During this time period, the employers of the parents taking leave are not required to pay the employees. However, the parents may be entitled to receive supplemental income from the German government (Federal Government Commissioner for Migration, Refugees and Integration—Office for the Equal Treatment of EU Workers, n.d.).

Another interesting aspect of German labor law is that it allows for trial and probationary employment periods that allow for both employees and employers to determine if a job and organization are a good fit for one another. The shorter of the two is the trial period (*Probearbeit*), which may last from one to five days and is unpaid. The probationary period (*Probezeit*), which is paid, may last several months and be part of a permanent employment contract or fixed-term contract. Employees on a permanent contract may be offered continuing employment after the probationary period. Employers must grant a new contract to those employees on a fixed-term contract once the probationary period has expired. In both cases, the employee is eligible for vacation leave (Federal Government Commissioner for Migration, Refugees and Integration—Office for the Equal Treatment of EU Workers, n.d.).

Wayne Finley

Further Reading

Federal Government Commissioner for Migration, Refugees and Integration—Office for the Equal Treatment of EU Workers "Working Conditions," n.d. https://www.eu-gleichbehandlungsstelle.de/eugs-en/eu-citizens/information-center/working-conditions/working-conditions-1894164. Accessed October 23, 2021.

Fürnthaler, Peter. "Employees' Rights in Germany," n.d. https://www.howtogermany.com/pages/employee-rights.html. Accessed October 23, 2021.

I Am Expat. "Working Hours in Germany," n.d. https://www.iamexpat.de/career/working-in-germany/working-hours. Accessed October 23, 2021.

OECD. "Better Life Index: Germany," n.d. http://www.oecdbetterlifeindex.org/countries/germany/. Accessed October 23, 2021.

Passport to Trade 2.0. "Work-Life Balance," 2019. https://businessculture.org/western-europe/business-culture-in-germany/work-life-balance-in-germany/. Accessed October 23, 2021.

CHAPTER 5

RELIGION AND THOUGHT

James Lund

OVERVIEW

The story of German religious history is marked by numerous periods of development, and at times, violent upheaval. Christianity, as first introduced in the fourth century to Germanic tribes who reportedly worshiped a pantheon of gods each overseeing a tribal region, slowly became the unifying movement in the creation of the Germanic people and the constitution of a new Medieval West.

The Christian conversion of the Gothic tribes to the east consummated rather quickly. Ulfilas, of Greek descent, was born in Gothic captivity in 311. Classically educated, Ulfilas was proficient in Greek and Latin and is credited with inventing the Gothic alphabet and translating the Bible into the Gothic language. His later missionary efforts led to the founding of the Gothic Christian Church.

The Christian conversion and baptism of King Clovis I of the Franks in 498 initiated the Christianization of the Frankish peoples. Guided by the assistance of missionaries from the Irish and Anglo-Saxon churches, including Saint Boniface (known as the "Apostle of the Germans"), the Frankish kingdom converted to Christianity over the next two centuries. The Christian conversion of the Saxons to the north began with Charlemagne's forced incorporation of the Saxons into the Frankish kingdom in 776. The Saxon's Christian conversion slowly progressed through the eleventh century.

The first hint of a distinct German identity amalgamated around a shared Christian faith. Saint Boniface, in the mid-eighth century, led the effort to organize churches in the south-central region of the emergent kingdom. As ecclesiastical organization expanded, political unity of the Germanic Christian tribes progressed. German church history then took a unique turn. With the anointing of the German King Otto I as Holy Roman Emperor in 962 by Pope John XII, Germany and Christendom become one. This union of German royalty and the Roman Empire would last until its dissolution by Napoleon in 1806.

The period commonly known as the High Middle Ages, eleventh and twelfth centuries, witnessed the revival of intellectual life primarily sponsored by the educational efforts of monasteries and local parishes. The clergy also saw their power and status increase throughout the kingdom as the papacy in Rome won numerous victories in conflicts with successive emperors. Locally, German bishops began strengthening their political power and ecclesiastical control by attaching themselves to the

THE OBERAMMERGAU PASSION PLAY

The Oberammergau Passion Play portrays the life of Jesus between his triumphal entry into Jerusalem on Palm Sunday until the Resurrection. The Passion Play dates from 1634 when the bubonic plague devastated many towns in Bavaria. The inhabitants of Oberammergau vowed to reenact the Passion of Jesus (his crucifixion and resurrection) every ten years if God would lift the scourge of the plague. The Passion Play consists of sixteen acts and sixty scenes with twenty tableaux, each of which describes an episode from the Hebrew Bible. Two thousand citizens of Oberammergau participate in the production, which includes 124 speaking roles, a sixty-five-member orchestra, and a forty-eight-voice choir.

The play is performed five times each week in an outdoor theater (capacity 4,700) and commences at 2:30 pm. The audience takes a dinner break at 5:00 and returns to the theater at 8:00 for the closing acts. The forty-second decennial presentation of the Passion Play was to take place between May 16 and October 4, 2020. Approximately 750,000 people were expected to attend the 102 scheduled performances. But the event had to be canceled in 2020 due to the pandemic. The Oberammergau Passion Play, while popular, has received its share of criticism. It was praised by Hitler and condemned by Jewish people as anti-Semitic.

Further Reading

Shapiro, James S. *Oberammergau: The Troubling Story of the World's Most Famous Passion Play*. New York: Pantheon Books, 2000.

---

developing feudal system and local magistrates. These developments further eroded the empire's ecclesiastical control in Germany. This period also saw an increased influence from burgeoning Jewish communities as moneylenders to non-Jews—a practice that greatly embittered Germans and led to recurrent conflicts.

In the later Middle Ages, thirteenth to fifteenth centuries, German urbanization increased. As towns sprung up across the regions, villagers found themselves under local princely rule. As to the Church, they were still officially operating independently of the local magistrates, yet as secular political power galvanized in local regions, many bishops seized the opportunity to assert their independence from Rome by aligning their futures with the local princes. In turn for their favor, the local magistrates sought influence over the governance of their local parishes. These developing and fragmenting relationships will play a crucial role in the coming religious revolution of the next century.

The Protestant Reformation in the early sixteenth century changed the course of European history. Martin Luther's objection to the Roman Catholic practice of selling indulgences ignited religious, political, and economic upheaval in the empire and across Europe. Luther, a German monk in the small town of Wittenberg, protested the arrival of Dominican preacher Johann Tetzel, who was out raising money through the sale of special plenary indulgences. These indulgences were to fund repayment of Archbishop Albert's debt to the pope and the construction of Saint Peter's Basilica in

---

IMMANUEL KANT (1724–1804)

Immanuel Kant, the philosopher of the German Enlightenment, laid the foundation for modern philosophy by removing the need for divine revelation in the pursuit of science and ethics. He expressed this Enlightenment philosophy in three critiques: *The Critique of Pure Reason* (1781), *The Critique of Practical Reason* (1783), and *The Critique of Judgment* (1790). In *Religion within the Limits of Religion Alone* (1793), he sought to strike a reasonable balance between science and religion. He cautioned against believing in miracles or religious mysteries, since neither can be proved scientifically. He also believed strongly that religious observances do not make people more righteous in God's eyes. Like many theologians and philosophers before him, Kant devised an argument for the existence of God. Kant's argument was based on morality: the goal of humankind is to achieve happiness or the "highest good" (the *sunnum bonum*). According to Kant, the highest good cannot be conceived apart from the possibility of an afterlife, which in turn demands the existence of God.

Kant's influence was immense and can be seen in nearly every philosophical movement that followed him.

Further Reading

Guyer, Paul. *Kant*. Cambridge, UK: Cambridge University Press, 1993.

Kuehn, Manfred. *Kant: A Biography*. Cambridge, UK: Cambridge University Press, 2009.

Scruton, Roger. *Kant: A Very Short Introduction*. Oxford, UK: Oxford University Press, 2011.

Rome. By the purchase of a special plenary indulgence, a parishioner would secure the forgiveness of all of their sins that deserved punishment in Purgatory. Luther believed the sale of indulgences exploited the people and misrepresented God's Word. He responded by writing a collection of ninety-five theses against the sale of indulgences and posted them on the church door in Wittenberg on October 31, 1517, with the aim of spurring academic debate. The theses were quickly translated from Latin and distributed in Germany and throughout Europe. Luther's conviction that God justifies sinners by faith alone contradicted the teaching of the Roman Catholic Church. He soon found himself excommunicated from the Church and a political fugitive in the empire. Reunion with Rome was no longer possible, and the "protesting" followers of Luther became the seed of Protestant congregations throughout Europe.

The Reformation triggered social and political upheaval as well. Bands of peasants, seeking economic reform and ecclesiastical rights, revolted in 1524 in what is known as the Peasants' War. The peasants were eventually defeated in 1526 by the forces of the ruling princes at a significant cost of life. As the Roman Catholic Church, allied with Catholic princes and their armies, pressed a "Counter Reformation," they encountered resistant Protestant territories and princes unwilling to surrender their new religious and political gains. The mounting political and ecclesiastical tensions resulted in the Thirty Years War from 1618 to 1648. The conflict drew in Protestant Sweden from the north and the French to the south as both countries desired to fend off a Holy Roman Empire victory. The long, bloody conflict ended in a stalemate with the Peace of Westphalia in 1648.

With the Peace of Westphalia, the boundaries of Germany stabilized until the empire's dissolution in 1806. Confessional territories materialized (with the addition of the Reformed or Calvinists), and a prohibition on forced conversion led to increased religious toleration. As attention turned from war to intellectual, economic, and cultural development, the emergent German Enlightenment began questioning the absolute authority of the Scriptures. Opposing this intellectualism on the one hand and Christian confessionalism on the other, German Pietism arose, emphasizing the subjective experiential Christian life, for example, the personal experience of conversion, private biblical meditation, and the sharing of Christian experiences in small groups. Additionally, conditions for the smallish Jewish communities improved with the granting of additional legal protections and access to enhanced economic opportunities.

The religious impact of the French Revolution on nineteenth-century Germany was profound. The dissolution of the Holy Roman Empire by Napoleon in 1806 was subsequently replaced by a confederation of thirty-eight states. Protestant regional churches (known as the Evangelical Church) and Roman Catholic dioceses lent ecclesiastical structure to the new German Confederation. Religious toleration, as included in the Peace of Westphalia, was accepted as a constitutional principle in the new Germany.

The brief German Revolution from 1918 to 1919 concluded with the adoption of the Weimar Constitution. The constitution granted regional churches their autonomy from state ecclesiastical structure. Around this time, a movement of conservative confessional Protestant churches arose in opposition to the liberalizing Evangelical Church. Under the Nazi dictatorship, the Evangelical Church in 1933 morphed into the German Evangelical Church (Deutsche Christen), aligning itself with the National Socialist movement. In opposition to this new statist church, a Confessing Church (Bekennende Kirche) emerged that soon included the majority of German Protestant congregations. Eventually, the Nazi regime turned hostile toward all expressions of Christianity, Protestant and Roman Catholic alike, intending to eliminate it after the "final victory." As is well documented and memorialized, the Nazi's murder of over 6 million people due to their Jewish faith and ethnic identification will forever be part of German religious history. After the war, the surviving Protestant churches in the West gathered to form the Evangelical Church of Germany. In the East, the Soviets allowed the Evangelical Church to exist, but with limited activity. Consequently, under atheist Soviet rule, three generations passed with little or no exposure to religion. Today, the former East German region reigns as the most "godless" in Europe. Jewish communities (*Jüdische Gemeinde*) quickly rebuilt in Allied-occupied Germany, increasing to its current membership of around 100,000.

After the collapse of East Germany and subsequent German reunification, Protestantism solidified its presence in the north and east with Catholic bishopric strongholds in the west and south. Currently, 35% of German adults identify as irreligious, 29% Roman Catholic, 27% Protestant, 2.4% Islamic, with the final number a mix of other faith expressions. In contrast to the 65% of German adults who affiliate with some form of religion, the majority of those in the age range of 16 to 29 claim no religious affiliation, mimicking a trend seen throughout twenty-first-century Europe.

James Lund

Further Reading

Betz, Hans Dieter. *Religion Past & Present: Encyclopedia of Theology and Religion.* Leiden, Netherlands: Brill, 2007.

Curta, Florin, and Andrew Holt, eds. *Great Events in Religion: An Encyclopedia of Pivotal Events in Religious History.* Santa Barbara, CA: ABC-CLIO, 2017.

Schulze, Hagen. *Germany: A New History.* Cambridge, MA: Harvard University Press, 1998.

Scribner, Robert W., and C. Scott Dixon. *The German Reformation.* Basingstoke, UK: Palgrave Macmillan, 2003.

Bonhoeffer, Dietrich (1906–1945)

Dietrich Bonhoeffer was a Lutheran pastor, theologian, political insurgent, and Christian martyr. Bonhoeffer's father, Karl, a leading psychiatrist in Berlin, provided upper-class benefits for his family. Consequently, Bonhoeffer was able to pursue an academic career in theology, earning a doctor of theology degree at age twenty-one from the University of Berlin, and he finished his *Habilitation*, which entitled him to teach at a university, when he was twenty-four. He also worked in Berlin as a *Privatdozent* (lecturer) at the Technische Hochschule, now Technische Universität. During his studies, he was greatly influenced by his professor, the liberal theologian Adolf von Harnack.

Bonhoeffer grew to disdain traditional religious expression, adopting Karl Barth's antithesis between faith and religion. Christian faith, for Bonhoeffer, could not be separated from obedience, as he famously states in his book *The Cost of Discipleship*—"only the believer is obedient, and only the obedient believes." Jesus, the suffering messiah, is the model for Christian discipleship—the weak and anguished Jesus of Gethsemane, not the triumphant Jesus of John's Revelation.

In 1935, Bonhoeffer assumed a position of leadership in the seminaries of the Confessing Church (a resistance movement to the "German Christians" who espoused Nazism). It was there that he penned his most widely read book, *Life Together*, an exposition of practical theology in the Christian community. Shortly after the Gestapo closed the seminaries in 1937, Bonhoeffer, banned from teaching, joined the insurgence against Hitler. In his travels throughout Europe, Bonhoeffer drummed up support for the resistance and led efforts to rescue Jews from the tentacles of the Third Reich. During this time, he penned *The Cost of Discipleship*, where he differentiated between the concepts of cheap and costly grace.

Bonhoeffer made a brief trip to the United States in 1939, but felt compelled to return to Germany, where he continued his resistance activities. He was arrested on April 5, 1943, and incarcerated at Tegel Prison, in a suburb of Berlin. While in prison, Bonhoeffer wrote *Letters and Papers from Prison*, where he expanded on his famous thesis of "Nonreligious Christianity." Nonreligious Christianity was his attempt to contextualize Christianity for the secular age. Traditional religion, as he defined it, was human dependence on God, leading to escapism for the individual and oppression of others by the organized church. Such a transcendent view of religion was unacceptable in an age of secularism and a hindrance to a messianic faith of suffering.

After an attempt on Adolf Hitler's life in July 1944, Bonhoeffer was accused of associating with the conspirators. He eventually ended up in Flossenbürg concentration camp, where he was condemned to death by Otto Thorbeck, the infamous SS judge. Bonhoeffer was hanged on April 9, 1945, and was most likely buried in a mass grave.

James Lund

See also: Chapter 2: Hitler, Adolf (1889–1945). Chapter 8: German Universities and *Fachhochschulen*.

Further Reading

Bonhoeffer, Dietrich. *The Cost of Discipleship*. New York: Macmillan, 1959.

Bonhoeffer, Dietrich. *Letters and Papers from Prison*. Minneapolis: Fortress Press, 2010.

Bonhoeffer, Dietrich. *Life Together*. New York: Harper, 1954.

Metaxas, Eric. *Bonhoeffer: Pastor, Martyr, Prophet, Spy: A Righteous Gentile vs. the Third Reich*. Nashville, TN: Thomas Nelson, 2010.

Contemporary Attitudes toward Religion

The Basic Law (*Grundgesetz*) guarantees religious freedom in Germany. As has been the case for over 1,300 years, Christianity remains the dominant religion in the country. Current polls consistently report that about 70% of Germans identify as Christian; however, only 20% of these respondents regularly attend church services. In post-communist eastern Germany, over half the population identify as atheists—belief in no God—where in western Germany that number is significantly lower (10%). Christians in Germany are evenly divided between Protestant and Roman Catholic. In a 2017 Pew Research Poll, "Being Christian in Western Europe," the majority of Germans who identify as nonpracticing Christians (approximately half the population) believe Christian churches still play an important role in society, such as helping the needy and the poor. Theologically, the nonpracticing Christian does not define God in a biblical sense, rather is inclined to refer to a "higher power" or "spiritual force in the universe."

A recent study exploring the religious attitudes among young European adults (those ages 16–29) found a dramatic turn away from organized religion: nearly half of young German adults do not identify with any religion. The study's author, Stephen Bullivant, observes that many children "will have been baptized and then never darken the door of a church again. Cultural religious identities just aren't being passed on from parents to children. It just washes straight off them."

Individuals who claim religious affiliation pay the church tax (*Kirchensteuer*), which is based on a percentage (8–9%) of an individual's income tax. Individuals may opt out of paying the church tax; however, those who do not pay it lose the opportunity to marry in a church or baptize their children.

There are an estimated 4–5 million Muslims in Germany. German attitudes toward Islam have shifted dramatically in recent years. Polls from earlier this century reported that two-thirds of Germans tolerated the practice of Islam and believed that Christianity is not a superior religion. That number has recently been inverted, where currently two-thirds of Germans believe Islam "does not belong in Germany." Jewish life in Germany was decimated by the Holocaust. Today, Germany is home to the fourth-largest Jewish population in Europe, some 100,000 people. Jews in Germany resettled quickly after World War II, finding safety in Allied-occupied territories. Yet Jewish communities are once again experiencing anti-Semitism. In 2017, German police recorded 1,453 anti-Semitic attacks, and over 60% of Jews polled reported experiencing anti-Semitism in their daily lives. The eastern religions of Buddhism and Hinduism continue to find new adherents from former German Christians and increased adherents via Asian immigration.

James Lund

See also: Chapter 3: Constitutions; Tax Policy. Chapter 5: Holocaust; Islam in Germany; Judaism in Germany. Chapter 6: Immigration; Jews in Germany. Chapter 10: Etiquette for Major Life Events.

Further Reading

Juergensmeyer, Mark. *The Oxford Handbook of Global Religions*. Oxford, UK: Oxford University Press, 2011.

Pew Research Center. "Being Christian in Western Europe." http://www.pewforum .org/2018/05/29/being-christian-in-western-europe/. Accessed July 9, 2020.

Vilaça, Helena, ed. *The Changing Soul of Europe: Religions and Migrations in Northern and Southern Europe*. London: Routledge, 2016.

Germanic Religions

Tracing pre-Christian religious practice in Germany is a challenging task due to the lack of primary literary sources and religious archaeological findings. This problem is compounded by the difficulty in defining "Germanic" ethnicity precisely in the period prior to the Roman Iron Age (1–200 CE). Consequently, much of the scholarship on Germanic religion is based on Icelandic myths from the thirteenth century. One exception is the ethnography *Germania* written in 98 CE by the Roman historian Publius Cornelius Tacitus. According to Tacitus, the German peoples sang hymns to the earth-born god Tuisco, whose son Mannus was the generator of the race. Mannus had three sons, each named for a tribal region: Ingaevones—the coastal area; Herminones—the interior lands; and Istaevones—the remainder. The coastal tribes united to worship Hertha or Mother Earth, who resided on an island in the ocean. During the time of worship, all peace breaks out and joy abounds until she is mortally wounded by her priest. Tacitus also described a second worship event by the Semnones, a self-proclaimed noble tribe, who gathered to perform a human sacrifice in celebration of their "barbarous rites." The Semnones revered a sacred grove, the residence of a deity who was considered to be the source of the nation.

Archaeologists have discovered few pre-Christian religious artifacts in Germany. Wooden idols that appear to be fertility gods as well as other cultic items were found in what appear to be ritual sites. As the German tribes began to convert to Christianity in the fourth century, Christian writers recorded little about the religious life they encountered. The Saxons are said to have worshipped a tree trunk that was believed to uphold the world. Charlemagne destroyed this religious site in 772, and Saint Boniface did the same to a relic oak tree outside the German village of Geismar in Thuringia.

The best-known account of Germanic mythology is preserved in the *Prose Edda,* written in 1220 by Icelandic historian Snorri Sturluson. Together, these two sources provide a broad narrative of Germanic mythology from creation to cosmological destruction. According to this saga, two tribes of gods make up the pantheon: the Vanir and the Aesir. Traditionally, the two tribes lived in peace until a great war erupted when the Aesir attacked the Vanir. The Vanir defended themselves vigorously to the point of a draw between the two tribes, when peace was made and hostages exchanged. Of the numerous gods in the pantheon, four are of note. Odin was the oldest and most revered leader of the Aesir; Thor, the son of Odin, was the god of thunder and a great warrior in the battles against the giants; Balder, another son of Odin, was thought to be immortal, but was murdered in a cunning plan by Loki, a "trickster" god who is able to change appearance and gender. Odin housed the honorable dead in Valhalla (the "hall of the fallen"), which was starkly portrayed in the Immolation Scene of Richard Wagner's opera the *Gotterdämmerung.*

James Lund

See also: Chapter 2: Overview; Charlemagne (748–814). Chapter 5: Saint Boniface (675–745).

Further Reading

The Poetic Edda. Carolyne Larrington, trans. Oxford, UK: Oxford University Press, 2014.

Sturluson, Snorri. *The Prose Edda: Norse Mythology.* Jesse L. Byock, trans. London: Penguin, 2005.

Tacitus, Cornelius. *Agricola and Germany.* Anthony Birley, trans. Oxford, UK: Oxford University Press, 2009.

Holocaust

The "Holocaust" refers to the attempted destruction of European Jewry during the era of the Third Reich (1933–1945). With the selection of Adolf Hitler as German chancellor on January 30, 1933, anti-Semitism became a central part of national policy under Nazi rule. In the ensuing months, the process of segregating Jews from the "national community" (*Volksgemeinschaft*) began in earnest. The Jewish populace, already suffering anti-Semitic violence, now suffered economic assault with the enactment of a national boycott of Jewish merchants, professionals, and the dismissal of all Jewish civil servants. On September 15, 1935, the adoption of the Nuremberg Laws, which banned marriage and sexual relations between Jews and Germans and declared only those of "German Blood" are citizens of the state, legalized the Nazi anti-Jewish program. By 1938, without means of employment and with continued violent exploitation, nearly two-thirds of German Jews had chosen to leave the country.

The outbreak of the Second World War only intensified the "Jewish Problem." Hitler was adamant that an expanded Reich be free of Jews (*Judenfrei*), but the adjacent territories had larger Jewish communities than Germany. With the quick conquest of Poland and France, the Jewish population under Nazi control exploded. Jews in Poland were incarcerated in ghettos as a transitory holding place for Jews awaiting a permanent solution.

Mourners attend the funeral of inmates who could not be saved or who were killed by the SS before the liberation of Auschwitz in Upper Silesia, Poland, 1945. The Holocaust claimed the lives of six million Jewish people. At Auschwitz, 960,000 Jews were murdered. (National Archives)

The Nazis, soon overwhelmed, planned for a "final solution" to the "Jewish question." One idea was to establish a Jewish reservation on the island of Madagascar and in the east at Lublin. With the number of Jews incarcerated growing exponentially after the invasion of Russia, a more sinister plan evolved—extermination. As German troops advanced on the Soviet Union, large Jewish communities, left defenseless in its wake, were marched into the forests, lined up naked next to large pits and executed, falling into mass graves. The Nazis, realizing these executions were openly public and that shooting mothers and babies had a negative emotional impact on the troops, consequently contrived a more private and impersonal method of killing.

At first, Jews in the ghettos were loaded into trucks and driven around with the exhaust redirected into the sealed compartment. When the screams had stopped, drivers dumped the bodies into mass graves concealed in the forest. Yet this also proved to be an inefficient method. Reinhard Heydrich, a high-ranking SS officer charged with solving the "Jewish Problem," convened a summit in Wannsee, a Berlin suburb, at a lakeside villa on January 20, 1942. The conclave of fifteen leaders from various government agencies coordinated a plan to exterminate 11 million European Jews in death camps—the Final Solution (*Endlösung*). Soon after the Wannsee summit, death camps opened in occupied Poland at Sobibor, Belzec, and Treblinka. Concentration camps such as Auschwitz added the capacity to exterminate.

SS troops orchestrated the roundup and deportation of Jews by train to the killing centers and concentration camps. When the trains arrived at Auschwitz, a physician separated the people. The aged, sick, children, handicapped, and pregnant women were dispatched directly to the gas chambers. The able-bodied became slave laborers in adjacent factories where they were worked to death. Carbon monoxide was the gas of choice in most camps, while Auschwitz deployed the lethal gas Zyklon B. Once dead, the bodies were burned in crematoria. At its peak capacity, Auschwitz could kill and dispose of nearly 9,000 people per day. It has been established that at least 6 million Jews died at the hands of the Nazis.

The war began to turn against the German army in the winter of 1942–43 when Soviet troops decimated the German forces at Stalingrad and went on the offensive. By December 1944, the Soviet army gathered on the banks of the Oder River ready to mount an attack on Berlin. The Soviets came first into contact with the Nazi atrocities at the concentration camp Majdanek in the Polish city of Lubin. News regarding the concentration camps spread to the West. The Nazis, not wanting the camps to be discovered, tried desperately to conceal their purpose. Wanting no witnesses, the German army forced prisoners to march west toward Germany. As the Soviets closed in on Auschwitz, the remaining prisoners were shipped to Germany by train—overwhelming the German camps. Allied troops, pressing in from the west, soon discovered other concentration camps, such as Dachau near Munich, and were confronted with the horrors of railcars full of dead bodies and starving prisoners. The unprepared troops quickly transitioned from a mission of destruction of the German military to one of mercy toward the prisoners in the concentration camps.

By the end of the Second World War, the Nazis had nearly exterminated the Jewish population in Europe. In Germany, an estimated 19,000 "free" Jews and 8,000 survivors of concentration camps populated the country. Surprisingly, the number of Jews in Allied-occupied Germany increased quickly in the postwar years. Yet few of the displaced Jews in the American and British Zones assimilated into the remnant German Jewish communities.

James Lund

See also: Chapter 2: Overview; Frank, Anne (1929–1944); Hitler, Adolf (1989–1945). Chapter 5: Judaism in Germany. Chapter 6: Jews in Germany.

Further Reading

Frankl, Viktor E. *Man's Search for Meaning*. Ilse Lasch, trans. Boston: Beacon Press, 2015.

Gilbert, Martin. *The Holocaust: The Jewish Tragedy*. Glasgow: Fontana/Collins, 1990.

Laqueur, Walter, and Judith Tydor Baumel-Schwartz, eds. *The Holocaust Encyclopedia*. New Haven, CT: Yale University Press, 2001.

Rees, Laurence. *The Holocaust: A New History*. New York: Public Affairs, 2017.

Wiesel, Elie. *Night*. New York: Hill and Wang, 2006.

Islam in Germany

In 1731, a small band of Turkish soldiers serving in the army of Prussian king Frederick William I became the first congregation of Muslims in Germany when the king, by decree, established a prayer room for his Muslim soldiers in Potsdam. The first mosque did not appear until the First World War in 1915, when the Wünsdorf Mosque was erected in a prisoner of war camp outside of Berlin. The Wünsdorf Mosque served nearly 15,000 Muslim soldiers interned by the Allies. The mosque fell into disrepair and was demolished around 1930.

Until the influx of temporary workers (*Gastarbeiter*) from Islamic countries in the 1960s (710,000 workers), Muslims were a minor cohort of the German population. When the program ended in 1973, many Muslims and their families remained in Germany. Islam, nearly overnight, became the third-largest religious community in Germany. Of the Muslims in Germany, less than 5% are members of a mosque. The three largest organizations are the Turkish-Islamic Union for Religious Affairs (DITIB)—the official Turkish State association—the Central Council of Muslims in Germany (ZMD), and the Islamic Council of Germany (Islamrat), a more conservative collection of mosques.

Since the mass immigration of the 1970s, Muslim organizations have fought for their constitutional right to have Islamic religious instruction included in the curriculum of public schools on par with Christianity and Judaism. Germany made religious instruction a constitutional obligation in state schools after World War II, yet the Muslim quest has met resistance since no single organization speaks religiously for the entire Islamic population—a condition of the law. It was only in 2012 that German states introduced such instruction in public schools. Nine of the sixteen German states now offer courses in Islam in more than 800 schools. Estimates from 2018 calculate the Muslim population at 6 million or 7% of the German population. This figure includes nearly 600,000 refugees from the Syrian Civil War.

James Lund

See also: Chapter 3: Regional Government/Federalism. Chapter 4: Guest Workers. Chapter 6: Immigration; Turks in Germany. Chapter 8: Primary and Secondary Education.

Future Reading

Al-Hamarneh, Ala, and Jorn Thielmann. *Islam and Muslims in Germany*. Leiden, Netherlands: Brill, 2014.

Cesari, Jocelyne, ed. *The Oxford Handbook of European Islam*. Oxford, UK: Oxford University Press, 2015.

Hernandez Aguilar, Luis Manuel. *Governing Muslims and Islam in Contemporary Germany: Race, Time, and the German Islam Conference*. Leiden, Netherlands: Brill, 2018.

Judaism in Germany

Jewish immigrants in the fourth and fifth centuries settled along trade routes in the German cities of Worms, Speyer, and Mainz. These cities grew as centers for Jewish commerce and religious education into the eleventh century.

During the First Crusade in 1096, Christian crusaders turned on Jewish communities in the Rhine Valley, killing over 10,000 Jews. This assault inaugurated a destructive shift in the history of German treatment of Jews. Jews, forced out of their trades and regular activities of commerce, turned to money lending to non-Jews as their main source of income, further escalating tensions.

Occasional persecutions continued in the twelfth and thirteenth centuries amid periods of growth and peace. Change came in the late thirteenth and fourteenth centuries when Jewish communities, accused of Host desecration (defiling the bread of the Catholic mass), were ransacked during the civil war in southwest Germany in 1298–99. Not long afterward, in 1336–37, Jews were caught in the wake of rioting by peasants, which destroyed over one hundred Jewish communities. Shortly thereafter, in 1348–50, Jews were accused of poisoning the water wells during the carnages of the Black Death, the bubonic plague. Three hundred Jewish communities across Germany were attacked and decimated.

Expulsion of Jews from Germany became the norm in the late fourteenth and fifteenth centuries, and many fled to Eastern Europe. The age of Christian Reformation in Germany (sixteenth century) brought upheaval to all areas of life. Society was in flux, and the leader of the Reformation, Martin Luther, viciously attacked Jews in the pamphlet *On the Jews, and Their Lies*, calling for such actions as destroying their homes, schools, and putting them into forced labor.

The end of the seventeenth and eighteenth centuries found renewed immigration (especially from Poland) reestablishing Jewish communities in Germany.

The new immigrants, not hindered by the past local customs, assimilated quickly into German mainstream culture. This was the time of enlightenment in Jewish circles led by religious philosophers Moses Mendelssohn and Rabbi Abraham Geiger.

The French Revolution prompted the conveying of equal rights to Jews that carried over into German territories captured by Napoleon. In the post-Napoleonic era, those rights were withdrawn across Germany. Yet certain Jewish enclaves progressed in their attempts to reform Judaism socially and religiously. Samuel Holdheim (1806–1860), meeting great resistance from conservatives, sought to reshape the faith by making it more palatable to contemporary society. Political reforms in the late nineteenth century granted full legal equality to Jews. Many Jews served in the army during World War I and achieved full emancipation during the years of the Weimar Republic.

Jewish emancipation would come to an abrupt end with the Nazi ascent to power in 1933. Anti-Jewish sentiment flourished, and their lives were thrown into disarray. By the end of World War II, 160,000–180,000 German Jews were murdered by the Nazis. Shortly after the war, Jewish communities began to repopulate. As of 2018, approximately 100,000 Jews are members of the *Jüdische Gemeinden* (Jewish congregations) in Germany; the actual number of Jews living in Germany is estimated to be at least double. Despite extensive political and educational campaigns, many continue to be the victim of anti-Semitic activity.

James Lund

See also: Chapter 2: Overview. Chapter 5: Holocaust; Luther, Martin (1483–1546); The Reformation. Chapter 6: Jews in Germany.

Further Reading

Gay, Ruth. *The Jews of Germany: A Historical Portrait*. New Haven, CT: Yale University Press, 2000.

Meyer, Michael A., Michael Brenner, Mordechai Breuer, and Michael Graetz. *German-Jewish History in Modern Times*. New York: Columbia University Press, 1996.

Mounk, Yascha. *Stranger in My Own Country: A Jewish Family in Modern Germany*. New York: Farrar, Straus & Giroux, 2014.

Statista. "Anzahl der Mitglieder der jüdischen Gemeinden in Deutschland von 2002 bis 2020." https://de.statista.com/statistik/daten/studie/1232/umfrage/anzahl-der-juden -in-deutschland-seit-dem-jahr-2003/. Accessed October 23, 2021.

Luther, Martin (1483–1546)

Martin Luther, the father of the Protestant Reformation, can be considered one of the most extraordinary figures in human history. Luther was born into an ordinary middle-class family in Eisleben and studied law until a frightful storm moved him to

Three years after he posted his 95 Theses on the church door at Wittenberg, the Catholic Church branded Luther a heretic. The reformer Martin Luther (1483–1546) burns the papal bull and the canon law near Wittenberg in 1520. (Library of Congress)

plead with Saint Anne to save him; vowing to become a monk if he survived. Luther did survive, and thus left his law studies to join an Augustinian monastery in Erfurt where he devoted himself to the study of the Bible with monastic devotion. He earned a doctor of theology degree in 1512 and joined the faculty at the University of Wittenberg, lecturing on numerous books of the Bible and preaching in local congregations. In 1517, in an attempt to support the construction of Saint Peter's Basilica in Rome, Johann Tetzel, a Dominican preacher, began selling indulgences (a pardon for sins) outside of Wittenberg. Luther was so troubled by the sale of indulgences that he posted ninety-five theses on the door of All Saints' Church (*Schlosskirche*) in Wittenberg to invite academic debate. Simultaneously, Luther, burdened by his own sense of unworthiness before God, embraced the doctrine of justification by faith alone, as he believed was taught in the epistles of Saint Paul. Although intended for a limited audience, Luther's theses circulated broadly, drawing the attention of Pope Leo X. Luther became a prolific writer during these contentious times, penning three titles of note: *Appeal to the Christian Nobility of the German Nation*—imploring German leaders to reform the Church; *On the Babylonian Captivity of the Church*—challenging the corruption of the Church's sacramental system; and *On the Freedom of the Christian*—an exposition of the doctrine of justification and the consequential freedom of the Christian conscience.

Luther's writings elevated the conflict with the Roman Catholic Church, leading to his excommunication by Pope Leo X in 1521. Summoned to the Diet of Worms, a meeting of the German parliament, Luther was implored to recant the errors in his writings. After taking twenty-four hours to contemplate his reply, he answered with his most famous speech: *"I consider myself convicted by the testimony of Holy Scripture, which is my basis; my conscience is captive of the Word of God. Thus I cannot and will not recant, because acting against one's conscience is neither safe nor sound. God help me. Amen."* In response, Emperor Charles V declared Luther a heretic. On his return trip to Wittenberg, Luther was seized by his sympathetic prince, Frederick of Saxony, and taken to Wartburg Castle, where he resided in secret, translating the New Testament and most of the Old Testament into German. When circumstances permitted, Luther returned to Wittenberg and took charge of the reform movement. He married Katharina von Bora, a former nun; had numerous children; and continued his writing. Luther died in 1546 in Eisleben, the city of his birth, at the age of sixty-two.

James Lund

See also: Chapter 5: Judaism in Germany; The Reformation. Chapter 6: Jews in Germany.

Further Reading

Hairline, Craig. *A World Ablaze: The Rise of Martin Luther and the Birth of the Reformation*. New York: Oxford University Press, 2017.

Leppin, Volker. *Martin Luther: A Late Medieval Life*. Grand Rapids, MI: Baker Books, 2017.

Oberman, Heiko A. *Luther: Man between God and the Devil*. New Haven, CT: Yale University Press, 2006.

Rex, Richard. *The Making of Martin Luther*. Princeton, NJ: Princeton University Press, 2017.

Pope Benedict XVI (1927–)

Born Joseph Ratzinger April 16, 1927, in Marktl am Inn, Germany, Ratzinger was elected Bishop of Rome (Pope of the Roman Catholic Church) on April 19, 2005, and retired February 28, 2013. Raised in a middle-class Catholic home, Ratzinger was gifted academically, and entered preparatory school in 1939. After the Nazis' seizure of power in 1933, Ratzinger could not escape involvement in the war preparations. He was forced to join the Hitler Youth in 1941, and was drafted in 1943, serving as a gunner in an antiaircraft unit for the German military.

When the war ended, Ratzinger continued his preparations for entering the priesthood and was ordained in 1951. He pursued advanced theological education, earning a doctorate in theology. Moving to the academy, his teaching career blossomed with successive teaching and administrative assignments in prestigious universities such as Bonn, Münster, Tübingen, and Regensburg. Ratzinger gained a reputation not only as a gifted lecturer, but also as a productive scholar, writing over sixty books.

As a churchman, Ratzinger served with rigor. His theological expertise provided clarity and direction for church leaders as they wrestled with reforms at the Second Vatican Council (1962–65). In 1977, Pope Paul VI chose Ratzinger to hold the office of Archbishop of Munich and then, three months later, promoted him to the College of Cardinals.

After the death of Pope John Paul II on April 2, 2005, Cardinal Ratzinger chaired the conclave to elect the next pope. A day into deliberations on April 19, 2005, Ratzinger was elected the 265th Bishop of the Roman Catholic Church. Ratzinger, at age seventy-eight, chose the name "Benedict" and became Pope Benedict XVI.

Benedict XVI was popular with conservative church members who anticipated a strong defense of the Church's teachings on abortion, homosexuality, and birth control. His detractors feared his conservative theological convictions and dogged approach, dubbing him "God's Rottweiler" and "The Enforcer." Those fears subsided, to an extent, as time passed. By most accounts, Benedict was gentle in speech, kind of heart, reflective in thought, and quick-witted.

Benedict visited the United States in 2008, where he expressed his opposition to the Iraq war and U.S. measures to curb illegal immigration. He celebrated Catholic Mass with 46,000 in attendance at National Park in Washington, D.C. and then met privately with leading interfaith dignitaries and scholars at the Catholic University of America. During a Mass in Saint Patrick's Cathedral, he spoke of the burgeoning clerical sexual abuse scandal and met privately with victims.

After two reports by the Irish government in 2010 exposed a wide range of sexual abuse in Catholic schools and by parish priests, Benedict apologized to victims in an eight-page letter and criticized Irish bishops for "grave errors of judgment and failures of leadership."

In a surprising announcement in February 2013, Benedict revealed he would resign at the end of the month, being only the second pope ever to do so. He resigned on February 28, 2013, and took the title Pope Emeritus.

James Lund

See also: Chapter 2: Hitler, Adolf (1889–1945). Chapter 7: Overview; LGBTQ Life in Modern Germany.

Further Reading

Benedict, Pope, and Peter Seewald. *Last Testament: In His Own Words.* Jacob Phillips, trans. London: Bloomsbury, 2016.

Benedict, Pope, John F. Thornton, and Susan B. Varenne. *The Essential Pope Benedict XVI: His Central Writings and Speeches.* New York: Harper San Francisco, 2007.

Guerriero, Elio. *Benedict XVI: His Life and Thought.* San Francisco: Ignatius, 2018.

The Reformation

The Reformation is widely regarded as one of the signature events in world history. It marked the culmination of the medieval world and initiated the current modern era. As part of the Holy Roman Empire, Germany was ruled by Emperor Charles V, who had expressed religious loyalty to the Roman Catholic Church and Pope Leo X. In 1517, Martin Luther, a monk and professor of theology, posted ninety-five theses on the door of All Saints' Church in Wittenberg protesting the special sale of indulgences by Johann Tetzel—an agent of the Catholic Church. Although intended for a limited academic audience, the theses were quickly translated from Latin into German and distributed throughout Germany. Luther's opposition to the Holy Roman Empire's theology and ecclesiastical governance ultimately led to his excommunication from the Church and being declared a heretic by the Empire.

What did Luther believe that was so controversial? Luther was convinced that the New Testament taught salvation or justification by faith alone, not by or combined with good works; it is a gift of God by faith in Jesus Christ. In Luther's view, it was the Scripture, not church tradition or the Pope, that was the final authority in matters of faith and practice. He contended that all believers have access to God's grace without an intermediary priest; hence the saying, "the priesthood of all believers." His aggressive challenge to church theology, government, and ministry disrupted the Church and threatened an already fragile empire.

The papal excommunication of Luther in 1520 and the empire's condemnation in 1521 did little to calm the religious movement. Nearly two-thirds of German cities had adopted the Reformation by the early 1530s. Outside of Germany, and independent of Luther, the movement spread quickly to the Swiss city of Zurich, where Ulrich Zwingli pressed the cause. Unable to unite the German and Swiss reform movements over disagreements with Luther on the presence of Christ's body in the Lord's Supper, Zwingli led an independent reform movement in Zurich until his death in 1531. In the Swiss city of Geneva, French reformer John Calvin preached and wrote to the point of exhaustion. Calvin is recalled eminently for his theology of predestination—God decrees to save some and not to save others. His most famous work, *Institutes of the Christian Religion*, is considered one of the finest summaries of Protestant Christian doctrine.

Back in Germany, the turmoil of the religious movement began to affect secular concerns. Peasants and other townspeople, feeling unfairly taxed, revolted in what is known as the Peasants' War (Bauernkrieg). From 1524 to 1526, bands of peasants took up arms demanding economic, religious, and social reform. After initial success, the German princes quelled the uprising, leading to some 100,000 peasant casualties.

On the religious front, numerous attempts at religious reconciliation with the Roman Church failed. In 1530, Emperor Charles V called the Diet of Augsburg to deal with the "German situation," particularly the rift within Christianity. At the Diet,

Lutheran reformers composed a confessional document, subsequently signed by German Protestant princes, creating official toleration for the Reformation's expression of Christianity. The document, known as the Augsburg Confession, continues to be the confessional basis for the Lutheran faith.

Although attempts at reconciliation between Lutherans and the Roman Catholic Church continued, it became increasingly evident that the split was permanent. The continued loyalty of Lutherans to the local Protestant princes infuriated the emperor. Soon after Luther's death in 1546, Charles V declared war on the Protestant princes and captured Wittenberg. A loose peace agreement in 1546 eventually led to the 1555 Peace of Augsburg—recognizing the existence of Lutheranism and the right of princes to determine the religious practice in their territories (*cuius regio, eius religio,* or "Whose realm, his religion"). The Protestant Reformation had split the political unity of the empire.

The Peace of 1555 left widespread Catholic discontent. In response to the Protestant Reformation and in an effort at internal reform, Pope Paul III convened a council in the northern Italian city of Trent in 1545. The Council of Trent met over an eighteen-year period, which included numerous extended breaks. At Trent, the Catholic Church clarified its positions on matters challenged by the Protestants—Biblical authority, apostolic tradition, justification, and the sacrament of the mass. To counter the Protestant reform movement, the council formed the Society of Jesus or Jesuits, who became aggressive promoters of Roman Catholicism within German Protestant territories. This Counter-Reformation proved quite effective. The Peace of Augsburg left Protestant territories in a state of disunity as fissures erupted within Protestantism. The Jesuits seized this opportunity, claiming many converts to the newly reformed and energized Roman Catholic Church.

The debate on the lasting broader implications of the Reformation (economic, scientific, political, etc.) continues to this day. Max Weber, the twentieth-century German sociologist, proposed the Protestant Ethic Thesis, that the pious character of the Protestant Christian (particularly Calvinism) is the foundation for modern capitalism. American sociologist Robert K. Merton suggested that the new science of seventeenth-century England owed its founding and accomplishments to the "Puritan ethos." Luther's doctrine of the "Two Kingdoms" reassessed the relationship of church and state, overturning the Middle Ages' practice of the Roman Church that granted the pope authority over secular authorities. Although provincial churches became the norm during the Reformation, local princes generally granted autonomy to the churches to conduct their own affairs.

James Lund

See also: Chapter 5: Luther, Martin (1483–1546); Religious Wars.

Further Reading

Brady, Thomas A. *German Histories in the Age of Reformations, 1400–1650.* Cambridge, UK: Cambridge University Press, 2009.

Hairline, Craig. *A World Ablaze: The Rise of Martin Luther and the Birth of the Reformation*. New York: Oxford University Press, 2017.

Marshall, Peter *1517: Martin Luther and the Invention of the Reformation*. Oxford, UK: Oxford University Press, 2017.

Scott, Tom. *The Early Reformation in Germany: Between Secular Impact and Radical Vision*. London: Routledge, 2013.

Religious Wars

The German Peasants' War of 1524–1526 was one of the greatest political, social, and religious uprisings in modern European history prior to the French Revolution. The revolt began in the summer of 1524 in the Black Forest region of southwest Germany when a band of peasants refused to pay fees and to provide services to their overlord. What started as an unarmed public demonstration quickly grew into a violent resistance as peasants under adjacent lordships joined forces. At its peak, an estimated 300,000 peasants took up arms with surprising success. The uprising ended abruptly when armies of the southwest German princes returned from battle in Italy, crushing the uprising with brutal force. Some 100,000 peasants died in the uprising with many more left injured.

Considerable controversy surrounds the cause of the Peasants' War. The list of grievances found in the "Twelve Articles of the Swabian Peasantry" is perhaps the best evidence for the source of discontent. Of notable interest is the peasants' application of Luther's standard for religious reforms to their social reforms: *"it is our conclusion and final resolution that if any one or more of the articles here set forth should not be in agreement with the word of God, as we think they are, such article we will willingly retract if it is proved really to be against the word of God by a clear explanation of the Scripture."* The peasants desired to choose their own pastors, be freed from serfdom, have rights to natural resources, and not be overburdened with taxes. Although the surviving peasants were severely punished by their local princes, concessions by their overlords restored stability.

Even more complex were the causes of the Thirty Years War (1618–1648). One hundred years after Luther posted his ninety-five theses and ignited the Reformation, escalating religious and political tensions led inexorably to conflict. With the Roman Catholic Church rallying to halt Protestant expansion and Protestants ready to defend their territory, war between ecclesiastically aligned military–political forces seemed inevitable. The first conflict, known as the "defenestration of Prague," began when an entourage of Protestant noblemen from Bohemia entered the Hradčany Castle in Prague to protest the attempt by the Catholic King Ferdinand of Bohemia to restore Roman Catholicism to the region. When the king's representatives proved inflexible, the Protestant noblemen threw them out a window. Ferdinand, now emperor, responded to the rebellion by gathering a strong coalition of Catholic military might, defeating the Protestants at the Battle of White Mountain in 1620. Bohemia was restored to Catholic control. The Catholic military campaign stretched northward, gaining control of the majority of German territory. Ferdinand's ambitions alarmed Protestant Sweden to the north, who in 1630 invaded Germany and, under Gustavus Adolphus, delivered a decisive military defeat to the emperor at the Battle of Breitenfeld. As the Swedes advanced from the north, the French, also not wanting a Germany dominated by the emperor, invaded from the south. With no single army strong enough to control central Europe, the conflict ended in a stalemate with the Peace of Westphalia in 1648.

James Lund

See also: Chapter 5: The Reformation.

Further Reading

Baylor, Michael G. *The German Reformation and the Peasants' War: A Brief History with Documents.* Boston: Bedford/St. Martin's, 2012.

Parker, Geoffrey, Simon Adams, Gerhard Benecke, and Richard J. Bonney. *The Thirty Years' War.* London: Routledge, 2007.

Wilson, Peter Hamish. *The Thirty Years War: Europe's Tragedy.* Cambridge, MA: Belknap Press of Harvard University Press, 2011.

Saint Boniface (675–745)

Saint Boniface (birth name Wynfrith or Winfrid) was a relentless missionary and church reformer who introduced Christianity to large swaths of northern Germany and the Netherlands. Wynfrith was born in England ca. 675 to a noble family. Educated in English monasteries, he subsequently was ordained as a priest in the Benedictine Order at the age of thirty and began teaching at the monastery's school. At the age of forty, he felt called to the mission field and ventured into Frisia, a Frankish kingdom hostile to Christianity. This trip failed, and in preparation for his next missionary effort, in 718 he made a pilgrimage to Rome, where Pope Gregory II granted him broad authority to evangelize the pagans in the Frisian region. Before he set out, Pope Gregory II conferred on him the name Boniface.

On his return to the Frankish kingdom, Boniface once again attempted to evangelize the Frisians with little success. He then turned his missionary efforts toward the Hessians, a notorious pagan people. By his passionate care for the poor and a clear Christian message, he found great success baptizing thousands of converts. In 722, he reported his success to the pope, who then consecrated him a missionary bishop. Additionally, the pope provided Boniface with numerous church canons (religious laws and instructions) to deliver to the clergy and civil rulers in the German region.

In 723, Bishop Boniface returned to the Hessians, where the Christian converts pressed him to deliver a final blow to the pagans by chopping down their relic oak tree at Geismar. This he did, turning its planks into a Christian chapel commemorating Saint Peter.

Over the next ten years, Boniface ministered in Thuringia, evangelizing and imposing order on the existing Christian church. In 732, Boniface was promoted by Pope Gregory III to archbishop, granting him authority to consecrate missionary bishops and instill church hierarchies.

On his final pilgrimage to Rome in 737, Pope Gregory III commissioned Boniface to organize churches throughout Germany. On his return to German regions, Boniface established bishoprics (church districts under a bishop) in Salzburg, Freising, Regensburg, Passau, Erfurt, and Buraburg in Hesse. With bishoprics established, Boniface in 742 gathered the bishops for the first council meeting to establish church hierarchy, confront moral issues in the priesthood, and remove pagan relics. Subsequent councils continued the practice of church discipline and resolved discrepancies over church properties.

Boniface retired from church politics in 747 but continued his missionary pursuit of the Frisians. In 753, the Frisians murdered Boniface and fifty-three companions on Pentecost Sunday. He is buried at the monastery in Fulda.

James Lund

See also: Chapter 2: Overview. Chapter 5: Overview.

Further Reading

Boniface. *The Letters of Saint Boniface*. Ephraim Emerton, trans. New York: Columbia University Press, 2000.

Greenaway, George William. *Saint Boniface: Three Biographical Studies for the Twelfth Centenary Festival*. London: Black, 1955.

Watkins, Basil. *The Book of Saints: A Comprehensive Biographical Dictionary*. London: T&T Clark, 2016.

Willibald. *The Life of Saint Boniface*. George W. Robinson, trans. Cambridge, MA: Harvard University Press, 1916.

CHAPTER 6

SOCIAL CLASSES AND ETHNICITY

OVERVIEW

German Sociology

German sociology differentiates between *Gemeinschaft* (community) and *Gesell-schaft* (society) (Tönnies, 1957). "Community" is based on organic relationships such as mother–child, husband–wife, and brothers and sisters. Its constituent unit is the nuclear family but may include the extended family as well as village(s) and profession(s). "Society" presupposes ideal relationships where individuals with arbitrary goals are brought together, and hence, they are governed by obligatory rights. Societies may be capitalistic (such as West Germany) or socialistic (former East Germany), open or closed, pluralistic, and so on.

At the turn of the twentieth century, Germany society was divided into clearly identifiable social classes. The industrial or working classes included both skilled and unskilled labor and were associated with labor unions and the Communist Party of Germany (KPD). Small business owners and white-collar employees made up the middle class, typically linked to various bourgeois parties and patriotic societies. The upper classes, namely, industrialists, financiers, and large landowners, identified with the government. After the Second World War, societal boundaries were relaxed in West Germany, and more individuals were able to attain the trappings of middle-class life. The DDR (Deutsche Demokratische Republik, German Democratic Republic) described itself as a "workers' and peasants' state." The government nationalized larger private enterprises and forced farmers into agricultural cooperatives (Eidson, 2001).

Over thirty years after the fall of the Berlin Wall and the political reunification, rifts remain in German society. While regional differences are expressed in variations of food, dialect, and religion, the greatest differences within German society are between the former East and West Germany. The Federal Republic of Germany (West Germany) became a liberal democracy committed to atoning for Nazi war crimes, often subjugating its own national interests to facilitate European integration. East Germany identified itself with the communist Soviet Union who resisted Nazi Germany, thus denying any role in the atrocities committed by the Third Reich. Behind the wall, the German Democratic Republic was frozen in time, a predominantly white country where nationalism endured. The Berlin Wall not only prevented people from leaving the GDR, but also served as a reminder that the totalitarian nation was not a destination for immigration. Since reunification, one in every seven East Germans either migrated to the western part of the country or left Germany altogether. The population in the five Eastern states (Brandenburg, Mecklenburg-Western Pomerania, Saxony, Saxony-Anhalt, and Thuringia) has dropped 10%. Gross domestic product in the east remains at 75% of that in the west. Only sixteen of the top 500 German companies are based in the east, and none of these businesses are listed on the DAX, Germany's main stock exchange. Tellingly, one in five people in the east consider themselves "East German" rather than "German." There is no equivalent regional identity in the western part of the country. Citizens from the East refer to West Germans as "Wessies," and consider them materialistic and self-centered. In the eyes of many West Germans, the "Ossies" (East Germans) are unsophisticated and harbor unrealistic expectations of immediate economic equality with the West.

Social Classes

The German nobility enjoyed numerous privileges prior to World War I. These were abolished in 1919 by the Weimar Republic, which declared all Germans equal under the law. While the status of nobility is no longer recognized by the German government, hereditary titles are permitted as part of the surname, for example, the aristocratic particles *von* and *zu*. At the present time, the German elites number less than 1% of the populations, and their status as such is based on economic and political performance and is rarely inherited. In the GDR, entrance into the elite strata of society was determined by ideological considerations. Hence, most of the GDR's elite lost their status with the fall of the Berlin Wall.

German society contains a large, prosperous middle class, comprising 60% of the population. This middle class includes mid-level civil servants, the majority of salaried workers, skilled blue-collar workers, and a shrinking pool of farmers. Civil servants (such as teachers and university professors) enjoy job security, generous pensions, and relatively higher incomes than other salaried employees. Members of the working class are both skilled (those who have completed occupational training) and unskilled workers (25% of whom are foreigners) as well as their supervisors. Blue-collar workers are an important component of the workforce, due in part to the influence of trade unions in Germany. Salaried workers other than civil servants generally earn one-third higher salaries than the working class.

Although Germany is a prosperous country, it contains an alarming level of poverty. Households with less than half the average net income are classified as poor. At the time of reunification, 7.5% of households in West Germany and 14.8% in East German were considered poor. Financial assets are distributed unequally in Germany, so that the upper 10% of the populace control 60% of the nation's wealth while the lower 50% control just 2.4% of the wealth. Half of German households have €60,000 (approximately $70,000) or less in assets, and households in East Germany still have only half the assets of their counterparts in the West. Twenty percent of the population lives on social benefits: unemployment compensation, social welfare, and statutory minimum pensions. Those most likely to receive *Sozialhilfe* are households with three or more children or those headed by a single parent. The remaining 30% are the working poor, who work full time yet are looking at permanent financial insecurity.

Ethnicity

Eighty percent of the population of Germany are ethnic Germans. The Grundgesetz (Basic Law) defined citizenship according to the principle of *Jus Sanguinis* ("right of blood"), that is, citizenship is determined by the nationality of the parents. As a result of this stipulation, children born outside of Germany to German expatriates are considered to be "German" while others born in Germany to noncitizens such as guest workers are not. The law was changed in 2000, which granted the right of dual

---

AFRO-GERMANS

Africans were first brought to Germany in the seventeenth century as household servants. African migration increased in the nineteenth century when Germany established colonies in areas now ruled by six African countries: Burundi, Cameroon, Namibia, Rwanda, Tanzania, and Togo. During the Weimar Republic, Africans were displayed in zoos and mixed-race children were disparagingly called *Rheinlandsbastarde* (believed to have been fathered by French soldiers of African descent after the First World War). Many of those were secretly sterilized starting in 1937 during the Third Reich, and naturalized Afro-Germans lost their passports. Historians have estimated that about 2,000 people of African descent were murdered in concentration camps.

After the end of the Nazi reign, discrimination and persecution officially ended; however, Afro-Germans continue to face many prejudices. The children fathered by African American soldiers and German mothers, so called *brown babies*, faced an uncertain future. Many of them were taken away from their unwed mothers and forcibly adopted to families in Denmark, the United States, and other countries. Today, between 500,000 and 800,000 Afro-Germans (Afro-Deutsche, schwarze Deutsche, Schwarze Deutsche) live in Germany, mostly in bigger cities, and still face discrimination. For example, the right-wing politician Alexander Gauland (deputy chairman of the AfD) claimed in 2016 that people do not want to live next to Jérôme Boateng, a famous Afro-German soccer player. The remarks caused a huge outcry, Gauland was scorned, and the AfD was forced to apologize.

Katharina Barbe

Further Reading

Bundeszentrale für politische Bildung. "African Diaspora in Germany." https://www.bpb.de/gesellschaft/migration/afrikanische-diaspora/. Accessed July 11, 2020.

Lennox, Sara, ed. *Remapping Black Germany: New Perspectives on Afro-German History, Politics, and Culture.* Amherst and Boston: University of Massachusetts Press, 2016.

citizenship to children born in Germany to foreign parents. However, at least one of the parents must have resided in Germany legally for at least eight years and must be in possession of a *Unbefristete Aufenthaltsgenehmigung* (comparable to a resident alien in the United States) before birth of the child.

Germany recognizes four national minorities: the Danes, Frisians, Sinti and Roma, and Sorbs. As such, these groups receive special protection and funding from the German government. However, the federal government does not keep official statistics on national minorities. In order to qualify as a federally recognized minority, a population group must meet five criteria. They

- are German nationals;
- have their own language, culture, and history;
- seek to retain their cultural identity;
- have been traditionally residents in Germany;
- live in their traditional settlement area (does not apply to Roma and Sinti).

The Sorbs, numbering 60,000–70,000 people, are a western Slavic people located about 100 km southeast of Berlin in the Lusatian (Lausitz). The area includes the Spreewald and now lives mainly on tourism. The Sorb homeland did not fare well under the Communist government, which destroyed their villages in order to extract the coal located underneath them. The *Länder* (states) of Saxony and Brandenburg pay subventions to help finance Sorb schools.

The duchies of Schleswig and Holstein straddle the Danish–German border. The nations fought two wars over the duchies until the border was settled peacefully by the Schleswig Plebiscite in 1920. Southern Schleswig, with its majority German and minority Danish and Frisian populations, remained part of Germany. Approximately 50,000 Danes and 10,000 Frisians live in Schleswig-Holstein. Both ethnic groups are represented by the South Schleswig Voter Federation in the state legislature.

Germany differentiates between the *Sinti* (Romani who migrated to the area in the fifteenth century) and the *Roma* (East European Romani who arrived after 1870). After the war, German authorities contended that the Romani faced *social*, not racial discrimination, and hence they received no compensation from German courts. Romani were not recognized as victims of the Holocaust until 1982, many years after the end of the Second World War. Many Romani do not have German citizenship but hold temporary residency status, which must be renewed periodically. This status, however, includes restrictions on freedom of movement, access to employment, and social assistance (*Sozialhilfe*). In 2003, the European Commission on Racism and Intolerance noted that Romani in Germany who are not citizens face discrimination.

Wendell G. Johnson

Further Reading

Auswärtiges Amt. "Staatsangehörigkeitsrecht." http://web.archive.org/web/20170516130924 /www.auswaertiges-amt.de/DE/EinreiseUndAufenthalt/Staatsangehoerigkeitsrecht _node.html. Accessed July 11, 2020.

Bennhold, Katrin. "Germany Has Been Unified for 30 Years. Its Identity Is Not." *New York Times*, November 8, 2019. https://www.nytimes.com/2019/11/08/world/europe /germany-identity.html?action=click&module=Top%20Stories&pgtype=Homepage. Accessed July 11, 2020.

Deutsche Welle. "The Ticking Timebomb of German Poverty." https://www.dw.com/en /the-ticking-timebomb-of-german-poverty/a-41379481. Accessed July 11, 2020.

Eidson, John. "Germany." In Melvin Ember and Carol R. Ember. *Countries and Their Cultures,* 847–865. New York: Macmillan Reference USA, 2001.

Federal Ministry of the Interior, Building, and Community. "National Minorities." https://www.bmi.bund.de/EN/topics/community-and-integration/national-minorities /national-minorities-node.html. Accessed July 11, 2020.

Lennox, Sara, ed., *Remapping Black Germany: New Perspectives on Afro-German History, Politics, and Culture.* Amherst and Boston: University of Massachusetts Press, 2016.

Rising, David. "30 Years after Berlin Wall Fell, East-West Divides Remain." *Washington Post*, November 4, 2019. https://apnews.com/article/ap-top-news-international-news -communism-berlin-business-bc1cc1f3ca0a479cbfd817a51a910611. Accessed October 23, 2021.

Tönnies, Ferdinand. *Community and Society (Gemeinschaft und Gesellschaft).* East Lansing: Michigan State University Press, 1957.

Aristocracy and the Elites

German aristocracy (*Adel*) was a privileged group of people, who were involved in government, society, economy, and the arts and whose titles were inherited, ensuring their continuation. Historically, the term "aristocracy" denoted a form of government where an advantaged group is in power; today the term indicates members of the nobility who no longer have special rights in a democracy. There are many types, but the biggest division is into high and low nobility; the former, also called *Hochadel*, included the emperor (*Kaiser*), king (*König*), and counts (*Fürst*). Persons were either born into nobility or named by an emperor or king. In Prussia, for example, the landed nobility, known as the *Junker*, were politically conservative, supported the monarchy, and advocated for protectionist agricultural policies. The proportion of land held by the aristocracy in Prussia was high by European standards—approximately 60%. By contrast, the respective figures were 20% for the French and 14% for the Russian nobility. In 1871, the unification of the German principalities into the German Empire, dominated by Prussia, raised the prestige of the Prussian officer corps and Prussian nobility. Otto von Bismarck, chancellor of Imperial Germany, was himself a Junker and often protected their interests.

The aristocracy maintained its social position through an unofficial "marriage policy." The sons of aristocratic families were free to marry the daughters of wealthy industrialists, thereby ensuring financial gain for their families. Their daughters, however, only married the sons of other aristocrats, thereby ensuring their lofty social

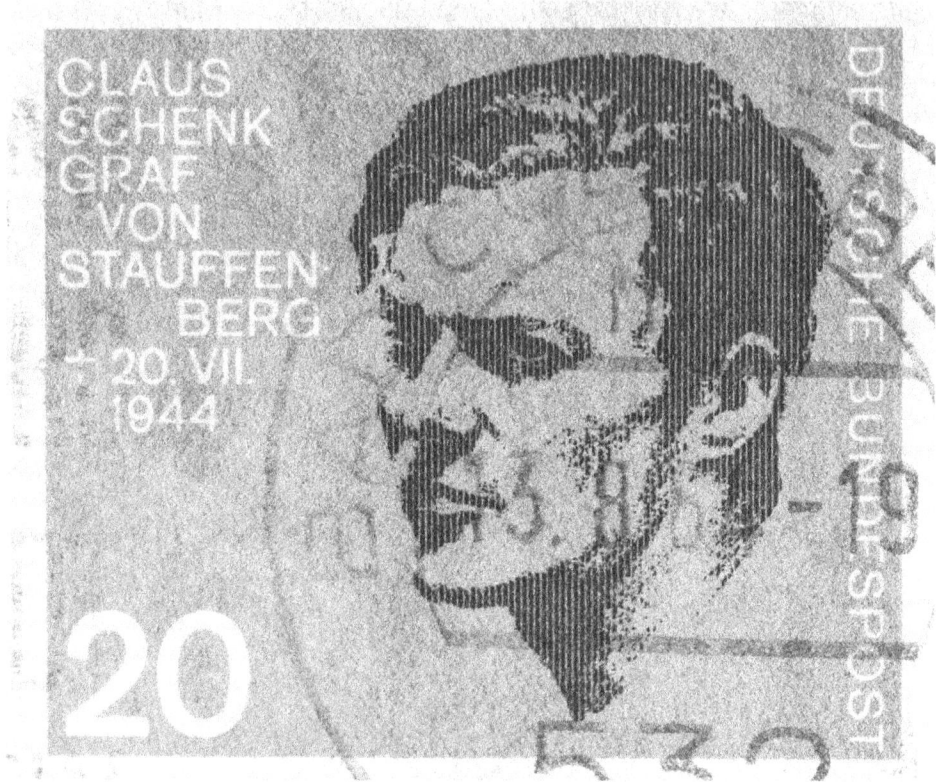

Claus Schenk Graf von Stauffenberg was a resistance fighter who was involved in the failed assassination attempt on Hitler on July 20, 1944. He was murdered by the Nazis on July 21, 1944, just 36 years old. (Matthias Zabanski/Dreamstime.com)

status. Thus, very few members of the industrial and economic elite were able to acquire aristocratic status.

After the First World War, the German Empire was dissolved, its monarch eliminated, and the political power of the aristocracy officially diminished. The Junkers retained their influence in the officer corps and diplomatic service but were otherwise hostile toward the Weimar Republic. Many young nobles became fervent Nazis, with the notable exception of Claus Philipp Maria Schenk Graf von Stauffenberg (1907–1944), a decorated war veteran. Claus von Stauffenberg was a leading figure in the German resistance to Hitler and took part in the July 20, 1944, plot to assassinate the German leader. He was executed by firing squad the next day.

The reconstruction of the West German economy after its destruction during the Second World War (the *Wirtschaftswunder*) created a society much different than that of class-based imperial society. The nobility retained their titles in West Germany, but their social status depended on their contributions to the nation's capitalist economy and body politic. In the German Democratic Republic, land reform served to eliminate

ARISTOCRACY

Adel/Aristokratie	Nobility/Aristocracy	
Kaiser	Emperor	Hochadel High Nobility
König	King	
Fürst	Prince/Count	
Kurfürst	Elector	Niederer Adel Gentry
Herzog	Duke	
Graf	Earl	
Freiherr/Baron	Baron	
Ritter	Knight	

Katharina Barbe

the economic and political power of the elites. Power was exercised originally by a small cadre of approximately 350 persons who in time produced a self-generating elite, whose stated goal was the equalization of the nation's material prospects for its population.

At the present time, the German aristocracy number about 80,000, less than one-tenth of 1% of the country's population. They are disproportionally represented in Germany's diplomatic corps and the upper echelons of its military. There is still the tendency among the *Adel* to remain among themselves, intermarry and attend invitation-only balls and other festivities, and, of course, to fill the pages of Germany's abundant tabloids.

Wendell G. Johnson

See also: Chapter 2: Overview; Bismarck, Otto von (1815–1898); Hindenburg, Paul von (1847–1934); Hitler, Adolf (1889–1945). Chapter 4: Overview. Chapter 16: Boulevard Press.

Further Reading

Baranowski, Shelley. "Aristocracy." In Dieter K. Buse, and Juergen C. Doerr, eds. *Modern Germany: An Encyclopedia of History, People, and Culture, 1871–1990*, 41–42. New York: Garland, 1998.

Hagen, William W. *Ordinary Prussians: Brandenburg Junkers and Villagers, 1500–1840*. Cambridge, UK; New York: Cambridge University Press, 2002.

Hoffmann, Peter. *Stauffenberg: A Family History, 1905–1944*, 3rd ed. Montreal: McGill-Queen's University Press, 2008.

Planet Wissen. "Geschichte des Adels." https://www.planet-wissen.de/geschichte/adel /adel_frueher/index.html. Accessed July 11, 2020.

The Grey Culture

Germany faces an unprecedented demographic aging of its population. The nation indeed is aging more rapidly than comparable nations: its median age of 46.1 years is the highest in the world. Germans fear that this situation affects not only the strength but perhaps the survival of the nation. A major contributing factor is Germany's TFR, or total fertility rate, which presently stands at 1.3% (by comparison, the rate in the United States is 1.9%), below the replacement rate of 2.1% established by the Population Reference Bureau. It is estimated that the size of the labor force in German will be reduced by 20% by the year 2050, from the current level of 50 million to 40 million workers.

The increasing median age of the German population has a profound impact on public finances. The Public Retirement Insurance System (the German equivalent of the Social Security system in the United States) is a pay-as-you-go program. Germany maintains a high level of "income adequacy" for its pensions, generally 66% of preretirement earnings, and provides other generous benefits, including comprehensive, high-quality medical care. As of 2017, the average pension in Germany was €1,263/month. Unfortunately, many pensioners in German live in poverty, and pensions in the former GDR are lower than those in the former BRD. The government of Chancellor Angela Merkel has thus proposed a "solidarity pension," meant to buttress the retirement income of those receiving below-average pensions despite their long employment and also to establish pension parity between the two regions of the country by 2025. Currently, the official pension age for men and women is sixty-five. This will increase gradually to sixty-seven years by 2029. At the present time, the ratio of workers to retirees is 2.9 to 1. If current population trends continue, this figure is projected to drop to 1.4 to 1 by the year 2100.

Aging has become a prominent topic in German film, television, and literature. Michael Haneke's *Love* (2012) won both the Palme d'Or at the Cannes Film Festival and an Oscar for Best Foreign-Language Film for its portrayal of a man unable to cope with his wife's dementia. On television, Jörg Lühdorff's 2007 dystopian thriller *2030: Aufstand der Alten* ("2030: Uprising of the Old") shows the elderly housed in barracks waiting to die, seemingly equating Germany's treatment of its senior citizens with its Nazi past (Taberner, 2015). Novelists examine love and sex in old age, such as Barbara Bronnen's *At the End, a Beginning* (2006), and the sense of isolation experienced by seniors who feel that society has moved on without them, in Gerhard Kopf's *An Elderly Gentlemen* (2007). Older writers themselves often reflect less on the biological process of aging than on their involvement in German history, such as Nobel Prize laureate (and former member of the Waffen SS at age seventeen) Günter Grass's (1927–2015) old age trilogy: *Peeling the Onion* (2007), *The Box* (2010), and *Grimm's Words* (2010).

The "grey culture" highlights a generational divide in Germany. Those who lived through and survived the events of the Third Reich and postwar division of the nation have a different view of German society and the role played by its senior citizens than do those born more recently.

Wendell G. Johnson

See also: Chapter 1: Demographics. Chapter 3: The German Welfare State; Merkel, Angela (1954–); Tax Policy. Chapter 6: Poverty. Chapter 16: Overview; Film.

Further Reading

Grass, Günter. *The Box: Tales from the Darkroom.* Krishna Winston, trans. Boston: Houghton Mifflin Harcourt, 2010.

Grass, Günter. *Grimms Wörter: Eine Liebeserklärung.* Göttingen, Germany: Steidel, 2010.

Grass, Günter. *Peeling the Onion.* Michael Henry Heim, trans. Orlando, FL: Harcourt, 2007.

How to Germany. *The German Retirement and Pension System—Basic Facts.* https://www.howtogermany.com/pages/german-retirement.html. Accessed July 11, 2020.

Taberner, Stuart. "'Grey' Culture." In Sarah Colvin and Mark Taplin, eds. *The Routledge Handbook of German Politics & Culture*, 268–282. London: Routledge, 2015.

Immigration

Between 1951 and 1988, over 1.5 million *Aussiedler* ("emigrants") entered Germany. As many as 750,000 Turkish guest workers arrived in the country during the period 1964–1973. In 1988 alone, the year before the fall of the Berlin Wall, 375,000 emigrants came to Germany. The end of the Cold War opened the way for further mass migration across Europe, much of which headed for Germany. Many East Germans headed westward and settled in the Federal Republic. The Federal Republic of Germany also attracted ethnic Germans from the former Soviet Union, Poland, Czechoslovakia, and Hungary. Asylum seekers fleeing conflicts in southern and eastern Europe, particularly from the former Yugoslavia, sought refuge in Germany. By 1995, 1.5 million asylum seekers had settled in Germany, 220,000 from Yugoslavia alone. At the turn of the century, Germany was the most generous asylum-granting nation in Europe.

By 2010, 13% of Germany's population were born outside of the country. Approximately 7.2 million people residing in Germany were not German citizens (*Ausländer*), and 4.7 million of these also were not EU citizens. During the ongoing Syrian civil war, nearly 800,000 Syrian refugees arrived in Germany.

The Federal Office for Migration and Refugees (BAMF) enforces immigration law in Germany. According to BAMF regulations, those who have held a residence title in Germany for at least five years without interruption may be eligible for a German EU open-ended residence permit (subject to certain conditions). In order to receive such a permit, an applicant must have an income, knowledge of German, and be integrated into Germany. This long-term residence permit also allows the holder to settle in other EU member states.

Immigrants from the European Union, the European Economic Area (which includes Iceland, Liechtenstein, Norway, and the EU countries), and Switzerland may remain in Germany for three months based on their national identity cards. These individuals may stay longer than three months if they are employed or looking for work. Members of an EU national's family are fundamentally entitled to immigrate to Germany.

Ethnic German resettlers are descendants of Germans from the former Soviet Union and other countries in Eastern Europe who have established their residence in Germany. The designation is open to those born no later than December 31, 1992, and is also available to spouses and descendants on the condition that they have a basic knowledge of German.

Extenuating circumstances apply to the admission of Jewish immigrants from the former Soviet Union into the Federal Republic of Germany. Persons born in this region before January 1, 1945, are assumed to be the victims of persecution by the National Socialist government of Germany, and special arrangements have been made to allow them to migrate into the country.

Wendell G. Johnson

See also: Chapter 1: Demographics. Chapter 2: Berlin Wall. Chapter 3: Citizenship; Constitutions; Germany and the European Union. Chapter 4: Working in Germany. Chapter 6: Jews in Germany; Sudeten Germans. Chapter 8: Goethe-Institut. Chapter 9: Gesellschaft für deutsche Sprache; Institut für deutsche Sprache.

Further Reading

Bundesamt für Migration und Flüchtlinge. https://www.bamf.de/DE/Startseite/startseite_node.html. Accessed July 11, 2020.

Eule, Tobias G. *Inside Immigration Law: Migration Management and Policy Application in Germany*. Farnham, UK: Ashgate, 2014.

Geißler, Rainer, and Thomas Meyer. *Die Sozialstruktur Deutschlands*, 7th ed. Wiesbaden, Germany: Springer VS, 2014.

Mau, Steffen, and Nadine M. Schöneck. *Handwörterbuch Zur Gesellschaft Deutschlands*, 3rd ed. Wiesbaden, Germany: Springer VS, 2013.

Panayi, Panikos. *Ethnic Minorities in Nineteenth and Twentieth Century Germany: Jews, Gypsies, Poles, Turks and Others*. London: Routledge, 2014.

Jews in Germany

Prior to the establishment of the Federal Republic of Germany, the country demonstrated a long history of antipathy toward its Jewish population. Stereotypical portrayals of Jews accused them of sacrificing their children in obscure rituals and linked them to the devil. Luther's treatise *Against the Jews and Their Lies* (1524) codified many of the religious fears Christians felt toward Jewish people. Composer Richard Wagner, in his essay "Das Judenthumm in der Musik" (1850, Judaism in Music), contended that Jews represented a cultural threat to Germany. Wagner's contemporary, the philosopher Friedrich Nietzsche, condemned him as an anti-Semite, and for decades after the Second World War, Israeli orchestras refused to play works by Wagner. Publications such as Wilhelm Marr's *Victory of Jewry over Germandom* (1879) and *The Protocols of the Elders of Zion* (1903, a document forged by the Russian czar's secret police) circulated in Germany, fanning resentment against Jews. Both works have been translated into English and are available online as well as in newer printings; incidentally, Henry Ford paid for the initial printing and distribution of *The Protocols* in the 1920s.

The German defeat in World War I accelerated anti-Semitism in Germany. The general staff produced the excuse that the nation was "stabbed in the back" by Jews and communists, leading to the defeat of 1918. No one embraced the stab-in-the-back theory more fervently than Adolf Hitler, who called for the annihilation of the Jewish race in Europe. To accomplish this goal, Hitler and the Nazi government established a series of death camps throughout Europe, where millions of Jews were murdered. It is estimated that 520,000 Jewish people were living in Germany when Hitler came to power in 1933, 300,000 had emigrated from the country by the dawn of the Second World War, and 180,000 were murdered by the Nazi regime.

After the war, Nazi symbols were explicitly banned in the Federal Republic of Germany, although the ban has been lifted on Nazi symbols in video games, and it is against the law to deny the Holocaust. Jews began to immigrate back to Germany (particularly from the former Soviet Union) shortly after the reunification of the country. There are perhaps 150,000- 200,000 Jewish people in Germany today, many holding prominent positions in the fields of media, government, and culture. Unfortunately, anti-Semitic activity has reemerged in German as well, with anti-Semitic demonstrations taking place in Kassel, Nuremberg, and Mainz. In 2019, during Yom Kippur, a right-wing extremist opened fire in a synagogue in Halle, killing two worshippers. While a return to the violence of the Nazi era is unlikely, the revival of extreme right-wing parties in Germany provides evidence that the assimilation of Jewish people into German society will continue to be a difficult and tumultuous process.

Christian Jimenez

See also: Chapter 2: Overview; Hitler, Adolf (1889–1945). Chapter 5: Holocaust; Judaism in Germany; Luther, Martin (1483–1546). Chapter 6: Immigration.

Further Reading

"Anti-Semitism in Germany: History Background." http://web.mnstate.edu/shoptaug /AntiFrames.htm. Accessed July 11, 2020.

Aschheim, Steven E. *The Nietzsche Legacy in Germany, 1890–1990*. Berkeley: University of California Press, 1992.

Peck, Jeffrey M. *Being Jewish in the New Germany*. New Brunswick, NJ: Rutgers University Press, 2006.

Nationalism

In the nineteenth century, Otto von Bismarck (1815–1898) sought to unify the German territories into a single nation-state. Prior to this time, nationalism in Germany was relatively weak. Bismarck's attitude toward political consolidation was characterized by his bellicose *Eisen und Blut* ("Blood and Iron") speech, delivered in 1862. Bismarck proclaimed "*Nicht durch Reden und Majoritätsbeschlüsse werden große Fragen der Zeit entschieden, . . . sondern durch Eisen und Blut.*" (The great questions of the time will not be resolved by speeches and majority decisions . . . but by iron and blood.) He often resorted to war to further his objectives. The Prussian victory over France in the Franco-Prussian War (1870–1871) and the subsequent proclamation of the German Empire led to an outbreak of national exuberance. Between unification and the First World War in 1914, Germany became the leading industrial power of Europe. The German nation's identity during this period included strong economic overtones. The late nineteenth century also saw the emergence of the *Völkisch* Movement, a virulent anti-Semitic, anti-Slavic nationalism movement that posited the superiority of the German language, race, and religion above those of other ethnic groups.

German nationalists became obsessed with imperial expansion, and the nation established colonies in Africa (in present-day Namibia and Tanzania) and obtained colonial concessions in China and other countries. On the eve of the First World War, Germany had a standing army and reserve corps numbering 4,500,000 men (the largest in Europe) and mustered a total of 11 million troops during the war. After its defeat, the German military was reduced to 100,000 troops by the Treaty of Versailles, and the nation was prohibited from building submarines or establishing an air force. In a further affront to its national pride, the treaty stripped Germany of its colonies and ceded German territory to France, Belgium, Lithuania, and Czechoslovakia. During the Weimar Republic (1919–1933), this gave birth to the "stab in the back" myth (*Dolchstoßlegende*), propagated in part by Paul von Hindenburg (1847–1934), the commander of the army and president of the country from 1925 until his death. This revisionist interpretation of history argued that Germany had not been defeated militarily in the First World War but had been betrayed by socialists. Further, the poor economic performance of the German economy during the Weimar Republic paved the way for National Socialism (the most tragic expression of German nationalism). Adolf Hitler promised to restore Germany's national honor and security and to revive the economy. He believed in the concept of a united German people standing behind one leader in a united German empire (***ein** Volk **ein** Reich **ein** Führer*). German nationalism produced the Holocaust—the tragic destruction of European Jews—and the Holocaust became identified with German nationalism.

Germany lost its national identity after the Second World War when the country was divided into four zones of occupation: the French, British, Soviet, and American, each administered by commanders in chief of the respective armies. The French, British, and American zones eventually united as the Federal Republic of Germany (FRG), while the Soviet zone became the German Democratic Republic. Expressions of nationalism remain muted in the FRG. Germans do not fly the national flag in their front yards, post decals of it on their automobiles, and the flag is never displayed in a church, albeit they have started to do so during soccer tournaments. Since 1952, Germany uses the third stanza of the Deutschlandlied (Song of Germany) "Einigkeit und Recht und Freiheit" (Unity and Justice and Freedom), written in 1841 by August Heinrich Hoffmann von Fallersleben with music by Joseph Haydn, as the national anthem. The anthem is played sparingly, mainly during official political and also sporting events, the latter, however, only when a national team is involved. East Germany had a different national anthem, "Auferstanden aus Ruinen" (Arisen from Ruins), from 1949 until the reunification. Recently, renascent German nationalism has found expression in right-wing political parties such as the Alternative für Deutschland (Alternative for Germany).

Wendell G. Johnson

See also: Chapter 2: Overview; Bismarck, Otto von (1815–1898); Hindenburg, Paul von (1847–1934); Hitler, Adolf (188–1945). Chapter 3: Political Parties; Sports and Government. Chapter 5: Holocaust. Chapter 15: Leisure and Sports in the German Democratic Republic.

Further Reading

Berger, Stefan. "Germany." In Guntram Henrik Herb and David H. Kaplan, eds. *Nations and Nationalism: A Global Historical Overview*, 609–622. Santa Barbara, CA: ABC-CLIO, 2008.

Doerr, Jurgen C. "Nationalism." In Dieter K. Buse and Juergen C. Doerr, eds. *Modern Germany: An Encyclopedia of History, People, and Culture, 1871–1990*, 700–702. New York: Garland, 1998.

German Bundestag. "The German National Anthem." https://www.bundestag.de/en /parliament/symbols/anthem. Accessed October 17, 2021.

Poverty

In the European Union, adults are considered vulnerable to poverty if their incomes are 60% or less than the national median income. In Germany, the minimum wage for full-time work, €1,500 ($1,700)/month, is nearly identical to the poverty line. Germany's Federal Statistics Office estimates that 15.5 million people (19% of the population) are threatened by the risk of poverty. An additional 3.4% of the population meet the EU definition of material deprivation, meaning that they have difficulty paying their rent and heating their homes, are food insecure, and spend their accrued vacation time at home. While these figures are lower than the EU average, they are concerning because—before the corona pandemic—Germany was experiencing historically low unemployment and had some of the lowest energy and food costs on the continent.

The German government provides "social help" (*Sozialhilfe*) to individuals living at or below the poverty line. Many individuals do not take advantage of this assistance and exist in a situation termed *Verdeckte Armut* ("hidden poverty"), either because they are ignorant of government programs designed to assist them or are too embarrassed to accept government aid.

The Enduring Problem of Poverty in East Germany

Poverty, as measured in the Federal Republic of (West) Germany, did not officially exist in the Democratic Republic of (East) Germany. In most cases, housing was provided by the state, as was a subvention that ensured a rather low standard of living. In 1970, nearly 30% of the East German population suffered from a lack of food. The elderly subsisted on meager pensions that provided only a minimal standard of living (Küster, 1998).

The reunification of Germany in 1990 and the subsequent currency union had a catastrophic effect upon the economy of eastern Germany and its populace. The gross domestic product of the five so-called **new** states, namely Mecklenburg Western-Pomerania, Brandenburg, Saxony, Saxony-Anhalt, and Thuringia, in 1991 contracted to 60% of its pre-reunification level in 1989. By 1993, employment in the former German Democratic Republic had plummeted by a third, from 9.7 million gainfully employed people in 1989 to 6.2 million. An additional 1.7 million citizens fled the GDR and headed west in search of improved living conditions (Ulrich, 2019).

A tent filled with the belongings of a homeless person in Stuttgart, Germany. Nearly 16% of the Germany's population live at or below the poverty line (defined as 60% of the national median income). The government provides "social help" (Sozialhilfe) for these individuals. (Salih Kuelcue/Dreamstime. com)

In 2017, 15.8% of the German population lived in poverty. Thirty years after reunification, differences remain in the poverty rates in East and West Germany. According to the *Wirtschafts- und Sozialwissenschaftliches Institut* (Economic and Social Sciences Institute), 17.8% of East Germans and 15.3% of West Germans live in poverty. The gap between those living in the West and East has eased gradually since 2005. However, this situation is not due to rising incomes in the East, but rather to increased poverty in the West.

Wendell G. Johnson

See also: Chapter 1: Demographics. Chapter 3: *Die Wende*; The German Welfare State; Germany and the European Union; Regional Government/Federalism. Chapter 4: Currency; Gross Domestic Product (GDP). Chapter 6: The Grey Culture.

Further Reading

"Development of Relative Income Poverty (in Per Cent) in Germany, East and West Germany, 2005–2017." https://www.wsi.de/en/poverty-in-east-and-west-germany-2005-2017-14394.htm. Accessed October 17, 2021.

Geissler, Rainer, and Thomas Meyer. *Die Sozialstruktur Deutschlands*. Wiesbaden, Germany: Springer VS, 2014.

Herbert, Ulrich. *History of Twentieth-Century Germany*. Oxford, UK: Oxford University Press, 2019.

Küster, Thomas. "Poverty." In Dieter K. Buse and Juergen C. Doerr, eds. *Modern Germany: An Encyclopedia of History, People, and Culture, 1871–1990*, 784–785. New York: Garland, 1998.

Refugees

Throughout the twentieth and into the twenty-first century, waves of refugees have fled to Germany. Prior to the First World War, 2 million Russian Jews, fleeing anti-Semitism in their home country, transited through Germany on their way to Great

Gemeinsam gegen die Angst—together against fear. People protest in support of a welcoming culture for refugees in Frankfurt, Germany. By 2021, 800,000 Syrian refugees had settled in Germany. Such a large influx strained the nation's infrastructure and caused resentment in certain quarters. (Meinzahn/Dreamstime.com)

Table 6.1: ASYLUM SEEKERS—SNAPSHOT JANUARY 2020

Country of Origin	Number of Asylum Seekers
Syria	3,498
Iraq	1,240
Afghanistan	881
Turkey	826
Iran	524
Nigeria	445
Republic of Georgia	419
Moldavia	339
Russia	322
Unknown	328
Others	3,390
Total	12,212

Source: Bundesamt für Migration und Flüchtlinge. Asylgeschäftsstatistik January 2020. https://www.bamf.de/SharedDocs/Meldungen/ DE/2020/20200207-asylgeschaeftsstatistik-januar.html;nn=284830. Accessed 11 July 11, 2020.

Britain and the United States. During the Third Reich, the Nazi government enacted anti-Semitic legislation, particularly the Nuremburg laws, which denied basic civil rights to Jews. German policy encouraged emigration from the country, and by 1938, two-thirds of German Jews had left Germany (90,000 of whom had settled in the United States). Shortly after the start of the Second World War, German authorities began levying onerous emigration taxes on Jews and severely restricted the amount of money they could take when leaving the country. Most of the Jews remaining in Germany were murdered during the Holocaust.

After the Second World War, many ethnic Germans were expelled from their traditional homelands in Eastern Europe. According to the first postwar census conducted in Germany (1946), 9.5 million of these ethnic Germans settled in the country. An additional 1.6 million displaced persons were settled in Germany under the auspices of the International Refugee Federation. From the end of the war until August 1961, ca. 3.5 million East German citizens fled to West Germany. As a result of this mass emigration, East German authorities built the Berlin Wall to staunch the flow of economic refugees to the Bundesrepublik. During the time when Germany was divided, the Federal Republic of Germany extended a generous welcome to both *Übersiedler* (Germans from East Germany) and *Aussiedler* (ethnic Germans from Eastern Europe and the Soviet Union). Thus between 1950 to 1988, nearly 6 million such Germans settled in West Germany.

In 1989, Prague, the capital of Czechoslovakia, became the scene of an inter-German refugee crisis. During the summer of that year, thousands of East Germans entered Czechoslovakia, one of the few countries to which they were allowed to travel, and took refuge on the grounds of the West German embassy in Prague. The West German foreign minister, Hans-Dietrich Genscher, traveled to the embassy on September 30, 1989, and arranged for the refugees, perhaps 20,000 strong, to transit through Czechoslovakia, originally against the wishes of the German Democratic Republic, in order to settle in the Federal Republic of Germany. Forty days later, the Berlin Wall fell, and with it the German Democratic Republic. From 1989 to 2011, a further 2.6 million East Germans moved to western Germany in search of greater economic opportunities.

Over 1 million asylum seekers sought refuge in the European Union in 2015, with Germany accepting more of these refugees than any of its European neighbors. By 2021, an estimated 800,000 refugees from the Syrian civil war had sought refuge in Germany. The influx of so many refugees stoked resentment. The right-wing populist party Alternative für Deutschland (AfD) incorporated an anti-immigrant plank in their political platform and saw its proportional representation rise in the Bundestag, although they suffered losses in the 2021 election.

Wendell G. Johnson

See also: Chapter 2: Overview; Berlin Wall. Chapter 3: Government and Politics in the German Democratic Republic; Political Parties. Chapter 5: Holocaust; Islam in Germany. Chapter 6: Jews in Germany.

Further Reading

De Zayas, Alfred M. *A Terrible Revenge: The Ethnic Cleansing of the East European Germans*, 2nd ed., rev. and updated. New York: Palgrave Macmillan, 2006.

Schenderlein, Anne C. *Germany on Their Minds: German Jewish Refugees in the United States and Their Relationships with Germany, 1938–1988*. New York: Berghahn Books, 2020.

Roma and Sinti

The Roma and Sinti are one of the four nationally recognized minority groups in Germany. The *Sinti* migrated to the area in the fifteenth century and the *Roma*, coming from Eastern Europe, arrived after 1870. Since the fourteenth/fifteenth century, they have been called by others *Zigeuner* (gypsies), a term that is discriminatory, and that was further racialized during the Nazi time. On the one hand, the Roma and Sinti are perceived as romantic figures, characterized by a free and sensual nature. On the other hand, they are viewed as uncivilized and prone to criminal acts, averse to work, and given to begging, prostitution, and drunkenness. They have been marginalized and persecuted; a 2009 study by the European Union Agency for Fundamental Rights found that they are one of the most discriminated-against groups.

During the Nazi time, the discrimination accelerated beginning in 1933 with new laws set to disenfranchise them. In 1936, Sinti and Roma were deemed alien, and

MEMORIAL TO
THE SINTI AND ROMA
OF EUROPE
MURDERED UNDER
NATIONAL SOCIALISM

Nearly 500,000 Roma and Sinti were murdered by the Nazis. A memorial to these victims is located near the Reichstag in Berlin. (Claudiodivizia/Dreamstime.com)

marriage to Germans was prohibited. Starting on October 17, 1939, the *Festsetzungserlass* (fixation ordinance) decreed that Roma and Sinti had to remain and reside where they were registered, ripping apart families. This is how they lost the freedom of mobility and had to petition to visit relatives in different locales. It was all part of a plan, which emerged completely in 1942, to send all Sinti and Roma to Auschwitz. In 1943, arrests and deportations commenced. Sinti and Roma married to Germans were able to remain in Germany; however, they and their children were sterilized. In the *Zigeunerfamilienlager* (gypsy family camps) of Auschwitz, 20,078 Sinti and Roma were murdered. Altogether, the Nazis murdered about a half a million Sinti and Roma.

Immediately after the war, German authorities contended that they had faced *social*, not racial discrimination during the Nazi time, and hence they were not eligible to receive compensation. Not until 1982, many years after the Second World War, were they recognized as victims of the Holocaust.

Today, between 70,000 and 150,000 Sinti and Roma live in Germany, 8–12 million live in Eastern and Southeastern Europe. In Germany, several organizations such as the Zentralrat Deutscher Sinti und Roma (Central Council of German Sinti and Roma) advocate for their interests.

Many Sinti and Roma do not have German citizenship, but only temporary status, which must be renewed periodically. This status, however, includes restrictions on freedom of movement, access to employment, and social assistance (*Sozialhilfe*). In 2003, the European Commission on Racism and Intolerance noted that Roma and Sinti in Germany who are not citizens face discrimination. And still, in the collective German memory, Sinti and Roma remain outsiders, a despised and poorly understood minority existing on the fringes of society.

Wendell G. Johnson

See also: Chapter 2: Overview. Chapter 5: Holocaust. Chapter 6: Overview.

Further Reading

Bundeszentrale für politische Bildung. "Sinti und Roma in Europa." https://www.bpb.de/internationales/europa/sinti-und-roma-in-europa/. Accessed July 11, 2020.

European Union Agency for Fundamental Rights. "Second European Union Minorities and Discrimination Survey—Roma. Selected Findings. 2016." https://fra.europa.eu/sites/default/files/fra_uploads/fra-2016-eu-minorities-survey-roma-selected-findings_en.pdf. Accessed July 11, 2020.

Margalit, Gilad. *Germany and Its Gypsies: A Post-Auschwitz Ordeal.* Madison: University of Wisconsin Press, 2002.

Milton, Sybil. "Gypsies and the Holocaust." *The History Teacher* 24(4), 375–387, 1991. https://www.jstor.org/stable/494697. Accessed March 15, 2020.

Tebbutt, Susan, ed. *Sinti and Roma: Gypsies in German-Speaking Society and Literature.* New York: Berghahn Books, 1998.

Zentralrat deutscher Sinti und Roma. https://zentralrat.sintiundroma.de/. Accessed July 11, 2020.

Sudeten Germans

Sudeten Germans (Sudetendeutsche) are a diasporic population of ethnic Germans historically living mostly in the mountainous borderland regions of Bohemia (Deutschböhmen), Moravia (Deutschmähren), and Czech Silesia (Deutschschlesien). The term itself, derived from the Sudeten Mountains lining northern Bohemia, is geographically inaccurate and ethnically charged, becoming widespread in the early twentieth century after the fall of the Austro-Hungarian Empire and the formation of Czechoslovakia. Ethnic Germans initially migrated into the lands of the Bohemian Crown on the invitation of Czech nobility to help with the settlement of hilly regions. They played a substantial role in the politics and economy of these areas, contributing to their industrial development—they were particularly active in the manufacturing of forest glass, porcelain, paper, and textiles ("Sudetes" 2017).

Despite occasional flare-ups, Sudeten Germans and Czechs coexisted peacefully for centuries, often even intermixing regionally. However, their relations deteriorated significantly with the rise of nationalism in the second half of the nineteenth century, with Czechs becoming increasingly resistant to the German linguistic and cultural domination they experienced since the 1620 Battle of White Mountain. The battle resulted in the ruling of the Lands of the Bohemian Crown by the pro-German Habsburgs, including the alleged confiscation and handing over of the estates of the Czech nobility to German and other foreign aristocrats (Cornwall, 1997). After the revolutions of 1848, Czechs and Germans maintained separate sociopolitical institutions in regions of their majority in efforts to create equality.

The tensions further intensified after the dissolution of the Habsburg monarchy and the founding of Czechoslovakia in 1918. Sudeten Germans, numbering approximately 3 million and constituting 23% of the new republic's population, feared that the Czechoslovak government would discriminate against them as a payback for prior perceived inequalities (Jenne, 1999). Therefore, many of them originally refused to recognize Czechoslovakia (now Czech Republic) as a sovereign state, setting up provisional governments in Reichenberg, Troppau, Krumau, and Znaim and pushing for the creation of a pan-German state that would include the Sudetenland. However, their separatist efforts were not successful at that time, with Czechoslovak authorities occupying the Sudetenland, and Germany and Austria giving up their territorial claims on Czechoslovakia by signing the 1919 Treaty of Versailles (Jenne, 1999).

The situation further escalated after the 1930s' Depression with its more pronounced economic impact on ethnic Germans than Czechs in Czechoslovakia. Sudeten Germans, feeling discriminated against, began to embrace a radical nationalistic agenda in growing numbers, as most significantly represented by the rising popularity of Konrad Henlein's Sudetendeutsche Heimatfront that was transformed into the strongly pro-Nazi Sudetendeutsche Partei in 1935. Henlein promoted open resistance to the Czech government, demanding the "[f]ull self-government for the German areas (and) . . . [r]ecognition of the principle: within the German area German officials" ("The Demands of the Sudeten Germans," 1938). With the signing of the Munich Agreement by Britain, France, Germany, and Italy on September 29, 1938, these demands materialized: Sudetenland was annexed to Germany, resulting in Czechoslovakia losing approximately 38% of its area. Consequently, many Czechs left Sudetenland.

The Czechoslovak state recovered the lost Sudeten districts at the end of World War II, with most of the ethnic Germans speedily and forcefully expelled and their property confiscated ("Sudeten Germans to Meet," 2018; "Sudetes," 2017). The Sudetes were then gradually resettled mostly by Czechs from the state's inland areas. The pain associated with these historic events lingers on both sides of the Czech–German border to this very day, even though both ethnic groups have taken gradual steps toward reconciliation and healing. Thus, in a 2011 survey, 42% of Czechs surveyed still considered the post-World War II expulsion of ethnic Germans to be just (down from 52% in 1995), with 39% believing the opposite (up from 28% in 1995) ("The Expulsion of Sudeten Germans," 2013). Along the same lines, Sudetendeutsche Landsmannschaft, the organization representing the interests of deported Sudeten Germans and their offspring, voted to drop its territorial claims against the Czech Republic only as recently as 2016 ("Sudeten Germans Drop Claim," 2016).

Ladislava Khailova

See also: Chapter 4: Manufacturing. Chapter 6: Aristocracy and the Elites; Nationalism. Chapter 15: Becker, Boris (1967–).

Further Reading

Cornwall, Mark. "'National Reparation'?": The Czech Land Reform and the Sudeten Germans 1918–38." *The Slavonic and East European Review* 75(2): 259–280, 1997.

"The Demands of the Sudeten Germans." *Bulletin of International News* 15(9): 10–12, 1938.

"The Expulsion of Sudeten Germans Is Still Raw." *The Economist: Eastern Approaches,* May 7, 2013.

Gerlach, David W. *The Economy of Ethnic Cleansing: The Transformation of the German-Czech Borderlands after World War II.* Cambridge, UK: Cambridge University Press, 2017.

Houžvička, Václav. *Czechs and Germans 1848–2004: The Sudeten Question and the Transformation of Central Europe.* Prague: Charles University in Prague Karolinum Press, 2015.

Jenne, Erin K. "The Impact of Group Fears and Outside Actors on Ethnic Party Demands: Comparing Sudeten Germans in Inter-war Czechoslovakia with the Post-1989 Moravian Movement." *Czech Sociological Review* 7(1): 67–90, 1999.

"Sudeten Germans Drop Claim to Territory in Czech Republic." *Canadian Press*, February 28, 2016.

"Sudeten Germans to Meet in Czechia in Early 2020s." *CTK National News Wire*, May 18, 2018.

"Sudetes." In *Columbia Electronic Encyclopedia.* New York: Columbia University Press, 2017.

Turks in Germany

Nearly 4 million Turks live in Germany (approximately 5% of the nation's population), the largest such concentration outside of Turkey. The Turkish population took root in Germany during the postwar economic boom. Many German multinational corporations (such as VW, Siemens, and Bosch) were in need of cheap, low-skilled labor to work in their factories, and Turks aged eighteen to forty-five years old were invited to come to West Germany as *Gastarbeiter* (guest workers). Many of these laborers were housed in company-owned on-site dormitories. In 1964, the West German government removed the two-year limit on employee contracts and permitted Turkish laborers to bring their families with them. West Germany ceased the guest worker program during the oil crisis of 1973. By that time, 700,000 Turks had settled in West Germany. The country, however, at that time, lacked an immigration process that would have allowed the Turks to acquire German citizenship and integrate into German society. In the year 2000, Germany finally granted citizenship to the children of Turkish parents, and many second- and third-generation German

Turks have become citizens. Despite acquiring the right to German citizenship, Turks today tend to earn lower wages than ethnic Germans, and their children are less likely to attend a university.

Approximately 1.5 million German Turks have retained their Turkish citizenship. As citizens, these individuals have the right to vote in Turkish elections. President Recep Tayyip Erdogan of Turkey campaigned in Germany during the 2014 Turkish presidential election. He called for Turkish integration into German society and encouraged German Turks to retain their language and culture. Erdogan's inflammatory rhetoric led German officials to ban future political rallies by Turkish politicians. In response, Erdogan accused Germany of using "Nazi" tactics, infuriating German politicians. Nearly 140,000 Turks turned out in Berlin's Olympic Stadium to vote in the 2014 Turkish presidential election.

Over 175,000 Turkish people live in Berlin, with large concentrations in the districts Mitte (38,000), Neukölln (37,000), and Kreuzberg (29,000). These areas are rife with Turkish small businesses, cafes, and döner kebab stands. Many Turkish women today don the traditional garb of head scarves and wide pants under their skirts. On market days (twice a week), the stretch of the Landwehr Canal between Neukölln and Kreuzberg (known as "Little Istanbul") resembles a giant souk. Berlin has a vibrant Turkish-language broadcasting landscape and in 1999 became the first city outside of Turkey to host its own twenty-four-hour Turkish-language radio station. The Turkish Union in Berlin Brandenburg (Türkischer Bund Berlin Brandenburg, or TBB) is the largest Turkish community organization in the area. The UUTBB is concerned exclusively with events in Germany and does not comment on Turkish political issues.

Turkish residents are prominent in all walks of German life. Cem Özdemir (b. 1965), cochair of the German Green party, was the first person of Turkish descent to be elected to the Bundestag. Asli Bayram (b. 1981) was crowned Miss Germany in 2005 and represented the county in the Miss Universe pageant. Mesut Özil (b. 1988), a third-generation German Turk, born in Gelsenkirchen, was a member of the 2014 World Cup Champion German national soccer team. After Germany was eliminated from the 2018 World Cut, he left the nation team, claiming "I am German when we win and am immigrant when we lose." He played attacking midfielder for Arsenal in the English Premier League and has played for Fenerbahçe Spor Kulübü in Istanbul since 2021.

The Turkish experience in Germany has also been reflected through the media; there are many German artists of Turkish descent. The comedian Kaya Yanar with his show *Was guckst du?* often deals with his observations; Yasemin Samdereli's 2011 movie *Almanya: Welcome to Germany* is about the experience of a Turkish family coming to Germany. Fatih Akin is one of the most famous German directors, with a wide variety of movies from very serious *(In the Fade)* to very light *(Soul Kitchen)*. Emine Sevgi Özdamar is an author and actor, and Feridun Zaimoğlu deals with the situation of Turks in Germany in his books, such as *Kanak Sprak*. He also received numerous awards and scholarships.

Wendell G. Johnson

See also: Chapter 3: Citizenship; Political Parties. Chapter 4: Guest Workers. Chapter 5: Islam in Germany. Chapter 6: Immigration. Chapter 14: Overview. Chapter 15: FIFA World Cups.

Further Reading

Hinze, Annika. *Turkish Berlin: Integration Policy and Urban Space*. Minneapolis: University of Minnesota Press, 2013.

Kosnick, Kira. *Migrant Media: Turkish Broadcasting and Multicultural Politics in Berlin*. Bloomington: Indiana University Press, 2007.

"Mesut Özil Walks Away from Germany Team Citing 'Racism and Disrespect.'" *The Guardian*, July 23, 2018. https://www.theguardian.com/football/2018/jul/22/mesut-ozil-retires-german-national-team-discrimination. Accessed October 10, 2019.

Reay, David. "Why German Turks Are Numerous, Divided, and Bitter." Handelsblatt Global, April 13, 2017. https://global.handelsblatt.com/politics/why-german-turks-are-numerous-divided-and-bitter-748329. Accessed January 5, 2018.

CHAPTER 7

GENDER, MARRIAGE, AND SEXUALITY

OVERVIEW

Gender

Historically, German society has been patriarchal, as was the case with European societies in general. Men were active in the labor force and exercised authority over the household, while women were expected to concern themselves with the three K's of *Kinder* (children), *Kirche* (church), and *Küche* (kitchen). During the nineteenth century, German civil code distinguished between *male* citizens, who were denoted as self-determining owners of property, and *female* citizens, who were defined by their status as wives and mothers. According to the Prussian General Code of 1791, girls remained under the authority of their fathers until marriage, and a wife did not exist as a legal person. In most German states, women were proscribed from entering a university. Several organizations devoted to the plight of women arose in Germany after the unification of the country in 1871, such as the Federation of German Women's Organizations (BDF, or the Bund Deutscher Frauenvereine), which was committed to the issue of women's suffrage and the Federation for the Protection of Mothers (BfM, or the Bund für Mutterschutz), which sought material security for unwed mothers and their children.

German women finally gained the right to vote in 1918 and entered the workforce in greater numbers during the Weimar Republic (1919–1933). A lesbian subculture took root and flourished until the National Socialists assumed power in 1933. The Nazis stressed that a German woman's primary duty was bearing children, and they excused ethnic German women from compulsory labor service during the Second World War. Throughout the persecution of Jews in Hitler's Germany, Jewish women entered forced labor camps and were ultimately deported to concentration camps, where they were exterminated.

Both Germanys endorsed gender equality in their postwar constitutions. However, the West German government fostered the ideal of the male head of household as the breadwinner and considered his wife a homemaker. This "housewife marriage" was deemed a bulwark against Nazism and Communism. As a result, fewer married women entered the workforce in West Germany than in other Western countries. The East German government, on the other hand, encouraged women to enter the workforce and provided child-care centers for the offspring of those who did so. Both countries liberalized abortion laws and offered paid maternity leave to counter low birth rates. It is probably safe to conclude that the policies of the East German government after the Second World War enhanced the resources available to women in the GDR, whereas the FRG introduced policies that reinforced women's economic dependence on a male breadwinner. Not until 1958 could women work outside the home without their husband's approval. Even after reunification, husbands in the East spend on average four hours per week more on household tasks than their Western counterparts.

At present, the Basic Law for the Federal Republic of Germany (the Grundgesetz, GG, or constitution) mandates equality before the law for men and women: "Men and women shall have equal rights. The state shall promote the actual implementation of equal rights for men and women and take steps to eliminate disadvantages that now exist" (Art. 3 Abs. 2, 2014). Although men and women are guaranteed equal rights by law, discrepancies exist between the sexes in many facets of German society. On average, German women have more education than do German men. During the school year 2014–2015, female students comprised 52% of *Gymnasium* (secondary school) students. Although half of university graduates are women, less than 10% of tenured professors are female. An increasing number of German women joined the labor forces in the decade 2004–2014. By 2014, nearly 40 million people (78% of inhabitants between the ages of twenty-four and sixty-four) were employed in Germany. Women comprised 45% of employed workers. Of these, 42% worked part-time. In 2014, half of men in higher education entered a STEM field (science, technology, engineering, or mathematics), while the percentage of women in the same fields was only one in four. A similar pattern was seen in apprenticeships: a majority of male trainees opted for technology-related professions, while many women opted for training in health care and social service. This choice of career and continuing education options is reflected in income levels. The non-adjusted gender pay gap in Germany (the average salary of all women compared to that of men) is 21%: a woman in Germany has to work an additional seventy-seven days a year to meet the annual income of a man. The adjusted figure, taking into account the income of men and women with comparable experience, is 6%. Women are also notably absent in the top tiers of German business—only 9.2% of upper- and middle-management positions are filled by women.

The German Family

After the Second World War, the rebuilding of western Germany included the political reconstruction of the family. In 1945, Germany was a society with more adult women than men. Three million soldiers did not return home from the war. The country suffered from an oversupply of women (*Frauenüberschuss*) and a scarcity of men (*Männermangel*). Given the large number of war widows and unmarried mothers, the status of women and the future of the nuclear family became a pressing political issue in immediate postwar Germany. In order to help reconstruct the family, the Bundestag (parliament) in the West approved the payment of *Kindergeld* (children's allowance) to parents to help defray the cost of raising children. In 1954, *Kindergeld* was paid only starting with the third child; that was changed in 1961, when parents received *Kindergeld* for the second child and all subsequent children. Since 1975, parents receive support for all children. In 2021, for example, parents receive €219 per month for each of their first two children, €225 per month for the third child, and €250 per month for each additional child. In Corona times, eligible families can receive an additional one-time €150 bonus per child.

The nuclear family remains important in German life, yet it is losing its monopoly as the basic structure for procreation. During the 1960s, 95% of adult Germans had been married at least once (and 94% of children were born to married couples). By 1994, only 53% of men and 60% of women had been married. During the last quarter of the twentieth century, Germans tended to remain single or adopt alternative methods of cohabiting, such as being *Lebensabschnittgefährten* ("temporary partners"). By 1995, 25% of single Germans between the ages of eighteen and fifty-five were in a partnership yet maintained separate households. Many of these couples were in so-called "commuter marriages" and did not marry until the birth of their first child. The German fertility rate (children born per women of childbearing age) is at a historic low of 1.4. This is due, in part, to Germany's high divorce rate. Overall, 30% of all German couples get divorced, and the figure is significantly higher, 50%, for couples in urban areas. Further, it is estimated that one-third of German women do not want to have children.

More than any other European nation, Germany continues to maintain that its mothers remain home with their children. Germany still seems to operate under the slogan that men *have* to go to work whereas women *choose* to do so. Only 20% of mothers in western Germany work full-time (by comparison, only 3% of employed fathers worked part-time). In the area of the former DDR, 48% are employed full-time. This statistical difference in employment figures demonstrates a continuing social divide between the western and eastern portions of Germany. In many parts of western Germany, there is a dearth of childcare facilities for children under the age of three, which makes it difficult for mothers to work outside of the home. They are expected to cook a warm meal at noon and care for preschoolers at home. In addition, women provide the bulk of the care for elderly relatives. In order to increase the compatibility and family life, Germany provides generous family-leave benefits: a parent receives 67% of their net income for twelve months. An additional two months are granted if the other parent takes leave as well.

Sexuality

Women in Berlin shared a massive and collective experience of sexual assaults after the Second World War, vividly recounted in the memoir *A Woman in Berlin* (Anonymous, 2017). By conservative estimates, 110,000 and perhaps as many as one-third of the city's 1.5 million women were raped by Soviet soldiers. At least 10,000 women died as a result of this large-scale assault. In Berlin's open election in 1946, female voters responded to the humiliation visited upon them by their Russian "liberators" by voting for the SPD (Social Democrats) over the eastern SED (Sozialistische Einheitspartei

Deutschlands, Socialist Unity Party), a party made up out of the eastern SPD and the Communist Party.

A conservative sexual ideology was reestablished in Germany following the Second World War. However, the student rebellions, women's liberation, and gay and lesbian emancipation movements of the 1960s (not to mention the development of birth control pills) introduced sexual liberalization. In 1966, 20% of German women and 30% of German men had sexual experience before marriage. By 1981, those figures had risen respectively to 60% and 80%. Presently, 86% of men and 82% of women describe themselves as exclusively heterosexual. A German man, on average, has 10.23 sexual partners during his lifetime, while the figure for German women is 5.46. Today, the average age at which Germans first have sex is 16.2 years, and German girls have sex, on average, at an earlier age than do German boys: 33.5% of fifteen-year-old girls have had sex, while the figure for boys is 22.5%. Despite this activity, the birth rate among sexually active German teens is quite low: 11.7 per 1,000 population (the rate is 21 in the United States, according to the World Health Organization).

Sex education is considered a public health issue in Germany and has been part of the school curriculum since 1970. Sexuality is regarded as a natural component of human development, and sex education aims to inform students on the reproductive cycle, the effectiveness of various methods of contraception, as well as the emotional, physical, legal, and social aspects of human sexuality. Other topics such as gender equality, sexual diversity, and reproductive rights also figure prominently in many German classrooms.

Other Issues: Prostitution and Abortion

Prostitution has been legal in Germany since 2002, and every major city has an official or unofficial red-light district. There are ca. 3,000 red-light establishments in Germany and 500 brothels in Berlin alone. It is estimated that 1 million men pay for sex every day in Germany. Prostitutes pay taxes in Germany and are entitled to the same employment benefits (unemployment and health insurance) as workers in other industries. The Prostitutes Protection Act (Prostituiertenschutzgesetz) of 2017 mandates the use of condoms and requires that prostitutes register with the government and obtain annual health checkups. Subsequently, owners of brothels were required to register their business, and restrictions were placed on advertising. The Green Party and two political consortia, HYDRA in Berlin and HWG in Frankfurt am Main, promote the rights of prostitutes. There are two troubling aspects to the legalized sex trade in Germany. First is the number of young women coming to wealthier European countries (such as Germany) to work in the sex trade. The second troubling aspect is the number of sex tours organized for German men to Southeast Asian nations such as Thailand. German law makes it illegal to have sex with minors outside of the country. However, very few German men have been arrested for violating this law.

In the DDR, prostitution was illegal and, according to the East German government, did not exist. Nonetheless, many high-class sex workers plied their trade in the hotels in East Berlin that catered to Westerners. In many cases, the Stasi (the East German secret police) employed these workers as spies and informants.

Abortion is permitted during the first trimester in Germany (and permitted later in cases of medical necessity). The current rate of abortions per 1,000 women aged fifteen to forty-four is 6.1. In 2017, 101,209 abortions were reported in the country, up from 98,721 in 2016 but down from the historic high of 134,964 in 2001. Ninety-seven percent of abortions in Germany are performed on demand. Before obtaining an abortion, a woman must visit a counseling center and receive a certificate of confirmation of pregnancy and then wait for three days.

Wendell G. Johnson

Further Reading

Anonymous. *A Woman in Berlin: Eight Weeks in the Conquered City*. New York: Picador, 2017.

Basic Law for the Federal Republic of Germany. https://www.btg-bestellservice.de /pdf/80201000.pdf, 1949 (amended 2014). Accessed March 29, 2020.

Brockschmidt, Laura, and Angelika Hessling. "Sexuality Education in Germany: An Effective Intervention to Support the Sexual and Reproduction Heath (SRH) of People across the Lifespan," 2015. http://www.euro.who.int/__data/assets/pdf_file/0018/292203/Sexuality -education-in-Germany.pdf?ua=1. Accessed March 29, 2020.

Cooke, Lynn Prince. "Persistent Policy Effects on the Division of Domestic Tasks in Reunified Germany." *Journal of Marriage and Society* 69(4): 930–950, 2007.

Facts about Germany. Germany at a Glance. https://www.tatsachen-ueber-deutschland .de/en. Accessed March 29, 2020.

Grossmann, Atina. "A Question of Silence: The Rape of German Women by Occupation Soldiers." *October* 72: 43–63, 1995. https://www.jstor.org/stable/778926. Accessed March 29, 2020.

Haversath, Julia, et. al. "Sexualverhalten in Deutschland." *aerzteblatt.de*. https://www .aerzteblatt.de/archiv/192871. Accessed March 29, 2020.

Kerbo, Harold R., and Hermann Strasser. *Modern Germany*. Boston: McGraw Hill, 2000.

Moeller, Robert G., ed. *West Germany under Construction: Politics, Society, and Culture in the Adenauer Era*. Ann Arbor: University of Michigan Press, 1997.

Proger, Uta. "Germany." In Bonnie G. Smith, ed. *The Oxford Encyclopedia of Women in World History*, vol. 2, 373–377. Oxford, UK: Oxford University Press, 2008.

Tuttle, Brad. "Germany Has Become the Cut-Rate Prostitution Capital of the World." *Time Online*. June 13, 2013. http://business.time.com/2013/06/18/germany-has-become -the-cut-rate-prostitution-capital-of-the-world/. Accessed March 29, 2020.

United Nations, Department of Economic and Social Affairs, Population Division. "World Abortion Policies 2013." https://www.un.org/en/development/desa/population /publications/policy/world-abortion-policies-2013.shtml. Accessed March 29, 2020.

Child Custody Laws

According to the German Civil Code (Bürgerliches Gesetzbuch), which covers family law and disputes, parents are obligated to care for children under the age of eighteen years whose habitual residence is in Germany. The citizenship of the child and the parents is irrelevant. Cases are generally decided before a District Court (Amtsgericht) judge in a private hearing. The decisions of the District Courts may be appealed to the regional Courts of Appeal (Oberlandesgericht), and in some cases, to the Supreme Court of Justice (Bundesgerichtshof).

Joint custody means that the parents must consult with each other and make joint decisions regarding long-term issues affecting the child. In very exceptional cases, the courts will give one parent sole parental custody. Married parents automatically have joint or shared custody of a child; this also applies if the parents were unmarried when the child was born but married afterward. When a child is born to unmarried parents, they may request joint custody. Unmarried fathers can petition the Family Court for a joint custody order when the mother refuses to sign a shared custody declaration. This petition is denied only when the court believes that joint custody is not in the child's best interests. A parent may ask the court to determine residential custody based on the welfare of the child. The court could decide to grant double residency/joint physical care of the child (the *Wechselmodell*) without both parents' consent. The parent who has residential custody (or independent visitation rights) makes the daily decisions regarding the child's welfare.

Unless the court rules otherwise, parents share custody of children after a divorce. The court may decide to end joint custody of a child and grant residential custody to one parent. The parent unlikely to win sole custody of a child (usually the father of a very young child) can petition the court for continued joint custody rights. In custody disputes, the court asks the Jugendamt (a government agency tasked with the oversight of children) to step in. If the government believes a child's welfare is endangered, it can order the child's removal from the family. This removal can be appealed in Family Court and is often overturned if it is determined that the government did not pursue all feasible alternatives.

The Jugendamt has been criticized for ignoring the rights of non-German parents. Both parents must agree before a child of a German and non-German parent is free to leave the country. If one parent does not agree, removal of the child from the country constitutes international child abduction, a violation of the Hague Convention on Civil Aspects of International Child Abduction. The German government will act to ensure that the child is returned to his or her habitual country as quickly as possible. German courts are reluctant to intervene unless the child is threatened with physical or psychological harm.

William P. Kladky

See also: Chapter 3: Citizenship. Chapter 7: Overview.

Further Reading

Kreidler-Pleus, Daniela. "Family Law in Germany: Overview." *Thomson Reuters Practical Law*, 2019. https://uk.practicallaw.thomsonreuters.com/8-575-0676?transitionType=Default&contextData=(sc.Default)&firstPage=true&bhcp=1#co_anchor_a919467. Accessed July 11, 2020.

Maydell, Marie von, and Sophie Beckers. "Germany: Family Law 2020." *International Comparative Legal Guides*. Global Legal Group, 2019. https://iclg.com/practice-areas/family-laws-and-regulations/germany. Accessed July 11, 2020.

Salmon, Jacqueline L. "Germany: International Child Custody." *Law Office of Jeremy D. Morley*, 2020. https://www.international-divorce.com/ca-germany_3.htm. Accessed July 11, 2020.

World Population Review. "Hague Convention Countries 2021." http://worldpopulation-review.com/countries/hague-convention-countries/. Accessed October 16, 2021.

Civil Unions and Same-Sex Marriage

Historical Overview

During the Medieval period, German town charters—along with feudal law—often specified a permissible age for marriage, impediments to marriage (such as existing promises to marry or inequality of rank), marital property law, inheritance law, and the status of illegitimate children. Many of these charters and laws did not coincide with canon law. In the early nineteenth century, the Napoleonic legal code required civil marriage in territories conquered by Napoleon. Following this period, and prior to the establishment of the German Empire in 1871, several sovereign German states instituted civil marriages, which could include either a religious or civil ceremony. Ecumenical civil marriages were available in the grand duchy of Saxe-Weimar-Eisenach, the German republic of the Free City of Frankfurt upon Main, the Free and Hanseatic cities of Hamburg and Lübeck, and in the Kingdom of Württemberg. In 1875, the Reichstag adopted the Civil Marriage Law, which bestowed legitimacy solely to civil ceremonies. Religious ceremonies were optional and carried no legal standing. It was not until 2009 that German couples were no longer required to marry in a civil ceremony before doing so in a religious one.

In 2001, the German legislature (Bundestag) passed the Act to End Discrimination against Same-Sex Unions, which legalized a "registered life partnership" (*eingetragene Lebenspartnerschaft*) for same-sex couples. As was the case for heterosexual couples, same-sex partners must care for and support one another, live jointly, and provide financial support for one another; either partner may petition the state to dissolve the relationship. The Federal Constitutional Court gradually extended the benefits of the act until registered life partners enjoyed nearly all of the benefits of heterosexual marriage. In 2008, the Court also ruled that transsexual persons could remain married and change their legal gender. In 2009, a ruling by the Constitutional Court mandated equal rights for same-sex registered couples concerning pension benefits as well as all rights and responsibilities of traditionally married couples.

Efforts to pass a same-sex marriage law in 2012 were supported by the Green Party, the Social Democratic Party, and the Left Party, but opposed by the CDU/CSU, the senior member parties of Germany's coalition government since 2005. A bill to legalize same-sex marriage was approved by the Bundesrat in 2015 but blocked in the Bundestag. Same-sex marriage in Germany was finally legalized as of October 1, 2017, with equivalent rights granted to same-sex partners in many areas including taxation, pensions, adoption, health insurance, and tenancy. Existing life-registered partnerships were permitted to convert their partnership into a marriage or to retain their status with all of the legal protections and obligations of heterosexual marriage.

Civil Unions

For all intents and purposes, civil unions are identical to civil weddings in Germany. Civil ceremonies are usually held at the local *Standesamt* (governmental registry office). Prior to 2009, when couples were required legally to enter into a civil union before getting married in a religious ceremony, the civil ceremony was held a few days or even months before the often larger traditional religious one. Today, a civil ceremony alone provides legal status to marriage in Germany. Many couples only have this simple ceremony with a few close relatives and/or friends as witnesses and dispense with a religious celebration altogether. Couples in Germany follow the same procedure whether getting married or establishing a civil partnership. The partners must visit the local registry office and provide proof of residency (for a minimum of twenty-one days) in the locality. Required documentation varies by region, and may

Civil unions are nearly identical to civil marriages in Germany. Ceremonies are held at the local governmental registry office. In 2019, 84% of Germans believed that same sex unions should be allowed throughout Europe. (Sergey Kohl/Dreamstime.com)

include a passport, residency statement, birth certificate with parents' names, birth certificates of any children, an affidavit that both are single, answer a marriage questionnaire, provide a certificate of finality of divorce if pertinent, marriage certificates from previous marriages, death certificate of a previous spouse, confirmation of name change(s), and a financial statement. The wedding ceremony must take place within six months after submitting the required documentation. Both spouses must attend the civil wedding ceremony held in the registry office, and witnesses are not required. If one of the partners is not German, the Higher Regional Court must verify that partner's legal status before the wedding ceremony can proceed.

Same-Sex Marriage

Germany has an ambivalent and contradictory history regarding homosexuality. While it has often been in the vanguard of gay culture, male homosexuality was illegal in the country after unification of the German states in 1871. Between 1945 and 1969, 100,000 men were indicted under the law's criminal code Paragraph 175 (Section 175), with nearly half of them imprisoned. Section 175 was known as 17. Mai or 17.5. (May 17). The first same-sex marriage in Germany was held in 2017 when Karl Kreile and Bodo Mende were married in Schöneberg's (a district of Berlin) town hall. The two men had been partners for thirty-eight years. Sixty guests and numerous journalists witnessed the occasion. The "Wedding March" by 19th-century German composer Felix Mendelssohn was played as the grooms entered the room. The two men said their vows and signed the marriage documents to the guests' applause and cheers. Their wedding cake had a rainbow flag and sported the motto "marriage for all." Following the passage of the same-sex marriage law, the Bavarian state government and the Alternative for Germany (AfD) party both considered petitioning the federal court for a judicial review. The court ruled that the AfD lacked standing to do so, and the Bavarian government, facing electoral defeat, withdrew its objection to same-sex marriage. Same-sex marriage continues to have very wide support in Germany. In June 2019, the AfD filed a motion in the Bundestag with the Legal Committee and the Family Committee in the Bundestag to abolish same-sex marriage. The motion was opposed by every other political party and failed to pass. The 2019 *Eurobarometer* found that 84% of Germans thought same-sex marriage should be allowed throughout Europe (only 12% were opposed).

William P. Kladky

See also: Chapter 3: Political Parties. Chapter 7: LGBTQ Life in Modern Germany; Weddings and Divorce.

Further Reading

Abrams, Lynn. "Finding the Female Self: Women's Autonomy, Marriage and Social Change in Nineteenth-Century Germany." In Jan Rüger and Nikolaus Wachsmann, eds. *Rewriting German History: New Perspectives on Modern Germany*, 142–157. Basingstoke, UK: Palgrave Macmillan, 2015.

Cichanowicz, Lily. "Unusual Wedding Traditions from Germany." Culture Trip, September 26, 2016. https://theculturetrip.com/europe/germany/articles/unusual-wedding-traditions-from-germany/. Accessed July 11, 2020.

Clark, Christopher. 2006. *Iron Kingdom: The Rise and Downfall of Prussia, 1600–1947.* Cambridge, MA: Harvard University Press, 2006.

Everything2. "Germany's Life Partnership Act," October 13, 2003. https://everything2.com/title/Germany%2527s+Life+Partnership+Act. Accessed July 11, 2020.

Expatica. "Getting Married in Germany," November 27, 2018. https://www.expatica.com/de/living/love/getting-married-in-germany-100926/. Accessed July 11, 2020.

Gleixner, Ulrike, and Marion W. Gray. "Introduction: Gender in Transition." In Ulrike Gleixner and Marion W. Gray, eds. *Gender in Transition: Discourse and Practice in German-Speaking Europe, 1750–1830,* 1–24. Ann Arbor: University of Michigan Press, 2006.

Jordans, Frank. "Germany Celebrates First Same-Sex Wedding." *The (London) Independent*, October 1, 2017. https://www.independent.co.uk/news/world/europe/germany-berlin-celebrates-same-sex-marriage-lgbt-angela-merkel-a7976576.html. Accessed July 11, 2020.

Maydell, Marie von, and Sophie Beckers. "Germany: Family Law 2019." https://iclg.com/practice-areas/family-laws-and-regulations/germany. Accessed July 11, 2020.

Rabuzzi, Daniel A. "Gender and Control in the Merchant's World: Stralsund, 1750–1830." In Ulrike Gleixner and Marion W. Gray, eds. *Gender in Transition: Discourse and Practice in German-Speaking Europe, 1750–1830,* 75–89. Ann Arbor: University of Michigan Press, 2006.

Von Schmädel, Judith. "The History of Marriage Law in Austria and Germany: From Sacrament to Civil Contract." *Hitotsubashi Journal of Law and Politics* 37: 41–47, 2009.

Woolsey, Barbara. "Why Germany Waited So Long to Legalize Gay Marriage." *Handelsblatt Today*, June 15, 2017. https://www.handelsblatt.com/today/handelsblatt-explains-why-germany-waited-so-long-to-legalize-gay-marriage/23570440.html?ticket=ST-1627397-ZTwRymg3BLL61Xd2ItBW-ap6. Accessed July 11, 2020.

Wunder, Heide. "Marriage in the Holy Roman Empire of the German Nation from the Fifteenth to the Eighteenth Century: Moral, Legal, and Political Order." In Seidel Menchi, Silvana, Emlyn Eisenach, and Charles Donahue, eds. *Marriage in Europe, 1400–1800,* 61–93. Toronto: University of Toronto Press, 2016.

Feminism

The first wave of feminism in Germany arose in Imperial Germany when women and women's rights groups pressured institutions to admit women. The Federation of German Women's Associations (Bund Deutscher Frauenvereine or BDF) was founded in 1894 as an umbrella organization of the middle- and upper-class women's movement in Germany. The members of the BDF advocated for equal access to education and equal political rights with men. At the beginning of the twentieth century, university study in the German Empire was limited to male students. Women were finally granted the right to enroll in a university in 1901 when two universities in Baden-Württemberg, Freiburg and Heidelberg, admitted female students. Women were first admitted to universities in Prussia in 1908. Women were finally granted the right to vote in 1918. The elections in January 1919 were the first in which women were allowed to vote and run for office. Female voter turnout exceeded 80%, and thirty-seven women were elected to the national assembly. After the Nazis came to power in 1933, the BDF disbanded and was replaced by a Nazi organization, the German Women's Front (Deutsche Frauenfront). The president of the BDF, Gertrud Baumer, refused to turn over the names of the Jewish members to the National Socialist government.

In West Germany, after the Second World War, the tendency emerged to return women to their "traditional" domestic role in the family. The East German government, on the other hand, viewed women as mothers and workers, and embraced *Muttipolitik* ("Mom politics") as a social policy that enabled mothers to function in the workplace.

A second wave of feminism emerged in West Germany when Alice Schwarzer orchestrated a campaign in which 374 women outed themselves as having had an abortion (technically illegal in Germany at the time) in 1971. Alice Schwarzer's name is synonymous with contemporary feminism in Germany. While working for the German media in the 1960s and 1970s, she forged a friendship with the French writer and feminist Simone de Beauvoir. Schwarzer and others founded the feminist magazine *Emma* (circulation ca. 50,000) in 1977; she remains its editor. *Emma* is published every two months and reports on a variety of women's and gender issues, including domestic violence, women in the military, and gay marriage.

A new, potential third wave of feminism is emerging in Germany. It is concerned with the living conditions of women, sexual violence, and the balance of power between men and women. However, widely divergent views remain about how to achieve this last goal.

Wendell G. Johnson

See also: Chapter 3: Government and Politics in the German Democratic Republic. Chapter 6: Jews in Germany. Chapter 7: LGBTQ Life in Modern Germany; Representation in Government; Women in the Workforce. Chapter 8: German Universities and *Fachhochschulen*. Chapter 16: Overview.

Further Reading

Fisher, Pamela. "Abortion in Post-Communist Germany: The End of *Muttipolitik* and a Still Birth for Feminism." *Womens's Studies International Forum* 28(1): 21–36, 2005.

Gruesbeck, Chloe. "Federation of German Women's Associations (Bund Deutscher Frauenvereine, BDF) (1894–1933)." http://hist259.web.unc.edu/federation-of-german -womens-associations/. Accessed March 30, 2020.

Mazón, Patricia M. *Gender and the Modern Research University: The Admission of Women to German Higher Education, 1865–1914.* Stanford, CA: Stanford University Press, 2003.

Sneeringer, Julia. *Winning Women's Votes: Propaganda and Politics in Weimar Germany.* Chapel Hill: University of North Carolina, 2002.

Gender Roles in Germany

As in other parts of Europe, gender roles in Germany have been renegotiated and reconfigured during the modern era. The early nineteenth century saw a major break in the Western tradition that had considered the categories of male and female as simply variations of a common human physiology in which gender roles were primarily shaped by culture. Instead, scientists and philosophers developed the notion that women and men were naturally biologically very different, and that this was the source of gender roles within society (Rosenhaft, 2004, pp. 209–211). These roles were confined to separate spheres in which men were to become the family's breadwinner and women would provide emotional support for the family while managing the household. This separation was maintained legally after the founding of the German Empire (1871), but as Germany continued to industrialize, more women gained employment outside of the household (Schaser, 2008, p. 135).

A high point in employment was reached during the First World War as women replaced men who had been sent to the front. The experience of independence during the war had profound effects on women's conceptions of citizenship during the Weimar Republic. Though equality was not achieved, the public sphere was no longer the preserve of men as women joined unions, voted, and campaigned for reproductive rights. The National Socialist era saw a backlash as the Nazis attempted to stabilize gender roles into two rigid categories: the male soldier and the female mother of the German race (Pine, 2017, pp. 103–116). Nevertheless, due to the high number of men fighting in the Second World War, women formed a larger proportion of the university and workplace populations.

The horrors and experiences of war set the stage for shifting gender roles that remain relevant in contemporary Germany. One of the most important shifts was the 1977 law that ended the requirement that women acquire the permission of their husbands to accept employment. This marked a profound alteration of the institution of marriage from "separate spheres" to the idea of a domestic partnership. In the same year, the divorce law was changed to remove the requirement of fault. A spouse no longer needed to prove that their partner had breached the marital agreement. This further destabilized the notion that there are particular roles that each spouse must fulfill legally and privately. Two other laws highlight the removal of such duties: the 1969 ending of adultery as a crime and, in 1997, the criminalization of marital rape. Both are notable for their emphasis on the emancipation of the physical body from prescribed general roles. Finally, in 2018, the German government approved official use of a third gender, labeled "other," primarily for intersex people. As can be seen from this final piece of legislation, contemporary Germany still links biological sex with gender. Nevertheless, the situation remains complicated. The German government has recognized the falling birth rate as a particular source of future problems (Bujard, 2015, p. 132). Germany has tried to balance a commitment to gender equality, especially in the workplace, with the need to raise birth rates to sustain the social welfare system. Men, however, tend to not use paternity leave and women are often dissuaded by employers from using their full maternity leave benefit (Reimer, 2017, p. 594). Many women choose to forgo having children in favor of pursuing a career. Among the general population, two competing conceptions of gender roles set the tone in contemporary Germany. The first is a revised version of the traditional formula in which women are no longer rigidly confined to the private sphere, but they are expected to eventually become a stay-at-home mother while men maintain a career. The second holds that gender roles are much more fluid or should not exist. Under this notion, either the man or the woman may be the stay-at home spouse, or society and the law should provide a means for both to pursue their careers while also being parents. This view is in the ascendancy, and German law in the previous several decades has tended to support it.

Christopher Thomas Godwin

See also: Chapter 7: Overview; Feminism; Weddings and Divorce; Women in the Workforce.

Further Reading

Bujard, Martin. "Consequences of Enduring Low Fertility: A German Case Study." *Comparative Population Studies* 40(2): 131–164, 2015.

Pine, Lisa. *Hitler's "National Community": Society and Culture in Nazi Germany*, 2nd ed. London: Bloomsbury Academic, 2017.

Reimer, Thordis. "Measuring German Fathers' Involvement in Childcare." *Men and Masculinities* 20(5): 588–608, 2017.

Rosenhaft, Eve. "Gender." In Jonathan Sperber, ed. *Germany 1800–1870*, 209–229. Oxford, UK: Oxford University Press, 2004.

Schaser, Angelika. "Gendered Germany." In James Retallack, ed. *Imperial Germany 1871–1918*, 128–150. Oxford, UK: Oxford University Press, 2008.

LGBTQ Life in Modern Germany

The history of LGBTQ people in Germany revolves around Paragraph 175 in the German Criminal Code of 1871. Although overt persecution of the LGBTQ community waned after the abolishment of the death penalty for sodomy in 1794 in Prussia, the 1871 law was the culmination of bourgeois middle-class attitudes and norms that developed over the course of the nineteenth century. The law explicitly criminalized male, but not female, homosexual acts. This specificity provided a leitmotif for much of the rest of LGBTQ history in Germany: while women also faced discrimination, the majority of legal and criminal action was directed toward men. Members of the

Germany is considered a "gay friendly" nation; 87% of the population believe that homosexuality should be accepted and several prominent politicians are openly gay. (Elena268/Dreamstime.com)

German Reichstag attempted several times to abolish Paragraph 175 in the decades after 1871, while some members attempted to broaden it to include lesbians (Giersdorf, 2000, pp. 1016–1017). It remained unchanged until the Nazi revision in 1935 that significantly broadened the scope of the law. While the mere rumor of being LGBTQ could cause scandal in Imperial Germany, the Weimar Republic had become the setting for greater public tolerance of the LGBTQ community. In contrast, the Nazi period was the community's darkest moment in German history as tens of thousands of gay men were subjected to incarceration, castration, scientific experimentation, and state-sanctioned murder. However, as in pre-Nazi Germany, lesbians and transvestites were primarily at risk only if they were "perceived to be breaching gender norms" (Marhoefer, 2016, pp. 1192–1193). After the Second World War, East Germany continued to criminalize homosexuality until 1987, though punishment was rare. A notable exception was women committing sexual acts with underage girls, marking a departure from German history's tendency to exclude women from consideration of homosexuality. In West Germany, Paragraph 175 was considered a pre-Nazi law and remained in effect, and tens of thousands of men were convicted and sentenced to prison (Whisnant, 2012, p. 29). Paragraph 175 was known colloquially as the 17th of May—17.5. In 1994, after the 1990 reunification, Paragraph 175 was abolished.

Contemporary Germany's cultural attitudes and social values toward the LGBTQ community are profoundly different from its history during the majority of the modern era. Germany consistently ranks as one of the most "gay friendly" countries in the world, and an estimated 87% of Germans in 2013 believed that society should accept homosexuality, up from 81% in 2007 (Pew Research Center, 2020). After 2000, homosexuality is, at least officially, no longer an impediment to serving in the armed forces (*Bundeswehr*), marking a distinct transition from approximately 200 years of the promotion of a "militarized masculinity" within German armies. Transgendered soldiers also serve in the *Bundeswehr*.

Since 2004, same-sex couples have been able to adopt children and same-sex marriage has been legal since 2017, after a decade of parliamentary debates. The turning point came when the traditional conservative party, the Christian Democratic Union, moderated its views on homosexuality. Other important legislation has abolished the need for transsexuals to have sex reassignment surgery in order to change their legal gender. Members of the LGBTQ community can donate blood. Several prominent politicians are openly gay, and even the conservative political parties are generally in favor of at least civil unions, if not even more LGBTQ rights, in contrast to the conservative parties of many non-European countries. Nevertheless, anti-LGBTQ stances and attitudes remain prominent among some religious communities that adhere to the idea that the purpose of marriage is procreation and that "marriage and family enjoy special protection"—with the implication that gay marriage is an attack on a heterosexual institution (Davidson-Schmich, 2018, p. 43). Furthermore, while the government has made strides to provide legal equality in civil administration with the non-LGBTQ population, there has been less support for inclusion in antidiscrimination laws, access to health care, and transgenderism/transsexuality (Davidson-Schmich, 2018, pp. 33–35).

Robert Ridinger

See also: Chapter 3: Political Parties. Chapter 7: Civil Unions and Same-Sex Marriage; Weddings and Divorce.

Further Reading

Davidson-Schmich, Louise K. "LGBTI Rights and the 2017 German National Election." *German Politics and Society* 36(2): 27–54, 2018.

Giersdorf, Jens Richard. "Paragraph 175." In George E. Haggerty, ed. *Gay Histories and Cultures: An Encyclopedia*, 1016–1017. New York: Garland, 2000.

Marhoefer, Laurie. "Lesbianism, Transvestitism, and the Nazi State: A Microhistory of a Gestapo Investigation, 1939–1943." *American Historical Review* 121(4): 1167–1195, 2016.

Pew Research Center. "Poll: The Global Divide on Homosexuality." *Pew Research Center*, June 4, 2013. https://www.pewglobal.org/2013/06/04/the-global-divide-on-homosexuality. Accessed July 11, 2020.

Whisnant, Clayton J. *Male Homosexuality in West Germany: Between Persecution and Freedom, 1945–69*. London: Palgrave Macmillan, 2012.

Representation in Government

Women feature prominently in the political life of the Federal Republic of Germany. Angela Merkel (of the CDU) is widely regarded as one of Europe's most influential leaders. In 2005, she became the first female chancellor (head of government) and was reelected in 2009, 2013, and 2017. During her time in office, she has dealt with the meltdown of the world's financial markets, the collapse of the Greek economy (which threatened the integrity of the European Union), a flood of refugees into Germany, the rise of right-wing nationalism in the country, and the global pandemic, Coronavirus.

In addition to Chancellor Merkel, Ursula Gertrud von der Leyen was the first woman to hold the portfolio of minister of defense, a post she held from 2013 to 2019, since then and until 2021 occupied by Annegret Kramp-Karrenbauer. Other female cabinet members in 2021 include Christine Lambrecht (SPD, since 2019—Justice and Consumer Protection and interim for Family Affairs, Senior Citizens, Women and Youth after Franziska Giffey's resignation), Julia Klöckner (CDU, 2018—Food, Agriculture and Consumer Protection), Franziska Giffey (SPD, 2018–2021—Family Affairs, Senior Citizens, Women and Youth), Svenja Schulze (SPD, 2018—Environment, Nature Conservation and Nuclear Safety), and Anja Karliczek (CDU, 2018—Education and Research). Women also occupy other influential positions in party politics in Germany, especially after the 2021 election.

Despite the diversity of Merkel's cabinet and the prominent role played by women in party politics, the percentage of female deputies in the Bundestag has reached a nineteen-year low, falling to 30.7%, or 218 deputies (the figures in the Bundesrat are slightly higher, twenty-seven members, or 39.1%). In large part, this decline is due to the rise of right-wing parties in Germany, particularly the AfD: of their combined ninety-two seats in the Bundestag, only ten are held by women, 83 after the 2021 election with nine women. The major political parties (CDU, SPD, Left Party, and the Greens) have adopted gender quotas in order to increase the number of women running for political office. The SPD, Greens, and Left Party have pledged that 50% of their candidates will be women, while the figure for the CDU is 33%. The CDU established an auxiliary association for women, the Frauen Union (Women's Union), which provides a guaranteed voice in party decision-making. The Frauen Union has shaped CDU polities on abortion, work and family issues, and female participation in the political process. Women occupy influential positions in party politics in Germany.

At the local level, two German *Länder* are headed by women: Manuela Schwesig of Mecklenburg-Vorpommern and Malu Dreyer of the Rhineland-Palatinate. As of 2018, several German cities had elected female mayors (*Oberbürgermeisterin*), including Cologne (Henrietta Reker) and Chemnitz (Barbara Ludwig).

Wendell G. Johnson

See also: Chapter 3: Merkel, Angela (1954–); Political Parties. Chapter 7: Overview; Women in the Workforce.

Further Reading

Bundestagswahl 2021. https://www.bundestagswahl-2021.de/ergebnis/#ergebnis. Accessed October 23, 2021.

Davidson-Schmich, Louise K. "Closing the Gap: Gender and Constituency Candidate Nomination in the 2013 Bundestag Election." *German Politics & Society* 32(2): 86–105, 2014. https://doi.org/10.3167/gps.2014.320206.

Eddy, Melissa. "Women Finding Their Way in German Politics." *New York Times,* March 7, 2013. https://www.nytimes.com/2013/03/08/world/europe/women-finding-their-way-in-german-politics.html. Accessed July 11, 2020.

Qvortrup, Matt. *Angela Merkel: Europe's Most Influential Leader.* New York: Overlook Duckworth, 2016.

Wiliarty, Sarah Elise. *The CDU and the Politics of Gender in Germany: Bringing Women to the Party.* Cambridge, UK: Cambridge University Press, 2010.

Weddings and Divorce

Historical Overview

From the early Medieval period through the latter part of the eighteenth century, Germanic law—based on Salic (Frankish) law—made women both subordinate to and dependent on men. Social status was based on traditional military and biological roles. Common marriage customs included arranged marriages, engagement rituals (such as the bride's family supplying alcoholic beverages), and the location of the marriage (the bride's hometown). Dispensations were necessary for blood relations marrying within the fourth degree or for marrying outside of one's religion. If either partner was a serf or divorced, the lord of the land had to give his permission for the wedding. Also, the town council could deny permission for a couple to marry. Marriage was a dowry-based contract. Wealthier families gave their daughters a dowry, but poorer women had to provide their own dowries. Wedding contracts regulated survivor benefits, the religious upbringing of children, and monetary support.

During the nineteenth century, when middle-class women were organizing for equality and greater civil rights, middle-class unions became love matches. Civil marriages were introduced in 1875, and purely religious unions were made illegal. Women's rights were curtailed during the Third Reich, when the Nazi government stressed the dual roles of women as wives and mothers. Gender equality in marriage was finally granted in 1977, when women in the Federal Republic of (West) Germany were first allowed to work outside of the home without the permission of their husbands. Further legislation revised rape laws, extended maternity leave, and legalized civil partnerships, bringing German law into compliance with other nations in the European Union. Today, marriage gives equal legal rights to couples in many areas including taxation, pensions, adoption, health insurance, and joint tenancy. Couples may marry in religious institutions or in a civil ceremony. A foreigner marrying a German citizen may apply for German nationality. As is the case throughout the European Union, the popularity of marriage in Germany has declined since 1960.

Weddings

Marriages and civil partnerships follow the identical process in Germany. The partners visit the local registry office and provide the required documentation: passport, residency permit, birth certificate (including those of any children), an affidavit swearing that both partners are single, a marriage questionnaire, certificates of divorce or death of a previous spouse (if relevant), and a financial statement. Not all couples exchange engagement rings, and those doing so move the ring from the left to the right hand after the marriage vows. Couples in Germany tend to wear identical gold bands rather than the more expensive varieties seen in the United States. A pre-wedding combination stag night and rehearsal dinner (*Polterabend*) is celebrated by the future bride, groom, family, friends, and neighbors. Traditional weddings in small villages—as depicted by painters like Pieter Brueghel de Jonge (1564–1638)—are still held where the groom and honored guests dress in local costumes. There is dancing or feasting at long tables, drummer and piper bands, fire brigade parades, and/or gun salutes. Some regions still follow the custom of the *Baumstamm sägen,* where the bride and groom ritualistically saw a (pretreated) log, indicating their willingness to stay together. In Southern Bavaria, the guests "kidnap" the bride at the reception and take her to a local pub, where the groom must pay a ransom to redeem his spouse. Many formal weddings take place in May. Traditionally, brides wear white gowns and the grooms black suits. During the reception, they dance beneath the bride's veil, which she tosses into the air after the dance. The single women at the reception tear the veil into pieces. Tradition holds that the woman with the largest piece of the veil will be the next to marry. The couple cuts the wedding cake together, and according to superstition, whichever spouse places his or her hand on the top of the knife will dominate the relationship. When the married couple leave the registry office or the church, witnesses and guests toss rice at them. The wedding party and guests then drive through town, with white ribbons attached to the car antennae and honking their horns.

Divorce

In the past, divorces were granted by a German court with the provision that partners were forbidden to remarry for several years. The Prussian General Law Code in 1794 ruled that an innocently divorced woman was entitled to financial compensation and that fathers had the obligation to provide children born out of wedlock with food and an education. Divorce was possible in Stralsund and other Protestant territories but remained difficult to obtain in Catholic areas of the country, since marriage and marital law were under the jurisdiction of the clergy until the eighteenth century.

In the modern era, Germany's divorce rate historically has been slightly higher than that of the European Union (EU) average, with a 2010 rate of 2.3 against an EU average of 2.0. German courts have jurisdiction over divorce cases if the couple are EU nationals and live permanently in Germany. Divorce applications are usually filed at the district or in the family court of joint residence. The sole legal ground for divorce in Germany is the disruption of the conjugal relationship with no expectation that it will be restored. It is presumed that the marriage is irreconcilably broken when the partners have been separated for at least one year and both agree to a divorce. If one party is opposed to a divorce, a mandatory period of separation for three years is enforced. In hardship cases (violence or other unreasonable behavior), a divorce is possible within one year. During the period of separation, spouses can petition for continued financial support to maintain their standard of living. This support, for both the spouse and children, includes housing, food, clothes, medical support, insurance, and housekeeping allowances. The level of support is decided by the presiding judge, who also rules on the division of marital property. When the divorce is uncontested by both parties, a divorce decree is usually granted after an initial hearing. Each spouse is given a month to appeal before the final decree is issued. In cases of a contested divorce, the judge must decide if the marriage is irretrievably broken, considering, for example, the trial separation of three years as evidence.

Any award of maintenance considers the financial means of the spouse and must be reasonable. Post-divorce, spouses are responsible for their own financial well-being. Alimony may be awarded to a parent looking after a child, one who is unable to work (due to illness, physical or mental weakness, or age), or when a spouse is pursuing education or training to compensate for marriage-related disadvantages. Each spouse is entitled to half of the couple's joint capital assets. The final divorce decree terminates any preexisting inheritance rights. A will favoring one spouse over the other is invalidated by the decree, unless the testator included divorce terms. Joint responsibility for childcare continues after the separation and divorce, as German law assumes that the interests of children are best served by contact with both parents. Joint care can be changed if the court determines that the child's welfare would benefit.

William P. Kladky

See also: Chapter 7: Child Custody Laws; Civil Unions and Same-Sex Marriage. Chapter 10: Etiquette for Major Life Events.

Further Reading

Abrams, Lynn. "Finding the Female Self: Women's Autonomy, Marriage and Social Change in Nineteenth-Century Germany." In Jan Rüger and Nikolaus Wachsmann, eds. *Rewriting German History: New Perspectives on Modern Germany*, 142–157. Basingstoke, UK: Palgrave Macmillan, 2015.

Rüger, Jan, and Nikolaus Wachsmann, eds. *Rewriting German History: New Perspectives on Modern Germany*. Basingstoke, UK: Palgrave Macmillan, 2015.

Women in the Workforce

Progress toward gender quality in the German workforce has been pursued but is still limited in recent years. Occupational segregation is an enduring feature of the German labor force, where female employees are highly concentrated in a few occupations. Between 50 and 60% of all women work in just eleven occupations: office workers, sales personnel, cleaners, typists, nurses, bank workers, medical assistants, seamstresses, house cleaners, bookkeepers/accountants, and cooks. Within these occupations, the median wage for women is 70% of that earned by men. Prior to 2007, minimum wages in Germany were implemented primarily in the male-dominated professions, such as construction. Unemployment has been declining in Germany in recent years, from 6.4% in 2015 to 5.0% in 2019. Since 2008, the unemployment rate for women has been slightly lower than the rate for men. In addition to traditionally defined gender roles, the main challenge to women's employment is the low quality of jobs. The recent growth in employment figures for German women is based on the rising number of part-time and "mini" jobs. Nearly 50% of women in Germany work part-time (the figure is 12% for men). One-fifth of all female employees in Germany work in marginal part-time jobs, and women account for two-thirds of mini jobbers.

Mini Jobs

Mini jobs are a form of marginal employment that was introduced in Germany in the 1960s to encourage housewives to take up part-time employment and help solve the nation's labor shortages in several industries. Presently, wages for mini jobs are capped at €450 per month, to which the employer pays an additional 20% to the social security system (8% for health insurance, 10% pension contribution, and 2% income tax). These jobs are typically cleaning and food-service jobs.

Low-Wage Employment and Minimum Wages

The German workforce is characterized by a weak relationship between low pay and skill levels: nearly 80% of German low-wage earners have completed vocational training or obtained an academic degree. Prior to 2007, minimum wages in Germany were implemented primarily in the male-dominated professions, such as construction. In recent years, minimum wages were extended to the commercial cleaning (700,000 employees) and care (800,000 employees) sectors, which are female-dominated industries. Since 2015, there has been a minimum wage that makes few exceptions.

Certain sectors have their own minimum wage; however, the amount depend on the *Land* and if it is in the East or the West. The minimum wage for the care industry, which

Table 7.1: MINIMUM WAGE

Date Effective	Amount in €
1/1/2015–12/31/2016	8.50
1/1/2017–12/31/2018	8.84
1/1/2019–12/31/2019	9.19
1/1/2020–12/31/2020	9.35
1/1/2021–6/30/2021	9.50
7/1/2021–12/31/2021	9.60
1/1/2022–6/30/2022	9.82
7/1/2022–	10.45

heavily employs women, increased after July 7, 2020, from €10.55 to €10.85 in the East and €11.05 to 11.35 in the West. In the cleaning industry, the hourly minimum for facilities cleaning (inside a building) is €10.55 in the East and €10.80 in the West. For exterior cleaning, the job pays at least €13.50 in the East and €14.10 in the West. Interior cleaning is mostly done by women, often migrants, and has a lot of part-time workers. Exterior cleaning companies employ predominantly men in full-time positions.

Female Employment in East and West Germany

In the GDR, employment rates for men and women were nearly identical. Hence, the employment rate for women in East Germany (87.4%) was much higher than that for West Germany (69.5%) at the time of reunification. Since then, the employment rate for women in East Germany has fallen (to 80.4%), while it has risen in West Germany (to 75.1%). Overall, there are limited childcare facilities, especially for children under the age of three, in 2018 about 300,000.

Entgelttransparenzgesetz and Quotas

On average, women earn 21% less than men, which has a host of explanations, such as type of work, interruption of work, part-time work. Looking at the same qualifications, women still earn 6% less than comparable men. Adopted in 2017, the *Entgelttransparenzgesetz* (salary transparency law) gives women the right to ask their employer for the comparable data. Additionally, a quota system was adopted in 2016 that gives women 30% presence on supervisory boards. In general, the Federal Ministry for Family Affairs, Senior Citizens, Women and Youth attempts to improve women's workplace experiences.

Wendell G. Johnson

See also: Chapter 1: Demographics. Chapter 3: Tax Policy. Chapter 4: Overview; Equal Pay Act. Chapter 7: Feminism.

Further Reading

Brückner, Hannah. *Gender Inequality in the Life Course: Social Change and Stability in West Germany, 1975–1995*. Hawthorne, NY: Aldine De Gruyter, 2004.

Bundesministerium für Familie, Senioren, Frauen und Jugend. "Sexismus im Alltag: Wahrnehmungen und Haltungen der deutschen Bevölkerung." https://www.bmfsfj .de/bmfsfj/service/publikationen/sexismus-im-alltag-141250. Accessed October 16, 2021.

Federal Government. "Minimum Wage to Rise—Important FAQs." https://www.bundes-regierung.de/breg-en/news/mindestlohn-faq-1765550. Accessed October 23, 2021.

Federal Ministry for Family Affairs, Senior Citizens, Women and Youth. "3rd Gender Equality Atlas for Germany." https://www.bmfsfj.de/bmfsfj/meta/en/publications -en/3rd-gender-equality-atlas-for-germany-114012. Accessed October 17, 2021.

Kleinert, Corinna. "Ostdeutsche Frauen häufiger in Führungspositionen." IAB-Kurzbericht. Nürnberg, March 2011. https://www.econstor.eu/bitstream/10419/158346/1 /kb2011-03.pdf. Accessed August 31, 2021.

Rose, Stephanie. *Das Reproduktionsregime: Sicherung von Arbeits- und Lebenskraft zwischen Effizienz und Resilienz.* Wiesbaden, Germany: Springer, 2018.

Weinkopf, Claudia. "Women's Employment in Germany: Robust in Crisis but Vulnerable in Job Quality." In Anne Eydoux, Antoine Math, and Hélène Périvier, eds. *European Labor Markets in Times of Crisis: A Gender Perspective, 189–214.* https://www.cairn .info/revue-de-l-ofce-2014-2-page-7.htm. Accessed October 17, 2021.

CHAPTER 8

EDUCATION

OVERVIEW

Not surprisingly, there was no uniform educational system in the German territories prior to the founding of the German Empire in 1871. Generally, education was available only to boys from wealthier families, who were often sent to monasteries to study. Martin Luther called for the education of girls in his "Discourse on the Duty of Sending Children to Schools" (1530).

In 1592, Pfalz-Zweibrücken, a small duchy in parts of present-day Rhineland-Palatinate and France, instituted compulsory schooling. The professor, teacher, and pietist August Hermann Francke (1663–1727) founded a school for the poor in 1695 with the goal of teaching about religion. His Frankesche Stiftung (Francke Foundations) still exists today. Johannes Julius Hecker (1707–1768) saw a dearth of teacher preparation opportunities and thus established a seminar where teachers could train for the *Realschule* he also started. Hecker's *Realschule*, a "realistic school," was so named because it accounted for the actual life circumstances of his pupils and combined the acquisition of knowledge with training in practical, vocational skills through internships. In 1763, Prussia introduced compulsory schooling, targeting both boys and girls aged five to thirteen/fourteen living in rural areas. The goal of these schools was to teach reading, writing, and good Christian values. Widespread opinion at that time held that if girls learned how to write, they would use that knowledge for nefarious reasons such as writing love letters. The situation in these *Volksschulen* (*Volk*—folk) was often not conducive to learning; too many children of all levels were packed together and taught by a teacher (usually a man) who was so poorly paid that he had to supplement his income with other jobs. Most children were needed to work on the family farm, and as a result, only about 60% of them were able to attend school regularly.

Starting in 1850, education became compulsory throughout the German areas. In German there is a difference between *Schulpflicht* (compulsory schooling) and *Unterrichtspflicht* (compulsory education); every child had to be educated, but it was not necessary to do so in a school setting. Parents who were well-off hired tutors to educate their children at home. By 1871, literacy had increased significantly to an estimated rate of 80–90% (older citizens comprised the bulk of the illiterate population). In a time of emerging industrialization, schooling was deemed especially important for the military, economy, and society in general. Parents who did not send their children to school were subject to fines. Although school attendance increased, it remained seasonal in rural areas as many children were needed for the harvest.

In 1772, the *Abitur* (an examination at the end of a student's secondary education) became the common entrance requirement for studying at a university. At this point, only men qualified for the *Abitur*. The *Lyzeums*, high schools for young women, did not offer the *Abitur* until 1908, the same year women were finally allowed to study at a university. Coeducation was not permitted at the secondary level until 1914. Comprehensive schooling for twelve years, including *Volksschule* (eight years) and *Fortbildungsschule* (continuing school, four years), was enshrined in the 1919 *Reichsverfassung* (imperial constitution) of the Weimar Republic. Beginning in 1933, the rights of Jewish students and professors were curtailed, and in 1942, Jewish children were completely prohibited from attending school.

After the war, East Germany instituted the *Einheitsschule* (single school type) after the Soviet model; in the West, the individual *Länder* became responsible for formal education, under the auspices of the KMK, Kultusministerkonferenz (The Standing Conference of the Ministers of Education and Cultural Affairs). In 1972, the *Oberstufenreform* (upper school reform) made the last two years *before* the *Abitur* more individual to prepare students for the university system. Students were still

STUDENT OR SCHÜLER?

The German language differentiates between students or pupils at a school (*Schüler* for boys, *Schülerin* for girls—*in* indicates feminine), and students at a university (*Student*, *Studentin*). The gender-inclusiveness of these terms in the plural is still widely debated: *Schüler und Schülerinnen*, *SchülerInnen*, *Schüler/innen*, *Schüler*innen*, or *Schüler_innen* are some of the options. The Gesellschaft für deutsche Sprache (GfdS) devoted its first *Sprachdienst* (a journal dealing with language issues) of 2020 to gender equity in language. Nonetheless, *Schüler* and *Schülerinnen* attend a *Grundschule* (elementary school) and then a secondary school, either *Hauptschule* (to Grade 9), *Realschule* (Grade 10), *Gymnasium* (Grade 12/13), or a *Gesamtschule*, combining all three types of secondary schools. In order to fulfill twelve years of school attendance, *Schüler* of a *Hauptschule* and *Realschule* still attend a *Berufsschule* for three or two years, respectively, while apprenticing in a company. *Studenten* study (*studieren*) at a university, *Fachhochschule* (university of applied science), or *Hochschule* (university, higher education institution). The verb *studieren* is not used for pupils.

Katharina Barbe

Further Reading

Deutscher Rechtschreibrat. "Empfehlungen zur geschlechtergerechten Schreibung," March 27, 2020. https://www.rechtschreibrat.com/DOX/rfdr_PM_2018–11-16 _Geschlechtergerechte_Schreibung.pdf/. Accessed October 17, 2021.

Kultusministerkonferenz. https://www.kmk.org/kmk/information-in-english.html https://www.kmk.org/kmk/information-in-english.html/. Accessed October 17, 2021.

required to study compulsory subjects, but electives were also added to the curriculum. There are five areas that each student must cover: (i) linguistic, literary, and artistic, (ii) social sciences, (iii) natural sciences and mathematics, (iv) religion or ethics, and (v) sports. These are graded via a point system. With reunification, the East German school system was *abgewickelt*, a euphemism for phased out, and absorbed into the Western system.

The 1999 Bologna process integrated the German higher education into a two-tier Europe-wide system of undergraduate and graduate education, in Germany termed "Bachelor" and "Master." Now students can transfer their earned *Leistungspunkte* (credit points) into the unified European Credit Transfer and Accumulation System (ECTS). In 2001, the so-called PISA Schock hit Germany. PISA (Programme for International Student Assessment) conducts an assessment of fifteen-year-olds in seventy-nine countries in reading, mathematics, and science. German students were shown to have major deficits, especially in reading competence. A large spread between the lowest and the highest achievers was revealed, as was a pronounced variation between achievements in the different *Länder*. Many students left school before attaining basic competencies, and students' academic success correlated with the economic prosperity of their home. The German educational system engaged in collective handwringing, instituted relevant reforms, and results have improved lately.

Less than 9% of all students attend private schools. For example, in 2010/2011, Lower Saxony had 2,902 public and 166 private schools. Of those 166 schools, 15.7% were Catholic, 6.6% Protestant, and 12.1% Waldorf Schools. Private schools must hire qualified teachers and offer a curriculum comparable to that in the public schools, especially if they intend to grant diplomas, such as the *Abitur*. Once a private school has operated successfully for three years, it receives a 75% *Finanzausgleich* (financial compensation) from the state; the remainder of the budget is privately funded.

Homeschooling is prohibited in Germany, as the basic law requires compulsory schooling. As EU citizens, families who want to homeschool their children have the option of moving to another EU country, such as Austria, where it is allowed. In 2013, the state of Hesse took four children of a family (Wunderlich) into custody because the family refused to send them to school. The children were eventually returned but were enrolled in a public school. The family sued and the case ended up in the European Court of Human Rights, which ruled against the family in 2019. Yet another family asked for asylum into the United States, where they now homeschool their children in Tennessee.

Katharina Barbe

Further Reading

Barz, Heiner. "Der PISA-Schock. Über die Zukunft von Bildung und Wissenschaft im Land der 'Kulturnation.'" In Gerhard Beier, ed. *20 Jahre neue Bundesrepublik: Kontinuitäten und Diskontinuitäten*, 215–237. Göttingen/Berlin: LIT, 2011.

Berg, Christa. *Handbuch der Deutschen Bildungsgeschichte*, 2 vols. München: C. H. Beck, 1987.

Bundeszentrale für politische Bildung. "Homeschooling." https://www.bpb.de /gesellschaft/bildung/zukunft-bildung/174625/bildungsrecht-wie-die-verfassung -unser-schulwesen-mit-gestaltet?p=all. Accessed March 27, 2020.

Engelsing, Rolf. *Analphabetentum und Lektüre*. Stuttgart: Metzler, 1973.

Hahn, H.-J. *Education and Society in Germany*. Oxford, UK: Berg, 1998.

Kultusministerkonferenz. "Vereinbarung zur Gestaltung der gymnasialen Oberstufe und der Abiturprüfung." https://www.kmk.org/fileadmin/Dateien/veroeffentlichungen _beschluesse/1972/1972_07_07-VB-gymnasiale-Oberstufe-Abiturpruefung.pdf. Accessed March 27, 2020.

Luke, Carme. *Pedagogy, Printing, and Protestantism: The Discourse on Childhood*. Albany, NY: SUNY Press, 1989.

Luther. Die allerbesten Schulen—auf für die Maidlein. https://www.monumente-online. de/de/ausgaben/2007/3/die-allerbesten-schulen-auch-fuer-die-maidlein.php# .XmZU8ahKg2w. Accessed March 27, 2020.

OECD. "PISA 2018—What Students Know and Can Do." https://www.Oecd-Ilibrary.Org /Docserver/5f07c754-En.Pdf?Expires=1583939993&Id=Id&Accname=Guest&Checks um=92D996B87B85B1B18E3ED02E37E065D3. Accessed March 27, 2020.

OECD. *Vocational Training in Germany: Modernisation and Responsiveness*. 1994.

Waldron, Ben. "Homeschooling German Family Allowed to Stay in the US." ABC News, March 5, 2014. https://abcnews.go.com/US/home-schooling-german-family-allowed -stay-us/story?id=22788876. Accessed March 27, 2020.

DAAD

The DAAD, Deutscher Akademischer Austauschdienst (German Academic Exchange Service) is a politically independent organization of German institutions of higher learning that fosters international exchange programs for students and researchers. In January 1925, Carl Joachim Friedrich (a student from Heidelberg) founded the DAAD, known at that time as the Akademischer Austauschdienst e.V. (AAD) or Academic Exchange Service. During his visits to the United States in 1922 and 1923, Friedrich worked with the New York Institute of International Education (IIE) to organize scholarships for German students. As a result of these efforts, an exchange program in political science was soon established in Heidelberg. The AAD moved to Berlin in 1925, where it joined with other organizations (including the Alexander von Humboldt Stiftung) to become the DAAD in 1931. This new organization expanded its reach beyond political science to include other fields of study. The DAAD lost its independence during the Third Reich and was dissolved in 1945. In an effort to end Germany's academic isolation, the Western occupying powers reconstituted the DAAD in 1946 to its current position as one of the most influential worldwide educational and research organizations.

Each year, the DAAD supports over 100,000 international researchers and since its inception has aided over 2 million academics. The DAAD works with the Institut für deutsche Sprache, the Gesellschaft für deutsche Sprache, and the Goethe-Institut, as a member of the Deutsche Sprachrat (German Language Council) with the goal to promote instruction and research in the German language. The DAAD accomplishes its mission by sending German researchers to educational institutions throughout the world and by providing financial support for foreign academics and leaders in Germany. Scholarships are available for completion of master's degrees, short-term research for doctoral students, one-year research for doctoral candidates (those who have passed their qualifying exams), and for doctoral work at a German university. Among the 250 programs supported by the DAAD are "3D Animation for Film and Games" at the Technische Hochschule Köln, "Academic Speech Therapy" at the Universität Würzburg, and "Accounting, Auditing & Taxation" at the Bochum University of Applied Sciences. Available short-term language classes sponsored by the DAAD include "Training for GFL (German as a Foreign Language) for Teachers and Graduates of German Studies," designed for non-native German speakers at the Universität Heidelberg, and "German for Technical Purposes" at the Technische Universität Ilmenau. The DAAD also finances binational universities, such as the German Jordanian University in Mushaqar, Jordan. In turn, the DAAD is financed predominantly by the Auswärtiges Amt (Federal Foreign Office) and the Bundesministerium für Bildung und Forschung (Federal Ministry of Education and Research). In 2020, its combined budget amounted to over €565 million, a significant increase from the 2015 figure of €417 million.

Katharina Barbe

See also: Chapter 8: German Universities and *Fachhochschulen*; Goethe-Institut. Chapter 9: Gesellschaft für deutsche Sprache; Institut für deutsche Sprache; *Sprachgesellschaften* (Language Societies).

Further Reading

Bundesministerium für Bildung und Forschung. "Deutscher Akademischer Austauschdienst." https://www.bmbf.de/bmbf/de/forschung/das-wissenschaftssystem /forschungspartner/deutscher-akademischer-austauschdienst-daad/deutscher-akade-mischer-austauschdienst-daad.html. Accessed October 23, 2021.

Deutscher Akademischer Austauschdienst. "Study Aussenblick." https://www.daad.de /en/. Accessed March 10, 2020.

Facts about Germany. "Working in Germany." https://www.tatsachen-ueber-deutschland .de/en. Accessed March 10, 2020.

Education in the German Democratic Republic

The German Democratic Republic (GDR or East Germany) followed the example of the Soviet Union in creating politically compliant and coeducational schools based on Marxist ideology. Religious and private schools were originally permitted (but not encouraged) by the East German government. In the 1950s, the GDR instituted a uniform educational system that was controlled by the state. Its main goal was to make education accessible to everyone and to educate all students to become qualified members of the workforce. This was especially important in the aftermath of the war, when the GDR needed a substantial workforce, male and female, to rebuild the state.

Teacher Training

Immediately after the war, an enormous need for teachers arose. Many of those who had taught during the Nazi time were no longer considered ideologically acceptable, and new teachers were quickly and often insufficiently prepared to teach in the different types of schools. Instruction was teacher-centered, and teachers often had to teach subjects for which they were not trained. Kindergarten teachers attended a pedagogical institution for three years. Elementary school teachers (grades 1–4) were educated

Table 8.1: STRUCTURE OF THE SCHOOL SYSTEM IN DDR

Age	Education and Continuing Education (adults)			years in school
	professional life	Technical school/University and Colleges		
19	↑	Vocational training with school leaving examination (*Abitur*)	↑	13
18	Vocational Training (two years)		Expanded upper level	12
17				11
16	Polytechnic secondary school	Upper Level		10
15				9
14				8
13				7
12		Mid Level		6
11				5
10				4
9		Lower Level		3
8				2
7				1
6	Nursery School			
5				
4				
3	Crèche			
2				
1				

Source: Mitteldeutscher Rundfunk. "Das Schulwesen in der DDR." https://www.mdr.de/zeitreise /schwerpunkte/eure-geschichte/themen/jugend-bildung/schulwesen/ddr-bildungssystem100.html. Accessed July 11, 2020.

at an *Institut für Lehrerbildung* (institute for teacher education) for four years, where they studied German, *Heimatkunde* (local history and geography), mathematics, and could opt for one *Wahlfach* (elective subject): music, sports, painting, or crafts. Every prospective teacher also was instructed in foundation of Marxism-Leninism, psychology, pedagogy, health education, speech training, and Russian. Secondary school teachers were required to study eight semesters at a university, where they had to specialize in two subjects.

Educational Institutions

In order to make it easy for women to enter the workforce, all children were entitled to a place in a *Krippe* (crèche, ages one to three) and then a *Kindergarten* (ages four to six). Those adopted flexible operating hours to accommodate the parents' differing work schedules. After eight years of *Grundschule* or elementary school, students followed with *Berufsschule* (vocational school), a *Fachschule* (technical school), or an *Oberschule* (high school, the sole gateway to university). In the *Oberschule*, students were placed in one of three tracks: *Neusprachlich* (modern languages), *Altsprachlich* (classical languages), or *Naturwissenschaftlich* (math and science). Advancement to the *Oberschule* was a political issue, where social background, the political orientation and reliability of the parents, and extracurricular activities played a more important role than did a student's academic performance. The *Polytechnische Oberschule* (POS, polytechnic secondary school) was introduced in 1959, which mandated instruction in mathematics, German, *Heimatkunde*, sports, music, and painting or other fine arts. Other topics, such as *Staatsbürgerkunde* (civics) and *Wehrkunde* (socialist military education), were included in the curriculum to enforce conformity with Marxist ideology.

Katharina Barbe

See also: Chapter 2: Marx, Karl (1818–1883). Chapter 3: Government and Politics in the German Democratic Republic. Chapter 8: German Universities and *Fachhochschulen*; Primary and Secondary Education; Vocational Training (*Duale Ausbildung*).

Further Reading

Bundeszentrale für politische Bildung. "Von der Krippe bis zur Hochschule: Das Bildungssystem der DDR." https://www.bpb.de/gesellschaft/bildung/zukunft-bildung/230383/von-der-krippe-bis-zur-hochschule-das-bildungssystem-der-ddr. Accessed March 20, 2020.

Deutschlandfunk. "DDR—Studieren in einer Diktatur." https://www.deutschlandfunk.de/ddr-studieren-in-einer-diktatur.1310.de.html?dram:article_id=398152. Accessed March 20, 2020.

Geissler, Gert. "Schule und Erziehung in der Deutschen Demokratischen Republik." *European Journal of Mental Health* 6(1): 56–82, 2011.

Günther, Karl-Heinz, and Gottfried Uhlig. *History of the Schools in the German Democratic Republic 1945 to 1968*. Aufl. Berlin: Volk und Wissen, 1973.

Rodden, John. *Repainting the Little Red Schoolhouse: A History of Eastern German Education, 1945–1995*. New York: Oxford University Press, 2002.

German Universities and *Fachhochschulen*

Institutions of higher education in Germany are commonly referred to as *Hochschulen* (not to be confused with the English "false friend" high schools). The ca. 400 *Hochschulen* in Germany are primarily state sponsored and generally do not charge tuition. Students pay only nominal fees to attend. Historically, higher education in Germany was a pursuit reserved for the elites.

There are three primary types of *Hochschulen*: *Universitäten* (universities), *Fachhochschulen* (applied technical colleges), and *Kunsthochschulen* (art-oriented institutions). In order to study at any of the *Hochschulen*, a student needs to have either the *Abitur* (general qualification for university entrance) from a *Gymnasium* or the *Fachhochschulreife* (a qualification to attend a *Fachhochschule*). Currently, about half of each cohort graduating with eligibility for university admission continue their studies at an institute of higher education.

Universities in Germany are research focused and offer coursework leading to bachelor's, master's, and doctoral degrees. *Fachhochschulen* have a technological, economic, social, or design focus and lead to the bachelor's or master's. The Beuth University of Applied Science in Berlin, for example, offers over eighty accredited BS and MS degrees in areas such as applied mathematics and project management. Students at a *Kunsthochschule* pursue studies in areas such as painting, music, and architecture.

One of Germany's 380 institutions of higher learning, Bonn University was founded in 1818. Currently ca. 35,000 students pursue studies in 200 degree programs. (Jan Kranendonk/ Dreamstime.com)

Eligibility for Admission

The primary qualification for admission to a German university is the *Abitur*; requirements vary for non-German students. American students, for example, must have graduated from high school and provide proof of German-language proficiency at least at the C1-level of the Common European Framework; but an AP score in German of 5 is also accepted by many

Table 8.2: UNIVERSITY DEGREES AND MAJORS

Bachelor's Degrees	Master's Degrees	Sample Majors
Bachelor of Arts (BA)	Master of Arts (MA)	Linguistics, sports, social sciences, economics
Bachelor of Science (BSc)	Master of Science (MSc)	Mathematics, natural sciences, medicine, nutrition science
Bachelor of Engineering (BEng)	Master of Engineering (MEng)	Engineering
Bachelor of Laws (LLB)	Master of Laws (LLM)	Law
Bachelor of Fine Arts (BFA)	Master of Fine Arts (BFA)	Arts
Bachelor of Music (BMus)	Master of Music (BMus)	Music
Bachelor of Education (BEd)	Master of Education (MEd)	Teacher education

universities. Certain areas of study, such as medicine and veterinary studies, also require a high GPA for admission, commonly known as *Numerus Clausus* (NC). The application process is conducted through hochschulstart.de, formerly ZVS (*Zentralstelle für die Vergabe von Studienplätzen*), that is, a central admissions service. Applicants may indicate their preferred university on their application, but there is no guarantee of admission to a specific school. Application deadlines are strictly enforced in Germany. Some disciplines accept students once a year, others twice a year. Students intending to enroll at a *Fachhochschule* apply directly to the school and not through a centralized portal.

Degrees

German universities offer several bachelor's and master's degrees (see Table 8.2).

German universities (not *Fachhochschulen*) also offer doctoral degrees, the doctoral degrees conferred indicating the topic studied: Dr. phil (Dr. of philosophy; includes humanities, psychology and others), Dr. ing. (Dr. of engineering), Dr. iur. (Dr. of law), Dr. rer. nat. (Dr. of natural sciences), or Dr. theol. (Dr. of theology). The Dr. med. (Dr. of medicine) is not automatically awarded at the end of a student's medical studies as is the case with the MD in the United States. Many German physicians do not have a doctoral degree; only those who successfully carry out an independent research program receive the degree.

BAföG

The *Bundesausbildungsförderungsgesetz* (*BAföG*), the Federal Law Concerning the Promotion of Education or Training, supports many students from low-income families. *BAföG* funds consist of grants and interest-free loans. The amount disbursed depends on factors such as household income and living situation (living with parents or not). In 2021, the highest award was €861/month. About 15% of students receive *BAföG*.

Katharina Barbe

See also: Chapter 8: Primary and Secondary Education.

Further Reading

Behmel, Albrecht, and Kelly Neudorfer. *The Foreigner's Guide to German Universities: Origin, Meaning, and Use of Terms and Expressions in Everyday University Life.* Stuttgart: ibidem-Verlag, 2016.

Breinig, Helmbrecht, Jürgen Gebhardt, and Berndt Ostendorf. *German and American Higher Education: Educational Philosophies and Political Systems.* Münster; Piscataway, NJ: LIT, 2001.

Bundeszentrale für politische Bildung. "Dossier: Bildung." https://www.bpb.de/gesellschaft /bildung/zukunft-bildung/. Accessed October 1, 2019.

The German Way and More. "The German School System." https://www.german-way .com/history-and-culture/education/the-german-school-system/. Accessed October 1, 2019.

Hochschulrektorenkonferenz (HRK). "Das Hochschulsystem in Deutschland." https:// www.hrk.de/fileadmin/_migrated/content_uploads/Das_Hochschulsystem _In_DEUTSCHLAND.pdf. Accessed October 1, 2019.

Nach dem Abitur. https://www.nach-dem-abitur.de/. Accessed October 1, 2019.

Süddeutsche Zeitung: Jurastudium und LL.M. https://bildung.sueddeutsche.de/llm /jurastudium-und-llm/. Accessed October 1, 2019.

Goethe-Institut

The Goethe-Institut (GI), a nonprofit, non-political, independent cultural organization, is headquartered in Munich. The GI operates 12 institutes in Germany and 159 others in ninety-eight countries under the motto *"Das Goethe-Institut bringt die deutsche Sprache in die Welt"* (The Goethe-Institute brings the German language into the world.) It takes its name from Johann Wolfgang von Goethe (1749–1832), the prolific author, natural scientist, lawyer, and politician, who was also conversant in several languages.

The GI was established in 1951 as the successor of the Deutsche Akademie (DA, or German Academy), which was founded in the 1920s to foster "Germanness." The German Academy became politicized during the Third Reich and expunged members such as Konrad Adenauer (first German chancellor from 1949 to 1963) and Thomas Mann (1875–1955; German author and 1929 Nobel Laureate). The DA was closed after the war, and its funding flowed to the GI, whose original task was to educate and support foreign teachers of German. The GI's language courses proved very popular and expanded quickly. Initially, courses were offered in smaller communities (generally in Bavaria), but in 1986, institutes were opened in larger cities. After the fall of the Berlin Wall, the GI expanded into Eastern Europe.

The tasks of the GI are multifaceted, following its slogan "Language. Culture. Germany." In the area of language acquisition, it offers language courses at all levels, develops and shares teaching materials and language tests, supports the continuing education of language teachers, provides stipends for teachers, and oversees ever-increasing online offerings. In addition, the GI sponsors many cultural activities, including screening movies, theater performances, and exhibits. Many Goethe-Institutes have a library.

Goethe-Institutes cooperate with local and regional associations of German teachers, such as the American Association of Teachers of Germans (AATG). The GI/AATG Certificate of Merit is a prestigious honor for teachers who have made a significant contribution to the profession. Worldwide, the GI employs approximately 3,650 people. Goethe-Institutes hire local staff; however, most upper-level positions, like directors, are staffed with employees who rotate to the various institutes and remain there for approximately five years. The GI receives the largest portion of its operating budget from the Federal Foreign Office. It also generates income from tuition from its language courses and examination fees. Worldwide, 270,000 students enrolled in its language courses in 2018, and that same year the GI administered 550,000 language exams (in the United States, the figures are 11,300 enrollees and 12,000 people sat for exams). Altogether 10 million people visited 30,000 cultural events at their local GI. The GI supported 282 book translations from German, the majority into Spanish, English, and Italian. The GI is a member of the Deutsche Sprachrat (German Language Council), whose common goal is to promote the instruction of German and support German-language research.

Katharina Barbe

See also: Chapter 8: DAAD. Chapter 9: Gesellschaft für deutsche Sprache; Institut für deutsche Sprache.

Further Reading

2018/2019 Goethe Institut Jahrbuch. https://www.goethe.de/resources/files/pdf179/jahrbuch-2018_2019.pdf. Accessed October 1, 2019.

Goethe-Institut. https://www.goethe.de/en/index.html. Accessed July 11, 2020.

Keilholz-Rühle, Nikky, Stephan Nobbe, and Uwe Rau. "Language Policies of the Goethe-Institut." In Andreas Gardt and Bernd Hüppauf, eds. *Globalization and the Future of German*, 245–52. Berlin: Mouton de Gruyter, 2004.

Michels, Eckard, *Von der Deutschen Akademie zum Goethe Institut: Sprach- und auswärtige Kulurpolitik 1923–1960*. München: R. Oldenbourg Verlag, 2005.

Libraries

Nearly all German cities with at least 5,000 inhabitants offer library services to their residents. The two main types of libraries, research libraries and public libraries, are politically independent. Public libraries, supported by municipalities

The German National Library was originally based in Leipzig. After the Second World War and the division of Germany into four occupation zones, the Western powers opened a second national library in Frankfurt am Main. Both libraries remain separate geographically but connected administratively today. (Robert Kühne/Dreamstime.com)

and churches, provide information resources and services to the public at no charge to patrons, while research libraries, funded by the federal states (*Länder*) and universities (*Hochschulen*), support teaching and research. Each German state has at least one university (the Saarland), and the state of North Rhine-Westphalia has the most with eighteen. All German institutions of higher learning provide library services for students and faculty. A larger and older university, for example, will have a central library and then often also supports more specialized institute libraries, whereas library services may be more centralized at newer and smaller universities.

By the latest count, about 12,000 public libraries (*Volksbibliotheken*, now *Öffentliche Bibliotheken*) are available to the public. In Berlin, for example, each district (*Bezirk*) has its own *Stadtbibliothek*, or municipal library. The *Bezirkszentralbibliothek* in the Berlin municipality Spandau (about 200,000 inhabitants) operates four *Stadtteilbibliotheken* (district libraries) spread out geographically. In addition, it offers a *Fahrbibliothek*, or mobile library, where patrons have access to about 19,000 items, of which 5,000 are on the bus. Every weekday, this mobile library is available at fifteen different locations for 1.5 hours each. In a *Stadtbibliothek*, patrons have free access to all the library's holdings. In order to check out items, patrons need a library card that shows they are registered residents. With their library card, they also have access and checkout privileges to all public libraries in Berlin; this comes at a nominal cost of €10/year for adults, €5/year for students and *Azubis* (trainees); children and the jobless do not incur any fees.

Deutsche Nationalbibliothek (DNB)

The DNB, or German National Library, was founded in 1913 in Leipzig as Deutsche Bücherei and is tasked with (i) the collection of German-language publications including music in Germany and abroad, as well as non-German output written in Germany; and (ii) the dissemination of this collection. The library lost its independence in 1933 when it became part of the Reichsministerium für Volksaufklärung und Propaganda (Reich Ministry of Public Enlightenment and Propaganda) under Joseph Goebbels, which had a predictably negative impact on collection development. Its building in Leipzig was closed in 1943 after being destroyed by an air raid. It reopened in 1946 as the Deutsche Bibliothek in Frankfurt am Main and the Deutsche Bücherei in Leipzig, thus providing divided Germany with two national libraries. After reunification in 1990, these two national libraries merged under the name *Die deutsche Bibliothek* (the German Library). In 2006, the facilities in Leipzig and Frankfurt received their current name—Deutsche Nationalbibliothek.

Katharina Barbe

See also: Chapter 1: Overview. Chapter 8: German Universities and *Fachhochschulen*; Goethe-Institut.

Further Reading

Bibliotheksportral. "Öffentliche Bibliotheken." https://bibliotheksportal.de/informationen/bibliothekslandschaft/oeffentliche-bibliotheken/. Accessed October 1, 2019.

Bücherei—ein Praxishandbuch. "Bibliotheken in Deutschland." http://www.buecherei-praxishandbuch.de/index.php?id=54. Accessed October 1, 2019.

Busse, Gisela von. *Das Bibliothekswesen der Bundesrepublik Deutschland: Ein Handbuch*, 3rd ed. Wiesbaden, Germany: Harrassowitz, 1999.

Deutsche Nationale Bibliothek. "History." https://www.dnb.de/EN/Ueber-uns/Geschichte/geschichte_node.html;jsessionid=5A3C6BE23040439651C0E27F2A0A772B.internet552. Accessed October 1, 2019.

Deutscher Bibliotheksverband (dbv). "Ziele und Themen des Deutschen Bibliotheksverbandes." https://www.bibliotheksverband.de/fileadmin/user_upload/DBV/ueber_uns/2015_Ziele_und_Aufgaben_des_dbv_endg.pdf. Accessed October 1, 2019.

Plassmann, Engelbert, Hermann Rösch, Jürgen Seefeldt, and Konrad Umlauf. *Libraries and the Information Society in Germany: An Introduction*. Wiesbaden, Germany: Harrassowitz Verlag, 2014.

Rau, Christian. *"Nationalbibliothek" im geteilten Land: Die Deutsche Bücherei 1945–1990*. Göttingen, Germany: Wallstein Verlag, 2018.

Max Planck Gesellschaft

The Max Planck Gesellschaft (MPG) maintains and supports eighty-four Max Planck Institutes, five of which are located outside Germany. The MPG is a non-profit organization whose mission is to support fundamental and original research in the sciences, humanities, and social sciences. The Gesellschaft is financed through federal and state funds (its budget was €1.7 billion in 2018), is not affiliated with any university, and conducts its research independently from any political influence. The MPG is Germany's most successful research organization. Since its founding, it has produced eighteen Nobel Laureates and produces more than 15,000 publications each year.

The MPG is a successor to the Kaiser Wilhelm Gesellschaft (KWG). Adolf von Harnack (1851–1930), a Lutheran theologian and professor, envisioned a reform of science and proposed research institutes independent from the university system. His efforts led to the founding of the Kaiser Wilhelm Gesellschaft in 1911 under the patronage of Kaiser Wilhelm II. Harnack led the KWG until 1930, when he was succeeded by the Physics Nobel Laureate Max Planck (1858–1947). Planck served as the president of the KWG until 1936, when he fell out of favor with the Nazi government because of his support for Jewish scholars, such as the chemist and Nobel Laureate Fritz Haber (1868–1934), who is known as the "father of chemical warfare."

The KWG carried out medical research on living subjects in the concentration camps under the National Socialist regime. Its postwar continuance was thus untenable, and it was superseded by and folded into the newly founded Max Planck Gesellschaft. After the war, Max Planck—officially classified as politically unobjectionable by the victorious powers—assisted in the founding of the new Max Planck Society and agreed to the use of his name. Otto Hahn (1879–1968), a Nobel Laureate and researcher of nuclear fission, was named the head of the organization and expanded the MPG to include forty institutes and research facilities. Today the Max Planck Institute for Chemistry in Mainz also bears his name, the Otto Hahn Institut. Following the motto of the society, "*Dem Anwenden muss das Erkennen vorausgehen*" (Insight must precede application), Hahn focused on the sponsorship and support of young researchers independent of any political influence.

After reunification in 1990, eighteen institutes were established in East Germany. Currently, there are MPGs in every German state, from one in Bremen to fourteen in North-Rhine-Westphalia. Outside of Germany, there are the Max Planck Florida Institute for Neuroscience; two institutes in Italy (Max-Planck-Institute for Art History in Rome and the Art Historical Institute in Florence); the Max Planck Institute Luxembourg for International, European and Regulatory Procedural Law; and the Max-Planck-Institute for Psycholinguistics in Nijmegen, Netherlands. The MPG also has connections with the Weizmann Institute in Israel and the Chinese Academy of Sciences. Scholars affiliated with the MPG are given complete autonomy. These top researchers determine their topics themselves, work under the optimal conditions, and hire their staff following the so-called Harnack principle (*Harnack Prinzip*), namely, to give exceptional scholars the tools they need to carry out creative research.

Katharina Barbe

See also: Chapter 2: Wilhelm II (1859–1941). Chapter 3: *Die Wende.* Chapter 6: Jews in Germany.

Further Reading

Brown, Brandon R. *Planck: Driven by Vision, Broken by War.* New York: Oxford University Press, 2015.

Bundeszentrale für politische Bildung. "Gründung der Max Planck Gesellschaft." http://www.bpb.de/geschichte/zeitgeschichte/deutschlandarchiv/53409/gruendung-der-max-planck-gesellschaft?p=all. Accessed October 1, 2019.

Heilbron, J. L. *The Dilemmas of an Upright Man: Max Planck as Spokesman for German Science.* Berkeley: University of California Press, 1986.

Hoffmann, Klaus. *Otto Hahn: Achievement and Responsibility.* New York: Springer, 2001.

"The Max Planck Approach." https://www.mpg.de/39596/MPG_Introduction.pdf. Accessed October 23, 2021.

Max-Planck-Gesellschaft. "A Portrait of the Max Planck Society." https://www.mpg.de/short-portrait. Accessed October 1, 2019.

Max-Planck-Gesellschaft. "Our History." https://www.mpg.de/183298/history. Accessed October 1, 2019.

Primary and Secondary Education

In most federal states, students attend the *Grundschule* (primary school) for four years, except in Berlin and Brandenburg, where primary school lasts six years. There is no compulsory kindergarten in Germany. The German term *Kindergarten* refers to preschool, while the term *Vorschule* corresponds to the American kindergarten, the school year immediately preceding first grade. Following primary school, students attend school in the so-called *Sekundärbereich I* from Grades 7 (Berlin and Brandenburg) or Grades 5 (all other states) to Grades 9 or 10.

After elementary school, students are placed in a *Gymnasium* (a secondary school leading to university studies, not to be confused with the English gymnasium), *Realschule* (akin to junior high) or *Hauptschule* (Grades 5/7–9). After Grade 10, students move to the *Sekundarbereich II.* For students in the *Gymnasium* this is referred to as Upper Level (*Oberstufe*) and lasts two to three years. Students of the *Realschule* pursue further studies in the so-called dual system; and those in the *Hauptschule*, who have not found an apprenticeship, pursue further studies for vocational preparation. The *Gesamtschule*, or comprehensive school, combines the three types of schools in one building; students can still get their certificates after 10th grade, but

On the first day of school, pupils proudly carry around a *Schultüte*, a cone filled with goodies, that is designed to "sweeten" the start of many years of school. (Gunold/Dreamstime.com)

qualified students may also pursue the *Abitur*. Students who drop out before a qualifying certificate still have the opportunity to finish *Hauptschule, Realschule,* or pursue the *Abitur* (once they are in the workforce) via Germany's *Zweiter Bildungsweg* (adult education as a second chance). A variety of schools such as *Abendschulen* (evening schools) or *Abendgymnasien* offer part-time studies. A full-time option, the *Kolleg* (an institution for adult education) leads to the *Abitur.* While attending the *Kolleg*, students are only allowed to work part-time; however, their jobs cannot interfere with the daily lessons.

Compulsory education in Germany begins with the first grade. To "sweeten" their entrance into the educational system, students get a *Schultüte*, a cone filled with goodies, on their first day of school. During their years in the *Grundschule*, students are instructed in groups of *twenty to thirty*; children with disabilities are taught in separate schools or mainstreamed, depending on the school district. The cohort stays together and keeps the same teacher until they matriculate at the next level. In general, elementary students are in class daily for four to six periods of forty-five minutes each with breaks. Table 8.3 shows a typical lesson plan for elementary school.

Table 8.3: ELEMENTARY SCHOOL LESSON PLAN

Time	Monday	Tuesday	Wednesday	Thursday	Friday
8:00–8:45	German	German	German	German	Math
8:45–9:30	German	German	Music	German	Social Studies
9:30–10:00	Break				
10:00–10:45	Math	Art	Math	Math	Deutsch
1045–11:30	Social Studies	Math	Physical Education	Physical Education	Music
11:30–11:45	Break				
11:45–12:30		Religion/ Ethics	Physical Education		

Table 8.4: VACATION

School Holidays 2021/2022	Fall 2021	Christmas 2021/2022	Winter 2022	Easter 2022	Pentecost 2022	Summer 2022
Baden-Württemberg	11/2-6	12/23-1/8	district specific	4/19-23	6/7-18	7/28-9/10
Bavaria	11/2-5, 11/17	12/24-1/8	2/28-3/4	4/11-23	6/7-18	8/1-9/12
Berlin	10/11-23	12/23-31	1/29-2/5	4/11-23	5/27 and 6/7	7/7-8/19
Brandenburg	10/11-23	12/23-31	1/31-2/5	4/11-23	5/27	7/7-8/20
Bremen	10/18-30	12/23-1/8	1/31-2/1	4/4-19	5/27 and 6/7	7/14-8/24
Hamburg	10/4-15	12/23-1/4	1/28	3/7-18	5/23-27	7/7-8/17
Hesse	10/11-23	12/23-1/8	—	4/11-23	—	7/25-9/2
Mecklenburg-Western Pomerania	10/2-9, 11/1-2	12/22-31	2/5-18	4/11-20	5/27 and 6/3-7	7/4-8/13
Lower Saxony	10/18-29	12/23-1/7	1/31-2/1	4/4-19	5/27 and 6/7	7/14-8/24
North Rhine-Westphalia	10/11-23	12/23-1/8	—	4/11-23	—	6/27-8/9
Rhineland-Palatinate	10/11-22	12/23-31	2/21-25	4/13-22	—	7/25-9/2
Saarland	10/18-29	12/23-1/3	2/21-3/1	4/14-22	6/7-10	7/25-9/2
Saxony	10/18-30	12/23-1/1	2/12-26	4/15-23	5/27	7/18-8/26
Saxony-Anhalt	10/25-30	12/22-1/8	2/12-19	4/11-16	5/23-25	7/14-8/24
Schleswig-Holstein	10/4-16	12/23-1/8	—	4/4-16	5/27-28	7/4-8/13
Thuringia	10/25-11/6	12/23-31	2/12-19	4/11-23	5/27	7/18-8/27

Working parents enroll their children in a pre- and after-school program called *Hort* for a nominal fee (between €70 and €150/month, dependent on parents' income). There, students are served a lunch and finish their homework. Unfortunately, demand for placement in the program outstrips supply.

Grades

The most common grading system in Germany has six numerical levels as compared to the five letter grades (A, B, C, D, and F) assigned in the United States. German grades are expressed in three different ways, as numbers, descriptors, or points (*Sekundarstufe II*).

- "1" is "outstanding" and provides 15–13 points;
- "2"—"good"—12–10 points;
- "3"—"satisfactory"—9–7 points;
- "4"—"sufficient"—6–4 points;
- "5"—"not sufficient"—3–1 points;
- "6"—"fail"—0 points.

Twice a year, students receive their report cards, which usually include a teacher's general written evaluation.

Vacation

Typically, German schoolchildren enjoy at least five breaks of varying length per year: Winter-, Easter-, Summer-, Fall-, and Christmas-Vacation. The six weeks in the summer are staggered in the Federal States in order to avoid overtaxing the mass transit system or causing huge traffic jams on the *Autobahn* (see Table 8.4).

Katharina Barbe

See also: Chapter 1: Transportation. Chapter 8: *Schultüte*; Vocational Training (*Duale Ausbildung*).

Further Reading

Bundeszentrale für politische Bildung. "Das Bildungssystem in Deutschland." https://www.bpb.de/gesellschaft/bildung/zukunft-bildung/163283/das-bildungssystem-in-deutschland. Accessed October 1, 2019.

Familienportal. "Betreuung im Kinderhort." https://www.familie-und-tipps.de/Kinder/Kinderbetreuung/Kinderhort.html. Accessed October 1, 2019.

Newcombe, Norman. *Europe at School: A Study of Primary and Secondary Schools in France, West Germany, Italy, Portugal, & Spain.* London and New York: Routledge, 2019.

Wong, Kenneth K., Felix Knüpling, Mario Kölling, and Diana Chebenova. *Federalism and Education: Ongoing Challenges and Policy Strategies in Ten Countries.* Charlotte, NC: Information Age Publishing, 2018.

Schultüte

On their first day of school, German children get a *Schultüte*, a large decorated paper cone filled with goodies meant to "sweeten" the start of school. The ritual harks back to the late eighteenth century when the *Schultüte* was a smaller cone-shaped device akin to a pastry bag. The bag was stuffed with sweets, and thus the word *Zuckertüte* (sugar cone) often appears as an alternative term. The custom spread following the publication of the children's book *Der Zuckertütenbaum* (1928, the sugar cone tree), which claimed that the basements of schools have a special tree, where teachers pick a *Schultüte* for all the well-behaved children. Today 98% of students receive a *Schultüte*. Many prominent authors have written about the *Schultüte* or *Zuckertüte* they received on their first day of school. Erich Kästner, the author of *Das Doppelte Lottchen* (The double Lottchen, the basis for the *Parent Trap* movies in the United States) found a silken bow attached to his cone. He accidentally dropped his *Zuckertüte*, and the content that spilled out included dates, chocolate Easter bunnies, figs, oranges, tartlets, waffles, and other assorted other sweets. In Hans Peter Richter's novel *Damals war es Friedrich*, the chapter "Schulanfang 1931" (First Day of School) shows the Jewish protagonist Friedrich with a slightly larger *Schultüte* than that of the narrator. Discouraged by his mother from checking the content in public, the narrator notices later that his *Schultüte* contained mostly newspaper. As reflected in the book, during times of war or austerity, many children found mostly paper stuffing in their opaque cone and very few sweets. And still today only two out of one hundred beginning students do not get one.

The *Schultüte* has become a status symbol in Germany. Parents can purchase *Schultüten* filled with sweets, school supplies, and toys. Many parents also add money, clothes, and even smartphones to the cones. Refugees and immigrant families may not be familiar with the German custom of a *Schultüte*, and poor families may lack the means to purchase them. In Leipzig, for example, the Aktion Zuckertüte supplies *Schultüten* to needy children. In 2007, the supermarket chain Kaufland offered a special for the first day of school when parents and their children could stop by a store to fill their cones. In 2015, a newspaper conducted a survey and published a *Schultüten* Ranking. On average, parents spend about €72 for the cone and the content, with parents in the new *Länder*, the former East Germany, being more generous than parents in the old West German states. On average, a *Schultüte* in Saxony cost €105 (highest) and €56,45 in Niedersachsen (lowest).

Katharina Barbe

See also: Chapter 2: Overview. Chapter 4: Overview. Chapter 6: Immigration; Poverty. Chapter 8: Primary and Secondary Education.

Further Reading

Deutsche Welle. "Die *Schultüte*: Wie der Schulanfang in Deutschland Gefeiert Wird." https://www.dw.com/de/die-schult%C3%BCte-wie-der-schulanfang-in-deutschland -gefeiert-wird/a-19492315. Accessed October 1, 2019.

Deutsche Welle. "Why Germans Give Their Kids Paper Cones on the First Day of School." https://www.dw.com/en/why-germans-give-their-kids-paper-cones-on-the-first-day-of-school/a-19492362. Accessed June 9, 2020.

Die Bild. "Die Bundesländer im Schultüten-Ranking 2015." https://www.bild.de/ratgeber/kind-familie/erziehung/schultueten-bundeslaender-ranking-kosten-inhalt-42073164.bild.html. Accessed October 1, 2019.

Die Welt. "Wie die Schultüte in die Welt kam." https://www.welt.de/welt_print/kultur/article4358724/Wie-die-Schultuete-in-die-Welt-kam.html. Accessed October 1, 2019.

Fraser, Catherine C., and Dierk O. Hoffmann. *Pop Culture Germany! Media, Arts, and Lifestyle*. Santa Barbara, CA: ABC-CLIO, 2006.

Richter, Hans Peter. *Damals War Es Friedrich*. 65. Auflage. München: Deutscher Taschenbuch Verlag, 2016.

Schmideler, Sebastian, and Johan Zonneveld. *Erich Kästner, so noch nicht gesehen: Impulse Und Perspektiven: Internationales Kolloquium Aus Anlass Des Erscheinens Der Bibliographie Erich Kästner Von Johan Zonneveld: Tagungsband*. Marburg, Germany: Tectum Verlag, 2012.

Vocational Training (*Duale Ausbildung*)

Germany (as well as Switzerland and Austria) offers vocational training, the so-called *Duale Ausbildung*, to students who have finished the ninth or tenth grade. The *Duale Ausbildung* consists of further study in a *Berufsschule* (or vocational school) combined with a paid apprenticeship in a company. The curriculum for the *Duale Ausbildung* is developed by the Standing Conference of Ministers of Education (Kultusministerkonferenz) of the German states (*Länder*) in consultation with employers and trade unions.

Each year, approximately half of all students finishing their secondary education opt to pursue this dual vocational training. The apprentices, the *Auszubildende* (often abbreviated as *AZUBIS*), are simultaneously employees and students. Approximately 300 occupations in Germany require this type of training, from *Anlagenmechaniker* (automotive systems mechanic) to *Zweiradmechatroniker* (bicycle mechanic). In 2018, the favorite apprenticeship training for women was *Kauffrau für Büromanagement* (office clerk), followed by *Medizinische Fachangestellte* (medical assistant) and *Verkäuferin* (shop assistant); for men the preferred programs were *Mechatroniker* (mechanic), *Elektroniker* (electronic technician), and *Einzelhandelskaufmann* (retailer).

To become an office clerk, for example, students are required to attain Mittlere Reife, certifying ten years of schooling. The apprenticeship lasts an additional three years, during which the students earn a monthly salary of €760 in the first year, €810 in the second, and €860 in the final year. Typically, apprentices spend eight to twelve hours per week in school and the rest of the workweek on the job, learning such tasks as office management, acquisitions, accounting, and project management. Companies such as ALDI and the German Post pay monthly salaries of €1,500–2,500 to *Azubis* who have completed their *Ausbildung*.

To become a mechanic, students must complete the Mittlere Reife and spend an additional 3.5 years as an *Azubi*. The compensation during the apprenticeships starts with € 830–930/month and increases to €1010–1120 by the final year. The profession, once termed *Mechaniker*, has been renamed *Mechatroniker* to reflect the large amount of electronic skills it requires. Like the office clerks, the mechanics split their time between a vocational school, where they learn quality management, and a company, where they conduct repairs. On completion of the vocational training at companies such as the German Railroad or German Post, mechanics can expect a starting monthly salary of €1,800–2,100.

Students must pass two tests during their apprenticeship: the *Zwischenprüfung* (intermediate test) halfway through their internship and then the final examination. The examinations are organized by the Chamber of Commerce and Industry (Industrie- und Handelskammer) and designed by *Prüfungsausschüsse* or examination boards. The tests are standardized throughout the country and provide assurance to employers that the *Azubis* have the requisite skills and knowledge to become successful employees. The 2021 winter final examination for the office clerk test is scheduled for November 23–24 and for the mechanic on December 7–8.

Katharina Barbe

See also: Chapter 2: Wilhelm II (1859–1941). Chapter 3: Overview. Chapter 8: Primary and Secondary Education. Appendix A: A Day in the Life of a Mechatronic Technician (Dieter M.).

Further Reading

Ausbildung.de. "Kauffrau für Büromanagement." https://www.ausbildung.de/berufe /kauffrau-fuer-bueromanagement/. Accessed October 1, 2019.

Ausbildung.de. "Mechatroniker." https://www.ausbildung.de/berufe/mechatroniker/. Accessed October 1, 2019.

Bundesinstitut für Berufsbildung. "Prüfungen in der dualen Berufsausbildung," https:// www.bibb.de/veroeffentlichungen/de/publication/show/8276. Accessed October 1, 2019.

Hoeckel, Kathrin, and Robert Schwartz. "OECD Reviews of Vocational Education and Training: A Learning for Jobs Review of Germany 2010." Paris: OECD Publishing, 2010.

Hoffman, Nancy. *Schooling in the Workplace: How Six of the World's Best Vocational Education Systems Prepare Young People for Jobs and Life*. Cambridge, MA: Harvard Education Press, 2011.

Industrie- und Handelskammer. "Aufgabenstelle für kaufmännische Abschluss- un Zwischenprüfungen." ihk-aka.de. Accessed October 1, 2019.

Senatsverwaltung für Bildung, Jugend und Familie. "Duale Ausbildung." https://www .berlin.de/sen/bildung/schule-und-beruf/berufliche-bildung/berufliche-schulen /duale-ausbildung/. Accessed October 1, 2019.

CHAPTER 9

LANGUAGE

Katharina Barbe

OVERVIEW

Nearly 100 million people speak German as their native language. German is an official language in six countries (Germany, Austria, Switzerland, Belgium, Luxembourg, Liechtenstein) as well as in the autonomous province of South Tyrol in Italy. It is the most widely spoken mother tongue in the European Union.

Linguists classify German and English as West Germanic languages. Both languages share a linguistic history and belong to the Indo-European language family. German as a language is first mentioned in a 786 Latin document as *theodisce*, which refers to a language actually in use. The German word for the language initially appears in the ninth century as *diutisce* (related to *deutsch*).

Based on textual evidence. the development of German can be divided into several periods that show shared linguistic features. The linguistic terminology still in use originated with Jacob Grimm, who identified four distinct periods in the development of German: *Althochdeutsch* (OHG, Old High German) from 600 to 1050, *Mittelhochdeutsch* (MHG, Middle High German) from 1050 to 1350, *Frühneuhochdeutsch* (Early New High German) from 1350 to 1650, and *Neuhochdeutsch* (NHG, New High German) from 1650 to today.

The primary characteristic of **Old High German** is a sound shift in consonants that occurred in German but not English (this is still noticeable in the differences between contemporary German and English. It is important to note the sounds rather than the spelling of the consonants; for example, [χ] is pronounced like the **ch** in Lo**ch** Lomond (see Table 9.1).

Table 9.1:   SOUNDSHIFT

	Pronounced	English	German
p -> pf	[p]—[f]	**p**ound	**Pf**und
p -> ff	[p]—[f]	slee**p**	Schla**f**
t -> ts	[t]—[ts]	**t**wo	**z**wei
t -> ss	[t]—[s]	ea**t**	e**ss**en
k -> ch	[k]—[χ]	**c**ook	Ko**ch**
d -> t	[d]—[t]	**d**aughter	**T**ochter

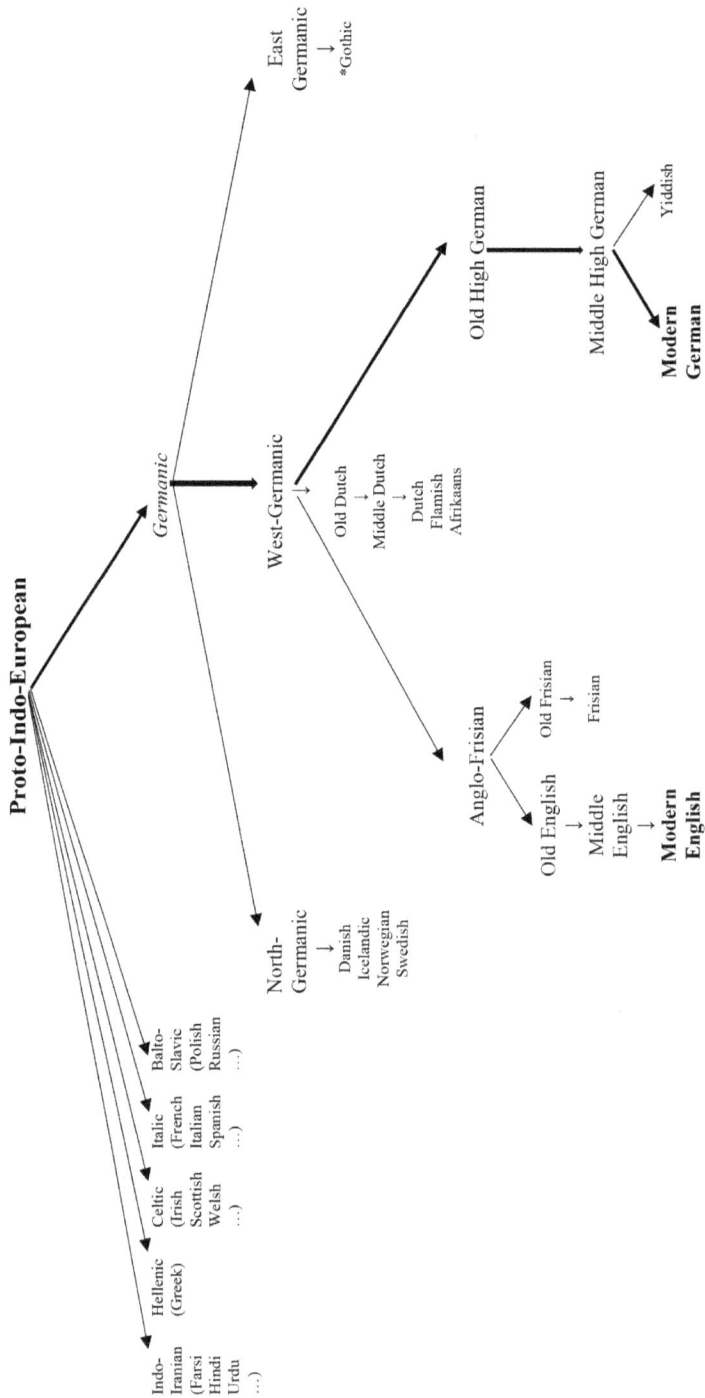

Proto-Indo-European

Indo-Iranian (Farsi Hindi Urdu ...)

Hellenic (Greek)

Celtic (Irish Scottish Welsh ...)

Italic (French Italian Spanish ...)

Balto-Slavic (Polish Russian ...)

Germanic

East Germanic
→
*Gothic

North-Germanic
→
Danish
Icelandic
Norwegian
Swedish

West-Germanic
→

Old Dutch
→
Middle Dutch
→
Dutch
Flamish
Afrikaans

Old High German
→
Middle High German
→
Yiddish
Modern German

Anglo-Frisian

Old Frisian
→
Frisian

Old English
→
Middle English
→
Modern English

Figure 9.1

THE GERMAN SOUNDSYSTEM

German and English share in the pronunciation of most consonants. Both differentiate between voiced and unvoiced consonants; for example, the **b** in **b**an is voiced, the **p** in **p**an is unvoiced. There are a few consonants in German that are not used in English and vice versa. Some consonant combinations provide difficulties for English speakers; for example, in **Kn**ie (knee), both the **k** and the **n** are pronounced in German and the k is silent in English; similarly, **Ps**ychologie, with **p** and **s**.

The **ch** in i**ch**, which is transcribed phonetically (as a sound) as [ç] and the **ch** in Na**ch**t (night) [χ] are not used in English. [ç] is unvoiced and [χ] voiced. English speakers have a sound approximating the [ç] word initially in **h**uge or **H**ugh. [χ] is close to the pronunciation of the **ch** in Lo**ch** Lomond. Many English speakers substitute a **k** for the **ch** in Na**ch**t, which produces the German word *nackt* (naked). Also [ts] as in **Z**eit (time) is a sound that English does not have at the beginning of a word, but at the end—ra**ts**—or in the middle—pi**zz**a. Sounds that are not found in German but in English are unvoiced [tʃ] like in **ch**air, voiced [dʒ] like in **J**ane, unvoiced [θ] like in e**th**er, and voiced [ð] like in ei**th**er.

Further Reading

Moulton, William G. *The Sounds of English and German*. Chicago: University of Chicago Press, 1962.

Middle High German (MHG) sees three major changes. (1) Vowels at the end of words, in the final syllable, became unstressed, while the primary stress on the *Stammsilbe* (syllable of the stem of a word) became stronger. So, vowels at the end of a multisyllable word started being pronounced by the so-called schwa; the phonetic transcription for schwa [ə] indicates a neutral unstressed vowel that can be represented in writing by any vowel. In English, the "a" in machine is pronounced with a schwa in normal speech; the "e" in the German word "Tage" is another example. (2) In addition, the *umlaut*, even though already present in OHG, spread further. An *umlaut*, another term coined by Jakob Grimm, also called *i-mutation*, is an assimilation of a vowel to a vowel in the following syllable, that is, the vowel is raised when the following syllable contains an "i". *Gast* (guest) was originally pluralized as "gasti." The final "i" "pulled" the "a" toward it, and as a result today we have *Gast* and its plural *Gäste*. (3) *Auslautverhärtung* denotes the devoicing of a final sound (a "b" is a voiced sound, whereas a "p" is unvoiced; both sounds are spoken using the upper and lower lip (bilabial) but are differentiated by voice). The English words **b**an and **p**an have different meanings, and the only difference is +/– voice. Final devoicing does not occur in English. In Standard German words like *lieb* (kind), *Fußweg* (path), or *Hund* (dog), the **b**, **g**, and **d** are pronounced [p], [k], or [t] respectively.

Early New High German's largest divergence from MHG is the vocabulary coming into German usage through Martin Luther's Bible translations. Before that, the Bible was primarily available to individuals who could read Latin or Greek. This excluded most people, as before 1520 the literacy rate was quite low (between 5% and

Table 9.2: HISTORY OF GERMAN

Name	Approximate Duration	Main Features
Old High German (OHG) *Althochdeutsch*	ca. 600–ca. 1050	High German Consonant Shift/Second Consonant Shift (2. *deutsche Lautverschiebung*)
Middle High German (MHG) *Mittelhochdeutsch*	ca. 1050–ca. 1350	Development of schwa (∂) in unstressed syllables
Early New High German *Frühneuhochdeutsch*	1350–1650	Expansion of the vocabulary through Luther's translations and other written works
New High German *Neuhochdeutsch*	since 1650	German grammar becomes standardized

30% depending on location). The invention of the printing press in 1439 and the subsequent printing of Luther's 1522 New Testament translation contributed to increased literacy as well as the formation of a common German dialect. Luther's German Bible translations had a unifying influence: his translation was far superior to any previous ones, and writers in other dialectal areas borrowed freely from his translations, thus spreading Luther's language.

Germany consisted of many small states and principalities that had taxing authorities and spoke their own dialect. A person from one area of Germany may not have been able to understand a person from another area. Germans living at the border to the Netherlands better understood a Dutch trader than one from Bavaria. Merchants who traveled through the land used Latin and French as the lingua franca rather than German. German universities taught in Latin, it was not until 1687, that German was first used. Until the nineteenth century, the ruling classes considered German to be unscientific, uneducated, and basically the language for the common people.

In the seventeenth and eighteenth centuries, *Sprachgesellschaften* (language societies) were formed after the French model. Members of these societies were interested in keeping the German language pure and free from foreign influences. The ultimate goal was to achieve a standard language with rules and to exchange *Fremdwörter* (foreign terms) with German ones. Regardless of these developments in the pursuit of a standardized German, the use of dialects was widespread, and most speakers, especially in rural areas, spoke a dialect.

A unified German state did not appear until 1871. Consequently, efforts to normalize German spelling appeared rather late, starting with the authoritative publication of *Regeln für die deutsche Rechtschreibung nebst Wortverzeichnis* (rules for the German orthography with a glossary). The reform movement has had a longer history. Around 1500, first spelling rules were discussed. Until the eighteenth century the spelling principles were *Schreibe so, wie du sprichst* ("Write as you speak") and consider the history of the words. Capitalization of nouns appeared in the seventeenth century. Konrad Duden (1829–1911), a schoolteacher, was asked to pursue the standardization of German orthography. He published the first *Duden Wörterbuch* in 1880. The *Duden* is currently in its twenty-seventh edition.

During the Third Reich, the Nazis (1933–45) attempted to unify the language. In this new Germany, there was only supposed to be *"ein Volk, eine Nation und ein Führer"* (one people, one nation and one leader). Dialects were considered an impediment to this goal. Numerous official prescriptions stipulated the sole use of standard German. In 1941, printing in *Fraktur* (black letter) and the use of the so-called German script, Sütterlin, in cursive were prohibited. The Nazis wanted to raise a new generation of citizens who considered themselves primarily German and not Bavarian or Hessian. Despite government pronouncements, schools continued to use dialect, and newspapers only changed gradually to the Antiqua script.

After the Second World War, the use of dialects became unpopular and was considered old-fashioned, especially during the *Wirtschaftswunder* (economic miracle) in the 1950s when people left their traditional home areas and moved freely around the country. The 1970s gave rise to a resurgence of interest in dialects. Plays and songs were written in dialect. Still, all German dialects do not have equal prestige.

English and German are both considered pluricentric languages: they are spoken in different countries with several standard varieties. Other countries such as Luxembourg and Belgium also use German, albeit in limited geographical areas, situations, and functions. Aside from Germany, German is the *Amtssprache* (official language) and the predominantly spoken language in Austria, Liechtenstein, and parts of Switzerland, the so-called DACH-L countries (D—**D**eutschland; A—**A**ustria; CH—**C**onfoederatio **H**elvetica, i.e. Switzerland; L—**L**iechtenstein).

Katharina Barbe

Further Reading

Besch, Werner et al., eds. *Sprachgeschichte: Ein Handbuch zur deutschen Sprachgeschichte und ihrer Erforschung.* Berlin: De Gruyter, 2004.

Braun, Peter. *Tendenzen der deutschen Gegenwartssprache: Sprachvarietäten.* Stuttgart: Kohlhammer, 1993.

Eggers, Hans. *Deutsche Sprachgeschichte III: Das Frühneuhochdeutsche.* Reinbek bei Hamburg: Rohwohlt, 1969.

Russ, Charles V. J. *The German Language Today: A Linguistic Introduction.* London: Routledge, 1994.

Schmidt, Wilhelm, ed. *Geschichte der deutschen Sprache: Ein Lehrbuch für das Germanistische Studium.* Stuttgart: Hirzel Verlag, 2008.

Von Polenz, Peter. *Deutsche Sprachgeschichte vom Spätmittelalter bis zur Gegenwart.* Berlin: De Gruyter, 1994.

Waterman, John T. *A History of the German Language.* Prospect Heights, IL: Wavelength Press, 1991.

Development of the Script

The first items written in German appeared relatively late (around the eighth century). Inscriptions on monuments use the so-called Carolingian minuscules, that is, non-capitalized letters written in the time of Charlemagne (742–814). These were clear, unified letters that were not connected or non-cursive, except for a few letter combinations such as "nt" or "rt."

Wessobrunner Gebet

Before the advent of the printing press, everything was written by hand, whether on parchment like the ninth-century book of spells and charms, the *Merseburger Zaubersprüche*; or chiseled into stone like the *Wessobrunner Gebet* of 790, the first Christian prayer (*Gebet*) in Old High German. This monument can still be found in the former Benedictine Monastery in Wessobrunn, southwest of Munich.

The development of writing is closely related to the materials available at the time. Most writing during the Middle Ages was done in the monasteries; the monks

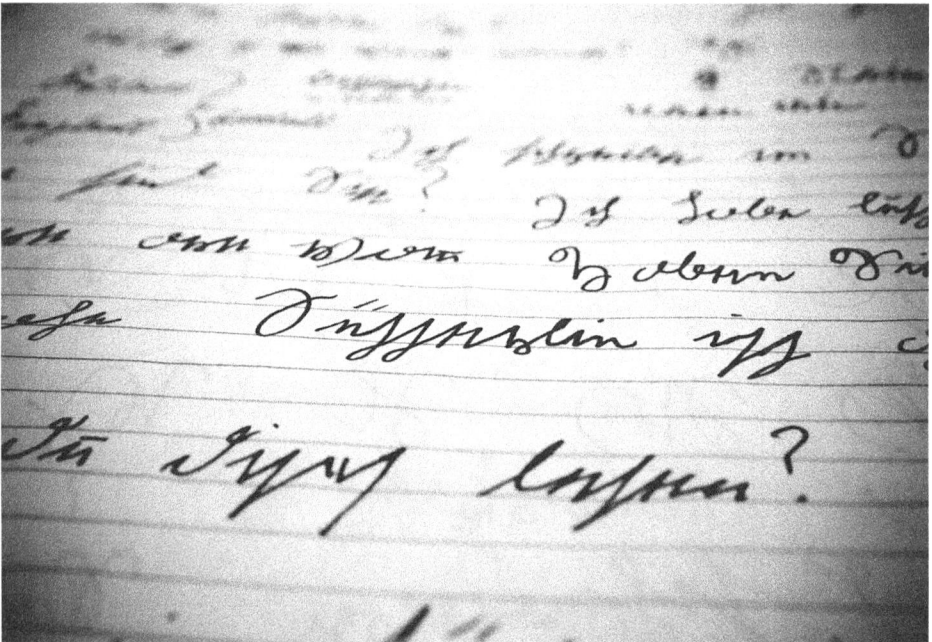

The pictured script is a sample of the Sütterlin script, developed by the graphic artist Ludwig Sütterlin (1865–1917) on behalf of the Royal Prussian Ministry of Culture in order to unify the different existing scripts. Sütterlin was used in schools officially from 1915–1941, and was also taught up until the 1970s as so-called Schönschrift (calligraphy) in some schools. (Ian Kahn/Dreamstime.com)

used quills (specially prepared goose feathers), which they dipped into ink. Until the fourteenth century, the monks wrote on parchment, made from animal skin. Later, they used paper, an invention imported from China, which was much more inexpensive to produce. Mistakes often occurred when scribes copied texts. Edited documents show strikethroughs or the errors were scraped out and corrected. At times, scribal errors remained uncorrected and can still be seen in medieval documents.

Gothic minuscules began appearing in the twelfth century. Letters in this script were written closer together than in Carolingian times, indicating the beginning of cursive. In the fifteenth century during the Renaissance, the so-called Latin script or Antiqua was rediscovered throughout Europe, except for Germany. With the invention of the printing press, printers had to learn to distinguish the various fonts and scripts to be used for different languages. Thus, in Germany, *Fraktur* or black letter, was employed for printed texts. *Fraktur*, formed from the document script of the chanceries, was a so-called broken script, where the curvature of the minuscules became angular. During the 1936 Olympic Games, newspapers printed in *Fraktur* included extras printed in Antiqua for the foreign guests.

In handwriting, the different Old German cursive scripts, called *Kurrent* (from the Latin *currere*, "run"), were normalized in the nineteenth century. The Prussian School and Culture Ministries asked the graphic artist Ludwig Sütterlin (1865–1917) to develop a script that elementary students could easily learn. His so-called Sütterlin script was in use from about 1900 to 1942 (the script was prohibited by the Nazis) and then again for a brief time after 1954. Since 1953, the *Lateinische Ausgangsschrift* (Latin basic letterform) has been taught to children throughout Germany except in Bavaria, where it was not introduced until 1966. Sütterlin was taught as *Schönschrift* (calligraphy) in schools until ca. 1970. As is the case in Finland, German educators are debating whether to teach two types of handwriting: cursive and non-cursive.

Katharina Barbe

See also: Chapter 2: Charlemagne (748–814). Chapter 9: Orthography and Reforms. Chapter 12: Carolingian Renaissance. Chapter 15: Olympic Games.

Further Reading

Bright, William, and Peter T. Daniels. *The World's Writing Systems*. New York: Oxford University Press, 1996.

Freunde der deutschen Kurrentschrift. "Deutsche Schreibschriften." http://www.deutsche-kurrentschrift.de/index.php?s=index_fraktur. Accessed February 11, 2020.

Read Sütterlin/Read Black Letters. http://www.suetterlinschrift.de/Englisch/Sutterlin.htm. Accessed February 11, 2020, in English.

Schneider, Karin. *Paläographie und Handschriftenkunde für Germanisten: Eine Einführung*, 3rd ed. durchgesehene Auflage. Berlin; Boston: De Gruyter, 2014.

Foreign Influences on German

Historically, the German language has been open to the lexical influence of other languages, predominantly Latin, French, and English. Latin has had a large influence on the development of the German language, particularly on its lexicon. Terms borrowed from other languages appeared in the areas of religion, warfare, administration, food, and architecture. Emperor Charles IV (1316–1378) decreed that anything written on religion had to be written in Latin. Thus, the Latin influence was immense and manifested itself not only in grammar (early German grammars incidentally were written in Latin) but also in many terms that entered the German spoken by the public.

Latin, a language unknown to the general public, was the lingua franca (the language used for teaching and research) at German universities. It was not until 1687 that Christian Thomasius (1655–1728) first used German in public in a university lecture, a revolutionary act at that time. It took another twenty-four years until lectures were held generally in German and thus made available to those who did not know Latin. In 1530, Luther advocated strongly for the ecclesiastical use of German in his *Sendbrief vom Dolmetschen*, or *An Open Letter on Translating*. The figure of the Latin scholar was mocked in plays like Gryphius's (1616–1664) *Horribilicribifax Teutsch,* which satirized the minimal knowledge of foreign languages by self-important scholars.

The influence of Latin diminished in the eighteenth and nineteenth centuries when the German aristocracy fell under the spell of everything French. As was the case with Latin, the use of French was largely restricted to a small group of people, the ruling classes and the aristocracy, who often spoke only rudimentary German. This practice was noted in the musings of the French philosopher Voltaire (1694–1778), who after visiting the Prussian emperor Frederick the Great, wrote "L'allemand est pour les soldats et pour les chevaux" (German is only for the soldiers and the horses).

French influence on the German vocabulary can be found predominantly in the areas of architecture, food, fashion, and social life. German verbs that end in *-ieren* are of French origin, such as *telefonieren* (to phone), *frisieren* (to fix one's hair), and *verlieren* (to lose). Many other French lexical terms have been Germanized, for example, der *Frisör/Frisöse* (hairdresser, male/female, from Fr. *friseur*), *blümerant* (feeling ill, from *bleu mourant*, a sickly blue color), and *Budike* (boutique). People who did not know French but wanted to sound French—and by extension educated—added as many French words as possible to their vocabulary. The migration of French Huguenots to Berlin also contributed to the widespread popularity of French. By 1700, nearly every fifth inhabitant was of French heritage.

A cartoon from around 1830 shows a boy with a lantern just having lit a man's cigar with the caption "Zigaro, mit avec du feu," or a cigar with fire. The phrase shows a curious mix: "Zigaro" refers to the German word for cigar, *Zigarre*; "mit" is German and "avec" is French for with; "du feu" is French for fire (Harndt, 1990).

Predominantly after the Second World War, British and American English constitute the third major wave of foreign contact with the German language. As was the

Table 9.3: **GERMAN, LATIN, AND ENGLISH COMPARISON**

German Term	Latin Term	English Term
Keller	celarius	cellar
Kloster	claustrum	cloister
Küche	coquina	kitchen
Mönch	monachus	monk
Pfeffer	piper	pepper
Strasse	stratum	street
Wein	vinum	wine
Zoll	tolonium	toll

case with French, the use of English words—*Anglizismen* and *Amerikanismen*—was and still is to an extent considered prestigious. Broder Carstensen distinguishes five types of lexical borrowings:

- Simple or direct loan—*smart, cool*
- Loan translation—flood light -> *Flutlicht*
- Loan creation or approximate translation—air conditioning -> *Klimaanlage* (climate system); note that the term *die Air Conditioning* is also used as a simple loan
- Semantic borrowing—existing word gets a new or additional meaning—*feuern* originally meant to light a fire but extended its meaning to let someone go from a job (to fire someone)
- Pseudo-loans—these are English words in German that do not exist in that meaning in English such as *das Handy* (cell phone) or *der Longdrink* (mixed drink)

English influences are largely limited to lexical items and pronunciation. Loans are adapted to German orthography, grammar, and word formation. Thus, the plural of *die Party* is *die Partys*; *das Girl* is neuter based on *das Mädchen* (the girl); *Mall* is usually feminine; *cool* gets adjective endings in *die coole Detektivin* (the cool detective) or *ich gebe der coolen Detektivin das Buch* (I am giving the book to the cool detective). Speakers often attempt to pronounce the terms in English, and occasionally the English pronunciation is made evident in terms like *Big Mäc*. The mingling of German and English has received a mixed reception. The so-called *Denglish* (**D**eutsch-**Eng**lish) is often lampooned, and artists like Gayle Tufts, who recently sent "Happy Greetings from Zuhause" (*Zuhause*—home), made a career out of it.

Katharina Barbe

See also: Chapter 6: Aristocracy and the Elites. Chapter 8: German Universities and *Fachhochschulen*. Chapter 9: Important Figures in the Study of the German Language; Orthography and Reforms. Chapter 16: Americanization.

Further Reading

Brunt, Richard James. *The Influence of the French Language on the German Vocabulary*. Berlin: De Gruyter, 1983.

Carstensen, Broder. *Amerikanismen der deutschen Gegenwartssprache; Entlehnungsvorgänge und ihre stilistischen Aspekte*. Heidelberg: C. Winter, 1963.

Eisenberg, Peter. *Das Fremdwort im Deutschen*. Berlin: De Gruyter, 2018.

Harndt, Ewald. *Französisch im Berliner Jargon*. Berlin: Stapp Verlag, 1990.

Russ, Charles V. J. *The German Language Today: A Linguistic Introduction*. London; New York: Routledge, 1994.

Schlobinski, Peter. *Berlinisch für Berliner und alle, die es werden wollen*. Berlin: Arana, 1984.

Schulz, H. *Die Bestrebungen der Sprachgesellschaften des XVII. Jahrhunderts für die Reinigung der deutschen Sprache*. Göttingen, Germany: Vandenhoeck & Ruprecht's Verlag, 1888.

Gesellschaft für deutsche Sprache

The Gesellschaft für deutsche Sprache (GfdS, or Association for the German Language) is a member of the Deutsche Sprachrat (German Language Council). Along with its other members, the Institute for the German Language, the Goethe-Institut, and the German Academic Exchange Service, the GfdS promotes instruction and research in the German language.

In 1885, the Allgemeine Deutsche Sprachverein (ADSV, General German Language Union) was founded with the goal of protecting the purity of the German language. The ADSV grew quickly and soon published the journal Muttersprache (*Mother Tongue*). Renamed the Deutscher Sprachverein (DSV) in 1935, the DSV was sympathetic to the Nazi regime until its doors were closed in 1943. The GfdS was founded as a successor organization to the DSV in 1947. Two years later, the GfdS restarted the publication of Muttersprache, which today is a very prestigious journal.

Starting in 1952, the GfdS published Der Sprachfreund (language friend), later renamed *Der Sprachdienst* (language service), which contains the organization's calendar and miscellanea that deal with German language issues. The GfdS's mission and main tasks are to deepen public awareness of the German language, cultivate and maintain it (*Sprachpflege*), critically observe its development, and provide advice based on sound research. The GfdS fields questions from the public regarding the proper use of German and, for a fee, assists patrons in writing letters, choosing an acceptable name for a child, and determining an appropriate name for a new product. The GfdS also has an office in the German Parliament (Deutscher Bundestag), where the editorial staff assists the government in the writing of understandable legislation.

In 1977, the GfdS started to publish the "Words of the Year." Many people in East Germany (*Ossies*, or Easterners) considered their Western counterparts (*Wessis*) arrogant and condescending. Hence, the first "Word of the Year" following the reunification of Germany in 1990 was *Besserwessi*, a play on the German words *Besserwisser* ("know it all") and *Wessi*. The GfdS was also involved in the publication of *100 Wörter*

BABY NAMES 2020

Starting in 1977, the GfdS has queried local registries to provide baby names. With an over 90% response rate, the GfdS has published a list of the most favorite first names.

	2020 Favorite First Names
Girls	Boys
1. Emilia	1. Noah
2. Hanna/Hannah	2. Leon
3. Emma	3. Paul
4. Sophia/Sofia	4. Matteo
5. Mia	5. Ben
6. Lina	6. Elias
7. Mila	7. Finn
8. Ella	8. Felix
9. Lea/Leah	9. Henry/Henri
10. Klara/Clara	10. Louis/Luis

---

des Jahrhunderts (100 words of the century), a book that reads like a lexical history of twentieth century. Starting in 1991, the GfdS selects the *Unwort des Jahres* (worst word of the year), which was *ausländerfrei* (free of foreigners) and referred to a rallying cry of xenophobic demonstrations in Hoyerswerda, Germany (September 17–23, 1991).

The GfdS has grown quickly since its inception. Each German federal state has a branch, and the organization opened its one-hundredth affiliate in London in 2010. Worldwide, the GfdS is represented in thirty-seven countries on four continents.

Katharina Barbe

See also: Chapter 8: DAAD; Goethe-Institut. Chapter 9: Grammar; Institut für deutsche Sprache.

Further Reading

Deutscher Bundestag. "Leichte Sprache." https://www.bundestag.de/leichte_sprache /was_macht_der_bundestag. Accessed February 11, 2020.

Gesellschaft für deutsche Sprache. "Gfds." https://gfds.de/ueber-die-gfds/. Accessed February 11, 2020.

Gesellschaft für deutsche Sprache. "GfdS in Geschichte und Gegenwart." https://gfds.de /wp-content/uploads/2018/02/Brosch%C3%BCre-70-Jahre-GfdS-Doppelseiten -geringe-Gr%C3%B6%C3%9Fe.pdf. Accessed February 11, 2020.

Parlamentsdeutsch. "Grundbegriffe des Bundestages in einfacher Sprache." https://www .btg-bestellservice.de/pdf/40351010.pdf.

Schneider, Wolfgang, ed. *100 Wörter des Jahrhunderts*. Frankfurt am Main: Suhrkamp, 1999.

Wirth, Karoline. *Der Verein deutsche Sprache. Hintergrund, Entstehung, Arbeit und Organisation eines deutschen Sprachvereins*. Bamberg, Germany: University of Bamberg Press, 2010.

Grammar

Many speakers are perfectly happy using their language and expressing themselves without being explicitly aware of its grammar. The rules of grammar are generally descriptive, in that they are based on observations of the regular use of language. While English and German are both classified as West Germanic languages, and thus share many grammatical similarities, significant differences remain.

Both English and German nouns indicate number (singular and plural) through changes on the nouns, usually by adding plural endings, such as an **-s** or an **-en**. German also inflects, that is, changes the form of a word, for gender (masculine, feminine, neuter) and cases (nominative, genitive, dative, and accusative). In both languages, the subject or nominative indicates the "doer," the direct object or accusative the "object" and the indirect object or dative the object that something is done to. In English, the relationships of the parts of speech are indicated through their relative position in a sentence (e.g., the subject appears in first position). German has much more flexible word order because the relationships are shown on the nouns through the case endings (Table 9.4).

Another feature of German nouns that is also often lampooned is compounding, that is, the formation of new with existing words. Compounding has proved very productive to the German language, leading to an increase in its lexicon. Simply, a

Table 9.4: WORD ORDER

Der Hund	*beißt*	*den Mann.*	=>	Der Hund (dog) is the biter
Nominativ		Akkusativ		
The dog	bites	the man.	=>	The dog is the biter
Subject		Direct Object		

What happens when the nouns are exchanged?

Den Mann	*beißt*	*der Hund.*	=>	Der Hund is still the biter.

The articles—*den* and *der*—indicate the functions of the nouns.

The man	bites	the dog.	=>	The man is the biter.

MARK TWAIN ON THE GERMAN LANGUAGE

In my note-book I find this entry:

. . . the length of German words. Some German words are so long that they have a perspective. Observe these examples:

Freundschaftsbezeigungen. Dilettantenaufdringlichkeiten. Stadtverordnetenversammlungen.

These things are not words, they are alphabetical processions. And they are not rare; one can open a German newspaper at any time and see them marching majestically across the page. . . . "Freundschaftsbezeigungen" seems to be "Friendship demonstrations," which is only a foolish and clumsy way of saying "demonstrations of friendship." "Unabhaengigkeitserklaerungen" seems to be "Independencedeclarations," which is no improvement upon "Declarations of Independence," so far as I can see. "Generalstaatsverordnetenversammlungen" seems to be "General-statesrepresentativesmeetings," as nearly as I can get at it—a mere rhythmical, gushy euphuism for "meetings of the legislature," I judge.

---

compound is a word that has more than one root. For example, *Hausarbeit* (housework, also homework) contains two nouns, *Haus* (house) and *Arbeit* (work). A noun and an adjective *hundemüde* (dog + tired, very tired) or a verb and a noun as in *Lesebuch* (read + book, reader) can also be joined. In addition, prefixes, suffixes, connecting elements, and so on are involved in word formation.

Germans apparently like these long words, which is evidenced by contests such as the one from the late 1980s conducted by the Gesellschaft für deutsche Sprache. The GfdS gave the task to form the longest German word without repeating any letter. The winner was *Heizölrückstoßabdämpfung*, which according to the winner means *die Abdämpfung des Rückstoßes, der beim Leitungstransport von Heizöl entstehen kann* or the minimization of the recoil, which can appear during the pipeline transport of heating oil. Mark Twain bitterly complained about German compounding.

In 1999, one of the GfdS's words of the year was *Rindfleischetikettierungsüberwachungsaufgabenübertragungsgesetz*, a legitimate word that is, however, no longer in use after EU law changes. In order to decode a word like this one must start at the end. So, it is a law (*Gesetz*) that governs "the delegation of monitoring beef labeling." A term written about a lot is *Lebensabschnittsgefährte*, which denotes a partner for a particular phase of one's life, that will sooner or later be concluded, that is, the relationship's end is foreseeable.

Leben—	*s—*	*abschnitt—*	*s—*	*gefährte*
Life—	(genitive s)—phase—		(genitive s)—partner	
Lebensabschnitt—phase of life				

Katharina Barbe

See also: Chapter 9: Development of the Script; Gesellschaft für deutsche Sprache; Orthography and Reforms.

Further Reading

Dartmouth. "Compound Words (Komposita). Word-Formation in German." http://www .dartmouth.edu/~deutsch/Grammatik/Wortbildung/Komposita.html. Accessed February 11, 2020.

Fox, Anthony. *The Structure of German*. Oxford, UK: Clarendon Press, 1990.

The Telegraph. "Germany Drops Its Longest Word." https://www.telegraph.co.uk/news/ worldnews/europe/germany/10095976/Germany-drops-its-longest-word-Rindfleischeti. . . .html. Accessed February 11, 2020.

Important Figures in the Study of the German Language

Many individuals promoted the study of the German language. Christian Thomasius (1655–1728) was the first to use German—and not Latin—in his university lectures. Johannes Gutenberg (1400–1468)—through the invention of the printing press in the fifteenth century—made it possible that research could be published and thus find a wider audience. Wilhelm von Humboldt (1767–1835) advanced the study of language in general. Three other outstanding figures were instrumental in the development of German, namely Martin Luther, who is often called the founder of German, and the Brothers Grimm, who are widely known for their collection of fairy tales.

Martin Luther (1483–1546)

Martin Luther touched a national nerve with his translation of the Bible. Prior to his time, German translations of the Bible—such as Johan Mentel's in 1461, which appeared in fourteen editions—were cumbersome to read and thus not attractive to the general public. In contrast, Luther sought to write a translation for a wide audience. He used the popular German of the time and laid out how he translated the Bible in his *Tischreden* (after-dinner speeches) and his famous *Sendbrief vom Dolmetschen (An Open Letter on Translating)*. In the latter he thundered against his Catholic adversaries and how they use his slightly adjusted Bible translation as their own, using choice language, calling adversaries colorful names. Luther was thus aware that his translations formed the basis for the work of other translators, often without attribution (which today would be a violation of copyright law). His Bible sold over 100,000 copies between 1534 and 1584, a significant figure given that the literacy rate of the time hovered around 16%. In other dialect areas, Luther's Bible was often printed with a glossary, and people used it as a pattern for their own language. His translation of the Bible formed the basis of Early New High German, the dominant literary language of the land by the end of the sixteenth century.

LUTHER ABOUT THE LANGUAGE IN HIS BIBLE TRANSLATION

When talking about his Bible translation and why he used German, Luther said in his *Sendbrief vom Dolmetschen* and his *Tischreden*:

"We do not have to ask about the literal Latin or how we are to speak German—as these asses do. Rather we must ask the mother in the home, the children on the street, the common person in the market about this. We must be guided by their tongue, the manner of their speech, and do our translating accordingly. Then they will understand it and recognize that we are speaking German to them."
(http://www.gutenberg.org/cache/epub/272/pg272-images.html)

Excerpt from *Tischreden:*

"I haven't any certain, special language of my own, but I use the common German language so that both North and South Germans can understand me. I speak according to the Saxon Chancery, which all the princes and kings in Germany follow; all Imperial Towns, princely courts write according to the Saxon Chancery of our prince, therefore that is the most common German language. Emperor Maximilian and Elector Frederick, Duke of Saxony have thus drawn together the German languages into one." (op cit. Russ, 15)

Brothers Grimm

A product of their time in the Romantic period, Jacob (1785–1863) and Wilhelm (1786–1859) Grimm compiled fairy tales, advancing the study of both German folklore and the German language. The Brothers Grimm are widely accepted as the founders of not only German philology but also philology in general. The second German sound shift is often referred to as Grimm's Law. Jacob Grimm in his meticulous *Deutsche Grammatik* (*German Grammar*, 1818) took a descriptive approach, that is, he wanted to *describe* how the language worked and *not prescribe* how speakers were supposed to use the language. Stylistically, Grimm capitalized words only at the beginning of a sentence and used lowercase letters elsewhere (modern German grammar capitalized all nouns). Both brothers began work on the *Deutsches Wörterbuch* (German Dictionary) in 1838. The entries *A–Frucht* (A–Fruit) were published during

Renowned throughout the world for their peerless collection of fairy tales, Jacob Grimm and Wilhelm Grimm were also innovative philologists and professors of German language whose works still influence scholars today. (Library of Congress)

their lifetime. The entire dictionary was not completed until 1961 and essentially remains a work in progress.

Katharina Barbe

See also: Chapter 5: Luther, Martin (1483–1546). Chapter 9: Foreign Influences on German.

Further Reading

Füssel, Stephan. *The Book of Books: The Luther Bible of 1534. A Cultural-Historical Introduction*. Köln: Taschen, 2003.

Grimm, Jacob. *Deutsche Grammatik*, 1822. https://archive.org/details/deutschegrammati01grim/page/n4. Accessed February 11, 2020.

Grimm, Jacob, and Wilhelm Grimm. *Deutsches Wörterbuch*. http://dwb.uni-trier.de/de/. Accessed February 11, 2020.

Hettinga, Donald R. *The Brothers Grimm: Two Lives, One Legacy*. New York: Clarion Books, 2001.

Luther, Martin. *An Open Letter to Translation*. Gary Mann, trans. http://www.gutenberg.org/cache/epub/272/pg272-images.html. Accessed February 11, 2020.

Luther, Martin. "Sendbrief vom Dolmetschen." https://www.bibel-in-gerechter-sprache.de/wp-content/uploads/sendbrief.pdf. Accessed February 11, 2020.

Institut für deutsche Sprache

Founded on April 19, 1964, the Leibniz Institut für deutsche Sprache (IDS, Leibniz Institute for German language) in Mannheim, Baden-Württemberg, is together with the Deutscher Akademischer Austauschdienst, the Gesellschaft für deutsche Sprache and the Goethe-Institut a member of the Deutscher Sprachrat, the German Language Council. Originally, the IDS arose as West Germany's response to East Germany's founding of a linguistic institute as part of the DDR Akademie der Wissenschaften (Academy of Sciences). The IDS is an independent and extramural organization that is financed partly by the state Baden-Württemberg and partly by the federal government. Such freedom from financial considerations provides the IDS with independence from economic and political interests. Currently, the IDS employs a staff of 140.

The IDS understands itself primarily as an interface between language usage and language research and thus focuses its inquiries on three areas of the German language, namely, grammar, the lexicon, and pragmatics (i.e., the actual use of language in context). In grammar, they support research projects into the description of written and spoken German, potential changes that can be observed, grammatical structures of current German, and focus on language technology and information systems. In the lexicon, they investigate the changes that are easily observable with the influx of vocabulary from other languages; scholars research the lexical inventory of German as it is currently used and as it was used in its most recent history. In pragmatics, scholars affiliated with the IDS observe basically who speaks how, where, and when. In order to have materials for this research, the IDS maintains a number of corpora, that is, collections of natural occurring language samples. For example, Das Deutsche Referenzkorpus (DeReKo, the German reference corpus) contains 28 billion words collected from literary, scientific and popular scientific texts, newspapers and other text types and is accessible for free. Like other organizations dealing with German language in research and teaching, the IDS does not pursue a prescriptive approach to German but rather a descriptive one.

The Rat für deutsche Rechtschreibung, the commission for German orthography, also has a seat at the IDS. As such, it coordinates the activities, prepares the meetings, is the public face for questions and inquiries, functions as the connection to the media and the responsible government institutions, advises in questions of the current orthography and coordinates the investigation into the development of orthography, and archives and administers materials related to orthography.

Katharina Barbe

See also: Chapter 8: DAAD; Goethe-Institut. Chapter 9: Gesellschaft für deutsche Sprache.

Further Reading

IDS. Leibniz-Institut für deutsche Sprache. http://www1.ids-mannheim.de/index.php?id=1. Accessed February 9, 2020.

Wirth, Karoline. *Der Verein deutsche Sprache. Hintergund, Entstehung und Organisation eines deutschen Sprachvereins*. Bamberg, Germany: University of Bamberg Press, 2010.

Language Development in Divided Germany

After the Second World War, the victorious allies divided Germany and its capital, Berlin, each into four separate zones of occupation. The French, British, and American zones became the Federal Republic of (West) Germany (the FRG or *BRD*), and the Soviet zone became the (East) German Democratic Republic (GDR or *DDR*). Berlin had a separate status. These two parallel political and educational systems each produced their own terminology, understandably due to different conditions. Scholars investigating the vocabularies of the two Germans rely on *Duden*, a standard dictionary of German and its orthography. The Duden was first published in 1880 and has now appeared in twenty-seven editions. Each edition of the Duden reflected the written and spoken German of its time, thus the eleventh and twelfth editions, published during the Third Reich, contain newly developed Nazi-related vocabulary. After the postwar formation of separate German states, East and West Germany each compiled their own edition of the Duden, published, respectively, in Leipzig and Mannheim. After reunification, an *Einheits-duden* (common Duden)—the twentieth edition—appeared in 1991.

Comparisons of the two Duden published in the East and the West demonstrate terminological differences, as different political and societal experiences led to new coinages in vocabulary. Some terms signified disparate ideological viewpoints of the same event. On the one hand, in the West, individuals who provided *Fluchthilfe* (assistance to escape) were considered heroes when they assisted East German citizens in their quest to reach the West. In the East, on the other hand, the same action was considered *Menschenhandel* (human trafficking).

Of the 150,000 entries in the East Duden, ca. 300, and thus a relatively small number, are unique vocabulary items. These include:

- New formations from existing words (250 items); the term *Autorenkollektiv, a* "group of authors," borrowed the term *kollektiv* from Russian.
- New meanings for old terms (41 items); *Brigade*, once used solely in a military context, referred to a group of workers.

In addition, the seventeenth edition of the East *Duden* contains a further 300 borrowings from Russian (and very few from English). In the eighteenth edition of the West *Duden*, ca. 1,400 English borrowing can be found. The common twentieth edition of the *Duden* retained the items unique to the East *Duden* but included the designation *besonders DDR* (especially DDR) in the entries.

For ideological reasons, some linguists in the GDR sought to demonstrate that the German spoken in the East developed separately from that spoken in the West. Although the two Germanies were separated for forty years, a very brief period in terms of language development and change, linguistic contact between the two nations persisted. West German television was watched throughout East Germany with the exception of the areas sarcastically referred to as the *Tal der Ahnungslosen* or the valley of the clueless, two areas in the northeast and southeast of the GDR.

Katharina Barbe

See also: Chapter 2: Overview. Chapter 3: Government and Politics in the German Democratic Republic. Chapter 16: Overview; *Ostalgie*.

Further Reading

Ammon, Ulrich. "The Differentiation of the German Language into National Varieties of the Federal Republic of Germany (FRG), the German Democratic Republic (GDR), Austria and Switzerland." *History of European Ideas* 13 (1–2): 75–88, 1991.

Auflagen des Duden (1880–2020). https://www.duden.de/ueber_duden/auflagengeschichte. Accessed February 11, 2020.

Clyne, Michael. *Language and Society in the German-Speaking Countries*. Cambridge, UK: Cambridge University Press, 1984.

Hellmann, Manfred W., and Marianne Schröder, eds. *Sprache und Kommunikation in Deutschland Ost und West. Ein Reader zu 50 Jahren Forschung.* Hildesheim, Germany: Germanistische Linguistik, 2008.

Jackman, Graham. *Finding a Voice: Problems of language in East-German Society and Culture*. Amsterdam; Atlanta, GA: Rodopi, 2000.

Matthees, Regina. "Elternaktiv zur DDR-Zeit." http://research.uni-leipzig.de/fernstud /Zeitzeugen/zz144.htm. Accessed February 9, 2020.

Röhl, E. "Deutsche Sprache der DDR. Nostalgischer Rückblick." *Sprachpflege und Sprachkultur 3, 83–85, 1990.*

Wojtak, Barbara. *"Rede—Wendungen" in "Wende—Reden." Deutsch als Fremdsprache,* 47–51, 1991.

Wolf, Birgit. *Sprache in der DDR: Ein Wörterbuch.* Berlin: De Gruyter, 2000.

Wolf-Bleiß, Birgit. "Sprache und Sprachgebrauch in der DDR," 2010. http://www.bpb.de /politik/grundfragen/sprache-und-politik/42769/ddr-sprache. Accessed February 9, 2020.

Language Development in the Third Reich

The language of the Third Reich (1933–1945) was characterized by changes in meanings of existing words, euphemisms (the use of innocuous words for embarrassing or unpleasant occurrences), new terminology, and copious abbreviations. The Nazis thought that the use of uniform language would lead to uniform thought and thus strengthen their control of the country. The Jewish intellectual Victor Klemperer (1881–1960) kept diaries that included meticulous linguistic observations. Klemperer was constantly harassed, and his home was frequently raided. However, he managed to survive the Third Reich because of his so-called *Mischehe* (intermarriage to a non-Jewish spouse). Klemperer noticed how people, even those opposed to the regime, slowly incorporated Nazi words into their vocabulary. He considered the language of Nazism a breeding ground for Nazi ideology, which he compared to a poison that one is unknowingly ingesting, slowly making its way through an individual's language.

Soon after the Nazis seized power in 1933, they issued two decrees that strictly limited press freedom. Rather than censor articles after they had been written, they resorted to issue prepublication directives during daily press briefings. These confidential instructions appeared under a variety of names, such as *Sprachregelungen* (language regulations/instructions), *Presseanweisungen* (press briefings), *Pressebestellungen* (press messages), and *Verlautbarungen* (bulletins). The recipients were a select audience of journalists who were tasked with incorporating this information into their respective papers. Under the threat of retribution, journalists were ordered to treat their handwritten notes as confidential, to share them with selected and trusted colleagues, and to destroy them regularly. Over time, the newspapers became so similar that many readers dropped their subscriptions (which resulted in follow-up instructions to make the papers less uniform).

The language instructions included very precise, granular directives down to single terms. A 1939 directive instructed that the term *tapfer* (courageous) was only to be applied to German soldiers. Similarly, a 1941 directive demanded that the term *Kampfflugzeug* (combat aircraft) was only to be used for German planes.

Because the state had control over all media, dictionaries were also modified to reflect the new, approved terminology. The *Duden*, the semiofficial German dictionary, appeared in its eleventh (1934) and twelfth (1941) editions during the Nazi reign. Each edition added new items, 180 in 1934 and 883 in 1941. The twelfth edition added such terms as *Rassenschande* (racial defilement), *Volljude* (fully Jewish), and *Volksschädling* (pest of the people). Most of these terms were deleted in the thirteenth edition, the first postwar edition in 1947.

Katharina Barbe

YIDDISH IN GERMAN

Yiddish appeared over nine centuries ago in areas around the Rhine. Hebrew, German, and Romance languages contributed in the beginning, and since about the thirteenth century, Slavic elements were added. In addition, the lexicon increases through words from places where the speakers reside. Today, Yiddish retains words that are no longer used in German. In the beginning of the twentieth century, Yiddish was spoken by about 11 million speakers; today, after the Holocaust, there are about 4–5 million speakers all over the world. Yiddish is written with the Hebrew script and from right to left.

German	Yiddish Origin	English
ausgekocht (kochen—cook)	kocherem—to prepare, plan	crafty
dufte	toff(te), taff—good, lovely	neat, smashing
Kaff, das	kefar—village	dump, Hicksville
malochen	melochnen—work	slave away
Mischpoke/Mischpoche, die	mischpocho—family	clan, awful company
Moos, das	moo—penny moos (plural)—money	loot, money
Pleitegeier, der (Geier—vulture)	plejta—flight gejer—someone, who goes/runs away	bankruptcy vulture (as a sign for impending bankruptcy)
Schlamassel, das	schlamassel—misfortune (massel—fortune)	mess
Tinnef, der	tinnef—dirt, feces	useless stuff
Zoff, der	zoff—Ende	trouble

Further Reading

Althaus, Hans Peter. *Chuzpe, Schmus & Tacheles. Jiddische Wortgeschichten.* München: Beck'sche Reihe, 2004.

Bastian Sick. "Jiddische Wörter in der deutschen Sprache." https://bastiansick.de/kolumnen/zwiebelfisch/von-abzocke-bis-zoff-jiddische-woerter-in-der-deutschen-sprache/. Accessed February 9, 2020.

Yudel, Mark. "The Yiddish Language: Its cultural impact." In Joshua Fishman, ed. *Never Say Die! A Thousand Years of Yiddish in Jewish Life and Letters.* Berlin: De Gruyter, 1981.

See also: Chapter 6: Jews in Germany. Chapter 9: Grammar; Orthography and Reforms. Chapter 16: Journalism under the Nazi Regime.

Further Reading

Brackmann, Karl-Heinz, and Renate Birkenhauer. *NS-Deutsch. "Selbstverständliche" Begriffe und Schlagwörter aus der Zeit des Nationalsozialismus.* Straelen, Germany: Straelener Manuskripte Verlag, 2001.

Hutton, Christopher. *Linguistics and the Third Reich: Mother-Tongue Fascism, Race, and the Science of Language.* London: Routledge, 1999.

Klemperer, Victor. *The Language of the Third Reich: LTI, Lingua Tertii Imperii: A Philologist's Notebook.* Martin Brady, trans. London: Athlone Press, 2000.

Michael, Robert, and Karin Doerr. *Nazi-Deutsch/Nazi-German: An English Lexicon of the Language of the Third Reich.* Westport, CT: Greenwood Press, 2002.

Schmitz-Berning, Cornelia. "Sprache und Sprachlenkung im Nationalsozialismus." https://www.bpb.de/politik/grundfragen/sprache-und-politik/42752/sprache-zur-ns-zeit?p=all. Accessed July 15, 2020.

Schmitz-Berning, Cornelia. "Vokabeln im Nationalsozialismus." http://www.bpb.de/politik/grundfragen/sprache-und-politik/42759/ns-vokabeln?p=all. Accessed July 15, 2020.

Schmitz-Berning, Cornelia. *Vokabular des Nationalsozialismus.* Berlin: De Gruyter, 2000.

Orthography and Reforms

"Unter Orthographie verstehen wir die Norm der Schreibung einer Sprache."
As orthography, we understand the norm of writing of a language.

Dieter Nerius, 1994

German orthography remains a work in progress. Historically, because Germany was comprised of many fiefdoms, the country's orthography was not unified but consisted of numerous so-called *Hausrechtsschreibungen* (orthographies according to local conventions). The First Orthographic Conference met in 1876 to codify the spelling of German words. The conference considered

- Language usage and norms
- Observations about the development of writing
- The relationship between sounds and the corresponding letters
- Contentious cases, such as the spelling of foreign words
- Inconsistencies in spelling

The 1876 conference failed to adopt a national orthography. In attendance, however, was Konrad Duden (1829–1911), who would go on to write and give his name to the authoritative German dictionary that bears his name. Konrad Duden persisted; working under the principle *Schreibe, wie du sprichst* ("Write like you speak"), he published the *Vollständiges Orthographisches Wörterbuch der deutschen Sprache*

(Complete Orthographic Dictionary of the German Language) in 1880. Duden's dictionary had appeared in six editions by the time the Second Orthographic Conference was convened in 1901 when he was tasked with overseeing the orthographic reform of the German language. The Duden Verlag became a semiofficial (*halbamtliche*) institution, and its publication of the seventh edition (1903) of Duden's orthographie became the first dictionary of the German language. The *Duden* is in its twenty-seventh edition (2017) with 145,000 items and contains the official orthography for Germany, Austria, and Switzerland.

The Spelling Reform of 1996 added 112 new rules governing German orthography. Germany, Austria, Switzerland, and Liechtenstein pledged to implement the changes by 1998. Controversy regarding the Spelling Reform ensued and was only resolved when the courts ruled that the reforms were lawful. The reforms were finally implemented in 2010 by the Rat für deutsche Rechtschreibung (RdR—Council for German Orthography). The RdR is comprised of academics, educators, and publishers with representatives from Germany (eighteen members), Austria (nine), Switzerland (nine), Liechtenstein (one), German-speaking Belgium (one), Südtirol in Northern Italy (one), and an ex-officio representative from Luxembourg.

Katharina Barbe

See also: Chapter 9: Development of the Script; Foreign Influences on German; Grammar.

Further Reading

Duden, Konrad. *Vollständiges Orthographisches Wörterbuch der deutschen Sprache*, 1888. https://archive.org/details/vollstndigesort03dudegoog/page/n11. Accessed February 9, 2020.

Duden Wörterbuch. https://www.duden.de. Accessed February 9, 2020.

Graf, Peter. *Was nicht mehr im Duden steht: Eine Sprach- und Kulturgeschichte*. Berlin: Dudenverlag, 2018.

Johnson, Sally A. *Spelling Trouble? Language, Ideology and the Reform of German Orthography*. Clevedon, UK: Multilingual Matters, 2005.

Rat für deutsche Rechtschreibung. "Regel- und Wörterverzeichnis." https://www.rechtschreibrat.com/DOX/rfdr_Regeln_2016_redigiert_2018.pdf. Accessed February 9, 2020.

Schimmel-Fijalkowytsch, Nadine. *Diskurse zur Normierung und Reform der deutschen Rechtschreibung*. Tübingen, Germany: Narr, 2018.

Sprachgesellschaften (Language Societies)

Sprachgesellschaften (language societies) appeared in Germany in the seventeenth century and were patterned after similar societies in France and Italy. One of the most important and well-known *Sprachgesellschaft* was the Fruchtbringende Gesellschaft

(Fruitbearing Society), founded by Prince Ludwig von Anhalt-Köthen (1579–1650). The *Sprachgesellschaften* had many stated goals, above all the *"Reinhaltung der deutschen Sprache"* (maintaining the purity of the German language). This society took significant pride in the original German language (*Ursprache*).

The Fruitbearing Society was composed of aristocrats and influential scholars such as the poet Martin Opitz (1597–1639), the grammarian Justus Georg Schottel or Schottelius (1612–1676), and the poet and author Andreas Gryphius (1616–1664). In his 1617 speech "Aristarchus sive de contempt linguae Teutonicae," the twenty-year-old Opitz lamented, in Latin no less, the careless use of German and its reliance on foreign words. He also advocated for German to be used in poetry. His 1624 *Buch von der Deutschen Poeterey* prescriptively guided the way from Latin to German poetry. Opitz prescribed rules for the different types of poems. With this publication, he exerted considerable influence on German literature, though not necessarily on the spoken language. Opitz faced his own challenges in becoming a member of the society since he was not a member of the aristocracy.

Language societies tried to *eindeutschen* the so-called *Fremdwörter*, that is, to coin new German words out of foreign ones. They were successful to a certain degree. Many of the foreign words and German words serve as synonyms in contemporary German.

Latin grammatical terms are used for German, not surprisingly, as most early German grammars were written in Latin. It is at that time that they get a German equivalent. Both words are still in use:

Nomen	*Hauptwort* (main word)
Verb	*Tuwort* (do word)
Singular/Plural	*Einzahl* (one number)/*Mehrzahl* (more than one number)
Adjektiv	*Eigenschaftswort* (a word denoting characteristics)

Other attempts at "Germanizing" terms such as *Gesichtserker* (literally "face bay") for nose were and still are ridiculed.

One form of *Überfremdung* (foreignization) was the so-called *alamode* language, namely the imitation of the language of the French court. The term implies a critique of the usage of contrived and exaggerated French. A further goal was to solidify *Hochdeutsch* ("High German"), which was the language of Upper Saxony, as the standard for written and oral communication. To this end, Schottel wrote a prescriptive

Table 9.5

Foreign Words (*Fremdwörter*)	German Term
Adresse	Anschrift
Moment	Augenblick
Dialekt	Mundart
Bibliothek	Bücherei

grammar, *Teutsche Sprachkunst* (German language arts), in 1641, using as the basis of his work the language of educated people. For Schottel, mastery of German grammar was the basis for the mastery of the language, hence he emphasized written German over the German spoken in everyday use by the general population.

Katharina Barbe

See also: Chapter 6: Aristocracy and the Elites. Chapter 9: Foreign Influences on German; Goethe-Institut.

Further Reading

Brown, Hilary. "Women Translators in the Sprachgesellschaften." *Daphnis: Zeitschrift für Mittlere Deutsche Literatur und Kultur der Frühen Neuzeit (1400–1750)* 38(3–4): 621–46, 2009. https://doi.org/10.1163/18796583-90001113. Accessed October 23, 2021.

Newman, Jane O. "Redemption in the Vernacular: The Language of Language Theory in Seventeenth-Century Sprachgesellschaften." *Monatshefte für deutschen Unterricht, deutsche Sprache und Literatur* 79(1): 10–29, 1987.

Opitz, Martin. *Buch von der Deutschen Poeterey*, 1624/2011. https://www.gutenberg.org/files/34806/34806-h/34806-h.htm. Accessed February 9, 2020.

Otto, Karl F. *Die Sprachgesellschaften des 17. Jahrhunderts*. Stuttgart: J. B. Metzler, 1972.

Wawrzynek, Markus. *Deutsche Sprachgesellschaften im 17. Jahrhunderts*. München: GRIN Verlag, 2000.

Standard and Dialect

"A language is a dialect with an army and a navy." (attributed to Max Weinreich)

In Germany, there are three major dialectal areas that coincide with geographic areas. In the North, it is *Niederdeutsch* (Low German), in the middle, *Mitteldeutsch* (Central German), and in the South, *Süddeutsch*, *Oberdeutsch* or *Hochdeutsch* (Upper German). Examples of Low German dialects are *Schleswigisch* and *Ostfriesisch*; of Middle German, *Hessisch* and *Ripuarisch* (Cologne) in the West and *Sächsisch* and *Thüringisch* in the East; of High German, *Bairisch*, *Schwäbisch*, and *Alemannisch*. Dialects differ primarily in pronunciation and the lexicon, and to a lesser extent grammar. So the final sound of *der Tag* (day) is realized in the North as [x], a German "ch"-sound (like the first sound in huge) or as [k] in other areas. Lexically, we find *die Schrippe* in Berlin, *das Rundstück* in Hamburg, and *die Wecke* in the South, all denoting the morning roll. In Standard German, *Joghurt* is masculine, *der Joghurt*. In Austria and Switzerland, speakers use *das Joghurt*, and in Eastern Austria even *die Joghurt*.

A standard is basically the dominant dialect or language variety; it is superregional and informs the written and spoken language and is understood by all speakers. One can think of dialects on a continuum. Dialect A is geographically close to Dialect B, and the speakers of A understand the speakers of B. Similarly, with Dialects B and C,

Table 9.6: GERMAN DIALECTS

Standard German	Hamburg Niederdeutsch	Berlin Ost-nieder-deutsch	Köln Mitteldeutsch	München Oberdeutsch	Wien Oberdeutsch	Basel Oberdeutsch
sprechen speak	schnacken	sprechen	schwaade	Sprecha	reden	reden
klein small	lütt	kleen	köppelig	Kola	kla(n)	chlei
Schnupfen sniffles	Schnöw	Schnuppen	Schnuppe	Katarrh	Stranka	Pfnüsel
Junge boy	Junge	Jung(e)	Junge, Fant	Bua	Bua/Bui	Bueb
Mädchen girl	Deern	Mädchen	Mädche, Weech	Diandl	Madl	Maidli
Kartoffel potato	Kartoffel	Kartoffel	Äädäppel	Erdapfel	Erdapfel	Herdapfel
nichts nothing	nix	nischt	nix	Nix	nix	nüt
Fleischer butcher	Schlachter	Fleischer	Metzger	Metzger	Fleischhacker/Fleischhauer	Metzger

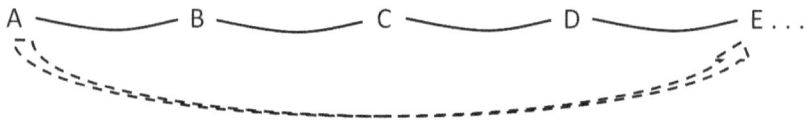

Figure 9.2

and C and D, and D and E. However, even though they are dialects of the same language, speakers of A may no longer understand speakers of E.

Altogether, more than fifty dialects of German can be differentiated, some with over a million speakers, others with as few as thirty. In some areas, dialect is only used by older people, so it may disappear. Schools usually demand use of the standard that is influenced by the local variety. Speakers have strong feelings about their own language and the language of the others. A 2015 survey yielded the popularity of dialects: *Bairisch* is by far the favorite dialect with about 25% of the respondents agreeing, *Kölsch* garners about 15%, the so-called *Berliner Schnauze* (Berlin bluntness, *Schnauze*—snout) 13%, and the least favorite dialect was *Sächsisch* with only 6%.

The study of dialects, dialectology, has its origin in Germany. In the nineteenth century, Georg Wenker (1852–1911) started investigating dialect boundaries, also called isoglosses (Greek *iso*—same and *gloss*—tongue or language). He sent out surveys in 1876 to 50,000 schoolmasters across Germany, where he asked them to indicate variations from standard words as closely as possible. Amazingly, he received about 45,000 replies and subsequently published the data in *Deutscher Sprachatlas* (German language atlas). Later, others followed in his footsteps and looked for the boundaries of certain words, often by traveling around and quizzing people about their language use. The results of these studies are freely available.

Katharina Barbe

See also: Chapter 10: Formal and Informal; Regional Clothing.

Further Reading

Barbour, Stephen, and Patrick Stevenson. *Variation in German: A Critical Approach to German Sociolinguistics*. Cambridge, UK: Cambridge University Press, 1990.

Braun, Peter. *Tendenzen der deutschen Gegenwartssprache*. Kohlhammer, 1998.

Dtv Atlas zur deutschen Sprache. München: dtv, 1985.

Mattheier, Klaus J. "Varibilität zwischen Dialekt und Standardsprache." *Zeitschrift für Germanistik* 8(55): 544–558, 1987.

Russ, Charles V. J. *The German Language Today: A Linguistic Introduction*. London: Routledge, 1994.

Statista. "Survey German Dialects." https://de.statista.com/statistik/daten/studie/100/umfrage/beliebte-dialekte/. Accessed February 9, 2020.Stedje, Astrid. *Deutsche Sprache gestern und heute*. Stuttgart: UTB, 2001.

Statista. "Survey German Dialects." https://de.statista.com/statistik/daten/studie/100/umfrage/beliebte-dialekte/. Accessed February 9, 2020.

CHAPTER 10

ETIQUETTE

Katharina Barbe

OVERVIEW

Germans are often maligned; typical American stereotypes portray them as aggressive, pedantic, assertive, stiff, unapproachable, unfriendly, inconsiderate, and humorless. Two key concepts in German life are "order" (*Ordnung*) and "clarity" (*Klarheit*). Germans also have the reputation of being efficient and punctual people. Germans and Americans do not think and act alike in many social and business situations. Germans have the right to act as Germans, and their behavior needs to be viewed against national expectations. The best advice that can be given regarding German etiquette is "When in Germany, do as the Germans do."

German Values

It is important to differentiate between the public and private behavior of Germans. In general, they appear to be most comfortable when they can compartmentalize their daily lives into discrete units. Many Germans engage in clear, unambiguous communication. They will say what they mean even at the expense of offending somebody. The extensive system of laws and regulations in the country add both *Ordnung* and *Klarheit* to daily life. Life is taken seriously (*ernsthaft*). Many Germans consider Americans to be superficial because of their propensity toward small talk and easily acquiring friends. Germans differentiate between *Freund* (friend) and *Bekannter* (casual acquaintance).

Many Germans are very handy and have no qualms putting up entire kitchens (often purchased at Ikea) in their homes or apartments. *Heimwerken* (DIY) is considered a less expensive and faster alternative to calling a handyman. However, residents may not engage in noisy home improvements during evening hours or on Sundays. "Quiet hours" are for the most part strictly observed in Germany. Apartment residents do not take showers or vacuum their apartments in the evening after 22:00. Homeowners do not use power tools or mow their lawns on Sunday. German restaurants located in residential areas post signs requesting that patrons respect the privacy of area residents. Restaurants may find themselves unable to set up tables and chairs on sidewalks if rowdy customers violate acceptable limits on noise. Germans generally frown on public commotion—except for Oktoberfest and Bundesliga soccer matches.

Gestures and Forms of Address

Germans smile less frequently than do Americans; gratuitous smiling can be misunderstood. When Walmart opened in Germany, the company required its sales staff to smile at the customers. The company had to halt this practice because many male shoppers interpreted this gesture by female employees as flirting. Germans do not cross their fingers for good luck. Rather, they cover their thumb with the index and middle fingers (*Daumen halten*). Counting begins with the thumb and not the index finger (which is added for the number two). In university settings, applause is expressed by knocking on the table (rather than clapping hands).

Germans shake hands when meeting each other and again when departing, a habit that may be adjusted after the pandemic. When speaking, they employ surnames prefaced by Herr (Mr.) or Frau (Ms.), unless the individual is a *Professor* (professor) or *Doktor* (doctor). A professor with an earned doctorate is addressed as Frau Professor Doktor. Phones are answered simply by stating their surnames; however, that custom is slowly disappearing with the advent of robocalls. There are two forms of address: informal (*Du/Ihr*) and formal (*Sie*). When meeting new people, it is advisable to use the formal address "*Sie*." Even after decades of collaboration, many Germans may remain on formal terms with colleagues; however, more frequent business meetings using English seem to be levelling that custom. If and when people decided to address each other by their given names, they will drop the formal *Sie* and adopt the informal *Du/Ihr*.

Dining Etiquette

When invited to a German home to dine, it is considered proper to bring a gift such as a bottle of wine or bouquet of flowers; not roses however, which would be considered a romantic gesture. For a dinner party, many Germans do not recognize "fashionably

---

MAHLZEIT!

In most German businesses, the lunchtime greeting is *Mahlzeit*! By itself, it means mealtime, but is an abbreviation of *Gesegnete Mahlzeit* (blessed mealtime). The brief sketch *Mittagspause* (lunch break) by the German comedian Gerhard Polt makes fun of this habit. Two colleagues' conversation at the lunch counter is interrupted by about thirty-five *Mahlzeit* greetings. When finally, someone wishes them *Guten Appetit*, both gasp and remark that the speaker must be new. The term *Mahlzeit* is also used ironically when something has gone wrong or as a sign of anger, then in the combination *Prost Mahlzeit*!

Further Reading

"Gerhard Polt: Mittagspause." https://www.youtube.com/watch?v=vC4t3NPT6gc. Accessed November 11, 2019.

The German Way & More. "Mahlzeit!" https://www.german-way.com/mahlzeit/. Accessed November 11, 2019.

late," so it is imperative for guests to arrive on time. Everyone will be seated at the table and before the meal commences, it is customary for the host to say *Guten Appetit*. Diners are not to take more food than they expect to consume, as it is impolite to leave food on the plate. If wine or beer is served with the meal, guests will wait for the host or propose a toast, *Prost* (Cheers) or *Zum Wohl* (to your health), before imbibing. While dining, Germans hold their fork in their left hand and their knife in their right; the American habit of switching hand and putting down and picking up the knife is considered to be an inefficient practice. When finished with their meal, Germans place the knife and fork parallel to each other across the right side of the place. It is a sign of good manners to follow-up the dinner invitation with a thank-you note.

When coming to a restaurant, it used to be the custom for diners to find their own seats. A single patron occupying a table with seating for four may be joined by a hungry couple. Although sharing a table, the single patron and hungry couple may ignore each other for the duration of the meal, except for an initial polite nod. Patrons will encounter two exceptions to the general practice of seating themselves in German establishments: tables with a small placard marked *Reserviert* (reserved) and the *Stammtisch*, a large circular table in the front of a bar that is reserved for regulars.

It is unusual for the staff at a German restaurant to hustle customers out the door. When customers are finished eating and socializing and want to leave the restaurant, they are expected to ask the server for the *Rechnung* (bill). The *Rechnung* usually includes a service fee (ca. 15%), but tipping is still expected but at a lower rate than is customary in the United States. The usual tip (*Trinkgeld*) is 5 to 10% in a sit-down restaurant, and customers round up to the nearest euro or two at a café. The *Trinkgeld* is not left on the table but added to the total by the customers themselves.

Shopping in Germany

The shopping experience in Germany differs from that in the United States. Customer service used to be an entirely foreign concept to those employed in the German retail sector. However, in order to remain competitive, service and retail businesses had to change their approach, and today one finds mostly friendly service. Customers in grocery stores are expected to bring shopping bags and sack their own groceries as the cashiers sit; if they forget to bring a bag, they will be charged for a plastic bag. In the United States, the German store ALDI has this policy and thus saves money on packaging.

It also used to be difficult to return items, even if defective, after they have been purchased. As a case in point, in 2000, in a famous court case, the American vendor Lands' End actually ran afoul of a 1932 German retail law when it advertised its standard return policy, namely, refunding a disgruntled customer's money at any time for any reason. A German court held that Lands' End was engaged in unfair retail practices because its return policy represented a product given away for free, and thus placing its competitors at a disadvantage. Land's End used this ruling as an advertisement for its practice. Today, most German companies have also made it easier to return merchandise. At the checkout, customers are now made aware of the return policy.

Schuld (debt) is a bad word, Homeownership incurs debt, and the number of renters versus owners shows this. In 2018, 51% owned their domicile; in comparison, there was 61% ownership in the United States at that time. Many establishments (including restaurants) do not accept regular credit cards but do accept EC cards. However, the trend toward accepting regular credit cards is going up so that most grocery stores now accept credit cards in order to stay competitive. Smaller establishments may not accept cards and often have signs advising the customer about this; these proprietors prefer not to pay the service charge (often 5%) levied by the credit card companies. The original German reticence to use credit affected the emergence of e-commerce in the country.

Personal Hygiene

Germans use fewer euphemisms than do Americans when discussing personal hygiene. The room in which business is conducted is called *die Toilette* or *das Klo* (toilet), not the powder or restroom. Some households have separate toilets and bathrooms; few toilets also contain a bidet. The toilet door is *always* closed, even when unoccupied. Public toilets are identified as either *Herren (men), Damen* (women), or Unisex. In department stores and even in some fast-food restaurants, toilets are often run by independent contractors, and customers are charged a fee by the attendant. In facilities for *Herren*, the attendant is often a woman. Access to toilets in train stations and many tourist attractions is through a turnstile, where the customer pays to get in. In recent years for better customer service, many malls have done away with charging for restroom use.

As soon as the first sunshine appears, one can see people disrobing and lying in the parks. Germans are by far less private about their bodies than Americans. In a sauna, for example, everyone walks around naked; however, using a towel when sitting down is considered good sauna etiquette.

Go Green

Germans have embraced the concept and practice of recycling with gusto, and proper observance of this concept and practice is considered good environmental etiquette. Unlike the United States, where most communities have two bins, one for trash and one for recycling, Germany uses up to six different bins: black (for general waste), blue (for paper), yellow (for plastic), white (for clear glass), green (for colored glass), and brown (for composting), although the colors may vary in different communities. The municipal authorities distribute booklets to residences explaining in detail the protocols of recycling. Individuals who improperly dispose of refuse are likely to be scolded by onlookers and instructed in the proper use of the bins. Further, many glass and plastic bottles are not discarded in Germany. Beer, water, and soft drink containers are sold with a deposit of as much as €0.25 per container. Container-return automats can be found in most grocery stores. Customers deposit the bottles in the automat and get a receipt for the deposit, which can be redeemed at the cashier.

Katharina Barbe

Further Reading

Baxmann, Matthias, and Matthias Eckoldt. *Typisch Deutsch? Von A wie Ämter bis Z wie Zuverlässigkeit—Wie Ausländische Korrespondenten Deutschland und die deutschen sehen.* München: Travelhouse Media GmbH, 2017.

Flippo, Hyde. *When in Germany, Do as the Germans Do: The Clued-in Guide to German Life, Language, and Culture.* Chicago: McGraw-Hill, 2002.

Fraser, Catherine C., and Dierk O. Hoffmann. *Pop Culture Germany! Media, Arts, and Lifestyle.* Santa Barbara, CA: ABC-CLIO, 2006.

Statista. "Homeownership Germany." https://www.statista.com/statistics/543381/house-owners-among-population-germany/. Accessed November 11, 2019.

Stern, Susan, and Hans Traxler. *These Strange German Ways and the Whys of the Ways.* Bonn: Atlantik-Brücke, 2000.

UNESCO. "Nationwide Inventory of Intangible Cultural Heritage." https://www.unesco.de/en/culture-and-nature/intangible-cultural-heritage/nationwide-inventory-intangible-cultural-heritage. Accessed November 11, 2019.

Zeidenitz, Stefan, and Ben Barkow. *The Xenophobe's Guide to the Germans*, rev. ed. London: Ravette, 1997.

Etiquette for Major Life Events

Birthdays

In Germany it is considered back luck to wish people "Happy Birthday!" (*Herzlichen Glückwunsch zum Geburtstag!*) or give a gift before the actual birth date. Germans organize their own birthday parties. It is customary for the person celebrating a birthday to provide food and drink for a party, both at home (guests are not expected to bring refreshments) and at the workplace (where coworkers expect to be served a piece of cake and a glass of sparkling wine). In northern Germany, predominantly in rural areas, single people celebrating their thirtieth birthday are expected to do household chores: men sweep a messy hallway, and women clean doorknobs with a toothbrush.

Baptisms

About 50 % of Germans belong to either a Catholic or Protestant church. Thus, not all children are baptized; of those who are, some are baptized before their first birthday in Germany, but others at their confirmation. The parents ask a friend or relative to be the *Taufpate* (godfather/-mother), a person to witness the baptism. A private celebration may take place after the baptism. Infants to be baptized usually wear a white gown. Other participants wear semiformal clothes and avoid jeans, t-shirts and sneakers.

Konfirmation, Firmung, and Jugendweihe

The Protestant *Konfirmation* (confirmation), the Catholic *Firmung* (confirmation), and the secular *Jugendweihe* (youth dedication) indicate entry into adulthood.

Adolescents preparing for confirmation in Protestant churches are around fourteen years old, have undergone religious instruction, and are ready to become members of a church and partake in Communion/the Lord's Supper. Children are customarily baptized as infants in Germany, and confirmation affords them a chance to confess their faith by their own volition. The confirmand often receives gifts of money.

In the Catholic church, *Firmung* is preceded by the *Erstkommunion* (First Communion). The children are usually between six and eight years old and have also participated in religious instruction before taking communion for the first time. Traditionally, girls wear white dresses and boys wear dark suits for the ceremony, where each receives a communion candle. Youth between fourteen and eighteen dedicate their lives to Jesus during the *Firmung*. The *Jugendweihe*, a secular coming-of-age ceremony observed predominantly in East Germany, has been around since the nineteenth century. The number of youths who participate in the religious and secular ceremonies has been decreasing steadily.

Engagements

A *Verlobung* (engagement) was once a very formal affair, where the husband-to-be asks the parents of the bride for her hand in marriage. The engagement was often sealed with an official announcement in a newspaper. Today, one can still find *Wir haben uns verlobt* (we are engaged) notices in the newspapers, but it is no longer customary, and Facebook has become the preferred way to share the news. Engaged couples wear rings engraved with each other's names and the date of the engagement on their left ring finger. However, many contemporary couples forgo this custom.

Weddings

The *Hochzeitsfeier* (wedding celebration) is a large family affair preceded by the *standesamtliche Trauung* (civil wedding), a *Polterabend* (eve of the wedding celebration), and culminating in, if desired, a church wedding.

The *Polterabend* used to be celebrated the night before the wedding, but today couples take liberty with the date. The numerous guests bring old dishes to this casual gathering (often collected especially for these events), which are smashed with fanfare in an attempt to ward off bad luck and bring good fortune. The civil ceremony is usually a smaller affair, which takes place in a government office, attended by a few witnesses. Brides often wear white festive gowns to their weddings (whether civil or religious) and both the groom and attendants are elegantly attired. Wedding parties typically include food and drink, speeches, dancing, and the throwing of a bouquet. Same-sex marriages have been legal since October 2017.

Funerals

Mourners who attend funerals in Germany customarily wear black clothes. After the funeral service, the casket is carried out and then taken to its last resting place or the crematorium. In a Christian burial, the religious official walks behind the casket followed by close relatives. At the burial site, the casket is lowered into the ground, and the official prays and puts some dirt on the casket. All the attendants do the same and share their condolences with the family. The burial is followed by a *Leichenschmaus* (funeral feast). It is vital that participants not arrive late, as this could be understood as a disregard for the deceased and his or her family.

These days, there is a tendency to opt for cremation (nearly 50% of Germans do so) or green burials and to forgo many traditional rituals.

Katharina Barbe

See also: Chapter 5: Overview. Chapter 7: Civil Unions and Same-Sex Marriage; Weddings and Divorce. Chapter 10: Regional Clothing.

Further Reading

Knigge2day. "Die Taufe." http://www.knigge2day.at/anlaesse/die-taufe. Accessed November 11, 2019.

Schwinghammer, Herbert. *Der neue Taschenknigge. Gute Umgangsformen in jeder Lebenslage*. Murnau, Germany: Mankan, 2013.

Süddeutsche Zeitung. "Kommunion, Konfirmation und Jugendweihe." https://www.sueddeutsche.de/leben/familie-kommunion-konfirmation-und-jugendweihe-was-ist-was-dpa.urn-newsml-dpa-com-20090101-190401-99-634686. Accessed November 11, 2019.

Tomalin, Barry. *Germany—Culture Smart! The Essential Guide to Customs & Culture*. London: Kuperard. 2015.

Formal and Informal

Brown and Gilman in their seminal article "The Pronouns of Power and Solidarity" discuss how languages express power symmetry and asymmetry in social interactions. Languages like Italian, French, Spanish, and German articulate power differentials among speakers by means of informal or formal pronouns, the *T-V*; *T* stands for the Latin singular *tu*, indicating informal address; in German *T* is realized as *DU*. Similarly, *V* signifies the Latin plural *Vos*, the formal, which is *SIE* in German. English used to indicate the difference with *Ye* (plural) and *Thou* (singular), in today's English "you."

Duzen (to use the informal) and *Siezen* (to use the formal) is guided by rules. A mutual *DU* or *SIE* implies persons of similar, a nonreciprocal *SIE/DU* of unequal status. Factors that determine address include age, social status, employment status, wealth, and context. Thus, a child will be addressed with *DU* but is expected to address an adult with *SIE*. Inside a family, children will use *DU* with relatives, although children in the upper classes used to address their parents formally. In many schools, students are addressed informally until about tenth grade. In the Third Reich, Jews like Victor Klemperer reported that they were addressed with the informal pronoun; here the *DU* was used to discriminate, and a mutual *DU* could have had dire consequences.

Violating these guidelines can lead to repercussions as a market woman found out in 1976. She had to pay DM 2,250 (at that time about $900) because she insisted on addressing a policeman informally. Her argument was that if you use the informal in addressing God, you should be able to address a policeman in the same way. In 2010, the president of the German Hells Angels addressed a policeman with the informal and called him a buffoon, which ended up costing him €2,400 ($3,200 in 2010 exchange).

Today there is a definite increase in *DU* in business. This may be partly due to the Swedish furniture store IKEA, which prescribes its use, the *Möbelhaus-DU* (furniture store). Another issue may be internationalization. In a business where a lot of meetings happen with foreign partners and thus in English with the use of first names, it would be peculiar if colleagues then address each other formally back in a German-speaking context.

Still, the usual address for persons who are not familiar with each other is Frau (Ms. or Mrs.)/Herr (Mr.) + optional title(s) + Last Name + *SIE*, like Frau Professor Dr. Cord. For persons familiar with each other, it is First Name + *DU*. "Violations" happen in certain contexts, like the so-called *Münchener Du*, which is the use of Frau or Herr + Last Name and the informal address (*du, Frau Müller*) and the Hamburger Sie, First Name and formal address, Lea + SIE.

A change from formal to informal is usually initiated by the more powerful person in terms of age and status. *Brüderschaft trinken* (to drink for brotherhood) is one ritual to realize this. To indicate closeness, Germans talk about *Wir sind Duzfreunde* (we are good friends, i.e., friends who speak to each other using informal pronouns). Urban legend has it that the former federal president Heinrich Lübke, who was prone to malapropisms, offered the queen the informal address with "You can say you to me." Supposedly former chancellor Helmut Kohl made the same offer to Bill Clinton.

When a person does not know what kind of address to use, he or she tries to talk without addressing the other person. Werner Lansburgh dealt with that in his 1977 book Dear Doosie, a *Denglish* (**Deutsch-English**) love story, where he does not know if he should address his beloved using *DU* or *SIE*.

Katharina Barbe

See also: Chapter 4: Overview. Chapter 6: Aristocracy and the Elites; Jews in Germany. Chapter 9: Standard and Dialect. Chapter 10: Greetings and Leave-Taking.

Further Reading

Brown, R., and A. Gilman. "The Pronouns of Power and Solidarity." In T. A. Sebeok, ed. *Style in Language*, 252–281. Cambridge, MA: MIT Press, 1960.

Hickey, Raymond. "The German Address System: Binary and Scalar at Once." In Irma Taavitsainen and Andreas H. Jucker, eds. *Diachronic Perspectives on Address Term Systems*, 401–425. Amsterdam: John Benjamins, 2003.

Lansburgh, Werner. *"Dear Doosie" Eine Liebesgeschichte in Briefen*. Frankfurt: Fischer Taschenbuchverlag, 1981.

Stern. Sprechen Sie Dus? https://www.stern.de/kultur/musik/sprachkultur-sprechen-sie -dus—3509236.html. Accessed November 11, 2019.

Der Tagesspiegel. "Beamtenbeleidigung." https://www.tagesspiegel.de/berlin/beamten-beleidigung-3200-euro-strafe-fuer-einen-witzbold/3938602.html. Accessed November 11, 2019.

"Was soll denn am Duzen schon ehrenrührig sein? Man ist doch schliesslich auch mit Gott per Du." https://www.nzz.ch/feuilleton/duzen-oder-siezen-hoeflichkeit-ist-nicht-mehr-angesagt-ld.1477782. Accessed November 11, 2019.

Greetings and Leave-Taking

Expressions of greetings and leave-taking marking the beginning and end of an interaction are ritualized and depend on a myriad of contextual features, such as the occasion, time of day, and social hierarchy. They can be verbal or nonverbal, or a combination thereof, and refusal to comply with these rituals is considered a breach of social conventions.

Greetings

Nonverbal greetings can be acknowledging a person from a distance by nodding the head. Embraces and kisses are frequently exchanged among friends and family members. *Verbal greetings* change with the time of day. Until about 11:00, people greet each other with [*Guten*] *Morgen!* (good morning), from about 11:00 until 17:30 one hears [*Guten*] *Tag!* (good day), and after that [*Guten*] *Abend!* (good evening). In business and offices, the lunchtime greeting is *Mahlzeit!* (have a good meal).

Different iterations of these greetings can be less formal, such as *Grüß dich! Sei gegrüßt! Hallo! Hi!* The diminutive of *Hallo, Hallöchen!* (hi there) is very colloquial and denotes a close relationship of the speakers. Questions of well-being like *Wie geht es?* (How are you?) are understood as empty phrases with a predetermined answer of *Danke, gut!* (fine, thanks). If questioners really want to know about the person's well-being, they ask two more times or say *Und wie geht es dir wirklich?* (and how are you really doing?). These greetings can be accompanied by a handshake using the right hand, an old ritual that originally signified that the people who greeted each other show no aggression (they were weaponless). The handshake is supposed to be firm with one pump: repeated pumping is interpreted as weakness. In the public and business sphere, the person higher in rank, social standing, or age initiates the handshake by extending the right hand. However, when a person enters a room, it is incumbent on them to initiate the greeting. Similarly, a host or hostess always extends greetings to guests regardless of other circumstances. Studies have shown that the handshake is used more often in Germany than in the United States, although this may be changed in a post-COVID-19 era. Among family members and friends, the handshake is uncommon and is often replaced with hugs and/or kisses.

Greetings for special occasions include those during religious and other holidays. Even though Germany is a rather secular country, one still hears *Frohe Weihnachten* (Merry Christmas), *Frohes Fest* (basically Happy Christmas Eve), *Frohe Ostern* (Happy

Easter), and *Frohe Pfingsten* (Happy Pentecost). Religious holidays are often accompanied by school holidays. *Frohe Festtage* is comparable to Happy Holidays, and *Frohes neues Jahr* (Happy New Year) or *Guten Rutsch* (literally have a good slide into the new year) can be heard near the end and beginning of a year.

So Long, Farewell, auf Wiedersehen, Goodbye

Leave-takings are dependent on time of day, personal relationships, duration of the separation, and time of the next meeting. Waving is a nonverbal type of leave-taking that can also happen at a distance. Verbal forms of leave-taking include explicit speech acts such as *Ich möchte mich jetzt verabschieden* (I'd like to say goodbye now), implicit goodbyes *Mein Bus kommt in 10 Minuten* (My bus arrives in 10 minutes), *Gruß an die Familie* (Greetings to your family), or *Fahr vorsichtig* (Drive carefully). More formalized items contain *Auf Wiedersehen!* and *Auf Wiederhören!* (said at the end of a phone conversation: "Hear you again"). Informal goodbyes can be expressed as:

> *Tschüss!* now often also *Ciao* or *Tschau* (See ya)
> *Bis dann/bald/später/morgen (until then/soon/later/tomorrow)*
> *Halt die Ohren steif!* (Keep a stiff upper lip)
> *Schönen Tag/Abend noch.* (Have a good day/evening!)
> *Gute Nacht.* (Goodnight.)
> *Schlaf gut!* (Sleep well!)
> *Viel Glück!* (Good luck.)
> *Alles Gute!* (All the best.)

Katharina Barbe

See also: Chapter 6: Aristocracy and the Elites. Chapter 10: Formal and Informal. Chapter 14: Overview.

Further Reading

Baldauf, Ana-Lucia. *Geschäftsleute unter sich: Die Internationalität der Business Culture.* Berlin: De Gruyter, 2015.

Bingan, Charles Boris Diyani. *Begrüßung, Verabschiedung und Entschuldigung in Kamerun und Deutschland: Zur linguistischen und kulturkontrastiven Beschreibung von Sprechakten in der Alltagskommunikation.* Frankfurt: Peter Lang, 2010.

Flippo, Hyde. *When in Germany, Do as the Germans Do: The Clued-in Guide to German Life, Language, and Culture.* Chicago: McGraw-Hill, 2002.

Karrierebibel. "Knigge-ABC für fast alle Lebenslagen." https://karrierebibel.de/wp-content/uploads/2018/03/Knigge-ABC-Alltag-Lebenslagen.pdf. Accessed November 11, 2019.

Mulo Farenkia, Bernard. "Grusshandlungen im Kultur Vergleich." *Grazer Linguistische Studien* 57: 71–88, 2002.

Schneider-Flaig, Silke. *Der neue große Knigge: Gute Umgangsformen—Privat und im Beruf.* Augsburg, Germany: Weltbild, 2012.

Stern, Susan, and Hans Traxler. *These Strange German Ways and the Whys of the Ways.* Bonn: Atlantik-Brücke, 2000.

Zeidenitz, Stefan, and Ben Barkow. *The Xenophobe's Guide to the Germans*, rev. ed. London: Ravette, 1997.

Knigge

From an early age, German children hear the adages "don't cut a (hot) potato with a knife," "don't point with your naked finger on clothed people," and "do not speak with your mouth full." These and other rules of behavior can be found in the so-called "Knigge," an eponymous term that has come to be identified with rules of etiquette. In 1788, Adolf Freiherr von Knigge (1752–1796), a baron and member of the lesser nobility, published *Über den Umgang mit Menschen* (On Human Relations), a work that gave him wide exposure and made him a household name. Knigge did not set out to write an etiquette guide; his book became such after his death when updated editions advised readers which hand holds the knife while eating and what clothes to wear to a funeral, and so on.

Knigge wrote during the Enlightenment, and his original collection of observations and instructions has often been considered a work of applied sociology. Knigge studied his fellow human beings and wrote in general about interactions between people of different backgrounds, temperaments, and ages, such as among family members, lovers, with women, neighbors and guests, scholars, people of dissimilar social positions, and even animals. In Western culture, many of his remarks are deemed timeless. In the centuries since his death, Knigge unwittingly spawned a multitude of books—with no end in sight. Recent titles include

In 1788, Adolf Freiherr von Knigge (1752–1796), a baron and member of the lesser nobility, published *Über den Umgang mit Menschen* (On Human Relations), a work that gave him wide exposure and made him a household name. The work was mistaken as a guide for how to behave and over the centuries his name became synonymous with etiquette. (Georgios Kollidas/Dreamstime.com)

BARON KNIGGE ABOUT HUMAN RELATIONS

In *Allgemeine Bemerkungen und Vorschriften über den Umgang mit Menschen* (general remarks and instructions about human relations), Knigge writes on page 17:
"Be on time, tidy, hard-working, diligent in your profession! Keep your papers, your keys and everything thus, that you can at any time find each piece even in the dark! Proceed even more carefully with items that do not belong to you! Never lend books or other things that were lent to you. Everyone likes to interact with a person, if one can rely on his punctuality in word and deed." (translation KB)

- *Knigge für Dummies*
- *Der Schweizer Knigge—Familienkalender 2015: Mit vielen tollen Tricks und Tipps* (The Swiss Knigge—Family Calendar 2015: With Many Great Tricks and Tips)
- *Knigge für freche Frauen* (for Sassy Women)
- *Business-Knigge: Stilsicher durch Büro und Alltag* (Confidence in Office and Daily Life)
- *China Knigge: Business und Interkulturelle Kommunikation*

And even a Knigge on how to put a cavession and other bridles onto horses:

- *Kappzaum Knigge: Der Passform-Ratgeber rund um den Kappzaum (und andere Zäume)* (Cavession-Knigge: The Fit Guide around the Cavession Bridle (and Other Bridles))

Two organizations provide online Knigge advice. In place of rigid rules of etiquette, the Deutsche Knigge Gesellschaft (DKG, http://deutsche-knigge-gesellschaft.de/), based on Knigge's book, claims that perfect style, the knowledge of current manners, and personal moral responsibility are vital elements of human interaction. The DKG offers seminars and maintains blogs about business etiquette. Similar goals are pursued by the Deutscher Knigge Rat (https://knigge-rat.de/), which boasts a descendent of Baron Knigge as one of its founding members.

Katharina Barbe

See also: Chapter 6: Aristocracy and the Elites. Chapter 10: Overview. Chapter 11: The Enlightenment (*Aufklärung*) (1680–1789). Chapter 15: *Vereine*.

Further Reading

Fraser, Catherine C., and Dierk O. Hoffmann. *Pop Culture Germany! Media, Arts, and Lifestyle*. Santa Barbara, CA: ABC-CLIO, 2006.

Knigge, Adolf. *Practical Philosophy of Social Life: Or the Art of Conversing with Men: After the German of Baron Knigge*, 2 vols. By P. Will, Minister of the Reformed German Congregation in the Savoy. London: Printed for T. Cadell, jun. and W. Davies, 1794.

Knigge, Adolf Freiherr von. *Über den Umgang mit Menschen*. Berlin: Treptower Verlagshaus GmbH, 1991.

Yuill, W. E. "A Genteel Jacobin: Adolf Freiherr von Knigge." In Hinrich Siefken, ed. *Erfahrung und Uberlieferung:Festschrift for C. P. Magill*, 42–56. Cardiff: University of Wales Press.

Die Zeit. Hellmuth Vensky. "Knigge war kein Freund von Anstandsregeln," April 23, 2013. https://www.zeit.de/wissen/geschichte/2013-04/knigge-ueber-den-umgang-mit-menschen. Accessed November 11, 2019.

Punctuality

A German proverb states that *Pünktlichkeit ist die Höflichkeit der Könige* (punctuality is the courtesy of kings). Another one says *Fünf Minuten vor der Zeit ist des Deutschen Pünktlichkeit* (arriving five minutes before the time is the German's punctuality). That Germans are always punctual is a time-honored stereotype. Germans—like Americans—live in a culture that is time-oriented, a culture that organizes around time. In both cultures, punctuality is seen as a common good expressed as "let's not waste anybody's time,"

Punctuality is acquired; it was "invented" during the Industrial Revolution in the nineteenth century, says famed German sociologist Karl-Heinz Geißler. Workers needed to be scheduled to operate expensive machines in an efficient manner. Incidentally, the mass production of clocks and watches started around the same time. Prior to this time, clocks were produced manually in small shops. In the United States, the watchmaker Ely Terry (1772–1852) started mass-producing clocks, which had a detrimental effect on small productions in two German-speaking areas known for clock production, the *Schwarzwald* (Black Forest) and Switzerland. Fritz Lang's 1927 film *Metropolis* shows how robot-like workers are dependent on the clock, even in their private time.

Several recent scandals bear witness that Germans are not always efficient and on time: In 2007, construction started for the Elbphilharmonie in Hamburg with a projected opening date in 2010; it finally opened in 2017 with a huge cost overrun. BER, the new airport in Berlin, was supposed to open in 2011, five years after construction began; it was finally opened in October 2020. Construction on the Stuttgart 21 railway station started in 2010 with a projected opening date of 2019. The station is now scheduled to open in 2025.

In a 2011 survey, the *Apotheken Umschau*, a free magazine available in pharmacies, found that nearly every fourth German likes to arrive early in order to not be late. More than 90% of respondents believed that children should be instructed to be punctual; however, more than 90% would accept tardiness if it has been announced in advance. About three-quarters of those surveyed tolerated occasional lateness, and a similar number accepted the so-called *akademisches Viertel*, arriving up to 15 minutes late (*Viertel*—quarter). The *akademisches Viertel* was once common practice at universities, where classes started 15 minutes later than listed in the schedule of classes. The schedule indicated *c.t.*—*cum tempore*—a 15-minute delay or *s.t.*—*sine tempore*—class starts on time. Finally, a little less than half of those surveyed strongly dislike *Pünktlichkeitsfanatiker*, those that are zealots about punctuality.

The daily paper Tagesspiegel in Berlin recently reported about appointments at the local *Bürgerämter* (municipal offices). In order to register a new residence after a move, one must visit the Bürgeramt. Online allocations for appointments are very precise—down to the minute, for example, 11:36 am. Staff members would wait two minutes before calling the next client. The *Bürgerämter* complained because nearly 20% of those scheduling appointments did not appear on time and did not call ahead to cancel.

As in the United States, Germany is adopting increased tolerance toward unpunctuality and focusing on individual time management in the appropriate context. Online learning, flextime at work, home office, TV on demand, cell phone use are all indications that attitudes toward time and punctuality are slowly changing.

Katharina Barbe

See also: Chapter 1: Transportation. Chapter 6: Overview. Chapter 8: Overview; German Universities and *Fachhochschulen*. Chapter 16: Overview; Film.

Further Reading

Hall, E. T. *Beyond Culture*. Garden City, NY: Anchor Press. 1976.

Lüber, Klaus. "German Punctuality. Imposing an Artificial Beat on Life." https://www.goethe.de/en/kul/mol/20436485.html. Accessed November 11, 2019.

Ringelstein, Ronja. "Wenn Bürger nicht zu Terminen erscheinen." *Der Tagesspiegel*, September 28, 2019. https://www.tagesspiegel.de/berlin/wenn-buerger-nicht-zu-terminen-erscheinen-ueberlastung-der-bezirksaemter-verschaerft-sich/25064712.html. Accessed November 11, 2019.

Schramm, Stefanie. "Wie wir ticken." *Die Zeit*, December 6, 2012. https://www.zeit.de/2012/50/Zeitwahrnehmung-Psychologie. Accessed November 11, 2019.

Stern, Susan. *These Strange German Ways and the Whys of the Ways*. Bonn: Atlantik-Brücke, 2000.

Zudeick, Peter. "Der Deutsche und die Pünktlichkeit." *DW*, July 12, 2012. https://www.dw.com/de/der-deutsche-und-die-p%C3%BCnktlichkeit/a-16398754 Accessed October 19, 2021.

Regional Clothing

Tracht (dress/traditional costume)

Old High German	*draht(a)*
	tragen (to wear)
Middle High German	*traht(e)*

Until the middle of the nineteenth century, all clothing was termed *Tracht*. Today, *Tracht* denotes regional clothing, such as folk costumes, and national, ethnic, and

This stereotypical picture depicts the traditional attire in the southern part of Germany. *Trachten* were initially work clothes that were adopted by wealthy vacationers and thus made popular. (Arne9001/Dreamstime.com)

traditional dress. *Trachten* are a form of communal and not individual dress. They are timeless and do not follow the dictates of fashions.

The German *Tracht* everyone knows is the dirndl, which evolved out of the working dress of young female servants in Austria and the South of Germany. In the local dialects, *Dirndl* is a diminutive of *Dirn*, denoting a young woman. In the late nineteenth century, summer visitors to the Alps adapted this simple attire, traditionally made up of a dress (*Leibchenrock*), undershirt (*Unterhemd*), and apron (*Schürze*), and wore it during their vacation in the mountains. Subsequently, this dirndl became increasingly fashionable in German cities, when vacationers took it back home. During the Nazi time, the concept of the dirndl was exploited because of its connection to *Heimat* (home), *Germandom*, innocence, and fortune. In 1938, all Jewish citizens of Salzburg were barred from wearing dirndl, lederhosen, and *Trachten* in general. A violation was punishable with a fine of 133 reichsmarks. The Salzburger Volksblatt wrote:

> *Diese Verfügung wird zweifellos von allen Kreisen begrüßt werden, die es seit langem hinnehmen müssen, dass z.B. das Dirndl—man erinnere sich nur an Bad Ischl früherer Jahre!—geradezu als ein jüdisches Nationalkostüm erschien.*

Without doubt, this ruling should be welcomed in all circles, that had for a long time to accept, that, for example, the dirndl—one should only recall Bad Ischl in prior years!—appeared to be a Jewish national costume. (translated by the author)

Although it was abused for ideological purposes in the Nazi time, the dirndl experienced a reassessment after the war and is now even more popular. Its popularity may have been helped by the 1965 movie *The Sound of Music*, which pictured the female Von Trapp members in dirndls, or the 1972 Munich Olympic Games, where all the hostesses wore dirndl. The British designer Vivienne Westwood was enamored of dirndls; during a visit to Austria in 2001, she is said to have remarked, "I do not understand you Austrians. If every woman wore a dirndl, there would not be any more ugliness." Today dirndls are not only offered in discount stores such as TK Maxx (a subsidiary of the U.S. chain TJ Maxx), but also in designer stores, where couture dirndls with the names Happy Heidi, *Rotkäppchen* (Little Red Riding Hood), and Think Pink bring in top euros.

Strictly speaking, a dirndl is not a *Tracht* but can certainly be part of one. A *Tracht* is a standardized form of clothing that delimits groups from each other (rural—urban, farmer—craftsman, physician—tradesman, Bavarian—Sorb). Up to the middle of the eighteenth century, what now is called *Tracht* was a characteristic of heritage and class membership and showed to which group or social class the wearer belonged. Until the French Revolution, clothing was strictly regulated by *Kleiderordnungen* or dress codes; violations of this code were punished.

In Germany, different *Trachten* styles are associated with geographical regions, from the *Schwarzwald* (Black Forest) in the West with its iconic *Bollenhut* with eleven red or black *Bollen* (pompons) to the Sorbian *Niederlausitz* in the East. Located to the Southeast of Berlin, the Sorbs have not only proudly maintained their language (close to Czech and Polish), but also their traditional ways, even throughout the time they spent under East German rule. In the relatively small area of *Niederlausitz*, we can find several iterations of *Trachten*. Differentiated geographically and by function, many elements influence the way the *Tracht* looks such as characteristics related to the wearer (married, single, widowed, "honorable") to the church year and ritual (Easter, Pentecost, Christmas, regular service, Eucharist), social class, major life events, and holidays. Thus, a *Tracht* shows the wearer's affiliation to a unit and as such is a standardized form of clothing that delimits social and regional groups.

Katharina Barbe

See also: Chapter 6: Jews in Germany. Chapter 9: Standard and Dialect. Chapter 10: Etiquette for Major Life Events. Chapter 15: Olympic Games. Chapter 16: Fashion Designers.

Further Reading

Bell, Bethany. "Lederhosen and Dirndl Dresses Make a Comeback." BBC News, October 22, 2012. https://www.bbc.com/news/magazine-19976271. Accessed November 11, 2019.

Condra, Jill, ed. *Encyclopedia of National Dress: Traditional Clothing around the World*, vol. 1. Santa Barbara, CA: ABC-CLIO, 2013.

Hollmer, Heide, and Kathrin Hollmer. *Dirndl: Trends, Traditionen, Philosophie, Pop, Stil, Styling*. Berlin: Edition Ebersback, 2011.

Lehnert, Gertrud. *Mode*. Köln: DuMont, 1998.

Loschek, Ingrid. *Reclams Mode- und Kostümlexikon*. Stuttgart: Reclam, 2005.

Moritz, Marina. *Alles Tracht? Ländliche Kleidung im 19. und beginnenden 20. Jahrhundert*. Erfurt, Germany: Museum für Thüringer Volkskunde, 2013.

Müller, Daniela, and Susanne Trettenbrein. *Alles Dirndl*. Salzburg: Anton Pustet Verlag, 2013.

Tostmann, Gexi. *Das Alpenländische Dirndl: Tradition und Mode*. Wien/München: Verlag Christian Brandstätter, 1998.

Wagner, Enrico. *Die Nationaltrachtdebatte im 18. und 19. Jahrhundert*. Berlin: LIT Verlag, 2018.

Wandinger, Alexander. *Tracht ist Mode*. Oberbayern, Germany: Trachteninformationszentrum, 2002.

Shopping

At one time, shopping was more of a challenge in Germany than it is today. Store hours were set to accommodate the salespeople and not necessarily the shoppers. Regulations were enacted and enforced that granted generous free time to retail employees. The *Ladenschlussgesetz* (store closing law) of November 28, 1956, stated that shops must be closed on Sundays and holidays, Monday–Friday from 18:30 to 7:00, Saturday from 14:00 to 7:00 Monday. Should Christmas Eve (December 24), fall on a regular workday, stores could remain open until 14:00. Over the course of the years, the *Ladenschlussgesetz* was changed, much to the chagrin of smaller businesses, so-called *Tante Emma Läden* (small corner shops). The shopkeepers contended that they lacked adequate staff and feared they would not stay competitive with larger retail outlets. Store hours were increased gradually. "Long Thursdays" were implemented in 1989, when stores were permitted to remain open until 20:30. In 2006, the matter of store hours was left to the individual states. In most states, grocery stores now are open until 22:00. The regulations regarding Sunday and holiday hours are still in place, with exceptions. The laws permit so-called "emergency rations" to be sold at train and gas stations. Soon, larger grocery stores with very liberal opening hours appeared in train and subways stations.

Little corner stores called *Spätis* or *Späthis* (*Spätkauf*—late shopping) are now found in neighborhoods throughout the country. In Berlin alone there are over 1,000 such stores. Most *Spätis* sell alcohol, emergency supplies, sweets, tobacco, papers, milk, and so on. Some *Spätis* also provide tables and chairs so that customers can drink beer outside on the sidewalk. In East Germany, *Spätverkaufsstellen* were widely available so that shift workers could purchase necessary items after late shifts.

Many Germans have relatively small refrigerators; they go shopping frequently and buy food such as cold cuts in small quantities, starting with 50–100 g. There are no baggers at supermarket checkouts, and the cashiers all sit and just push the wares down a conveyor belt. Shoppers put the groceries in their cloth shopping bag or purchase plastic, paper, or tote bags. Each supermarket has a bottle recycling machine that takes the recyclable bottles (*Mehrweg*—reusable). *Einwegflaschen* (disposable bottles) are not accepted and will be returned. The machine provides a receipt that can either be cashed or applied to a purchase.

Asides from supermarkets, many municipalities also have weekly or biweekly markets that sell produce, meats, breads, and other items. In Munich, the *Viktualienmarkt* is a permanent market filled with locals and tourists, the latter especially in the summer months. In Berlin, there are permanent *Markthallen* (market halls) all over the city, some very traditional, others appealing to a hip clientele.

In 1997, Walmart tried to participate in the lucrative German discounter market, opening about eighty-five stores. Amazingly, Walmart failed: Germany has a strong pro-labor union culture, salespeople are rather reserved, and forced smiles and "happy" greetings did not go over well with them and the customers. Walmart also underestimated the competition. About 40% of the supermarkets are discount stores such as ALDI, LIDL, Netto, and Penny. Walmart left Germany in 2006 without having turned a profit.

Katharina Barbe

See also: Chapter 1: Climate Policy and Recycling. Chapter 10: Overview. Chapter 14: Overview; Beer; Food Laws in Germany.

Further Reading

Baret, Christophe, Steffen Lehndorff, and Leigh Sparks. *Flexible Working in Food Retailing: A Comparison between France, Germany, the United Kingdom, and Japan.* London: Routledge, 2000.

Berlin.de. "Späti: Treffpunkt, Supermarkt und Seelentröster." https://www.berlin.de/special /immobilien-und-wohnen/neu-in-berlin/4971123-744080-spaeti-treffpunkt-markt -seelentroester.html. Accessed November 11, 2019.

Gabler Wirtschaftslexikon. "Ladenschlussgesetz." https://wirtschaftslexikon.gabler.de /definition/ladenschlussgesetz-ladschlg-40482. Accessed November 11, 2019.

Huffpost. "Why Did Walmart Leave Germany?" August 29, 2011. https://www.huffpost .com/entry/why-did-walmart-leave-ger_b_940542. Accessed November 11, 2019.

MDR. "Der umstrittene späte Feierabend." https://www.mdr.de/zeitreise/sechzig-jahre -ladenschlussgesetz-100.html. Accessed November 11, 2019.

Der Spiegel. "Walmarts Rückzug." https://www.spiegel.de/wirtschaft/wal-marts-rueckzug -warum-der-us-titan-scheiterte-a-429017.html. Accessed November 11, 2019.

CHAPTER 11

LITERATURE AND DRAMA

Jessamine Cooke-Plagwitz

OVERVIEW

Germany's literary history dates back to the eighth century, when most writing was in Latin and took place in monasteries. Short pieces, such as the *Hildebrandslied* and the *Muspilli*, written in the vernacular Old High German, did appear, though it was not until the beginning of the Middle High German period (ca. 1050–1350) that an increase in German texts, particularly a type of lyric poetry called *Minnesang*, began to materialize. Walter von der Vogelweide (ca. 1170–1230) was doubtless the most important and the most prolific of these lyric poets, with thirty-two surviving manuscripts of his work. The same period saw the rise of the courtly romance, with Wolfram von Eschenbach's (ca. 1160–1220) *Parzival*, and epics like the *Nibelungenlied*, as probably the best-known of these works.

Toward the end of the fourteenth and the beginning of the fifteenth centuries, popular literature began to take the form of folk songs, fables, and short plays. During this period, *Meistersänger*, like Hans Sachs (1494–1576), dominated, while the Reformation brought the development of the printing press and Martin Luther's (1483–1546) translation of the Bible into German. The combination of these two elements led to a unified High German Language and to a rapid increase in the public's desire for thought, discussion, and more reading material. Thus what is categorized as the Early Modern Period is marked by an exponential increase in the writing and distribution of printed texts. This period lasted from approximately 1500 to 1789 and is characterized by humanism and the Reformation, which favored a new freedom of expression, particularly in religious matters. During this era, German writings began to show greater variety in both form and genre, though the subject matter remained largely religious.

The beginning of the seventeenth century in Germany is the beginning of its Baroque period in literature and drama. The Thirty Years War was often contemplated in poetry and in prose, with Grimmelshausen's (1621–1676) picaresque novel *Simplicius Simplicissimus* (1668) generally viewed as the most famous novel of the period.

The German Enlightenment period, which lasted from ca. 1680 to 1789, was characterized by reason and an admiration of French principles encouraging belief in the senses. The literature of the period is often didactic and practical. Emotions were controlled and often expressed through measured sentimentality. Writers such as

---

GERMAN LITERARY PRIZES

The *German Book Prize* is Germany's most prestigious literary award. Established in 2005, the German Book Prize (the equivalent of the Booker Prize) is awarded each October at the Frankfurt Book Fair for the best novel written in German. In 2019, twenty novels were nominated for the prize. The winner (Arno Geiger) received €25,000.

The *Georg Büchner Prize* was established in 1923 by the State of Hesse to recognize writers, artists, actors, and musicians. Since 1951, the Büchner Prize has been awarded annually by the German Academy for Language and Literature to an author "writing in the German language whose work is considered especially meritorious and who has made a significant contribution to contemporary German culture." The prize is awarded in Darmstadt and includes a stipend of €50,000. Four winners of the Büchner Prize have gone on to win the Nobel Prize in literature: Günter Grass (1965), Heinrich Böll (1967), Elias Canetti (1972), and Elfriede Jelinek (1998).

The German Crime Prize has been awarded since 1985. A panel of journalists and critics award two prizes each year: one for the best crime novel (*Krimi*) written in German and the other for the best international crime novel. American author Ross Thomas has won the award four times. Other well-known international winners include John le Carré, Michael Connelly, and others.

Sources: https://www.deutscher-buchpreis.de/en/. Accessed January 7, 2020.
https://www.deutscheakademie.de/en/awards/georg-buechner-preis. Accessed January 6, 2020.

Barthold Heinrich Brockes (1680–1747), Christoph Martin Wieland (1733–1813), and Gotthold Ephraim Lessing (1729–1781) advocated the application of common-sense principles to the creation of poetry and drama and wrote pieces expressing this more civilized approach.

The Enlightenment period ended with a backlash against this controlled, regimented approach to writing in the brief period of *Sturm and Drang* (Storm and Stress), in which writings were aimed at shocking readers and audiences or producing strong, uncontrolled emotions. Perhaps the most representative work of the period is Johann Wolfgang von Goethe's (1749–1832) *Die Leiden des jungen Werthers* (*The Sorrows of Young Werther,* 1774), an epistolary novel detailing the unfortunate fate of a sensitive young artist when confronted with an unrequited love.

Goethe remains Germany's towering intellectual figure. He was born in Frankfurt. He studied at the Universities of Leipzig and Strasbourg before finally settling in Weimar. In 1789, he embarked on an extended journey to Italy, recounted in his *Italienische Reise* (1816–1817). While in Italy, he acquired an appreciation for the principles of classical art, reflected in his *Romische Elegien* (*Roman Elegies*) and *Venezianische Epigramme* (*Venetian Epigrams*). Goethe's epic poem *Faust* (in which the protagonist, Johann Georg Faust sells his soul to the Devil in exchange for knowledge and worldly pleasures) is considered the finest example of German Romantic poetry. His scientific writings include *Beiträge zur Optik* (*Essays on Optics*) and *Farbenlehre* (*A Theory of Color*). His autographical works include *Dichtung und Wahrheit* (*Poetry and Truth*) and *Gespräche mit Eckermann* (Goethe's secretary) *in den Letzten Jahren seines Lebens* (*Conversations with Eckermann in the Last Years of His Life*). Goethe died in Weimar. Germany's worldwide cultural and linguistic organization, the Goethe Institut (GI), is named after Goethe.

The *Sturm und Drang* movement with its expression of strong emotions and subjectivity, coupled with the violence of the French Revolution and subsequent Reign of Terror, pushed the pendulum back toward the more structured literature and drama of German Classicism. Figures like Goethe and Friedrich Schiller (1759–1805), who featured prominently in the *Sturm und Drang* period, also contributed to the literature of German classicism. This period focused on a reevaluation of earlier concepts of art and beauty. No longer guided by questions of rules and reason, German classicism introduced a new idealistic theory of art and literature, outlining the duty of all who create art or literature to better mankind through the depiction of the classical hero, who embodied the perfect balance between sensuality and rationality.

The final decade of the eighteenth and early decades of the nineteenth centuries were characterized by the Romantic movement, in which literature and drama pondered questions of individual liberty and exalted nature as a source of inspiration. Philosophers like Friedrich Schelling (1775–1854) and Friedrich Schlegel (1772–1829) considered issues of nature, mind, and human creativity and inspired writers like Friedrich "Novalis" von Hardenberg (1722–1801), Ludwig Tieck (1773–1853), and Joseph Freiherr von Eichendorff (1788–1857), who believed that writers and artists were able to discern the hidden inner workings of nature, and that it was their duty to translate this hidden language for the edification of mankind.

Much of nineteenth-century German literature after 1840 is characterized by a focus on realism. For many, this realism grew from a desire for social and political improvements. Indeed, many writers of the period were prohibited from publishing their work in Germany because of their promotion of liberal ideas. Prominent German figures of the realist school include Heinrich Heine (1797–1856), Georg Büchner (1813–1837), and Adalbert Stifter (1805–1868). The various schools of realism include *Biedermeier, Vormärz* (Pre-March), *Junges Deutschland* (Young Germany), poetic realism, and naturalism.

In the latter years of the nineteenth century up to World War I (1914–1918), naturalism, symbolism, and expressionism are perhaps the most readily recognizable literary genres in German literature. Naturalism removed the veil from depictions of life and showed readers and audiences the unseemly side of life by presenting the wretched truth of life among the poorer classes, while symbolism came as a direct rejection of naturalism by conveying a mystical meaning to all of life's components. Where naturalism depicted the "brutal truth" of life, symbolism attempted to discover the secrets of life and nature.

Expressionism as a literary movement existed during and immediately after the First World War. Its art and literature focused on inner truths as opposed to external forms. Not surprisingly, given its time frame, expressionist works often depicted the utter disintegration of the world, though with a hopeful emphasis on the regeneration of humankind.

The Second World War (1939–1945) and its chaos forms the backdrop of *Exilliteratur* (exile literature). This term refers to that literature and drama produced by German authors such as Bertolt Brecht and Thomas Mann who sought political asylum outside of Germany during the National Socialist regime. The term applies to literature and drama written by exiled authors from the early 1930s until approximately 1949. Not surprisingly, the works of these authors tend to express an anti-Nazi sentiment. Many of these authors were Jewish or Communist sympathizers.

In that part of Germany that became West Germany in 1949, the immediate aftermath of World War II was known as the *Stunde Null* (zero hour). At this point, German writers hoped to begin again after the horrors of Nazism. In many ways, the period represented an attempt to create a Germany that was in direct opposition to the nation Hitler had hoped to build. Many writers felt the need to reflect on the war and its aftermath in order to heal. Some of the more influential voices of the period include Gottfried Benn (1886–1956), whose *Probleme der Lyrik* (*The Problems of Lyric Poetry,* 1951) represented an important revitalization of German poetry within the larger European tradition. The writings of Heinrich Böll (1917–1985) and Wolfgang Borchert (1921–1947), whose works were often negatively termed *Trümmerliteratur* or rubble literature also teemed with social criticism. However, these works were instrumental not only in documenting events in Germany during and after the war, but also the evolution of German values that resulted.

Perhaps not surprisingly, the dominant trend in German literature and drama of the later twentieth century was marked by a tendency to turn inward and examine questions of human motivation. This movement became known as *Neue Subjektivität* (New Subjectivity). Popular topics included issues affecting the Third World, frequently in the context of its abuse at the hands of the First. Human emotions were often the focus of this inner examination. Important authors of New Subjectivity in Germany include Walter Kempowski (1929–2007), Sarah Kirsch (1925–2013), and Martin Walser (b. 1927).

After the fall of the Berlin Wall in 1989 and German Reunification, many German authors were cautious regarding the future of a united Germany. Some from the former East Germany were loath to give up on the promises of Communism, while others were skeptical that East Germans could ever adapt to a capitalist system. These doubts, however, gradually gave way to a new generation of writers and dramatists who wrote from a less political vantage point and whose works were written primarily to entertain.

While the work of these writers has remained popular through the first twenty years of the twenty-first century, other themes have begun to emerge. As concepts such as national or cultural identity have become more fluid, so too the field of German literature has come to include migrant literature to reflect new questions of Germanness. Writers such as Emine Sevgi Özdamar (*Mutterzunge* [*Mother Tongue*], 1990]) and Feridun Zaimoglu (*Kanak Sprak* [*Kanake-Talk*], 1995) have won literary prizes and amassed critical acclaim for their examinations of language and identity, migration, racism, and German-Turkish identity.

Jessamine Cooke-Plagwitz

Further Reading

Beutin, Wolfgang, et al. *A History of German Literature: From the Beginnings to the Present Day*. London: Routledge, 2005.

Garland, Henry, and Mary Garland, eds. *The Oxford Companion to German Literature*. Oxford, UK: Oxford University Press, 1997.

Biedermeier (1815–1830), *Junges Deutschland* (1830–1850), and *Vormärz* (1830–1848)

The nineteenth century in Germany was a time of political upheaval and hopes for democracy. For a considerable amount of the century, censorship and authoritarianism permeated almost all aspects of daily life. After Napoleon's defeat at Waterloo in 1815, the Congress of Vienna established the *Deutscher Bund* (German Confederation), which remained in place until German unification in 1871.

Against this backdrop, three major literary movements evolved. The period 1815–1848, the so-called *Biedermeier* period, is characterized by a fairly conservative literature, marked by political conformity and a general preference for the comfortable and the familiar. *Biedermeier* subject matter held to nonpolitical topics, and authors of the era retreated to the home and the simple country life as popular literary themes. As the middle class became more educated, interest in reading among "ordinary people" steadily increased, so novels and short stories focused on the comforts of the unpretentious *bürgerlich* (middle-class) lifestyle, and sentimental reflections on nature became increasingly popular. Key to this literature was the maintenance of the social status quo.

Biedermeier authors include Adalbert Stifter (1805–1868), known for his brand of poetic realism. Stifter's short story collection *Bunte Steine* (*Colored Stones*, 1853) proposed that inspiration can come from the small and insignificant things one finds in one's natural environment. His novel *Nachsommer* (*Indian Summer*, 1857) is a *Bildungsroman* in the tradition of Goethe's *Wilhelm Meister*. Stifter emphasizes the object world, both natural and manmade, in this serene and largely uneventful novel that traces the narrator's youth, education, and tranquil later life. Eduard Friedrich Mörike's (1804–1875) poetry is rife with personifications and striking descriptions of the natural world. His 1856 novel *Mozart auf der Reise nach Prag* (*Mozart on the Way to Prague*) employs such natural objects as a rosebush and a pine sapling to foretell of Mozart's early death, pairing a sense of danger with the possibility of a life filled with harmony. Annette von Droste-Hülshoff's (1797–1848) works can fall into the *Biedermeier* movement, but she has been placed in the Romantic school as well. Her compelling descriptions of nature focus on the minutiae of the world around her. Her collection of nature poetry *Gedichte* (*Poems*) was published in 1844, and her novella *Die Judenbuche* (*The Jews' Beech*), her most famous work, was published in 1842.

The periods known as *Junges Deutschland* (Young Germany) and *Vormärz* (Pre-March) are generally interchangeable and refer to a trend toward more liberal ideas in the face of growing threats of censorship, repression, and absolutism. What differentiates these movements from *Biedermeier* is the overt expression of their authors' political and social leanings. In general, the works of these writers moved away from the trends of Romanticism and encouraged political reform and sexual and religious toler- ance. Though *Junges Deutschland* and *Vormärz* are often placed under the same umbrella, the literature of the former movement calls for the establishment of a liberal society, while that of the latter is likelier to advocate political change, in some cases through whatever means necessary. *Vormärz* refers to the period prior to the March Revolution of 1848 when calls for political and social change became increasingly stri- dent. Thus, August Heinrich Hoffmann von Fallersleben's (1798–1874) *Lied der Deutschen* (*Song of the Germans,* 1841) or Georg Herwegh's (1817–1875) *Aufruf* (*Appeal,* 1841) with their political sentiment present fitting examples of *Vormärz* literature.

Representative writers and works of *Junges Deutschland* include Heinrich Heine's *Reisebilder* (*Travel Pictures,* 1826–1827), while Karl Gutzkow's (1811–1878) *Wally, die Zweiflerin* (*Wally the Doubter,* 1835) and *Uriel Acosta* (1847) are particularly notewor- thy for their defense of women's rights and the Jewish emancipation respectively. Works of *Vormärz* literature include Heinrich Heine's poem *Die schlesischen Weber* (*The Silesian Weavers,* 1844) in which the vast discontent of workers is expressed. and his satirical epic poem *Deutschland. Ein Wintermärchen* (*Germany. A Winter's Tale,* 1844), which articulates his dissatisfaction with German nationalism, while simulta- neously affirming his love for the country. Georg Büchner's (1813–1837) dramas *Dan- tons Tod* (*Danton's Death,* 1835) and *Woyzeck* (published posthumously in 1879 and did not debut until 1913) reflect both pessimism at society's disarray and compassion for its victims. Carl Ludwig Börne's satirical *Briefe aus Paris* (*Letters from Paris,* 1830– 1833) vehemently criticized oppressive conditions in Germany.

During the overlapping *Biedermeier, Junges Deutschland,* and *Vormärz* move- ments, women writers were also speaking out. Louise Otto-Peters (1819–1895), a founder of the German women's movement, published the *Frauen-Zeitung* (Women's Newspaper), in which women aired their views on a variety of political objectives. With the increase in social engagement prevalent in the latter two literary move- ments, women writers now felt compelled to document the issues women faced within German society. Louise Aston (1814–1871), a champion of women's rights, describes the plight of poor women in her *Lied einer schlesischen Weberin* (*Song of Silesian Weaver*). Her novel *Aus dem Leben einer Frau* (*A Woman's Life,* 1847) calls for women's emancipation, while her *Revolution und Contrerevolution* (1849) is a depiction of the Revolution of 1848 from a woman's perspective. Meanwhile, Fanny Lewald's (1811–1889) three-volume autobiography, *Meine Lebensgeschichte* (*The Edu- cation of Fanny Lewald: An Autobiography,* 1861–1862) provides an eye-opening account of a woman's life, excluded from higher education and raised solely for pur- poses of marriage and motherhood.

Jessamine Cooke-Plagwitz

See also: Chapter 6: Overview; Jews in Germany. Chapter 7: Women in the Work- place. Chapter 12: Artists; Decorative Arts *Biedermeier* and *Jugendstil.*

Further Reading

Beutin, Wolfgang, et al. *A History of German Literature: From the Beginnings to the Present Day.* London: Routledge, 2005.

Garland, Henry, and Mary Garland. *The Oxford Companion to German Literature.* Oxford: Oxford University Press, 1997.

Koelb, Clayton, James Hardin, and Eric Downing, eds. *German Literature of the Nineteenth Century, 1832–1899*, vol. 9. Rochester, NY: Camden House, 2005.

Morris-Keitel, Helen G. *Identity in Transition: The Images of Working-class Women in Social Prose of the Vormärz (1840–1848)*, vol. 15. New York: Peter Lang, 1995.

Nemoianu, Virgil. *The Taming of Romanticism: European Literature and the Age of Biedermeier.* Cambridge, MA: Harvard University Press, 1984.

Tipton, Frank B. *A History of Modern Germany Since 1815.* Berkeley: University of California Press, 2003.

Zajdowicz, Rebecca Ann. *Engaging with the Nation: German Women Writers of the Vormärz and Constructions of National Identity.* Pennsylvania State U, PhD dissertation, 2010. https://etda.libraries.psu.edu/files/final_submissions/5092 Accessed October 19, 2021.

The Early Modern Period (ca. 1550–1750)

The line of demarcation between the late Medieval period and the beginning of the Early Modern period of German literature is not a clear one. Some scholars place it at the middle of the fifteenth century, while others place it almost one hundred years later. Because the period spans such a wide time frame, its literature is also understandably wide-ranging in nature. Nevertheless, the early works of the period tended to center on religious themes.

Renaissance humanism in Germany began in the early to mid-fifteenth century and can be associated with the invention of the printing press around 1450. It lasted until the early sixteenth century, when it was supplanted by the Reformation. German humanism is marked by attempts to advance mankind through reaching back and renewing the knowledge of the Ancients. German humanists focused on classical verse forms and Latin prose. The German humanists built a sort of spiritual elite through a variety of approaches. Scholars such as Ulrich von Hutten (1488–1523), Conrad Celtis (1459–1508), and Johannes Reuchlin (1455–1522) made important contributions through their critical writings and linguistic studies. Perhaps the most influential scholar of the humanist school was Erasmus von Rotterdam (1466–1536) and his belief in an active and tolerant Christianity. In 1516, he published a version of the New Testament in Ancient Greek with translation in Latin, which became the model for the Lutheran Bible. His *Moriae Encomium Seu Laus Stultitiae (In Praise of Folly,* 1511) illustrates his wit and religious tolerance.

In 1517, the German monk Martin Luther nailed his Ninety-Five Theses to the door of the All Saint's Cathedral in Wittenberg. Thus began, according to many scholars, the Protestant Reformation. Initially, this period of change focused on Martin

Luther's (1483–1546) religious ideas. Luther's ambition was the production of a "true" version of the New Testament translated into German for the benefit of the German-speaking public. His ideas spread rapidly and were adopted and adapted by other reformers in the 1520s. The Reformation's consequences were extensive not only in terms of altering the public's relation with the Church and with God, but also as they applied to the status of the individual within society.

The *Barock* (Baroque) period of the Early Modern era is loosely dated between 1600 and 1720. This was a time of abundant production in German literature, with frequent emphasis on themes of life's transience and admonitions of remaining faithful in the face of death's inevitability. Key figures of the period include Hans Sachs (1494–1576; *Die Wittenbergisch Nachtigall* [*The Wittenberg Nightingale*],1523), Andreas Gryphius (1616–1664), and Catharina Regina von Greiffenberg (1633–1694; *Geistliche Sonnette* [*Spiritual Sonnets*], 1662). Of these writers, the best known and probably most versatile is Andreas Gryphius, whose works run the gamut from Latin poetry (*Olivetum*, 1646) to tragedies (*Leo Arminius*, 1646; *Cardenio und Celinde oder unglücklich Verliebte* [*Cardenio and Celinde or The Unhappy Lovers*], 1647–1649), to comedies (*Absurda Comica oder Herr Peter Squentz*, 1657; *Horribilicribrifax Teutsch oder Wählende Liebhaber* [*Horribilicribrifax or Choosing Lovers*], 1663). Gryphius's tragedies feature stoic characters who represent Christian redemption, while his comedies also show virtue rewarded as lighter fare. His works emphasize constancy and fortitude, two recurring themes, in the face of life's cruelty.

Daniel Casper von Lohenstein (1635–1683), another significant literary figure of the period, wrote (among his other works) six plays: *Ibrahim*, 1649–1650; *Cleopatra*,1661; *Agrippina*, 1665; *Epicharis*, 1665; *Ibrahim Sultan*, 1673; *Sophonisbe,* 1680, all set in "exotic" lands and focused on ideas of power. Powerful women figure prominently in his dramas, most notably Cleopatra and Agrippina, who use their sensuality to enslave men. Though Lohenstein's tragic figures ultimately see the error of their ways, their redemption and true understanding in most cases only comes through death.

The drive toward the use of German as the language of poetic expression is well exemplified in Martin Optiz's (1597–1639) *Buch der deutschen Poeterey* (*Book of German Poetry*, 1624). During the seventeenth century, literary societies dedicated to promoting the use of the German language in literature began to spring up around Germany. For example, the *Fruchtbringende Gesellschaft* (Fruitbearing Society) was founded in 1617 by members of the Weimar court, and the *Pegnesischer Blumenorden* (Pegnitz Flower Society) was founded in 1644. The latter remains active today.

Seventeenth-century German literature is colored by the tragedy of the *Dreißigjähriger Krieg* or Thirty Years War, which lasted from 1618 to 1648. The war began as a religious conflict between Protestants and Catholics, but soon encompassed much of Western Europe and involved political, dynastic, and national interests in addition to purely religious motivations. The war devastated the European continent, and its effects are reflected in the literature of the era. Perhaps the best-known piece of the period is Hans Jakob Christoffel von Grimmelshausen's (1621/22–1676) sweeping picaresque novel *Der abenteuerliche Simplicissimus Teutsch* (*Simplicius*

Simplicissimus, 1668), in which the hero's adventures unfold against the backdrop of the Thirty Years War. With vividly drawn characters and coarse humor, the novel follows the hero through year of experiences, some hilarious and some horrific, at the end of which he renounces the corrupt world to become a hermit. The novel is considered by many literary scholars to be the first German-language novel of importance. It was adapted as an opera in the mid-1930s by Karl Amadeus Hartmann, and one of the novel's characters became the inspiration for Bertolt Brecht's *Mutter Courage und ihre Kinder* (1938–1939, *Mother Courage and Her Children*).

Jessamine Cooke-Plagwitz

See also: Chapter 5: Luther, Martin (1483–1546); The Reformation; Religious Wars. Chapter 9: *Sprachgesellschaften* (Language Societies). Chapter 13: Musical Periods and Composers.

Further Reading

Brandt, George W., and Wiebe Hogendoorn, eds. *German and Dutch Theatre, 1600–1848*. Cambridge, UK: Cambridge University Press, 1993.

Cameron, Euan. *The European Reformation*. Oxford, UK: Oxford University Press, 1991.

Garland, Henry, and Mary Garland. *The Oxford Companion to German Literature*. Oxford, UK: Oxford University Press, 1997.

Hardin, James, ed. *German Baroque Writers, 1661–1730*. Detroit: Thomson Gale, 1996.

Roeck, Bernd. *Civic Culture and Everyday Life in Early Modern Germany*. Leiden, Netherlands: Brill, 2006.

Skrine, Peter. *The Baroque: Literature and Culture in Seventeenth-Century Europe*. London: Methuen, 1978.

Wiggin, Bethany. *Novel Translations: The European Novel and the German Book, 1680–1730*. Ithaca, NY: Cornell University Press, 2011.

Woodford, Charlotte. "Women as Historians: The Case of Early Modern German Convents." *German Life and Letters* 52(3): 271–280, 1999.

The Enlightenment (*Aufklärung*) (1680–1789)

The Enlightenment in Europe began in the early seventeenth century with René Descartes (1596–1650) in France and in the mid-seventeenth century with Samuel von Pufendorf (1632–1694) in Germany. The epoch encompasses many different and often contradictory ideas, yet the overarching theme of the period is that of reason and rationalism.

The concept of Enlightenment was defined for the first time by Immanuel Kant (1724–1804) in his 1784 essay *Was ist Aufklärung?* (*What Is Enlightenment?*) in which he described the movement as a person's liberation from self-imposed immaturity.

This immaturity, he clarified, was the inability to use one's mind without another's guidance. The literature of the Enlightenment changed dramatically from the early to the late periods. As the era progressed, portrayals of the middle class replaced those of the nobility and courtly society. Important themes and ideas prevalent throughout Enlightenment works include critical thinking regarding religion and absolutism; the veneration of science and rejection of superstition; appeals for religious tolerance; the belief that man can be educated (nurture above nature); belief in the importance of human virtue; human reason as a component of human perception; and the belief in human reason as a virtue.

One of the earliest intellectuals to influence the development of the German Enlightenment was the philosopher Gottfried Wilhelm Leibniz (1646–1716), and the first literary figures to popularize his ideas were the poet Barthold Heinrich Brockes (1680–1747) and the prose satirist Gottlieb Wilhelm Rabener (1714–1771). During the first half of the eighteenth century, Johann Christoph Gottsched (1700–1766) and his wife, Luise Adelgunde Victorie Gottsched (1713–1762), authored several enlightened tragedies and comedies. Gottsched attempted to establish new canons in the theater of his day and helped in formulating rules for judging the quality and content of literature. Though his rules were highly restrictive, he did amass a number of followers, one of whom was Friedrich Gottlieb Klopstock (1724–1803), who gained renown with his epic poem *The Messias* (1749–1773). Klopstock's contribution to Enlightenment poetry came through his liberation of lyric poetry from long-standing restrictive rules and formulas and incorporating his own innovative language and meters.

In his work *The Messias*, Friedrich Gottlieb Klopstock contributed to the ideas of the Enlightenment. (Library of Congress)

Ultimately, Gottsched's rather narrow views were surpassed by the broader views of the Swiss theorists Johann Jakob Bodmer (1698–1783) and Johann Jakob Breitinger (1701–1776), who advocated the expression of controlled emotions through sentimental language while at the same time continuing to reject any expression of uncontrolled emotion. The high point of this literary Enlightenment came with the works of the literary theorist and playwright Gotthold Ephraim Lessing (1729–1781), who created a new type of German drama with his *Bürgerliches Trauerspiel* (bourgeois tragedy). His plays *Miss Sara Sampson* (1755) and *Emilia Galotti* (1772) focused on middle-class protagonists, ignored aesthetic prejudices, and advocated for religious tolerance. While earlier comedies had always placed ordinary people in comedies, tragedies had, up to this point, been reserved for the nobility, as according to Aristotle's *Ars Poetica*, only the higher classes were capable of suffering the kind of loss worthy of the tragedy.

Christoph Martin Wieland (1733–1813) was another important writer of the period. His novel *Die Abentheuer des Don Sylvio von Rosalva* (*The Adventures of Don Sylvio von Rosalva,* 1772) was based on the model of Cervantes' *Don Quixote* and featured a visionary hero, who eventually triumphs after many failures by adopting an enlightened attitude toward his life. Wieland also translated the works of Shakespeare into German prose, thereby inspiring later playwrights of the *Sturm und Drang* and Romantic periods.

The author and philosopher Gottfried von Herder (1744–1803) contributed a sense of German identity with his *Journal meiner Reise im Jahr 1769* (*The Journal of My Travels in the Year 1769*), notable for its descriptions of states of mind and profound thinking on language, art, and education. Here the author describes the concept of *Volksseele* (ethnic soul), which he felt could help to prevent the *Volk* from being dominated by or subsumed under the influence of other nations. His theory led to a study of folk literature, which in turn would become extremely important for later *Sturm und Drang* writers.

Jessamine Cooke-Plagwitz

See also: Chapter 10: Knigge. Chapter 11: Romanticism (*Romantik*) (1788–1835); Storm and Stress (*Sturm und Drang*) (1767–1785).

Further Reading

Boyle, Nicholas. *Goethe, the Poet and the Age*, vol. 1: *The Poetry of Desire, 1749–1790.* Oxford, UK: Clarendon, 1991.

Boyle, Nicholas. *Goethe, the Poet and the Age*, vol. 2: *Revolution and Renunciation, 1790–1803*. Oxford, UK: Clarendon, 2000.

Bruford, Walter Horace. *Theatre, Drama and Audience in Goethe's Germany*. London: Routledge, 2018.

Gay, Peter. *The Enlightenment: An Interpretation*, vol. 1. New York: Norton & Company, 1995.

Reill, Peter Hanns. *The German Enlightenment and the Rise of Historicism*. Berkeley: University of California Press, 1975.

Robertson, Ritchie, ed. *Lessing and the German Enlightenment*. Oxford, UK: Voltaire Foundation, 2013.

Sharpe, Lesley, ed. *The Cambridge Companion to Goethe*. Cambridge, UK: Cambridge University Press, 2002.

Watanabe-O'Kelly, Helen, ed. *The Cambridge History of German Literature*. Cambridge, UK: Cambridge University Press, 2000.

Exile Literature *(Exilliteratur)*

German *Exilliteratur* is that body of literature produced by anti-National Socialist writers who fled from Nazi Germany and those countries and/or territories sympathetic to the Nazi cause between 1933 and 1945 (the period is extended by some literary scholars to 1949, the year in which the two new German states were founded). Many of these writers were Jewish and/or held communist views. Between 1933 and 1939, many German exiled authors settled in Paris, Amsterdam, Stockholm, Zürich, Prague, Moscow, and London. Many others emigrated to the United States or Mexico.

The works of *Exilliteratur*'s authors often expressed their resistance to National Socialism either directly or indirectly. Many autobiographical works dealt with the authors' own experiences or those of their families or acquaintances in Nazi Germany. These writers were determined to make the world aware of the horrors transpiring in Germany. Some wrote novels detailing life in Nazi Germany, while others wrote of the "other" Germany for which they longed that had existed prior to the Nazi regime. Many of these authors were never able to feel at home in their adopted countries and were unable to establish themselves outside of Germany because of the language barrier.

While *Exilliteratur* does not possess any formal characteristics, certain genres were prominent during this period. Key among these was the continued development of Bertolt Brecht's Epic Theater and a variety of novel categories, including historical novels, most notably those of Lion Feuchtwanger, who employed historical material as parables, thus raising his novels from mere storytelling to a literary analysis of contemporary issues. Additional genres included the exile novel, used to describe the situation of exiles and to provide information about the Third Reich and National Socialism, for example, Anna Seghers's (1900–1983) novel *Transit* (1944); contemporary novels, which were generally social critiques; and utopian novels, which depicted an imaginary future as a way of counteracting the pessimism brought about by the oppressive regime of the National Socialists, such as Hermann Hesse's final full-length novel, *Das Glasperlenspiel* (*The Glass Bead Game*, 1943).

Prominent *Exilliteratur* authors include the pacifist Oskar Maria Graf (1894–1967), whose novel *Die Eroberung der Welt* (*The Conquest of the World*, 1949), retitled *Die Erben des Untergangs* (*The Inheritors of the Ruins*), tells the story of mankind's efforts to rebuild the world after an atomic catastrophe. The novel is a utopian look at mankind's promise and a stark criticism of National Socialism. Thomas Mann's older brother Heinrich (1871–1950) fled Germany to France and finally to the United States, where he died penniless in Los Angeles in 1950. He is best known for his 1905 novel *Professor Unrat* (*Small Town Tyrant*), which was the basis for the 1930 movie *Der Blaue Engel* (*The Blue Angel*). Sadly, he did not flourish in his new country, nevertheless continuing to write some of his greatest works in exile. Among these works is his memoir *Ein Zeitalter wird besichtigt* (*Review of an*

The authors of Exile Literature left Germany during the Third Reich and wrote about the horrors transpiring in Nazi Germany. Prominent proponents include Erich Maria Remarque, Berthold Brecht, and Anna Seghers. (Alexander Mirt/Dreamstime.com)

Age, 1945), which examines the history of Europe from the French Revolution through the Third Reich. Concerned for his own safety in Germany due to his anti-National Socialist writings, Thomas Mann fled first to Switzerland in 1933 and to the United States in 1938. He, too, settled in Los Angeles, but under conditions far superior to those of his older brother. Here he completed his novel *Doktor Faustus* (1947), a retelling of the Faust legend set against the tumultuous backdrop of early twentieth-century Germany.

Additional important authors of the exile period include Erich Maria Remarque (1898–1970), who is perhaps best known for his novel *Im Westen nichts Neues* (*All Quiet on the Western Front,* 1928), and whose writings on post-World War I Germany were declared unpatriotic. He fled to the United States in 1939. Bertolt Brecht, whose political stance made him an early target of the Nazis, fled to the United States in 1941 where he spent six years in Los Angeles trying with limited success to become a Hollywood screenwriter. During his period of exile in Europe and the United States, Brecht wrote some of his most famous works, including *Mutter Courage und ihre*

Kinder (*Mother Courage and Her Children*, 1939), *Das Leben des Galilei* (*The Life of Galileo*, 1943), and *Der gute Mensch von Sezuan* (*The Good Person of Szechwan*, 1953). However, even though his works were translated, he never became truly popular in the United States.

Several female writers fled Germany during the Third Reich. Among the most well-known are Anna Seghers (1900–1983), whose Jewish heritage and Communist Party membership forced her to flee Germany, first to France in 1934 and then to Mexico in 1941. While in Paris, she wrote *Das siebte Kreuz* (*The Seventh Cross*, 1939), relating the tale of seven prisoners who escaped from a concentration camp. Her 1944 novel *Transit* (*Transit Visa*), set in France after the German invasion, relates a series of interwoven stories of refugees trying to escape German-occupied France. Annette Kolb (1870–1967) was an outspoken pacifist author who criticized Germany's political climate openly. She fled Germany to Paris in 1933 and to New York in 1941. Her 1940 autobiographical work *Glückliche Reise* (*Happy Journey*) outlines her emigration (often in ironic terms). Hannah Arendt (1906–1975) was primarily a philosopher and political theorist. From a Jewish family, her writings on anti-Semitism in 1930s Germany forced her to flee first to Paris in 1933 and to the United States in 1941, where she settled in New York. She was a visiting professor at many prestigious U.S. universities. Her writings deal primarily with the nature of power and authority and how they threaten human freedom. Though most of her writing was theoretical, Arendt also published poetry, most of which exudes a deep sense of sadness and yearning.

Jessamine Cooke-Plagwitz

See also: Chapter 2: Overview. Chapter 5: Holocaust. Chapter 6: Overview; Jews in Germany; Refugees. Chapter 7: Overview. Chapter 11: Expressionism (*Expressionismus*) and Its Successors (1905–1925). Chapter 16: Film.

Further Reading

Brunnhuber, Nicole. "Explaining the Enemy: Images of German Culture in English-Language Fiction by German-Speaking Exiles in Great Britain, 1933–45." *Seminar—A Journal of Germanic Studies* 42(3): 277–287, 2006.

Mauthner, Martin. *German Writers in French Exile, 1933–1940*. London: Vallentine Mitchell. 2007.

Mews, Siegfried. "Exile Literature and Literary Exile: A Review Essay." *South Atlantic Review* 57(1): 103–109, 1992.

Rosenthal, Michael A. "Art and the Politics of the Desert: German Exiles in California and the Biblical Bilderverbot." *New German Critique: An Interdisciplinary Journal of German Studies* 118: 43–64, 2013.

Roy, Pinaki. "Patriots in Fremden Landern: 1939–45 German Émigré Literature." In G. N. Ray and J. Sarkar, eds. *Writing Difference: Nationalism, Identity, and Literature*, 367–391. New Delhi: Atlantic Publishers, 2014.

Expressionism (*Expressionismus*) and Its Successors (1905–1925)

Works of German expressionism are filled with feelings of isolation, death, and extremes of emotion. This period in Germany was one of rapid change and resulting social upheaval. With the country's defeat in World War I (1914–1918), the overthrow of the kaiser (emperor) in 1918, and the political instability that followed, uncertainty and a desire for new beginnings became prevalent literary themes. In order to express these changes, expressionist writers developed new techniques and began to work with new media. While expressionist works do reveal the inner reality of their authors, at the same time they represent a new way of using words as art. Expressionism often reflects feelings of being lost and disillusioned by the anonymity of Germany's rapidly expanding cities. The familiar was frequently shown in an unfamiliar environment, thus encouraging a new perception of the world. Authors strove to achieve liberation from the rigid political, social, and aesthetic ideas of the past, and themes involving death and the end of the world accompanied by the promise of new beginnings became prevalent. In many expressionist works, the protagonists sought escape from the rationality and boredom of their everyday lives through intoxicating dream worlds and ecstatic experiences that enable a sensual experience.

Georg Heym's (1887–1912) 1910 poem "Der Gott der Stadt" ("The God of the City") reflects his belief that the unchecked urbanization and industrialization of the era were deleterious to Germany's future. Heym employs unorthodox descriptions and strange metaphors to create a sense of unease. The city is portrayed as a living being, but one bent on harming both the people living in it and the nature destroyed through its creation. The expressionist poetry of Gottfried Benn (1886–1956) in his collection *Morgue und andere Gedichte* (*Morgue and Other Poems*, 1912) shocked bourgeois sensibilities. Here Benn juxtaposes love and beauty with illness and death; instead of praising the beautiful features of a woman, for example, he describes diseases of erogenous body parts. Nothing is as expected. The poetry's subject matter is dreadful; the poems themselves are beautiful.

Expressionist novels include Hermann Hesse's (1877–1962) masterpiece *Der Steppenwolf* (1927), which details the experiences of Hesse's semi-autobiographical hero on his journey of self-discovery. The novel is a mix of fiction and fantasy that criticizes modern industrial society and its excesses while attempting to reconcile the protagonist's role within it; the desire for bourgeois comfort versus the individualistic facet of his character, which recognizes the inherent vanity and absurdity of these desires.

Alfred Döblin's (1878–1957) *Berlin Alexanderplatz* (1929), set in 1920s Berlin, traces the fate of a petty criminal recently released from prison as he attempts to navigate his return to a decaying society and lead an honest life during the years leading up to World War II. The novel is written from a variety of viewpoints, constantly shifting perspectives and incorporating such elements as press clippings, weather reports, and period songs to establish setting. In addition, Döblin incorporated stream-of-consciousness interior monologues and periodic breaking of the fourth wall through narrator commentary. The novel is Döblin's best-known work and has been adapted for film and radio and translated into twenty-two different languages.

The famous Bohemian author Franz Kafka's (1883–1924) work spans the literary movements of expressionism and modernism. His early stories, "Das Urteil" ("The Judgement," 1913) and "Die Verwandlung" ("The Metamorphosis," 1915) lean toward the former, while later works, such as the novels *Der Prozess* (*The Trial*, 1925) and *Das Schloß* (*The Castle*, 1926), are more easily categorized as early modernist works. The thread that runs through much of Kafka's work, however, is the uncertainty of human perception. Kafka's protagonists are often passive and dominated by authority figures or inexplicable bureaucratic processes. His works abound with a sense of hopelessness and inadequacy in a world that has become increasingly absurd. It is this very absurdity, so prevalent in Kafka's fiction, that inspired the common term "Kafkaesque" to refer to situations grotesque enough to seem appropriate to his stories.

Expressionist drama is dominated by the works of Georg Kaiser (1878–1945) and Ernst Toller (1893–1939). The expressionist dramatic style frequently involved unrealistic lighting and bizarre décor, a combination that lent a nightmarish atmosphere to the plays. Plots were disjointed, and characters often lacked names in favor of designations like "The Man," alluding to their lack of individuality. Actors tended to exaggerate their words and movements as exemplified in Ernst Toller's (1893–1939) drama *Die Wandlung: Das Ringen eines Menschen* (*The Transformation: A Man's Struggle*, 1919), whose hero undergoes a spiritual metamorphosis from patriotic volunteer to revolutionary leader by turning his horrifying war experiences into an appreciation of human unity.

Georg Kaiser's (1878–1945) expressionist dramas *Die Bürger von Calais* (*The Citizens of Calais*, 1914) and *Von morgens bis mitternachts* (*From Morn till Midnight*, 1916) criticized capitalism and nationalism, endorsing instead new communities and value systems. While Kaiser's plays appealed to like-minded audiences alarmed and drained by war, his work was ultimately banned by the National Socialists. He fled Germany to Switzerland in 1938.

Expressionist drama would eventually evolve into a new dramatic form in the Epic Theater of such dramatists as Bertolt Brecht (1898–1956), who wrote some forty plays during his lifetime. While this style maintained certain elements of expressionist theater, Brecht criticized that style for being too abstract. As in expressionist theater, there are interruptions and a sense of fragmentation to Epic Theater, but here the purpose of these intrusions lies in distancing the audience from the drama. This technique, called the *Verfremdungseffekt* (estrangement effect), encouraged the use of documentary effects, audience interaction, and explanatory placards. Brecht espoused Marxist ideology and used his plays to critique contemporary society. For a time, he collaborated with Kurt Weill, who set Brecht's lyrics to music in *Die Dreigroschenoper* (*The Threepenny Opera*, 1928) and *Aufstieg und Fall der Stadt Mahagonny* (*Rise and Fall of the City Mahagonny*, 1927–1929). Because of his political leanings, Brecht would also become an important figure among the writers of German *Exilliteratur* (exile literature).

Else Lasker-Schüler (1869–1945) is the best-known female writer of the male-dominated expressionist movement. Lasker-Schüler composed poetry, short stories, novels, and plays. Between 1910 and 1930, she contributed to the expressionist journal *Der Sturm,* and in 1911 she published her poetry collection *Meine Wunder* (*My Miracles*). Her work is filled with rich visual imagery, and prevalent themes include religious experience (particularly regarding Judaism), love, and Middle Eastern influences. Her play *Arthur Aronymus und seine Väter* (*Arthur Aronymous and His Fathers,* 1932) focused on the question of religious tolerance as the Nazis rose to power in Germany. Lasker-Schüler fled to Switzerland in 1933, settling in Palestine in 1937.

Jessamine Cooke-Plagwitz

See also: Chapter 2: Overview; Wilhelm II (1859–1941). Chapter 11: Exile Literature (*Exilliteratur*).

Further Reading

Benjamin, Walter. *Understanding Brecht.* Anna Bostock, trans. London, New York: Verso, 2003.

Benson, Renate. *German Expressionist Drama: Ernst Toller and Georg Kaiser.* London: Macmillan, 1984.

Brown, Hilary, ed. *Landmarks in German Women's Writing,* no. 39. New York: Peter Lang, 2007.

Donahue, Neil H., ed. *A Companion to the Literature of German Expressionism.* Rochester, NY: Camden House, 2005.

Falkenberg, Betty. *Else Lasker-Schuler: A Life.* Jefferson, NC: McFarland, 2003.

Furness, Raymond, and Malcolm Humble. *A Companion to Twentieth-Century German Literature.* London: Routledge, 2003.

Krause, Duane. "An Epic System." In Phillip B. Zarrilli, ed. *Acting (Re)considered: Theories and Practices,* 262–274. Worlds of Performance Series. London: Routledge, 1995.

Lawrie, Steven W. "Bertolt Brecht." *The Literary Encyclopedia.* December 17, 2004. https://www.litencyc.com/php/speople.php?rec=true&UID=554, Accessed October 19, 2021.

Literature of the German Democratic Republic

The literature of East Germany, that portion of Germany under Soviet control from 1945 to 1990, was controlled by a communist government. The literature of the German Democratic Republic (GDR) went through two major phases in the immediate aftermath of World War II: first from 1945 to 1947, it was characterized by anti-fascism and the hope of German reunification. During these years, several authors of *Exilliteratur* returned to the Soviet zone of Germany: Anna Seghers in 1947 and Bertolt Brecht in 1948 among them. At this time, the ruling party declared that literature should portray workers as heroes who triumph over the evil of capitalism. This

Aufbauliteratur (development literature) presented an optimistic outlook for the future and would focus on building socialism.

Second, with the construction of the Berlin Wall in 1961, GDR literature began to develop a measured note of criticism. Authors cautiously began to express concerns over the construction of the wall and the *Staatssicherheitspolizei* (Stasi), and by the 1970s, authors had begun turning their attention to the issues faced by the individual within this communist society. In 1976, the nonconformist singer and poet Wolf Biermann was stripped of his GDR citizenship while on a concert tour in West Germany. This action elicited protests from GDR authors, and the government began to clamp down on writers and intellectuals, many of whom left for the West. Increasingly, GDR writers ignored party guidelines, published their works with Western presses, and by the fall of the Berlin Wall in 1989, the differences between the literatures of East and West Germany had become far less evident.

Notable GDR authors include Uwe Johnson (1934–1984), who published *Mutmaßungen über Jakob* (*Speculations about Jacob*) in 1959, the same year he left the GDR for West Germany. The novel is filled with scathing criticisms of the GDR and its political system. Jurek Becker (1937–1997) wrote *Jakob der Lügner* (*Jacob the Liar*, 1969) initially as a film script and then as a novel, which relates the story of a Jew in a Nazi ghetto who tells increasingly convoluted stories in order to raise the hopes and spirits of his friends. The novel ponders the malleable nature of truth. Ulrich Plenzdorf (1934–2007) caused a sensation with his novel *Die neuen Leiden des jungen W.* (*The New Sufferings of Young W.*, 1973). The novel and play, based on Goethe's *Werther*, is constructed in a montage format, and the reader must piece together the protagonist's story. The story abounds with questions regarding the search for identity and individualism in the context of the communist system.

Christa Wolf (1929–2011) published her novel *Der geteilte Himmel* (*Divided Heaven*) in 1963, in which she describes problems of life in the GDR. In 1968, she published *Nachdenken über Christa T.* (*The Quest for Christa T.*), which examines a woman's experience of societal pressure to conform. Anna Seghers (1900–1983), well known as an *Exilliteratur* author, settled in the GDR in 1947, where she was required to adhere to state guidelines in her writing. At this time, she composed her novel trilogy detailing the rise of German socialist society: *Die Toten Bleiben Jung* (*The Dead Stay Young*, 1949); *Die Entscheidung* (*The Decision*, 1959); and *Das Vertrauen* (*Trust*, 1960).

Jessamine Cooke-Plagwitz

See also: Chapter 2: Berlin Wall. Chapter 3: Citizenship; Government and Politics in the German Democratic Republic. Chapter 9: Language Development in Divided Germany.

Further Reading

Bathrick, David. *The Powers of Speech: The Politics of Culture in the GDR*. Lincoln: University of Nebraska Press, 1995.

Fehervary, Helen. "The Literature of the GDR (1945–1990)." In Helen Watanabe-O'Kelly, ed. *The Cambridge History of German Literature*, 393–439. Cambridge, UK: Cambridge University Press, 1997.

Herminghouse, Patricia. "Whose German Literature? GDR-Literature, German Literature and the Question of National Identity." *GDR Bulletin* 16(2): 6–11, 1990.

Leeder, Karen, ed. *Rereading East Germany: The Literature and Film of the GDR*. Cambridge, UK: Cambridge University Press, 2015.

Robinson, Benjamin. *The Skin of the System: On Germany's Socialist Modernity*. Stanford, CA: Stanford University Press, 2009.

Saunders, Anna, and Debbie Pinfold, eds. *Remembering and Rethinking the GDR: Multiple Perspectives and Plural Authenticities*. Basingstoke, UK: Palgrave Macmillan, 2013.

Silberman, Marc. "Writing What—for Whom? 'Vergangenheitsbewältigung' in GDR Literature." *German Studies Review* 10(3): 527–538, 1987.

The Middle Ages (ca. 718–1500)

The generally accepted time span of medieval German literature runs from the Carolingian Dynasty (ca. 718–1122) to the time of the Reformation (ca. 1517) and is commonly divided into three distinct periods: Old High German (ca. 700–1050); Middle High German (ca. 1050–1350); and Renaissance Transition (ca. 1350–1500). Because most poetry or storytelling was spoken and not written, there is little surviving writing of the Old High German Period. The oldest existing text written in German, *Die Merseburger Zaubersprüche*, consists of two charms named for the town in which they were discovered (Merseburg). The texts are still preserved there. The manuscript in which the charms appear was written in the tenth century, but the origin of the charms extends back to pre-Carolingian times. The charms' subject matter consists of gods and goddesses from Germanic myth.

Dating from the seventh century and believed to be of Langobardic origin, the *Hildebrandslied* represents the only remaining example of epic poetry. The manuscript relates the tale of the tragic encounter between Hildebrand and his son Hadubrand, who meet on opposing sides of battle. Though the monks ran out of space and did not complete the story, it is generally believed that the tale ends with Hildebrand killing his son. Because monks did the bulk of the writing during this time, most existing texts of the period are liturgical in nature; for example, passages from the *Heliand* and the *Evangelienbuch* of Otfried von Weißenburg as well as the *Wessobrunner Gebet* (late 8th century) and *Muspilli* (early 9th century). Toward the end of the ninth century some shorter poems appeared that were essentially Old High German adaptations of Latin poems. Of these, the *Ludwigslied* is probably the most significant. The most notable author of period writing in Old High German is Notker der Deutsche (950–1022), who was a schoolmaster at St. Gallen. Much of his writing consists of translations from Latin into Old High German, but his greatest accomplishment is his creation of the first systematic orthography of Old High German.

Beginning in the middle of the eleventh century and increasingly throughout the period of the Crusades (1096–1291), religious life in Germany began to take on immense significance. This was especially true during the Second Crusade (1147–1149), when

The Middle Ages in German literature extends from the time of Charlemagne to the Reformation. The oldest existing texts written in German are the eleventh-century Merseburger Charms. (Mikhail Markovskiy/Dreamstime.com)

the German emperor Conrad III (1093–1152) allied with Louis VII of France (1120–1180), exposing German nobles (knights) to French manners and culture as they fought side by side. This contact contributed to the emergence of the courtly epic poetry of the Middle High German period (1050–1350). The first significant works exhibiting this French influence are Alberich de Briançon's *Alexanderlied* (ca. 1150) and Pfaffe Konrad's *Rolandslied* (ca. 1170). Both works employ secular material in order to impart a religious message, and both are important for their portrayal of characteristics generally attributed to the heroes of the courtly epic.

Probably the best known of the German courtly epics is Wolfram von Eschenbach's (1160–1220) *Parzival* (ca. 1205), which tells the tale of the knight Parzival and his quest for the Holy Grail. Other famous courtly epics written during the same period include Gottfried von Strassburg's (?–1210) *Tristan* (ca. 1210) and Hartmann von Aue's (ca. 1160–1210) *Erec*, *Gregorius*, and *Der arme Heinrich* (*Poor Henry*), all believed to have been written in the 1190s.

The French influence also made itself known through lyric poetry, which slowly replaced earlier songs with the *Minnesang*, or courtly songs of love and honor. This was the tradition of the love song (in this context generally meaning pure affection and service), which was written and performed by the *Minnesänger* who wandered throughout the countryside. The most famous and prolific of the *Minnesänger* was Walther von der Vogelweide, who lived from approximately 1170 to 1230. According to historians, von der Vogelweide composed more than one hundred love songs and was an extremely important performer in the princely courts of medieval Germany. Though several of his written manuscripts survive, little is known about their musical accompaniment.

The late Middle Ages in Germany saw the gradual dwindling of the chivalric themes of the court epic and the *Minnesang*. At this time, the beginnings of German drama emerged and *Schwänke*, short comedies, became popular entertainment. These short pieces ranged from the silly to the obscene, often focusing on the foolish farmer who becomes the butt of every joke. The most famous character to result from this tradition was Till Eulenspiegel, a German peasant and trickster. Poetry and stories of the period contained a strong didactic element. Sebastian Brant's (1458–1521) *Narrenschiff* (*Ship of Fools*) of 1494 is a well-known example of the genre. The story is a satirical allegory in which Brant ridicules humankind's weaknesses, portraying them as fools traveling in a ship to a fool's paradise. The work is particularly critical of corruption within the Catholic Church.

Finally, the late Middle Ages saw a rise in religious devotion among ordinary citizens in Germany. Adherents of this intense spiritualism followed the teachings of Meister Eckhart (ca. 1260–1328), whose treatises outline the stages of the mystical union of the soul with God. This interest in Christian mysticism would become a significant impulse behind the literature of the Reformation, the Baroque, and German Romanticism.

Jessamine Cooke-Plagwitz

See also: Chapter 2: Overview; Charlemagne (748–814). Chapter 5: The Reformation. Chapter 9: Overview; Foreign Influences on German. Chapter 11: Romanticism (*Romantik*) (1788–1835). Chapter 12: Carolingian Renaissance. Chapter 13: Musical Periods and Composers.

Further Reading

Classen, Albrecht. Review of "The Tristan Story in German Literature of the Late Middle Ages and Early Renaissance. Tradition and Innovation." *Studies in German Language and Literature* 5; *Studies in Russian and German* 5: 415–418, 1992.

Classen, Albrecht. "Whatever Happened to Courtly Love? The Role of Love in Late Medieval German Literature, with Emphasis on the 'Volksbuch.'" *Fifteenth Century Studies* 20: 35, 1993.

Gibbs, Marion, and Sidney M. Johnson. *Medieval German Literature: A Companion*. London: Routledge, 2002.

Murdoch, Brian, and James N. Hardin, eds. *German Literature of the Early Middle Ages*, vol. 2. Rochester, NY: Camden House, 2004.

Ozment, Steven. "Eckhart and Luther: German Mysticism and Protestantism." *The Thomist: A Speculative Quarterly Review* 42(2): 259–280, 1978.

Watanabe-O'Kelly, Helen, ed. *The Cambridge History of German Literature*. Cambridge, UK: Cambridge University Press, 2000.

Wellbery, David E., Joseph Leo Koerner, and Anton Kaes, eds. *A New History of German Literature*. Cambridge, MA: Harvard University Press, 2004.

Wimmer, Albert K. *Anthology of Medieval German Literature: Synoptically Arranged with Contemporary Translations*. Berrien Springs, MI: Vande Vere, 1991.

Post-Wall Literature (ca. 1989–2005)

With the fall of the Berlin Wall in 1989, emotions among Germany's intellectuals were mixed. Some were cautiously optimistic, while others mourned the loss of socialism's promise to conquer what they perceived to be capitalism's evil empire. The question of German identity took on prominence and held the public's attention throughout the 1990s. Literary soul-searching explored life in communist East Germany and attempted to come to terms with actions and inaction committed in the name of political indoctrination. Still other works questioned whether the idea of a unified Germany was even possible in light of the nation's Nazi past. Much of the popular literature of the 1990s centered on Berlin as Germany's metaphorical center, and throughout that decade and the early 2000s a new generation of writers produced works that focused on the popular. These *neue Archiviste* (New Archivists) focused on fashion and trends; they named specific brands, designers, or songs in their works and emphasized the superficial, avoiding questions of politics or emotion.

In 1991, Monika Maron (b. 1941) explored the nature of inherited guilt in her *Stille Seile Sechs* (*Silent Close No. Six*), while Christa Wolf's novella *Was bleibt* (*What Remains, 1990*) created controversy not only with its revelations of the author's own Stasi collaboration, but also in her perceived opportunism in waiting to publish the work until after the fall of communism rather than in 1979 when it was originally written.

Writers of the New Archivist school include Thomas Brussig (b. 1964), whose novels *Helden wie wir* (*Heroes Like Us*, 1995) and *Am kürzeren Ende der Sonnenallee* (*At the Shorter End of Sonnenallee*, 1999) provide satirical insights on life in East Germany before, during, and after the fall of the wall. Elke Naters's (b. 1963) early novels *Königinnen* (*Queens*, 1998) and *Lügen* (*Lies*, 1999) are both set in 1990s Berlin and provide the reader with a close look at the city's cultural milieus, the local dialect, and its role as a consumer paradise. Meanwhile, Thomas Meinecke's 1998 novel *Tomboy* explores the role of gender and sexuality within contemporary German life.

During this period, a new group of female writers emerged whose works emphasized women's perspectives of newly unified Germany. Their works are no longer concerned with assuaging past guilt but rather examine the state of Germany going forward.

Here we find such authors as Sibylle Berg (b. 1968), whose numerous novels and plays include *Ein paar Leute suchen das Glück und lachen sich tot* (*A Few People Search for Happiness and Laugh Themselves to Death*, 1997), a comic consideration of life's banalities told through a multiperspective narrative. Alexa Henning von Lange's (b. 1973) 1997 novel *Relax* is considered one of the founding works of the pop literature movement, while Judith Hermann (b. 1970) (*Sommerhaus, später* [*Summerhouse, Later*, 1998]), Jana Hensel (b. 1976) (*Zonenkinder* [*Zone Children*, 2002]), and Juli Zeh (b. 1974) (author of the award-winning *Adler und Engel* [*Eagles and Angels*, 2001]) all continue to produce popular works of high literary quality.

Jessamine Cooke-Plagwitz

See also: Chapter 2: Berlin Wall. Chapter 3: Government and Politics in the German Democratic Republic. Chapter 6: Overview. Chapter 7: Overview. Chapter 9: Standard and Dialect. Chapter 13: Overview; Contemporary Popular Music. Chapter 15: Leisure and Sports in the German Democratic Republic. Chapter 16: Fashion Designers.

Further Reading

Costabile-Heming, Carol Anne, Rachel J. Halverson, and Kristie A. Foell, eds. *Textual Responses to German Unification: Processing Historical and Social Change in Literature and Film.* Berlin; Boston: De Gruyter, 2013.

Gerstenberger, Katharina. *Writing the New Berlin: The German Capital in Post-Wall Literature,* vol. 21. Rochester, NY: Camden House, 2008.

Niven, Bill. "Literary Portrayals of National Socialism in Post-Unification German Literature." In Helmut Schmitz, ed. *German Culture and the Uncomfortable Past,* 19–36. London: Routledge, 2017.

Steding, Elizabeth Priester. *Re-membering the Father: Constructions of the Father and the Authoritarian State in Post-Unification East German Literature,* 2005. Michigan State University, PhD Dissertation. https://search.proquest.com/docview/305425943?pq -origsite=gscholar

Taberner, Stuart. *German Literature of the 1990s and Beyond: Normalization and the Berlin Republic.* Rochester, NY: Camden House, 2005.

Twark, Jill E. *Humor, Satire, and Identity: Eastern German Literature in the 1990s.* Berlin, Boston: De Gruyter, 2007.

Twark, Jill E., ed. *Strategies of Humor in Post-Unification German Literature, Film, and Other Media.* Newcastle upon Tyne, UK: Cambridge Scholars Publishing, 2011.

Postwar Literature

Immediately following the end of World War II, German writers and intellectuals found themselves at *Stunde Null* (zero point), which refers to the desire for complete social reformation. Authors returning from exile and those who had weathered the war in Germany aspired to rebuild a Germany free of the elements that could lead to dictatorship.

Trümmerliteratur, or rubble literature, dominated Germany's literary landscape from the end of the war well into the 1950s. This literature employed simple, realistic language to depict the central theme of destruction, both of the cities and of the lives and dreams of their inhabitants. Many authors probed questions of guilt for the war and for their own roles in it. A popular genre for this literature was poetry, which writers employed to report their concise and unembellished observations. Earlier poetic conventions, like meter or rhyme, were abandoned. The leading voices behind the movement were those of Gruppe 47, who worked to provide authors of the period with a critical base from which to pursue their efforts to recreate German literature.

Key writers of Postwar German literature include Wolfgang Borchert (1921–1947), whose play *Draußen vor der Tür* (*The Man Outside*, 1947) was one of the first to address existence in a defeated and traumatized country. During the period between 1947 and 1950, Heinrich Böll (1917–1985), who was forced to serve in Hitler's army during the war, wrote short stories centered on the daily lives of ordinary soldiers; and his 1953 novel *Und sagte kein einziges Wort* (*Acquainted with the Night*) focuses on the problems faced by ordinary Germans after the war during the period of restoration. Nelly Sachs (1891–1970), who was both a playwright and a poet, published her volume of poetry *In den Wohnungen des Todes* (*In the Dwellings of Death*) concerning the Holocaust and the Nazi death camps in 1947.

Prominent authors of the later postwar period include Günter Grass (1927–2015), whose debut novel, *Die Blechtrommel* (*The Tin Drum*, 1959), the first novel of his *Danziger Trilogie* (*Danzig Trilogy*), relates elaborate tales of World War II, the Russian influx, and the later postwar reformation years; and Peter Weiss (1916–1982), whose play, *Die Ermittlung* (*The Investigation*, 1965) recreates the trials of the men who committed mass murders at Auschwitz.

As memories of the war faded, literature through the later decades of the twentieth century began to examine new topics and take on fresh forms. The postmodernist movement of the late twentieth century was also greatly influenced by the works of Günter Grass, with his *Der Butt* (*The Flounder*, 1977) and *Die Rättin* (*The Rat*, 1986). Postmodernist works are often marked by unreliable and contradictory narration and self-reflexivity. These works often contain multiple narratives and can seem at times disjointed. However, many postmodern authors have been praised for creating literary masterpieces, such as Rainald Goetz's (b. 1954) *Irre* (*Insane*, 1983), a semi-autobiographical work which details the struggles of a psychiatrist-in-training who suffers a mental breakdown when confronted with the daily reality he finds working in a psychiatric hospital, and Patrick Süskind's (b. 1949) *Das Parfum* (*Perfume: The Story of a Murderer*, 1985), which employs lavish descriptions to explore the sense of smell and its connection to human emotions.

Anne Duden's (b. 1942) 1985 novel *Das Judasschaf* (*The Judas Sheep*) employs rich language to present the tale of a woman's personal trauma and its inextricable link with the trauma of the German past. Meanwhile, much of Herta Müller's (b. 1953) writing (*Niederungen* [*Nadirs*], 1982; *Herztier* [*The Land of Green Plums*], 1994) focuses on the oppressive atmosphere and censorship endured during Nicolae Ceausescu's regime in Romania; and the Turkish-German author Emine Sevgi Özdamar (b. 1965) explores the connection of identity with language in her short story collection *Mutterzunge* (*Mothertongue*, 1990). Her novel *Das Leben ist eine Karawanserei, hat zwei Türen, aus einer kam ich rein, aus der anderen ging ich raus* (*Life Is a Caravanserai: Has Two Doors I Went in One I Came out the Other*, 1992) is a tale of the narrator's life in Turkey and departure for Germany.

Jessamine Cooke-Plagwitz

See also: Chapter 2: Overview; Hitler, Adolf (1889–1945). Chapter 5: Holocaust. Chapter 6: Turks in Germany.

Further Reading

Bartram, Graham, and Philip Payne, eds. *The Cambridge Companion to the Modern German Novel*. Cambridge, UK: Cambridge University Press, 2004.

Bray, Joe, Alison Gibbons, and Brian McHale, eds. *The Routledge Companion to Experimental Literature*. London: Routledge, 2012.

Fowler, Douglas. "Millhauser, Süskind, and the Postmodern Promise." *Journal of the Fantastic in the Arts* 1(4): 77–86, 1988.

Grange, William. *The A to Z of Postwar German Literature*. Metuchen, NJ: Scarecrow Press, 2010.

Horton, Aaron Dennis. *Catastrophe and Identity in Post-War German Literature*, 2005. East Tennessee State University, MA thesis. https://dc.etsu.edu/cgi/viewcontent.cgi?article=2218&context=etd. Accessed October 19, 2021.

Keele, Alan Frank. *The Apocalyptic Vision: A Thematic Exploration of Postwar German Literature*. Madrid: J. Porrúa Turanzas Scripta Humanistica, 1983.

McCormick, Richard W. *Politics of the Self: Feminism and the Postmodern in West German Literature and Film*, vol. 1150. Princeton, NJ: Princeton University Press, 2014.

Nicholson, Linda. *Feminism/Postmodernism*. London: Routledge, 2013.

Paul, Georgina. *Perspectives on Gender in Post-1945 German Literature*. Rochester, NY: Camden House, 2009.

Roberts, David. "Nullpunkt und kein Ende? Perspectives and Theses on Postwar German Literature." *Orbis Litterarum* 35(3): 250–273, 1980.

Schäfer, Martin Jörg, and Elke Siegel. "The Intellectual and the Popular: Reading Rainald Goetz." *The Germanic Review: Literature, Culture, Theory* 81(3): 195–201, 2006.

Stoehr, Ingo Roland. *German Literature of the Twentieth Century: From Aestheticism to Postmodernism*, vol. 10. Columbia, SC: Camden House; Woodbridge: Boydell & Brewer, 2001.

Stone, Katherine. *Women and National Socialism in Postwar German Literature: Gender, Memory, and Subjectivity*. Rochester, NY: Camden House, 2017.

Realism and Naturalism (*Realismus* and *Naturalismus*) (1848–1899)

The authors of German realism endeavored to observe the world objectively and to reproduce it as realistically as possible. Early realists adopted a relatively optimistic view of the world, while later adherents were more pessimistic, particularly in their portrayals of the social issues brought about by industrialization. Many realist authors focused on historical subjects and social issues, particularly questions regarding the inner life of the individual and their role in society. While these themes were to be replicated as accurately as possible, the perception of beauty was understood to be subjective, and the author's role was to imbue the represented world with beauty through these depictions.

Major figures of German realism include Theodor Fontane (1819–1898), whose novels contain detailed descriptions of nineteenth-century bourgeois German life and manners. His 1888 novel *Irrungen, Wirrungen* (*Trials and Tribulations*) portrays the limitations placed on a pair of lovers from different social classes, while his masterpiece, *Effi Briest* (1894–1895), addresses the theme of adultery in its portrayal of a woman who begins an extramarital affair. Fontane describes the heroine's feelings of guilt in powerful detail and notes the absurdity of the tale's inevitable tragic end as the direct consequence of social convention.

Gustav Freytag (1816–1895) authored the novel *Soll und Haben* (*Debit and Credit*, 1855), in which he praises the integrity and efficiency of the German middle class, extolling its virtues as pillars of the German nation. Wilhelm Raabe's (1831–1910) work spans the genres of realism and modernism. Much of his early fiction concerns social problems; for example, his *Der Hungerpastor* (*The Hunger Pastor*, 1864) analyzes the difficulties faced by the individual when confronted with his limited control of his own life. His *Stopfkuchen* (*Tubby Schaumann*, 1891), with its frequent interruptions and tangential narratives, suggests the beginnings of modernism, while its descriptions paint a clear picture of a world of modernization and colonization.

Theodor Storm (1817–1888) was a liberal thinker and one of Germany's most important realist writers. His two best-known works are his novellas *Immensee* (1849), with its rich symbolism and almost painful nostalgia, and *Der Schimmelreiter* (*The Rider on the White Horse*, 1888), probably his greatest work, in which the rugged North Sea coast is the setting for Storm's tale of a man's struggles with social pressures within a small, conservative community. A late addition to the realist novel genre is Thomas Mann's (1875–1955) *Buddenbrooks: Verfall einer Familie* (*Buddenbrooks: The Decline of a Family*, 1901), which traces several generations of a commercial family, including precise depictions of social events, home and school settings, and business practices of the mid-nineteenth century. Louise von François (1817–1893) wrote on historical subjects in the realist style. Her novel *Die letzte Reckenburgerin* (*The Last Lady of Reckenburg*, 1870) presents an interesting glimpse into female psychology in its presentation of the fates of two women whose lives are damaged by marriage and the prosperous life of their unmarried contemporary.

While realism and naturalism both strived to represent the world objectively, realist literature attempted for the most part to avoid negative depictions. Naturalism, on the other hand, reproduced the disagreeable in detail. While realism tended to stay with the (fairly) comfortable existence of the middle class for its subject matter, naturalism removed the filter and revealed the misery and suffering endured by the lower classes. Naturalist themes often concern physical and mental illness, class struggle, and disillusionment. Influenced by Charles Darwin's theory of evolution, naturalists believed that one's heredity and environment determined one's character and that ultimately, individuals were locked in a struggle against baser instincts to retain a civilized appearance.

Die Familie Selicke (*The Selicke Family*, 1890), a play coauthored by Arno Holz (1863–1929) and Johannes Schlaf (1862–1941), is illustrative of the naturalist style. Set in a Berlin tenement, the novel depicts a daughter, terrorized by her drunken father, as the victim of environmental determinism who finds herself unable to cut the ties to her oppressive environment when given the chance. Gerhart Hauptmann (1862–1946) was a prolific writer of naturalist poetry, novels, and dramas. His controversial social drama *Vor Sonnenaufgang* (*Before Dawn*, 1889) shocked theater audiences in its day, but brought him renown and encouraged him to continue writing. *Die Weber* (*The Weavers*, 1892) dramatized the Silesian Weavers' Revolt of 1844. Its stark portrayal of the weavers' wretched circumstances plus Hauptmann's use of common speech made this one of his most riveting dramas, while his *Fuhrmann Henschel* (*Drayman Henschel*, 1898) portrayed the personal decline of a workman due to domestic stress. Finally, Hauptman's comedy *Der Biberpelz* (*The Beaver Coat*, 1893) was a work of social criticism featuring characters speaking in Berlin dialect and a dishonest but clever cleaning woman who outwits the local authorities. Hauptmann was awarded the Nobel Prize for Literature in 1912.

Women of the naturalist school provide unique insights into the female experience in novels such as Gabriele Reuter's (1859–1941). *Aus guter Familie* (*From a Good Family*, 1895) details the growing desperation of a young woman in the face of social conventions. Lou Andreas-Salomé depicts independent women in her stories "Fenitschka" (1898) and "Eine Ausschweifung" ("A Debauch," 1898). Finally, Franziska Gräfin zu Reventlow's (1871–1918) novel *Ellen Olestjerne* (1903) relates the story of a woman who realizes her own self-worth while gaining worldly experience and finding happiness as a single mother.

Jessamine Cooke-Plagwitz

See also: Chapter 7: Feminism. Chapter 9: Standard and Dialect. Chapter 12: Naturalism.

Further Reading

Campbell, Donna. "Naturalism." *The Encyclopedia of the Novel*, 2010. https://doi .org/10.1002/9781444337815.wbeotnn008. Accessed October 19, 2021.

DeMair, Jillian. "Unsettled Soil and Uncertain Stories in Wilhelm Raabe's 'Stopfkuchen.'" *Colloquia Germanica* 47(4): 351–370, 2014.

Downing, Eric. *Double Exposures: Repetition and Realism in Nineteenth-Century German Fiction*. Stanford, CA: Stanford University Press, 2000.

Kontje, Todd Curtis, ed. *A Companion to German Realism, 1848–1900*. Rochester, NY: Camden House, 2002.

Osborne, John. *Gerhard Hauptmann and the Naturalist Drama*. London: Routledge, 2005.

Root, Winthrop H. "German Naturalism and Its Literary Predecessors." *The Germanic Review: Literature, Culture, Theory* 23(2): 115–124, 1948.

Walker, John. *The Truth of Realism: A Reassessment of the German Novel 1830–1900*. London: Routledge, 2017.

Romanticism (*Romantik*) (1788–1835)

While Romanticism was not a direct reaction against the literature and aesthetics of the Enlightenment, it was certainly a reaction to the chaos and revolution in Europe at the end of the eighteenth century. In place of the Enlightenment's emphasis on reason, Romanticism presented a poetic world and portrayed individual experience in the search for a greater truth. In the works of this period, it is the artist who is divinely inspired and through whom individuals and nature can find their true voices. What was revolutionary in this work was the writer's refusal to obey predetermined rules of composition, with the resulting creation of new forms of thought and expression.

Major themes and leitmotifs of the period include the wanderer, who searches for new places, both physically and metaphorically, through the portrayal of exotic lands, the depths of the human psyche, and the indescribable beauties of nature, which is endowed by the Romantics with a mystical essence and a secret language to which only the true artistic soul is permitted access. The early Romantics included Ludwig Tieck (1773–1853), Wilhelm Heinrich Wackenroder (1773–1798), August Wilhelm von Schlegel (1767–1845) and his younger brother Friedrich (1772–1829), and Novalis (Friedrich, Freiherr von Hardenberg, 1772–1801). Characteristic works of the early movement are Wackenroder's *Herzensergießungen eines kunstliebenden Klosterbruders* (*Confessions of an Art-Loving Friar*, 1797) and Tieck's fairy-tale-like novellas *Der blonde Eckbert* (*Blond Eckbert*, 1797) and *Der Runenberg* (*The Runic Mountain*, 1804). These editions contain the eerie atmosphere, complicated plotline, and mysterious occurrences that have become synonymous with Romanticism. Among Tieck's best-known stage plays is *Der gestiefelte Kater* (*Puss in Boots,* 1797).

During this period, the Schlegel brothers along with Novalis and Tieck strove to define Romantic poetry in their periodical, *Athenaeum* (1798–1800), which published Novalis's masterpiece *Heinrich von Ofterdingen* (1802) posthumously. The novel, set in the Middle Ages, follows the hero's journey inspired by his dream of the Blue Flower— the symbol of Romantic longing. Though the novel remained unfinished at the time of Novalis's death in 1801, it has come to be appreciated as one of the key works of the early Romantic period and served as the inspiration for later Romantic novels. The second phase of Romanticism (1805–1815) features such writers as Heinrich von Kleist (1777–1811), Achim von Arnim (1781–1831), Clemens Brentano (1778–1842), Joseph Freiherr von Eichendorff (1788–1857), Adelbert von Chamisso (1781–1838), and Friedrich de la Motte Fouqué (1777–1843).

During this period, the literary focus was on the creation of a German national identity in direct opposition to the turmoil inflicted on Europe through the Napoleonic Wars from 1803 to 1815. To this end, much literary work aimed to highlight this national identity through *Volkspoesie* or folk poetry. Arnim and Brentano published traditional folk songs in *Des Knaben Wunderhorn* (*The Boy's Magic Horn*, 1805–1808). It was at this time as well that the Grimm Brothers Jakob (1785–1863) and Wilhelm (1786–1859) began collecting their fairy tales, *Volksmärchen,* the first collection of which, *Kinder- und Hausmärchen* (*Children's and Home Fairytales*), was published in 1812. Other works of particular note created during this period include Eichendorff's poetry and his prose works *Das Marmorbild* (1819) and *Aus dem Leben eines Taugenichts* (*On the Life of a Good-for-Nothing*, 1826); Kleist's dramas *Amphitryon* (1807) and *Der zerbrochene Krug* (*The Broken Jug,* 1808); Chamisso's novella *Peter Schlemihls wundersame Geschichte* (*Peter Schlemihl's Wondrous Story*, 1814); and la Motte Fouqué's novella *Undine* (1811), which was adapted as an opera by E. T. A. Hoffmann (1776–1822), the author famous for such tales as *Der goldene Topf* (*The Gold Pot*, 1814), *Der Sandmann* (*The Sandman*, 1816), *Das Fräulein von Scuderi* (*Mademoiselle Scudéry*, 1819), and *Lebensansichten des Katers Murr* (*The Life and Opinions of the Tomcat Murr*, 1819).

The writers of the later Romantic period were, to a certain extent, somewhat critical of the movement. However, a number of prominent writers continued to publish works incorporating Romantic facets. Friedrich Hölderlin (1770–1849) and Heinrich Heine (1797–1856) contributed such works as Hölderlin's epistolary novel *Hyperion* (1797–1799) and Heine's poetry, particularly his two volumes *Reisebilder* (*Travel Pictures*, 1826) and *Buch der Lieder* (*Book of Songs*, 1827), in which a sense of irony and even occasional disillusionment permeate otherwise Romantic themes.

Women of the Romantic age were quite influential within literary circles. Among the most significant are those who were in some way connected to important male authors of the period: Caroline Böhmer (1763–1809) married and divorced A. W. Schlegel and later married the philosopher F. W. J. Schelling (1775–1854). Most of Böhmer's work consisted of literary reviews and correspondence with important Romantic figures. Dorothea Veit (1764–1839), daughter of the philosopher Moses Mendelssohn and wife of Friedrich Schlegel, published two novels, *Lucinde* (1799) and *Florentin* (1801). Bettina Brentano (1785–1859), the sister of Clemens Brentano and later wife of von Arnim, assisted with the collection of songs for *Des Knaben Wunderhorn*, and published *Goethes Briefwechsel mit einem Kind* (*Goethe's Correspondence with a Child*, 1835) and *Die Günderode* (*Miss Günderode*, 1840), among other works. Sophie Mereau (1770–1806), who was married to Clemens Brentano, initially published anonymously, later publishing her novel *Amanda und Eduard* (1803) under her own name.

Jessamine Cooke-Plagwitz

See also: Chapter 9: Important Figures in the Study of the German Language. Chapter 12: Artists.

Further Reading

Behler, Ernst. *German Romantic Literary Theory*. Cambridge, UK: Cambridge University Press, 1993.

Beutin, Wolfgang, et al. *A History of German Literature: From the Beginnings to the Present Day*. London: Routledge, 2005.

Garland, Henry, and Mary Garland. *The Oxford Companion to German Literature*. Oxford, UK: Oxford University Press, 1997.

Lacoue-Labarthe, Philippe, and Jean-Luc Nancy. *The Literary Absolute: The Theory of Literature in German Romanticism*. Albany, NY: SUNY Press, 1988.

Mahoney, Dennis. *The Literature of German Romanticism: History of German Literature*, vol. 8. The Camden House History of German Literature. Rochester, NY: Camden House, 2004.

Saul, Nicholas, ed. *The Cambridge Companion to German Romanticism*. Cambridge, UK: Cambridge University Press, 2009.

Tymms, Ralph. *German Romantic Literature*. London: Routledge, 2019.

Storm and Stress (*Sturm und Drang*) (1767–1785)

The period of *Sturm und Drang* (Storm and Stress) began with Friedrich Maximilian Klinger's (1752–1831) *Wirrwarr*, whose title was later changed to *Sturm und Drang*. At the time, the expression described a movement that was something of a reaction against the rationalism of the Enlightenment, but which still represented an affirmation of its aesthetic principles. During this relatively brief period (ca. 1767–1785), many writers attempted to exalt the character of the noble man—aristocratic not necessarily by birth, but rather through a strong and uncompromising nobility of character. The resulting conflict between the principled individual and societal conventions was a frequent theme in the literature and drama of the period.

One key characteristic of *Sturm und Drang* drama is the relaxation of earlier classical literary forms such as the generally accepted dramatic rules regarding unity of time and place within a dramatic plot. *Sturm und Drang* dramatists favored multiple scene changes and side plots resulting in theater that was somewhat more complex than that to which audiences had become accustomed. Language in many dramas of the period moved to a natural expression, with many plays for the first time written in prose instead of verse. Tragedies of the period attempted to evoke fear and terror as opposed to the earlier expected fear and compassion, for the new middle-class dramatic hero could represent any of the plays' audience, and the protagonist's misfortunes might just as easily be their own. Reason could not protect them from an arbitrary God.

Sturm und Drang authors and playwrights produced works exalting personal freedom and the perfection of nature. Representative works of the period include von Goethe's epistolary novel *Die Leiden des jungen Werthers* (*The Sorrows of Young Werther*, 1774), his poem "Prometheus" (1789), and his play *Götz von Berlichingen mit der eisernen Hand* (*Götz of the Iron Hand*, 1773). During this period in Goethe's career, his works reflect a pure and innocent joy in nature and the natural world and in love. At times his work suggests feelings that are too deep for mere words to express, and he then relies on descriptions of

Storm and Stress (*Sturm und Drang*) represented a reaction against the rationalism of the Enlightenment. Wolfgang Johann von Goethe and Friedrich von Schiller were two of its most prominent authors. (Perry-Castaneda Library)

nature to impart his meaning. Indeed, the writings produced by Goethe during this period would prove inspirational to the later writers and poets of the German Romantic school. Such is certainly the case with his *Werther*, with its tale of unrequited love ending in suicide—all detailed in passionate descriptions of unrestrained (and unrestrainable) emotions. *Werther* would inspire a number of later epistolary novels relating events and emotions from the narrator's perspective, among them Jakob Michael Reinhold Lenz's (1751–1792) *Der Waldbruder* (*The Friar of the Forest*, 1776) and Friedrich Heinrich Jacobi's (1743–1819) *Eduard Allwills Papiere* (*Eduard Allwill's Papers*, 1781).

Like Goethe's, Friedrich Schiller's (1759–1805) career spanned several literary movements. His dramas *Die Räuber* (*The Robbers*, 1781) and *Kabale und Liebe* (*Intrigue and Love*, 1784) are representative of his *Sturm und Drang* period with their strong elements of social criticism and melodrama. Each play involves complicated plots in which attempts to deceive end badly for those involved. While *Die Räuber* was by far the more violent of the plays with its depictions of bloody violence, both this play and *Kabale und Liebe*, a retelling of the *Romeo and Juliet* narrative critical of artificial class divisions, catapulted Schiller to fame as a dramatist.

Other authors of the *Sturm und Drang* period include the aforementioned Friedrich Maximilian Klinger (1752–1831; *Faustus*, 1791; *Sturm und Drang*, 1776), Johann Gottfried Herder (*Journal meiner Reise im Jahr*, 1769, 1846; *Italienische Reise*, *1788*), and Marianne Ehrmann (1755–1795), whose novel *Amalie, eine wahre Geschichte in Briefen* (*Amalie, A True Story in Letters*, 1796) depicts intelligent women who are capable of both strong reason and powerful emotion.

Jessamine Cooke-Plagwitz

See also: Chapter 6: Aristocracy and the Elites. Chapter 8: Goethe-Institut. Chapter 11: The Enlightenment (*Aufklärung*) (1680–1789); Romanticism (*Romantik*) (1788–1835).

Further Reading

Baldick, Chris. *The Concise Oxford Dictionary of Literary Terms*. Oxford, UK: Oxford University Press, 1990.

Boyle, Nicholas. *German Literature: A Very Short Introduction*, vol. 178. Oxford, UK: Oxford University Press, 2008.

Dawson, Ruth P. *The Contested Quill: Literature by Women in Germany, 1770–1800*. Newark: University of Delaware Press, 2002.

Hill, David, and James N. Hardin, eds. *Literature of the Sturm und Drang*, vol. 6. Rochester, NY: Camden House, 2003.

Leidner, Alan C. *Sturm Und Drang: The German Library*, vol. 14. New York: Continuum, 1992.

Niekerk, Carl. "'Spätaufklärung': Rethinking the Late Eighteenth Century in German Literary History." *Journal of English and Germanic Philology* 102(3): 317–335, 2003.

Pascal, Roy. *The German Sturm und Drang*. Manchester, UK: Manchester University Press, 1967.

Turn-of-the-Century Literature (*Jahrhundertwende*) (1880–1920)

The latter years of the nineteenth century and early years of the twentieth saw a dizzying array of literary movements, from naturalism to impressionism to symbolism to expressionism and more. The only real common thread among these movements is in their rejection of positivism. In terms of content, much of the literature of the period revolves around cultural decay and can also be understood as a counter movement to naturalism, which, above all in art and literature, regarded the scientifically exact shaping of empirical reality as an ideal. Many of the period's authors were strongly influenced by Friedrich Nietzsche's (1844–1900) cultural pessimism and criticism of Christian morality. Around the same time, Sigmund Freud (1856–1939) published his *Traumdeutung* (*Interpretation of Dreams*, 1900), which shone a light on the inner workings of the human psyche, particularly in regard to experiences and ideas suppressed by the subconscious, subjects that would also figure prominently in the works of period authors.

The literature of German impressionism (ca. 1890–1920) refers to the representation of subjective, fleeting impressions. The momentary perception of a subject determines how it is depicted. The emphasis is on subjectivity and on capturing the tiniest details of sensation and mood. While the impressionists were also concerned with realistic representation, their definition of reality differed significantly from that of the naturalists. For the impressionists, reality was not determined by political or social conditions, but by the artist's subjective feelings. Thus, reality was not the objective world in and of itself, rather the world as perceived by the viewer through the filter of inner experience. Thus, impressionism is directed against the ideals of naturalism, which was primarily concerned with the most objective, realistic representation possible of existing social conditions. Major themes of impressionist literature are love and yearning, while death and life's transience are also frequent topics.

Perhaps the most prominent writer of the impressionist school is Thomas Mann (1875–1955), whose novella *Tonio Kröger* (1903) provides the reader with insight into the protagonist's psyche and motivations, while his novel, *Der Tod in Venedig* (*Death in Venice*, 1912), long considered one of Mann's masterpieces, presents a writer's descent into obsession and his resulting mental and physical demise. Here, too, Mann describes the protagonist's psychological deterioration as his mania grows. Both works feature a common theme in Mann's work, namely the artist's inability to reconcile the two sides of his dual nature: the passionate and the rational. Frequently, as in these two examples, the artist becomes ill—either metaphorically, as in *Tonio Kröger*, or physically, as in *Tod in Venedig*. Another important author of the movement is Stefan George (1868–1933), whose poetry reflects his belief that language should be not only a means of communication, but also a means of overcoming imperfect reality, a principle he illustrated in his poetry collection *Der Siebente Ring* (*The Seventh Ring*, 1907).

The symbolist movement in German literature coincided roughly with that of impressionism, ca. 1890–1920. The symbolists rejected the idea of direct imitation of reality and declined to connect the meaning of art to social conditions. They did not believe that these conditions could change, but through abstraction and disembodiment, they sought to allow a deeper truth to become recognizable behind visible reality. Thus, the aim of symbolism was not only to stimulate the mind of the reader, but also to increase their emotional receptivity to things that are behind the reality they think they see. Frequent themes of German symbolist literature are the transience of human existence as well as loneliness, imprisonment, and hopelessness.

Germany's most influential symbolist writer is Karl Gustav Vollmöller (1878–1948), whose titles include archaeologist, philologist, poet, author, playwright, screenwriter, translator, race car driver, aircraft designer, and silent-film pioneer. Though perhaps best known for authoring the screenplay for the film *Der blaue Engel* (*The Blue Angel*, 1930), the film adaptation of Heinrich Mann's novel *Professor Unrat* (*Small Town Tyrant*, 1905), Vollmöller's early plays *Catherina, die Gräfin von Armagnac und ihre beiden Liebhaber* (*Catherina, Countess of Armagnac and Her Two Lovers*, 1903) and *Assüs, Fitne und Sumurud* (1904) are both considered important works of symbolist drama. Stefan George (1868–1933) wrote in a variety of styles, and in addition to his impressionist works, composed several collections of symbolist poetry: *Hymnen* (*Hymns*, 1890), *Pilgerfahrten* (*Pilgrimages*, 1891), *Algabal* (1892), and *Das Jahr der Seele* (*The Year of the Soul*, 1897). Richard Dehmel's (1863–1920) first collection of poems, *Erlösungen* (*Redemptions*, 1891), exhibits his inner struggle between sensuality and self-restraint. His poetry, rife with emotion, touched on themes of art, beauty, and erotic love. Due to the frankness of his expressions of human sexuality, his works were often censored. Nevertheless, Dehmel's collected works of poetry, stories, and dramas (ten volumes) were published during his lifetime, and famous composers such as Richard Strauss, Jean Sibelius, and Arnold Schönberg set his poetry to music.

Jessamine Cooke-Plagwitz

See also: Chapter 12: Naturalism. Chapter 13: Bausch, Pina (1940–2009); Musical Periods and Composers. Chapter 16: Film.

Further Reading

Bithell, Jethro. *Modern German Literature: 1880–1950*. London: Routledge, 2019.

Blackbourn, David, and Richard Evans. *The German Bourgeoisie (Routledge Revivals): Essays on the Social History of the German Middle Class from the Late Eighteenth to the Early Twentieth Century*. London: Routledge, 2014.

Dougherty, Jude P. Review of Stromberg, Roland N. *Realism, Naturalism, and Symbolism: Modes of Thought and Expression in Europe, 1848–1914*. *The Review of Metaphysics* 73(2): 383–384, 2019.

Furness, Raymond, and Malcolm Humble. *A Companion to Twentieth-Century German Literature*. London: Routledge, 2003.

Levesque, Paul. "'Jahrhundertwende, Fin de Siécle,' Wilhelminian Era: Re-Examining German Literary Culture 1871–1918." *German Studies Review* 13(1): 9–25, 1990.

Mundt, Hannelore. *Understanding Thomas Mann*. Columbia: University of South Carolina Press, 2004.

Riechel, Donald C. "Monet and Keyserling. Toward a Grammar of Literary Impressionism." *Colloquia Germanica*, vol. 13. Tübingen, Germany: Francke Verlag, 1980.

Robertson, Ritchie, ed. *The Cambridge Companion to Thomas Mann*. Cambridge, UK: Cambridge University Press, 2002.

Twenty-First-Century German Literature

It is difficult to isolate a particular literary movement in twenty-first-century German literature, primarily because it is still relatively young. Nevertheless, certain themes do emerge. Naturally, many of the authors of post-Wall literature continue to publish; thus, their names belong on the list of important twenty-first-century authors, but new authors have joined them, bringing with them new themes, new approaches, and thanks to developments in computer and internet technologies, new media as well. Some prevalent themes in twenty-first-century German literature include the analysis of the immigrant/migrant experience in Germany. These works are frequently autobiographical, and many examine questions of identity, homeland, and "Germanness." Artur Becker's (b. 1968) 2003 novel *Kino Muza*; Eleonora Hummel's (b. 1970) novel *Die Fische von Berlin* (*The Fish of Berlin*, 2005), and Marica Bodrožić's (b. 1970) short story collection *Der Windsammler* (*The Wind Collector*, 2007) all belong to this category.

Meanwhile, the experiences of Turkish-Germans in novels, dramas, and films are often thematically similar to those of migrant literature, but because many Germans of Turkish descent have been in the country for generations, Germany is the only home they have ever known; thus relationships can be further complicated when they attempt to navigate their own identity issues. Well-known writers of Turkish-German literature include Feridun Zaimoglu (b. 1964), whose *Kanak Sprak* of 1995 became the de facto label for a generation of German-Turkish adolescents, has continued to be a prolific writer of novels and short stories. Additional authors of the genre include Yadé Kara (b. 1965) with her *Selam Berlin* (2003); Yüksel Pazarkaya (1940) for his story collection *Die Weidengasse* (*Meadow Lane*, 2001); and Selim Özdoğan (b. 1971) with his 2016 novel *Wieso Heimat, ich wohne zur Miete* (*Who Said Heimat? I'm Only Renting*).

Finally, themes centered on contemporary concerns such as environmental crises, LGBTQ issues, and the rise of right-wing political movements, as well as personal topics including relationships, lifestyle, mental or physical illness, and the ever-popular crime fiction, are all components of contemporary German literature and dramas, as are the science-fiction and fantasy works of such authors as Andreas Eschenbach (b. 1959) with *Herr aller Dinge* (*Lord of All Things*, 2011) and *Eine Billion Dollar* (*A Trillion Dollars*, 2001); and Frank Schätzing (b. 1957) with *Keine Angst* (*Have no Fear*, 1999), and *Der Schwarm* (*The Swarm*, 2004), who have published best-selling works in these genres.

Jessamine Cooke-Plagwitz

See also: Chapter 1: Climate Policy and Recycling. Chapter 2: Berlin Wall. Chapter 3: Citizenship; Political Parties. Chapter 6: Immigration; Turks in Germany. Chapter 7: LGBTQ Life in Modern Germany. Chapter 16: *Tatort*.

Further Reading

Adelson, Leslie. *The Turkish Turn in Contemporary German Literature: Towards a New Critical Grammar of Migration*. Basingstoke: Palgrave Macmillan, 2005.

Breger, Claudia. *An Aesthetics of Narrative Performance: Transnational Theater, Literature, and Film in Contemporary Germany*. Columbus: The Ohio State University Press, 2012.

Cheesman, Tom. *Novels of Turkish German Settlement: Cosmopolite Fictions*. Rochester, NY: Camden House, 2007.

Herrmann, Elisabeth, Carrie Smith-Prei, and Stuart Taberner, eds. *Transnationalism in Contemporary German-Language Literature*. Rochester, NY: Camden House, 2015.

Langenbacher, Eric, and Friederike Eigler. "Memory Boom or Memory Fatigue in 21st Century Germany?" *German Politics and Society* 23(3): 1–15, 2005.

Marven, Lyn, and Stuart Taberner, eds. *Emerging German-Language Novelists of the Twenty-First Century*. Rochester, NY: Camden House, 2011.

Shortt, Linda. *German Narratives of Belonging: Writing Generation and Place in the Twenty-First Century*. Oxford, UK: Legenda, 2015.

Taberner, Stuart. *Transnationalism and German-Language Literature in the Twenty-First Century*. Basingstoke: Palgrave Macmillan, 2017.

Venkat Mani, B. *Cosmopolitical Claims: Turkish-German Literatures from Nadolny to Pamuk*. Iowa City: University of Iowa Press, 2007.

Weimar Classicism (*Weimarer Klassik*) (ca. 1772–1805)

Weimar classicism is generally considered to have lasted from 1772 to 1805, though some scholars argue that its duration was shorter, from 1786, when Johann Wolfgang von Goethe (1749–1832) first visited Rome, to 1805 with the death of Friedrich Schiller (1759–1805). Still other scholars argue that the period should extend to the death of Christoph Martin Wieland (1733–1813), or even until the death of Goethe himself in 1832. Regardless of any distinct time period, however, the movement represents an attempt, primarily through Goethe and Schiller, to achieve a new form of humanism or aesthetic totality, which would unite expressions of strong emotion with rational thought. This new form was based on an idealization of the aesthetics of ancient Greece particularly as described by Joachim Winckelmann (1717–1768) in his *Gedanken über die Nachahmung der griechischen Werke in der Malerei und Bildhauerkunst* (*Reflections on the Imitation of Greek Works of Art in Painting and Sculpture*, 1755). Many of this movement's publications came in the form of journals, with Schiller's *Die Horen* (*The Horae*, 1795–1798) and Goethe's *Die Propyläen* (1798–1800) being of particular significance. Schiller's long essay *Über die ästhetische Erziehung des Menschen* (*On the Aesthetic Education of Mankind,* 1795) is considered the framework of classicism. In this treatise, Schiller proclaims that art is the answer to humankind's woes, and as such, humanity is in desperate need of aesthetic education.

The writers and dramatists of Weimar classicism advocated the use of classical forms and themes in their work. Both Goethe and Schiller, who had become friends and collaborators during the period, were remarkably productive, authoring several works in antique meter or re-conceiving material from Greek myth. Other works, for example Goethe's *Wilhelm Meisters Lehrjahre* (*Wilhelm Meister's Apprenticeship,* 1795), while not employing overtly classical themes or forms, display the movement toward resolution through aesthetic measures, thus embodying the classical ideals advocated by the movement.

Representative dramas of Weimar classicism include Schiller's *Wallenstein* (1798–1799), *Maria Stuart* (1800), *Die Jungfrau von Orleans* (*The Maid of Orleans,* 1801), *Wilhelm Tell* (1804), and *Die Braut von Messina*; Goethe's *Iphigenie auf Tauris* (*Iphigenia on Tauris,* 1787), *Egmont* (1788), *Torquato Tasso* (1790), *Die natürliche Tochter* (*The Natural/Bastard Daughter,* 1803) as well as his *Faust* Part I and C. M. Wieland's *Alceste* (1773). Here, too, we can include August Wilhelm Schlegel's (1767–1845) *Ion* (1803) and Heinrich von Kleist's (1777–1811) tragedy *Penthisilea* (1808).

Classical models are to be found in classical verse epics based on the models of Homer's *Iliad* and *Odyssey,* such as Goethe's *Luise* (1783–1784) and *Reineke Fuchs* (*Reynard the Fox,* 1794) and his *Hermann und Dorothea* (1797). In addition, significant works of poetry such as Goethe's *Römische Elegien* (*Roman Elegies,* 1795), Schiller's *Die Götter Griechenlandes* (*The Gods of Greece,* 1788), and Johann Christian Friedrich Hölderlin's (1770–1843) *Gedichte* (*Poems,* 1826) were also modeled on classical themes and ideals.

In addition to Goethe's *Wilhelm Meister,* several important novels of the period contain classical themes or models. These include such works as Johann Heinrich Voss's (1751–1826) *Luise* (1783–1784), Karl Philipp Moritz's (1756–1793) *Anton Reiser* (1785), Jean Paul Richter's (1763–1825) *Titan* (1800–1803), and Hölderlin's epistolary *Bildungsroman* (educational novel), *Hyperion oder der Eremit in Griechenland* (*Hyperion or the Hermit in Greece,* 1797–1799).

It is also worth noting that the Weimar period featured a number of women writers, among them Schiller's sister-in-law, Caroline von Wolzogen (1763–1847), whose works include the novel *Agnes von Lilien* (1796–1797); Sophie Merau (1770–1831), who published two novels, four volumes of poetry, and two letter exchange collections; and Luise Brachmann (1777–1822), who was also a prolific writer of novels, short stories, and poetry.

Jessamine Cooke-Plagwitz

See also: Chapter 8: Goethe-Institut.

Further Reading

Gelus, Marjorie, and Benjamin Bennett. "Modern Drama and German Classicism: Renaissance from Lessing to Brecht." *Theatre Journal* 40(1): 133–136, 1988.

Holmgren, Janet Besserer. *The Women Writers in Schiller's Horen: Patrons, Petticoats, and the Promotion of Weimar Classicism.* Newark: University of Delaware Press, 2007.

Kerry, Stanley Sephton. *Schiller's Writings on Aesthetics*, vol. 11. Manchester, UK: Manchester University Press, 1961.

Lamport, Francis John. *German Classical Drama: Theatre, Humanity and Nation 1750–1870*. Cambridge, UK: Cambridge University Press, 1992.

Richter, Simon, ed. *The Literature of Weimar Classicism*, vol. 7. Rochester, NY: Camden House 2005.

Watanabe-O'Kelly, Helen, ed. *The Cambridge History of German Literature*. Cambridge, UK: Cambridge University Press, 2000.

Wilkinson, Elizabeth M., and L. A. Willoughby. "'The Whole Man' in Schiller's Theory of Culture and Society." In S. S. Prawer, R. Hinton Thomas, and Leonard Forster, eds. *Essays in German Language, Culture and Society, London,* 177–210. London: Institute of Germanic Studies, 1969.

Wilson, Katharina M. *An Encyclopedia of Continental Women Writers*. Chicago: St. James Press, 1991.

CHAPTER 12

ART AND ARCHITECTURE

OVERVIEW

German archaeology has unearthed artifacts dating back the Upper Paleolithic era (beginning ca. 40,000 years ago). The Venus of Hohle Fels was discovered near Schleklingen in 2008, The Venus, constructed of mammoth ivory approximately 35,000 years ago, is likely the oldest extant depiction of a human being and one of the earliest examples of figurative art. Major finds of Celtic art, dating from the Iron Age (from the tenth century BCE onward), have been discovered in Reinheim and Hochdorf. The Roman Empire expanded its borders into German territory, and a significant cache of Roman pottery was located in Reinzabern.

Carolingian Renaissance

The beginnings of medieval German art can be traced to the time of Charlemagne (d. 814), who, although illiterate, was directly responsible for the Carolingian Renaissance. He invited Alcuin, an English scholar and clergyman, to his court, who introduced the liberal arts into the Frankish Kingdom. Alcuin was accompanied by Irish monks, who in turn introduced artistic painting into the realm. The practice of illuminated manuscripts flourished in Germany until the inventing of the printing press in the fifteenth century. The period ushered in many new artistic artifacts, blending Mediterranean and Northern German elements. An early example of Carolingian architecture is the Palatine Chapel (now part of the Aachen Cathedral) built by Otto of Metz (ca. 800).

Middle Ages

Two great art forms are evident on the medieval German artistic landscape. The development of Romanesque art in Germany corresponds to the ruling dynasties of the era. The artistic achievements of the Ottonian period (950–1050, named after three emperors who bore the name Otto) rest on the foundations established during the Carolingian Renaissance, and hence, sacred buildings of this time were based on early Christian architecture. The Benedictine Abbey of St. Michael of Hildesheim (ca. 1020) was designed by Bishop Bernward of Hildesheim, who drew inspiration from his travels in Byzantium and Rome. The church features a three-aisle basilica nave between symmetrical transepts (in a church shaped like a cross, transepts are the two extending sides that form the arms of the cross). Its exterior is also arranged in strict geometrical order. The large bronze doors of the church, featuring biblical scenes, are the most important such surviving works of medieval German craftsmen. The Cathedral at Speyer (officially the Imperial Cathedral Basilica of the Assumption and St. Peter) was consecrated during the Salian Dynasty (1050–1150). Previously, cathedrals were covered by flat, timbered ceilings, which had the unfortunate tendency to catch fire. The Cathedral of Worms was perhaps the greatest architectural achievement of the Hohenstaufen dynasty (1150–1250). It is taller than earlier Romanesque cathedrals, and its new structural design is characterized by two turrets or small ornamental towers flanking an octagonal central tower. The second major artform of medieval German was the Gothic style, so named because it was introduced by the Goths. The first major Gothic cathedral was built in Strasbourg (now in France) during the thirteenth century. Perhaps the best-known Gothic cathedral is the Cologne Cathedral, begun in 1248 by Master Gerhard. Construction on the cathedral continued for centuries, and it was not completed until 1880. Many German Gothic churches are so-called hall churches, where the naves and the aisles are of equal height.

The Renaissance

The Renaissance, the "rebirth" of European cultural life following the Middle Ages, is often associated with Italian painters (Leonardo Da Vinci, 1452–1519), sculptors (Michelangelo, 1475–1564), and architects (Filippo Brunelleschi, 1377–1446). The Italian Renaissance exercised surprisingly little influence on German art. After the Reformation, church architecture in Germany suffered a period of decline. Rather than build new churches, the Protestants in Germany adapted existing structures to their liturgical needs. However, that is not say that German artists were not active in other areas during the Renaissance. Albrecht Altdorfer (1480–1538) is credited with founding the tradition of European landscape painting. In his famous painting *Battle of Alexander* (housed in Munich's Alte Pinakothek), the battle on the ground between two opposing armies is portrayed as a mere reflection of the conflict in the picture's celestial landscape. Altdorfer's work is the prototype of the Danube style, which emphasizes the importance of landscape over human portraiture. Lucas Cranach (the Elder; 1472–1553), although an avid Protestant, painted altarpieces for Catholic churches. He incorporated angels into every portrait of the Virgin Mary. In his *Flight into Egypt*, angels are pictured as the playmates of the infant Jesus. In addition to painting, Cranach was an established printmaker and woodcutter. Another noted woodcutter was Albrecht Dürer (1471–1528), whose work includes *The Apocalypse*, a series of fifteen woodcuts taken from the Book of Revelation in the New Testament. Finally, Hans Holbein (the Younger; 1497–1543) painted three portraits of the great humanist Erasmus of Rotterdam.

The Baroque and Rococo

After the creative stagnation of the Reformation, the Baroque (1600–1750) era transformed artistic expression. St. Michael, a Jesuit church in Munich designed by the Italian-Dutch architect Federico Sustris (1540–1599), was the first sacred structure in Germany to feature Baroque elements. It featured an oval floor plan, a vaulted nave without aisles, and large openings in the side chapels that permitted the interior to be bathed in light. Baroque interiors showcase a blend of architectural details, such as arches, sculptures, and paintings. The painted ceilings of Baroque churches contain celestial figures, which seek to unite architecturally the realms of heaven and earth. The architecture of civil structures acquired prominence during the Baroque period. During the age of Absolutism, powerful monarchs built elaborate palaces (e.g., Versailles, built by the French king Louis XIV). Notable German Baroque palaces in Germany include Sanssouci in Potsdam (the summer residence of Emperor Frederick the Great), the Zwinger in Dresden, and Nymphenburg in Munich. The Rococo art movement dominated the late Baroque period. Frederick the Great himself oversaw the interior decoration of Sanssouci palace in Potsdam. Sanssouci features white stucco marble columns, painted ceilings, and over-door reliefs, a style known as Frederician Rococo. In sacred buildings, the Bavarian pilgrimage church Wieskirchen features pure white pillars with gilt cornices, painted ceilings, and frescoes in the nave.

The Nineteenth Century

Following the Baroque period, the wide variety of nineteenth-century German art included architecture, painting, sculpture, and interior decoration. Karl Schinkel (1781–1841) was one of nineteenth-century Germany's most prominent architects, and his surviving work can still be seen in Berlin. Schinkel, a proponent of Greek Revival, adapted classical forms to meet modern requirements. He designed the Altes Museum (Old Museum), Neue Wache (New Guardhouse), and renovated the Berlin Dome. Caspar David Friedrich (1774–1840) is known for his allegorical landscapes. His Romantic masterpiece *Wanderer above the Sea of Fog* (1818) is displayed in Hamburg's Kunsthalle. Friedrich's work fell out of favor during his later years but gained newfound appreciation in the early twentieth century. His *Monk by the Sea* (1808–1810) and *The Abbey in the Oakwood* (1809–1810), the most famous pair of paintings from the German Romantic period, have been recently restored and can be viewed in Berlin's Alte Nationalgalarie. Christian Davis Rauch (1777–1857) was the founder of the Berlin school of sculpture and nineteenth-century Germany's foremost sculptor. Among his iconic work is the equestrian statue of Friedrich the Great on Unter den Linden in East Berlin. The early designs for the statue were done by Johann Gottfried Schadow (1764–1850), who designed the chariot atop the Brandenburg Gate, and finally executed by Rauch in 1851. Rauch also created numerous public statues, including Dürer in Nuremberg, Luther in Wittenberg, and General Blücher in Breslau (present day Wroclaw) in Poland. *Biedermeier*, a term applied to middle-class life and art in Germany and central Europe between the end of the Napoleonic Wars (1815) and the European revolutions of 1848, is known best perhaps for its furniture design and interior decoration. Biedermeier interior design created *Wohninseln* (residential islands), small informal areas conducive to family life (and a term still used as a proper noun by German furniture retailers).

Modern German Art

Founded by Walter Gropius in Weimar in 1919, the Bauhaus remains the signature artistic movement in the history of German art. Its architecture is best described as functional, with its geometrical construction and marked lack of ornamentation. After the Bauhaus was relocated to Dessau, the separate workshops for stone and wood sculpture were conjoined into a single shop. A well-known Bauhaus sculpture is the *Monument to the March Dead* (by Walter Gropius). The monument memorializes those workers killed in the Kapp Putsch, an attempt by monarchist and nationalist factions to overthrow the Weimar Republic. The sculpture was destroyed by the Nazis in 1936 and reconstructed ten years later. Famous Bauhaus painters such as Paul Klee (*The Red Balloon*, 1922) and Wassily Kandinsky (*Yellow-Red-Blue*, 1925) are well-known adherents of the expressionist movement, an artistic style based on pure luminous color. These artists attempted to express their own emotional experience in their art, rather than impressions of the external world. In response, the *Neue Sachlichkeit* (New Objectivity) arose, characterized by unsentimental realism. Painters such as Max Beckmann, Georg Grosz, and Otto Dix portrayed the political and social turmoil of Weimar Germany. After the National Socialists came to power in 1933, they initiated a series of attacks on modern art. The Degenerate Art (*Entartete Kunst*) Law of 1937 sanctioned the disposal of modern art in state collections. The government collected over 600 works by notable artists such as Klee, Grosz, and Dix (works by Pablo Picasso, Piet Mondrian, and Marc Chagall were also considered degenerate) and staged presentations in Munich, Berlin, Leipzig, Düsseldorf, Weimar, and the Austrian cities of Vienna and Salzburg. The travelling degenerate art exhibition devastated the modern art collections of many German museums. The widespread destruction of Germany's social fabric during the Second World War extended to the nation's art scene. Following the war, German artists engaged in often vitriolic debates regarding their artistic practices and its relationship to national identity. The exhibit *Inventur—Art in Germany 1943–55* (at the Harvard Art Museum, 2018) chronicled how fifty artists reconstituted German art after the war. Postwar sculpture certainly reflected German history. During the Weimar Republic, public commissions were generally confined to monuments to those killed during WWI. The commercial market for sculpture essentially dried up during the Third Reich. In the aftermath of the Second World War, German sculpture followed the division of the nation. Sculpture in the Federal Republic of Germany followed developments in Western Europe, while sculpture in the German Democratic Republic was more political in nature. Waldemar Grzimek's (1918–1984) *Through Death and Struggle to Victory* in the Buchenwald concentration camp exemplifies postwar Soviet realism. Grzimek also executed a sculpture in the ruins of Sachsenhausen concentration camp (north of Berlin): a statue of two inmates holding a cloth containing the remains of a fellow inmate. The early 1960s spawned Fluxus, an international coterie of avant-garde artists who emphasized the artistic process over the finished product. Joseph Beuys (1921–1986) was perhaps its best-known German adherent. Recent years have witnessed the ascendance of the New Leipzig School of Art (characterized by a mastery of technique), which sought to protect German art against the influence of Beuys. Neo Rauch, from the Leipzig

School, has seen his paintings exhibited widely throughout Europe and the United States.

Wendell G. Johnson

Further Reading

Andersson, Christiane, Charles W. Talbot, and Martin Luther. *From a Mighty Fortress: Prints, Drawings, and Books in the Age of Luther, 1483–1546*. Detroit: Detroit Institute of Arts, 1983.

Asvarishch, B., Vincent Boele, and Femke Foppema. *Caspar David Friedrich & the German Romantic Landscape*. Aldershot, UK: Lund Humphries, 2008.

Barron, Stephanie, and Peter W. Guenther. *Degenerate Art: The Fate of the Avant-Garde in Nazi Germany*. New York: Abrams, 1991.

Forster, Kurt Walter. *Schinkel: A Meander through His Life and Work*. Basel: Birkhäuser, 2018.

Hartog, Arie. "Germany: 20th Century-Contemporary." In Antonia Böstrom, ed. *The Encyclopedia of Sculpture*, 647–650. New York: Fitzroy Dearborn, 2004.

Keuning, Ralph, et al. *Neo Rauch: Dromos: Paintings 1993–2017*. Berlin: Hatje Cantz Verlag, 2018.

King, Anthony. *Roman Gaul and Germany*. Berkeley: University of California Press, 1990.

Kries, Mateo, et al. *The Bauhaus: #itsalldesign*. English ed. Weil am Rhein, Germany: Vitra Design Museum GmbH, 2015.

Lindemann, Gottfried. *History of German Art: Painting, Sculpture, Architecture*. New York: Praeger, 1971.

Ottomeyer, Hans, Klaus Albrecht Schröder, and Laurie Winters. *Biedermeier: The Invention of Simplicity*. Milwaukee, WI: Ostfildern, Germany: Milwaukee Art Museum; Hatje Cantz, 2006.

Roth, Lynette, ed. *Inventur: Art in Germany, 1943–55*. Cambridge, MA: Harvard Art Museums, 2018.

Schutz, Herbert. *The Carolingians in Central Europe, Their History, Arts, and Architecture: A Cultural History of Central Europe, 750–900*. Boston: Brill, 2004

Tadgell, Christopher. *Transformations: Baroque and Rococo in the Age of Absolutism and the Church Triumphant*. London: Routledge, 2013.

Architecture

Every major European architectural style can also be found in Germany. A fine example of Romanesque architecture is the Palatine Chapel (Pfalzkapelle) in Aachen, a large, sixteen-sided polygon built by Charlemagne (d. 814). During this period, the Germans constructed several hall churches, a type of church in which the nave and aisle are of equal height. Gothic architecture, originating in France, arrived in Germany around 1200; the Magdeburger Dom was the first church built in the Gothic style. The cathedral in Cologne (consecrated in 1322) is the second-largest Gothic

The 18th-century Brandenburg Gate is one of the most iconic German buildings, symbolizing both the separation of the two Germanys from 1961 to 1989 and Germany's subsequent reunification. (Corel)

cathedral in the world (after the Milan Cathedral). In secular work, the castle in Meissen (rebuilt 1417–1485) represents the Gothic transition from castle to palace. Baroque architecture in Germany is exemplified by Schloss Charlottenburg in Berlin (inaugurated 1699), the Zwinger Palace in Dresden (1710–1719), and Potsdam's New Palace (*Neues Palais*, 1763–1769). Classicism took root in Berlin, where its design can be seen in the iconic Brandenburger Tor (Brandenburg Gate, completed 1791). The Altes Museum (Old Museum, 1823–1830) was conceived by German classicism's most famous architect, Friedrich Schinkel (1781–1841).

Bauhaus was an influential German school of art, design, and architecture founded by Walter Gropius in Weimar in 1919. The Bauhaus movement originally intended to promote the ideals of the Arts and Crafts movement and unify art and technology with the motto, originating with the American architect Sullivan (1856–1924), "Die Form folgt der Funktion" (FFF) or form follows function, indicating the renunciation of any type of ornamentation. The school moved from Weimar (1919–1925) to Dessau (1925–1932) and then to Berlin (1932–1933), where it was headed by Ludwig Mies van der Rohe (1886–1969) until it was closed in 1933 by the Nazi authorities, who regarded it as a hotbed of left-wing agitation.

In 1937, the architect Albert Speer (1905–1981) was tasked by Adolf Hitler to transform Berlin into a gleaming new capital: Germania. The neoclassic plans were ambitious, and included a Grand Hall meant to hold 180,000 people and a 350-foot-tall

Arch of Triumph inscribed with the names of Germany's 1.8 million casualties from the First World War. Plans for the capital also included broad avenues, an artificial lake, and vast commercial and residential developments. Germania proved more than an idealist vision. Several buildings were completed, including the 1,200-foot-long Reich Chancellery (destroyed during the Russian siege of Berlin in 1945); the Olympic Stadium, site of the 1936 Olympic Games; and the headquarters of the Luftwaffe (Air Force), which presently houses the German finance ministry.

Many German cities suffered widespread devastation during the Second World War. Reconstruction efforts varied across Germany. Many cities restored well-known landmarks to their classical form, such as the Frauenkirche in Dresden, originally a Baroque church. In Berlin, on the other hand, the bell tower of the ruins of the Kaiser Wilhelm Memorial Church are a memorial to the horrors of war. It is difficult to describe a typical, modern German architectural style. Many buildings in the north of the country reflect the influence of Scandinavian design, while those in the south pay tribute to their Austro-Hungarian heritage.

German architects have achieved international renown while working in the United States. Mies van der Rohe emigrated to the United States in 1937 and settled in Chicago, where he was appointed director of the Architecture School of the Illinois Institute of Technology. His work is characterized by cubic simplicity and a precision of detail where each element of the structure makes its own individual statement. German-born architect Helmut Jahn (1940–2021) also settled in Chicago. Jahn's notable designs include the James R. Thompson Center and the United Airlines Terminal in Chicago, the Messeturm in Frankfurt, and the Sony Center in Berlin (erected near the site of the former Reich Chancellery).

Wendell G. Johnson

See also: Chapter 1: Cities. Chapter 2: Charlemagne (748–814); Hitler, Adolf (1889–1945). Chapter 3: Germany and the United States. Chapter 11: Weimar Classicism (*Weimarer Klassik*) (ca. 1772–1805). Chapter 12: Overview; Bauhaus and Walter Gropius; Carolingian Renaissance; Museums. Chapter 13: Musical Periods and Composers. Chapter 15: Olympic Games.

Further Reading

Fleming, John, Hugh Honour, and Nikolaus Pevsner. *The Penguin Dictionary of Architecture and Landscape Architecture*. London: Penguin Books, 1998.

Kitchen, Martin. *Speer: Hitler's Architect*. New Haven, CT: Yale University Press, 2015.

Artists

Since Albrecht Dürer (1471–1528), the most influential artist of the "German Renaissance," German artists have played an important role in the canon of art history and reflect an ever-present tension between existing cultural ideologies and the evolving trends of the international art world. Anton Raphael Mengs (1728–1779), although more accomplished as a portrait painter, was an early pioneer of neoclassicism through his classical and religious scenes. In response to this style, artists such as Caspar David Friedrich (1774–1840), who painted powerful and symbolic landscapes, moved toward the subjective and emotional forms of Romanticism. Rejecting emotional intensity, Adolph Menzel (1815–1905), most famous for his paintings of Frederick the Great, was also a proponent of the objectivity and contemporary subjects of realism, as depicted in his later industrial scenes and interior studies.

The clash between "German art" and international influences becomes particularly significant starting in the late nineteenth and early twentieth century with the advent of modernism. Artists rebelled against the realism and naturalism favored by the art academies to form the Munich Secession in 1892 and the Berlin Secession in 1898. Max Liebermann (1848–1935), Lovis Corinth (1858–1925), and Max Slevogt (1869–1932), leading artists of German impressionism, would become central figures in the Berlin Secession, the premier venue for avant-garde art. Also associated with the Berlin group was Käthe Kollwitz (1867–1945), the first woman to be admitted to the Prussian Academy of Art.

The birth of expressionism comes in 1905 when Erich Heckel (1883–1970), Ernst Ludwig Kirchner (1880–1938), Karl Schmidt-Rottluff (1884–1976), and Fritz Bleyl (1880–1966) founded Die Brücke (The Bridge). These artists sought to break from the past by evoking men's emotional, inner life through simplified or distorted forms and strong, unnatural colors. In 1911, the Blaue Reiter (The Blue Rider) was founded at the house of artist Gabriele Münter (1877–1962), Wassily Kandinsky (1866–1944), and Franz Marc (1880–1916). More interested in nature and mystical spiritualism than their Die Brücke counterparts, members also included August Macke (1887–1914), Paul Klee (1879–1940), and Marianne von Werefkin (1870–1938). Both groups were initially met with public bewilderment and criticism; however, expressionism would become the unofficial national style of art academies and museums during the Weimar Republic.

After World War I, artists rejected expressionism for more anti-establishment movements. Raoul Hausmann (1886–1971) and Hannah Höch (1889–1978), part of the Berlin Dada, created photomontage as an alternative to art academy styles. Max Ernst (1891–1976), also an early member of the Dada movement, was a pioneer of surrealism in Paris. However, Neue Sachlichkeit (New Objectivity) became the dominant art of this period with such artists as Max Beckmann (1884–1950), Otto Dix (1891–1969), and George Grosz (1893–1959), whose social criticism was characterized by caricature; and Käthe Kollwitz (1867–1945) and Otto Nagel (1894–1967), both proletarian revolutionaries.

The rise of Hitler and Nazism led to a campaign against modern art, deemed "degenerate," and many artists were forced into exile. Adolf Ziegler (1892–1959), a favorite painter of Hitler, was president of the Reich Chamber of Visual Arts, which regulated "German art," favoring paintings in the style of Romantic realism representing the "Blood and Soil" ideology.

Many postwar German artists were influenced by American and British pop art of the 1950s and 1960s. Although inspired by the imagery of mass media, Sigmar Polke (1941–2010), Gerhard Richter (b. 1932), and Konrad Lueg (1939–1996, also known as Konrad Fischer) founded "capitalist realism," a movement and political ideology critical of the consumer culture. Georg Baselitz (b. 1938), with his signature upside-down motif, influenced the raw, figurative style of painters considered part of *Die Neuen Wilden* (neo-Expressionism), like Elvira Bach (b. 1951) and Helmut Middendorf (b. 1953). Joseph Beuys (1921–1986), perhaps the most influential artist of post-World War II Germany, expanded the concept of art to include all creative activity, which culminated in his concept of "social sculpture."

Contemporary German artists, such as Anselm Kiefer (b. 1945), who explores the construction of history, myth, and Germany's post-Nazi identity; Rosemarie Trockel (b. 1952), a pioneer of feminist art with her knitted pictures; and Isa Genzken (b. 1948), an important figure in postmodernist sculpture, continue to achieve international recognition, underscoring the significant role of German artists in the ongoing creative discourse.

Larissa Garcia

See also: Chapter 11: Expressionism (*Expressionismus*) and Its Successors (1905–1925); Romanticism (*Romantik*) (1788–1835); Weimar Classicism (*Weimarer Klassik*) (ca. 1772–1805). Chapter 12: Degenerate Art; Kollwitz, Käthe (1867–1945). Chapter 13: Contemporary Popular Music.

Further Reading

Barron, Stephanie, and Sabine Eckmann. *New Objectivity: Modern German Art in the Weimar Republic, 1919–1933*. Los Angeles: Los Angeles County Museum of Art, 2015.

Behr, Shulamith. *Expressionism*. London: Tate Gallery, 1999.

Joachimides, Christos M., Wieland Schmied, Werner Becker, and Norman Rosenthal. *German Art in the 20th Century: Painting and Sculpture, 1905–1985*. London: Royal Academy of Arts; Weidenfeld and Nicolson, 1985.

Michaud, Eric, and Janet Lloyd. *The Cult of Art in Nazi Germany*. Stanford, CA: Stanford University Press, 2004.

Myers, Bernard S. *The German Expressionists: A Generation in Revolt*, concise ed. New York: McGraw-Hill, 1963.

Tisdall, Caroline. *Joseph Beuys*. New York: Thames and Hudson, 1979.

Bauhaus and Walter Gropius

The Bauhaus was perhaps the most influential modernist art school of the twentieth century. The school's name refers to medieval mason's lodges (or *Bauhütten*). The school was founded in Weimar, Germany, by the architect Walter Gropius in 1919 after he returned from service in the German army during the First World War.

In 1919, the Bauhaus was founded in Weimar by Walter Gropius, a renowned architect. It moved to Dessau in 1925 and finally to Berlin, where it was closed by the Nazis in 1933. (Sérgio Nogueira/Dreamstime.com)

Gropius was born in 1883 to an affluent family in Berlin. His great-uncle (also named Walter Gropius) was an internationally recognized disciple of the neoclassical architect Karl Friedrich Schinkel (1781–1841). Gropius briefly studied architecture in Munich and apprenticed in a local firm. He moved to Berlin and worked for Peter Behrens designing modern factories for Krupp. He soon set out on his own, and one of his first projects was the Fagus Shoe Factory, which demonstrated his personal architectural vocabulary of form and material. He went on to employ this vocabulary in the production of prefabricated mass housing.

Bauhaus was founded on the goal of creating a total work of art (or *Gesamtkunstwerk*). Students who attended the Bauhaus were expected to become both artists and craftspeople. Women were admitted to Bauhaus but were originally prevented from studying architecture and were moved to weaving, pottery, and bookbinding. The Swiss painter Johannes Itten (1888–1967) developed Bauhaus's first compulsory course, designed to purge novices of academic tendencies and stimulate artistic creativity. The Hungarian designer and photography László Moholy-Nagy (1895–1946) joined Bauhaus in 1923, and under his tutelage the school became a laboratory for combining art and technology. During this period, the school concentrated on designing and producing items for everyday use.

In 1928, Bauhaus moved to Dessau, where Ludwig Mies van der Rohe subsequently became director of the school and the curriculum in time emphasized teaching over production. Among the influential painters associated with Bauhaus are Paul Klee (1879–1940) and Wassily Kandinsky (1866–1944). Klee was born in Switzerland and was invited by Walter Gropius to join Bauhaus in 1920. While at Bauhaus, he adopted many innovative techniques for creating pictures, including oil transfer drawing (a process that involves tracing a pencil drawing over a page covered with black ink onto a third sheet). Klee taught color theory at Weimar and achieved international fame. His well-known paintings from 1922 along include *Senecio* (oil on gauze, 1922), *Fright of a Girl* (oil transfer drawing), and *Red/Green Architecture* (oil on canvas). Paul Klee left Bauhaus in 1931 and returned to Switzerland. Wassily Kandinsky was a pivotal figure in the transition from representation to abstract art during the early twentieth century. During his Bauhaus residency (1922–1933), he experimented with geometric form, as shown in his *Circles in a Circle* (1923). He was also active in theater, directing Mussorgsky's *Pictures at an Exhibition* for the Friedrich Theater in Dessau (1928). After leaving Bauhaus, Kandinsky moved to Paris.

The Bauhaus moved to Berlin 1932. However, the Nazi government viewed the Bauhaus school as a nest of left-wing agitation and closed it in 1933. The Bauhaus architects dispersed, taking their principles of design with them. Walter Gropius accepted a position at Harvard's Graduate School of Design, Ludwig Mies van der Rohe became the director of the College of Architecture at the Illinois Institute of Technology, and László Moholy-Nagy formed the Institute for Design in Chicago, Illinois.

Wendell G. Johnson

See also: Chapter 2: Overview. Chapter 11: Weimar Classicism (*Weimarer Klassik*) (ca. 1772–1805). Chapter 12: Architecture; Artists.

Further Reading

Barnett, Vivian Endicott, ed. *Kandinsky*. New York: Guggenheim Museum Publications, 2009.

Ferrier, Jean Louis. *Paul Klee*. Paris: Terrail, 1999.

Weber, Nicholas F. *The Bauhaus Group: Six Masters of Modernism*. New York: Alfred A. Knopf, 2009.

Carolingian Renaissance

The Carolingian Renaissance is the term for a variety of cultural phenomena characteristic of the reign of Charlemagne (742–814), who was King of the Franks from 768 to 814, the Lombards (774–814), and also Roman emperor (800–814), and of his son and successor Louis the Pious (778–840) and continuing through the ninth century. Their reign includes the building of educational institutions, an organized program for the copying of ancient manuscripts, both Christian and non-Christian and a revival of ancient literature. In art and architecture, the Carolingian period was marked by the creation of many new art objects and a blending of classical Mediterranean and Northern European, including German, elements. Carolingian art was also influenced by British and Irish art and Byzantine art. The Carolingian Empire saw itself as a revival of the Western Roman Empire. The Carolingian Renaissance sought to produce art worthy of that claim.

Carolingian art includes illuminated manuscripts, miniatures, statues, coins, and frescoes. Much Carolingian work was religious, dedicated to the glory of God in the Christian tradition and setting forth the ideology of the Carolingian Empire as a holy empire. Monasteries and bishoprics served as centers of artistic and cultural production. The most ornately decorated manuscripts were sacred texts. Numerous sacred objects, such as reliquaries, were richly adorned. Pre-Carolingian Germanic art traditions, such as that of ornate metalwork incorporating gems and abstract designs, continued to influence Carolingian art. However, there was a growing presence of the human figure, based on Roman and Early Christian art.

Although the Carolingian Empire presented itself as a continuation or revival of the Roman Empire, its capital was not Rome but Aachen, also known as Aix-la-Chapelle and located in the German region of Upper Rhine-Westphalia. Part of Charlemagne's artistic and architectural program was to make Aachen worthy of being an imperial capital on the level of Rome or Constantinople. One of the few buildings of the Carolingian Renaissance remaining is the chapel at Aachen, formerly part of a palace complex built by Charlemagne. The chapel is modeled on a late Roman basilica at Ravenna and is basically continuous with late Roman design. Like much Carolingian art, it employs *spolia* (related to "spoil"), ancient objects taken from their original settings and incorporated into new buildings and works of art. Other Carolingian Renaissance buildings in Germany surviving in part include the Abbey of Lorsch and the Abbey of Corvey, a UNESCO World Heritage site. One Carolingian innovation found in some churches including Lorsch and Corvey is a "westwork," an elaborate entrance on the west framed between two towers. This feature would be adopted and elaborated in subsequent medieval sacred architecture.

The Carolingian Renaissance ended with the breakup of the Carolingian Empire under pressure from invaders around the end of the ninth century, but it continued to influence medieval civilization in Germany and elsewhere.

William E. Burns

See also: Chapter 2: Overview; Charlemagne (748–814). Chapter 9: Development of the Script. Chapter 12: Overview.

Further Reading

McKitterick, Rosamond, ed. *Carolingian Culture: Emulation and Innovation*. Cambridge, UK: Cambridge University Press, 1994.

Nees, Lawrence. *Early Medieval Art*. Oxford, UK: Oxford University Press, 2002.

Decorative Arts *Biedermeier* and *Jugendstil*

Biedermeier

Biedermeier is a term applied to middle-class life and art in Germany and Central Europe between the end of the Napoleonic Wars (1815) and the European revolutions of 1848. The name refers to a thrifty and small-minded cartoon character, Gottlieb Biedermeier, featured in a weekly satirical magazine, who led an uneventful life, filled with order and simplicity. Biedermeier artists, such as Carl Spitzweg (1808–1885) and Georg Friedrich Kersting (1785–1847), avoided religious subjects and painted family portraits, landscapes, and still lifes. Although their work was panned by academic art critics, it was in high demand by the middle- and upper-middle-class public.

The Biedermeier period is best known perhaps for its furniture design and interior decoration. This furniture, characterized by thrift, comfort, and practicality, while still elegant, was influenced by the French Empire style, with neoclassical symmetry, flat surfaces, and simple geometric shapes. Biedermeier furniture rejected ornate decorative details and expensive materials, using locally available timbers such as cherry, oak, and ash. The furniture was comfortable, and its chairs featured upholstery and curved backs. Biedermeier interior design created "residential Islands" (*Wohninsel*), small informal areas conducive to family life (and a term still used as a proper noun by German furniture retailers). The furniture in these "islands" was not aligned against interior walls but organized in sofa-table-chair combinations. Toward the end of the period, wallpaper, parquet floors, and carpet became popular furnishings. Before the fall of the Berlin Wall in 1989, antique furniture dealers would pay $30,000 or $40,000 to visit warehouses in East Germany, where they were allowed to select thirty or forty pieces of Biedermeier furniture of varying quality, which they could sell for much higher in the West.

Jugendstil

Jugendstil (youth style), as Art Nouveau was known in the German-speaking regions of Europe, began in the mid-1890s and continued until the First World War. Art Nouveau arose from the desire to create a new artistic style that could be incorporated into the objects of everyday household use. *Jugendstil* takes its name from the periodical *Die Jugend* founded in Munich in 1896. Many *Jugendstil* designers were originally painters who gave up painting to pursue decorative art. After Otto Eckman (1865–1902) ceased painting, he took up natural history. His favorite animal was the swan, and through his influence this bird became the leitmotif of *Jugendstil*. He also designed the characteristic *Jugendstil* fonts that bear his name (*Eckman* and *Fette Eckman*), which are still in use today. *Jugendstil* is associated closely with Henry Van de Velde (1863–1957), a Belgian-born artist who was influenced by the English and American Arts and Crafts movement. Van de Velde received numerous commissions in Berlin for interior design. He was the first furniture designer to apply curved lines to an abstract style.

Jugendstil benefitted from the largesse of ruling families and leading industrialists, such as Ernst Ludwig, Grand Duke of Hesse-Darmstadt (1868–1937). He commissioned several rooms in Darmstadt's New Palace to be decorated in Art Nouveau style. The Grand Duke subsequently established a colony at Mathildenhöhe, Darmstadt, with the goal of transforming the Arts and Crafts movement. Artists were invited to settle there and build houses, which were to combine architecture with interior design. One of the artists who took up residence in Mathildenhöhe was the architect Peter Behrens (1868–1940), who not only designed his own house, but all of the household furnishings (furniture, paintings, pottery) within it. Mathildenhöhe hosted *Jugendstil* exhibitions in the past, the last of which took place in 1914, and is today a museum open to the public.

Wendell G. Johnson

See also: Chapter 11: *Biedermeier* (1815–1830), *Junges Deutschland* (1830–1850), and *Vormärz* (1830–1848). Chapter 12: Artists.

Further Reading

Chase, Linda, Karl Kemp, and Lois Lammerhuber. *The World of Biedermeier*. New York: Thames & Hudson, 2001.

Lavallee, Michele. "Art Nouveau." In Jane Turner, ed. *The Dictionary of Art*, vol. 2, 561–568. New York: Grove Dictionaries, 1996.

Morton, Marsha. "Biedermeier." In Jane Turner, ed. *The Dictionary of Art*, vol. 4, 39–41. New York: Grove Dictionaries, 1996.

Ottomeyer, Hans, Klaus Albrecht Schröder, and Winters, Laurie. *Biedermeier: The Invention of Simplicity*. Milwaukee, WI: Milwaukee Art Museum, 2006.

Wolf, Norbert. *Art Nouveau*. Munich: Prestel, 2011.

Degenerate Art

The term *degenerate art* (*Entartete Kunst*) refers to modern art confiscated during the Third Reich (1933–1945), which was regarded as worthless, unhealthy, and against the rules of the German vision of the pure Aryan race and its ideals. This purge was conducted in line with Hitler's idea of reform and rehabilitation of Germany, which extended beyond the political and economic into the cultural and artistic. Confiscations were partially motivated by an attack on Jewish art for its contribution to the decline of the German cultural scene. Works of art that did not comply with German lofty ideals were banned from public institutions and public consumption. Prohibited from teaching at universities, degenerate artists were generally considered a threat and an enemy to the German government and people. Some artists were forced into exile, such as Paul Klee, and others, like Otto Dix, agreed to work within the set restrictions and parameters laid out by the Nazi government. Among the artistic movements banned under Nazi rule were dada and surrealism, cubism, impressionism, fauvism,

Ernst Ludwig Kirchner (1880–1938, died by suicide) was a German Expressionist painter and founding member of Die Brücke. Thirty-two of his paintings were part of the Degenerate Art Exhibit of 1937. (Contemporary Collection of The Cleveland Museum of Art and Bequest of William R. Valentiner)

New Objectivity, and Bauhaus. German expressionism was the most censored art under Nazi rule, with artists such as Emil Nolde (1867–1956) banned from buying art material and forbidden to paint. Nolde, although a party member, was still the most censored artist under this purge, with 1,052 of his art works seized and confiscated. In the novel *Deutschstunde* (*The German Lesson*), German author Siegfried Lenz (1926–2014) based Max Nansen, a painter harassed by the Nazis through local officials, on Emil Nolde. Artists deemed degenerate and subjected to varying degrees of censorship by the Nazis included Henri Matisse, Juan Miró, Pablo Picasso, Salvador Dalí, Gustav Klimt, George Grosz, Max Beckmann, Marc Chagall, Oskar Kokoschka, Marg Moll, Elfriede Lohse-Wächtler, Paul Klee, and Ernst Ludwig Kirchner. Art that was experimental and promoted putative racial impurity or decadence was deemed abnormal. In contrast, approved art promoted a vision of the Caucasian muscle–bulging male as the desired archetype, exemplified in Josef Thorak's 1937 sculpture *Kameraden*

(*Comradeship*), which depicted two muscular men clasping hands. Thorak, a committed Nazi, divorced his Jewish wife in 1933.

The term degenerate art also refers to an art exhibition held by the Nazis in Munich in 1937 that featured 650 confiscated works by 112 artists including works by Wassily Kandinsky and Cesar Klein. The exhibition was structured in a way to elicit a negative response from the audience. The space of the venue, the Institute of Archeology, was dimly lit and crammed, its walls marked by derogatory terms. Works were divided in rooms by category, Jewish art, art contemptuous of women, and art that assaulted religion. Pieces from the degenerate art exhibition were subsequently auctioned, burnt, or stored away. The degenerate art exhibition catalogue featured a photo of Otto Freundlich's sculpture "*Der Neue Mensch/The New Man* (1912), which was featured in the exhibition and later destroyed. Emil Nolde had numerous paintings on exhibit there. The exhibition attracted more than a million visitors, at least three times more than the concurrent exhibition that showed sanctioned, sober, and "decent" German art right across the street at the House of German Art Museum and titled *Great German Art Exhibition* (*Große Deutsche Kunstausstellung*). In his speech at the opening of the exhibition in which he declared fierce war on decadence, Hitler remarked that the two contrasting exhibitions were instructional on how to turn away from degeneracy and embrace purity. He regarded degenerate artists as talentless and deceitful as their art was not self-explanatory and needed contextualization. Hitler himself had been an aspiring artist during the years he lived in Vienna (1908–1913) before rising to power. His realistic art was dismissed in favor of more imaginative endeavors; he was twice denied entry into the Academy of Fine Arts Vienna. His assault on modern art is deemed by many as his revenge for his own previously censored aspirations. The Victoria and Albert Museum in London holds the only hard copy of the complete inventory of confiscated art. The list can be accessed through the museum's website.

Alia Soliman

See also: Chapter 2: Hitler, Adolf (1889–1945). Chapter 11: Expressionism (*Expressionismus)* and Its Successors (1905–1925). Chapter 12: Architecture; Artists; Bauhaus and Walter Gropius; Museums.

Further Reading

Barron, Stephanie. *Degenerate Art: The Fate of the Avant-Garde in Nazi Germany.* Los Angeles: Los Angeles County Museum of Art, 1991.

"*Entartete Kunst*": The Nazis' Inventory of "Degenerate Art." Digital reproduction of a typescript inventory by the Reischministerium für Volksaufklärung und Propaganda, ca. 1941/1942. (V&A NAL MSL/1996/7). London: Victoria and Albert Museum, January 2014. http://www.vam.ac.uk/entartetekunst. Accessed July 15, 2020.

Explore "*Entartete Kunst*": The Nazis' Inventory of "Degenerate Art." https://www.vam.ac.uk/articles/explore-entartete-kunst-the-nazis-inventory-of-degenerate-art. Accessed July 15, 2020.

Kaiser, Fritz. *Degenerate Art: The Exhibition Catalogue Guide in German and English.* San Bernardino, CA: lulu.com, 2018.

Peters, Olaf, et al. *Degenerate Art: The Attack on Modern Art in Nazi Germany*. Munich: Prestel, 2014.

Smilingoff. "1937 Munich Exhibition of Degenerate Art." YouTube. https://www.youtube.com/watch?v=NmdO9tWeptY. Accessed October 18, 2021.

East German Art

Art in the GDR, or East Germany, was dominated by the VBK (Verband Bildender Künstler der DDR). In order to receive commissions or exhibit their work, artists had to be members of the VBK. The officially sanctioned form of art in the GDR was socialist realism. According to the principles of socialist realism, an acceptable work of art must be *proletarian* (relevant and understandable to the working class), *typical* (portray scenes of everyday life), *realistic* (not representationally abstract), and *partisan* (support the East German government and its ruling party, the SED).

Artists in East Germany were also employed to produce propaganda posters, which explained the policies of the government and announced important activities. Shortly after the Second World War, posters in East Berlin focused on maintaining law and order, rebuilding towns and cities, reforming agriculture along Soviet lines, and generally portraying the SED (the Socialist Unity Party of Germany) as the foundational party in the Soviet occupation zone and the pathway to a new Germany. The political posters of the day emphasized the differences between communism and capitalism and presented an emotional appeal to war-weary East Germans, urging them to work together to rebuild their shattered country. The 1950s were the high point of poster art in the GDR.

The postwar economic recovery was well under way in West Germany, and tens of thousands of East Germans crossed into West Berlin every month. The East German government needed to show its citizens that life could be better under the SED than in the West. The standard of living gradually began to rise in the East, and the propaganda posters heralded the increased availability of consumer goods. During the 1960s, propaganda posters touted the achievements of the USSR, and by extension, the GDR. The posters also announced solidarity with other communist regimes and condemned the militarism of the United States and West Germany, which the GDR blamed for the construction of the Berlin Wall in 1961. The propaganda posters of the 1970s adopted a more optimistic tone. While extolling the virtues of communism over capitalism, East German propaganda also called for the normalization of relations between the two German states and praised the benefits of détente. In place of strict socialist realism, pop art and geometric design began to appear on the posters. Labor strikes in Poland during the early 1980s led to a hardening of the East German regime. Propaganda posters warned of the dangers of nuclear weapons and announced important events in the life of the country, such as the thirty-fifth anniversary of the GDR in 1984.

The posters show how the East German authorities promulgated the message of the SED and tried to influence the thinking of their citizens. The posters also provide a contemporary lens into the day-to-day life of the East German citizens. East German propaganda posters met their demise on November 9, 1989, with the fall of the Berlin Wall. The final poster of the era simply read "40 Years of the GDR—Good-bye SED."

After the demise of the GDR, the artistic merit of the work of many East German artists was called into question. Willie Sitte (1921–2013), for example, was a member of the Central Committee of the SED, which gave him a role in determining which artists in the GDR were granted official recognition and could display their work. His paintings portrayed the working class and also dealt with the themes of war, fascism, and the oppression of minorities. Bernhard Heisig (1925–2011) was head of the Leipzig Academy of Visual Arts. He received commissions from Erich Honecker and other senior East German politicians. Heisig painted portraits of Lenin, and his scenes depicted a leftist historical perspective. He served in the SS during the Second World War and considered himself both a perpetrator and victim of the era in which he lived. The Museum Barberini in Potsdam has a large collection of East German artists.

Wendell G. Johnson

See also: Chapter 2: Berlin Wall. Chapter 3: Government and Politics in the German Democratic Republic. Chapter 4: Overview. Chapter 16: *Ostalgie.*

Further Reading

Barron, Stephanie, Sabine Eckmann, and Eckhart Gillen, eds. *Art of Two Germanys—Cold War Cultures*. New York: Abrams, 2009.

Heather, David, and Mechthild Barth. *DDR Posters: Ostdeutsche Propagandakunst/The Art of East German Propaganda*. Munich: Prestel, 2014.

Kelly, Elaine, and Amy Lynn Wlodarski, eds. *Art outside the Lines: New Perspectives on GDR Art Culture*. Amsterdam: Rodopi, 2011.

Tannert, Christoph, Eugen Blume, Martin-Gropius-Bau (Berlin), Deutsche Gesellschaft, and Künstlerhaus Bethanien. *Gegenstimmen: Kunst in der DDR 1976-1989; Ausstellung 16.7.-26.9.2016 = Voices of Dissent*. Berlin: Deutsche Gesellschaft e. V., 2016.

Kollwitz, Käthe (1867–1945)

Käthe Kollwitz (née Schmidt) ranks among Germany's best-known and most beloved artists. She began her professional education studying painting in Königsberg, Germany (present-day Kaliningrad, Russia) in 1881. After studying the prints of Max Klinger (1857–1920), she gave up painting in 1890 in favor of etching and lithography. In 1891, she married the physician Dr. Karl Kollwitz and moved to Berlin, where she experienced her initial professional success. Her *Ein Weberaufstand* (*A Weaver's Revolt),* based on Gerhard Hauptmann's play *Die Weber* (*The Weavers*), a portfolio of three lithographs and three etchings, was shown at the Grosse Berliner Kunstaustausstellung in 1898. She was supposed to receive a prize, but the emperor Wilhelm II did not support it. Soon thereafter, she was appointed to a teaching post at the Künstlerinnen-schule, a school for female artists, in Berlin. She joined the Berlin Secession, a group of artists who consciously "seceded" from the city's art establishment (particularly the Berlin Academy of Art) in order to champion new forms of contemporary art. She also visited Paris, where she attended sculpture classes at the Julien Academy and met the French sculptor Auguste Rodin (1840–1917).

While in Berlin, her prints were primarily black and white, and she concentrated on different ways of portraying the human form. Her best-known work from this period was the etching *Women with Dead Child*, which depicts a crouching female figure with a child on her lap. At this time, she became acutely aware of the condition of the working class, whose plight informed her work. She completed a second cycle of works, *The Peasant War* (1902–1908), based on the violent peasant uprising during the Reformation (1525) in which nearly 100,000 peasants were killed. Pieces in this collection included *Plowing, Raped, Sharpening the Scythe, Arming in the Vault, The*

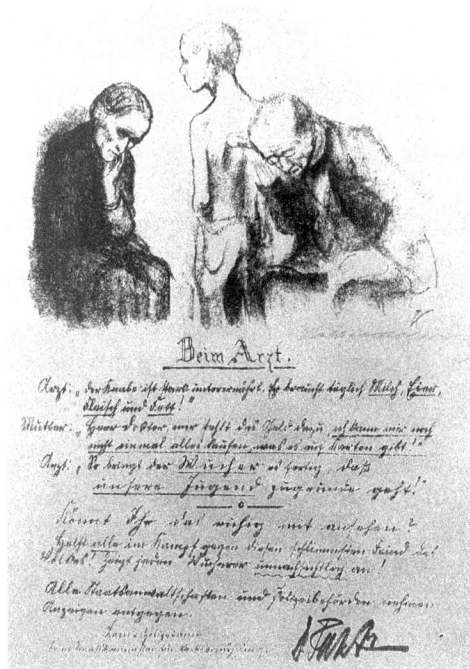

Käthe Kollwitz's (1867–1945) drawings were often critical of society. In this 1920 poster, the young boy is malnourished, but his mother cannot afford the doctor-recommended necessary foods (milk, eggs, meat, and fat) for him, even though she has a ration card. The poster asks people to turn in extortionists ("Wucherer") who profit from people's misfortune. (Charcoal drawing of a physician examining a boy, by Kollwitz. Wellcome Collection. Attribution 4.0 International [CC BY 4.0])

Prisoners, and presciently, *After the Battle* (which featured a mother searching corpses for the body of her son). Her younger son Peter was killed in a battle at Diksmuide, Flanders, in 1914. Kollwitz was overcome with grief, and her preoccupation with death was reflected in her work. She sculpted a tribute to her son, *The Grieving Parents*, which was dedicated at the Vladslo military cemetery in Flanders in 1932. She subsequently created the series *Death*, a collection of eight lithographs.

During the Weimar Republic (1919–1933), Kollwitz became the first woman to be admitted to the Prussian Academy of Art, where she was also the first woman to receive the Prussian award Pour le Mérite for her printmaking. She helped found the Society for Women Artists and Friends of Art and visited the Soviet Union as a guest of the government. Kollwitz and her husband issued an appeal to left-wing parties imploring them to unite in opposition to Adolf Hitler. By 1933, she was forced to resign her teaching position and was unable to exhibit her work. Kollwitz's grandson was killed in Russia during the Second World War. She left Berlin in 1943, and much of her work was lost when her house was bombed. Kollwitz died at Moritzburg (near Dresden) on April 22, 1945.

Käthe Kollwitz's work directly confronted human suffering in the first half of the twentieth century. Her sculpture *Mother with Her Dead Son* (based on her etching) resides in the Neue Wache in Berlin's central memorial to the victims of war and tyranny. Two hundred of her works are on display at the Kollwitz Museum in Berlin. Kollwitz's works are also on display in the Museum of Modern Art in New York as part of its exhibit on German Expressionism.

Wendell G. Johnson

See also: Chapter 5: The Reformation; Religious Wars. Chapter 7: Women in the Workforce. Chapter 11: Expressionism (*Expressionismus*) and Its Successors (1905–1925); Weimar Classicism (*Weimarer Klassik*) (ca. 1772–1805). Chapter 12: Artists; Degenerate Art; Museums.

Further Reading

Gabler, Josephine. "Kollwitz, Käthe." In Jane Turner, ed. *The Dictionary of Art*, vol. 18, 205–207. New York: Grove Dictionaries, 1996.

Kearns, Martha. *Käthe Kollwitz: Woman and Artist.* Old Westbury, NY: Feminist Press, 1976.

Museums

Located behind the Berlin Dome, Museum Island in the former East Berlin is the home to five museums. The Pergamon Museum is Berlin's most popular museum, with nearly 1 million visitors each year. Its main attractions are the Pergamon Altar, the Ishtar Gate of Babylon, and the Market Gate of Miletus. The museum is undergoing a significant renovation and will open fully in 2025. It was damaged during the Second World War, and its collection was looted by the Soviet Army. Significant relics from the collection are still stored in the Pushkin Museum in Moscow and the Hermitage in St. Petersburg.

The Bode Museum is home to two major collections: sculpture and Byzantine art. It contains one of the largest collections of ancient sculpture in the world. The Byzantine works range from the third to fifteenth century, with emphasis on Roman sarcophagi. The Old Museum (Altes Museum), a stunning neoclassical structure designed by Schinkel, was originally built to house the art collection of the Prussian royal family. At present it contains the largest collection of Etruscan art outside of Italy and portrait busts of Caesar and Cleopatra. The New Museum and the Old National Gallery were designed by Friedrich August Stüler (1800–1865), the Prussian court architect. The construction of the New Museum was a sensation, built of prefabricated cast and wrought iron. It was also severely damaged during the Second World War and remained in ruins until rebuilding began in 1999. The famous bust of the Egyptian queen Nefertiti (formerly displayed in the Egyptian Museum) can now be seen in the New Museum. The Old National Gallery was inspired by the Acropolis in Athens. It shows paintings and sculptures from the Romantic through Biedermeier period. The collection includes works by the German artist Caspar David Friedrich (1774–1840) and Johann Gottfried Schadow's *Princesses Luise and Friedericke*, perhaps the most beautiful sculpture ever executed by a Prussian artist. Museum Island was designated a UNESCO World Heritage Site in 1999.

Elsewhere in Germany, patrons of the arts can visit the Zwinger in Dresden. Originally part of the Dresden fortress, the Zwinger is situated between the inner and outer defensive walls of the city. It presently houses the Dresden Porcelain Collection, which display both Asian and Meissen porcelain (the Meissen porcelain factory is located approximately twenty miles from Dresden) and the Old Masters Picture Gallery, which features Renaissance and Baroque paintings by artists such as Raphael, Titian, Correggio, Rembrandt, and Vermeer. Many of the artistic treasures of the Zwinger were placed in storage during the Second World War and survived the first bombing of Dresden in 1945.

The German Photo Museum in Leipzig is the largest of its kind in Germany. It showcases 70,000 historic photographs and 3,000 vintage cameras. The museum contains a permanent exhibit of East German photography. The Museum of the Printing Press (Druckkunst-Museum) combines a working print shop with a museum. In commemoration of the 500th anniversary of the Protestant Reformation, the museum recently hosted the exhibit "Luther—Leipzig—Letterpress!" Johann Sebastian Bach is buried in the Thomaskirche in Leipzig. Across the street, in the Bose House, are the Bach Museum and Bach archives. The Museum of Musical Instruments, in the city center, owns over 10,000 artifacts, making it one of the largest collections in Europe.

The Bavarian State Picture Collection Munich is comprised of three art galleries, each specializing in a different era of European art. The Old Gallery (Alte Pinakotheck) contains the largest collection in the world of German paintings from the fourteenth to the seventeenth centuries, including *The Four Apostles* by Albrecht Dürer and *Lamentation beneath the Cross* by Lucas Cranach. The New Gallery (Neue Pinakotheck) has a strong emphasis on German Romanticism, the Munich School, and artists of the Biedermeier movement. Many of the art movements of the twentieth century are represented in the Modern Gallery (Moderne Pinakotheck), including expressionism, New Objectivity (Neue Sachlichkeit), and Bauhaus.

Wendell G. Johnson

See also: Chapter 11: Expressionism (*Expressionismus*) and Its Successors (1905–1925). Chapter 12: Architecture; Artists; Decorative Arts *Biedermeier* and *Jugendstil*. Chapter 13: Musical Periods and Composers. Chapter 16: Media Photography.

Further Reading

Rohde, Elisabeth, ed. *The Altar of Pergamon*. Berlin: Berlin State Museum, Antiquities Collection, 1981.

Sheehan, James J. *Museums in the German Art World from the End of the Old Regime to the Rise of Modernism.* New York: Oxford University Press, 2000.

Websites

https://www.visitberlin.de/en/museum-island-in-berlin
https://www.der-dresdner-zwinger.de/en/home/
http://www.druckkunst-museum.de/home.html
http://www.fotomuseum.eu/
http://www.bachmuseumleipzig.de/en/bach-museum
https://www.pinakothek.de/en

Naturalism

Considered the first modern movement of literature and the arts in Germany, naturalism can be traced to France and the novelist Emile Zola, who likened his literary style to the scientific method. Naturalist artists and writers, also influenced by the development of photography, sought to faithfully record their subjects without idealization or stylization. Significant for promoting social criticism as a legitimate artistic concern, naturalism was primarily dominant in the last two decades of the nineteenth century.

The first manifestation of German naturalism appeared in *Kritische Waffengänge* (*Critical Passage of Arms*), a series of six theoretical pamphlets published from 1882 to 1884 by the brothers Heinrich (1855–1944) and Julius (1859–1930) Hart in Berlin. While criticizing the literary establishment, these works balanced realism and idealism, showing little interest in the social criticism that would be reflective of later naturalists. In 1885, Michael Georg Conrad (1846–1927) founded the Munich journal *Gesellschaft* (*Society*), which would become an important publication for naturalist writing until 1890, favoring prose from a variety of writers emphasizing social problems.

The literature of naturalism is exemplified in the *Sekundenstil* (second-by-second style) prose sketches of Arno Holz (1863–1929), the movement's best-known theorist, and Johannes Schlaf (1862–1941), where characters' actions are captured in minute detail. Other writers of the movement portraying working-class life included Max Kretzer (1854–1941), Helene Bohlau (1859–1940), Wilhelm von Polenz (1861–1903), and Clara Viebig (1860–1952).

Drama was the most important genre of the German naturalism movement and was best represented by Gerhart Hauptmann (1862–1946), who received the Nobel Prize in Literature in 1912. His masterpiece of the period, *Die Weber* (1892; *The Weavers*, 1899), which depicted the 1844 weavers' revolt in Poland, premiered at the Freie Bühne (Free Stage), a significant venue for naturalist theater founded in 1889 by Otto Brahm. Brahm, also the editor of the 1890 periodical *Freie Bühne für modernes Leben*, is credited with guiding the movement to prominence.

In the visual arts, naturalism has been used synonymously with realism, referring to the objective style and focus on everyday subjects and scenes. Naturalist painters sought to depict nature with the least amount of distortion or interpretation. In Germany, artists associated with naturalism or realism were largely influenced by the French painter Gustave Courbet (1819–1877) and his works depicting peasants and laborers. Thus, Wilhelm Leibl (1844–1900) asserted the principle of "absolute painting" with his depictions of the local peasantry of the Bavarian countryside. Although Leibl's reputation was greater in France, where he exhibited regularly, he did have a group of dedicated German followers known as the Leibl Circle, which included Carl Schuch (1846–1903), Johann Sperl (1840–1914), and Wilhelm Trübner (1851–1917). Fritz von Uhde (1848–1911) often painted working-class subjects in non-studio settings with natural light. Although he was considered a major figure of the naturalist movement, he became a founding member of the Munich Secession and served as its president from 1899 to 1904.

While short-lived, naturalism remained the dominant aesthetic mode in Germany until 1898 and is significant for connecting art and social criticism, which would influence future generations of writers and artists in Germany.

Larissa Garcia

See also: Chapter 11: Realism and Naturalism (*Realismus* and *Naturalismus*) (1848–1899). Chapter 12: Artists.

Further Reading

Eisenman, Stephen, and Thomas E. Crow. *Nineteenth Century Art: A Critical History*, 4th ed. New York: Thames & Hudson, 2011.

Koelb, Clayton, and Eric Downing. *German Literature of the Nineteenth Century, 1832–1899*. Rochester, NY: Camden House, 2005.

Osborne, John. *The Naturalist Drama in Germany*. Totowa, NJ: Rowman & Littlefield, 1971.

CHAPTER 13

MUSIC AND DANCE

OVERVIEW

Germany has a storied musical tradition extending back to the Middle Ages. Hildegard of Bingen (1098–1179) wrote dramatic and lyrical poetry that survives in musical form. Taken together, Hildegard's music forms a liturgical cycle, including a Kyrie and an Alleluia. Walther von der Vogelweide (ca. 1170–1230) was a *Minnesänger* (minnesinger) whose most important works include the love song "*Herzeliebez vrouwelin*" (*herzliebstes Fräulein*, "Darling Girl"). The Protestant reformer Martin Luther (1483–1546) was an accomplished performer on both the lute and the flute. Luther also wrote thirty-six hymns. His most famous hymn, "*Ein feste Burg ist unser Gott*" ("A Mighty Fortress Is Our God"), is still sung in Protestant churches in Germany and the United States. Many of the themes in Luther's hymns were subsequently taken up by Johann Sebastian Bach.

In classical music, the "Three Bs" refer to the preeminence of three German composers: Johann Sebastian Bach, Ludwig van Beethoven, and Johannes Brahms. J. S. Bach (1685–1750), the musical genius of the Baroque period, served as *Kapellmeister* in Cöthen and cantor at the Thomaskirche and teacher at the Thomasschule in Leipzig. He composed the Brandenburg Concertos, Weihnachtsoratorium (Christmas), and numerous motets, among other works. Ludwig van Beethoven (1770–1827), the preeminent composer of the classical period, was born in Bonn and studied composition with Joseph Haydn in Vienna. He wrote nine symphonies, thirty-two piano concertos, and numerous chamber works. "Ode to Joy" ("*An die Freude*") from his Ninth Symphony is the anthem of the European Union. Johannes Brahms (1833–1897), composer and pianist during the Romantic period, was born in Hamburg but spent much of his professional life in Vienna. Brahms admired the classical composers Wolfgang Amadeus Mozart and Joseph Haydn. He composed symphonies and chamber music but is perhaps best known for his "Lullaby" (or the "*Wiegenlied*," op. 49 no. 4). Orchestras throughout Europe and North America continue to include music by Bach, Beethoven, and Brahms in their repertoires. In particular, Beethoven remains one of the most frequently performed composers in the world. Bonn, Beethoven's birthplace and the former capital of the Federal Republic of Germany, hosts an annual festival in the composer's honor.

Kabarett, turn of the century German musical theater, was introduced to American audiences through Bob Fosse's 1972 film *Cabaret*. *Kabarett* was staged in nightclubs where patrons could eat and drink while enjoying a show. It was originally low-key and featured song, dance, comedy, and political satire. By the 1920s, *Kabarett*'s political satire had evolved into outrageous dance routines and maudlin ballads.

Jazz became very popular in Germany following the First World War. The Swing Kids (*Swingjugend*), the subject of the 1993 movie of the same name, were Weimar-era swing and jazz aficionados from middle- and upper-middle-class households in Hamburg and Berlin. They admired the American way of life and affected British clothing styles. These youth adopted swing music as a protest against Nazi ideology. Jazz was considered degenerate music by the Nazi authorities because it was often performed by Black musicians. The government clamped down on the Swing Kids: many were arrested and sent to the juvenile concentration camp in Moringen.

Anglo-American music dominated the landscape of popular music in postwar Germany after 1945. American Forces Network and British Forces Broadcasting Services filled the airwaves with American and British popular music; and Elvis Presley's tour of duty as an American GI in Bad Neuheim stirred considerable "Elvis mania" among German teenagers. Both the Beatles and the Rolling Stones performed in Germany in the early 1960s, and their music inspired many German artists who in turn performed only in English.

Schlager, the most conservative and parochial genre of German popular music, was the easy-listening music of postwar Germany and played a vital role in the social psychology of the traumatized nation. Schlager evoked consoling images of prewar Germany and provided the soundtrack to the new national self-esteem of the Economic Miracle. The political turbulence of the 1960s gave rise to the Liedermacher movement, protest songs in the tradition of German folk music with artists such as Wolf Biermann, Reinhard Mey, and Konstantin Wecker. Many of them played their string instruments in the finger-plucking style of Pete Seeger and Woody Guthrie.

Krautrock (one term among many used to describe West German electronic popular music) stood in stark contrast to traditional folk music and Schlager. Numerous Krautrock musicians were classically trained and discarded many elements of American and British rock and roll. They used a steady metronomic beat in place of the backbeat of traditional rock and deliberately played on German stereotypes such as efficiency and engineering prowess. Kraftwerk, the best-known Krautrock group, released its breakthrough album *Autobahn* in 1974. Cosmic rock, following on the heels of Krautrock and often overlapping with it, describes the synthesizer-heavy sound of composer Klaus Schulz and groups such as Ash Ra Tempel and Tangerine Dream.

West German punk rock in the 1970s followed the mantra of British punk, "no future," with one crucial difference. In British punk, the mantra signified a rejection of social stratification and expressed the hopelessness of Britain's crumbling postwar (and pre-Brexit) economy. To West German punks, "no future" was a rejection of the legacy of German fascism. The punk movement, and its music, emerged against the backdrop of the remilitarization of West Germany and the domestic terrorism of the Baader-Meinhof Gang. The music of Mittagspause (Lunch Break) protested

German law curtailing civil liberties under the ruse of combatting terrorism. Two of the members of the band, singer Peter Heim and guitarist Thomas Schwabel, eventually spun off from the group and founded Fehlfarben (off-color), which served as a bridge to the Neue Deutsche Welle (NDW, New German Wave).

Following the British and American punk revolution in the late 1970s, the Neue Deutsche Welle, new wave music with the addition of the term German, reformulated Krautrock for the post-punk generation. Prior to the appearance of the NDW, German pop musicians who wanted to appeal to younger audiences often sang in English. However, German speech rhythms do not always adapt themselves well to the structure of English-language rock. NDW musicians such as Nina Hagen and Nena (99 *Luftballons*) changed this dynamic and recorded their music in German. NDW skipped over Krautrock and transported German pop music back to the 1950s and 1960s. Many critics viewed the NDW as modernized Schlager.

German techno music is characterized by massive speed and scale. Techno is closely identified with the Berlin of the late 1980s. Set against the dramatic conditions following the fall of the Berlin Wall, techno became the soundtrack of the end of the Cold War. It was embraced by the youth of East Berlin, and techno clubs sprung up in abandoned factories, bunkers, and power stations in the former capital of the German Democratic Republic. Tresor, the nightclub and record label, proved to be the primary vehicle for techno music in Berlin. Its breakout release was *Der Klang der Familie* (1992). Techno turned out to be a significant economic and cultural force in the newly unified capital. The Loveparade festival took place in Berlin and other German cities in the 1990s and early 2000s, attracting between 500,000 and 1.6 million partyers. The Loveparade was ended after the death of twenty-one participants in Duisburg in 2010 in a stampede. The Goethe-Institut used the international appeal of techno to market and advertise German culture.

German "industrial" music dates to 1980 when the group Einstürzende Neubauten (Collapsing New Buildings) was formed in West Berlin. Einstürzende Neubauten developed an anti-pop approach to its music and eschewed traditional instruments, using instead power tools and industrial detritus (such as sheet metal, fencing, and steel drums) found on construction sites. The band's music is marked by sonic excess and the apocalyptic lyrics of singer Blixa Bargeld (née Christian Emmerich). Rammstein, also from Berlin (founded 1994), is commercially the most successful and well-known German industrial band. Their inaugural album, *Herzleid* (*Heartbreak*), remained on the German charts for nearly two years. In concert, the band appears in futuristic outfits or bondage gear, and their lyrics refer to social deviance and sexual violence.

Unterhaltungsmusik (light or popular music), *Ernste Musik* (serious music, usually classical music), and *Funktionsmusik* (functional music, such as film or theater music) are commonly differentiated. More than 70,000 artists are members of GEMA, the Gesellschaft für musikalische Aufführungs- und mechanische Vervielfältigungs-srechte (Society for Musical Performing and Mechanical Reproduction), an institution that basically makes sure that artists are getting paid when their works are performed or heard.

Wendell G. Johnson

Further Reading

Adelt, Ulrich. *Krautrock: German Music in the Seventies.* Ann Arbor: University of Michigan Press, 2016.

Bent, I., and M. Pfau. "Hildegard of Bingen." *Grove Music Online,* 2001. https://www .oxfordmusiconline.com/grovemusic/view/10.1093/gmo/9781561592630.001.0001 /omo-9781561592630-e-0000013016. Accessed December 9, 2019.

Die Gema. https://www.gema.de. Accessed July 15, 2020.

Hall, Mirko M., Seth Howes, and Cyrus Shahan. *Beyond No Future: Cultures of German Punk.* New York: Bloomsbury Academic, 2016.

Kater, Michael H. *Different Drummers: Jazz in the Culture of Nazi Germany.* New York: Oxford University Press, 1992.

Leaver, R. (2001). Luther, Martin. *Grove Music Online.* https://www.oxfordmusiconline .com/grovemusic/view/10.1093/gmo/9781561592630.001.0001/omo-9781561592630-e -0000017219. Accessed December 9, 2019.

Lexikon der Musik—Instrumente, Musikrichtungen, Veranstaltungen. https://www .lexikon-der-musik.de/. Accessed July 15, 2020.

Schütte, Uwe. *German Pop Music: A Companion.* Berlin; Boston: De Gruyter, 2017.

Bausch, Pina (1940–2009)

Pina Bausch, arguably one of the most influential performance artists and choreographer of the twentieth century, died June 2009 in Wuppertal, Germany, merely five days after being diagnosed with lung cancer. Born Philippine (Pina) Bausch on July 27, 1940, in Solingen, Germany, she performed at a very young age for guests of her parents' hotel and restaurant in Solingen. She started studying dance at the age of fourteen under Kurt Jooss at the Essener Folkwang Hochschule. In 1958, she moved to study ballet at the Juilliard School of Music in New York with a one-year scholarship from the German Academic Exchange Service (DAAD). She stayed for a second year, which she financed with an engagement at the Metropolitan Opera. Her two years in New York were formative ones, and she partially credited the city's energy and chaos for her early creative epiphany.

After appearances in Italy, Bausch returned to Germany and became a soloist under her teacher Kurt Jooss at the Folkwang *Tanztheater.* In 1973, she established her company *Tanztheater Wuppertal Pina Bausch.* Tanztheater (dance theatre), a fusion form of dance characterized by its defiance of classical dance protocols that strictly differentiate between *ernster* (serious) and *unterhaltender* (entertaining) music. *Tanztheater* emanates from German expressionism creating a heavily metaphoric, interdisciplinary performative art form that blends elements of speech, movement, singing, speaking, and fragmented narrative. Her dance creations echoed the experience of the Second World War.

The body in Bausch's art was situated between the specific and the collective, mapping the social and cultural significance of the human body through movement. Bausch's pieces trump social dichotomies of male/female, often commenting on gender dynamics through gender-role reversal and cross-dressing. Her radical vision elicited strong responses from her audience that ranged from awe and admiration to rejection and shock. Her pieces were non-hierarchical, and her dancers were from all age groups between twenty-three and sixty-three. She created an exchange of experiences between bodies that defied taboos and prejudices and reflected her philosophy: "I'm not interested in how people move; I'm interested in what makes them move." Her modernized dance routines mirrored the urgency of her motto "dance, dance otherwise we are lost." Her disruptive radical dance pieces were corporeal, performative, and theatrical, and their *mise-en-scène* played an integral role in the message conveyed. Dirt, rocks, and water are some of the elements included in her performances. In her iconic *The Rite of Spring*, the stage is covered with soil.

Stylistically and thematically, she used the repetition of gestures and words as a narrative device that sought to convey the uncanny feeling emanating from human attempts to repeatedly and absurdly navigate life. *Cafe Müller* (1978), arguably her most enduring creation, employs the repetitive movement of its dancers to navigate a stage strewn with black chairs and tables with their eyes closed. The dance was inspired by her own experience and ensuing memories watching her father work during World War II. Bausch herself and *Cafe Müller* are featured in Pedro Almodóvar's film *Talk to Her* (2002).

Before her death, Bausch collaborated with German director Wim Wenders to create the Oscar-nominated documentary *Pina*, which was completed posthumously and was first screened during the Berlin Film Festival in 2011. The film became a homage to her enduring artistic vision, highlighting the radical humanism of her dance and her life interpreted through her craft.

Among her numerous awards, Bausch received the UK's Laurence Olivier Award (2006), Japan's Kyoto prize (2007), the Golden Lion for Lifetime Achievements (2007), and Germany's Goethe Prize (2008). On July 27, 2015, the seventy-fifth anniversary of her birth, Germany issued a postage stamp in her honor. Bausch created forty-six original pieces. Her creative legacy is carried out by the *Tanztheater Wuppertal*. Pina Bausch married Rolf Borzik, who died in 1980 of leukemia. She is survived by her son Rolf and her life partner Ronald Kay.

Alia Soliman

See also: Chapter 2: Overview. Chapter 7: Overview. Chapter 8: DAAD; Goethe-Institut. Chapter 16: Film.

Further Reading

Climenhaga, Royd. *Pina Bausch*. London: Routledge, 2008.

Meyer, Marion. *Pina Bausch*. Penny Black, trans. London: Oberon Books, 2018.

Pina. 2011. Wim Wenders. Germany. Film.

"Tanzend vom Menschen sprechen—Pina Bausch Biographie." http://www.pinabausch .org/de/pina/biografie. Accessed July 15, 2020.

Bayreuth

Bayreuth (population ca. 73,000), located in Bavaria, is internationally renowned as the site of composer Richard Wagner's Festspielhaus and the home of the Bayreuth Festival. Wagner (1813–1883) sought a locale suitable for staging his *Der Ring der Nibelungen,* a cycle of four operas: *The Rhinegold, The Valkyrie, Siegfried,* and *Twilight of the Gods.* A full performance of the cycle takes place over the course of four evenings, with a total playing time of nearly fifteen hours. The final scene of *Twilight of the Gods,* often referred to as the "Immolation Scene," contains one of the longest arias in the operatic corpus.

Wagner laid the foundation stone for the Festspielhaus in 1872 and commemorated the event by conducting a performance of Beethoven's Ninth Symphony. Subsequently, Wagner set out to raise funds to complete the structure. The auditorium originally had 1,460 seats, and the orchestra was hidden from sight. The first performance of *The Ring* took place in 1876, with Emperor Wilhelm I, Friedrich Nietzsche, and Pyotr Ilyich Tchaikovsky in attendance. The production was a financial disaster, and another festival was not staged until 1882, when Wagner himself conducted *Parsifal,* the only opera written specifically for the Festspielhaus.

After Wagner's death in 1883, leadership of Bayreuth fell to his widow Cosima Liszt Wagner (1837–1930). Early productions of *The Ring* attempted to replicate Wagner's original staging, based on Norse mythology. The Bayreuth festival was presented sporadically until 1936, when Adolf Hitler decreed that it was to be held annually. The festival was not held 1945–50 but reopened to widespread acclaim in 1951. The leadership remained in the Wagner family until today.

Perhaps the most noteworthy modern performance was the centennial production of 1976 conducted by Pierre Boulez. This presentation departed from Wagner's

---

LEADERSHIP OF THE BAYREUTH FESTIVAL

1876–1882	Richard Wagner (1813–1883)
1886–1906	Cosima Liszt Wagner (1836–1939), second wife of Richard Wagner, daughter of Franz Liszt
1908–1930	Siegfried Wagner (1869–1930), son of Richard and Cosima
1931–1944	Winifred Wagner (1907–1980), British-born wife of Siegfried and unapologetic close friend of Hitler
1951–1966	Wieland (1917–1966) and Wolfgang Wagner (1919–2010), sons of Winifred and Siegfried
1967–2008	Wolfgang Wagner
2008–	Eva Wagner-Pasquier (b. 1945) and Katharina Wagner (b. 1978), daughters of Wolfgang

original scenery and was set during the industrial revolution, with a hydroelectric dam replacing the Rhine River as the background for the music. Avant-garde presentations of *The Ring* continue to deconstruct Wagner's original opera. The backdrop for Frank Castdorf's 2013 production was the global quest for oil. *The Rhinegold* was set in a Route 66 gas station; *The Valkyrie* was set in the Caspian oil fields; *Siegfried* used Mount Rushmore as a backdrop, but substituted the images of Marx, Lenin, Stalin, and Mao for those of Presidents Washington, Jefferson, Roosevelt, and Lincoln; and *Twilight of the Gods* took place in the New York Stock Exchange. This 2013 staging incensed patrons, who booed for ten minutes after the final curtain fell.

The Bayreuth Festival has become one of Germany's great cultural events. A new staging of *The Ring* is produced every five to seven years. The annual demand for tickets (500,000) far exceeds supply (58,000). Applicants can expect to spend ten years on a waiting list until tickets become available.

Wendell G. Johnson

See also: Chapter 2: Hitler, Adolf (1889–1945). Chapter 13: Musical Periods and Composers.

Further Reading

Hartford, Robert. *Bayreuth, the Early Years: An Account of the Early Decades of the Wagner Festival as Seen by the Celebrated Visitors & Participants*. London: Cambridge University Press, 1980.

Millington, Barry. *The Sorcerer of Bayreuth: Richard Wagner, His Work, and His World*. New York: Oxford University Press, 2012.

Skelton, Geoffrey. *Bayreuth* (opera). *Grove Music Online*. Oxford, UK: Oxford University Press.

Cabaret

Cabaret (*Kabarett*) designates both a genre (a revue of songs, skits, and monologues satirizing politics and social attitudes) and a venue (the theater where cabaret is performed). Cabaret was popularized in the United States by the Broadway musical of the same name (1966), based loosely on Christopher Isherwood's novel *Goodbye to Berlin*. The screen adaptation of *Cabaret* (1972) won eight Academy Awards. Perhaps the best-known film depiction of German *Kabarett* was *Der blaue Engel* (*The Blue Angel*), starring Marlene Dietrich and Emil Jannings. At the present time, "cabaret" has become nearly synonymous with a "nightclub," where variety shows are staged and patrons are seated at tables.

Strictly speaking, cabaret originated in Paris in the 1880s when Rodolphe Solis opened Le Chat Noir (The Black Cat). Solis viewed his nightclub as a venue where artists and musicians could meet and confront the public. The first German cabaret,

Based on Christopher Isherwood's 1939 book *Goodbye to Berlin, Cabaret* was a musical first performed in 1966. In 1972, the movie of the same name, starring Liza Minnelli under the direction of Bob Fosse, garnered eight Oscars and many more accolades. (Markwaters/Dreamstime.com)

Ernst Wolzogen's Überbrettl (a play on words on Nietzsche's *Übermensch, über*—super, *Brettl*—stage), was opened in Berlin in 1901. This venture proved to be a success, and other cabarets were soon opened, including Max Reinhardt's well-known Schall und Rauch (Sound and Smoke). Cabaret also thrived in Munich, where the Eleven Executioners (Die Elf Scharfrichter) danced onstage and performed a mixture of songs, puppet plays, and literary parodies. One of the Executioners' founding members and stars was Marya Delvard (1874–1965), who dressed in black, sported a chalk-white face, and sang in a highly stylized manner. The Executioners were the most famous pre-World War I cabaret in the country and set the stage for the dynamic cabaret culture of Weimar Germany.

The *Revue* was Weimar Berlin's most popular form of live entertainment. Cabaret also featured the *Conferencier*, an orator who provided satirical commentary on the contemporary situation featuring political satire and gallows humor (in the movie version of the musical *Cabaret*, this role was played by Joel Grey). Cabaret during the Weimar Republic became "Americanized," or influenced by what Germans perceived to be African American culture. While well-intentioned, it reinforced prevailing stereotypes. Perhaps the most notorious act at the time was the Ballet Celly de Rheide, which featured near-naked women "hopping around" (*Hopserei*) on the stage. Another well-known act was the Comedian Harmonists, a close ensemble sextet and one of Europe's most popular recording groups. Other famous cabaret artists include Claire Waldorf, who sang using Berlin dialect. Werner Finck and Karl Valentin were also part of the cabaret scene. The Nazis considered cabaret degenerate, outlawing the conferenciers and closing the theaters, which is depicted in the musical *Cabaret*.

The tradition of Berlin cabaret is carried on by *Max Raabe und das Palast Orchester* (founded 2006) and many others. The orchestra is comprised of men, except for the violin player, who has always been a female. Cabaret made a comeback in postwar Germany. Venues, such as *Die Wühlmäuse* (voles) and *Die Stachelschweine* (porcupines) in Berlin and the *Lach- und Schießgesellschaft* in Munich, show live performances. Many contemporary cabaret artists like Dieter Hallervorden, Dieter Nuhr, Bülent Ceylan and Anke Engelke perform on television.

Wendell G. Johnson

See also: Chapter 9: Standard and Dialect. Chapter 13: Dietrich, Marlene (1901–1992). Chapter 16: Film.

Further Reading:

Appignanesi, Lisa. *The Cabaret*, rev. and expanded ed. New Haven, CT: Yale University Press, 2004.

Fechner, Eberhard. *Die Comedian Harmonists: Sechs Lebensläufe*. 4. Aufl. München: Wilhelm Heyne Verlag, 1998.

"The German Cabaret." The Guide to Musical Theater. http://www.guidetomusicaltheatre.com/shows_c/cabaret_essay.htm. Accessed May 1, 2019.

Jelavich, Peter. *Berlin Cabaret*. Cambridge, MA: Harvard University Press, 1996.

Contemporary Popular Music

Two events promoted the spread of American and British pop music in Germany after the Second World War. To many young Germans, Elvis Presley represented the incarnation of American rock and roll music, and his time as a GI in Germany 1958–1960 received extensive media coverage. Second, the British invasion of the Beatles and Rolling Stones in the early 1960s spawned many German imitators who sang in English.

Contemporary popular music in Germany is highly paradoxical, often characterized as *Heulsusen-Pop* (crybaby pop) and shallow yet receives constant airplay and occupies high positions on the nation's pop charts. At the present, these pop charts are dominated by German entertainers, including established artists such as Herbert Grönemeyer, Peter Maffay, and the heavy metal band Scorpions. Grönemeyer's album *Mensch* (2002) is the best-selling German album of all time (his album *4630 Bochum* is third). The singer Udo Lindenberg (b. 1946) has been active since the early 1970s. His 1983 album *Sonderzug nach Pankow* (*Special Train to Pankow*, a district in East Berlin) was a reaction to East Germany and by extension to Erich Honecker banning

Table 13.1: POP CHART TOP 10—GERMANY JUNE 2021

#	Artist	Song	Language/Country
1	Olivia Rodrigo	"Good 4 U"	English/USA
2	Måneskin	"Beggin'"	English/Italy
3	Måneskin	"I Wanna Be Your Slave"	English/Italy
4	Nathan Evans, 220 KID & Billen Ted	"Wellerman (Sea Shanty)"	English/Scotland
5	Riton, Nightcrawlers, Mufasa & Hypeman	"Friday"	English/various
6	Shirin David	"Ich darf das"	German/Germany
7	PA Sports, Kianush & Jamule	"Shawty"	English/Germany
8	Justin Wellington & Small Jam	"Iko Iko"	English/Germany
9	Kollegah	"Rotlichtsonate"	German/Germany
10	Jamule	"Liege wieder wach"	German/Germany

his performance. In 2020, the biopic *Lindenberg! Mach dein Ding* (*Do Your Thing*) opened in theaters.

International artists manage to chart in Germany, but with the exceptions of global phenomena such as Adele and Ed Sheeran they drop off the charts rather quickly. American rock music is popular, giving bands like Linkin Park, Metallica, and Foo Fighters a strong fan base. However, country music is practically nonexistent in Germany. Neither Brad Paisley nor Faith Hill or Tim McGraw have come close to Germany's Top 100 in recent years.

Two genres of German popular music have spawned criticism: *Deutschrock* (German rock) for its perceived right-wing affiliation, and indigenous hip-hop for its aggressive lyrics against homosexuals and women, leading the Bundesprüfstelle für jugendgefährdende Medien (the Federal Review Board for Media Harmful to Young People) to ban certain recordings. Rammstein's 2009 *Liebe ist für alle da* was pulled off the shelf weeks after its release due to glorification of violence in one song. Die Ärzte (the Physicians) and Die toten Hosen (the Dead Pants) established themselves as left-wing punk-rock band. Madsen is an indie band, whose music can be found on the Goethe-Institut website. In the 1970s and 1980s, *Ton Steine Scherben* with Rio Reiser was a very political band, whose first song "Macht kaputt, was euch kaputt macht" ("Destroy What Destroys You") captured the mood of the time.

German hip-hop artists, such as Bushido and Sido, have gained popularity among teenagers. More recently, female rappers like Schwesta Ewa and non-gangster rappers like Cro have broadened the genre's appeal. Hip-hop, in particular, suffers the vagaries of Germany's entertainment charts, which ranks songs and albums by gross receipts rather than units sold. Music labels tend to release hip-hop in boxed sets, costing €30–60, which initially resulted in increased sales and higher chart positions.

Schlager, a uniquely German genre loosely equivalent to American country music, combines catchy instrumental arrangements with sentimental lyrics. Schlager arose in the 1950s in response to American rock and roll. Perhaps the best-known early Schlager artist was Freddy Quinn, whose first hit "Heimweh" (the German version of Dean Martin's "Memories Are Made of This") sold 8 million copies and stayed atop the German charts for five months in 1956. The genre has enjoyed a renaissance of late. Sarah Connor's first German album, *Muttersprache* (2015), Helene Fischer's *Farbenspiel* (2013), and Mark Forster's *Bauch und Kopf* (2014) each stayed on the German charts for more than one hundred weeks.

Randy Fink

See also: Chapter 13: Overview.

Further Reading

Ahlers, Michael, and Christoph Jacke, eds. *Perspectives on German Popular Music*. New York: Routledge, 2017.

Scholz, Harald. *"Ein Hoch auf uns . . .": Facetten deutschsprachiger Populärmusik*. Berlin: LIT Verlag, 2017.

Schütte, Uwe, Ed. *German Pop Music. A Companion. Companion to Contemporary German Culture,* vol. 6. Berlin; Boston: De Gruyter, 2017.

Dietrich, Marlene (1901–1992)

Born in Berlin at the beginning of the twentieth century, Marie Magdalene Dietrich was best known as "Marlene" Dietrich to millions of fans worldwide. She was most famous for her German cabaret style in song, dance, and acting performances. As an artist, she began her early career playing the violin and acting on stage and the silent screen. However, it was her first sound film, *Der blaue Engel* (*The Blue Angel*), directed by Josef von Sternberg, that launched her international film career. *Der blaue Engel* debuted in 1930 as one of Germany's first sound films. It highlighted the hedonistic lifestyle of the late 1920s German cabaret scene, easily capturing wider audiences than could previously only be reached in small, live venues. It was a great success, and Marlene left Germany for Hollywood to pursue a major film career, starring in six other von Sternberg films within five years. This move would initially be merely geographical but would later also prove to be quite political.

No matter the role, Marlene Dietrich "embodied . . . cabaret itself in all of its glory and infamy" (Farina 2013, p. 53). For American audiences, her portrayal of the femme fatale was dazzling, desirable, and dangerous all at once. "Dietrich . . . had bravely imported the wildness and freedom of German *Kabarett* onto the Hollywood big screen" (Farina 2013, p. 58). Her stylish dress, sexualized image, and sultry song and dance performances became her trademarks. Her fame led her to work on films with notable actors like Cary Grant, Jimmy Stewart, and John Wayne, and directors like Alfred Hitchcock.

Despite still being a German citizen at the onset of World War II, Marlene Dietrich used her fame and wealth to assist the United States during the war. She supported the American troops by visiting the front lines with USO shows, touring the United States to sell war bonds, and donating her own money to war and refugee efforts. In 1939, in a strong stance to separate herself from Nazi Germany and avoid being used by its media, Marlene Dietrich officially became an American citizen. Her wartime work was notably recognized by the United States, France, and Israel in subsequent peace-time years.

After the war, Marlene continued to work on films, but returned to live performance cabaret acts beginning with a Las Vegas show in the 1950s. This opened the door to a worldwide cabaret tour, which was quite successful throughout Europe. However, in 1960, the tour met with mixed reviews in her native Germany because the public still felt as though she had abandoned her country during the war. Marlene Dietrich performed twice on Broadway in the late 1960s. Her film career ended with a singing cameo role in *Just a Gigolo* in 1979, a movie with David Bowie. Due to her failing health, Dietrich withdrew from the public, living mainly in Paris for the remainder of her life.

Josianne Campbell

See also: Chapter 3: Citizenship; Germany and the United States. Chapter 13: Cabaret. Chapter 16: Film; Journalism under the Nazi Regime.

Further Reading

Farina, William. "The Long, Strange Journey of Marlene Dietrich." In *The German Cabaret Legacy in American Popular Music*. Jefferson, NC: McFarland & Company, 2013.

Johnson, Wendell G. "Dietrich, Marlene." In Lisa Tendrick Frank, ed. *An Encyclopedia of American Women at War*, vol. I: A–L. Santa Barbara, CA: ABC-CLIO, 2013.

Marlene. Directed by Maximillian Schell. Bayerischer Rundfunk (BR), DVD, 1984.

Riva, Maria. *Marlene Dietrich: The Life*. New York: Knopf, 1993.

German Folk Music and Dance

Volksmusik is the German term for "the people's music" or "folk's music." It typically refers to traditional types of music from rural areas in Germany, many of which are accompanied by a traditional form of dance and attire. These folk music songs and dances have been passed down for centuries, and still retain contemporary popularity in much their original form across the world.

The traditional *Volksmusik* is not to be confused with *volkstümliche Musik*, a type of commercial music using traditional *Volksmusik* features. *Volksmusik* is crafted, using dialect, incorporates tradition passed down orally, and only thrives on interaction with the audience. *Volkstümliche Musik* works with—often inadequately—full playback and uses simple texts suitable for mass consumption (another name could be popular entertainment music—*populäre Unterhaltungsmusik*).

Growing out of *Volksmusik*, the *Schuhplattler* is one of Alpine Germany's oldest and most famous dance traditions. The name of the dance is derived from a description of the dance itself; "the dancer strikes the soles of his shoes (*Schuhe*) with his hands held flat (*platt*)" ("History" 2018). At times, it was used as a courtship dance, where women danced in a circle around the men. However, it is also performed as solely a men's dance, all depending on the variation, of which there are over 150. The *Schuhplattler* is characterized by the dancers' leaps; a series of intricate slaps to hands, feet, and thighs; and even acrobatics to entertain and impress the audience. Depending on the location, the *Schuhplattler* took on different forms "or imitated the various professions of the performers, such as the *Mühlradl* (Miller's Dance), the *Holzhacker* (wood cutter), and the *Glockenplattler* (Bell Dance)" ("History" 2018).

The music for a *Schuhplattler* usually took the form of a *Landler* or *Ländler* type of composition in slow three-quarter time accompanied by a variety of instruments such as guitar, zither, accordion, or even a small band. The rhythm of the slapping and stomping of the dance often with yodeling lent itself to helping drive the beat and tempo of the music.

German folk music and dance, especially in the form of the traditional *Schuhplattler*, has retained its popularity to this day. Clubs across the world perform it as a way to retain and reflect their German heritage. *Schuhplattler* was captured most famously in American popular culture when Clark Griswold (played by Chevy Chase), in the 1985 movie *National Lampoon's European Vacation*, participated in a *Schuhplattler* dance while visiting his relatives in Germany. Intensity, laughter, originality, and improvisation are all a part of German *Volksmusik*.

Wendell G. Johnson

See also: Chapter 13: Contemporary Popular Music. Chapter 15: *Vereine*.

Further Reading

Historisches Lexikon Bayerns. https://www.historisches-lexikon-bayerns.de/Lexikon/Volksmusikpflege. Accessed October 19, 2021.

"History of the Schuhplattler Dance." http://isartalerpittsburgh.org/history-of-the-schuhplattler-dance/. Accessed October 19, 2021.

National Lampoon's European Vacation. Directed by Amy Heckerling, 1985; Warner Bros. DVD.

Oswald, Sonja. "Volkstümliche Musik." Oesterreichisches Musiklexikon online. https://www.musiklexikon.ac.at/ml/musik_V/Volkstuemliche_Musik.xml. Accessed July 15, 2020.

Volksmusik Glossar. https://volxmusik.de/glossar.html. Accessed July 15, 2020.

Williams, Victoria. "Schuhplattler and Landler, Germany and Austria." In *Celebrating Life Customs around the World: From Baby Showers to Funerals*, vol. 1. Santa Barbara, CA: ABC-CLIO, 2017.

Musical Periods and Composers

Germany has produced many of the world's most renowned composers. The origins of "German" music can be traced to the abbess Hildegard of Bingen (1098–1179), whose best-known composition, *Ordo Virtutum*, is a Latin morality play with eighty-two songs. The reformer and Bible translator Martin Luther (1483–1546) regarded hymns as an important avenue for the development of the Christian faith. He was a prolific hymnodist, and among his works is the iconic "A Mighty Fortress Is Our God."

Classical music in Germany is often associated with the three "Bs": Bach (1685–1750), Beethoven (1770–1827), and Brahms (1833–1897), who were active in different eras. Johann Sebastian Bach is perhaps the best-known German composer of the Baroque era (1600–1750). Baroque music was characterized by tonality (musical compositions written in a particular key) and counterpoint (a combination of simultaneously sounding musical lines). Bach was born in Eisenach and established himself as a keyboard virtuoso at an early age. Among his well-known works are the *Brandenburg Concertos*, which exerted a lasting influence on chamber music. Bach died of a stroke in July 1750 and was buried in the Thomaskirche in Leipzig. Such was his influence on Western music that the year of his death is considered the end of the Baroque era. Other famous German composers of the Baroque era include Georg Philipp Telemann (whose vast oeuvre contained at least 3,000 pieces), Georg Friedrich Händel ("*The Messiah*"), and Charles Theodore Pachelbel (Canon in D).

The Baroque era was followed by the Classical era, which extended until ca 1820/25. Music of this era is characterized by a clear melody line overlaid on a subordinate chordal arrangement. During the classical era, the piano replaced the harpsichord as the dominant keyboard instrument, and the orchestras were larger than during the Baroque era. This era is closely associated with the life and work of Ludwig van Beethoven. Beethoven was born in Bonn and moved to Vienna, where he studied with Joseph Haydn. Among his works are nine symphonies, five piano concertos, thirty-two piano sonatas, and sixteen string quartets. Beethoven's prolific career is all the more astonishing given the fact that he had lost 60% of his hearing by 1801 and was completely deaf by 1816. In his Ninth Symphony (1824), Beethoven became the first major composer to include chorus and vocal soloists in the final movement of a symphony. This final movement, "Ode to Joy," is the anthem of the European Union.

The Romantic era (1830–1900), taking its cue from the literature of German Romanticism, followed the classical era. Romantic music was marked by expansive symphonies and dramatic operas. Johannes Brahms was born in Hamburg and produced several large-scale orchestral works from 1873 to 1887, including four symphonies. He was considered Beethoven's successor to such a degree that his own "First Symphony" was "the Tenth" (adding to the nine written by Beethoven). Richard Wagner (1813–1883) was born in Leipzig and viewed opera as musical drama. He drew on German and North mythology for his leitmotivs. *The Ring der Nibelungen*, abbreviated as *The*

Ring, Wagner's cycle of four operas, is performed annually at the Bayreuth Festival. Wagner is one of the most controversial figures in the history of German music. His essay "Das Judentum in der Musik" ("Jewishness in Music") was highly critical of the influence of Jewish people in German culture. Adolf Hitler held Wagner's work in high esteem, and Wagner's daughter-in-law Winifred was an unapologetic Nazi supporter. Israeli orchestras boycotted his music and refused to play it until 2012.

The strong German tradition of classical music continued into the twentieth century. Highly regarded composers include Carl Orff (1895–1982), who wrote "Carmina Burana," and Paul Hindemith (1905–1963), whose best-known work is "Symphonic Metamorphosis of Themes by Carl Maria von Weber." The prolific Karlheinz Stockhausen (1928–2007), a composer and teacher, was a pioneer in new music, experimenting with electronic music and influencing musicians across genres, such as Björk.

Wendell G. Johnson

See also: Chapter 5: Luther, Martin (1483–1546). Chapter 11: Romanticism (*Romantik*) (1788–1835). Chapter 13: Overview; Bayreuth; Orchestras.

Further Reading

Cooper, Barry. *Beethoven*. Oxford, UK; New York: Oxford University Press, 2008.

Erickson, Raymond. *The Worlds of Johann Sebastian Bach*. New York: Amadeus Press, 2009.

Schulenberg, David. *Music of the Baroque*, 2nd ed. New York: Oxford University Press, 2008.

Orchestras

Germany is the home of several internationally recognized orchestras. The Berlin Philharmonic (founded in 1882), widely regarded as one of the world's finest symphony ensembles, has been led by two of the greatest conductors of the twentieth century. Wilhelm Furtwängler (1886–1954) was named chief conductor of the orchestra in 1922 (he also led the Leipzig Gewandhausorchester from 1922 to 1928), a post he held until 1945, with one interruption in 1934/35 and then again from 1952 to 1954. He aligned himself with the Nazis and was acquitted after the war in his denazification trial. He was admired for his interpretations of Beethoven, Brahms, and Bruckner. Furtwängler was succeeded by the Austrian Herbert von Karajan (1908–1989), who was named conductor of the Berlin Philharmonic in 1954. Karajan had been a member of the Nazi party and was not able to work briefly before he was denazified. Karajan had an affinity for music from the first half of the twentieth century, including works by Mahler, Prokofiev, Debussy, Hindemith, and Stravinsky. Under his direction, the Berlin Philharmonic continued to be identified with the works of Beethoven; the orchestra made three recordings of Beethoven's complete cycle of symphonies for Deutsche Grammophon. Since 1963, the Berlin Philharmonic has played in the Philharmonie, built by Hans Scharoun, originally located just west of the Berlin Wall, now in the center.

The Leipzig Gewandhausorchester traces its origin back to 1479 when the Leipzig City Council appointed three musicians as municipal employees. The orchestra takes its name from the Gewandhaus, which was the trading hall of the city's cloth merchants. Construction of a concert hall on the site was completed in November 1781. Mozart played his own works here, and luminaries such as Berlioz, Brahms, and Wagner conducted the Gewandhausorchester. The Gewandhaus Orchestra took its first foreign tour in 1916 when it accepted an invitation to perform in Switzerland. The orchestra made an extensive tour of Europe in 1931 but did not leave Germany again until 1951. The Gewandhaus was destroyed during the Second World War, leaving the Leipzig Orchestra to play in locations throughout the city until its New Gewandhaus, the only genuine concert hall constructed in the German Democratic Republic, opened its doors in 1981.

The highly esteemed Dresden Staatskappelle, founded in 1548, is one of the world's oldest orchestras. The Staatskapelle accompanies the Dresden State Opera and for thirty years was closely linked to Richard Strauss, whose operas *Salome*, *Elektra*, and *Der Rosenkavalier* all premiered in Dresden. The current venue of the Staatskapelle is the Semper Opera House, which was severely damaged by the firebombing of the city in 1945 and restored in 1985. Since 2013, the Staatskappelle (under the direction of Christian Thielemann) has been the resident orchestra of the Salzburg Easter Festival.

Wendell G. Johnson

See also: Chapter 2: Overview; Berlin Wall; Hitler, Adolf (1889–1945). Chapter 13: Bayreuth; Musical Periods and Composers.

Further Reading

Aster, Misha. *The Reich's Orchestra: The Berlin Philharmonic 1933–1945*. Oakville, Ontario: Mosaic Press, 2012.

Gewandhaus Orchester. "History." https://www.gewandhausorchester.de/en/gewandhaus /history/. Accessed October 18, 2021.

Jung, Hans-Rainer, and Claudius Böhm. *Das Gewandhaus Orchester: Seine Mitglieder und Seine Geschichte seit 1743*. Leipzig: Faber & Faber, 2006.

Lebendiges Museum Online. "Wilhelm Furtwängler 1886–1954." https://www.dhm.de /lemo/biografie/wilhelm-furtwaengler. Accessed October 18, 2021.

Music and the Holocaust. "Herbert von Karajan." http://holocaustmusic.ort.org/politics -and-propaganda/third-reich/karajan-herbert-von/. Accessed October 18, 2021.

The Staatskappelle Dresden. http://www.staatskapelle-dresden.de/en/staatskapelle/history/. Accessed October 18, 2021.

Stresemann, Wolfgang. *The Berlin Philharmonic from Bülow to Karajan: Home and History of a World-Famous Orchestra*. Berlin: Stapp, 1979.

CHAPTER 14

FOOD

Wendell G. Johnson and Katharina Barbe

OVERVIEW

German food is *deftig* (hearty or substantial), heavy on meat, and does not lack in calories. The German food most familiar to foreigners hails from Bavaria in the southern part of the country.

Foods

Bread (*Brot*) occupies a central role in German cuisine, and many German expats in the United States complain of their difficulty in finding suitable bread. German bakers employ a variety of whole grains in their breads: wheat, rye, oats, spelt, linseed, millet, and so on. Next to bread, potatoes (*Kartoffeln*) are the most important staple in the German diet; the Germans eat about 60 kg/year per capita. This is down from a high of 180 kg in 1950. *Pellkartoffeln* (small potatoes boiled in their jackets) are served with warm meals. Leftover *Pellkartoffeln* often show up in the next day's meal as *Bratkartoffeln*, potatoes often fried with bacon and onions. Another form of starch, dumplings, features prominently in southern German cuisine. Pork is the meat favored by Germans and can be found in the overwhelming variety of German sausages and cold cuts. Drinking alcoholic beverages, particularly beer and wine, is a part of daily life for many Germans. Fourteen- and fifteen-year-old children are permitted to drink alcohol if accompanied by a parent. People at least sixteen years of age may purchase beer and wine, but a customer must be at least eighteen years old to buy hard liquor.

German Meals

Germans begin their day with *Frühstück* (breakfast), which typically consists of hot coffee or tea, rolls (*Brötchen*) with butter, cold cuts (salami or thinly sliced ham), and cheese, and a soft-boiled egg eaten with a spoon. Bakeries open early, so it is possible to pick up fresh-baked bread daily. A quick meal between breakfast and lunch is not uncommon in Germany. In Bavaria, it is common to have a *Hefeweizen* (wheat beer) during *Brotzeit* (bread time) or *Zweites Frühstück* (second breakfast). In the late morning, Bavarians sit down to a meal of bread, cheese, veal sausage, and a beer. When President Barack Obama visited Bavaria in 2015 for the G7 summit, Chancellor Angela Merkel served him a Bavarian breakfast, complete with (in this case, nonalcoholic) *Hefeweizen*. German schoolchildren generally do not get served meals in school, so provision is made for *Pausenbrot* (recess bread). Students bring a small sandwich or piece of fruit to tide them over until the end of the school day, when they return home for the main meal of the day. Adults take a midday break for a cup of coffee. In rural areas and traditional households, the main meal of the day is eaten between the hours of 12:00 and 14:00. In this case, *Mittagessen* (lunch) consists of meat or fish, starch, a vegetable, and may be preceded by either soup or a salad. Dessert is *Kompott* (stewed fruit). Sunday midday meals are sumptuous family affairs, often accompanied by a glass of wine. Germans frequently break for coffee and cake (*Kaffee und Kuchen*) in the afternoon. *Kaffee und Kuchen* is especially popular on the weekends, and many households have special china coffee sets for these afternoon festivities. Substitute an evening beer for the morning coffee and *Abendessen* or *Abendbrot* (the evening meal) essentially mirrors breakfast without the soft-boiled egg: bread, sausage, and cheese.

Traditional German Dishes

A restaurant serving traditional German good will likely have the following dishes on its menu.

Kassler: salted and salted pork chops served with mashed potatoes and sauerkraut. To augment the flavor, the chops are often warmed up with the kraut.

Schweinebraten: traditional Bavarian roast pork with beer sauce, served with potato dumplings and red cabbage. *Schweinebraten* is served in beer halls and is also a popular Oktoberfest dish.

Sauerbraten: meat marinated in vinegar, water, onions, and spices and then baked. The meat becomes more sour the longer it marinates. *Sauerbraten* is served with potatoes or dumplings, gravy, and mixed vegetables.

Schnitzel: a breaded and fried cutlet (either pork or veal) served with potatoes (either fries or potato salad).

Currywurst: a Berlin favorite, a fried sausage topped with ketchup and curry powder and accompanied by fries or a roll.

Weisswurst: boiled white sausage served with sweet mustard and a pretzel. According to tradition, *Weisswurst* should be consumed shortly after it has been made and should thus only be available before 11:00 a.m.

Königsberger Klopse: meatballs cooked in hot water or broth and topped with a caper-studded white roux. *Königsberger Klopse* are served with red potatoes peeled at the table.

Maultauschen: pasta squares filled with meat, spinach, and spices and served in a broth.

Spaetzle: made from flour and eggs, *Spaetzle* are boiled and are a side to a variety of meat dishes. They are also served with chanterelle mushrooms (*Pfifferlinge*).

Kaiserschmarrn: a pancake, usually with raisins, that can be served with applesauce and topped with vanilla sauce or powdered sugar.

Spargel: Springtime in Germany is *Spargelzeit* (asparagus time). The sandy soil surrounding Berlin is ideal for growing asparagus. Germans eat white asparagus with butter or a hollandaise accompanied by cold, sliced ham or a *Schnitzel*.

For many Germans, the ideas of health and diet are closely linked. The German Nutrition Society (DGE) periodically surveys the culinary habits of German and issues nutritional guidelines. The DGE has determined that overall, Germans consume too much meat and not enough plant-based foods. Further, Germen men consume six times more beer than do women. Based on its most recent survey (2015), the DGE issued "10 Guidelines for a Wholesome Diet":

- Enjoy food diversity: eating a balanced diet ensures proper nutrition;
- Vegetables and fruit—take 5 a day: a balanced diet includes three servings of vegetables and two servings of fruit each day;
- Choose whole grain foods over those produced with white flour;
- Complete your diet with animal-based foods, particularly milk and other dairy products such as yogurt and cheese. Eat fish twice a week and limit consumption of other meat to 600 grams per week;
- Opt for healthy fats such as vegetable oil and avoid the hidden fats in processed food and sausage;
- Reduce sugar and salt intake. Sugar contains unnecessary calories and salt may increase blood pressure;
- Water is the best choice for hydration. Drink 1.5 liters of water per day and avoid soft drinks and alcohol;
- Carefully prepare cooked dishes. Neither overcook nor undercook food, which preserves its natural taste and preserves its nutrients;
- Eat slowly;
- Watch your weight and stay active. Moderate physical activity helps prevent obesity.

Grocery Shopping in Germany

Grocery shopping in Germany is not a 24/7 possibility as it is in the United States. Most grocery stores in Germany are open from 7:00 to 20:00, recently even up to midnight Monday through Saturday and are closed Sunday (desperate customers can usually find an open grocery store or kiosk Sundays in larger train stations). Grocery stores in Germany are generally smaller than those in the United States, which means the aisles are narrower and the selection of items more circumscribed. Employees expect customers to move out of the way when they stock the shelves. Many grocery stores in Germany have two or three cashier stations, where cashiers are seated, and customers are expected to bring their own shopping bags and bag their own groceries. Those who forget to bring their own bags can buy plastic ones at the checkout lane for €0.10 to 0.25 apiece. Because of the waste, customers are strongly encouraged to bring their own bags. Most glass and plastic bottles are sold with a small deposit (*Pfand*), which can be redeemed when the bottles are returned.

Germany has several grocery chains. Edeka, with a 26% market share, is the country's largest supermarket corporation. Aldi was founded in Germany after the Second World Wars. It was owned by brothers Karl (1920–2014) and Theo Albrecht (1922–2010), both notoriously reclusive. In 1961, the company split into Aldi Nord (Theo) and Aldi Süd (Albrecht); the dividing line is jokingly known as the *Aldi Äquator*. Most German towns have at least one Aldi (which stands for **AL**brecht **DI**scount) store, the first discount chain in the country. Aldi has 4,100 stores in Germany and 1,600 in the United States. Lidl is another German discount chain; it belongs to the Schwarz

Unternehmensgruppe (consortium) that operates more than 10,000 stores in Europe and the United States; of that number, over 3,000 are in Germany, nearly 100 in the United States. Schwarz *Unternehmensgruppe* also operates *Kaufland*, a "hypermarket," a combination of a supermarket and department store (similar to a Super Walmart or Super Target). Other well-known chains include Penny Markt, Netto Marken-Discount, and REWE.

Organic Food

Germany has played a pioneering role in the organic food movement in the European Union. Organic foods in Germany are marked with the *Bio-Siegel*, indicating that these products conform to EU standards. Among the major chains featuring organic products are Denn's, Alnatura, Bio Company, and Basic. Germany hosts the largest agricultural consumer show in the world, International Green Week (Grüne Woche), held every January in Berlin. The show attracts 1,600 exhibitors and nearly 400,000 visitors annually. The country is also home to the world's largest organic food trade show: BioFach. BioFach takes place in Nuremburg in February. Each year 3,000 exhibitors present organic products to international representatives.

Further Reading

German Nutrition Society. "10 Guidelines of the German Nutrition Society (DGE) for a Wholesome Diets." https://www.dge.de/ernaehrungspraxis/vollwertige-ernaehrung/10-regeln-der-dge/en/. Accessed March 18, 2020.

Heinzelmann, Ursula. "Germany." In Ken Albala, ed. *Food Cultures of the World*, vol. 4, 133–145. Santa Barbara, CA: ABC-CLIO, 2011.

Heuer, Thorsten, et al. "Food Consumption of Adults in Germany: Results of the German National Nutrition Survey II Based on Diet History Interviews." *British Journal of Nutrition* 113(10): 1603–1614, 2015.

Kohl, Hannelore, and Helmut Kohl. *A Culinary Voyage through Germany*. New York: Abbeville Press, 1997.

Oetker, August. *Schul-Kochbuch*. Bielefeld, Germany: Ceres, 1972.

Statista. "Potato Consumption from 1950–2016/." https://de.statista.com/statistik/daten/studie/175422/umfrage/pro-kopf-verbrauch-von-kartoffeln-in-deutschland/. Accessed March 18, 2020.

Beer

Germans love to drink beer—nearly twenty-eight gallons annually per person (in Europe, only the Czechs drink more). Germany is home to the world's largest beer festival, Oktoberfest, held every year in Munich. According to the regulations of the European Union, only beers licensed by breweries in Munich can be labeled as Oktoberfest beers. These beers are golden in color with alcohol by volume (ABV) between 5.8% and 6.3%. Beer brewed in Germany conforms to the nation's *Reinheitsgebot*

Germans drink an annual average of twenty-eight gallons of beer per person, which puts them in 4th place in the world. The country is home to many distinctive styles of beer, including *Kellerbier*, *Schwarzbier*, and *Bockbier*. (Oleksii Anatskyi/Dreamstime.com)

(purity law) of 1516 and its newer iterations, which states that beer must be composed of three ingredients: barley, hops, and water and nothing else. At that time there was no awareness of yeast; today it is water, hops, malt (from barley), and yeast.

German pilsner, known as *Pils* in Germany, a pale golden lager, is the archetype of most beer brewed in the world today, comprising 95% of global beer consumption by volume. Pilsner was originally brewed in Pilzen (in the present-day Czech Republic) in 1842 by the Bavarian brewmaster Josef Groll. It represents the fortuitous union of Czech ingredients (sweet Moravian barley, bitter Bohemian hops, and soft sandstone-filtered water) with German brewing technology.

Many of the best-known varieties of German beer (*Kellerbier*, *Rauchbier*, *Schwarzbier*) as well as the myriad varieties of *Bockbier* (*Doppelbock*, *Maibock*, *Weizenbock*, and *Eisbock*) originated in Bavaria, as did the world's most popular wheat beer: *Hefeweizen* (wheat ale with yeast).

- *Kellerbier* (cellar beer) is a summer favorite in beer gardens in Franconia in central Bavaria. *Kellerbier* is unfiltered, unpasteurized, and usually served in earthenware mugs.

REINHEITSGEBOT

The so-called *Reinheitsgebot* of 1516 has been widely touted as the first and still valid consumer protection legislation. This Bavarian beer law was actually not the first decree about beer; there were numerous before from the fourteenth century. It did restrict the ingredients of beer to *Gerste* (barley), *Hopfen* (hops), and *Wasser* (water). Yeast was at that time considered a by-product. Implementation of the law was driven primarily by economic and health reasons. In the Middle Ages, all kinds of herbs and spices, such as thorn apple, belladonna, henbane, and even soot, found their way into beer, some of them poisonous, others hallucinogenic. One intended to use wheat for baking primarily; barley was not a good grain for baking, but was found to be excellent for beer brewing. By 1541, ingredients like coriander and laurel became accepted additives, and by 1616, salt, juniper, and caraway could legally be added. The *Reinheitsgebot* has only been valid for all of Germany since 1906; until then it was a law enforced only in Bavaria. After the First World War, Bavaria made it a condition for joining the Weimar Republic that the *Reinheitsgebot* had to be applied all over Germany. Interestingly, the term *Reinheitsgebot* itself was not used until 1918. After the Second World War, the *Reinheitsgebot* was embedded in the *Biersteuergesetz* (Beer Tax Law) of 1952. An EU law that was litigated with Germany on the losing end forced other beers into Germany under the principle of mutual recognition. German brewers who wanted to name their beverage beer still had to abide by the *Reinheitsgebot*.

- *Rauchbier* (smoked beer) is a medium-strength lager brewed with smoked malt. It is typically served with smoked meats and is enjoyed by cigar smokers. Perhaps the most famous *Rauchbier* Aecht Schlenkerla is brewed by Heller-Trum in Bamberg, a brewery whose history dates back to the fourteenth century.
- *Schwarzbier* (black beer), a German porter, is brewed from roasted malt. By definition *Schwarzbier* should be brewed in Munich. However, after reunification the output of this type of beer soared in the eastern part of the country, and the largest producer is now the Köstritzer Schwarzbierbrauerei in Thuringia.
- *Bockbier* is a stronger beer, with an alcohol content above 6% ABV. Many British, Belgian, and American ales are more properly bock beers according to European standards.

Other areas of Germany also produce distinctive brews. *Kölsch* is a light-colored, strongly hopped beer from Cologne served in a distinctive six-ounce glass, a *Stangen*. *Altbier* (old beer) is an indigenous ale produced near Düsseldorf. *Berliner Weisse*, from Berlin, is a sour beer with a relatively low ABV (3%). It is often served with a shot of red (raspberry) or green (woodruff) syrup as a *Berliner Weisse mit Schuß* (shot).

Wendell G. Johnson

See also: Chapter 6: Sudeten Germans. Chapter 10: Shopping. Chapter 14: Overview; Beer; Food Laws in Germany; Oktoberfest. Chapter 15: Overview.

Further Reading

Braukulturland Franken. https://www.braufranken.de/html/bkgeschichte.html. Accessed March 18, 2020.

Dornbusch, Horst D. *Prost! The Story of German Beer.* Boulder, CO: Siris Books, 1997.

Gretzschel, Moritz. "Das Reinheitsgebot ist tot—lang lebe das Reinheitsgebot: Ein paar kritische Fragen vor dem großen Jubiläum." *Brau! Magazin*, Spring 2015. http://braumagazin.de/article/reinheitsgebot-ist-tot/. Accessed March 18, 2020.

Oliver, Garrett. *The Oxford Companion to Beer.* Oxford, UK; New York: Oxford University Press, 2012.

Unser Reinheitsgebot. https://www.reinheitsgebot.de/startseite/. Accessed March 18, 2020.

Bread

Bread has been around for millennia. Nearly 11,000 years ago, people were eating a type of gruel made up of two grains, einkorn and wild emmer. The first "bread" was most likely discovered accidentally when the gruel that was left in the pots over fire hardened to a flatbread. Sourdough bread was probably discovered inadvertently 3,500 years ago in Egypt.

Germans began incorporating more cereals and cultivated grains into their diet in the Middle Ages. Poorer people ate dark bread, while the rich ate the finer white bread, which was more labor-intensive to produce but also less nutritious. Rye became the most important crop in the land. A thirteenth-century table manual stated that a good German meal includes bread and wine. In the fourteenth and fifteenth centuries, *Botterbroth* (*Butterbrot*), a sliced dark sourdough rye bread with salted butter, became a staple in Northern Germany, while in the South lighter bread made from wheat, was consumed without a topping. Even at this early date it was recognized that darker bread had more nutrients than white bread. Bread became commercially available in the eighteenth century when bakers opened shops and sold their bread. Class differences remained in the consumption of bread: the poorer masses ate dark bread and the wealthier opted for white bread. Bread became a staple in in German prisons in the nineteenth century, where a typical meal consisted of bread and thickened soup.

Because of a huge increase in population in Berlin, the *Backfabrik* was founded there in 1856. This baking factory was able to process up to 250 tons of rye flour per day and baked about one-third of all rye breads sold in Berlin. Smaller bakeries were able to coexist by producing *Brötchen* (small rolls) in addition to loaves of bread. Grain production was nationalized during the First World War. In October 1914, the use of potatoes was encouraged in all kinds of products including bread. The so-called *K-Brot* left the consumer wondering if **K** stood for *Krieg* (war) or *Kartoffel* (potato). Supplies soon dwindled, and beginning in June 1915 bread was rationed. The Nazis promoted *Vollkornbrot* (whole wheat bread), which was easier to produce but harder to digest. Food (which included bread) became very scarce after the Second World War, and many people subsisted on 400–1,000 calories per day. Heinrich Böll

Table 14.1: FAMOUS BREAD

Each German area boasts at least one, if not more, local varieties

Areas	Bread Specialty	Explanation
Baden-Württemberg	*Schwarzwälder Landbrot*	Black Forest Farmers bread—mixed wheat, with a firm crust and a slightly sour taste
Bavaria	*Bayrisches Urbrot*	a really old recipe made with spelt, emmer wheat, einkorn wheat, and kamut grain
Berlin/Brandenburg	Kommissbrot	originally made for the military (Kommiss—army), a square sourdough rye bread
Hamburg	*Hamburger Schwarzbrot*	coarse dark bread, mostly made with rye and the addition of rye malt and barley malt
Hessen	*Kasseler Brot*	multigrain wheat bread with at least 51% wheat
Mecklenburg-Western Pomerania	*Pommersches Landbrot*	Pomeranian farmers bread, predominantly rye flour
Lower Saxony	*Gersterbrot*	multigrain rye bread made with sourdough and yeast with a very crisp crust
Rheinland	*Rheinisches Schwarzbrot*	very dark bread with cracked rye and wheat flour and seeds
Saxony-Anhalt	*Altmärkerbrot*	mild sourdough bread
Saxony	*Malfabrot*	from GDR times, a multigrain bread with a malted beverage
Schleswig-Holstein	*Rosenstuten*	light sourdough bread, 85% wheat, 15% rye
Thuringia	*Thüringer Kartoffelbrot*	a very light bread using equal parts flour and potatoes
Westphalia	*Westfälischer Pumpernickel*	really dark and substantial all-rye bread
Wurttemberg	*Genetztes Brot*	baked with wheat and rye and equal parts water

Sources: Lehman, Peter. *Deutschland. Die Bibel der Feinschmecker: Deutsche Küche*. BookRix, 2017.
Der Brotexperte Brotblog. https://www.brotexperte.de. Accessed March 18, 2020.
Deutsches Brotinstitut. https://www.brotinstitut.de/. Accessed March 18, 2020.

(1917–1975), the German author and winner of the 1972 Nobel Prize for Literature, lamented his constant hunger and the yearning for bread in "Das Brot der frühen Jahre" ("The Bread of Those Early Years"). Once Germany improved its food distribution and production in the 1950s, supplies increased and a four-person household typically consumed about 23 kg non-white and 5 kg white bread per month. Once again, white bread was considered a delicacy and not as readily available as rye bread.

Bread remains a staple at every German meal, whether at breakfast (*Frühstück*), lunch (*Mittagessen*), or supper (*Abendessen*). In many parts of the country, the evening meal is referred to as *Abendbrot* or evening bread. Typically, breakfast involves *Brot* or *Brötchen* (roll); lunch or dinner can either be a cooked meal (Germans typically eat one cooked meal per day) or simply *Brot*: bread with cold cuts and cheese.

Throughout the country, *Brötchen*, like *Brot*, come in many different shapes and with many different ingredients: *Brötchen* is the generic term, but each area has its own word: *Wecke* in the Saarland, *Rundstück* in the North, *Schrippe* in Berlin, and *Semmel* in Bavaria. In Cologne, a *halve Hahn* is half a roll with cheese and mustard. *Brot* (bread) is thus a major aliment for Germans, and one can easily overhear Germans in the United States discussing where adequate *Brot* can be purchased. While the American approach to bread may be described as "bread is what holds my sandwich together," in Germany the bread is primary; what is put on it is secondary, signified in the Berlin expression *Stulle mit Brot* (where *Stulle* is a Berlin term for *Brot,* here in terms of sandwich). A *Stulle mit Brot* is basically an open-faced sandwich with toppings (cold cuts, cheeses).

In 2014, the German bread culture was recognized by the UNESCO as an intangible cultural heritage (and "World Bread Day" is celebrated each year on October 16). The over 3,200 different types of bread are strictly regulated. The German Food Stuff Commission (Deutsche Lebensmittelbuch-Kommission) defined bread as food that "is mostly or partly produced from cereals and cereal products, generally by adding liquid, as well as other foodstuffs, such as legume and potato products, usually prepared by kneading, forming, loosening, baking, or hot extruding of the bread dough. Bread contains less than 10% weight parts fat and/or sugars on 90% parts cereals and/or cereal products." (KB translation)

A big change has occurred in German bread consumption. *Dark* break is now preferred by well-to-do people, and to satisfy the demand, artisan bakeries have appeared that offer rye bread in many varieties. So the light bread that used to be called *Schönbrot* or *Schönroggen* (*schön*—beautiful, *Roggen*—rye) a few centuries ago and preferred by the well-to-do has given way to the darker bread with more nutrients.

Katharina Barbe

See also: Chapter 14: Overview; Food Laws in Germany; German Sausages; Regional Specialties; Wine.

Further Reading

Atlas zur deutschen Alltagssprache. "Brötchen/Semmel." http://www.atlas-alltagssprache .de/brotchen/. Accessed March 18, 2020.

Deutsche Lebensmittelbuchkommission. "Leitsätze für Brot und Kleingebäck." https:// www.bmel.de/SharedDocs/Downloads/DE/_Ernaehrung/Lebensmittel-Kennzeichnung /LeitsaetzeBrot.html. Accessed March 18, 2020.

Deutsches Brotinstitut. https://www.brotinstitut.de/. Accessed March 18, 2020.

Heinzelmann, Ursula. *Beyond Bratwurst: A History of Food in Germany*. London: Reaktion Books, 2014.

Weiss, Luisa, and Aubrie Pick. *Classic German Baking: The Very Best Recipes for Traditional Favorites, from Pfeffernüsse to Streuselkuchen*. Berkeley, CA: Ten Speed Press, 2016.

Cake and Coffee (*Kaffee und Kuchen*)

Coffee is immensely popular in Germany. More than 80% of the population aged fourteen or older are coffee drinkers. The consumption of coffee in the country dates to the seventeenth century, when coffeehouses were opened in larger cities. Women were permitted to meet and drink coffee in these establishments, which led the less-enlightened burghers to dub these gatherings *Kaffeeklatsch* (coffee and gossip). Presently, Jakob's Krönung is the most popular supermarket brand of coffee in Germany. Two other well-known brands, Eduscho and Tchibo, also operate small retail outlets that offer an array of non-coffee products that change weekly. Eduscho was founded by Eduard Schopf in 1924 in Bremen and was acquired by Tchibo in 1997. Germany is number 8 in coffee consumption in the world with 6.65 kg/person, Finland is the highest with 10.35 kg/person, and the United States is number 18 with 4.43 kg/person.

During the workweek, colleagues often meet at a local bakery for a cup of coffee and piece of cake. In the Turkish quarter of larger cities, Turkish coffee is served with baklava. Coffee and cake are a more elaborate ritual on weekend afternoons. Family and friends meet between 15:00 and 16:00 o'clock to drink coffee, eat cake, and socialize (and it is not unusual to begin the festivities with a glass of sparkling wine). Guests invited to someone's home for afternoon coffee usually bring a bouquet of flowers for the hostess.

Among the baked goods served at afternoon coffee are

1. *Berliner*: yeast pastry filled with red jam (in Berlin those are called *Pfannkuchen*), akin to doughnuts;
2. *Schwarzwälder Kirschtorte* (Black Forest cake): chocolate cake with cherries and cherry liqueur;
3. *Käsekuchen*: cheesecake made with *Quark* (curd cheese), not cream cheese; Cheesecakes in Germany are less sweet than those generally available in the United States;
4. *Strudel*: puff pastry filled with apples and walnuts;
5. *Streuselkuchen*: sheet cakes with or without fruit but topped with *Streusel* (crumbles);
6. *Frankfurter Kranz*: butter cream cake with brittle.

Many of those are now also available in gluten-free or vegan varieties.

Coffee culture in Germany is undergoing a sea change as is illustrated by the famed and iconic Café Kranzler on Berlin's main boulevard (the Ku'damm or Kurfürstendamm) in West Berlin. The Café Kranzler is an old institution that opened at its present place in 1932. It was destroyed in the war, reopened in 1951, and was completely rebuilt in 1957/58 into its current two-story form, with a rotunda and red-and-white awnings on the upper floor. Designated as a national monument and placed under legal protection, it was not razed in the interest of urban development. Instead, the famed architect Helmut Jahn incorporated it into a mixed-use office and shopping project in 2001. The coffee company The Barn kept the iconic—The Barn Café Kranzler—name but completely changed its focus. The Café Kranzler lost its traditional identity and became a place for urban hipsters. In place of the customary *Schwarzwälder Kirschtorte* and *eine Tasse* (cup) or *ein Kännchen* (pot) *Kaffee,* guests now experience a very different type of coffee culture, one where the preparation of the coffee has become the focus. However, throughout Berlin and other cities, the traditional *Konditoreien* (pastry shop), such as Frau Behrendts Torten in Berlin, Café Luitpold in Munich, or Café Bormuth in Darmstadt, continue to draw customers.

Katharina Barbe

See also: Chapter 6: Turks in Germany. Chapter 12: Architecture; Artists. Chapter 14: Overview; Regional Specialties. Chapter 15: Overview.

Further Reading

Berliner Zeitung. "Café Kranzler." https://www.berliner-zeitung.de/mensch-metropole /berlin-kurfuerstendamm-neueroeffnung-vom-cafe-kranzler-wird-zum-kulturschock -li.22693. Accessed March 18, 2020.

Egelkraut, Ortrun, and Johann Scheibner. *Bruckmann Reiseführer Berlin: Zeit für das Beste*. Bruckmann Verlag, 2019.

Statista. "Top Coffee Drinking Nations." https://www.statista.com/chart/8602/top-coffee -drinking-nations/. Accessed March 18, 2020.

Visit Berlin. "Kranzler Eck." https://www.visitberlin.de/en/kranzler-eck. Accessed March 18, 2020.

Food and Drink in the German Democratic Republic

After the Second World War, food rationing in East Germany continued until 1958, at which time the Politbüro announced that food production in the DDR would surpass that of the Federal Republic by 1961 (coincidently the year the Berlin Wall would be built). In an attempt to increase food production, market-driven private farms were eliminated and replaced by centrally managed state agricultural enterprises. Food thus became a direct responsibility of the state, which was blamed for food shortages (potatoes and coffee in the 1970s, fruit in the early '80s). The government's responsibility for food extended to cooked meals: in 1978, between one-half and one-third of the population had their main meal of the day at school or work.

The government believed that people with full stomachs seldom rebel and kept food prices artificially low and subsidized them by increasing the prices on other consumer goods. Shopping for food in East Germany could be quite an ordeal. As soon as foodstuffs appeared in the stores, such as bananas or oranges, long lines materialized. East Germans with access to hard currencies (such as West German deutsche mark, French or Swiss francs, American dollars, and British pounds sterling) could shop at Intershop, a chain of stores where the East German mark was not accepted. Two other chains, Exquisit and Delikat, accepted East German currency and sold goods not available at other state-run outlets.

Wir Kochen Gut (*We Cook Well*), the standard East German cookbook, provided recipes based on ingredients readily available to East German shoppers, such as *Berliner Leber* (liver), *Thüringer Rostbrätl* (grilled pork cutlet), *Königsberger Klopse* (meatballs), and *Goldbroiler* (roasted chicken). Each citizen consumed on average 96 kilos of meat, 43 kilos of sugar, 15.7 kilos of butter, and 307 eggs annually. Alcohol consumption in East Germany surpassed that in the West. Brands such as Rotkäppchen ("Little Red Riding Hood") sparkling red wine and Radeberger Pilsner beer endure to the present. As Jutta Voigt noted, the East Germans spent their money on food because there was little else to buy. The GDR Museum in Berlin offers recipes for typical East German cuisine, including Broiler mit Pommes (chicken with fries) and smoked pork with potatoes and sauerkraut.

Wendell G. Johnson

See also: Chapter 2: Berlin Wall. Chapter 3: Government and Politics in the German Democratic Republic. Chapter 4: Overview. Chapter 14: Regional Specialties.

Further Reading

Fulbrook, Mary. *The People's State: East German Society from Hitler to Honecker*. New Haven, CT; London: Yale University Press, 2005.

Heinzelmann, Ursula. *Beyond Bratwurst: A History of Food in Germany*. London: Reaktion Books, 2014.

Jampol, Justinian, Benedikt Taschen, and Ina Pfitzner. *Beyond the Wall: Art and Artifacts from the GDR = Jenseits Der Mauer: Kunst und Alltagsgegenstände aus der DDR*. Köln: Taschen, 2014.

Voigt, Jutta. *Der Geschmack des Ostens. Vom Essen, Trinken und Leben in der DDR*. Berlin: G. Kiepenheuer, 2006.

Food Laws in Germany

As a member of the European Union, Germany follows EU guidelines regarding the production and marketing of food. All EU nations abide by the "Home Country Principle," which states that any product produced and placed into commerce in one country of the European Community may be exported into other members of the EU.

Processed food must be clearly labeled in German and include

- nutrition table;
- list of ingredients in descending order of weight;
- labeling of origin of meat (whether of pigs, sheep, poultry, etc.). If the product is not a whole piece of meat and composed of mixed pieces, the label must state that it is a "formed meat/fish" product;
- if water is added to the product, it must be noted if water makes up more than 5% of its total weight;
- if frozen, the date of the initial freezing;
- allergens (e.g., peanuts or milk products);
- the net quantity of the food.

The label must be printed legibly (with a minimum font) and include a use-by date (minimum durability), the name and address of the business that produced the food, and instructions for use. Certain exceptions apply, such as products comprised of a single ingredient (even if processed), carbonated water, coffee, herbs and spices, and so on.

Animal Products

The EU has more stringent regulations regarding the raising and slaughtering of livestock than the United States. In the EU, live birds may be transported for a maximum of twelve hours; in the United States the limit is twenty-eight hours. The birds become more susceptible to infection during the extra sixteen hours of transport. In the United States, chicken is washed in chlorinated water to kill microorganisms and mask the unhygienic production methods of American poultry producers. The EU also has more restrictions on the use of growth hormones and antibiotics in livestock than does the United States.

Many suspected carcinogens (cancer-causing agents) found in American products are not considered safe for human consumption in the EU. One such agent is potassium bromate, added to American flour to make dough rise faster. It has been found to cause tumors in laboratory animals.

The EU and the United States have different regulatory approaches to their food chain. The EU will pull a product from its shelves if it believes the product would cause harm to consumers. In the United States, on the other hand, the manufacturers of the food themselves are responsible for policing potential harmful products.

Country of Origin/Trademarks

The EU protects the provenance of its products. For example, German Black Forest Ham, a dry cured smoked ham, must be produced in the Black Forest region of Germany if it is to be sold in the EU. Knockoffs produced in the United States and labeled as "Black Forest Ham" may not be sold in Germany or anywhere else in the EU. Sparkling wine cannot be sold as "Champagne" in Germany unless it was produced in the Champagne region of France. German bubbly is sold as *Sekt*. Likewise, American vintners may not label their wine as "Champagne" and sell it in the European market.

Wendell G. Johnson

See also: Chapter 3: Germany and the European Union; Germany and the United States. Chapter 14: Beer; Wine.

Further Reading

European Commission. "Food Safety." https://ec.europa.eu/food/overview_en. Accessed March 18, 2020.

German Federal Ministry of Food and Agriculture. "Safe Food and a Healthy Diet." https://www.bmel.de/EN/Food/Safe-Food/_Texte/GermanImportconditionsforFood.html;nn=522306. Accessed March 18, 2020.

German Sausages

Germany is home to a bewildering array of sausages—perhaps 1,500 different varieties. It often seems that Germans eat sausage morning (breakfast), noon (lunch), and night (dinner). German sausage can bear the name of its geographical provenance; although the terms "frankfurter" and "wiener" are used interchangeably in the United States, these two German sausages have very different origins. The *Frankfurter*, made of pork, was created by the Coburg butcher Johann Georghehner, who traveled to Frankfurt am Main to promote his product (hence its name). *Wieners*, named after Wien, the capital of Austria, are made of both beef and pork. In Germany, wieners are usually boiled or steamed and resemble American foot-long hot dogs. In contrast to American hot dogs, German *Frankfurters* and *Wieners* are 100% meat and contain no fillers, such as up to 3.5% corn starch, corn syrup, dried milk, and binders made from cereals or grain. *Braunschweiger*, in the United States a sausage that contains smoked pork liver, is actually a different type in Germany. The spreadable and smoked *Braunschweiger Mettwurst* does originate in Braunschweig in Lower Saxony, but it is made of pork and beef and does not contain liver. The *Thüringer* (*Rostbratwurst*), a brat from Thuringia, boasts Protected Geographical Status by the European Union—only sausages originated from Thuringia can be identified as *Thüringer*. According to a 2002 EU order, it must be at least 15 cm long, weigh about 100–150 grams, and at least 51% of its content has to have their origin in Thuringia.

Currywurst is one of Germany's favorite fast foods, with upwards of 800 million consumed annually in the country. In an attempt to enliven her family's bland postwar diet, Berlin housewife Herta Heuwer put ketchup (instead of mustard) and sprinkled curry powder on a grilled pork sausage. Her concoction proved a hit, and soon she was selling it to workers reconstructing the bombed-out capital. *Currywurst* has always been associated with the working class, and each election cycle German politicians pose in front of their favorite sausage stand. The cities Berlin and Hamburg both claim the invention of the *Currywurst*. In popular culture, Herbert Grönemeyer, a German singer and actor (*Das Boot*), released his song "Currywurst" in 1982; and Uwe Timm's 1993 book *Die Entdeckung der Currywurst* puts the *Currywurst* invention into Hamburg. The Berlin Currywurst Museum closed its doors after ten years in 2018.

American picnic-goers are very familiar with *Bratwurst*, a sausage made of finely chopped beef, veal, and pork. The areas of Thuringia and Franconia are in a gastronomic dispute over the provenance of *Bratwurst*, with each locale claiming original ownership. Brats can be grilled, pan-roasted, or simmered in beer before grilling.

Other favorite German sausages:

Knackwurst (from the German verb *knacken*, to crack, the sound made when biting into the casing) is often served with sauerkraut and mustard.

Bockwurst, meant to be consumed with bock beer, is made from ground veal and pork and served with sharp yellow mustard.

Weißwurst, a white Bavarian spiced sausage also made from veal and pork and filled into pork casings, is usually served with pretzels and sweet whole-grain mustard. There are several ways to eat *Weißwurst*, as the casings are not eaten. *Zuzeln* basically means sucking out the content; another way is cutting the skin and then opening the sausage and taking out its content.

Landjäger, made of pork and beef, resemble beer sticks sold at American deli counters and are eaten in dried form.

Blutwurst (blood sausage) is one of the oldest sausages known, Homer is said to have mentioned it in *The Odyssey*. Made from blood and pork bacon with spices, it is usually eaten warm together with a *Leberwurst* and sauerkraut and potatoes. Other countries also have this kind of sausage, which uses slaughter by-products; in France it is *boudin noir* (Louisiana boudin) and in England, English Black Pudding.

Katharina Barbe

See also: Chapter 3: Germany and the European Union. Chapter 14: Beer; Food Laws in Germany; Regional Specialties.

Further Reading

Heinzelmann, Ursula. *Beyond Bratwurst: A History of Food in Germany*. London: Reaktion Books, 2014.

Netzwissen. "Ihr Wissensportal im Netz." https://www.netzwissen.com/ernaehrung /blutwurst.php. Accessed March 18, 2020.

Wolff, Otto. 2017. *WURST! The Very Best of German Food*. Collingwood, Victoria, Australia: Smith Street Books, 2017.

Oktoberfest

Oktoberfest, one of Germany's most important events and the largest beer festival in the world, is held each year in Munich during the last two weeks in September to the first weekend in October. The annual festival dates to 1810, when Crown Prince Ludwig of Bavaria (1786–1868) married Princess Therese of Saxe-Hildburghausen (1792–1854). To commemorate the event, Ludwig invited the citizens of Munich to a celebration held in the *Wiesn* (field) outside of the city. Oktoberfest soon became an annual gala, held in Theresienwiese (Therese's field).

At noon on the first day of Oktoberfest, the mayor of Munich taps the first keg and intones *"O'zapft is"* (It is tapped'), thus kicking off the festival. According to tradition, the first glass of beer is served to the Bavarian prime minister.

Each year over 7 million people attend Oktoberfest, congregating in huge beer tents that seat up to 10,000 guests. Revelers consume over 66,000 barrels of beer, served in a *Masskrug* (one-liter glass). Only large breweries that operate within Munich are permitted to provide beer to the festivities: Augustinerbräu, Hacker-Pschorr, Hofbräu, Löwenbräu, Paulaner, and Spaten-Franziskaner-Bräu. According to European law, only beer brewed by these authorized breweries can label their beer "Oktoberfest." These breweries produce a beer called *Märzenbier* (March Beer), so named because it was traditionally brewed in March and lagered or stored over the summer. Beer sold at Oktoberfest is lagered for at least thirty days and has a higher

Oktoberfest is the world's largest beer festival. Each year, seven million guests crowd into beer tents and consume sixty-six thousand barrels of beer. (Shutterstock)

alcohol content than other brews: nearly 6% ABV (alcohol by volume). Each year, food served during the festival includes fried chicken (half a million birds), sausages (over 200,000 pairs), ox on a spit (more than 125 oxen), accompanied by potato salad with bacon, *Brez'n* (soft large pretzels), or cheese spaetzle, and finished off with a dessert of *Kaiserschmarrn* (a pancake-like dish) or dumplings. All this food is very fatty, but recently the Oktoberfest also serves vegetarian and vegan fare. While dining and drinking, Oktoberfest visitors are serenaded by polka bands.

The Costume and Riflemen's Procession takes place on the first Sunday of Oktoberfest. This parade features 7,000 participants, clad in traditional costumes and historical uniforms marching through the streets of Munich. The following Sunday features an open-air big band concert with the musicians from the various Oktoberfest bands.

Octoberfest 2020 was scheduled to open on September 19 and conclude on October 4; however, it had to be canceled because of the pandemic, as has the 2021 celebration. Other festivals modeled on the Bavarian original are held in Kitchener-Waterloo, Canada, and Cincinnati, Ohio.

Wendell G. Johnson

See also: Chapter 14: Beer; Food Laws in Germany; Regional Specialties.

Further Reading

Muenchen.de. "Oktoberfest." https://www.muenchen.de/int/en/events/oktoberfest/schedule.html. Accessed March 18, 2020.

Oktoberfest.de. https://www.oktoberfest.de/en. Accessed March 18, 2020.

Oliver, Garrett. *The Oxford Companion to Beer.* Oxford, UK: New York: Oxford University Press, 2012.

Skowronek, Julia, and Brigitte Sporrer. *Oktoberfest Cookbook.* New York: DK Publishing, 2015.

Regional Specialties

Many regions throughout the country enjoy the same food. What northerners, and especially Berliners, know as *Eisbein mit Sauerkraut*, is a *Schweinshaxe* in Bavaria. Both dishes use the same cut of meat—pork knuckle—but it is simmered on top of sauerkraut (*Eisbein*) in the north and roasted (*Schweinshaxe*) in the south. One national craze is the *Spargelzeit* (asparagus time) in the spring. Germans take *Spargelzeit* very seriously, and each region lays claim to the best asparagus. *Spargel* is harvested from the middle of April until June 24. Asparagus is grown under the soil and thus does not develop the chlorophyll that turns the spears green. When it is harvested, the spears are white and they are served with melted butter or hollandaise sauce, accompanied by ham or *Schnitzel,* and the seemingly ubiquitous potatoes.

Southern Germany

One of the best-known meals is Munich's *Weisswurst* ("white sausage"), served with pretzels, sweet mustard, and washed down with *Hefeweizen* (wheat beer with yeast). Bavarian pretzels have a thin, crisp crust and a soft, chewy center. They are also eaten as a snack and served with *Obazda*, a mixed cheese prepared out of ripe Camembert, butter, spices and sometimes even spiked with a dash of beer. *Leberkäse* (liver cheese) contains neither liver nor cheese. Rather, it is meatloaf comprised of beer, pork, and bacon and seasoned with marjoram. *Leberknödelsuppe* (liver dumpling soup), however, does contain liver, combined with breadcrumbs, shaped into dumplings, and served in beef broth. Roasted bratwurst from Nuremberg (the city is also famous for its *Lebkuchen*, or gingerbread) is another specialty that can also be found at a *Weihnachtsmarkt* (Christmas market) in the United States.

The state of Baden-Württemberg is home to the Black Forest (*Schwarzwald*) from whence comes the eponymous Black Forest ham (*Schwarzwälder Schinken*), a smoked ham akin to prosciutto, and Black Forest cake (*Schwarzwälder Kirschtorte*), where the dough is drizzled with *Kirschwasser* (cherry brandy). Southwestern Germany abuts the French border, and its food has been influenced by its neighbor's cuisine. The Alsatian dish *Flammkuchen* has a cracker-like crust covered with crème fraiche, layered with thinly sliced onions and strips of prosciutto, and then is baked in a wood-fired oven. People in the Saarland are fond of outdoor grilling, known locally as *Schwenkbraten*, which is similar to a rotisserie. However, instead of rotating on a spit, the meat swings (*schwenken*) back and forth over a fire.

Central Germany

Sauerbraten (literally "sour roast") from the Rhineland is perhaps Germany's most iconic dish. *Sauerbraten* is a beef roast that has marinated in vinegar (or wine) and water for at least three days (the meat becomes increasingly sour as it marinates). Gingerbread may be added to the pan drippings to make a sweet-and-sour gravy. *Kasseler Rippchen* are smoked pork loin chops with an unknown origin. They may have originated in the city Kassel (Hesse), or, according to another theory, they were first introduced by a butcher named Cassel. Frankfurt (Hesse) is well known for its *Grüne Soße,* a sauce served cold with eggs and made from a variety of herbs and sour cream. The local *Äppelwoi* (*Apfelwein*, cider) is the Hessian state beverage. The *Westfälischer Knochenschinken* is a salted, smoked, and cured ham that gets its special flavor from the bone (*Knochen*).

Königsberger Klopse are meatballs from Königsberg, a city once located in eastern Prussia (today called Kaliningrad in Russia). These poached meatballs served in a white sauce flavored with lemon and capers were already served to guests by Königsberg's most famous citizen, the philosopher Immanuel Kant. They are still a staple in several states and Berlin, and incidentally the favorite food of Chancellor Angela Merkel. Saxony is the home of many sweet yeast cakes, among them the Christmas favorite Dresdner *Christstollen* (basically a Christmas fruitcake), that are shipped all over the world and that have been made since at least 1474. The Dresdner *Christstollen* are a registered trademark and protected by the Stollen Association.

WHAT ARE THE FAVORITE FOODS OF THE GERMANS?

1. Spaghetti bolognese
2. Spaghetti with tomato sauce
3. *Schnitzel* (breaded cutlets)
4. Pizza
5. *Rouladen* (rolled-up beef with filling of pickles, onions, bacon, mustard)
6. Asparagus
7. *Sauerbraten* (in vinegar- or wine-marinated beef roast)
8. Lasagna
9. Steaks
10. Pasta casserole
11. *Kohlroulade* (cabbage roll)
12. Fish
13. *Kasslerbraten* (smoked pork roast)
14. Spinach
15. *Königsberger Klopse* (meatballs in a white sauce with capers)
16. Kale with hearty meat and potatoes

Source: https://www.naanoo.style/blog/was-essen-die-deutschen-am-liebsten, based on an EMNID survey. Accessed March 18, 2020.

Northern Germany

Schleswig-Holstein is the northernmost region of Germany, and its cuisine resembles that of its Scandinavian neighbors. The area provides 10% of the country's milk and is the home of *Holsteiner* Tilsit cheese. Tilsit has a high milk fat content, 30–60%, and is often flavored with peppercorns or carraway seeds. A dish that is known all over the seafaring area is *Labskaus*. Made of salted meat, pickles, onions, red beets, and potatoes, all mashed together, it was easy to eat for sailors who often had teeth troubles due to lack of Vitamin C in their diet. Hamburg, a major port city, is connected to the North Sea by the Elbe River. Many of the city's specialties contain seafood, for example *Rollmöpse* (rolled herring with pickles), smoked eel, and eel soup. For dessert, Hamburg offers *Rote Grütze*, a kind of red fruit jelly of raspberries, currants, and sour cherries served with vanilla sauce.

The Hanseatic city of Lübeck is famous for its marzipan. The designation *Lübecker Marzipan* is protected by the European Union and its quality monitored by the German Institute for Quality Assurance and Classification. Any product marketed as "Lubeck Fine Marzipan" may contain no more than 10% sugar.

Wendell G. Johnson

See also: Chapter 14: Beer; Food Laws in Germany; German Sausages; Oktoberfest.

Further Reading

Fulson, Gerhild. *German Meals at Oma's: Traditional Dishes for the Home Cook*. Salem, MA: Page Street Publishing, 2018.

Kohl, Hannelore, and Helmut Kohl. *A Culinary Voyage through Germany*. New York: Abbeville Press, 1997.

Stollen Association. https://www.dresdnerstollen.com/en/dresdner-christstollen. Accessed March 18, 2020.

Wine

Germany is the northernmost of the classic European wine-producing countries, and thus its grapes ripen slowly with an extended growing season stretching into November. Viniculture in Germany dates to the time of the Roman emperor Probus (ca. 276–282 CE). The production of wine became an economic mainstay of the Frankish Empire under Charlemagne, and in time Cologne became the most important wine market of the Hanseatic League. In the fifteenth century, Cistercian monks discovered that Riesling was ideally suited to Germany's climate and soil (Reinhardt, 2012). Wine was often the preferred beverage of the day as a lot of the water was dirty. The Thirty Years War (1618–1648) destroyed nearly all vineyards. In the nineteenth century, the non-native *Reblaus* (aphid wine pest) was accidentally introduced when wines were imported from America and the native vines could not withstand this pest. The *Reblaus* remains a major problem as there are no pesticides that could destroy it. The solution was to graft German wines onto American rootstock. Thus, most German wines today have American roots.

Germany exports about one-third of the wines it produces. Today, nearly 80,000 vintners produce approximately 10 million hectoliters (1 hl is 100 liters) of wine per year. Over 20% of the wine grown in Germany is Riesling, which thrives in the red and blue slate of the country's river valleys. Germany produces over 60% of the world's Riesling, which is generally not aged in barrels and remains drinkable for a decade after bottling. Other varietals include *Grauburgunder* (Pinot Gris), *Weissburgunder* (Pinot Blanc) Gewürztraminer, and a red wine, *Spätburgunder* (Pinot Noir).

There are thirteen wine-growing regions in Germany, each with its own appellation (legally defined geographical indication).

- Ahr
- Baden
- Franken
- Hessische Bergstrasse
- Mittelrhein
- Mosel
- Nahe
- Pfalz
- Rheingau
- Rheinhessen
- Saale-Unstrut

- Sachsen
- Württemberg

Each year, the German Wine Institute elects a "German Wine Queen" from one of the nation's thirteen wine-growing regions (the two runners-up are referred to as "Wine Princesses"). The Deutsches Weinbaumuseum (viticulture museum) in Oppenheim, Rhineland-Palatinate, was opened in 1980 and is a comprehensive source for everything that has to do with wine.

German wine is classified as either "German Wine" (*Deutscher Wein*) or "quality wine" (*Qualitätswein*). German Wine is produced from underripe grapes, not subjected to geographical appellation regulations, and generally not exported to the United States. *Qualitätswein* is tested for compliance with regional appellation laws. These wines are made from approved grape varietals which have reached a specific level of ripeness. According to this graduated level of ripeness, these "wines with special attributes" (*Prädiktatswein*) are classified as

Kabinett—light wines made from fully ripe grapes
Spätlese—superior wines made from late-harvested grapes
Auslese—wine made from specially selected very ripe grapes
Beerenauslese—a dessert wine made from individually selected overripe grapes
Trockenbeerenauslese—wine made from individual selected grapes that have dried
   almost to the point of becoming raisins
Eiswein—ice wine, made from grapes harvested and pressed while frozen.

Interesting facts about German wine:

- Germans drink more sparkling wine (*Sekt*) per capita than any other nation.
- Germany is the world's eighth-largest producer of wine (Italy is the world's largest producer of wine; the United States fourth).
- *Liebfrauenmilch* (beloved lady's milk), a sweet, rather low-quality wine, was mostly produced for export. It was best known in the United States as Blue Nun, with its characteristic blue bottle. The wine fell out of favor in the 1990s.

Wendell G. Johnson

See also: Chapter 2: Charlemagne (748–814). Chapter 14: Overview; Food Laws in Germany; Regional Specialties.

Further Reading

Deutsches Weinbaumuseum. https://www.dwm-content.de/. Accessed March 18, 2020.

Foulkes, Christopher. *Larousse Encyclopedia of Wine*, updated ed. New York: Larousse, 2001.

Reinhardt, Stephen, Jon Wyand, and Hugh Johnson. *The Finest Wines of Germany: A Regional Guide to the Best Producers and Their Wines*. Berkeley: University of California Press, 2012.

Robinson, Jancis. *The Oxford Companion to Wine*. Oxford, UK; New York: Oxford University Press, 1994.

Schoonmaker, Frank, and Peter M. F. Sichel. *The Wines of Germany: Frank Schoonmaker's Classic*. Completely rev. ed. by Peter M. F. Sichel. New York: Hastings House, 1980.

Statista. "Wine Production." https://de.statista.com/statistik/daten/studie/73337/umfrage /weinproduktion-bestimmter-laender-und-regionen/. Accessed March 18, 2020.

CHAPTER 15

LEISURE AND SPORTS

OVERVIEW

Germans have more official holidays (eleven national holidays plus other regional and religious holidays), longer paid vacations (thirty to thirty-five days per year), and shorter average work weeks (thirty-five hours) than citizens of most other nations. Germans take advantage of their holidays to travel, and one-third of them spend their vacation time in Germany. A favorite domestic destination are the Baltic Beaches in Mecklenburg-Western Pomerania. The northern Hanseatic cities of Stralsund, Wismar, and Rostock are also popular vacation spots. Neuschwanstein Castle, the inspiration for Cinderella's castle at Disney World and Sleeping Beauty's Castle at Disneyland, in Bavaria is Germany's second most popular tourist attraction. Approximately half of German citizens spend part of their vacation in Europe. Spain, particularly the Balearic Island Mallorca, is their favorite European destination, followed by Italy and Austria. About 2 million Germans visit the United States each year, the sixth-largest yearly contingent of international visitors to American shores. German citizens may travel to the United States without a visa provided they have obtained an ESTA (Electronic System for Travel Authorization) visa waiver prior to their trip. Travelers who are denied an ESTA visa waiver may apply for a traditional B1 Business Visa or B2 Tourist Visa for entry into the United States.

Germany has a very comprehensive spa culture. Chancellor Otto von Bismarck (1815–1898) sponsored social insurance laws that made it possible for the working class to seek spa treatments at government expense. Each worker had the right to spend four weeks in a spa every three years. This benefit has been curtailed recently, but many German citizens still have the right to three weeks of spa treatment every four years. Germany offers a variety of spa treatments: mineral, marsh, sea, and saltwater spas, depending on location and type of treatment. Kneipp spas, developed by the naturopath Sebastian Kneipp (1821–1897), offer a holistic regimen for those suffering from high blood pressure, rheumatism, and arthritis. The treatment at a Kneipp spa incorporates hot and cold showers, rinses, and compresses; its diet includes fresh fruits and vegetable, whole grains, and herbal supplements. Many towns in Germany have affixed the prefix "*Bad*" (Bath) to their names, such as **Bad** Kreuznach in Rhineland-Palatinate that boasts the Salinen Inhaltorium, an outdoor Breathing Park. These towns have met strict air- and water-quality standards and have extensive medical facilities. Bad Kreuznach has five health and

HUNTING AND GOLF IN GERMANY

Many popular leisure activities are strictly regulated in Germany. Hunting has a long tradition in Germany, and over 350,000 registered hunters live in the country. A hunting license is required to hunt in Germany, and an additional permit is needed for specific seasons. In order to qualify for a hunting license, hunters must pass both a written and an oral exam and demonstrate knowledge of basic animal biology, firearms laws and techniques, and awareness of wildlife and landscape conservation regulations. Germany has stringent laws regarding ownership of firearms. Gun owners carry liability insurance, and authorities may request access to the premises of owners to monitor whether the weapons are being properly stored.

Germany is home to more than 600 golf courses (with the highest concentration in Bavaria) and 500,000 golfers. Unlike the United States, where golfers of any ability can simply show up at a public course, pay a greens fee, and play, golfers in Germany are required to book a tee time in advance and present a handicap certificate recognized by the German Golf Association (DGV) before teeing off. In lieu of a certified handicap, a golfer must present a golf license, or *Platzreife*. In order to obtain a golf license, a player must demonstrate driving, putting, and chipping skills; play a round in 108 strokes or less with a DGV professional; and pass a written examination on the rules and etiquette of golf. Many golf clubs in Germany offer three- to five-day courses for obtaining the *Platzreife*. These sessions are relatively expensive, so many golfers head to Austria or Switzerland to obtain their golf license.

wellness spas; all over Germany there are over 900. Currently, nearly 20% of all spas in Europe are located in Germany. Germans seeking spa treatment often travel to other European countries. They find the spas in Eastern Europe less expensive than in Germany, but also go to Southern Europe for treatment in a sunnier and warmer climate.

Outdoor Activities

Germans love the outdoors and are avid gardeners. Gardening is considered a key component of a healthy lifestyle. The local *Schwimmbad* (swimming pool) is also important to outdoor life. Adjacent to the pool is an area known as the *Liegewiese*, a public space for sunbathing and socializing. During the winter months, many Germans head to Bavaria to ski in the Alps, particularly resorts around Garmisch-Partenkirchen and the Zugspitze. Garmisch-Partenkirchen was the site of the 1936 Winter Olympics, and visitors today can ski down three mountains: Hausberg, Kreuzeck, and Alpspitze. The Zugspitze, Germany highest peak at 2,962 m or 9,718 ft, has thirteen miles of downhill slopes. During the summer, the ski resorts remain open for hiking and mountain climbing. Cycling is another favorite outdoor activity; more than 80% of Germans use a bicycle, making it one of the leading cycling nations in the world. The city of Münster in Nordrhein-Westfalen calls itself a *Fahrradstadt* (bicycle town). There more citizens use bicycles than cars on the about 300 km bike paths; there are over 500,000 bicycles for 310,000 inhabitants.

The Federal Ministry of Transport and Digital Infrastructure has developed a National Cycling Plan, which emphasizes the health benefits of cycling as well as its positive impact on the environment.

Bars and Cafes

Germans often head to bars and cafés for *Gemütlichkeit*, an untranslatable word referring to a feeling of contentedness, friendliness, and relaxation. In the industrial *Ruhrgebiet*, workers often head to a *Stehkneipe* (stand-up bar) after work for a beer. In Berlin of the late nineteenth and early twentieth century, *Eckkneipen* (corner bar) functioned as a living room as apartments were at a premium and apartment sharing among unrelated people was common.

Munich is the home of many *Bierhallen* (beer halls), including the Löwenbräukeller and the Augustinerbräukeller. Perhaps the most famous beer hall in Germany is the Hofbräuhaus, which serves 4,500 patrons daily. In the summer, people head to a *Biergarten* (beer garden) to slake their thirst al fresco. The largest beer garden in the country is the Hirschgarten, located in Munich, which can seat up to 8,000 customers and serves beer solely in one-liter mugs. Germans frequent cafes and bakeries for coffee and pastries. The average German drinks 160 liters of coffee yearly. Germany's coffee culture now includes Starbucks with over 150 outlets and McCafes in 800 McDonald's restaurants. Still, many local independent coffee bars, some specializing in vegan baked goods, can be found throughout the country.

Sports

Germany is both an enthusiastic and successful sporting nation. The country has hosted three Olympiads, the Summer Games in 1936 (in Berlin) and 1972 (in Munich), and the Winter Games in 1936 (in Garmisch-Partenkirchen). Germans have won 1,757 Olympic medals, trailing only athletes from the United States and the Russian Federation. Germany has hosted both the men's and women's FIFA World Cups (in 2006 and 2011 respectively). The German men won the World Cup in 1954, 1974, 1990, and 2014, while the German women hoisted it in 2003 and 2007.

Germany is the home to several professional sports leagues. The most popular by far is the Bundesliga, the federal soccer league. Eighteen soccer clubs play in the Bundesliga. With attendance averaging ca. 45,000 per match, the Bundesliga has the highest average attendance of all European soccer leagues. Bayern München is one of the world's iconic sports franchises. Many of Germany's most illustrious players have played for Bayern München, including "the Kaiser" Franz Beckenbauer. Germany also boasts a competitive women's soccer league, the Frauen-Bundesliga with twelve teams. Longtime FFC Turbine Potsdam midfielder Ariane Hingst is a soccer analyst for Fox Sports and provided color commentary to American audiences during the 2019 women's World Cup.

The German Ice Hockey League was founded in 1994. The league has fourteen teams and averages 6,200 spectators per match. Very few German players have played in the National Hockey League in the United States and Canada. Forward Walt

Tkachuk of the New York Rangers was the first German-born player to appear in an NHL game. Defenseman Uwe Krupp was a member of the Colorado Avalanche when the team won the Stanley Cup in1996. Krupp went on to coach the German national team.

The Basketball Bundesliga is Germany's professional basketball league. The most successful team to date has been the Bayer Giants Leverkusen with fourteen league titles. The German national team has not fared well in international competition with the exception of the 1993 FIBA European Championships when the Germans beat the heavily favored Russian team 71–70. Several German players have played in the National Basketball Association. Dirk Nowitski (from Würzburg) and the Dallas Mavericks won the NBA championship in 2011, beating LeBron James and the Miami Heat in the finals.

The Deutscher Handball Bund (German Handball Federation) is the organization overseeing all handball clubs, for men and women. The Handball Bundesliga Frauen has twelve teams and the DKB Handball Bundesliga is comprised of eighteen teams, many from smaller cities such as Lemgo, Melsungen, and Wetzlar. THW Kiel has won twenty titles, making it the most successful team in the men's league; on the women's side, Bayer Leverkusen is the winningest club. Germany has enjoyed success on the world stage, winning eight World Cups. One of the most recognizable players was and still is Stefan Kretzschmar, who played from 1991 to 2009 in the Bundesliga and in many international meets. He is now a handball expert on TV.

German players have won multiple Grand Slam titles in tennis. Steffi Graf won twenty-two major titles during her career and the Golden Slam in 1988 (only the Australian Margaret Court and Serena Williams of the United States have won more Grand Slam titles), Boris Becker six, and Angelique Kerber three. Germany hosts four international tournaments each year: the Halle Open, German Open (in Hamburg), the Bavarian Open (Munich), and the Stuttgart Open. The German men have won the Davis Cup three times (1988, 1989, 1993) and finished second twice (1970 and 1985). The German women have prevailed at the Federation Cup twice (1987 and 1992) and finished second five times (1966, 1970, 1982, 1983, and 2014).

Golf flies under the radar in Germany. The country has relatively few public courses, and weekly tournaments are not broadcast by subscription-free television providers. Two German players have won major tournaments: Bernhard Langer won the Masters tournament in 1985 and 1993, and Martin Kaymer was the PGA champion in 2010 and the U.S. Open titlist in 2014. Kaymer was the top-ranked player in the world for eight weeks in 2011.

Wendell G. Johnson

Further Reading

Deutscher Handballbund DHB. https://www.dhb.de/. Accessed June 9, 2020.

Fahrradstadt Münster. https://www.stadt-muenster.de/tourismus/fahrradstadt.html. Accessed June 9, 2020.

Fraser, Catherine C., and Dierk O. Hoffmann. *Pop Culture Germany! Media, Arts, and Lifestyle*. Santa Barbara, CA: ABC-CLIO, 2006.

Gaab, Jeffrey S. *Munich: Hofbräuhaus & History: Beer, Culture, & Politics.* New York: Peter Lang, 2006.

Kurklinik Verzeichnis. "Rehakliniken und Kurkliniken in Deutschland." https://www.kurklinikverzeichnis.de/. Accessed June 9, 2020.

Beckenbauer, Franz (1945–)

Franz Beckenbauer is considered Germany's greatest soccer star. Beckenbauer was born in Bavaria and grew up a fan of soccer club München 1860. He eventually joined Bayern München (a second-division team at the time) and helped it win promotion (*Aufstieg*) to the Bundesliga during his first full season with the club. Beckenbauer's fluid play earned him the nickname "*Der Kaiser*" (The Emperor). He reinvented the position of center-back. He not only excelled as a defender but was able to attack from the back line. Together with forward Gerd Müller (1945-2021) and goalie Sepp Maier (b. 1944), he led Bayern München to victory in the German Cup in 1967 and the European Cup the following year. By the early 1970s, Bayern München was the dominant team in Europe. With Beckenbauer, the club won the Bundesliga title 1972, 1973, and 1974 and the European Cup 1974, 1975, and 1976. During this time, Beckenbauer was named European Footballer of the Year in 1972 and again in 1976. Along with Brazilian legend Pelé and the Italian striker Giorgio Chinaglia, he played for the New York Cosmos from 1977 to 1979 and then transferred back to the Bundesliga in 1980, where he played for Hamburger SV for three years. After playing one final year for the Cosmos in 1983, he retired from club soccer. Success followed Beckenbauer to New York, as the Cosmos won the American Soccer Bowl three times during his stay.

Internationally, Beckenbauer played in 103 matches and scored fourteen goals for West Germany. He was a member of three World Cup squads, losing to England in 1966 and to Italy in 1970. Beckenbauer finally hoisted the World Cup in 1974 when West Germany bested the Netherlands. He went on to coach the West German national team in 1984, when it lost to Argentina 3-2, and again in 1990, when the Germans beat Argentina 1-0. With the German victory in the 1990 World Cup, Beckenbauer became the first person to win the World Cup as both a player and a coach (a feat since matched by Mario Zagallo of Brazil and Didier Deschamps of France).

After his playing career, Beckenbauer enjoyed success as the manager of Bayern München. Under his tutelage, the club won the Bundesliga title in 1994 and the UEFA Cup in 1996. In 1998, he was nominated vice president of the Deutscher Fußball-Bund (DFB, German Football League). He headed Germany's successful bid to host the 2006 FIFA World Cup. Beckenbauer was investigated for fraud as a result of his activities connected with the bidding process and was fined 7,000 Swiss francs for failing to cooperate with the investigation.

Beckenbauer has been married three times and has five children.

Wendell G. Johnson

See also: Chapter 15: Overview; Bundesliga; FIFA World Cups; *Vereine.*

Further Reading

Dempsey, Luke. *Club Soccer 101: The Essential Guide to the Stars, Stats, and Stories of 101 of the Greatest Teams in the World.* New York: W. W. Norton & Company, 2014.

Parrish, Charles, and John Nauright. *Soccer around the World: A Cultural Guide to the World's Favorite Sport.* Santa Barbara, CA: ABC-CLIO, 2014.

Becker, Boris (1967–)

Boris Becker was born in Leimen in the state of Baden-Württemberg, the son of Elvira and Karl-Heinz Becker. His father was an architect who built the tennis club where Boris learned to play. He remembers his father spanking him after he greeted him with a Hitler salute. Becker's mother was a refugee from the Sudetentland (Czech Republic). Elvira was initially skeptical of Boris's pursuit of a tennis career and wanted him to stay in school and attend a university. In his own words, Becker considered his hometown to be the epitome of provincial Germany: "clean, smug, a little sterile, but also pretty secure" (Becker, 2004, p. 19).

Becker won Wimbledon at the age of 17, the youngest men's singles champion ever. At the champions' dinner that evening he danced with Martin Navratilova (the women's champ). His victory that day inspired future Wimbledon champions Michael Stich of Germany and Pete Sampras from the United States. During his career, Becker won forty-nine singles titles, fifteen doubles titles, and six Grand Slam championships. He and Michael Stich won 1992 Olympic gold medals in men's doubles. Becker became Germany's most famous male athlete. As reported on *60 Minutes,* Becker was "the first German national hero since the defeat of the German army in the Second World War" (Becker, p. xiii). He found the pressure unbearable at times, carrying the weight of expectations of the entire nation of Germany and feeling forced to grow up under its microscopic gaze. He felt that he achieved success too rapidly, at too young an age, and believed he would have become a better tennis player had he won his Wimbledon tournament at twenty-three.

Becker married Barbara Feltus, the daughter of an African American father and a German mother in 1993. The couple had two sons, Noah and Elias. At the time, the marriage of Germany's most famous athlete to a black woman was viewed as a symbol of racial tolerance in the country. However, he received a series of racist threats and was forced to hire bodyguards to protect his family. The breakdown of the marriage shocked the nation. The couple divorced in 2001. In addition to his divorce, Becker cites other considerable challenges he has faced: the death of his father in 1999, a conviction for tax fraud in 2002 (Becker received a two-year suspended jail sentence), and a daughter conceived out of wedlock (the result of a tryst in a broom closet). Becker has a home near Wimbledon, the site of his first Grand Slam title. He married Dutch model Sharley Kerssenberg in 2009 and the couple had one son, Amadeus. The couple separated in 2018.

Wendell G. Johnson

See also: Chapter 6: Sudeten Germans. Chapter 15: Graf, Steffi (1969–).

Further Reading

Becker, Boris. *The Player*. London: Bantam Press, 2004.

Morgan, Peter. "Germany Gripped by Becker Case." *BBC News*. http://news.bbc.co.uk/2 /hi/europe/1108344.stm. Accessed December 3, 2019.

Bundesliga

Professional soccer in Germany is divided into three tiers: the Bundesliga, Bundesliga 2, and 3. Liga. The top two tiers, Bundesliga and Bundesliga 2, each have eighteen clubs. Twenty teams compete in the 3. Liga. The Bundesliga season extends from August through May, with each club playing a home and away match against the other clubs. At the close of each season, the bottom two teams of the Bundesliga are relegated to Bundesliga 2, and the top two teams of Bundesliga 2 are promoted to the Bundesliga. In addition, the third team from the bottom of the Bundesliga plays the third-place team from Bundesliga 2 to determine which team qualifies to play in the Bundesliga the following year. Teams in the 3. Liga compete for promotion to Bundesliga 2. Each summer the teams compete in the DFB Pokal, an annual knockout competition (**D**eutscher **Fußball-B**und, German Soccer Federation, where all clubs are members).

The Bundesliga began operation in 1963 and has the highest average attendance per match of all the European leagues: ca. 45,000, albeit not in COVID-19 times. Even the top five teams competing in Bundesliga 2 draw between 30,000 and 50,000 spectators per match (by comparison, attendance in the English Premier League averages 39,000). According to the 2019 Economic Report of the Deutsche Fußball Liga (DFL German Soccer League, the professional soccer alliance), the Bundesliga and Bundesliga 2 clubs generated a total revenue €4.42 billion for the year. German soccer teams are not privately owned but operate on the *Verein* (club) structure. The fans are dues-paying members of the club and have voting rights on club policies.

FC Bayern München has been the most successful soccer club in the Bundesliga, having won twenty-nine national titles and nineteen national cups. Bayern München has also won the UEFA (Union of European Football Associations) Champions League finals five times, most recently in 2013. Several of Germany's iconic soccer stars have played for Bayern München, including Franz Beckenbauer, Lothar Matthäus, Gerhard "Gerd" Müller, and goalies Oliver Kahn and Josef "Sepp" Maier.

Germany also boasts a competitive women's soccer league, the Frauen-Bundesliga with twelve teams. VfL Wolfsburg has won the league championship the past three years. Birgit Prinz, from FFC Frankfurt, is recognized as one of the greatest female soccer players in history. She was voted the FIFA Player of the Year for three consecutive years, 2003–2005, and appeared in five FIFA World Cups and four Olympic Games.

Wendell G. Johnson

See also: Chapter 15: Beckenbauer, Franz (1945–); FIFA World Cup; *Vereine.*

Further Reading

Gammelsæter, Hallgeir, and Benoît Senaux, eds. *The Organisation and Governance of Top Football across Europe: An Institutional Perspective.* New York: Routledge, 2011.

Parrish, Charles, and John Nauright. *Soccer around the World: A Cultural Guide to the World's Favorite Sport.* Santa Barbara, CA: ABC-CLIO, 2014.

FIFA World Cups

The German men's and women's national soccer teams have experienced success in the FIFA (Fédération Internationale de Football Association) World Cup, soccer's grandest stage. The German men have won the World Cup four times (1954, 1974, 1990, and 2014), while the German women prevailed twice (2003 and 2007). Following the Second World War, the German men were banned from playing in the 1950 World Cup. In the 1954 final, played in Switzerland, the Germans beat the favored Hungarians 3-2, in what became known as the Wunder von Bern (Miracle of Berne), captured in the 2003 movie of the same name. West Germany was the host nation for the 1974 World Cup. In the final, played in West Berlin's Olympiastadion (Olympic Stadium), Germany defeated the Netherlands 1-0 for its second title. The Germans made it to the championship matches in both the 1982 and 1986 World Cups, losing respectively to the Italians and Argentines. In a rematch of the 1986 final, Germany defeated Argentina 1-0 to claim the 1990 World Cup. Germany played in the 2002 final, losing to Italy, but hoisted the championship trophy for the fourth time in 2014, defeating Argentina 1-0. Germany hosted the men's World Cup in 2006. The Germans opened the tournament in Munich with a 4-2 victory over Costa Rica. They advanced to the semifinal match, where they lost to eventual champions Italy. The match was tied at the end of regulation time, but the Italian squad netted two goals in extra time to earn the trip to the final, where they defeated France. Germany was a pre-tournament favorite for the 2018 World Cup, but the team was already eliminated during group play, losing to Mexico (1-0) and South Korea (2-0), necessitating a lot of soul-searching and bad press.

In the 2003 women's World Cup, held in the United States, Germany beat the host team 3-0 and went on to win the title by virtue of a 2-1 victory over Sweden. The Germans repeated as champions in 2007, defeating Brazil 2-0 in the final. Germany was the host nation for the 2011 women's World Cup. The official opening game was played in Olympic Stadium in Berlin, where the hosts prevailed over Canada. Germany lost to eventual champion Japan 1-0 in the knockout stage; Japan went on to defeat the United States by virtue of penalty kicks. Approximately 845,000 tickets were sold for the thirty-two matches played in the tournament. In the two most recent World Cups, Germany lost to the United States 2-0 in the 2015 semifinal and fell to Sweden 2-1 in the first game of the knockout stage in 2019.

Wendell G. Johnson

See also: Chapter 15: Beckenbauer, Franz (1945–); Olympic Games.

Further Reading

Lisi, Clemente Angelo. *A History of the World Cup: 1930–2018*, new ed. Lanham, MD: Rowman & Littlefield, 2019.

Parrish, Charles, and John Nauright. *Soccer around the World: A Cultural Guide to the World's Favorite Sport*. Santa Barbara, CA: ABC-CLIO, 2014.

Graf, Steffi (1969–)

Stefanie ("Steffi") Maria Graf (b. 1969), one of the greatest tennis stars of the twentieth century, was born in Mannheim, the first child of Peter and Heidi Graf. Graf began playing tennis when she was three years old. Her first professional tournament victory came in 1986 when she defeated Chris Evert in the Family Circle Cup finals in South Carolina. The following year she won the French Open and by the end of the year was the top-ranked female tennis player in the world. Her powerful forehand led her to be nicknamed "Fräulein Forehand."

In 1988, she won the "Golden Grand Slam." In addition to prevailing at Wimbledon, the Australian, French, and U.S. Opens, she won the women's singles at the Olympics in Seoul, South Korea. The following year she won three of the four Grand Slam titles, losing only to Arantxa Sanchez Vicario in the finals of the French Open. Overall, Graf won twenty-two Grand Slam singles finals and one Grand Slam doubles title (with Gabriela Sabatini). She retired in 1999 after losing

During her career, Steffi Graf was one of the greatest tennis stars of the twentieth century. She won twenty-two Grand Slam titles. She is married to former tennis star Andre Agassi. (Jerry Coli/Dreamstime.com)

to Lindsay Davenport at Wimbledon. During her career, Graf was the number-one ranked player in the world for 377 weeks.

Steffi Graf's tennis career was not without drama. In 1993, Monica Seles had supplanted Graf as the top-ranked player in the world. That year the two players were both competing in the Citizen Cup Tennis tournament in Hamburg. Günter Parche, a fan obsessed with Graf, stabbed Seles during her quarterfinal match against Magdalene Maleeva. Parche was irritated that Seles had supplanted Graf as the number-one female tennis player in the world. Incredibly, officials did not cancel the tournament, nor did Graf withdraw. Sanchez Vicario defeated Graf in the final, but Graf soon reappeared at the top of the rankings. Monica Seles never regained the form that catapulted her to the top of the tennis world and vowed never to play tennis again in Germany. Two years later, Peter Graf was charged with tax evasion. He was convicted of illegally sheltering $28 million of Steffi's earning to avoid paying tax on them and served a brief term in prison. Steffi denied knowledge of the scheme and was never charged with the crime.

In 1998 Graf founded Children for Tomorrow, a foundation devoted to helping children and their families recover from the trauma of war, violence, and persecution. She married American tennis star Andre Agassi in 2001. The couple have two children and reside near Las Vegas, Nevada.

Wendell G. Johnson

See also: Chapter 15: Becker, Boris (1967–); Olympic Games.

Further Reading

Levinson, David. "Graf, Steffi." In Karen Christensen, Allen Guttmann, and Gertrud Pfister, eds. *International Encyclopedia of Women and Sports*, vol. 3, 470–471. New York: Macmillan Reference USA, 2001.

L. J. W. "Steffi Graf." *Sports Illustrated for Women* 1(4): 88, 1999.

Leisure and Sports in the German Democratic Republic

While West Germans enjoyed the freedom to travel, international travel was more difficult for East Germans. Those who could afford to travel were permitted to visit the "fraternal socialist states" of Czechoslovakia, Hungary, Romania, Bulgaria, the Soviet Union, and Poland; however, after 1981, travel to Poland was proscribed because East German authorities feared the spread of the Solidarity movement. Otherwise, East Germans had two domestic options for their vacations. First, they could visit state-owned vacation settlements on the Baltic Sea. To do so, they obtained trade-union coupons (called "vacation checks") from the FDGB (Freier Deutscher Gewerkschaftsbund, the Free German Trade Union Confederation). Unfortunately, the FDGB only had enough vacation checks for 20% of the population, and as a result, East German families often could not vacation together. The second option was camping, which many East German vacationers considered essential to a healthy lifestyle.

Walter Ulbricht, first secretary of the ruling Socialist Unity part of (East) Germany, famously stated, "Everybody, everywhere, should play sports every week" (Johnson, 2008, p. 65). The government founded mass organizations, such as the German Sports Association and the German Gymnastics and Sports Federation (Deutscher Turn- und Sportbund), to mobilize the citizenry through sports. These organizations had three functions: to transmit party goals to the population, integrate citizens into state-sponsored activities, and control the population by requiring reports on these activities. The government believed that participating in collective sports activities would build socialism by fostering both greater productivity at work and the development of paramilitary skills. Emblematic of the emphasis that the GDR placed on collective athletic endeavors were the Sports Shows, such as the spectacle staged in Leipzig's 100,000-seat Central Stadium in 1956. The Sports Shows featured choreographed gymnastics and other synchronized exercises, among other activities.

The East German Olympic teams gained notoriety both for their athletic successes and for the endemic state-sponsored doping associated with them, doping that at times was hidden from the athletes. East German athletes did not compete under their own national banner until the 1968 Mexico City Olympics. They were tremendously successful. During its forty-year existence, East Germany amassed 755 Olympic Medals, 768 world championship and 747 Europe championship titles, winning 406 medals (including 153 gold) in the summer games and 110 medals (39 gold) in the winter games during the period 1968–1988. According to the East German propaganda, this athletic success was proof of the superiority of its government and social structure. East German Olympic athletes were recruited out of local sports clubs. One of the most (in)famous clubs was Sport Club (SC) Dynamo Berlin. The club sought out young girls whose motor skills and physique were especially suited for swimming. The key to this Olympic dominance was the doping control laboratory in Kreischa, Saxony, which developed both performance-enhancing drugs and masking agents. An official plan from 1974 stipulated the secret doping of 15,000 athletes as well as illegal research on unsuspecting athletes. Many surviving athletes today are fighting the long-term health effects of the doping. After reunification, Manfred Ewald (1926–2002), the GDR's minister of sport, was convicted of providing illicit drugs to athletes and thereby causing them intentional bodily harm.

Wendell G. Johnson

See also: Chapter 3: Government and Politics in the German Democratic Republic. Chapter 15: Olympic Games; *Vereine.*

Further Reading

Crowley, David, and Susan Emily Reid, eds. *Pleasures in Socialism: Leisure and Luxury in the Eastern Bloc.* Evanston, IL: Northwestern University Press, 2010.

Dennis, Mike, and Jonathan Grix. *Sport under Communism: Behind the East German "Miracle."* New York: Palgrave Macmillan, 2012.

Geipel, Ines. "Staatsplan 'Sieg.' Die Stasi im Leistungssport," 2017. https://www.bpb.de/geschichte/deutsche-geschichte/stasi/219625/sport. Accessed June 9, 2020.

Johnson, Molly. *Training Socialist Citizens: Sports and the State in East Germany.* Leiden, Netherlands: Brill, 2008.

Ungerleider, Steven. *Faust's Gold: Inside the East German Doping Machine.* New York: Thomas Dunne Books/St. Martin's Press, 2001.

Olympic Games

Germany has hosted the Olympic Games three times: the Summer Olympics in Berlin (1936) and Munich (1972) and the Winter Olympics in Garmisch-Partenkirchen (1936). The nation was also selected to host the 1916 Summer Games (Berlin) and 1940 Winter Games (Garmisch-Partenkirchen), but these games were canceled due to World Wars.

The 1936 Winter Games provide an early example of the politicization of the Olympics. Adolf Hitler opened the games on February 6, accompanied by 6,000 SS (*Schutzstaffel*) and SA (*Sturmabteilung*) troops. The German organizers wanted to control the international image of the games and did not grant credentials to foreign photographers. The Nazi government used the games as a propaganda in defense of its regime. With 427 athletes, Germany fielded the largest contingent, followed by the United States with 376 participants. While Germany also won the most medals (89), the star of the 1936 Berlin games was Jesse Owens, an African American track and field athlete. Owens won four gold medals and set world records in the 100- and 200-dashes, long jump, and as a member of the 400-meter relay. Leni Riefenstahl produced the 1938 propaganda film *Olympia* with footage from the Berlin Olympics.

The 1972 Summer Games in Munich are best remembered for an act of terrorism. On the morning of September 5, eight Palestinians took hostage eleven members of the Israeli team, killing two of the hostages in the process. The terrorists demanded the release of 200 Palestinians imprisoned in Israel. Eventually, a gun battle between the terrorists and police resulted in the deaths of the remaining Israelis and three of the terrorists.

After the First and Second World Wars, Germany was barred from participating in the Olympic Games in 1920, 1924, and 1948. In 1951, the International Olympic Committee (IOC) recognized the national Olympic Committee for Germany, based in West Germany, as the official Olympic Committee for both West and East Germany. As a result, athletes from both West and East Germany competed on the United Team of Germany (EUA, Équipe Unifiée Allemande) until the East German Olympic Committee was recognized by the IOC in 1968. The two countries competed separately from 1968 until 1988. Following the invasion of Afghanistan by the Soviet Union in 1979, West Germany joined other Western democracies in boycotting the 1980 Olympic Games held in Moscow. In response, East Germany joined the Soviet boycott of the 1984 games staged in Los Angeles. East German athletes enjoyed considerable success in the Olympic Games, but their achievements were clouded by their government's state-sponsored doping regimen. Many former East German athletes continue to suffer the health effects of government-mandated steroid consumption and other drugs, of which they often were not aware. Following national reunification in 1990, Germany fielded a unified team in the 1992 Barcelona Summer Games.

Wendell G. Johnson

See also: Chapter 2: Overview; Hitler, Adolf (1889–1945). Chapter 10: Regional Clothing. Chapter 15: Leisure and Sports in the German Democratic Republic; Witt, Katarina (1965–). Chapter 16: Film.

Further Reading

Findling, John E., and Kimberly D. Pelle, eds. *Encyclopedia of the Modern Olympic Movement.* Westport, CT: Greenwood Press, 2004.

Hilmes, Oliver. *Berlin 1936: Sixteen Days in August.* Jefferson S. Chase, trans. New York: Other Press, 2018.

Schiller, Kay, and Christopher Young. *The 1972 Munich Olympics and the Making of Modern Germany.* Berkeley: University of California Press, 2010.

Schrebergärten

Tourists travelling by train through Germany will often see little gardens alongside the train tracks. These small gardens are *Schrebergärten*, a small allotment of land where lessors can grow fruits and vegetables and spend leisure time. *Schrebergärten* are named after Dr. Daniel Schreber, who wanted to create more outdoor space in Leipzig and convinced the civic authorities to lease small plots of land to apartment dwellers. During the First World War, when food became scarce, the gardens became an area for people to grow their own food. Subsequently, during the Second World War, many people constructed small sheds on their plots to ease the housing shortage caused by Allied bombing. After the war, *Schrebergärten* took on the look and feel of a "staycation," a bucolic getaway for the urban populace. The East German authorities attempted to collectivize the gardens in the 1950s, but soon abandoned the project.

The use of *Schrebergärten* is regulated by the Federal Small Garden Act (Bundeskleingartengesetz—or BKleinG). The size of the lot may not exceed 400 square meters and must be divided between one-third plants and flowers, one-third lawn (kept free of weeds), and one-third recreational area. The use of herbicides is banned as is the burning of vegetation (although composting is allowed). Tenants are free to build small cottages or sheds (*Lauben*) on the allotment, but are not permitted to erect garages, carports, or other parking spots nor install furnaces, wind generators, or radio and/or television antennae. The *Laube* can be no larger than twenty-four square meters (6% of the allotment) or higher than 8.5 feet. Tenants may install ponds (ten square meters maximum), playground equipment, and erect fences (no higher than four feet). The *Laube* may be connected to the municipal water supply, but not to the sewage system. Many gardeners hence install

Many Germans lease *Schrebergärten*, small plots of land with cottages where urban dwellers can grow fruits and vegetables. The use of *Schrebergärten* is regulated by the federal government. (PGregoryB/Dreamstime.com)

chemical toilettes or compost human waste. The *Schrebergärten* are often adorned with *Gartenzwerge* (garden gnomes), the German equivalent of pink flamingos.

To lease a *Schrebergarten*, one needs to become a member of a *Gartenverein* (garden club) that runs it. The initial membership fee is about €350, the lease is about €500/year, and the initial costs to take over a parcel can be about €6,000 and up. Even though the individual *Gartenvereine* boast many precise rules, *Schrebergärten* are in high demand. The Verein *Unter Uns* (entre nous) in Berlin-Tempelhof, for example, contains sixty garden plots and is known for its roses.

At the present time, there are approximately 1.5 million such small allotment gardens in Germany. Berlin has the most (over 70,000), followed by Hamburg (35,000), Leipzig (32,000), Dresden (23,000), Hannover (20,000), and Bremen (16,000). There is even a Schrebergarten Museum in Leipzig: Deutsches Kleingärtner Museum. The museum features three exhibits, a garden, a *Schuppen* (shed) and a garden from the DDR, as well as a historical playground and a beer garden.

Katharina Barbe

See also: Chapter 1: Cities. Chapter 15: Overview; *Vereine*.

Further Reading

Deutsche Welle. "A Brief Guide to German Garden Colonies." https://www.dw.com/en/a
-brief-guide-to-german-garden-colonies/a-39133787. Accessed December 5, 2019.

Senatsverwaltung für Stadtentwicklung und Umwelt. "Das bunte Grün. Kleingärten
in Berlin." https://www.berlin.de/senuvk/umwelt/stadtgruen/kleingaerten/downloads
/Kleingartenbroschuere.pdf. Accessed October 21, 2021.

Wahmen, Birgit. "Allotments and Schrebergärten in Germany." In Monique Mosser and Georges Teyssot, eds. *The History of Garden Design: The Western Tradition from the Renaissance to the Present Day*, 451–453. London; New York: Thames & Hudson, 2000.

Vereine

"If three Germans with the same interest get together, they will organize a club (*Verein*)" (Fraser and Hoffman, 2006, p. 155). Sporting clubs, charitable organizations, and hobby enthusiasts all form *Vereine* in Germany. There are 300,000 such clubs in Germany and 60% of adults in the country are members of at least one *Verein*. Over 15,000 of these clubs are *Schützenvereine* ("shooting clubs"), many of which were organized as local militias during medieval times. A true *Verein* is registered as such and appends the designation *e.V.* (*eingetragener Verein* or "registered association") after the club's official name, indicating that it is a nonprofit organization and as such remains exempt from taxation. Examples of German *Vereine* include:

- Bayern München, one of Germany's most successful soccer teams, is a registered *e.V.* with 290,000 members. Membership dues are €60 per year, and benefits include a 10% discount on club-related merchandise and the opportunity to enter a lottery for tickets to sold-out matches.
- Germany has many hiking *Vereine*. Deutscher Alpenverein, e.V. (DAV, or the German Alpine Club) is the eighth-largest sport *Verein* in the country. The DAV is a member of the German Olympic Sports Confederation with oversight for both hiking and mountaineering. With its 1.3 million members, the DAV is the umbrella organization for over 300 local chapters. It maintains mountain huts along hiking trails and fosters the conservation of alpine fauna and flora.
- The Deutsche Altbriefsammler-Verein e.V. (DASV) is a philatelic organization of individuals who collect postage stamps issued by the German *Länder* (states) prior to the establishment of the empire in 1871. The DASV has a long history of collaboration with the Royal Philatelic Society of London.
- The Verein für Reformationsgeschichte e.V. (VRG, or the Organization for the History of the Reformation) was founded in Magdeburg in 1884, the 400th jubilee of Martin Luther's birth. The VRG publishes research on the Reformation and is currently located at the University of Göttingen. It counts 423 members, 298 individuals, and 125 institutions.

Germans can join any number of quirky *Vereine*. The Sensenverein Deutschland e.V. is a club of scythe enthusiasts who consider the implement an environmentally friendly alternative to the gas-powered lawn mower. The Belle Moustache e.V. is a club for gentlemen who sport eccentric beards and mustaches. The club hosts the annual International South German Beard Championship, and German contestants are fixtures at annual competitions around the world. The Pinkbunnycrew e.V. is the largest charitable motorcycle club in Germany. During fundraising events, members ride their motorcycles dressed in pink bunny costumes. German clubs have not always been so benign. During the Third Reich, the Verein für Deutsche Kulturbeziehungen im Ausland (the Association for German Cultural Relations Abroad) used German minorities abroad to carry out espionage missions in foreign countries.

Wendell G. Johnson

See also: Chapter 5: The Reformation. Chapter 10: Knigge. Chapter 15: Overview; Bundesliga; *Schrebergärten*.

Further Reading

Deutsche Welle. "Get to Know the Concept of the German Verein." https://www.dw.com/en/get-to-know-the-concept-of-the-german-verein/a-48306152

Fraser, Catherine C., and Dierk O. Hoffmann. *Pop Culture Germany! Media, Arts, and Lifestyle*. Santa Barbara, CA: ABC-CLIO, 2006.

Witt, Katarina (1965–)

Katarina Witt (b. 1965) of the German Democratic Republic was the dominant female figure skater of the 1980s. She was born in Staaken, on the border between West Berlin and the GDR. Her father, Manfred Witt (b. 1938 in Kisil, Romania), was a farmer, and her mother, Kate Sonntag (b. 1936 in Schmolsin, Poland), was a physical therapist. Both of Witt's parent were deemed politically reliable by the East German authorities, who considered her upbringing to be "politically positive" (Witt, 1994, p. 44). She entered the Ernst-Thälman-Oberschule in Karl-Marx-Stadt (renamed Chemnitz after unification) in 1972 and as a result of her athletic potential soon transferred to the East Germany sports academy, where she was trained by Jutta Müller, a former ice skater who became a very successful coach. When Witt was fourteen, she placed tenth in the 1980 world championships. Two years later, she placed second and claimed her first European championship, which she won for six consecutive years (1982–1987). Witt won the gold medal at the 1984 Winter Olympic Games in Sarajevo and repeated as champion four years later at the Calgary Olympics.

As a world-class athlete, Katarina Witt traveled the world and represented her country in international competitions. However, before and after such trips, she was contacted by the authorities of the Stasi, the East German secret police. After the Berlin Wall fell on November 9, 1989, she applied to the German government to view the secret files that Stasi had compiled about her. The file consisted of 3,000 pages and indicated that the government had been spying on her since she was seven years old and included the most intimate details of her life.

She competed in the Olympics for the final time in Lillehammer in 1994, where she finished seventh. Following her retirement from competitive skating, Witt published an autobiography, launched a line of jewelry, appeared on television shows (*Everybody*

Loves Raymond, Biggest Loser), and made appearances in motion pictures (*Ronin* and *Jerry Maguire*). Witt was inducted into the World Figure Skating Hall of Fame in 1995. In 1998, she became the first prominent female athlete to pose for *Playboy* magazine.

Wendell G. Johnson

See also: Chapter 2: Berlin Wall; Honecker, Erich (1912–1994). Chapter 3: Government and Politics in the German Democratic Republic. Chapter 15: Olympic Games.

Further Reading

Painter, Wendy. "Katarina Witt." In Karen Christensen, Allen Guttmann, and Gertrud Pfister, eds. *International Encyclopedia of Women and Sports*, 1274–1276. New York: Macmillan Reference USA, 2001.

Witt, Katarina. *Meine Jahre zwischen Pflicht und Kür.* Munich: C. Bertelsmann, 1994.

Witt, Katarina, and E. M. Swift. *Only with Passion: Figure Skating's Most Winning Champion on Competition and Life.* New York: Public Affairs, 2005.

CHAPTER 16

MEDIA AND POPULAR CULTURE

OVERVIEW

Print Media

The German print market is the largest in Europe and the fifth largest in the world. Daily newspaper circulation in Germany was 13.5 million copies in 2019, a sharp drop from the 1991 total of 27.3 copies. Readership of print newspapers among older readers (fifty to seventy years of age) remains strong in the country, hovering between 72 and 79 percent. Younger consumers, however, have turned to online news providers, and 9.6 million readers have news delivered by a publishing house to a mobile device.

Dailies. Many German newspapers make a hard and fast distinction between the news on the front pages of the paper and the opinions expressed by the editorial page in the back. One exception to this practice is the mass circulation *Bild Zeitung (BZ)*, Germany's biggest newspaper. The *BZ* is modeled after Britain's *Daily Mirror*. It contains pictures of scantily clad women and columns of strident prose. Axel Springer Verlag publishes three of the leading German dailies. *Die Welt*, published in Berlin, is often considered the German newspaper of record. *Die Welt* adopted an editorial policy of featuring two articles (one British, one German) on each major topic. The *Frankfurter Allgemeine Zeitung (FAZ)* reports on politics and the economy from a moderately conservative editorial outlook. The *FAZ* is also known for its feature section containing information on German culture. *Süddeutsche Zeitung (SZ)*, published in Munich, is a center-left paper that also features a Friday magazine. The leading financial daily is the *Handelsblatt*, published in Düsseldorf.

Weeklies. The leading weekly newspaper, the centrist *Die Zeit,* is published in Hamburg and is known for its extensive reporting on politics and public affairs and for its selection of podcasts. Each issue of *Die Zeit* also contains a sixty-page supplement, *Leben* (Lifestyle). The three most widely circulated news magazines are *Der Spiegel*, *Stern,* and *Focus. Der Spiegel* is one of the foremost news publications in the world. *Der Spiegel* is noted for its strong investigative reporting and features stories on both national and international affairs. Recently, the magazine has published interviews with former president Barack Obama and Senator Bernie Sanders. *Stern* has been in circulation since 1948, when Henri Nannen received a license from British military authorities to rename the youth-oriented *Zick-Zack* to *Stern*. The magazine soon ran afoul of the military authorities when it accused the occupying powers of wasting money and resources during the occupation of the country, and it was forced to suspend publication for a week. In 1983, *Stern* published the so-called "Hitler Diaries." The diaries proved to be a hoax, and the journalistic reputation of the magazine was severely tarnished. *Focus* was founded in 1993 as an alternative to *Der Spiegel*. In 2006, *Focus* became embroiled in a scandal when it was revealed that their journalists had been cooperating with the German Intelligence Service.

Broadcast Media

With 38 million households, Germany's television market is the largest in Europe. Every household in Germany pays the *Rundfunkbeitrag* ("TV tax"). After consumers purchase either a television or radio in Germany they go to a bank or post office and obtain a registration form for the device. The registration authorizes the broadcast tax (*Rundfunkbeitrag*) to be deducted from the consumer's bank account. It is difficult to pirate radio and television broadcasts: the authorities drive trucks around neighborhoods that determine how many devices are in a building. Each year the *Rundfunkbeitrag* raises €8 billion that is split among state media authorities, the radio Deutschlandradio, the television stations ARD and ZDF, internet service providers, and various media centers; the top commercial networks operated by RTL, ProSieben, and Sat 1 do not receive public funds. The purpose of the fee is to ensure high-quality public services broadcasting independent of commercial and political interests. Most Germans prefer cable television to satellite service. Residents in multifamily buildings are not able to contract for service independently. The owner of the building has the responsibility for obtaining cable service for all residences and assesses a monthly fee. Satellite television in Germany is often less expensive than cable. Customers pay for the dish and a one time-installation fee (most satellite service is free from additional monthly fees). Tenants must obtain the permission of the landlord before installing a satellite dish. Deutsche Welle (DW or "German Wave") is Germany's international broadcast service. DW is publicly funded, but as a member of the European Broadcasting Union its content remains free from government interference. Its flagship service is its twenty-four-hour English-language television channel broadcast around the world. DW seeks to provide a comprehensive view of Germany and provide access to the German language.

Social Media

In 2019, WhatsApp was the most widely used social media platform in Germany, followed by YouTube, Facebook, and Instagram. Facebook proved such a success that it drove the German site Wer-kennt-wen out of business. When Facebook sought to acquire WhatsApp in 2014, the merger caught the attention of the German government, which expressed antitrust concerns. Facebook has run afoul of the German government on numerous occasions. The government contends that Facebook has been complacent in addressing its role in election meddling and the spread of misinformation. In 2019, Facebook was ordered to stop combining data it collects about Germans' use of apps and websites with user consent.

Hamburg-based Xing is the largest professional networking site in the German-speaking market (Germany, Austria, Switzerland) with 16 million users in 2019. In contrast to LinkedIn, which is oriented toward digital natives and dependent on user-generated content, Xing is geared toward the corporate culture of the German middle class.

The Federal Data Protection Act (Bundesdatenschutzgesetz) regulates the use of personal data by internet providers and social media platforms. Other regulations require internet companies to flag far-right propaganda, graphic portrayals of violence, and posts indicating that someone is preparing a terrorist attack, and recently the German cabinet approved a bill that requires social media sites to report hate speech.

German Television Series/Shows

ARD produces the popular crime drama *Tatort* (*Crime Scene*). *Tatort* has been broadcast on Sunday evenings since 1970, making it the longest-running franchise on German television. ZDF commissioned the World War II miniseries *Unsere Mütter Unsere Väter* (*Our Mothers Our Fathers*), which has been likened to HBO's *Band of Brothers*. The English version of the series was screened in American theaters under the title *Generation War*. *Babylon Berlin*, based on a series of best-selling novels by Volker Kutscher, is set in the Weimar Republic. It is the most expensive television series ever filmed in Germany and stars Volker Bruch, who was also featured in *Generation War*.

Many popular German reality television series are based on shows broadcast in the United States (see Table 16.1).

Germany automatically qualifies for the Eurovision international song competition because it is broadcast by the ARD consortium. Each participating country submits an original song to be performed on television and radio. The audience votes for the best song via telephone or text message. German contestants have won the Eurovision contest on two occasions: Nicole in 1982 in Harrogate, UK, for "Ein bisschen Frieden" ("A Little Peace") and Lena in 2010 in Oslo for "Satellite."

Broadcasting during the Cold War

During the Cold War, Radio Free Europe (RFE) and Radio Liberty (RL), based in Munich and funded by the U.S. government, broadcast news and commentary into Eastern Europe (RFE) and the Soviet Union (RL). RFE combined its broadcasts with Operation Prospero, a balloon campaign that dropped leaflets into Czechoslovakia

Table 16.1: TELEVISION SERIES

Germany's Next Top Model	America's Next Top Model
Deutschland sucht den Superstar (Germany seeks the Superstar)	*American Idol*
Der Bachelor	*The Bachelor*
The Masked Singer Germany	*The Masked Singer*

and Hungary. RIAS (Radio in the American Sector) was founded by the U.S. occupational forces after World War II in Berlin. RIAS had a huge following in East Germany. The East German government also engaged in frequency wars. In response to Western broadcasting, the authorities launched Der Schwarze Kanal (The Black Channel). Der Schwarze Kanal rebroadcast West German news reedited with Communist commentary. In 1988, RIAS TV began broadcasting along the inner German border. After the fall of the Berlin Wall, DW inherited RIAS's television facilities

German Pop Culture and the United States

Many accomplished German actors and actresses end up working in Hollywood. Franka Potenta starred in *Run Lola Run* (a screenplay written specifically for her by her longtime boyfriend Tom Tykwer) before appearing in *Blow* with Johnny Depp and *The Bourne Conspiracy* with Matt Damon. Diane Kruger (born as Heidkrüger) appeared in *Inglourious Basterds, Unknown*, and the FX crime drama *The Bridge*. Kruger won the Cannes Film Festival Award for Best Actress in 2017 for her role in *The Fade*. Michael Fassbender can be seen in several *X-Men* films and was cast as an American soldier in HBO's World War Two miniseries *Band of Brothers*.

David Hasselhoff, star of the American television series *Baywatch* and *Knight Rider*, has been a pop icon in Germany for over thirty years. His debut album, *Night Rocker* (1985), rose to the top of the Austrian charts. In 1989, RTL, the country's first privately owned television network, began broadcasting American television programs, including *Knight Rider*. That same year, Hasselhoff sang the title track of his new album *Looking for Freedom* at the Brandenburg Gate on New Year's Eve. That performance cemented his status as a cultural icon among some German youth.

American viewers of the long-running comedy show *Saturday Night Live* are familiar with the "Sprockets," a sketch parodying traditional German stereotypes. In the sketch "Dieter," Mike Myers, clad in a black turtleneck sweater and black tights, portrayed a bored West German expressionist. The background music for the sketches was Kraftwerk's 1986 song "Electric Café," and each sketch concluded with identically clad cast members dancing to techno music. A film adaptation of the sketch was scheduled for 2001, featuring Myers, Will Ferrell, Jack Black, and David Hasselhoff. Myers backed out of the project, setting off prolonged litigation.

Herbert Grönemeyer appeared in the 1981 German war movie *Das Boot* (*The Boat*). He soon thereafter turned his attention to music and released fifteen studio albums and forty singles (including "Männer" and "Currywurst"). According to the Bundesverband Musikindustrie, Herbert Grönemeyer is the best-selling German musical artist. Grönemeyer was the first non-English-speaking artist to appear on MTV's *Unplugged*, and he recorded songs for the Olympic Games in Athens (2004) and the FIFA World Cup in Germany (2006). He made his American debut at the Chicago Theater in 2013.

Wendell G. Johnson

Further Reading

Bönker, Kirsten, Julia Obertreis, and Sven Grampp. *Television beyond and across the Iron Curtain*. Newcastle upon Tyne, UK: Cambridge Scholars Publishing, 2016.

Deutsche Welle. "Profile." https://www.dw.com/en/about-dw/profile/s-30688. Accessed December 28, 2019.

Fraser, Catherine C., and Dierk O. Hoffmann. *Pop Culture Germany! Media, Arts, and Lifestyle*. Santa Barbara, CA: ABC-CLIO, 2006.

Hoffmann, Christian R., and Wolfram Bublitz. *Pragmatics of Social Media*. Berlin; Boston: De Gruyter, 2017.

Johnson, A. Ross. *Radio Free Europe and Radio Liberty: The CIA Years and Beyond*. Washington, DC; Stanford, CA: Woodrow Wilson Center Press; Stanford University Press, 2010.

"The License Fee." https://www.rundfunkbeitrag.de/welcome/englisch/index_ger.html. Accessed October 15, 2021.

Media Landscapes. "Germany." https://medialandscapes.org/country/germany/media/print. Accessed December 28, 2019.

Powell, Larson, and Robert R. Shandley, eds. *German Television: Historical and Theoretical Approaches*. New York: Berghahn Books, 2016.

Puddington, Arch. *Broadcasting Freedom: The Cold War Triumph of Radio Free Europe and Radio Liberty*. Lexington: University Press of Kentucky, 2000.

Statista. "Daily Newspaper Circulation." https://www.statista.com/statistics/380784/circulation-daily-newspapers-germany/. Accessed December 28, 2019.

Süddeutsche Zeitung. *Zum Geleit*. October 6, 1945. http://www.sueddeutscher-verlag.de/assets/sv_geschichte/451006_sz_erstausgabe.pdf. Accessed December 28, 2019.

Americanization

Like other countries in the world, Germany has been affected by *Amerikanisierung*, or Americanization. This is the process by which American cultural, political, and economic systems find their way into other countries and influence or change them. Many effects of Americanization in German culture coincide with the rise of modernization, particularly as it's related to industry in the beginning of the twentieth century. During this period, the United States often served as the paragon of industry and best practices. Fordism and Taylorism, in particular, played a large role in influencing German manufacturing. Taylorism, based on ideas by Fred Taylor (1856–1915), was the scientific management used to create efficiencies in production. Similarly, Henry Ford (1863–1947), the automobile maker, created well-known techniques to mass-produce his products on a large scale, for example, by mechanizing tasks that otherwise would have been performed by humans. One such innovation of this period was the assembly line. Germany began partial use of these methods during World War I. These methods were seen as the answer to post-World War I issues, which led to similar efficiencies in other areas of life, including housework. American inventions like the vacuum cleaner greatly reduced the difficulty of women's housework in the early and mid-twentieth century.

In the Weimar Republic (1918–1933, a democratic turn in Germany's history occurring after World War I and directly preceding the Third Reich), other effects of

Americanization were seen on German culture. American films were popular and demonstrated American customs and fashions. Jazz, too, (and later Swing) became popular forms of musical entertainment in this period. However, the Weimar Republic also saw a backlash against Americanization and modernization, sparking a back-to-nature movement. With the rise of the Third Reich, the United States' cultural influence slowed, although the efficiencies of scientific management as relating to production remained important to Nazi invasions and political expansion.

Americanization became more pronounced after the end of the Second World War. As one of the Allied powers, the United States helped govern immediately after the war and then would occupy a portion of the Federal Republic of Germany (FRG, West Germany). The influence the United States had over West Germany in the postwar period cannot be overstated. With the Marshall Plan, the United States aided the FRG in rebuilding a robust economy and industry. In occupying part of southwest Germany, the United States also brought in a significant number of soldiers and other civilian employees who performed a multitude of political and administrative roles in the aftermath of the war. The soldiers brought their own cultural products (films, music, print media) that disseminated into the areas in and surrounding their zone and sector in Berlin.

The American Forces Network (AFN) was a radio station started in Europe as a part of the War Department during World War II. It was maintained in the postwar period because of the large number of soldiers and civilians working in support of the U.S. government and would later become part of the broadcasting arm of the Department of Defense. The station was intended as a news and entertainment service "from home" for those serving in Europe, playing wherever troops were stationed, including southwestern Germany and Berlin. AFN broadcast popular American music, as well as jazz and classical, and it was instrumental in introducing the newest U.S. records and sounds, such as rock and roll, to broader Germany.

American cinema, too, continued to play a role in influencing film culture in the postwar period. A popular German film on youth culture, *Die Halbstarken* (1956, dir. Georg Tressler), for example, takes up narrative themes and visual elements found in *The Wild One* (1953, dir. László Benedek) and *Rebel without a Cause* (1955, dir. Nicholas Ray).

Today, Americanization still occurs. With the rise of the internet, culture can travel immediately from one country to another, and, thus, American music and other media (Hollywood films especially) can be found on German airwaves and in theaters. American chains and brands are important to the German *Alltag* (daily life). McDonald's, Starbucks, The Gap, Levi's, and Snickers are easily found in most German cities and towns, nestled alongside German and European stores and brands. Indeed, in the mid-twentieth century, another, slightly disparaging term for Americanization emerged: cocacolonization. The term refers to the distribution and market takeover of the Coca-Cola brand. German émigré Billy Wilder directed a brilliant English-language comedy about precisely this topic in 1961 entitled *One, Two, Three*.

Anglicisms or Americanisms—that is, words that are English in origin—have begun to appear more frequently in German writing, as well. For example, though the

German word for "to download," "*runterladen*" exists, it is just as common for someone to use the alternate verb "*downloaden*." It is also common to see English words in advertisements, such as McDonald's *Der Big Vegan*.

Nichole Neuman

See also: Chapter 2: Berlin Wall. Chapter 3: Armed Forces; Germany and the United States. Chapter 4: German Automobile Industry; Manufacturing. Chapter 9: Foreign Influences on German. Chapter 13: Overview. Chapter 14: Overview. Chapter 16: Film; *Rundfunkgebühren*.

Further Reading

Maulucci, Thomas W, and Detlef Junker, eds. *GIs in Germany: The Social, Economic, Cultural, and Political History of the American Military Presence*. Washington, DC; New York: German Historical Institute: Cambridge University Press, 2013.

Stephan, Alexander, ed. *The Americanization of Europe: Culture, Diplomacy, and Anti-Americanism after 1945*. New York: Berghahn Books, 2006.

Boulevard Press

The Boulevard Press (*Boulevardpresse*) in Germany is so named because its papers used to be sold in kiosks and newsstands along the busy thoroughfares/boulevards of German cities. The *Boulevardzeitungen*, comparable to British tabloids, often feature colorful headlines, scandalous stories, and sensationalistic visual material. Berlin's Boulevard Press traces its roots back to the *Lokal-Anzeiger,* launched in 1883 by August Scherl. Early editions of the *Lokal-Anzeiger* featured want ads and light entertainment. By 1889, its daily circulation reached 123,000, making it Berlin's largest newspaper. The success of the *Lokal-Anzeiger* prompted the publishing company Ullstein to launch *Die Morgenpost*, which featured illustrations by Heinrich Zille and incorporated elements of Berlin's unique dialect into its copy. Circulation of the *Morgenpost* soon surpassed that of the *Lokal-Anzeiger*. On the eve of the First World War, nearly half of all Berliners regularly read either the *Morgenpost* or *Lokal-Anzeiger*.

The most popular, and perhaps most notorious *Boulevardzeitung*, is the *B.Z.* (abbreviated from *Berliner Zeitung*; there is another left-leaning paper called *Berliner Zeitung*), published Monday through Saturday by Axel Springer SE. *BZ am Mittag* ("BZ at Noon") first appeared in 1904 and became popular because of its large sports section. By 1919, nearly half of every newspaper was devoted to sports and spectacular events, such as aviation rallies. After the Second World War, *B.Z.* included photographs of topless female models on its inside pages. This regular feature, once headlined as "Kitty," was included to entice male readers to purchase the newspaper. The editorial board of *B.Z.* acknowledged that many female readers found the pictures offensive, so the paper abandoned this practice in 2018 and substituted pictures of models in their underwear.

At the present, Axel Springer Publishing Company also publishes a Sunday edition, *Bild am Sonntag,* as well as regional editions, *Bild Hamburg* and *Bild Köln* (Cologne). *Bild's* combined daily circulation is nearly 5 million, making it Germany's most widely circulated daily. These papers are sold at newsstands and often have an online platform. These tabloids do not publish sensational exposés (as does *The Sun* in Great Britain or *National Enquirer* in the United States), nor are they condensed versions of their parent newspapers. Rather, their target audience are younger people aged eighteen to thirty-five who are not habitual newspapers readers.

Wendell G. Johnson

See also: Chapter 6: Aristocracy and the Elites. Chapter 9: Language Development in the Third Reich. Chapter 16: Overview; Springer, Axel (1912–1985).

Further Reading

Fritzsche, Peter. *Reading Berlin 1900.* Cambridge, MA: Harvard University Press, 1996.

Hessel, Franz. *Walking in Berlin: A Flaneur in the Capital.* Amanda DeMarco, trans. Cambridge, MA: MIT Press, 2017.

Newspapers in Germany. https://germanculture.com.ua/germany-facts/newspapers-in -germany/. Accessed December 28, 2019.

Fashion Designers

Karl Lagerfeld (1933–2019) was perhaps the world's best-known German designer. Born in Hamburg to a German mother and a Swedish father, Lagerfeld has designed for many of Europe's top fashion houses. He moved to Paris in 1953 and started working for several designers, first Pierre Balmain for approximately one year, and then Jean Patou, where he designed haute couture collections for five years. His later work for the upscale ready-to-wear house Chloe was known both for its high fashion and high camp. Lagerfeld designed furs for Fendi, shoes for Valentino, and was responsible for modernizing Chanel's line while maintaining its distinctive character. His designs won awards for the House of Chanel in 1982 and 1991.

Lagerfeld's own line, KL, combines bold tailoring with easy wearability. In 2004, he launched a signature collection for the mass-market retailer Hennes & Mauritz (better known in the United States as H&M) and went on to design outfits for Madonna's Re-Invention World Tour and Kylie Minogue's Showgirl tour. Personally, he was known for his distinctive individual style, sporting a stiff white collar, fingerless gloves, dark glasses, and a ponytail.

Wolfgang Joop was born near the Sanssouci Palace in Potsdam, Germany, in 1944. He studied art education, advertising, and psychology at the University of Braunschweig but never completed a degree. After entering a design competition in 1970, he won the top three prizes. In 1979, he launched his JOOP! line and presented his first ready-to-wear line in 1982. Joop's line of jeans ranks among his greatest successes. He sought to design his clothes according to the ethos of traditional American sportswear. Joop subsequently added eyewear, shoes, accessories, and perfume to his design collection before selling his company entirely in 2001.

Joop founded his high-end couture label Wunderkind in 2003 and was invited by the Council of Fashion Designers of America to premiere the collection internationally in New York the next year (it showed there for three seasons before moving to Paris). Currently, Joop works as a professional illustrator and has also appeared as a judge on the television show *Germany's Next Topmodel* (hosted by Heidi Klum). Joop's daughter Jette has designed products under her own name, notably fragrances and flatware.

Jil Sander was born in Wesselburen, Germany, in 1943. After studying textile design in Krefeld, she spent two years in the United States as an exchange student and worked as a fashion journalist before embarking on her career as a designer. At that

Karl Otto Lagerfeld (1933–2019) was a German fashion designer who worked for fashion houses such as Fendi and Chanel. (Fashionstock .com/Dreamstime.com)

time, Karl Lagerfeld was the only other German designer with an international reputation. Sander opened her first boutique in Hamburg, and her first collection under her own label debuted in 1973 (she subsequently added cosmetics and eyewear to her collection). Aside from her flagship store in Paris, her boutiques can also be found in Japan, Hong Kong, in Europe, and throughout the United States. Sander's style is best described as luxurious minimalism. Her designs are known for the high quality of their materials and craftsmanship, and clothes are perfectly proportioned with little or no decoration.

Prada purchased Sander's business in 1999. She stayed on as creative designer for the company but soon fell out with Prada's head, Patrizio Bertelli. She returned to the company in 2003 but left again in 2005. Sander joined forces with the Japanese company Fast Retailing to oversee both the women's and men's wear named +J for its Uniqlo label. The final collection for the collaborative label was its fall/winter 2011 line.

Wendell G. Johnson

See also: Chapter 10: Regional Clothing.

Further Reading

Alford, Holly Price, and Anne Stegemeyer. *Who's Who in Fashion.* New York: Fairchild Books, 2010.

Martin, Richard. *The St. James Fashion Encyclopedia. A Survey of Style from 1945 to the Present.* Detroit: Visible Ink, 1997

Mauriès, Patrick. *Chanel Catwalk: The Complete Karl Lagerfeld Collections.* New Haven, CT: Yale University Press, 2016.

O'Hagan, Andrew. "The Maddening and Brilliant Karl Lagerfeld." *New York Times Style Magazine.* October 12, 2015. https://www.nytimes.com/2015/10/12/t-magazine/karl-lagerfeld-interview.html. Accessed March 29, 2020.

Polan, Brenda, and Roger Tredre. *The Great Fashion Designers.* Oxford, UK: Berg, 2009.

Film

Characterized by many influential stylistic periods, film in Germany has a long and illustrious history. Exhibition of short, silent films dates back to 1895 and gained popularity among the working class, who would flock to *Kintopps* to watch short films with trivial subjects (Brockman, 2010, p. 13). As with other national cinemas of this period, German film would soon transition to telling longer-form stories. German cinema is also particularly known for its many visual and technical advances in cinematography.

German film rose to international prominence shortly before and during the Weimar Republic (1919–1933). The period was characterized by horror films (*The Student of Prague, Nosferatu,* and *The Cabinet of Dr. Caligari*), as well as in increased interest in psychology and changes within society. At a time of increased urbanization, changing gender roles, and a population recovering from a terrible war, cinema expressed many of the anxieties about these developments and their societal impacts. A production company, UFA (Universal Film AG), emerged in 1917 with a location in Babelsberg near Berlin and was soon responsible for producing many of the films of the early Weimar Republic. Many filmmakers of this era—Ernst Lubitsch, Robert Wiene, Fritz Lang, F. W. Murnau, G. W. Pabst—are still lauded today for their unique visions, producing some of the most memorable movies of all time. Lang's 1927 *Metropolis,* one of the earliest science-fiction movies, and Wiene's 1920 *Caligari,* which explores themes of madness, manipulation, and the after-effects of World War I (1914–1918), both consistently rank as two of the best movies ever made.

Expressionism emerged as a dominant cinematic style in dialogue with the changing times of the interwar period. This avant-garde style, which included *Caligari,* focused on the subjective (i.e., interior, emotional) experience, and the movies used high-contrast lighting, shadows, and abstracted sets. In addition to experimentation with style, others were investigating how to combine images and film to create animation. Lotte (Charlotte) Reiniger created one of the first feature-length animated film, *Die Abenteuer des Prinzen Achmed (The Adventures of Prince Achmed)* in 1926 utilizing paper cutouts. In addition to avant-garde films, a popular genre of this period was the *Bergfilm* or mountain film genre. These films showcased dazzling mountain landscapes and feats of mountain climbing.

Many stars of the era also acted intermittently in Hollywood, which often worked to lure German talent to the United States. Emil Jannings, for example, was an incredibly popular and respected actor during this period and was able to use his recognition in Europe to secure contracts in Hollywood, where he would go on to win the first Academy Award for Best Actor in 1929 for his work on two American productions. The rise of "talkies," or films with sound, compelled Jannings and other German-speaking actors to return to Europe.

However, with the rise of the National Socialists to power in January 1933, hundreds of cinema professionals (directors, cameramen, actors, producers, etc.) were forced to flee Germany. Indeed, almost immediately after the *Machtergreifung* in 1933, Jews as well as dissidents were banned outright from working in the film industry in Germany. Film during the Third Reich fell under the purview of Joseph Goebbels, the Minister of Propaganda. Whether outright propaganda—see, for example, Leni Riefenstahl's *Triumph of the Will* (1935) about the Nazi Congress in Nuremburg or the anti-Semitic faux documentary *The Eternal Jew* (1940) or popular entertainment films—all cinema served the State. Plainly, this meant glorifying Germany and its power and creating clear negative images of the country's internal (e.g., Jewish) and external enemies. This also meant that other popular national cinemas, most notably Hollywood exports, were now banned by the Nazi regime. *Die Feuerzangbowle* (*The Punchbowl*) was shot in Babelsberg in four months in 1943, in the middle of the war. Still regularly shown on TV, this movie remains very popular not the least because of his lead, the actor Heinz Rühmann, who went to the *Führerhauptquartier* (Führer Headquarters) to get permission to have the film shown. It premiered in January 1944 in the early afternoon as air attacks were expected at night.

Once the Allies won World War II (1945), they temporarily took control of overseeing cinematic fare in the immediate postwar period before the founding of the East and West German states in 1949. Initially, films during this time showed the devastation of the war. The *Trümmerfilm*—or rubble film—genre marked this period, which often showed cities in ruin and featured narratives of a slow and complicated return to normal life, for example, *The Murderers Are among Us* (1946). When Germany split into two countries—the Federal Republic of Germany (FRG, or West Germany, 1949–1990) and the German Democratic Republic (GDR, or East Germany, 1949–1990)—so, too, did their national cinemas.

In West Germany, popular film genres that dominated the 1950s through the 1970s were *Arztfilme* (medical dramas focusing on doctors and moral dilemmas), light comedies with romantic subplots, and *Heimatfilme* (films set in small villages and which focused on the local, natural, and bucolic, with emphases on folk costumes, folk songs, and traditional, conservative values). These films often employed escapism and ignored the atrocities of the war Germany had perpetrated.

As a protest of the noncritical, mainstream popular cinema of the FRG, a group of young, radical filmmakers gathered in 1962 to author the Oberhausen Manifesto.

This document, named for the short film festival in Oberhausen, Germany, declared a need for a new type of filmmaking that challenged conventional and generic norms. From this the New German Cinema (NGC, also known as the Young German Cinema) movement began. Perhaps the most well-known and critically acclaimed period of filmmaking since the Weimar period, NGC saw socially critical films that also departed stylistically from contemporary popular cinema. Filmmakers from this period, such as Rainer Werner Fassbinder, Alexander Kluge, Wim Wenders, Volker Schlöndorff, Margarethe von Trotta, and Werner Herzog, produced films that garnered international attention. Notable films of this period include *Abschied von Gestern* (*Yesterday Girl*, 1966), *Ali: Fear Eats the Soul* (1974), and *Germany in Autumn* (1978). Television movies or miniseries also gained in popularity throughout the 1970s and 1980s with well-known filmmakers Fassbinder and Edgar Reitz also producing fare for the small screen (*Berlin, Alexanderplatz* and *Heimat*, respectively).

In the GDR, the production company DEFA (Deutsche Film AG) took over operations of cinema in the Soviet Zone. Known for contributions to genre films (particularly children's films, science-fiction movies, and Eastern Bloc "westerns"), East German cinema was imbued with socialist values. Important East German filmmakers include Konrad Wolf (*I Was 19*, *Solo Sunny*) and Heiner Carow (*The Legend of Paul and Paula*). Carow's film *Paul and Paula* remains a cult favorite, though its initial release was threatened by its content. Indeed, politics governed not only content of DEFA films, but whether or not films could be distributed in the country. Many filmmakers and actors would eventually defect to the FRG in order to enjoy more artistic freedom or in opposition to communist principles.

Upon reunification in 1990, German cinema again rose to international prominence, in terms of both critical and popular reception. Florian Henckel von Donnersmarck's 2006 *Das Leben der Anderen* (*The Life of Others*) received the 2007 Oscar for Best Foreign Movie. Directors Tom Tykwer, Wim Wenders, and Werner Herzog routinely create films in the United States and other countries (*Cloud Atlas*, *Buena Vista Social Club*, and *Grizzly Man*, respectively). Germany is also home to many important production studios for both German and international cinema, including Babelsberg Studio and Bavaria Film, both of which have produced movies since the 1910s. Quentin Tarantino's *Inglourious Basterds* was mostly filmed in Babelsberg.

Nichole Neuman

See also: Chapter 2: Overview. Chapter 3: *Die Wende*. Chapter 6: Jews in Germany. Chapter 10: Punctuality. Chapter 11: Expressionism (*Expressionismus*) and Its Successors (1905–1925). Chapter 16: Overview.

Further Reading

Brockmann, Stephen. *A Critical History of German Film*. Rochester, NY: Camden House, 2010.

Hake, Sabine. *German National Cinema*. New York: Routledge, 2002.

Pflaum, Hans Günther. *Germany on Film: Theme and Content in the Cinema of the Federal Republic of Germany.* Detroit: Wayne State University Press, 1989.

Pinkert, Anke. *Film and Memory in East Germany.* Bloomington: Indiana University Press, 2008.

Journalism under the Nazi Regime

With a decentralized press and daily issues of local, regional, and national newspapers, Weimar Germany reflected on a long press tradition, albeit one that was accustomed to frequent government interference. The close relationship of press and government, the repeated threat to the freedom of the press through "emergency" decrees, and the dismal economic situation of most publishers in the early 1930s facilitated the Nazi attempt to direct the press. Less than a month after Nazi ascension to power, two decrees strictly limited press freedom, euphemistically called *Zum Schutz des deutschen Volkes* (for the protection of the German people, February 4, 1933) and *Zum Schutz von Volk und Staat* (for the protection of people and state, February 28, 1933). Since initially the mainstream press was not targeted, papers looked on directives rather passively and adopted a wait-and-see attitude. Journalists now also had to request accreditation explicitly, leading to increased regimentation and control. The institution of a *Berufsliste* (professional register) ensured that journalists and their spouses were of Aryan origin.

Instead of censoring articles after they had been written but before they were to be published, the Nazis started to give out pre-writing directives in June 1933 during daily press conferences. These confidential content instructions appeared under a variety of names, such as *Sprachregelungen* (language regulations/instructions), *Presseanweisungen* (press briefings), *Pressebestellungen* (press messages), and *Verlautbarungen* (bulletins). Recipients were a select audience of about 150 journalists, representatives of major papers that maintained offices in Berlin. The official interpretation of the news was to be incorporated into the respective papers and passed on to local papers. In a meeting that took place after the press conference, a limited number of journalists were informed in a much more open fashion; in this so-called *Nachbörse*, government representatives candidly justified news fabrications as indispensable. An estimated 50,000–100,000 instructions are available today solely because some journalists did not obey the disposal order.

A typical example is the instruction from the *Sammlung Brammer* of January 10, 1934, where the journalists, who had access to the instructions, signed with their initials and times of transmission, are indicated. Marinus van der Lubbe (1909–1934), a Dutch worker, had been convicted of starting the Reichstag fire and executed.

Kommentare zu der Hinrichtung Lubbes sind unerwünscht.
[Commentaries regarding Lubbes' execution are not welcome]

Gesehen [seen by]: *D.* (Dertinger), *Fa.* (Falk), *K.* (Kausch)
weitergegeben [passed on to]
an   Hb. (Hamburg, i.e., *Hamburger Nachrichten*) *um*   [at] *12.58 Uhr*
an   Bresl. (Breslau, i.e., *Schlesische Zeitung*) *um*   *1.08"*
an   Chmn. (Chemnitz, i.e., *Allgemeine Zeitung*) *um*   *12.58"*

The journalists took handwritten notes based on an oral presentation of the government representative. The instruction sounds like a wish, as *unerwünscht* (undesirable) does not indicate an order. However, in the context of the daily press briefings, it did amount to one. The Propaganda Ministry expected strict compliance with its orders and did not shy away from closing newspapers that did not follow instructions. Nazi-affiliated-papers could be closed just as easily.

Katharina Barbe

See also: Chapter 9: Language Development in the Third Reich.

Further Reading

De Mendelssohn, Peter. *Zeitungsstadt Berlin: Menschen und Mächte in der Geschichte der Deutschen Presse*. Berlin: Ullstein, 1982.

Denne, David B. *Inhumanities: Nazi Interpretations of Western Culture*. Cambridge, UK; New York: Cambridge University Press, 2012.

Fulda, B. *Press and Politics in the Weimar Republic*. Oxford: Oxford University Press, 2008.

Mühlberger, Detlef. *Hitler's Voice: The Völkischer Beobachter, 1920–1933*. Oxford, UK; New York: Peter Lang, 2004.

Müsse, W. *Die Reichspresseschule—Journalisten für die Diktatur? Ein Beitrag zur Geschichte des Journalismus im Dritten Reich*. München: Saur, 1995.

Oschinksi, N. *Inhalt und Umsetzung früher nationalsozialistischer Presseanweisungen— Drei Göttinger Zeitungen im Vergleich (1933–1935)*. München: GRIN Verlag, 2007.

Toepser-Ziegert, Gabriele, and Hans Bohrmann. *NS-Presseanweisungen der Vorkriegszeit: Edition und Dokumentation*. München; New York: Saur, 1984.

Ostalgie

Ostalgie or "fondly recalling the bad old days" (Zeitchick, 2003), is a surprising cultural development associated with the collapse of the former DDR. The term is a portmanteau from the German words *Ost* (east) and *Nostalgie* (nostalgia), signifying a longing for aspects of life under the communist regime in the German Democratic Republic. Many moviegoers in the United States were introduced to *Ostalgie* by the international hit movie *Good-bye Lenin* (2003). Following the release of *Good-bye Lenin*, several television shows about life in the GDR also appeared. The *Ostalgie Show* provided features of daily life in the GDR and interviews with East German entertainers. Nearly 5 million viewers tuned into the *Ostalgie Show* when it premiered, giving the program a market share of 21.8% of the viewing audience. The *DDR Show*, hosted by Olympic figure-skating champion Katarina Witt, highlighted some of the problematic areas of life in East Germany.

The Center for the Documentation of the East German Daily Life (in Eisenhüttenstadt) preserves 50,000 samples of the material culture of the DDR. It was not the intent of the East German government to provide an alternative to the material affluence of the West, but a successor to it. In the view of the *Wessies* or West Germans, these artifacts suggest a simpler, less materialistic time. For the *Ossies* or East Germans, they have become cultural icons of their rustic homeland. Despite their reputation for shoddy quality and gruesome styling, many East German products such as Mocha Fix Gold coffee, Rotkäppchen ("Little Red Riding Hood") sparkling wine, Spreewaldgurken (pickled gherkins from the Spreewald), and Zeha footwear, continue to attract customers. Wernesgrüner Bier, a traditional brewery since 1436, was expropriated in East Germany but still exported their beer to West Germany and all over the world. The Ampelmann stores in Berlin sell souvenirs based on facsimiles of the *Ampelmänner*—a red or green figure seen on crossing lights in East Berlin.

Several East German rock bands survived the demise of the GDR and enjoy success in reunited Germany. The Puhdys, perhaps East Germany's oldest and best-known rock band, continued to record and tour until 2016. City, founded in 1972, keeps on playing before sold-out crowds. The band's most famous record, *Am Fenster*, has sold 10 million copies. The Puhdys' *Geh zu ihr* (*Go to Her*) and *Wenn ein Mensch lebt* (*When a Person lives*) were featured prominently in the East German movie *Die Legende von Paul und Paula* (1973). Both the Puhdys and Karat, founded in East Berlin, were among the few bands granted permission by East German authorities to perform in the West.

Many infamous sites in Berlin, now turned into museums, caution against romanticizing life in the German Democratic Republic. The Stasi put millions of citizens of the GDR under surveillance. The archive in its former headquarters in Lichtenberg holds sixty-nine *miles* of files. The Stasi prison in Hohenschönhausen was feared for the physical (waterboarding) and psychological (prisoners were forced to sleep underneath bright lights) torture inflicted on its inmates. The prison was left off any East Berlin maps, and only people loyal to the regime were allowed to live around that location. The so-called Tränenpalast (Palace of Tears), adjacent to the Friedrichstrasse train station, displays the former border crossing between East and West Berlin where elaborate and intrusive customs checks were carried out, and where East German citizens said good bye to their West German relatives in tears.

Wendell G. Johnson

See also: Chapter 2: Honecker, Erich (1912–1994). Chapter 3: Government and Politics in the German Democratic Republic. Chapter 9: Language Development in Divided Germany. Chapter 14: Beer; Food and Drink in the German Democratic Republic. Chapter 15: Witt, Katarina (1965–). Chapter 16: Film.

Further Reading

Castillo, Greg. "East as True West: Redeeming Bourgeois Culture from Socialist Realism to *Ostalgie*." In György Péteri, ed. *Imagining the West in Eastern Europe and the Soviet Union,* 87–110. Pittsburgh: University of Pittsburgh Press, 2010.

Cooke, Paul. "*Ostalgie's* Not What It Used to Be: The German Television GDR Craze of 2003." *German Politics & Society* 22(4): 134–150, 2004. https://www.jstor.org/stable/23740783. Accessed February 24, 2020.

Deutsche Welle. "East German Brands Thrive 30 Years after Berlin Wall Fell." https://www.dw.com/en/east-german-brands-thrive-30-years-after-berlin-wall-fell/a-4752593. Accessed February 23, 2020.

Hodgin, Nick. *Screening the East: Heimat, Memory and Nostalgia in German Film Since 1989.* New York: Berghahn Books, 2011.

Zeitchick, Steven. "German Ostalgie: Fondly Recalling the Bad Old Days." *New York Times,* October 7, 2003.

Media Photography

The research of Alexander von Humboldt played a pivotal role in introducing photography to Germany. Humboldt viewed a number of daguerreotypes in Paris in 1839 and wrote several treatises about them. Shortly thereafter, the first photographic studios in the country were opened in 1845. The nineteenth century produced several noteworthy female practitioners. Bertha Wehner-Beckman (1815–1901) was Germany's first professional female photographer. She worked in daguerreotypes, and her pictures are on display in Leipzig's Stadtgeschichtliches Museum (Municipal Museum). Emilie Biever (1810–1884) was a successful portrait photographer in Hamburg who specialized in hand-tinted pictures. Sophia Goudstikker (1865–1924) attended art school in Dresden and was the first unmarried German woman to be granted a license for photography. Her work defied the contemporary depiction of women, and she has become a subject of gender studies by American scholars.

Many of the best-known German photographers of the early twentieth century worked in Berlin: Steffi Brandl shot the Weimar stars of the 1920s and 1930s; Heinz Hajek-Halk shot color montages and incorporated nudes into his work; Erich Saloman photographed Marlene Dietrich; Henrich Zille, also a gifted illustrator and caricaturist, documented working-class neighborhoods in the capital.

After the Second World War, photography continued to develop in divided Germany. In the West, the Düsseldorf School of Photography produced a coterie of artists who studied under Bernd and Hilla Becher at the Düsseldorf Academy of Art in the 1970s. The Bechers were adherents of the New Objectivity (Neue Sachlichkeit) of the 1920s. Responding to the "New Topographics" (an exhibition curated by William Jenkins in 1975), the Düsseldorf School photographed urban landscapes and interior environments. Their photographs minimized the human figure and blurred the boundaries between painting and photography.

In the East, Siegfried Wittenburg, from Rostock, documented daily life in the GDR. His exhibition "Greetings from the GDR: Daily Life in a Vanished State" included images of buildings and everyday streets scenes from the northern part of East Germany. Arno Fischer, Wittenburg's colleague, was commissioned to document the reconstruction of East Berlin. Ulrich Wüst's work includes images of mass-produced prefabricated apartment blocks (*Plattenbau*) and documents developments in East and West Berlin after the fall of the Berlin Wall. Helga Paris also shot photographs of East German houses and accepted a commission for an exhibition in 1986. The show was canceled, however, because her photographs portrayed derelict housing in the city of Halle. The German Photography Museum in Leipzig is the largest photographic museum in Germany. The museum houses 70,000 historic photographs, 3,000 vintage cameras, and a permanent exhibit devoted to GDR-era photography.

Wendell G. Johnson

See also: Chapter 2: Overview. Chapter 3: *Die Wende*. Chapter 12: Museums. Chapter 13: Dietrich, Marlene (1901–1992).

Further Reading

Gronert, Stefan. *The Düsseldorf School of Photography*. London: Thames & Hudson, 2009.

Sachsse, Rolf. "Germany." In John Hannavy, ed. *Encyclopedia of Nineteenth-Century Photography*, 581–586. New York: Routledge, 2008.

Rundfunkgebühren

The *Rundfunkgebühren*, also known as *Rundfunkbeitrag*, are fees that each German household and business is required to pay to fund public broadcasting. The scope of broadcasting covered by the fees includes television and radio, as well as some video and online offerings.

This method of support for broadcasting is regulated under public law and, as aforementioned, applies to both professional and private realms. Paid by bank transfer (which is how most bills, such as rent, utilities, and even online shopping, are paid in Germany), the fees in 2019 were €17,50 (around $20) per month. Each household must pay the fees, regardless of how many people live in it; whether they consume television, internet, or radio; or how many devices (radios, televisions, computers) they have. Similarly, businesses and institutions are also required to pay the tax, depending on how many sites of operation—including business vehicles—the company or organization has. The regulation of the fees aims for transparency. Indeed, 70.3% goes to ARD, a network with regional broadcasters; 24.9% to ZDF, a national public television broadcaster; 2.9% to *Deutschlandradio* (public radio); and 1.9% is reserved for *Landesmedienanstalten*, or the state media authorities. Although there are some exceptions allowed under the laws governing *Rundfunkgebühren*—for example, some second residences or unemployed qualify for a waiver—most Germans pay this tax as a matter of course.

The reasons behind mandatory support of public broadcasting in Germany are largely ideological. *Rundfunkgebühren* aim to provide the public with information, educational programming, advice, and entertainment, all investigated and presented independently. This approach protects not just content but also quality, and allows for a very diverse range of topics of interest to be represented. Indeed, the *Rundfunkbeitrag* website claims that there is a "quality program for each taste." The fees, then, allow for independent reporting and findings without stations and programmers needing to worry about sponsorship or corporate interests. The fees are also determined democratically: the Parliament of the 16 German states (Bundesrat) considers and accepts the fees each cycle.

Public financing for broadcasting is intended to help citizens create their own opinions from a factually sound base that is objective and neutral. The *Rundfunkbeitrag* website underscores this, claiming that such programming forms "the basis for [their] personal freedom of opinion, social plurality of opinion, and our democracy." To achieve this, programming strives to be timely, critical, and provide diversity, both in terms of content and to various audiences. Further, programming at *Rundfunkbeitrag*-supported broadcasters focuses on regional, national, and international investigative reporting.

The TV stations ARD and ZDF, and Deutschlandradio, which oversees multiple radio broadcasters, all support entertainment, sports, culture, and news and have extensive online presences. Included in this programming is extensive engagement with and programs for children (e.g., KIKA, Logo, *Die Sendung mit der Maus*). In its attempt to program for the citizenry, broadcasters supported by *Rundfunkgebühren* work to be *barrierefrei*, or accessible. That means that 70–95% of its television programming is subtitled, and they are working toward 100% for those who are deaf and hard of hearing.

Nichole Neuman

See also: Chapter 4: Overview. Chapter 10: Shopping. Chapter 16: Overview.

Further Reading

Nakamura, Kiyoshi, and Koichiro Agata. *Convergence of Telecommunications and Broadcasting in Japan, United Kingdom and Germany: Technological Change, Public Policy and Market Structure.* London: Routledge, 2001.

Potschka, Christian. *Towards a Market in Broadcasting: Communications Policy in the UK and Germany.* Basingstoke, UK; New York: Palgrave Macmillan, 2012.

Rundfunkbeitrag. https://www.rundfunkbeitrag.de/. Accessed December 28, 2019.

Springer, Axel (1912–1985)

Axel Springer refers to both a prominent and powerful publisher, and the publishing company he founded. He rose to notoriety in the postwar period as an outspoken critic of the student movement in the late 1960s in West Germany. He was also a

Axel Springer (1912–1985) set up a large publishing empire, including the tabloid *Bild-Zeitung*, which is still in circulation. (Cineberg Ug/Dreamstime.com)

severe critic of communism and, therefore, of the Deutsche Demokratische Republic (East Germany or the GDR), and used his influence to campaign for a reunited Germany.

Born in Altona near Hamburg on May 2, 1912, Axel Cäsar Springer would spend almost his entire life in the publishing industry. After a short period during his youth as a typesetter, he worked as a cub reporter. In 1933 (the same year the National Socialists took control of the German government), he returned to his hometown paper and soon became chief editor (1935). From 1941 to 1945, he was a literary publisher. After World War II, he established the publishing house that would bear his name with his father, Hinrich Springer.

The Springers began their career in 1946 producing the *Nordwestdeutsche Hefte*, a monthly magazine tackling a broad range of topics, from politics to household. Soon thereafter, they created *Hörzu* (initially *Hör Zu!*), a weekly magazine that highlights upcoming radio and television broadcasts. In 1948, they began publishing their first daily newspaper, the *Hamburger Abendblatt*. The publishing house (Axel Springer SE), initially based in Hamburg, then in Berlin (with a publishing house built next to the Berlin Wall in 1966), would become an important part of the West German *Wirtschaftswunder*, or the incredible economic growth and success of West Germany in the postwar period. Throughout the 1950s, Axel Springer grew the publishing house into an empire, which included the *Bild-Zeitung* (today one of the best-selling tabloid newspapers in Europe) and *Die Welt*. With these titles, Springer and his company acquired access to a national market and considerable power and recognition on a national level.

By the mid-1960s, the Springer publishing company had cornered 50–70% of the newspaper market in West Berlin, as well as 26% of the daily and 29% of the weekly markets across the country, and Axel Springer was one of the most powerful media figures in West Germany. It was during this period, too, that Axel Springer rose to notoriety. A student movement, critical of Germany's National Socialist legacy and the many political, educational, and social institutions that still had former Nazis in positions of power, began to demonstrate regularly and demanded accountability. These students also supported global social justice causes during that decade. On June 2, 1967, during a demonstration against the Shah of Iran's visit to West Berlin, a student named Benno Ohnesorg was shot in the back by Karl-Heinz Kurras, a police officer, and died. The next day, *Bild* printed of Ohnesorg's death that he was "a victim of riots, staged by aggressive youths," said nothing of the policeman who shot him, and blamed students for things having gone amok. This misrepresentation of the day's events was commonplace in Springer's publications, which largely protected police from criticism and made inflammatory claims about the student opposition. After this event, "*Enteignet Springer!*" ("Oust Springer!") became a popular slogan among the student collectives, with the Springer media continuing to paint student activists as terrorists. Therefore, when the spokesperson of the student movement, Rudi Dutschke, was shot in the head by Josef Bachmann on April 11, 1968, the blame was laid at the publisher's feet. To this day, Axel Springer is implicated in and shares the responsibility for Dutschke's attempted murder because of the strong agitations against the 68ers (as the student movement came to be known) that were regularly found in the pages of his publications.

Throughout the remainder of his life and involvement in the publishing house, Springer would continually push for the development of technology in new media, including the launching of the video disc (similar to a DVD). Of this venture, Springer said, "I for one will never become tired . . . of advocating that publishers have their share of the electronic media that exist to date, and even more, that in all new information systems that will come to us in the future." This marked the beginning of the transformation of the company from a traditional print media publisher to a digital media company. During this period, too, the company added titles for specific audiences, for example, women; became involved in television broadcasting; and began publishing titles in other parts of Europe.

Alex Springer died in West Berlin on September 22, 1985. He was preceded in death by his son, Axel Springer Jr., and survived by his fifth wife, Friede (his son's former nanny), and his children Barbara and Raimund Nicolaus. His legacy lives on in his media company, where his widow is the main owner. Even today, the company lives by the five mandates Springer authored in 1967 (twice revised) to guide his business:

1. We stand up for freedom, the rule of law, democracy, and a united Europe.
2. We support the Jewish people and the right of existence of the State of Israel.
3. We demonstrate solidarity with the free values of the United States of America.

4. We uphold the principles of a free market economy and its social responsibility.

5. We reject political and religious extremism.

Following the reunification of East and West Germany in 1990, Axel Springer SE began publishing almost immediately in the former GDR. In 1995, they incrementally began launching websites for their national titles. In 2014, the company sold some of their most recognized, founding papers, including the *Berliner Morgenpost* and *Hörzu*, in order to fund continued digital expansion in the twenty-first century.

Although Springer's legacy is inextricably linked to not only Germany's publishing industry in the twentieth century, but also the political and social turmoil of the late 1960s in West Germany, it also extends to charitable interests. The publisher donated a considerable amount of money to the Israel Museum in Jerusalem and engaged in life-long philanthropy to that country. He also created *"Ein Herz für Kinder"* in 1978, which focused on safety for children on the roads to prevent child death in traffic accidents.

Nichole Neuman

See also: Chapter 3: *Die Wende*; Government and Politics in the German Democratic Republic. Chapter 4: Corporations in Germany. Chapter 5: Judaism in Germany. Chapter 6: Jews in Germany. Chapter 16: Overview; Boulevard Press.

Further Reading

Berghahn, Volker R. *Journalists between Hitler and Adenauer: From Inner Emigration to the Moral Reconstruction of West Germany.* Princeton, NJ: Princeton University Press, 2019.

Müller, Hans Dieter, J. A. Cole, and Desmond Donnelly. *Press Power: A Study of Axel Springer.* London: Macdonald & Co., 1969.

Schwarz, Hans-Peter. *Axel Springer: Die Biografie.* Berlin: Propyläen, 2008.

Tatort

Tatort is a popular television series set in the German-speaking countries of Germany, Austria, and Switzerland. The series, whose title means "crime scene," is a police procedural drama and is the second-longest-running program in Germany. It has become a staple of Sunday night television, spanning generations of viewers, with over 1,000 episodes produced.

Airing without interruption since its premiere in 1970, *Tatort* was originally conceived for West German television. Gunther Witte created the program for Westdeutscher Rundfunk, a regional broadcaster based in Köln. Each episode follows different *Ermittler*, or investigators, as they work and solve crimes, often homicides. Part of the series' popularity owes to the unique settings and investigators throughout a season. For the first twenty years of the program, *Tatort* would take place in cities located in West Germany and Austria. After reunification in 1990, settings expanded to include cities in the former East, as well as Switzerland. Although *Tatort* has occasionally aired in other countries, it remains a domestic television phenomenon.

Each episode of *Tatort* lasts ninety minutes, beginning at 8:15 p.m. after the *Tagesschau* news program. Other similarities from program to program include the opening sequence and opening song (written by Klaus Doldinger for the original program). Both sequence and song have changed little since the series' debut.

Each regional broadcast partner produces its own *Tatort* segments, usually with one or two investigative teams in different cities throughout its region. So, while there are currently approximately thirty episodes per season, each investigative team may only reappear a handful of times. The show will visit cities all over the three featured German-speaking countries with different crimes. While recurring characters and subplots appear in each city-specific show, viewers still experience many different characters, cities, and crimes throughout a season. As such, part of the show's charm is that it foregrounds aspects of the cities in which the stories take place. Viewers get insight to each setting's cityscape and architecture, local customs, and unique vocabularies and accents.

Another reason for the series' popularity is the way in which crimes are investigated. Rather than focusing solely on the detectives' process in investigating the crime, *Tatort* employs a multifaceted approach to its storytelling. The show focuses on well-rounded narratives surrounding the criminal event and delves into personal aspects of the characters (criminals/perpetrators, victims, investigators) beyond immediate relevance to the story at hand.

Current social issues constitute an important discourse in *Tatort*. Beyond the more nefarious crimes such as homicides, the show's episodes center on other criminal activity including prostitution, drugs, and organized crime. However, the show also draws on national and international issues and frequently references political developments in both realms, for example, exploring social issues like youth-specific problems, domestic violence, migration and refugees, and class.

The latter theme—that of class—was best exemplified in the character of Chief Inspector Horst Schimanski, played by Götz George (1938–2016, son of the actor Heinrich George). Because each city is only featured a handful of times per year, there are multiple investigative teams, and some of the *Kommissare* and show's stars participate for years. Over the course of fifteen years, actor Peter Sodann played Kommissar Ehrlicher in Dresden in forty-five episodes. George, though only in twenty-nine episodes spanning a decade, portrayed one of the most beloved and complicated characters in the series. Schimanski marked the beginning of a new type of character—that of the gritty, street-smart police officer. At the time, the character proved controversial. Some appreciated the portrayal of an officer that represented the working class, while others contended it debased his station. Regardless, the character, who always wore a distinct M-1965 field jacket, became a cult figure, and that item of clothing became known as a "Schimanski Jacket." And like his colleague Til Schweiger, George's Schimanski enjoys the distinct honor of being in one of the only *Tatort* that made it to the big screen. In total, four *Tatort* films screened in cinemas before later playing on television.

In 1971, the GDR conceived its own version of the show, *Polizeiruf 110*. The show, which still runs today, partnered with *Tatort* in 1990 with a crossover episode featuring George's Chief Inspector Schimanski investigating criminal activities by former Stasi (East German secret police) members.

Nichole Neuman

See also: Chapter 3: *Die Wende*; Government and Politics in the German Democratic Republic. Chapter 6: Immigration; Refugees. Chapter 16: Overview; *Rundfunkgebühren*.

Further Reading

Das Fernsehlexikon. "Tatort." http://www.fernsehlexikon.de/208/tatort/. Accessed December 28, 2019.

Hämmerling, Christine, and Mirjam Nast. "Popular Seriality in Everyday Practice: Perry Rhodan and Tatort." In Frank Kelleter, ed. *Media of Serial Narrative*, 248–620. Columbus: The Ohio State University Press, 2017. Accessed June 8, 2020.

Kutch, Lynn M., and Todd Herzog. *Tatort Germany: The Curious Case of German-Language Crime Fiction*. Rochester, NY: Camden House, 2014.

Mattson, Michelle. "Tatort: The Generation of Public Identity in a German Crime Series." *New German Critique* 78: 161–81, 1999. https://doi.org/10.2307/488458. Accessed June 8, 2020.

A DAY IN THE LIFE

A DAY IN THE LIFE OF A SERVER AND COOK (DORIS O.)

I am a cook and occasional server at an American BBQ restaurant in a *Markthalle* in Berlin. I usually awaken at 8 or 9 in the morning, drink a cup of coffee, and eat fruit and yoghurt for breakfast. The restaurant gives me free meals, but I only eat there occasionally. The food is fairly heavy, so I pack a lighter, healthier lunch. I travel to my job via public transportation, and the trip from my two-room apartment in Schöneberg takes about forty-five minutes. Every month I buy a pass (for about $100.00) that allows me to ride the subway, busses, streetcars, the *S-Bahn* (S = *schnell*, fast train), and even ferries within Berlin. I try to get to work between 10 and 12 in the morning (depending upon when food is delivered to the restaurant). German hygiene regulations follow the international HACCP or Hazard Analysis Critical Control Points that forbid me from wearing outside shoes or clothes in a kitchen. As soon as I get to work, I wash my hands, pull up my hair, and don a chef's jacket. I grab another cup of coffee and ponder how to organize the kitchen in order to produce the food most efficiently, taking into account delivery time and staff meetings. After prepping the food, I do more office work for deliveries. Around 4 p.m. I start setting up the kitchen for service, and get everything from storage. I need to calculate how much food will be needed, taking into consideration the number of reservations and the day of the week (the restaurant is much busier on the weekends). I need to be vigilant about checking the temperature of various foods, as different foods require different temperatures. For example, a restaurant cannot warm up food, cool it, and reuse it. The restaurant uses a bain-marie to slowly warm foods and to keep them warm. The organization in the kitchen, especially, if there are more people working in it, needs a lot of communication, as the customers want all dishes brought out at the same time.

The kitchen closes at 9 p.m., often later. It takes about two hours to clean up, and I am usually done around 11 p.m. While I am officially supposed to have breaks, they often do not happen. I started smoking, so that I can take a break occasionally (restaurant work is backbreaking). After work, I sometimes hang out with colleagues for a *Feierabendbier* (after-hours beer). I am usually very tired after my nearly twelve-hour shifts. In order to decompress, I watch TV and take a shower when I get home.

A DAY IN THE LIFE OF A FOREIGN-LANGUAGE SECRETARY (MARIANNE S.)

I am a *Fremdsprachensekretärin* (foreign-language office worker) for a large German corporation. I live outside of Berlin and commute to the city every workday. The trip on the S-Bahn to downtown Berlin takes about an hour. I start work at 8, so I usually get up at 6 and eat my usual breakfast of fresh lemon juice, an egg, bread, butter, and jam.

I have a disability, so I work thirty hours per week. As soon as I get to work, I boot up my computer and share a pot of tea with my office mate. I am eagerly looking forward to retirement: I don't like the trend towards web conferences and multi-spaces offices. I consider them insufficient. My work includes a lot of routine and requires little creativity. I eat lunch in the company cafeteria with my colleagues. The cafeteria offers a large choice of meals, including vegetarian and vegan options. Each dish costs about $6.00. The company also has a bistro for small snacks and a gym I use a couple of times a week for a workout.

As a member of the *Betriebsrat* (workers' council), I represent other disabled colleagues during weekly council sessions. According to the law, the *Betriebsverfassungsgesetz*, the workers' council is tasked to participate in several important social, personnel, and economic decisions.

After leaving work, I often visit my physician and do my shopping before taking the train home. My husband usually cooks dinner, which I really appreciate. After dinner, I tidy the apartment, read, do yard work, or watch TV.

In my free time, I enjoy meeting my friends. My husband and I are enthusiastic dancers and participate in dance classes several times a month with an eye towards eventually participating in a competition. We also own several small apartment houses that we inherited and renovated. Most of the apartments are rented. Managing those properties takes another chunk of time: there are always repairs to oversee and then there is the occasional renter from hell.

A DAY IN THE LIFE OF A MECHATRONIC TECHNICIAN (DIETER M.)

My name is Dieter. I live in Erfurt, in Thuringia, with my girlfriend and our two children. I am a product of Germany's *Duale Ausbildung*, namely, I went to school while serving as an apprentice. I finished school with the *Mittlere Reife* certificate (ten years, secondary school) and started an apprenticeship as a *Mechatroniker*, a mechatronic technician with the Deutsche Bundesbahn (DB, German Railroad). After I completed my training (three and a half years), the DB hired me, and I have now been working there for over ten years.

My workdays start early, I get up at 5 and leave home around 6:15. I am fortunate: I live ten minutes by bicycle from my workplace. Work starts at 6:30. Upon arriving, I don orange pants, t-shirt, and jacket. I also wear steel-enforced boots.

There are ten people in my team, and we are responsible for work in the western part of Thuringia. My daily workplan is sent to my mobile phone. We work in small groups of two or three. We drive a specialized truck to sites that need to be inspected, serviced, or repaired. For example, the turnout heating at switches is conducted through electronic heating rods, and these need to be checked for potential malfunctioning. We also monitor RCDs (residual current devices) for functionality, which is important because they are needed to break the current in emergency situations. Recently, thieves have been removing copper coils to the tune of several million euros each year. This has subsided since 2013, when the railroad started marking the coils. Theft still happens, and we are tasked to inspect and repair such sites. Much of my job is routine. All switches must be inspected every four years with specialized instruments. When I find an issue, I repair it immediately.

I am a strict vegan. Usually, I pack my lunch, but occasionally I purchase a salad at a local supermarket. I get half an hour for lunch. When I am on call, I take my work truck home so that I can drive to disturbances without delay. I rarely work overtime, and then only when I am out on a repair and a problem arises or a scheduled repair requires extra time to be completed. We cannot leave a repair undone. My regular workday ends at 3:00 p.m. and I get home around 3:15, where I am greeted by my sons, both toddlers.

Like many Germans, my girlfriend and I are big believers in *Frische Luft* (fresh air). After work we take our kids for walk and head to the playground or the store. We return home and eat dinner and put the boys to bed by 7:30. We spend our evening watching TV or playing board games. My girlfriend is studying for her master's degree, so when she is busy, I enjoy gaming or meet my buddies for a beer.

A DAY IN THE LIFE OF A RETIRED ADMINISTRATOR (EVA L.)

I live in Munich with my second husband, a retired schoolteacher. Munich is a very expensive city, but our centrally located apartment is still a relative bargain since we have lived there for many years. Typically, I get up between 8 and 9 and fix lattes for myself and my husband. After the usual grooming, I prepare breakfast and we eat while listening to the news and reading the *Süddeutsche Zeitung*.

My pension is relatively small, so I try to supplement my income with a so-called *Minijob* or *450-Euro Job*. I am not allowed to earn more than €450 per month in order to keep my accrued benefits and avoid paying additional taxes. I used to work at a fashion store close to my apartment. I really liked the job because I also got a discount on clothes. However, I spent a lot of my extra money in the store. When the store closed, I started working at a research foundation as an administrative assistant. The foundation is located outside of Munich. My commute on Munich's subway is about one hour. I work at the foundation twice a week for six hours. My current task is to peruse old files to find materials that can be used in educational research and publication. When I return home, my husband is busy cooking dinner. After dinner we watch *Kulturzeit* on 3SAT (a German television network). On Thursday evenings I practice with my choir, where I sing soprano. My husband and I have remained politically active. I volunteer at a cultural institution in a Munich suburb, where I have chaired the board for many years. Among my duties are scheduling interesting speakers, chairing sessions, and updating the website, to name a few. Recently, I even put on a film festival; that was fun, but a lot of work. Because of all of my activities, I often do not get to bed before 11 p.m.

A DAY IN THE LIFE OF A STUDENT AND TEACHER (IRMA B.)

My days are full of working around the house, taking care of my family, my house, and my dogs and cats while being employed as a teacher of psychology and completing additional certification to teach mathematics. I am a so-called *Quereinsteiger* (lateral entrance) teacher. Originally, I studied psychology and earned my *Diplom* (degree in psychology). Several years ago, I started teaching psychology part-time at a *Gesamtschule* (integrated comprehensive school). Teachers in Germany generally provide instruction in two subject areas. Because of the dearth of mathematics teachers, I had the opportunity of going through *StEPS* (**Studienzentrum für Erziehung, Pädagogik und Schule**, Center of Study for Education, Pedagogy and School), a four-semester program where participants take classes in higher math and math teaching methods two days a week. The participants also teach their first subject, psychology in my case, at a school for three days a week.

My day starts before 6 a.m., when I get ready to leave our house in a rural suburb of Berlin. On a typical workday, I take my daughter to school before arriving at work around 8 a.m., about one hour by car if the traffic cooperates. I teach all levels from 8th to 12th grade. Students who are about to finish school with their *Abitur* (qualification for university entrance) need special attention, since they write papers and tests which I must correct in a timely fashion. In principle, I can be asked to substitute in a variety of subjects. Thus far, I have taught Ethics, German, and Chemistry, none of which lie in my area of expertise.

During the workday I am also expected to assume *Pausenbeaufsichtigung* (recess monitor), attend staff meetings and *Notenkonferenzen* (grading conferences). I am now in my last semester of my studies. I enrolled in stochastic theory, advanced geometry, and methods of teaching mathematics. As a student, I also regularly take tests and write exams. Thus far, it is going well. My day is not over after I leave work or the institute. I still have to prepare lessons, and correct tests and homework; in my role as a student, of course, I have to study and prepare my own homework. Recently, in order to avoid distractions, I actually go to a library. Unless I study at the library, I usually arrive home between 3 and 4.

After getting home, I often take the dogs for a walk, which help me to decompress. Across the street from our house is a large wooded area that is ideal for dog walking. Our dogs are well trained and walk off leash. My mother-in-law, who lives nearby, occasionally joins me. Upon returning home, my husband and I go shopping at a nearby LIDL or ALDI discount supermarket and then start cooking supper. It is important to me that our family shares at least one meal per day. After supper and tidying up, I feed the dogs and help my daughter with her homework. Unless I have to prepare lessons or do homework for the following day, my long day ends in front of the television set, where we play WII or watch a show on Netflix or Amazon (we do not subscribe to network TV).

GLOSSARY OF KEY TERMS

Abitur: Qualification to attend a university

Alternative fur Deutschland (AfD): An anti-immigration political party

Antiziganismus: Anti-"gypsy" sentiment

Arbeitlosenversicherung: Unemployment insurance

Armut: Poverty

Aufklärung: The Enlightenment

Ausbildung: Continuing education

Ausländer: Foreigners

Aussiedler: Emigrants

Autobahn: Highway. The German national highway system

Azubi: Apprentice

Bahn: Railway. Passengers also travel via subway (*U-Bahn*), suburban express train (*S-Bahn*), and streetcar or trolley (*Strassenbahn*).

Bauernkrieg: Peasants' War

Beerdigung: Funeral

Bekennende Kirche: The Confessing Church, those not aligned with the Third Reich

Berg (also Gebirge): Mountain (Mountains)

Berufsschule: Vocational school

Bibliothek or Bücherei: Library

Bildung: Education

Blut und Eisen: "Blood and Iron," a speech delivered by Bismarck in 1862

Bundesgericht: The supreme court of Germany

Bundeskabinette: Federal cabinet

Bundeskanzler: Chancellor

Bundesliga: Federal League. Also the German professional soccer league

Bundespräsident: The president (head of state) of Germany

Bundesrat: The upper house of the German legislature

Bundesrepublik Deutschland (BRD): Federal Republic of Germany

Bundestag: The German Parliament

Bundeswehr: Armed forces

Bürgerliches Gesetzbuch (BGB): German Civil Code

Bürgermeister: Mayor

Christlich Demokratische Union (CDU): The Christian Democratic Union. A center-right political party

Christlich Soziale Union (CSU): The Christian Social Union. The Bavarian affiliate of the CDU

DAAD—Deutscher Akademischer Austauschdienst: German Academic Exchange Service

Der Alte: "The Old Man," an affectionate term for Konrad Adenauer, the first chancellor of the Federal Republic of Germany

Der Alte Fritz: "The Old Fritz," Frederick II

Deutsche Christen: German Christians aligned with the Third Reich

Deutsche Demokratische Republik (DDR): The German Democratic Republic, or East Germany

Deutschemark (DM): The currency of the Federal Republic of Germany

Dolchstoß: "Stab in the Back." The theory that the German army did not lose World War I, but rather, was stabbed in the back

Drittes Reich: Third Reich (1933–1945)

Ernsthaft: Seriously (adv.)

Europäische Gemeinschaft (EG): European Union

Fachhochschule: University of Applied Sciences

Fachschule: Technical School

Flughafen: Airport

Fluss (pl. Flüsse): River

Freie Demokratische Partei (FDP): The Free Democratic Party, a center-right political party

Fremdwörter: Foreign words

Gastarbeiter: Guest workers

Gemeinschaft: Community

Gemütlichkeit: A state of well-being

Gesellschaft: Society

Gesellschaft für deutsche Sprache (GfdS): Association for the German Language

Grundgesetz: Basic Law, German constitution

Grundlagenvertrag: The "Basic Treaty" normalizing relations between East and West Germany in 1972

Grundschule: Elementary school

Grüne (also Bündnis 90/Die Grünen): The Greens, a grassroots movement comprised of environmental activists

Gymnasium: College preparatory school/high school

Heer: Army

Heimat: Homeland

Hochdeutsch: High German, the standard contemporary German dialect

Hochschule: University (not high school)

Hochzeit: Wedding

Holocaustleugnung: Holocaust denial

Innerdeutsche Grenz: Inner German border between East and West Germany

Insel: Island

Judenfrei: Free of Jews

Jugendstil: Art Nouveau

Kabarett: Originally, a turn-of-the-century (twentieth) musical and satirical revue; still popular

Kaiser: Emperor

Kaiserreich: The Wilhelmine Empire or Second Reich in German history

Kanzler: Chancellor

Karte: Ticket. Passengers can buy tickets for a single journey (*Einzelfahrkarte*) or passes valid for a day (*Tageskarte*), week (*Wochenkarte*), month (*Monatskarte*), or year (*Jahreskarte*)

Kindergarten: Preschool

Kirche: Church

Kirchensteuer: Church tax

Klarheit: Clarity

Konzentrationslager: Concentration camp

Krankenversicherung: Health insurance

Krautrock: West German electronic popular music

Kristallnacht: "Crystal Night" (November 9, 1938)

Kunst: Art

Land (pl. Länder): *State*

Lebensabschnittsgefährte: (Romantic) Partner during a particular period of someone's life

Lebensraum: Habitat

Lederhosen: Leather pants

Linke: The Left, an electoral alliance of two left-wing parties

Luftbrücke: The Berlin airlift 1948–1949 (literally airbridge)

Luftwaffe: Air Force

Machtergreifung: Seizure of power

Marine: Navy

Mauer: The Berlin Wall

Mittelstand: Small and medium-sized companies in German-speaking Europe; also, middle class

Oberschule: High school

Ordnung: Order

Ossies: East Germans

Pfand: Deposit. German consumers pay a deposit (€0.08–.25) on returnable glass and plastic bottles

Platz: Place

Reichskanzler: The imperial chancellor appointed by the emperor

Reichskommissar. Reich commissioner

Reichstag: Historic building in Berlin housing the Imperial Diet

Rentenversicherung: Pension insurance

Rotkäppchen: Little Red Riding Hood, a character from the Grimm brothers' fairy tales and the brand name of sparkling wine from East Germany

Rundfunkgebühren: Public broadcasting fees

Schlager: Parochial German popular music

Schnitzel: Breaded cutlet

Schrebergärten: Allotment gardens

Schultüte: A large decorated paper cone given to children on their first day of school

Schwarzfahrer: Fare dodger

See: Lake

Sozialdemokratische Partei Deutschlands (SPD): The Social Democratic Party of Germany, a center-left political party

Sozialhilfe: Social assistance or welfare

Sozialistische Einheitspartei Deutschlands (SED): The Socialist Unity Party, the ruling party of the German Democrat Republic

Spätis: Convenience stores

Sprachgesellschaften: Language societies

Sozialhilfe: Social assistance or welfare

Sprache: Language

Stadt: City

Stasi: Abbreviation for *Staatssicherheitsdienst* or State Security Service, the East Germany ministry for state security

Tatort: Scene of the crime

Taufe: Baptism

Tracht: Regional clothing

Verein (pl. Vereine): Club (clubs)

Vergangenheitsbewältigung: Coming to terms with the past

Verlobung: Engagement

Volksmusik: Popular music

Volkssturm: "People's Army" comprised of men between the ages of sixteen and sixty during the Second World War

Vorschule: Kindergarten

Wald: Forest

Wende: Turnaround. The series of events in 1980–1990 leading to the reunification of Germany

Wessis: West Germans

Wiedergutmachung: Reparations paid to survivors of the Holocaust

Wiedervereinigungsvertrag: The Reunification Treaty signed between the East and West German governments, uniting the Federal Republic of Germany and the German Democratic Republic

Wirtschaftswunder: Economic Miracle. The rapid postwar expansion of the German economy

Wörterbuch: Dictionary

U-Bahn: Subway

Zigeuner: A racist, pejorative term for a person of Roma heritage

Zollverein: A coalition of German states (notably Prussia, Bavaria, Württemberg, Saxony, Schleswig-Holstein, etc.) formed in 1833 to regularize tariffs and economic policies within their territories

APPENDIX C

FACTS AND FIGURES

Table 1:   GEOGRAPHY

Location	Located in north-central Europe, Germany is bordered by the Netherlands, Belgium, Luxembourg, and France to the west; Switzerland and Austria to the south; the Czech Republic and Poland to the east; and the Baltic Sea, Denmark, and the North Sea to the north.
Time Zone	6 hours ahead of U.S. Eastern Standard
Land Borders	2,250 miles
Coastline	1,485 miles
Capital	Berlin
Area	137,767 sq. miles
Climate	The climate is generally temperate, although there is much variation between the lowlands in the north and the highlands in Bavaria. The average annual temperature is about 48°F.
Land Use	70.62% arable land; 1.2% permanent crops; 34.24% cropland; 13.44% permanent meadows and pastures; 32.69% forest land. (2016)
Arable Land	46.7% (2017)
Arable Land per Capita	0.20 hectares per person (2017)

Table 2: POPULATION

Population	80,594,000 (estimate) (2017)
World Population Rank	19th (2017)
Population Density	231.1 people per square kilometer (2017)
Population Distribution	77.3% urban (2018)
Age Distribution	
0–14 years	12.82%
15–24 years	10.09%
25–54 years	40.45%
55–64 years	14.58%
65 years and over	22.06% (2017)
Median Age	47.1 years (2017)
Population Growth Rate	–0.2% per year (2018)
Net Migration Rate	1.5 (2018)
Languages	German
Religious Groups	Christian (72%)

Table 3: HEALTH

Average Life Expectancy	80.9 years (2018)
Average Life Expectancy, Male	78.6 years (2018)
Average Life Expectancy, Female	83.4 years (2018)
Crude Birth Rate	8.6 per 1,000 people (2018)
Crude Death Rate	11.8 per 1,000 people (2018)
Maternal Mortality	7 per 100,000 live births (2017)
Infant Mortality	3 per 1,000 live births (2017)
Doctors	4.2 per 1,000 people (2016)

Table 4: ENVIRONMENT

CO_2 Emissions	9.7 metric tons per capita (2017)
Alternative and Nuclear Energy	11.7% of total energy use (2014)
Threatened Species	116 (2017)
Protected Areas	159,169 sq. miles (2016)
Total Renewable H_2O Resources per Year	1,875 cubic meters, per person, per year (2017)

Table 5: ENERGY AND NATURAL RESOURCES

Electric Power Generation	588,500,000,000 kilowatt hours per year (estimate) (2018)
Electric Power Consumption	514,600,000,000 kilowatt hours per year (estimate) (2017)
Nuclear Power Plants	7 (2018)
Crude Oil Production	43,000 barrels per day (2017)
Crude Oil Consumption	2,460,000 barrels per day (2017)
Natural Gas Production	7,900,000,000 cubic meters per year (estimate) (2017)
Natural Gas Consumption	93,360,000,000 cubic meters per year (estimate) (2017)
Natural Resources	Coal, lignite, natural gas, iron ore, copper, nickel, uranium, potash, salt, construction materials, timber, arable land

Table 6: NATIONAL FINANCES

Currency	Euro
Total Government Revenues	$1,598,000,000,000 (estimate) (2017)
Total Government Expenditures	$1,573,000,000,000 (estimate) (2017)
Budget Deficit	0.7% of GDP (2017)
GDP Contribution by Sector	Agriculture: 0.6%; Industry: 30.1%; Services: 69.3% (2017)
External Debt	$5,326,000,000,000 (2017)
Economic Aid Extended	$19,458,430,000 (2018)
Economic Aid Received	$0 (2017)

Table 7: INDUSTRY AND LABOR

Gross Domestic Product (GDP)—official exchange rate	$3,597,965,000,000 (estimate) (2013)
GDP per Capita	$47,786 (estimate) (2019)
GDP—Purchasing Power Parity (PPP)	$4,170,790,000,000 (estimate) (2017)
GDP (PPP) per Capita	$50,425 (estimate) (2017)
Industry Products	Metals, electronics, coal, processed food, cement, chemicals, machinery, beverages, motor vehicles, bicycles, footwear, machine tools, textiles, petroleum.
Agriculture Products	Sugar beets, wheat, barley, potatoes, rapeseed, fruit, pork, beef, poultry, dairy products.
Unemployment	4.3% (2020)
Labor Profile	Agriculture: 1.4%; industry: 24.2%; services: 74.3% (2016)

Table 8: TRADE

Imported Goods	Machinery and transportation equipment, basic manufactures, agricultural products, fuels, raw materials, metals, chemical products, foodstuffs.
Total Value of Imports	$1,104,000,000,000 (estimate) (2017)
Exported Goods	Machinery and transportation equipment, machine tools, clothing, paper, chemicals and chemical products, fuels, metals, consumer goods.
Total Value of Exports	$1,401,000,000,000 (estimate) (2017)
Import Partners	Netherlands 13.8%, China 7%, France 6.6%, Belgium 5.9%, Italy 5.4%, Poland 5.4%, Czech Republic 4.8%, United States 4.5%, Austria 4.3%, Switzerland 4.2% (2017)
Export Partners	United States 8.8%, France 8.2%, China 6.8%, Netherlands 6.7%, United Kingdom 6.6%, Italy 5.1%, Austria 4.9%, Poland 4.7%, Switzerland 4.2% (2017)
Current Account Balance	$296,000,000,000 (estimate) (2017)
Weights and Measures	The metric system is in use.

Table 9: EDUCATION

School System	Schooling varies by state. Most states have four-year primary programs, with a variety of secondary programs that generally last for six to seven years. Secondary education can be academic, provided at gymnasiums, or vocational, at *Berufschules, Fachoberschules, or Berufsfachschules.*
Mandatory Education	9 years, from ages 6 to 15.
Average Years Spent in School for Current Students	17 (2016)
Average Years Spent in School for Current Students, Male	17 (2016)
Average Years Spent in School for Current Students, Female	17 (2016)
Primary School–Age Children Enrolled in Primary School	2,954,775 (2017)
Primary School–Age Males Enrolled in Primary School	1,520,256 (2017)
Primary School–Age Females Enrolled in Primary School	1,434,519 (2017)
Secondary School–Age Children Enrolled in Secondary School	7,028,713 (2017)
Secondary School–Age Males Enrolled in Secondary School	3,743,606 (2017)
Secondary School–Age Females Enrolled in Secondary School	3,363,869 (2016)
Students per Teacher, Primary School	12.2 (2016)
Students per Teacher, Secondary School	12.1 (2016)
Enrollment in Tertiary Education	2,977,781 (2016)
Enrollment in Tertiary Education, Male	1,592,025 (2017)
Enrollment in Tertiary Education, Female	1,499,669 (2017)
Literacy	99% (2016)

Table 10: MILITARY

Defense Spending (% of GDP)	1% (2017)
Total Active Armed Forces	180,000 (2017)
Annual Military Expenditures	$41,067,000,000 (2019)
Military Service	The German military uses a conscription system, with terms of service lasting ten months. (2016)

Table 11: TRANSPORTATION

Airports	539 (2013)
Registered Vehicles	52,391,000 (2015)
Paved Roads	100.0% (2016)
Railroads	33,590 miles (2017)
Ports	Major: 11 (including Bremen, Hamburg, Rostock, Wilhelmshaven, Bremerhaven).

Table 12: COMMUNICATIONS

Facebook Users	31,000,000 (estimate) (2017)
Internet Users	72,365,643 (2016)
Internet Users (% of Population)	88.0% (2019)
Land-Based Telephones in Use	44,400,000 (2017)
Mobile Telephone Subscribers	106,000,000 (2017)

HOLIDAYS

PUBLIC HOLIDAYS (2022)

- **1 January (Saturday):** New Year's Day (*Neujahrstag*)
- **15 April (Friday):** Good Friday (*Karfreitag*)
- **17 April (Sunday):** Easter (*Ostern*)
- **18 April (Monday):** Easter Monday (*Ostermontag*)
- **1 May (Sunday):** Labor Day (*Maifeiertag*)
- **26 May (Thursday):** Ascension Day (*Christi Himmelfahrt*, forty days after Easter)
- **5 June** (Sunday): Whit Sunday (*Pfingstsonntag*)—seventh Sunday after Easter, also called Pentecost Sunday
- **6 June (Monday):** Whit Monday (*Pfingstmontag*) seventh Monday after Easter, also called Pentecost Monday
- **3 October (Monday):** Day of German Unity (*Tag der deutschen Einheit*)
- **31 October (Monday):** Reformation Day (*Reformationstag*)—generally a regional holiday in Brandenburg, Mecklenburg-Western Pomerania, Saxony, Saxony-Anhalt, and parts of Thuringia
- **25 December (Sunday):** Christmas Day (*Weihnachtstag*)
- **26 December (Monday):** Saint Stephen's Day (*Stephanstag*)—also known as the second day of Christmas (2. *Weihnachtsfeiertag*)
- **31 December (Saturday):** New Year's Eve

REGIONAL HOLIDAYS (2022)

- **6 January (Thursday):** Epiphany (*Heilige Drei Könige*)—Baden-Württemberg, Bavaria, and Saxony-Anhalt
- **8 March (Tuesday):** International Women's Day—Berlin
- **16 June (Thursday):** Corpus Christi (*Fronleichnam*)—Baden-Württemberg, Bavaria, Hesse, North Rhine-Westphalia, Rhineland-Palatinate, Saarland, and some local authorities in Saxony and Thuringia
- **8 August (Monday):** Peace Festival (*Friedensfest*)—Bavaria (Augsburg)
- **15 August (Monday):** Assumption Day (*Maria Himmelfahrt*)—Saarland and some local authorities in Bavaria
- **20 September (Tuesday):** World Children's Day—Thuringia

- **1 November (Tuesday):** All Saints' Day (*Allerheiligen*)—Baden-Württemberg, Bavaria, North Rhine-Westphalia, Rhineland-Palatinate, and Saarland
- **16 November (Wednesday):** Day of Prayer and Repentance (*Buß-und Bettag*, Wednesday before 23 November)—Saxony

OTHER IMPORTANT DATES (2022)

- **28 February (Monday):** Shrove Monday (*Rosenmontag*)
- **1 March (Tuesday):** Shrove Tuesday (*Faschingsdienstag* or *Fastnacht*)
- **2 March (Wednesday):** Ash Wednesday (*Aschermittwoch*), end of the Carnival time and beginning of Lent
- **27 March (Sunday):** Clocks go forward one hour due to the start of daylight saving time
- **8 May (Sunday):** Mother's Day (second Sunday of May)
- **26 May (Thursday):** Father's Day (*Vatertag*, also known as *Männertag/Herrentag*, Men's Day)—coincides with Ascension Day and can be a family celebration or celebrated by an outing with male friends
- **10 September (Saturday):** German Language Day
- **11 September (Sunday):** European Heritage Days—when monument buildings are opened to the public
- **17 September (Saturday):** Oktoberfest starts
- **30 October (Sunday):** Clocks go back one hour due to the end of daylight saving time
- **9 November (Wednesday):** Fall of the Berlin Wall
- **11 November (Friday):** St. Martin's Day—a religious observance where children take part in lantern processions, also the start of the carnival season
- **13 November (Sunday):** National Day of Mourning (*Volkstrauertag*)– victims of war are remembered and, in some regions, music or dance events are illegal
- **6 December (Tuesday):** Saint Nicholas Day

Sources: https://www.expatica.com/de/lifestyle/holidays/german-holidays-105411/. Accessed October 5, 2021.

"Alle gesetzlichen Feiertage 2022 in Deutschland im Überblick." Berliner Morgenpost, October 4, 2021. https://www.morgenpost.de/vermischtes/article233458756/feiertage-deutschland-2022-ueberblick.html. Accessed October 5, 2021.

SELECTED BIBLIOGRAPHY

GENERAL WORKS

Buse, Dieter K., and Juergen C. Doerr. *Modern Germany: An Encyclopedia of History, People, and Culture, 1871–1990*. New York: Garland, 1998.

Colvin, Sarah, ed. *The Routledge Handbook of German Politics and Culture*. London: Routledge, 2015.

Jampol, Justinian, Benedikt Taschen, and Ina Pfitzner. *Beyond the Wall: Art and Artifacts from the GDR = Jenseits Der Mauer: Kunst Und Alltagsgegenstände Aus Der DDR*. Köln: Taschen, 2014.

Landsford, Tom, ed. *Political Handbook of the World, 2016–2017*, vol. 1. Thousand Oaks, CA: Sage, 2017.

Lewis, Derek, Johannes Schwitalla, and Ulrike Zitzlsperger. *Contemporary Germany: A Handbook*. London; New York: Arnold; copublished in the United States by Oxford University Press, 2001.

Sandford, John, ed. *Encyclopedia of Contemporary German Culture*. London: Routledge, 1999.

GEOGRAPHY

Bristow, Philip. *Through the German Waterways*, new rev ed. London: Nautical Books, 1988.

Coulmas, Florian, and Ralph Lützeler. *Imploding Populations in Japan and Germany: A Comparison*. Leiden, Netherlands: Brill, 2011.

Elkins, T. H. *Germany: An Introductory Geography*, rev. ed. New York: Praeger, 1968.

Gaab, Jeffrey S. *Munich: Hofbräuhaus & History: Beer, Culture, & Politics*. New York: Peter Lang, 2006.

Kibele, Eva U. B. *Regional Mortality Differences in Germany*. Dordrecht, Netherlands; New York: Springer, 2012.

Large, David Clay. *Berlin*. New York: Basic Books, 2000.

Miller, Gary. *The Rhine: Europe's River Highway*. New York: Crabtree Pub. Company, 2010.

HISTORY

Ahonen, Pertti. *Death at the Berlin Wall*. Oxford, UK: Oxford University Press, 2011.

Althoff, Gerd. *Otto III*. University Park: Pennsylvania State University Press, 2003.

Blanning, T. C. W. *Frederick the Great: King of Prussia*. New York: Random House, 2016.

Clark, Christopher M. *Iron Kingdom: The Rise and Downfall of Prussia, 1600–1947*. Cambridge, MA: Belknap Press of Harvard University Press, 2006.

Dennis, Mike. *The Rise and Fall of the German Democratic Republic, 1945–1990*. Harlow, UK: Longman, 2000.

Engel, Jeffrey A., ed. *The Fall of the Berlin Wall: The Revolutionary Legacy of 1989*. Oxford, UK: Oxford University Press, 2009.

Evans, Richard J. *The Third Reich in History and Memory*. Oxford, UK: Oxford University Press, 2015.

Fichtenau, Heinrich. *The Carolingian Empire*. Peter Munz, trans. Toronto: University of Toronto Press in Association with The Medieval Academy of America, 1995.

Frank, Anne. *The Diary of a Young Girl: The Definitive Edition*. Frank Otto and Susan Massotty, eds. New York: Doubleday, 1995.

Fried, Johannes, and Peter Lewis. *Charlemagne*. Cambridge, UK: Harvard University Press, 2016.

Fulbrook, Mary. *A Concise History of Germany*. Cambridge, UK: Cambridge University Press, 2004.

Giesinger, Adam. *The Story of Russia's Germans: From Catherine to Khrushchev*. Battleford, SK, Canada: Marian Press, 1974.

Goldhagen, Daniel Jonah. *Hitler's Willing Executioners: Ordinary Germans and the Holocaust*. New York: Alfred A. Knopf, 1996.

Kershaw, Ian. *Hitler*, 2 volumes. New York: W. W. Norton, 1999–2000.

Kitchen, Martin. *A History of Modern Germany, 1800 to the Present*. 2nd ed. Chichester, UK; Malden, MA: Wiley-Blackwell, 2012.

MacDonogh, Giles. *The Last Kaiser: The Life of Wilhelm II*. New York: St. Martin's Press, 2001.

Massie, Robert K. *Catherine the Great: Portrait of a Woman*. New York: Random House, 2012.

Miller, Melissa. *Anne Frank: The Biography*. New York: Metropolitan Books/Henry Holt and Company, 2013.

Nipperdey, Thomas. *Germany from Napoleon to Bismarck, 1800–1866*. Princeton, NJ: Princeton University Press, 1996.

Ozment, Steven E., Elliott Beard, and Adam G. Beaver. *A Mighty Fortress: A New History of the German People*. New York: HarperCollins Publishers, 2004.

Pommerin, Reiner, ed. *The American Impact on Postwar Germany*. Providence, RI: Berghahn Books. 1995.

Richie, Alexandra. *Faust's Metropolis: A History of Berlin*. New York: Carroll & Graf, 1998.

Röhl, John C. G. *Kaiser Wilhelm II: A Concise Life*. New York: Cambridge University Press, 2014.

Röhl, John C. G. *Wilhelm II: The Kaiser's Personal Monarchy, 1888–1900*. New York: Cambridge University Press, 2004.

Sarotte, M. E. *The Collapse: The Accidental Opening of the Berlin Wall*. New York: Basic Books, 2014.

Scales, Len. *The Shaping of German Identity: Authority and Crisis, 1245–1414*. Cambridge, UK: Cambridge University Press, 2012.

Shepherd, Ben. *Hitler's Soldiers: The German Army in the Third Reich*. New Haven, CT: Yale University Press, 2016.

Showalter, Dennis E. *The Wars of German Unification*. London: Arnold, 2004.

Smith, Helmut Walser. *The Oxford Handbook of Modern German History*. Oxford, UK; New York: Oxford University Press, 2011.

Smyser, W. R. *From Yalta to Berlin: The Cold War Struggle over Germany*. New York: St. Martin's Press, 1999.

Steinberg, Jonathan. *Bismarck: A Life*. Oxford, UK: Oxford University Press, 2011.

Stoker, Donald. *Clausewitz: His Life and Work*. Oxford, UK: Oxford University Press, 2014.

Todd, Malcolm. *The Early Germans*. Malden, MA: Blackwell, 2004.

Ulrich, Herbert. *History of Twentieth-Century Germany*. Oxford, UK: Oxford University Press, 2019.

Von der Goltz, Anna. *Hindenburg: Power, Myth, and the Rise of the Nazis*. Oxford, UK: Oxford University Press, 2009.

Watson, Alexander. *Ring of Steel: Germany and Austria-Hungary in World War I*. New York: Basic Books, 2014.

Weinfurter, Stefan. *The Salian Century: Main Currents in an Age of Transition*. Philadelphia: University of Pennsylvania Press, 1999.

Whaley, Joachim. *Germany and the Holy Roman Empire*. Oxford, UK: Oxford University Press, 2012.

Wheen, Francis. *Karl Marx: A Life*. New York: Norton, 2000.

Williams, Charles. *Adenauer: The Father of the New Germany*. New York: John Wiley, 2000.

Wolfram, Herwig, and Denise Adele Kaiser. *Conrad II, 990–1039: Emperor of Three Kingdoms*. University Park: Pennsylvania State University Press, 2006.

GOVERNMENT AND POLITICS

Bock, Jan-Jonathan, and Sharon Macdonald. *Refugees Welcome? Difference and Diversity in a Changing Germany*. New York: Berghahn Books, 2019.

Conradt, David P., and Eric Langenbacher. *The German Polity*, 10th ed. Lanham, MD: Rowman & Littlefield Publishers, 2013.

Corum, James S. *Rearming Germany*. Leiden, Netherlands; Boston: Brill, 2011.

Crawford, Alan, and Tony Czuczka. *Angela Merkel: A Chancellorship Forged in Crisis*. Chichester, UK: John Wiley & Sons, 2013.

Crosby, Margaret Barber. *The Making of a German Constitution: A Slow Revolution*. Oxford, UK: Oxford University Press, 2008.

Erb, Scott. *German Foreign Policy: Navigating a New Era*. Boulder, CO: Rienner, 2003.

Green, Simon, et al., eds. *The Politics of the New Germany*. London: Routledge. 2008.

Gunlicks, Arthur B. *The Länder and German Federalism*. Manchester, UK: Manchester University Press; 2003.

Jonas, Manfred. *The United States and Germany: A Diplomatic History*. Ithaca, NY: Cornell University Press. 1984.

Kolb, Eberhard. *The Weimar Republic*. London: Routledge, 2005.

Leiby, Richard A. *The Unification of Germany, 1989–1990*. Westport, CT: Greenwood Press, 1999.

Major, Patrick. *Behind the Berlin Wall: East Germany and the Frontiers of Power*. Oxford, UK: Oxford University Press, 2010.

Maull, Hanns, ed. *Germany's Uncertain Power: Foreign Policy of the Berlin Republic*. Basingstoke, UK: Palgrave Macmillan. 2006.

Mushaben, Joyce Marie. *Becoming Madam Chancellor: Angela Merkel and the Berlin Republic*. Cambridge, UK: Cambridge University Press, 2017.

Qvortrup, Matt. *Angela Merkel: Europe's Most Influential Leader*. New York: Overlook Duckworth, 2016.

Rowe, Carolyn, and Wade Jacoby. *German Federalism in Transition: Reforms in a Consensual State*. London: Taylor & Francis Group, 2013.

Schweigler, Gebhard, and Steven Muller, eds. *From Occupation to Cooperation: The United States and United Germany in a Changing World Order*. New York: Norton, 1992.

Stangl, Paul. *Risen from Ruins: The Cultural Politics of Rebuilding East Berlin*. Stanford, CA: Stanford University Press, 2018.

Umbach, Maiken. *German Federalism: Past, Present, Future*. Basingstoke, UK; New York: Palgrave, 2002.

Wallach, H. G. Peter, and Ronald A. *United Germany: The Past, Politics, Prospects*. Westport, CT: Greenwood Press, 1992.

ECONOMY

Berghoff, Hartmut, and Uta A. Balbier. *The East German Economy, 1945–2010: Falling Behind or Catching Up?* Washington, DC: New York: German Historical Institute; Cambridge University Press, 2013.

Bryson, Phillip J., and Manfred Melzer. *The End of the East German Economy: From Honecker to Reunification*. New York: St. Martin's Press, 1991.

ebrary, Inc. *Germany: Money & Banking*. Petaluma, CA: World Trade Press, 2010.

Glossner, Christian Ludwig. *The Making of the German Post-war Economy: Political Communication and Public Reception of the Social Market Economy after World War II*. London; New York: Tauris Academic Studies, 2010.

Kramer, Alan. *The West German Economy: 1945–1955*. New York: St. Martin's Press, 1991.

Miller, Jennifer A. *Turkish Guest Workers in Germany: Hidden Lives and Contested Borders 1960s to 1980s.* Toronto; Buffalo; London: University of Toronto Press, 2018.

Mody, Ashoka. *Germany in an Interconnected World Economy.* Washington, DC: International Monetary Fund, 2013.

Müller, Birgit. *Disenchantment with Market Economics: East Germans and Western Capitalism.* New York: Berghahn Books, 2007.

Overy, R. J. *War and Economy in the Third Reich.* Oxford, UK: Clarendon Press, 1994.

Smith, Owen E. *The German Economy.* London: Routledge, 2008.

Spicka, Mark E. *Selling the Economic Miracle: Reconstruction and Politics in West Germany, 1949–1957.* New York: Berghahn Books, 2007.

RELIGION AND THOUGHT

Al-Hamarneh, Ala, and Jorn Thielmann. *Islam and Muslims in Germany.* Leiden, Netherlands: Brill, 2014.

Baylor, Michael G. *The German Reformation and the Peasants' War: A Brief History with Documents.* Boston: Bedford/St. Martin's, 2012.

Brady, Thomas A. *German Histories in the Age of Reformations, 1400–1650.* Cambridge, UK: Cambridge University Press, 2009.

Gay, Ruth. *The Jews of Germany: A Historical Portrait.* New Haven, CT: Yale University Press, 2000.

Guerriero, Elio. *Benedict XVI: His Life and Thought.* San Francisco: Ignatius, 2018.

Hairline, Craig. *A World Ablaze: The Rise of Martin Luther and the Birth of the Reformation.* New York: Oxford University Press, 2017.

Hernandez Aguilar, Luis Manuel. *Governing Muslims and Islam in Contemporary Germany: Race, Time, and the German Islam Conference.* Leiden, Netherlands: Brill, 2018.

Kuehn, Manfred. *Kant: A Biography.* Cambridge, UK: Cambridge University Press, 2009.

Laqueur, Walter, and Judith Tydor Baumel-Schwartz, eds. *The Holocaust Encyclopedia.* New Haven, CT: Yale University Press, 2001.

Leppin, Volker. *Martin Luther: A Late Medieval Life.* Grand Rapids, MI: Baker Books, 2017.

Marshall, Peter. *1517: Martin Luther and the Invention of the Reformation.* Oxford, UK: Oxford University Press, 2017.

Metaxas, Eric. *Bonhoeffer: Pastor, Martyr, Prophet, Spy: A Righteous Gentile vs. the Third Reich.* Nashville, TN: Thomas Nelson, 2010.

Meyer, Michael A., Michael Brenner, Mordechai Breuer, and Michael Graetz. *German-Jewish History in Modern Times.* New York: Columbia University Press, 1996.

Oberman, Heiko A. *Luther: Man between God and the Devil.* New Haven: Yale University Press, 2006.

Parker, Geoffrey, Simon Adams, Gerhard Benecke, and Richard J. Bonney. *The Thirty Years' War.* London: Routledge, 2007.

Rees, Laurence. *The Holocaust: A New History.* New York: Public Affairs, 2017.

Rex, Richard. *The Making of Martin Luther*. Princeton, NJ: Princeton University Press, 2017.

Scott, Tom. *The Early Reformation in Germany: Between Secular Impact and Radical Vision*. London: Routledge, 2013.

Shapiro, James S. *Oberammergau: The Troubling Story of the World's Most Famous Passion Play*. New York: Pantheon Books, 2000.

Tacitus, Cornelius. *Agricola and Germany*. Anthony Birley, trans. Oxford, UK: Oxford University Press, 2009.

Willibald. *The Life of Saint Boniface*. George W. Robinson, trans. Cambridge, MA: Harvard University Press, 1916.

Wilson, Peter Hamish. *The Thirty Years War: Europe's Tragedy*. Cambridge, MA: Belknap Press of Harvard University Press, 2011.

SOCIAL CLASSES AND ETHNICITY

Aschheim, Steven E. *The Nietzsche Legacy in Germany, 1890–1990*. Berkeley: University of California Press, 1992.

Campt, Tina. *Other Germans: Black Germans and the Politics of Race, Gender and Memory in the Third Reich*. Ann Arbor: University of Michigan Press, 2003.

Clarkson, Alexander. *Fragmented Fatherland: Immigration and Cold War Conflict in the Federal Republic of Germany, 1945–1980*. New York: Berghahn Books, 2013.

Coulmas, Florian, and Ralph Lützeler. *Imploding Populations in Japan and Germany: A Comparison*. Leiden, Netherlands: Brill, 2011.

De Zayas, Alfred M. *A Terrible Revenge: The Ethnic Cleansing of the East European Germans*. 2nd ed., rev. and updated. New York: Palgrave Macmillan, 2006.

Diedrich, Maria I., and Jürgen Heinrichs, eds. *From Black to Schwarz*. East Lansing: Michigan State University Press, 2011.

Flockton, Christopher, Eva Kolinsky, and Rosalind M. O. Pritchard. *The New Germany in the East: Policy Agendas and Social Developments Since Unification*. London; Portland, OR: F. Cass, 2000.

Göktürk, Deniz, David Gramling, and Anton Kaes. *Germany in Transit: Nation and Migration, 1955–2005*. Berkeley: University of California Press, 2007.

Hagen, William W. *Ordinary Prussians: Brandenburg Junkers and Villagers, 1500–1840*. Cambridge, UK; New York: Cambridge University Press, 2002.

Hamm, Ingrid, Helmut Seitz, and Martin Werding. *Demographic Change in Germany: The Economic and Fiscal Consequences*. New York: Springer, 2008.

Herbert, Ulrich. *History of Twentieth-Century Germany*. Oxford, UK: Oxford University Press, 2019.

Hinze, Annika. *Turkish Berlin: Integration Policy and Urban Space*. Minneapolis: University of Minnesota Press, 2013.

Hoffmann, Peter. *Stauffenberg: A Family History, 1905–1944*, 3rd ed. Montreal: McGill-Queen's University Press, 2008.

Kolinsky, Eva, and Wilfried van der Will. *The Cambridge Companion to Modern German Culture*. Cambridge, UK; New York: Cambridge University Press, 1998.

Kosnick, Kira. *Migrant Media: Turkish Broadcasting and Multicultural Politics in Berlin*. Bloomington: Indiana University Press, 2007.

Lennox, Sara, ed. *Remapping Black Germany: New Perspectives on Afro-German History, Politics, and Culture*. Amherst and Boston: University of Massachusetts Press, 2016.

Margalit, Gilad. *Germany and Its Gypsies: A Post-Auschwitz Ordeal*. Madison: University of Wisconsin Press, 2002.

Panayi, Panikos. *Ethnic Minorities in Nineteenth and Twentieth Century Germany: Jews, Gypsies, Poles, Turks and Others*. London: Routledge, 2014.

Peck, Jeffrey M. *Being Jewish in the New Germany*. New Brunswick, NJ: Rutgers University Press, 2006.

Schenderlein, Anne C. *Germany on Their Minds: German Jewish Refugees in the United States and Their Relationships with Germany, 1938–1988*. New York: Berghahn Books, 2020.

Tebbutt, Susan, ed. *Sinti and Roma: Gypsies in German-Speaking Society and Literature*. New York: Berghahn Books, 1998.

Tönnies, Ferdinand. *Community and Society (Gemeinschaft und Gesellschaft)*. East Lansing: Michigan State University Press, 1957.

Vierra, Sarah Thomsen. *Turkish Germans in the Federal Republic of Germany: Immigration, Space, and Belonging, 1961–1990*. Cambridge, UK; New York: Cambridge University Press, 2018.

GENDER

Boehm, Philip, ed. *A Woman in Berlin: Eight Weeks in the Conquered City: A Diary*. New York: Metropolitan Books/Henry Holt, 2005.

Brückner, Hannah. *Gender Inequality in the Life Course: Social Change and Stability in West Germany, 1975–1995*. Hawthorne, NY: Aldine De Gruyter, 2004.

Flockton, Christopher, Eva Kolinsky, and Rosalind M. O. Pritchard. *The New Germany in the East: Policy Agendas and Social Developments Since Unification*. London; Portland, OR: F. Cass, 2000.

Giersdorf, Jens Richard. "Paragraph 175." In George E. Haggerty, ed. *Gay Histories and Cultures*, 1016–1017. New York: Garland, 2000.

Kerbo, Harold R., and Hermann Strasser. *Modern Germany*. Boston: McGraw Hill, 2000.

Mazón, Patricia M. *Gender and the Modern Research University: The Admission of Women to German Higher Education, 1865–1914*. Stanford, CA: Stanford University Press, 2003.

Moeller, Robert G., ed. *West Germany under Construction: Politics, Society, and Culture in the Adenauer Era*. Ann Arbor: University of Michigan Press, 1997.

Oertzen, Christine von. *The Pleasure of a Surplus Income: Part-time Work, Gender Politics, and Social Change in West Germany, 1955–1969*. New York: Berghahn Books, 2007.

Pine, Lisa. *Hitler's "National Community": Society and Culture in Nazi Germany*, 2nd ed. London: Bloomsbury Academic, 2017.

Qvortrup, Matt. *Angela Merkel: Europe's Most Influential Leader*. New York: Overlook Duckworth, 2016.

Rosenhaft, Eve. "Gender." In Jonathan Sperber, ed. *Germany 1800–1870*, 209–229. Oxford, UK: Oxford University Press, 2004.

Rüger, Jan, and Nikolaus Wachsmann, eds. *Rewriting German History: New Perspectives on Modern Germany*. Basingstoke, UK: Palgrave Macmillan, 2015.

Schaser, Angelika. "Gendered Germany." In James Retallack, ed. *Imperial Germany 1871–1918*, 128–150. Oxford, UK: Oxford University Press, 2008.

Sneeringer, Julia. *Winning Women's Votes: Propaganda and Politics in Weimar Germany*. Chapel Hill: University of North Carolina, 2002.

Whisnant, Clayton J. *Male Homosexuality in West Germany: Between Persecution and Freedom, 1945–69*. London: Palgrave Macmillan, 2012.

Wiliarty, Sarah Elise. *The CDU and the Politics of Gender in Germany: Bringing Women to the Party*. Cambridge, UK: Cambridge University Press, 2010.

EDUCATION

Alexander, Thomas. *The Prussian Elementary Schools*. New York: Macmillan, 1918.

Behmel, Albrecht, and Kelly Neudorfer. *The Foreigner's Guide to German Universities: Origin, Meaning, and Use of Terms and Expressions in Everyday University Life*. Stuttgart: ibidem-Verlag, 2016.

Breinig, Helmbrecht, Jürgen Gebhardt, and Berndt Ostendorf. *German and American Higher Education: Educational Philosophies and Political Systems*. Münster: Piscataway, NJ: Lit, 2001.

Brown, Brandon R. *Planck: Driven by Vision, Broken by War*. New York: Oxford University Press, 2015.

Günther, Karl-Heinz, and Gottfried Uhlig. *History of the Schools in the German Democratic Republic 1945 to 1968*. 1. Aufl. Berlin: Volk und Wissen, 1973.

Hahn, H.-J. *Education and Society in Germany*. Oxford, UK: Berg, 1998.

Heilbron, J. L. *The Dilemmas of an Upright Man: Max Planck as Spokesman for German Science*. Berkeley: University of California Press, 1986.

Hoffmann, Klaus. *Otto Hahn: Achievement and Responsibility*. New York: Springer, 2001.

Lamberti, Marjorie. *State, Society, and the Elementary School in Imperial Germany*. New York: Oxford University Press, 1989.

Luke, Carme. *Pedagogy, Printing, and Protestantism: The Discourse on Childhood*. Albany, NY: SUNY Press, 1989.

Plassmann, Engelbert, Hermann Rösch, Jürgen Seefeldt, and Konrad Umlauf. *Libraries and the Information Society in Germany: An Introduction*. Wiesbaden, Germany: Harrassowitz Verlag, 2014.

Rodden, John. *Repainting the Little Red Schoolhouse: A History of Eastern German Education, 1945–1995*. New York: Oxford University Press, 2002.

LANGUAGE

Barbour, Stephen, and Patrick Stevenson. *Variation in German: A Critical Approach to German Sociolinguistics*. Cambridge, UK: Cambridge University Press, 1990.

Bright, William, and Peter T. Daniels. *The World's Writing Systems*. New York: Oxford University Press, 1996.

Brunt, Richard James. *The Influence of the French Language on the German Vocabulary*. Berlin: De Gruyter, 1983.

Clyne, Michael. *Language and Society in the German-Speaking Countries*. Cambridge, UK: Cambridge University Press, 1984.

Fehringer, Carol. *German Grammar in Context*, 3rd ed. Oxon, UK; New York: Routledge, 2020.

Fox, Anthony. *The Structure of German*. Oxford, UK: Clarendon Press, 1990.

Füssel, Stephan. *The Book of Books: The Luther Bible of 1534. A Cultural-Historical Introduction*. Köln: Taschen, 2003.

Hawkins, John A. *A Comparative Typology of English and German: Unifying the Contrasts*. London: Croom Helm, 1986.

Hettinga, Donald R. *The Brothers Grimm: Two Lives, One Legacy*. New York: Clarion Books, 2001.

Jackman, Graham. *Finding a Voice: Problems of Language in East German Society and Culture*. Amsterdam; Atlanta, GA: Rodopi, 2000.

Johnson, Sally A. *Spelling Trouble? Language, Ideology and the Reform of German Orthography*. Clevedon, UK: Multilingual Matters, 2005.

Michael, Robert, and Karin Doerr. *Nazi-Deutsch/Nazi-German: An English Lexicon of the Language of the Third Reich*. Westport, CT: Greenwood Press, 2002.

Minert, Roger P. *Deciphering Handwriting in German Documents: Analyzing German, Latin, and French in Historical Manuscripts*, 2nd ed., rev. and exp. Provo, UT: GRT Publications, 2013.

Moulton, William G. *The Sounds of English and German*. Chicago: University of Chicago Press. 1962.

Pegelow, Thomas. *The Language of Nazi Genocide: Linguistic Violence and the Struggle of Germans of Jewish Ancestry*. Cambridge, UK; New York: Cambridge University Press, 2009.

Russ, Charles V. J. *The Dialects of Modern German: A Linguistic Survey*. London: Routledge, 1990.

Russ, Charles V. J. *The German Language Today: A Linguistic Introduction*. London: Routledge, 1994.

Sanders, Ruth H. *German: Biography of a Language*. New York: Oxford University Press, 2010.

Waterman, John T. *A History of the German Language*. Prospect Heights, IL: Wavelength Press, 1991.

Zorach, Cecile, and Charlotte Melin. *English Grammar for Students of German: The Study Guide for Those Learning German*, 3rd ed. Ann Arbor, MI: Olivia and Hill Press, 1994.

ETIQUETTE

Flippo, Hyde. *When in Germany, Do as the Germans Do: The Clued-in Guide to German Life, Language, and Culture*. Chicago: McGraw-Hill, 2002.

Fraser, Catherine C., and Dierk O. Hoffmann. *Pop Culture Germany! Media, Arts, and Lifestyle*. Santa Barbara, CA: ABC-CLIO, 2006.

Jefferies, Matthew. *Imperial Culture in Germany, 1871–1918*. New York: Palgrave Macmillan, 2003.

Stern, Susan., and Hans Traxler. *These Strange German Ways and the Whys of the Ways*. Bonn: Atlantik-Brücke, 2000.

Tomalin, Barry. *Germany: A Quick Guide to Customs and Etiquette*. London: Kuperard, 2003.

Zeidenitz, Stefan, and Ben Barkow. *The Xenophobe's Guide to the Germans*, rev. ed. London: Ravette, 1997.

LITERATURE

Adelson, Leslie. *The Turkish Turn in Contemporary German Literature: Towards a New Critical Grammar of Migration*. New York: Palgrave Macmillan, 2005.

Bartram, Graham, and Philip Payne, eds. *The Cambridge Companion to the Modern German Novel*. Cambridge, UK: Cambridge University Press, 2004.

Behler, Ernst. *German Romantic Literary Theory*. Cambridge, UK: Cambridge University Press, 1993.

Benjamin, Walter. *Understanding Brecht*. Anna Bostock, trans. London: Verso, 1983.

Beutin, Wolfgang, et al. *A History of German Literature: From the Beginnings to the Present Day*. London: Routledge, 2014.

Bithell, Jethro. *Modern German Literature: 1880–1950*. London: Routledge, 2019.

Boyle, Nicholas. *German Literature: A Very Short Introduction*, vol. 178. Oxford, UK: Oxford University Press, 2008.

Boyle, Nicholas. *Goethe, the Poet and the Age*, vol. 1: *The Poetry of Desire, 1749–1790*. Oxford, UK: Clarendon, 1991.

Boyle, Nicholas. *Goethe, the Poet and the Age*, vol. 2, *Revolution and Renunciation, 1790–1803*. Oxford, UK: Clarendon, 2000.

Brandt, Georg W., and Wiebe Hogendoorn, eds. *German and Dutch Theatre, 1600–1848*. Cambridge, UK: Cambridge University Press, 1993.

Bruford, Walter Horace. *Theatre, Drama and Audience in Goethe's Germany*. London: Routledge, 2018.

Dawson, Ruth P. *The Contested Quill: Literature by Women in Germany, 1770–1800*. Newark: University of Delaware Press, 2002.

Donahue, Neil H., ed. *A Companion to the Literature of German Expressionism*. Rochester, NY: Camden House, 2005.

Downing, Eric. *Double Exposures: Repetition and Realism in Nineteenth-Century German Fiction*. Stanford, CA: Stanford University Press, 2000.

Falkenberg, Betty. *Else Lasker-Schuler: A Life*. Jefferson, NC: McFarland, 2003.

Furness, Raymond, and Malcolm Humble. *A Companion to Twentieth-Century German Literature*. London: Routledge, 2003.

Garland, Henry B., and Mary Garland. *The Oxford Companion to German Literature*, 2nd ed. Oxford, UK; New York: Oxford University Press, 1986.

Gerstenberger, Katharina. *Writing the New Berlin: The German Capital in Post-Wall Literature*, vol. 21. Rochester, NY: Camden House, 2008.

Gibbs, Marion, and Sidney M. Johnson. *Medieval German Literature: A Companion*. London: Routledge, 2002.

Grange, William. *The A to Z of Postwar German Literature*. Lanham, MD: Scarecrow Press, 2010.

Hardin, James. ed. *German Baroque Writers, 1661–1730. Detroit:* Thomson Gale, 1996.

Hill, David, and James N. Hardin, eds. *Literature of the Sturm und Drang*, vol. 6. Rochester, NY: Camden House, 2003.

Holmgren, Janet Besserer. *The Women Writers in Schiller's Horen: Patrons, Petticoats, and the Promotion of Weimar Classicism*. Newark: University of Delaware Press, 2007.

Koelb, Clayton, James Hardin, and Eric Downing, eds. *German Literature of the Nineteenth Century, 1830–1899.* vol. 9. Rochester, NY: Camden House, 2005.

Kontje, Todd Curtis, ed. *A Companion to German Realism, 1848–1900*. Rochester, NY: Camden House, 2002.

Lacoue-Labarthe, Philippe, and Jean-Luc Nancy. *The Literary Absolute: The Theory of Literature in German Romanticism*. Albany, NY: SUNY Press, 1988.

Lamport, Francis John. *German Classical Drama: Theatre, Humanity and Nation 1750–1870*. Cambridge, UK; New York: Cambridge University Press, 1992.

Leeder, Karen, ed. *Rereading East Germany: The Literature and Film of the GDR*. Cambridge, UK: Cambridge University Press, 2015.

Mauthner, Martin. *German Writers in French Exile, 1933–1940*. London: Vallentine Mitchell, 2007.

Mundt, Hannelore. *Understanding Thomas Mann*. Columbia: University of South Carolina Press, 2004.

Murdoch, Brian, and James N. Hardin, eds. *German Literature of the Early Middle Ages*, vol. 2. Rochester, NY: Camden House, 2004.

Nemoianu, Virgil. *The Taming of Romanticism: European Literature and the Age of Biedermeier*. Cambridge, MA: Harvard University Press, 1984.

Osborne, John. *Gerhard Hauptmann and the Naturalist Drama*. London: Routledge, 2005.

Pascal, Roy. *The German Sturm und Drang*. Manchester, UK: Manchester University Press, 1967.

Reill, Peter Hanns. *The German Enlightenment and the Rise of Historicism*. Berkeley, CA: University of California Press, 1975.

Richter, Simon, ed. *The Literature of Weimar Classicism*, vol. 7. Rochester, NY: Camden House, 2005.

Robertson, Ritchie, ed. *The Cambridge Companion to Thomas Mann.* Cambridge, UK: Cambridge University Press, 2002.

Robertson, Ritchie, ed. *Lessing and the German Enlightenment.* Oxford, UK: Voltaire Foundation, 2013.

Robinson, Benjamin. *The Skin of the System: On Germany's Socialist Modernity.* Stanford, CA: Stanford University Press, 2009.

Safranski, Rüdiger, and David B. Dollenmayer. *Goethe: Life as a Work of Art.* New York: Liverwright, 2018.

Saul, Nicholas, ed. *The Cambridge Companion to German Romanticism.* Cambridge, UK: Cambridge University Press, 2009.

Sharpe, Lesley, ed. *The Cambridge Companion to Goethe.* Cambridge, UK: Cambridge University Press, 2002.

Skrine, Peter. *The Baroque: Literature and Culture in Seventeenth-Century Europe.* London: Methuen, 1978.

Stone, Katherine. *Women and National Socialism in Postwar German Literature: Gender, Memory, and Subjectivity.* Rochester, NY: Camden House, 2017.

Taberner, Stuart. *German Literature of the 1990s and Beyond: Normalization and the Berlin Republic.* Rochester, NY: Camden House, 2005.

Tautz, Birgit. *Translating the World: Toward a New History of German Literature Around 1800.* University Park: Pennsylvania State University Press, 2018.

Tymms, Ralph. *German Romantic Literature.* London: Routledge, 2019.

Walker, John. *The Truth of Realism: A Reassessment of the German Novel 1830–1900.* London: Routledge, 2017.

Watanabe-O'Kelly, Helen, ed. *The Cambridge History of German Literature.* Cambridge, UK: Cambridge University Press, 2000.

Wellbery, David E., Joseph Leo Koerner, and Anton Kaes, eds. *A New History of German Literature.* Cambridge, MA: Harvard University Press, 2004.

ART AND ARCHITECTURE

Andersson, Christiane, Charles W. Talbot, and Martin Luther. *From a Mighty Fortress: Prints, Drawings, and Books in the Age of Luther, 1483–1546.* Detroit: Detroit Institute of Arts, 1983.

Asvarishch, B., Vincent Boele, and Femke Foppema. *Caspar David Friedrich & the German Romantic Landscape.* Aldershot, UK: Lund Humphries, 2008.

Barnett, Vivian Endicott, ed. *Kandinsky.* New York: Guggenheim Museum Publications, 2009.

Barron, Stephanie, and Sabine Eckmann. *New Objectivity: Modern German Art in the Weimar Republic, 1919–1933.* Los Angeles: Los Angeles County Museum of Art, 2015.

Barron, Stephanie, and Peter W. Guenther. *Degenerate Art: The Fate of the Avant-Garde in Nazi Germany.* New York: Abrams, 1991.

Barron, Stephanie, Sabine Eckmann, and Eckhart Gillen, eds. *Art of Two Germanys—Cold War Cultures.* New York: Abrams, 2009.

Barron, Stephanie, and Wolf Dieter Dube. *German Expressionism: Art and Society*. New York: Rizzoli, 1997.

Behr, Shulamith. *Expressionism*. London: Tate Gallery, 1999.

Chase, Linda, Karl Kemp, and Lois Lammerhuber. *The World of Biedermeier*. New York: Thames & Hudson, 2001.

Eisenman, Stephen, and Thomas E. Crow. *Nineteenth Century Art: A Critical History*. 4th ed. New York: Thames & Hudson, 2011.

Ferrier, Jean Louis. *Paul Klee*. Paris: Terrail, 1999.

Forster, Kurt Walter. *Schinkel: A Meander through His Life and Work*. Basel: Birkhäuser, 2018.

Heather, David, and Mechthild Barth. *DDR Posters: Ostdeutsche Propagandakunst/The Art of East German Propaganda*. Munich: Prestel, 2014.

Jentsch, Ralph, Enrico Crispolti, and Philippe Dagen. *George Grosz: Berlin—New York*. New York: Skira, 2008.

Joachimides, Christos M., Wieland Schmied, Werner Becker, and Norman Rosenthal. *German Art in the 20th Century: Painting and Sculpture, 1905–1985*. London: Royal Academy of Arts: Weidenfeld and Nicolson, 1985.

Kaiser, Fritz. *Degenerate Art: The Exhibition Catalogue Guide in German and English*. San Bernardino, CA: lulu.com, 2018.

Kearns, Martha. *Käthe Kollwitz: Woman and Artist*. Old Westbury, NY: Feminist Press, 1976.

Kelly, Elaine, and Amy Lynn Wlodarski, eds. *Art outside the Lines: New Perspectives on GDR Art Culture*. Amsterdam: Rodopi, 2011.

Keuning, Ralph, et al. *Neo Rauch: Dromos: Painting 1993–2017*. Berlin: Hatje Cantz Verlag, 2018.

Kitchen, Martin. *Speer: Hitler's Architect*. New Haven, CT: Yale University Press, 2015.

Kries, Mateo, et al. *The Bauhaus: #itsalldesign*. English ed. Weil am Rhein: Vitra Design Museum GmbH, 2015.

Lindemann, Gottfried. *History of German Art: Painting, Sculpture, Architecture*. New York: Praeger, 1971.

McKitterick, Rosamond, ed. *Carolingian Culture: Emulation and Innovation*. Cambridge, UK: Cambridge University Press, 1994.

Michaud, Eric, and Janet Lloyd. *The Cult of Art in Nazi Germany*. Stanford, CA: Stanford University Press, 2004.

Myers, Bernard S. *The German Expressionists: A Generation in Revolt*, concise ed. New York: McGraw-Hill, 1963.

Nees, Lawrence. *Early Medieval Art*. Oxford, UK: Oxford University Press, 2002.

Ottomeyer, Hans, Klaus Albrecht Schröder, and Laurie Winters. *Biedermeier: The Invention of Simplicity*. Milwaukee, WI: Milwaukee Art Museum; Hatje Cantz, 2006.

Peters, Olaf, et al. *Degenerate Art: The Attack on Modern Art in Nazi Germany, 1937*. Munich: Prestel, 2014.

Petropoulos, Jonathan. *The Faustian Bargain: The Art World in Nazi Germany*. New York: Oxford University Press, 2000.

Rohde, Elisabeth. ed. *The Altar of Pergamon*. Berlin: Berlin State Museum, Antiquities Collection, 1981.

Roth, Lynette, ed. *Inventur: Art in Germany, 1943–55*. Cambridge, MA: Harvard Art Museums, 2018.

Schutz, Herbert. *The Carolingians in Central Europe, Their History, Arts, and Architecture: A Cultural History of Central Europe, 750–900*. Boston: Brill, 2004

Sheehan, James J. *Museums in the German Art World from the End of the Old Regime to the Rise of Modernism*. New York: Oxford University Press, 2000.

Tadgell, Christopher. *Transformations: Baroque and Rococo in the Age of Absolutism and the Church Triumphant*. London: Routledge, Taylor & Francis Group, 2013.

Tisdall, Caroline. *Joseph Beuys*. New York: Thames and Hudson, 1979.

Weber, Nicholas F. *The Bauhaus Group. Six Masters of Modernism*. New York: Alfred A. Knopf, 2009.

Wolf, Norbert. *Art Nouveau*. Munich: Prestel, 2011.

MUSIC

Adelt, Ulrich. *Krautrock: German Music in the Seventies*. Ann Arbor: University of Michigan Press, 2016.

Ahlers, Michael, and Christoph Jacke, eds. *Perspectives on German Popular Music*. New York: Routledge, 2017.

Appignanesi, Lisa. *The Cabaret*, rev. and expanded ed. New Haven, CT: Yale University Press, 2004.

Aster, Misha. *The Reich's Orchestra: The Berlin Philharmonic 1933–1945*. Oakville, Ontario: Mosaic Press, 2012.

Climenhaga, Royd. *Pina Bausch* (Routledge Performance Practitioners). London: Routledge, 2008.

Farina, William. *The German Cabaret Legacy in American Popular Music*. Jefferson, NC: McFarland & Company, 2013.

Frackman, Kyle, and Larson Powell. *Classical Music in the German Democratic Republic: Production and Reception*. Rochester, NY: Camden House, 2015.

Gardiner, John Eliot. *Bach: Music in the Castle of Heaven*. New York: Alfred A. Knopf, 2013.

Geck, Martin, and Stewart Spencer. *Richard Wagner: A Life in Music*. Chicago: University of Chicago Press, 2013.

Hall, Mirko M., Seth Howes, and Cyrus Shahan. *Beyond No Future: Cultures of German Punk*. New York: Bloomsbury Academic, 2016.

Hartford, Robert. *Bayreuth, the Early Years: An Account of the Early Decades of the Wagner Festival as Seen by the Celebrated Visitors & Participants*. London: Cambridge University Press, 1980.

Jelavich, Peter. *Berlin Cabaret*. Cambridge, MA: Harvard University Press, 1996.

Kater, Michael H. *Different Drummers: Jazz in the Culture of Nazi Germany*. New York: Oxford University Press, 1992.

Meyer, Marion. *Pina Bausch*. Penny Black, trans. London: Oberon Books, 2018.

Millington, Barry. *The Sorcerer of Bayreuth: Richard Wagner, His Work, and His World*. New York: Oxford University Press, 2012.

Riva, Maria. *Marlene Dietrich: The Life*. New York: Knopf, 1993.

Schulenberg, David. *Music of the Baroque*, 2nd ed. New York: Oxford University Press, 2008.

Schütte, Uwe. *German Pop Music: A Companion*. Berlin; Boston: De Gruyter, 2017.

Stresemann, Wolfgang. *The Berlin Philharmonic from Bülow to Karajan: Home and History of a World-Famous Orchestra*. Berlin: Stapp, 1979.

Wallace, Robin. *Hearing Beethoven: A Story of Musical Loss and Discovery*. Chicago: University of Chicago Press, 2018.

FOOD

Dornbusch, Horst D. *Prost! The Story of German Beer*. Boulder, CO: Siris Books, 1997.

Hassani, Nadia. *Spoonfuls of Germany: German Regional Cuisine*, expanded ed. New York: Hippocrene Books, 2013.

Heinzelmann, Ursula. *Beyond Bratwurst: A History of Food in Germany*. London: Reaktion Books, 2014.

Heinzelmann, Ursula. *Food Culture in Germany*. Westport, CT: Greenwood Press, 2008.

Kohl, Hannelore, and Helmut Kohl. *A Culinary Voyage through Germany*. New York: Abbeville Press, 1997.

Leader, Daniel, Lauren Chattman, Jonathan Lovekin, and Alan Witschonke. *Local Breads: Sourdough and Whole-Grain Recipes from Europe's Best Artisan Bakers*. New York: W. W. Norton & Company, 2007.

Oliver, Garrett. *The Oxford Companion to Beer*. Oxford, UK: Oxford University Press, 2012.

Reinhardt, Stephen, Jon Wyand, and Hugh Johnson. *The Finest Wines of Germany: A Regional Guide to the Best Producers and Their Wines*. Berkeley: University of California Press, 2012.

Schoonmaker, Frank, and Peter M. F. Sichel. *The Wines of Germany: Frank Schoonmaker's Classic*. Completely rev. ed. by Peter M. F. Sichel. New York: Hastings House, 1980.

LEISURE

Becker, Boris. *The Player*. London: Bantam Press, 2004.

Crowley, David, and Susan Emily Reid, eds. *Pleasures in Socialism: Leisure and Luxury in the Eastern Bloc*. Evanston, IL: Northwestern University Press, 2010.

Dempsey, Luke. *Club Soccer 101: The Essential Guide to the Stars, Stats, and Stories of 101 of the Greatest Teams in the World*. New York: W. W. Norton & Company, 2014.

Dennis, Mike, and Jonathan Grix. *Sport under Communism: Behind the East German "Miracle."* New York: Palgrave Macmillan, 2012.

Fritzche, Peter. *Reading Berlin 1900*. Cambridge, MA: Harvard University Press, 1996.

Gammelsæter, Hallgeir, and Benoît Senaux, eds. *The Organisation and Governance of Top Football across Europe: An Institutional Perspective.* New York: Routledge, 2011.

Hessel, Franz, ed. *Walking in Berlin: A Flaneur in the Capital.* Amanda DeMarco, ed. Cambridge, MA: MIT Press, 2017.

Hilmes, Oliver. *Berlin 1936: Sixteen Days in August.* Jefferson S. Chase, trans. New York: Other Press, 2018.

Johnson, Molly. *Training Socialist Citizens: Sports and the State in East Germany.* Leiden, Netherlands: Brill, 2008.

Lisi, Clemente Angelo. *A History of the World Cup: 1930–2018,* new ed. Lanham, MD: Rowman & Littlefield, 2019.

Mauriès, Patrick. *Chanel Catwalk: The Complete Karl Lagerfeld Collections.* New Haven, CT: Yale University Press, 2016.

McDougall, Alan. *The People's Game: Football, State and Society in East Germany.* Cambridge, UK: University Press, 2014.

Parrish, Charles, and John Nauright. *Soccer around the World: A Cultural Guide to the World's Favorite Sport.* Santa Barbara, CA: ABC-CLIO, 2014.

Schiller, Kay, and Christopher Young. *The 1972 Munich Olympics and the Making of Modern Germany.* Berkeley: University of California Press, 2010.

Ungerleider, Steven. *Faust's Gold: Inside the East German Doping Machine.* New York: Thomas Dunne Books/St. Martin's Press, 2001.

Wahmen, Birgit. "Allotments and Schrebergärten in Germany." In Monique Mosser and Georges Teyssot, eds. *The History of Garden Design: The Western Tradition from the Renaissance to the Present Day,* 451–453. London; New York: Thames & Hudson, 2000.

Witt, Katarina, and E. M. Swift. *Only with Passion: Figure Skating's Most Winning Champion on Competition and Life.* New York: Public Affairs, 2005.

MEDIA

Berghahn, Volker R. *Journalists between Hitler and Adenauer: From Inner Emigration to the Moral Reconstruction of West Germany.* Princeton, NJ: Princeton University Press, 2019.

Bönker, Kirsten, Julia Obertreis, and Sven Grampp. *Television beyond and across the Iron Curtain.* Newcastle upon Tyne, UK: Cambridge Scholars Publishing, 2016.

Brockmann, Stephen. *A Critical History of German Film.* Rochester, NY: Camden House, 2010.

Fraser, Catherine C., and Dierk O. Hoffmann. *Pop Culture Germany! Media, Arts, and Lifestyle.* Santa Barbara, CA: ABC-CLIO, 2006.

Führer, Karl Christian, and Corey Ross, eds. *Mass Media, Culture and Society in Twentieth-century Germany.* Basingstoke, UK; New York: Palgrave Macmillan, 2006.

Gronert, Stefan. *The Düsseldorf School of Photography.* London: Thames & Hudson, 2009.

Gumbert, Heather L. *Envisioning Socialism: Television and the Cold War in the German Democratic Republic.* Ann Arbor: University of Michigan Press, 2014.

Hake, Sabine. *German National Cinema.* New York: Routledge, 2002.

Hale, Oron J. *The Captive Press in the Third Reich*. Princeton, NJ: Princeton University Press, 1964.

Hoffmann, Christian R., and Wolfram Bublitz. *Pragmatics of Social Media*. Berlin; Boston: De Gruyter, 2017.

Powell, Larson, and Robert R. Shandley, eds. *German Television: Historical and Theoretical Approaches*. New York: Berghahn Books, 2016.

Puddington, Arch. *Broadcasting Freedom: The Cold War Triumph of Radio Free Europe and Radio Liberty*. Lexington: University Press of Kentucky, 2000.

Stephan, Alexander, ed. *Americanization and Anti-Americanism: The German Encounter with American Culture after 1945*. New York: Berghahn Books, 2005.

Willett, Ralph. *The Americanization of Germany, 1945–1949*. London; New York: Routledge, 1989.

INDEX

Italic page numbers indicate images; page numbers followed by *t* indicate tables.

ABOUT THE AUTHORS

Wendell G. Johnson is professor at Northern Illinois University, DeKalb, Illinois. Johnson's previous work for ABC-CLIO, *End of Days: An Encyclopedia of the Apocalypse in World Religions* (2017), was named an Outstanding Reference Source by the Reference and User Services Association of the American Library Association. He is the general editor of the *Journal of Religious and Theological Information*, published by Taylor and Francis.

Katharina Barbe, PhD, professor emerita, was chair of the Department of World Languages and Cultures at Northern Illinois University. A native of Berlin, she came to the United States originally on a scholarship from the DAAD (German Academic Exchange Service). She is author of *Irony in Context* (1995) and coauthor of *Prüfungstraining DaF: AP German Language and Culture* (2013). In 2013, she received the Goethe-Institut/AATG Certificate of Merit (AATG—American Association of Teachers of German). In 2016, she was named the Illinois German Teacher of the Year. She is also the 2019 AATG Outstanding German Educator.

THE CONTRIBUTORS

William E. Burns—George Washington University, Washington, D.C.

Josianne Campbell—Andrew Jackson High School, Kershaw, South Carolina

Jessamine Cooke-Plagwitz—Northern Illinois University, DeKalb, Illinois

Randy Fink—Independent scholar, Germany

Wayne Finley—Northern Illinois University, DeKalb, Illinois

Larissa Garcia—Northern Illinois University, DeKalb, Illinois

Christopher Thomas Godwin—University of Illinois Urbana-Champaign

Christiane Grieb—Global Humanistic University

Christian Jimenez—Independent scholar

Ladislava Khailova—Georgetown University, Washington, D.C.

William P. Kladky—American Institutes for Research, Washington, D.C.

James Lund—Westminster Seminary, California

Nichole Neuman—Indiana University-Purdue University, Indianapolis

Robert Ridinger—Northern Illinois University, DeKalb, Illinois

Alia Soliman—University College, London

John Stark—Illinois Math and Science Academy, Aurora, Illinois (retired)

www.ingramcontent.com/pod-product-compliance
Lightning Source LLC
Chambersburg PA
CBHW080409270326
41929CB00018B/2960